本成果同时受到北京外国语大学中国-非洲法律研究中心和北京外国语大学基本科研业务费青年学术创新团队支持计划《中国企业在非洲投资的法律风险控制研究》（编号2015JT007）支持出版

中非法律评论

China-Africa Law Review

主编：万猛 张海征
副主编：杨天娲

U0824547

3
第三卷

中国法制出版社
CHINA LEGAL PUBLISHING HOUSE

本书学术顾问 / 中国 – 非洲法律研究中心理事：

名誉理事长： 陈冀平

理　事　长： 张鸣起

副理事长： 黄　进　王利明　谷昭民　彭　龙　杜石平

理　　　事：

刘合华　罗东川　郭兴旺　林松添　李成钢　周渝波　于健龙

付子堂　贾　宇　何勤华　沈四宝　赵秉志　莫纪宏　刘晓红

张守文　王振民　周仲飞　王　铁　卢建平　丁　丁　李明德

朱慈蕴　李安山　孔庆江　李永辉　牛华勇　孙晓萌　万　猛

秘　书　长： 万　猛

主　　编： 万猛（Wan Meng）　张海征（Zhang Haizheng）

副 主 编： 杨天娲（Yang Tianwa）

主办单位： 中国 – 非洲法律研究中心

（China-Africa Legal Research Center）

中国 – 非洲法律培训基地

（China-Africa Legal Training Base）

北京外国语大学法学院

（School of Law, BFSU）

序　言

世界多极化、经济全球化和交往的深入化促使法律与规则在其国际交往中发挥比之于过往更加重要的作用。与此同时，如何切实促使法律与规则成为保障和稳固国家间关系的重要手段，理解彼此间经贸往来的安全标线，加快彼此间经贸往来，是全球法律智者们共同关注和思考的问题。

在我国所坚持的法治社会建设方向下，不断加强与包括所有非洲国家在内的世界各国法律界的交流、沟通和学习的方针，对于促进彼此间法律与实践的了解与相互借鉴，促成经贸、社会往来的合作与加速，共同维护世界政治经济新秩序与和平发展共同新未来，都将发挥无可替代的决定性作用。

因此，在“一带一路”国家战略大力推进，中非合作论坛进程不断加快的大趋势下，北京外国语大学法学院发挥长期以来的国际化法律教学、科研和交流的特色与优势，瞄准社会对专业化智力支持的需要，在中国法学会、北京外国语大学的大力支持下，开展了中非法律高端交流、非洲国家法律人才培训、非洲国别法律环境研究等一系列活动。

《非洲法律评论》系列，作为我院前期务实工作的部分成果，先行呈现给社会各界，以便共同交流、探讨。同时，也希望获得相关专业人士的支持和指导，以利于我院后续工作和相关成果的不断改进和提高。

万　猛

中国–非洲法律研究中心理事、秘书长

北京外国语大学法学院教授

目录

非洲各国投资法律规定之介绍

Introduction to Investment laws and Regulations of African Countries

在非投资的法律风险

Legal risks of Foreign Investment in African Countries

非洲各国法律对中国企业在非投资的影响及争端解决机制

The Influence of Laws and Regulations of African Countries on the Investment of Chinese Enterprises and Investment Dispute Resolution Mechanism between China and Africa

非洲国家劳动法规对中国企业投资的影响

作者：Abdoul Khadir DIOP 译者：徐伟刚

由于企业、个体企业家以及商人需要获得帮助以获取、设计、生产、实施他们的工作以及完成他们的目标，因此他们必须雇佣工人。这些工人就是职工劳动力。

一方面，由于企业需要劳动力完成各项任务，因此劳动力就成为了企业资源的一部分。劳动力是商业经营中十分重要的一个要素，并且被认为是企业的人力资源。每个企业意图控制它的职员，根据自己的意愿雇佣或开除工人，部署、分配任务，并根据需要使用企业的职工并使企业利益最大化。企业与个人为了利益在商业领域交汇在一起，因此他们都是以利益为导向并且尽其所能充分运用资源的。从这个角度讲，企业是按需使用劳动力的。

另一方面，职工是生产成本的一部分。实际上，根据法律对雇主的要求，职工享受着除工资之外的福利以及社会保障，而这些对雇主来说都是经济成本。

因此，职工既是生产工具也是生产成本，对职工的控制便成为企业平稳运行并实现其目标的重点。

由于对职工流动性的生硬限制以及法律赋予职工的保障和福利使雇主承受了过重的负担，企业已不再热衷雇佣员工，劳动立法或多或少成为了阻碍企业和投资发展的绊脚石。

劳动法的立法目的在于平衡劳动者和雇主之间不平等的地位，调和经济和社会问题（允许存在一定的灵活空间）以及保护就业，使得对劳动者的保护不再是企业的负担。

为了实现这一目的，非洲各国施行的劳动法都强调对劳动者的保护，这源于劳动者与雇主相比的弱势、依赖地位的现实。非洲各国的劳动法立法部门致力于实现保障劳动者劳动关系的连续性和稳定性。因此，立法部门倾向于规定永久雇佣制度并将解除劳动关系变得更加困难。此外，立法部门还设置了社会保障措施以使雇主承担更多的义务从而使劳动者受益。

然而，上述情况并非非洲国家所独有。事实上，劳动法具有社会法的本质，其基本精神在于为劳动者提供保护。中国的法律同样注重对劳动者提供保障（参见《中华人民共和国劳动法》）[①]。

劳动法规对投资企业会产生一定的影响。以当前广泛存在的企业迁移现象为例，大量企业从对劳动者实施严格的立法保护以及劳动力成本高昂的国家迁出，迁入劳动法规更加灵活、劳动力成本更加低廉的国家。

这一现象使得亚洲国家尤其受益，企业在这些国家可以找到技术娴熟、价格低廉的劳动力，从而控制劳动力成本，因此企业可以扩大规模并更加具有竞争力。然而，企业迁移在非洲并不罕见，如 H&M[②] 公司在埃塞俄比亚设立工厂；从 20 世纪开始，中国开始在埃及、毛里求斯、尼日利亚和赞比亚等地设立经济特区等。

国家为了吸引并获取投资，一定会调整劳动法规以适应企业的需求。但是，国家也承担着为劳动者提供社会保障措施的义务，以避免出现劳动者为了防止失业而任由企业支配的情况。

在塞内加尔，尽管劳动立法旨在保护劳动者，它仍然寻求保证企业的稳定。因此，平衡难以实现。这一点可以从雇主通过雇佣、解雇的规定控制职工规模以及职工报酬、福利以及劳动安全保障等方面得出结论。此外，旨在鼓励投资的特别法被采用，这在一定程度上减少了在职工雇佣和管理方面上的约束。

劳动法对投资的影响主要体现在雇佣、解雇劳动力和职工管理的经济负担等方面。笔者将从这两方面进行讨论：第一部分，阐述劳动法的一般规定以及其对投资的影响；第二部分，阐述劳动法的限制规则以及其对投资的影响。

一、劳动法的一般规定以及其对投资的影响

任何一家生产货物或提供服务的企业都在寻求一个目标，即通过调整资源分配以适应生产需求和通过控制开支等方式，从而控制职工数量和生产成本。塞内加尔

① Text in French. Translated by Hong Liang and Paul Kramer, under the supervision of Jérôme Patenotte Lefèvre Pelletier & Associés Firm, lawyers, available atwww.droitfrancechine.org/content/.../950101_loi_rpc_sur_le_travail.pdf, retrieved on May 13, 2016.

② http://skandikafrik.com/news/hm-set-to-begin-production-in-ethiopia, retrieved on May 8, 2016.

劳动法是建立在劳动法典、社会保障法典、特定领域内签订并适用的集体协议以及雇主和雇员签订的劳动合同等基础之上，此外法院对案件的审理也进一步对法规进行解释和完善。

（一）对企业职工数量的控制及其对投资的影响

企业应当有权控制其员工数量，适时雇佣职工以及解雇过量的职工。同样，企业可以根据职工的身体状况及专业技能为其安排相应的工作岗位。

如果考虑到企业作为其“商业活动”的所有者所具有的决定性权力，企业应当具有管理其业务的合法决定权，但事实上这一决定权常被束缚。企业必须遵守国内现行法规，换句话说就是必须尊重国家立法机关。因此，合同当事人根据合同自由原则享有缔约自由，一旦合同成立，双方应当遵守合同确定的义务。在这种情况下，即使合同当事人任何一方欲解除合同，为了使行为合法化，该方仍然应遵守已经确立的合同规则。

1. 关于雇佣的可适用规则

在塞内加尔，劳动合同分为两种。一种是固定期限劳动合同，该合同具有特定的期限或合同期限基于某一特定事件，如建筑工程因无法准确确定完工日期，但合同期限基于建筑工程的完工等。另一种是无固定期限劳动合同，合同由双方当事人决定，不受时间限制。

需要指出的是，合同是个人化的，仅在劳动者与雇主之间建立联系。塞内加尔不存在集体合同。

固定期限劳动合同必须以书面形式签订，否则推定为无固定期限劳动合同。另外，固定期限劳动合同的期限不得超过 2 年。(《劳动法》第 44 条）

在塞内加尔，立法者旨在确立无固定期限劳动合同这一法律规则，并限制同一劳动合同双方签订固定期限劳动合同的次数。

根据法律规定，劳动者不得与同一企业签订两次以上固定期限劳动合同，或将定期合同延期一次以上。法律强调除了法律另有规定的情形（容后述之），合同期间届满后劳动者继续提供劳动的视为订立无固定期限劳动合同①。

这一规定将成为投资的桎梏。因为事实上，企业不需要劳动者持续提供劳动，而仅在第二次固定期限劳动合同到期后，根据企业需要不再继续接受劳动者提供的

① S. L.42 of Law No.97-17 of December 1, 1997 on the Labor Code.

服务。如果不想受无固定期限劳动合同的约束，企业应当解雇劳动者，或者聘用新职工并为新职工提供培训以使其能够胜任工作。

法律对特定种类的劳动者规定了例外情形。这些劳动者包括：参加农业、商业、工业或艺术活动的日工或短期工人；在港口工作的码头工人；为企业不断增加的业务补充劳动力而雇佣的临时工；企业为暂时替代中止合同的劳动者而雇佣的劳动者；鉴于特定活动的性质，在习惯做法上虽不采用无固定期限劳动合同，但企业为完成暂时性工作而雇佣的劳动者。

例外情形的重要性在于其极大地削弱了与同一劳动者不得签订超过两次固定期限劳动合同的规定，然而这一限制仍然停留在原则层面。

根据《劳动法》第 49 条的规定，一切不属于固定期限劳动合同、学徒关系合同以及完成特定任务合同的劳动合同均推定为无固定期限劳动合同。

如果订立合同的自由受到了如此限制，终止合同自然也应当被严格限制。

2. 终止合同的可适用规则

如果雇主不再愿意接受劳动者提供的服务，雇主可随意地解除劳动关系。为了避免权力滥用以及考虑到公司的利益，塞内加尔劳动法规定了终止劳动合同的法定情形。

一般规则是，无论固定期限劳动合同还是无固定期限劳动合同，双方当事人均可依据合意而解除合同。

固定期限劳动合同期限届满前不得解除，但不可抗力以及重大过失的除外。(《劳动法》第 48 条)

无固定期限劳动合同的终止可以由一方当事人提出。劳动者可以辞职，雇主也可以开除劳动者。

除了因职工过错而解除劳动关系的情形，解除劳动合同必须事先通知。雇主未提前通知的应当向劳动者支付补偿金，补偿金数额应当与劳动者事先获得通知可能取得的一切收益相当。

考虑到公司可能面临经济困难以及需要因其经济地位和技术发展情况重整等情形，法律允许因经济原因解除劳动关系（《劳动法》第 60 条）。根据该条规定，因经济原因解除劳动关系是指雇主因经济困难或内部重整而与一个或数个劳动者解除劳动关系。在此情形中，出现资不抵债的经济或财产困难情形也可以视为因经济原因解除劳动关系，但解除劳动关系必须为迫不得已并经过破产法官（司法专员）的许可。

在任何情形下，解除劳动合同的正当事由的举证责任由雇主承担，举证不能的则推定雇主违反法律规定滥用解除权。

（二）由于职工而产生的经济成本及其对投资的影响

在劳动者提供劳动期间，雇主负有支付报酬或提供福利的义务，这些都是经济成本。

1. 管理职工的成本

劳动法及集体协议赋予了劳动者各种社会福利。这些福利包括：最低工资制度，工时制度，加班制度，休假制度，等等。雇主必须提高工作场所的安全等级以保障劳动安全并尽可能避免事故、职业病等对劳动者的潜在伤害。

塞内加尔实施了最低工资保障制度（SMIG）。根据颁布该制度的政令①，月最低工资为36.243法郎。除此之外，各专门领域的集体协议也提供了该领域相关工作的最低工资（SMIG），专门领域的最低工资要高于一般最低工资。然而，与生活成本相比，现有的工资仍然处于很低的水平。

塞内加尔领域内的雇主必须遵守上述规则，否则将被责令按照最低工资补足劳动者的工资。相关研究表明，这项要求在某些非洲国家并未得到落实，尤其是在安哥拉和南非。在这两个国家，中国工人的工资标准低于雇佣的当地工人。②

“安哥拉公司每天支付当地工人3～4美元，而中国工人仅有1美元。由于南非没有最低工资制度，导致对劳动者的剥削不断恶化，合理的工资水平被不断破坏。欧洲建筑公司每月向中国工程师支付大约130美元。”

在塞内加尔，工资可以在最低标准的基础上自由协商。劳动法禁止对劳动者的歧视并规定：有着同等资格和职业技能、工龄相同的劳动者的工资水平应当相等，不因其身份、性别、年龄及其他情况而有所差异。（《劳动法》第105条）

对劳动者应当实行同工同酬，其工资应当与工作时间相当。因此，工资不得与法律法规、集体协议或当事人之间的协议相抵触。（《劳动法》第105条）

除了这一规定，塞内加尔劳动法还规定了带薪休假制度，使得雇主有义务在劳动者享受法定休假期间向其支付报酬③。在因雇主或劳动者服兵役、劳动者患病等使

---

① Decree No.96-154 of February 19, 1996.

② Chinese Investments in Africa: A Labour Perspective, Anthony Yaw Baah and Herbert Jauch, Ed., p. 32-33.

③ Law No.74-52 of 4 November 1974 on the national holiday and statutory holiday, as amended by Law No.83-54 of February 18, 1983 and Law No.89-41 of December 26, 1989.

劳动合同中止的情形下，雇主应当在中止通知的期限内向劳动者支付补偿金。

另外，根据《劳动法》第65条的规定，当法定情形满足时，雇主可以使劳动者处于技术性失业的状态。在此情形下，双方应当签订协议以明确技术性失业的期间，双方还可以在协议中约定雇主在中止期间应当向劳动者支付的报酬。

其他与职工管理有关的成本由雇主承担。企业作为支付工资的雇主有义务缴纳税款。企业必须履行缴纳雇主支付工资一定比例的税款义务，税款数额应为企业支付工资总额的3%。

企业还应当根据调整社会福利机构的法律规定，向社会福利机构申报职工信息，并向社会福利机构缴纳法律规定的数额的款项以为职工提供福利。国家批准设立的社会福利机构包括社会保障基金以及塞内加尔养老金基金。

向社会保障基金缴纳的款项数额由职工工资数额决定，凡达到最低工资标准的劳动者，企业都应当为其缴纳社会保障基金。缴纳的社会保障基金上限为63000西非法郎/月或756000西非法郎/年。对于家庭工资的比率为7%，对工伤、职业病的比率根据该工作的情况分别为1%、3%、5%。

除此之外还有其他与合同违约有关的成本。

2. 合同违约产生的成本

违反劳动合同引起的当事人之间的争议应当向劳动法庭起诉。起诉与诉讼程序免诉讼费用。雇主与劳动者都无须支付争议解决程序的费用，无论是一审、二审还是上诉至最高法院。然而，尽管无须向国家支付费用，但是这并不包含当事人辩护所支付的费用，如委托律师的费用必须由当事人自行承担。

合同违约的情形中，雇主应当支付因损害劳动者权利而产生的一定数额的金钱赔偿。

除上述例外情形之外，固定期限劳动合同终止的，雇主应当向劳动者支付合同存续期间工资总额7%的补偿金。合同违约应适用相关法律规定，这些规定旨在审查解除合同的必要性及合法性，如果没有这些规定，合同解除就可能被滥用同时导致赔偿的产生。

劳动合同解除必须根据劳动性质确定相应期限提前通知劳动者。在通知期间，尚未离职的劳动者仍继续享受工资待遇。该通知期间用于让劳动者寻找新的工作。未提前通知的，雇主应当支付与劳动者的损失相当的赔偿。然而实际情况是，雇主为了尽快摆脱劳动者而倾向于向其支付赔偿而不是提前通知。

雇主违约并满足特定条件的，雇主应当支付解除合同赔偿金。该赔偿金应当向被解除劳动关系的所有劳动者支付，但劳动者有重大过失的除外。因此，劳动者的普通过失并不产生雇主支付赔偿金的豁免。

因经济原因与劳动者解除劳动关系的，除提前通知并支付赔偿金之外，雇主还应当额外支付劳动者一个月的工资，该部分工资免税。(《劳动法》第62条)

在上述劳动法一般条款之外，特别规定为雇佣及解除劳动关系提供了灵活性，但同时也有着经济方面的影响。

二、劳动法的限制规则以及其对投资的影响

为了吸引并鼓励投资，塞内加尔政府规定了对劳动法的限制以吸引投资者。这些限制体现在投资法、自由出口企业法、采矿法以及石油法中。

这些法律为投资提供了各种优待，包括税收和社会方面减少法律限制以及减轻企业负担。从用工权角度来说，对雇主的主要限制在于与同一劳动者可签订的固定期限劳动合同次数。一般规定是只能签订两次，然而实务中根据不同领域的情况存在着许多例外。企业除了在满足相应条件时可以主张享受法律规定对劳动法限制的特定优待之外，还有权享受投资优待部门提供的优待，但前提是企业经过国家许可[①]。

特别法律规定的优待可根据其影响分为两类。一方面它们影响雇佣及劳动关系的解除，另一方面它们也是管理职工所需的成本。

（一）关于雇佣及劳动关系解除的规则

我们可以将投资法的规则与自由出口企业法的规则进行区分。

1. 投资法的规则

投资法规定的社会优待，尤其是对于固定期限劳动合同，集中体现在两方面：

第一，被雇佣的劳动者自投资者通知并连续提供劳动之日起视为劳动法规定的提供劳动的劳动者。(《投资法》第19条)

第二，企业可以自批准之日或五年期固定期限劳动合同起雇佣劳动者。

2. 自由出口企业法的规则

自由出口企业法设置了对劳动法的限制，企业可以从海外自由雇佣职工。

---

① 经济与财政部。

此外，对于因周期性或意外性的原因而导致的停工，如设备故障、动力停止、自然灾害、天气状况以及稀有材料、工具、交通方式短缺，雇主与职工代表商议后可以决定全体职工停工。

职工管理所支出的成本究竟如何？

（二）管理职工所需的成本

雇主通常所负担的雇佣、解除劳动关系所需支出的成本在自由出口企业法中也不例外。雇主在上述情形中违约的必须向劳动者支付补偿金甚至赔偿金。

但是自由出口企业享受应当缴纳的3%税率的减免优待。

三、结论

塞内加尔劳动法旨在保护劳动者以及企业双方。因此它是一个平衡的系统，使劳动者不至于沦落到受雇主任意支配的地步，同时企业的经营及其利益得到保障。经营能够持续，就业也得以延续。

可适用于投资者的规则更加简单，以促进其安置并开展经济活动。塞内加尔政府还规定了雇主与劳动者之间的争议必须经过法院裁决。这些规则确保了雇主与劳动者双方的利益，从而满足了经营投资环境的需求。

The Influence of Labor Laws and Regulations of African Countries on the Investment of Chinese Enterprises

Author: Abdoul Khadir DIOP

Because companies, and even individual entrepreneurs or businessmen, need help in conceiving, designing, producing, executing their task or attaining their goal, they have to hire people. People working for them are their workforce.

On the one hand, the workforce of a company is a part of the resources implemented by this entity to achieve its results since the tasks are performed through it. It is an important element in the business operation and is regarded as the human capital of the company. To use their staff according to their needs and get the best benefit from it for their well-being, companies want to have control over their personnel and be able to recruit, deploy, assign tasks, and dismiss their workers according to their will. Companies and natural persons intervene in the business field for profit. So they are profit-oriented and try to optimize their resources. In this sense, they use their workforce according to their needs.

On the other hand, the staff is a part of production costs. Indeed, the worker is not only paid but also receives some benefits and some social protection imposed by the law to the employer, which have a financial cost.

So, the staff is both a production tool and a production expense. Therefore, its control is essential for the smooth running of the company and the attainment of its results.

Thus, depending on whether the staff's mobility is rigidly restricted or guarantees and advantages recognized to the workers by law weigh too much on the costs borne by the employer, the labor legislation may become more or less a brake on the development of enterprises and hence the investment by making enterprises reluctant to recruit.

The purpose of the labor law is to protect the employee against an employer dominant position, to reconcile economic and social imperatives (allowing some flexibility), and protect jobs, precision being made that the protection of the employee should not be at the expense of the company.

In compliance with this goal, African States have adopted Labor Laws which are protective for workers, considered as being in a position of weakness and dependence vis-à-vis the employer. In this sense, African Labor Legislations seek to guarantee to workers the continuity of their employment contracts. Thus they favor permanent hiring and make the dismissal of workers somewhat difficult. In addition, they organize some social protection which the workers benefit which has as a result some obligations borne by the employer.

However, this aspect is not specific and exclusive to African States. In fact, the spirit of Labor Law itself, also referred to as Social Law, tends to provide protection to the worker. The guarantees and protection granted to workers exist in Chinese law as well (See Act on The Labor Law of the People's Republic of China)①.

Legislation and regulation of labor can therefore affect investment companies. In this regard, and for illustrative purposes, we can invoke the increasingly widespread phenomenon of relocation of companies, leaving countries with strong legislation protective of workers associated with high personnel costs to countries where labor laws are more flexible and workforce is cheaper.

This phenomenon has particularly benefited Asian countries in which companies can find skilled and inexpensive workers, this situation allowing them to control their production costs, to increase their margins and to be more competitive. However, relocation is not totally absent in Africa since cases have been observed there particularly in Ethiopia with H & M②, as well as the initiatives of China with its Special Economic Zones established in the latter country but also in Egypt, Mauritius, Nigeria and Zambia.

To attract and retain investment, States certainly have interest to ease their Labor Legislation and regulation to adapt them to the needs of enterprises, but they are confronted with their obligation to ensure some social protection to the workers in order to avoid leaving them at the mercy of their employers.

In Senegal, although the Labor Legislation is protective of workers, it seeks also to ensure the sustainability of the company. So, a certain balance was struck, which can be observed both at the level of the control the employer have on the size of the workforce through recruitment and dismissal rules, and at the level of the remuneration, benefits and safety in the workplace. In addition, special laws intended to encourage investment by derogatory rules to the common law, have been adopted, which constitute a considerable relief of the constraints related to the recruitment and management of the staff.

Since the impact that Labor Law can have over the investment is mainly centered on the control of the workforce through recruitment and dismissal and on the financial burden related to the management of the personnel, we will discuss the subject focusing on these two points. However, we

① Text in French. Translated by Hong Liang and Paul Kramer, under the supervision of Jérôme Patenotte Lefèvre Pelletier & Associés Firm, lawyers, available atwww.droitfrancechine.org/content/.../950101_loi_rpc_sur_le_travail.pdf, retrieved on May 13, 2016.

② http://skandikafrik.com/news/hm-set-to-begin-production-in-ethiopia, retrieved on May 8, 2016.

will examine the ordinary rules of Labor Law and their influence on the investment in a first part and a second part the derogatory rules of Labor Law and their influence on the investment.

The Ordinary Rules of Labor Law and their influence on the investment

Having control over staff and production costs is the objective sought by any enterprise producing goods or services, by adapting its resources to its needs and by controlling its expenses. The labor Law in Senegal is essentially based on the Labor Code and the Social Security Code, but also on the Collective Agreements signed and applicable in specific sectors and on work contracts signed by employers and employees. The jurisprudence interprets and sometimes completes the rules by applying to cases submitted to courts the solution deemed applicable.

A- The Control of the Company Staff and its Influence on Investment

Companies should be able to control their workforce, recruit when they need it and fire workers who become unwanted. Similarly, they should be able to assign employees to positions corresponding to their physical or professional skills.

But if companies under their quality of owner of 'their business' and taking into consideration the power of direction that is attached to this character, should have the legitimate right to decide how to manage their business, they do not always have the hands free. They must comply with the rules in force in the country, in other words, respect national legislation. Thus, if the principle is freedom of contract, the parties to a contract have, on the other hand, once the agreement is reached, the duty to comply with what was agreed between them. One of them may want to untie him or herself but shall, in this case, comply with the rules laid down for that purpose to make their action legitimate.

1- The Rules Applicable to Hiring

In Senegal, two categories of Labor contracts exist. The contract may be subject to a specific duration or be determined approximately by taking into account, for example, the realization of an event such as the end of a construction site; this is the fixed-term contract. It may also be not subject to any limitation in time, which is determined by the parties, it is the permanent contract.

It is important to note that the contract is individual. It binds a worker to an employer. There is no collective contract in Senegal.

The fixed-term contract must be written. Otherwise, it is presumed to be concluded permanently. In addition, its duration cannot exceed two years (Art. L.44 CT).

The Senegalese lawmakers intended to make the permanent contract as the rule by facilitating its conclusion and by limiting the ability to contract several times a fixed-term between the same employee and the same employer.

According to the law, in fact, no worker can conclude with the same employer more than two fixed-term contracts, or renew more than once a fixed-term contract. The Act emphasizes that at the end of the term the continuation of services except for cases listed, which we will evoke infra, amounts to the execution of a permanent contract[①].

This may be an obstacle, or even a brake to the investment, due to the fact that companies which do not need a worker continuously but simply according to their needs will not continue to use the services of such an employee after the end of the second contract. They should let them leave if they don't want to be bound to them by a permanent contract, or replace them with a worker that they could have to give a training to make them operational.

The law affords exceptions for certain categories of workers. It is the daily worker or seasonal worker engaged for the duration of a campaign either agricultural, commercial, industrial or artisanal, the docker hired to perform handling tasks inside the ports, the handling worker engaged as complementing workforce due to an increased activity of the company, the worker hired to ensure the temporary replacement of another worker of the company in situation of legal suspension of their contract, the worker hired by companies within a sector of activity in which it is customary to not use permanent contracts due to the characteristics of the activity itself, when the employment of these workers is by nature temporary.

The importance of the number of exceptions attenuates considerably the no more than two fixed-term contracts with the same worker rule, but still the limitation is maintained as the principle.

Furthermore, according to article L.49 of the Labor Code (CT) any employment contract which does not meet the definitions of the fixed-term contract, the contract of apprenticeship or the contract of appointment subject to conclusive test should be considered as a permanent contract.

If the freedom to conclude a contract is regulated or restricted, the termination of contract is also strictly controlled.

2- The Rules Applicable to the Termination of the Contract

Faced with an employer who does not want anymore its services or its presence, the worker may get fired abusively. To avoid mistreatment and taking into account the interests of the company, the Senegal Labor Law has defined conditions to the termination of the Labor contract.

As a general rule, the termination of contract can always intervene by mutual agreement, be the contract permanent or concluded for a fixed-term.

The fixed-term contract cannot be broken before the term, except in cases of force majeure or gross negligence (Art. L.48 CT).

The indefinite contract may be terminated at the initiative of one or the other party. The worker may resign. It can also be fired by the employer.

① S. L.42 of Law No.97-17 of December 1, 1997 on the Labor Code.

Except in the case of dismissal for misconduct of the worker, the termination of the contract must be preceded by a notice. Lack of compliance with the notice rule involves the payment of a compensation equivalent to the amount of money corresponding to the all sums the worker would have received during the period of prior notice.

Conscious that the company can face economic difficulties or need to reorganize itself in light of its economic situation or technical developments, i.e., the law allows dismissals for economic reasons (Art. L.60 CT). According to the law, any individual or collective dismissal by an employer and motivated by economic difficulty or an internal reorganization is a dismissal for economic reasons. In this sense, the opening of collective (insolvency) proceedings, which is the consequence of a difficult economic and financial situation, may also justify a dismissal for economic reasons but isn't sufficient alone. The dismissal should appear necessary and authorized by the bankruptcy judge (Juge-Commissaire).

In all cases, the employer bears the burden of proof on the justification of the dismissal. Otherwise, the breach initiated by him is abusive.

B- The Financial Costs of the Personnel and its Influence on Investment

During the execution of the work and consequently to his breach the situation of the worker may involve the obligation for the employer to pay money as compensation or provide certain benefits, all generating a financial cost.

1- Costs Associated with the Management of the Personnel

Many social benefits are granted to workers by the Labor Code and by the Collective Agreements. Among them can be listed fit the policy of minimum wage, the regulation of working hours, overtime, vacation etc. Employers must also implement security standards to secure the work environment and ensure it is a potential source of injury, such as accidents or professional diseases, for workers.

Senegal introduced a policy of Guaranteed Minimum Wage (SMIG). Pursuant to a decree①, guaranteed minimum wage is 36.243 francs per month. Besides, the Collective Agreements in particular sectors of activities provide Categorical Minimum Wage (SMIC) for the branch of activity concerned, which are generally higher than the minimum wage. But, this is virtual because practical salaries remain very low, compared with the cost of living.

In all cases, employers settled in the Senegalese territory must abide by these rules. Otherwise, they may be condemned to complete the wages paid to the worker when it is less than the minimum allowed. In this regard, a study has shown that in some African countries this requirement was not applicable, especially in Angola and in South Africa where Chinese workers, for instance, are paid at

① Decree No.96-154 of February 19, 1996.

a lower level than workers recruited locally. According to the study[①]:

"Local companies in Angola are expected to pay US$ 3 - 4 per day for labourers as compared to US$ 1 that Chinese workers receive. The absence of a sectoral determination or minimum wage in South Africa tends to exacerbate the exploitation of workers, and undermines reasonable local wages. Chinese engineers are paid approximately US$ 130 per month, one sixth of what European construction firms pay Angolan engineers. "

In Senegal, the salary is freely negotiated, subject to authorized minima. It should be equal for all workers in the same situation with regard to their qualifications and professional skills, and after taking into account also the duration of their presence in the enterprise. The Act prohibits discrimination in this respect and provides: when they are submitted to equal working conditions, and have equal professional qualification and performance, the wage is equal for all workers, regardless of their origin, their sex, their age and their status (Art. L.105 CT).

The salary corresponds to the counterparty of the work performed and must be proportional to the time of work. Thus, no salary is due absent apart from the cases provided for by regulations, collective agreements or agreements of the parties (article L.105 CT).

But despite this rule, Senegal Labor Law experiences and applies the system of paid holidays, which impose the employer the obligation to maintain the remuneration of the worker for the corresponding days, which shall be determined by law[②]. In some cases the suspension of the labor contract, for reason of military service undergone by the employer or the worker, or illness of the worker, the employer is required to compensate the workers, within the time limits of the notice of suspension, by providing him the amount of his remuneration.

In addition, under the provisions of article L.65 CT, the employer may, if the conditions laid down by law are met, decide to place workers in technical unemployment. In this case it signs an agreement specifying the duration of technical unemployment and eventually, if the parties decide do, the remuneration that the employer owes to the workers during the period of suspension.

Other costs are borne by the employer relatively to the management of the workforce. The company is, indeed, bound to the payment of taxes due to the fact it is an employer paying wages. It must satisfy the obligation related to the fixed contribution paid by employers every year, which is equivalent to 3% of the payroll of the company.

The company must also, under the laws organizing the social welfare institutions, declare the workers and affiliate them to one of the regimes imposed by the Law and pay a contribution to those institutions for the benefit of workers. Two institutions have been established by the State: The

---

① Chinese Investments in Africa: A Labour Perspective, Anthony Yaw Baah and Herbert Jauch, Ed., p.32-33.

② Law No.74-52 of 4 November 1974 on the national holiday and statutory holiday, as amended by Law No.83-54 of February 18, 1983 and Law No.89-41 of December 26, 1989.

Social Security Fund (Caisse de Sécurité Sociale) and the Pension Fund of Senegal (Institution de Prévoyance Retraite du Sénégal).

The amount of the contribution to be paid to the Social security Fund depends on the level of remuneration and is due if the worker receives at least the minimum wage. Its maximum is set at 63 000 F CFA per month or 756 000 F CFA per year. Rates are of 7% for the branch of the family allowances, 1%, 3% and 5% for the branch of Work Accidents or Professional Diseases, depending on the primary activity of the establishment in question.

There are other costs related to the breach of contract.

2- The Costs Associated with the Breach of the Contract

The breach of the Labor contract in case of disagreement between the parties shall be submitted to Labor Courts. Referral to Labor Courts and the procedure is free of charge. Thus both the employer and the worker don't have to shell out money to pay for the proceedings related to their dispute, both in the first instance, on appeal and before the Supreme Court. However, even though a duty or tax is payable to the State, this does not extend to the costs necessitated by the defense of the parties, including the appointment of counsel, which must be borne by them.

Breach of the contract entails the payment by the employer of certain sums of money for the liquidation of the worker's rights.

The end of the fixed-term contract, in cases other than those constituted by the exceptions mentioned above, entails the obligation for the employer to pay the employee an amount of money equal to 7% of his or her gross remuneration for the duration of the contract. Similarly, the breach of contract is subject to rules designed to monitor the seriousness and legitimacy of the cause invoked without which it becomes abusive and can generate reparations.

The termination of the contract must be preceded by a period of notice whose duration depends on the categories of workers, during which, the worker who has not yet left the company, continue to receive his remuneration. Periods of time paid are granted to him or her to be used for looking for another job. Failure to comply with this notice period entails the obligation for the employer to pay to the worker the amount of money it would have received during the period of notice. However, the employer may prefer to get rid immediately of the worker and pay the corresponding compensation.

Breach of the contract at the initiative of the employer may also lead, under certain conditions, to payment of a termination indemnity. This compensation is due to any worker fired for cause other than their gross negligence. Thus, any kind of misconduct of the worker does not lead to exclusion of termination pay.

The worker fired for economic reasons has, in addition to the notice and the dismissal indemnity, as a special compensation, a non-taxable allowance paid by the employer and equal to one month's gross salary (Art. L.62 CT).

Besides these ordinary Labor Laws, there are special provisions introducing some flexibility in the regulation of recruitment and dismissal but also having a financial impact.

The Derogating Rules from the General Labor Law and their Influence on the Investment

To attract and encourage investment, the Senegalese Government introduced derogations from general Labor Law benefiting investors. These include, among others, the Investment Code and the Law on the Status of the Free Export Enterprise and to a lesser extent, the Mining Code and the Oil Code.

Plans established by these texts result in packages of various benefits, including tax or social advantages with a view of lifting legal constraints and easing the burden borne by companies. Regarding the right to work, the main drawback faced by employers is the limitation of the number of fixed-term contracts they can sign with a same worker. This number is fixed to two by the general rule, but in practice, many exceptions have been introduced according to the specificities of the various sectors of activity. In this context, in addition to having the right to claim the benefit of the rules providing derogations when they satisfy the conditions, enterprises are entitled to specific benefits provided for by the investment incentive scheme. To do so, the company must obtain the approval issued by the State[①].

Benefits from the special rules can be classified in two categories depending on impact. On the one hand, they impact the recruitment and dismissal, on the other hand, the cost associated with the management of the staff.

A- The Rules about Recruitment and Dismissal

We can distinguish the rules laid down by the code of investments to those laid down by the Act on the Status of Free Export Enterprise.

1- The Rules Laid Down by the Investment Code

The social benefits granted by the Investment Code, are reflected essentially in terms of possibility to conclude fixed-term contracts, and this, in two ways:

First, recruited workers, from the date of implementation of consecutive operating benefits to the notification by the investor of the start of their activities, are assimilated to workers engaged in staffing complement to perform work of a born increased activity within the meaning of labor law (Art. 19 Act).

Then, companies can conclude with recruited workers from the date of approval, fixed-term employment contracts for a limited period to five years.

---

① Ministry of Economy and Finance.

2- The Rules Laid Down by the Statute of Free Export Enterprise

The status of Free Export Enterprise sets up a derogatory framework that allows them to recruit staff from abroad freely.

In addition, in case of need for a work stoppage resulting from cyclical or accidental causes such as equipment failure, a stoppage of the driving force, a disaster, weather conditions, an accidental shortage of raw materials, tools, means of transport, the employer may, after consultation with workers' representatives, decide a collective interruption work of all or part of the staff.

What is the cost generated by the personnel management?

B- The Rules about the Cost Associated with the Management of the Personnel

Like in the ordinary case the occupation and dismissal of workers have a cost which the employer is not discharged under Status of the Free Export Enterprise. Indeed, the employer must remunerate the worker and pay him compensation or eventually damages for breach of the employment contract in the cases and circumstances described above.

But specifically, Free Export Companies enjoy an attenuation of the burden of costs normally supported with the exemption of Fixed Contribution to be paid by employers, which is based on the payroll and whose the amount is set at 3% of the latter.

Conclusion

The Senegalese Labor Law wants to be at the crossroads between the protection of the worker and the safeguard of the company. Thus it has enacted a balanced system which, while not letting the worker at the mercy of the employer, defends the interest of the latter and their business, whose continuity guarantees the preservation of jobs in general.

Applicable rules are even more simplified for investors, to facilitate their installation and the exercise of their activity.

The Senegalese Government has also established a mandatory procedure for individual dispute between employer and employee that must be settled exclusively by the courts.

These rules ensure security for both the employer and the worker, and thus fully meet the requirements of a business environment conducive to investment.

非洲劳动法律法规对中国企业投资的影响

作者：Moke Maye　译者：侯佳音

一、前言

几年来，我们见证了中国投资者大量涌入非洲大陆市场的盛况。这片市场曾被西方世界独占。我们国家和刚果共和国也不例外。最近的统计数据显示，中国在矿业、基础设施建设和能源开发上对非洲的投资已超过七百万美元。中国和非洲的一些国家是传统的合作伙伴。中国在非洲投资力度的加强与中非再次合作的计划紧密相关。

在20世纪90年代，西方国家对东非的支援是以对非洲经济政策的限制为前提的。他们打着带领非洲国家走向他们所称的“民主”和“善治”的旗号实行上述限制，同时要求非洲国家在面对恐怖袭击和移民问题时必须与西方国家协作一致。总体来说，这些约束条件被认为是殖民者的强制与压迫。

然而中国的情况则不同，中国并不以自身的政治经济政策为导向。中国与非洲国家的合作是建立在不干涉非洲国家内政的基础上，不要求非洲国家实现所谓民主，也没有在资金使用的透明度和反腐等内政问题上提出要求。

在劳动力市场上，中国企业获得了廉价的劳动力资源。最终，在最艰难的环境中创造更为有利条件的中国投资者取得了胜利。实践也证明了，在外资不足的情形下，中国提供的帮助是最实际有效的。

在经济方面，中国的投资对非洲的好处体现在很多方面。中国廉价的原材料出口至非洲，通过再加工出口，提高了非洲国家的出口获利。新中非合作关系使非洲重新出现在国际贸易市场，这是它在过去几十年里没有达到的。

在刚果（金），无论是从基础设施建设，如道路桥梁建设、宗戈(Zongo)大坝二期工程的建设，还是从采矿等大型项目上，都能看到中国的身影。中国的参与和影响十分显著。

但同时我们必须意识到中国的帮助是把双刃剑。

一方面，中国政府资金支持的合作计划项目由中国企业完成，这些企业主要招聘中国工人而非本地工人，同时也没有给本地工人提供合格的工作条件。

另一方面，中国基础建设项目的投资是与非洲对石油、矿藏开采的特许经营权有机联系的。

正如前文所言，中国投资企业主要聘用中国员工而非本地工人，这引发了当地工人的不满，也造成了当地人与中国投资者之间的紧张关系。

二、在非投资的中国企业用工现状及问题

接下来，我们将以刚果的中国投资企业为例，讨论在非投资的中国企业用工方面的问题。这些问题主要表现在工作条件与劳动关系两个方面。

事实上，中国企业给工人提供的工作条件，和与工人建立的劳动关系方面颇受争议。

我们将从以下几个方面进行分析：（1）工作条件、薪酬；（2）福利待遇；（3）劳动关系与工会；（4）压迫、侵犯工人权利的情形；（5）工人健康与工作安全；（6）歧视、虐待的情形；（7）工会的职责范畴。

（一）工作条件

劳动合同的缺失在中国企业中普遍存在。

《刚果共和国劳动法》[①]第36条第2款规定，劳动合同应当订立，并包含如下方面：劳动合同生效时间，劳动合同的期限，劳动者提供的劳动、服务类型，工作环境必须达到的标准，报酬，津贴，可偿还的支出和其他必要规定。劳动合同的订立要符合本法规定，在双方合意下订立，同时参考公司的制度和当地习惯。

但如果没有订立劳动合同，用人单位便可以灵活决定薪酬等事项。

实践中大部分中国投资企业都没有与工人订立劳动合同，这带来的问题是他们与劳动者之间的关系大部分是临时性的。

《劳动法》第39～43条对于劳动合同的期限规定了下列原则：

---

① 法字015/2002号，2002年10月16日施行，以下简称《劳动法》。

1. 劳动合同分为定期合同和不定期合同。

2. 按天雇佣的情况下，如果劳动者在2个月时间内工作了超过22天，则在2个月期限内新约定的雇佣关系将被视为不定期合同，否则，将面临惩罚。

3. 定期合同不得超过2年。但是，如果劳动者已婚并同家庭分离，或失去配偶、分居或离婚，或同他监护的孩子分离，该定期的期限不得超过1年。

4. 任何劳动者不得和同一雇主或同一企业签订2个以上的定期合同，也不得超过一次地续签定期合同。当劳动者为了企业或机构内某个固定的工作而受雇时，应签订不定期合同。

然而，很多中国企业无视上述规定，不重视他们本应获得的合法权利。

《劳动法》第119条规定，雇员和工人的法定劳动时间每周不得超过45小时；每天不得超过9小时。

然而，很多用人单位并不清楚这些条款，有些工人甚至连续不间断地工作12个小时。

（二）工作薪酬

《劳动法》第二章第86～118条是对劳动薪酬的规定。它的基本原则是工作薪酬可以在劳动者与工作单位的自由协商的劳动合同中订立，也可以在集体合同中订立。薪酬标准必须高于职工最低工资保障标准（SMIG）。

然而，中国企业经常压榨劳动者的薪酬。

（三）福利待遇

向职工提供福利待遇的中国企业很少，而且即使有些企业提供了福利待遇，也仅限于必要的几项。而且一般来说，这些福利待遇并不提供给非洲工人，非洲工人只能得到自己的工资。

原因很简单：大多数的非洲工人都被认为是临时工。即使他们订立了劳动合同，也往往被看作订立的是短期性的劳动合同。因此在极端少数的案例中，当地工人甚至获得不了交通补贴、养老保险、住房补贴，单位也不给工人提供医疗保障。然而，中国的工人却普遍受到良好的待遇，他们不仅享有诸多福利，而且工资高昂。

尽管《劳动法》赋予劳动者休年假的权利，但几乎所有的非洲工人都不能享有这个福利。更有甚者，女性的产假——这一在世界上普遍被承认的权利——都被剥夺。

工人的住宿条件差也是频繁发生的问题。工人的公寓一般与工厂建在同一片区域，但建在偏远的角落。工人们对公寓条件怨声载道。那些地方卫生通常不达标且拥挤。用人单位是不会在意这些的，劳动者只能自己去解决这些问题。然而与之同时，中国企业想尽一切办法去满足中国员工的住房问题。宗戈水坝二期工程旁一处住房就是为中国员工所建的。

（四）与工会组织的关系

大多数中国企业并不接受在企业中设立工会，一些企业甚至采取策略避免建立工会，工人可能会因参加工会而被解雇。不幸的是，由于经济危机和失业的原因，这些工人们总是能够接受这些近乎是剥削的条件，来维持这份可能是他们唯一生活来源的工作。

在这种情况下，工会的组织者被认为是“找麻烦的人”，因而人人避而远之。集体劳动合同的订立是非常少见的，雇佣单位在缺乏与工人和工会代表协商的程序下就自行制定了工资、工作条件的标准。即使是在极少数的订立集体合同的情况中，薪酬和工资条件也只能协商至国内的平均水平。

在设立工会的企业中，中国企业管理层往往不给工会代表上谈判桌发言的机会。即使他们允许工会代表参与讨论，他们也会以工会代表发言用的语言是法语或本地语言而非英语为借口，说他们的发言是无效的。

我们常听工会抱怨说谈判进行得太缓慢且无聊，因为中国企业认为工会的人只不过是工人的代理，真正具有最终决定权还是中国企业的股东和管理者。

以上表明，中国企业进驻非洲劳动力市场，对工人的权利造成了威胁，而工人的这些权利是他们通过年复一年艰辛的斗争得来的。

（五）对工人的压迫及对其权利的侵犯

中国企业违反了国际劳工组织的很多公约规定的义务，剥夺了工人的权利，包括工人具有参加工会的权利、订立集体合同的权利、获得公平报酬的权利和反歧视的权利。

尤其是在工作时间内限制工人人身自由这一条构成了对劳动者权利的严重侵犯。在工厂失火时，这种限制举措很可能会使工人遭受危险。

在尼日利亚的一个案例中，20 位劳动者在工厂中死亡。在肯尼亚的一个案例中，29 位劳动者因工作过度死亡。在报道的多个劳动者被强制工作的案例中，这些劳动者都遭受了身体和语言上的暴力。

（六）劳工健康和工作安全

劳动者工作中的生命健康问题从来没有得到过中国企业的重视。几乎所有的中国企业都没有为劳动者提供安全防护措施。

非洲有一套关于劳动者生命健康与工作安全的法律法规。但是企业中并没有形成对劳工的健康和工作安全的保障，只有少部分雇佣单位为劳动者提供了防护性的工作服和完善的安全设施。

工作场所的卫生间也存在问题。那些卫生间的卫生状况太糟糕了，甚至对劳动者的身体健康都造成了威胁。在一些极端的案例中，这些卫生间同时被用作更衣室，甚至和餐厅相连。

（七）歧视与虐待

在大多数中国企业中，干同一项工作，中国工人都享有比当地工人好得多的待遇。有些企业因为女职工怀孕而解雇她们，有些企业剥夺了法律赋予她们的休产假的权利。

中国投资力量在非洲的兴起时期正好与非洲工会主义的艰难时期相吻合。非洲工会主义的力量在 1980 年到 1990 年期间因国际货币基金组织和世界银行正在采取的整顿紧缩措施所削弱。

这些措施削弱了非洲工会可采取措施的力度。相关研究称，在撒哈拉以南的非洲，工会化的速率在减缓。一些专家称，南非的工会化程度不超过 10%。

此外，这些紧缩性措施对经济结构产生了负面影响，提升了劳动力市场的计算机化程度。

这种情况使工会化发展上升的速度明显减缓。

在上述各项因素的削弱下，工人运动无法对抗为了吸引外资而推动劳动法改革的政府，也不能遏制工作条件的恶化。

劳动法改革对劳动者权利保护的趋势和本应保障工人权利的劳动监察机关、工会的退化的趋势使中国企业家获利。这些因素都削弱了集体谈判中劳动者一方的力量。

尽管如此，还是有部分非洲工会成功组织起某些中国企业的工人。这些企业也尝试着听取职工的诉求。

为了应对上述问题，我们必须采取措施提高对在中国企业工作的工人的法律和社会保护。这些措施包括：

1. 非洲工会组织的成员要学习中文

语言问题是阻碍提升工人在中国公司的劳动关系的因素。法语是我国的官方语言，而中国企业的领导一般不会说法语。

为了降低培训的费用，非洲工会组织可以与中华全国总工会联合起来，共促目标的达成。非洲法律文件应被翻译成中文，以使中国企业熟知当地的法律制度。

2. 进一步完善劳动立法和最低工资制度

工会必须向政府施压，以免监督机构收了投资者的好处后就对他们的所作所为睁一只眼闭一只眼。

监督措施的良好实施会让监督机构更有存在感，便于他们对监督工作条件及工作报酬的执法。

工会应当更坚决地要求集体谈判，敦促中国投资者参与谈判。

3. 劳动立法在非洲大陆上的协调一致

非洲各国，特别是刚果（金），迫切需要吸引投资者到其国内投资。这种对吸引投资的需求引发了忽视立法的结果。因而各地的工会组织应当发挥作用，促进各国的劳动立法协调统一。

4. 为工会领袖在谈判方法上提供培训

工会谈判技巧的缺乏也是他们与中国企业谈判时遇到困难的原因，诚实地讲这在企业中很常见。

5. 拓宽对话事项范围

和大部分非洲国家一样，刚果（金）有自己的工人、用工单位和政府之间的协商机制，然而这个机制能处理的问题非常有限。因而工会应拓宽上述协商事项的范畴。协商的问题应涵盖工作时长、社会安全、病假、带薪休假、医疗保险和工作的健康与安全。

工会要有能力举证中国企业用工时的违规问题，使这些问题能够展现在用工单位代表、政府甚至是国际劳动组织面前。

在能够向他们提出对本地工人合法权利保护的问题之前，我们要坚持不懈地努力。中国的企业似乎并不在意我们的《劳动法》提出的对劳动者权利保护的内容。对本地工人的保护是我国立法者所关心的，也是执法者在执法过程中要达到的目标。

《劳动法》第 185 条第 8 款对可以参与工作的外国劳动力进行了限制。据此制定的行政法规[①]对企业内外国员工的比例规定了最高的限度。

在采矿行业，外国员工的雇佣比例应低于全体员工的2%，作为监管人员应低于2.5%，在高层管理人员中应低于2%。然而，由于某些特殊性工作需要专业人才，而刚果（金）本地的人才达不到标准，因此某些公司外国雇工的比例高出了上述限制。特别是在大型机械的操纵工作及制造、装配工作中，比例超标严重。

大多数中国投资者都无视刚果（金）政府为了保障本地劳动者而制定的法律法规。若比例超标是因为本地员工不具有相应工作能力的原因，还可以理解，但是一些企业雇佣超过法定限度的中国人，只是让他们从事刚果（金）人也可以轻松完成的工作。

企业并没有向东道国举证在哪些行业中当地的劳动者水平达不到要求。由此产生的印象是，中国投资企业以大批量中国工人替代雇佣本地非洲工人的理由只是为了牟利的借口。因此，刚果（金）公权力机关有义务设计一套防止此类情形继续发展的政策。确实，我们有相关的立法，但是立法本身不能完全解决目前的问题。

刚果民主共和国的国家职业介绍所，全称国家职业培训学院（INPP），是应本地劳动者就业的需求设立的。然而，目前这个机构亟须改革，改革应将科技进步的重要性考虑在内，注重培养学员的技术水平和能力

这在刚果（金）技术培训学校面临赤字很高的今天更为重要。这是由于技术教育的缺失和贸易类学校数目不足造成的。正是这种状况给外国企业在技术型工作上雇佣非本地工人提供了合理的理由。

2011年，在科卢韦齐（Kolwezi）建立的矿业公司KCC招聘了数百名印度蓝领工人，他们都是焊接领域的专家。公司雇佣他们的原因就是在刚果（金）本地没有能够完成这样任务的人才。有些公司雇佣了外国专家参与当地的铅工业、石造建筑行业，因为刚果（金）本地的学校并没有开设这些课程的能力。KCC公司的情形与其他矿业公司的情形一样，而矿业的现状与建造业和其他工程又大同小异。

三、中国企业投资的现状及问题

作为刚果（金）第一个经济合作者，中国在过去的25年中占据了刚果投资市场的巨大份额。中刚两国在基础设施建设项目以及工业矿产开发项目上共同合作发展。

① No.12 /CAB/MIN/ETPS/ of October 26th, 2005.

如今在刚果（金），中国人的身影无所不在，他们已经融入了本地人的生活。他们挤占了基础设施建设、道路建设的市场，也充斥在商店、中国餐馆和刚果（金）的大城市中。他们甚至已经开始进驻后发展的城市了。

在 2008—2014 年间，中国投资了刚果（金）的十项基础设施建设项目。完成这些项目要花费的总额大约为 4.6 亿美元。在 2015 年，项目规划已扩展至公共道路、学校的建设等。这些项目的花费预计是 2.5 亿美元。

在 2014 年年终，一共有 14 个采矿项目在进行，这大大加强了国家经济发展的实力。对这些采矿项目的投资总共是 37.2 亿美元，其中有 3.2 亿美元投向了刚果（金）中心的宗戈水力发电站的建设。

全国新闻报道了最近发生的中国栾川钼业集团股份有限公司对美国菲力普 · 麦克莫兰铜金公司（Freeport Mc Moran）的收购一事。该中国企业以 26.5 亿美元的价格收购了麦克莫兰公司在刚果（金）的坦科凡古鲁米矿（Tenke Fungurume Mining)的产业。根据对铜矿产业发展的预测，这项资产的价值在 2018 年将增长 1.2 亿美元。虽然我们看到了一些外国投资者，主要是西方投资者在刚果（金）市场的退出，但由于中国投资者一直在持续加强在刚果（金）投资市场上的投入。刚果（金）人对此是感到愉快的，因为这些投资者给刚果（金）带来了发展。

然而，坦科凡古鲁米的民众对此次回购的反映揭示了他们对在刚果（金）的中国投资者行为的忧虑。坦科凡古鲁米当地发展委员会主席 Venance MUMBA 说，中国投资者并不像美国人一样理解本地的社会运动。他强调说："很少有人能改变加丹加省（Katanga）的中国企业。他们对于社会的建设和当地的发展并不是很感兴趣。他们让我们感到害怕。"

加丹加所面临的尴尬情况也是刚果（金）其他省份的真实情况。

我们期望在非洲投资，尤其是在刚果（金）投资的中国企业能够致力于遵守本地法律法规，保障工人权益。否则，虽然我们国家需要他们，但人民对他们的看法会与对殖民者的看法并无二致。

四、结语

中国在非洲的经济崛起同时造成了复发的劳动关系和劳动者的权利问题。部分中国商人如同新的殖民者，像非洲曾经的殖民者一样剥削非洲工人。

工会的妥协是以其行为的可信度与合法度为代价的。这种妥协使中国企业对劳动者各项权利都有所侵害。尽管某些工会也采取行动改变现状，他们所做的改善很小，几乎不能保障劳动者的权利不受侵害。问题主要源于中国企业十分轻视工会，同时采取威胁工人的手段，不允许他们参加工会。

非洲工会必须将非洲的发展与工人权利的保护作为任何投资者来非洲投资都要接受的、没有协商余地的绝对条件。我们还应开展非洲工人运动组织与中国工人运动组织之间的直接对话，因为中国劳工在国内受的压迫与非洲工人在非洲受到的中国企业的剥削是类似的。这将为了解中国国内环境，了解其反对种族主义、反分裂的斗争创造条件。对中国国内环境的了解也可为非洲层面行动的协调提供思路。

在上述的文字中，我试图向您描绘了在非投资的中国企业为当地工人提供的工作条件的阴暗面。目前境况突出的特点是中国企业竟然无视《劳动法》中强制性法规为非洲工人提供的权利保障。甚至有观点认为，部分在非洲的中国投资者，尤其是在刚果（金）的中国投资者，仅仅把工人视为生产的机械工具。

中国企业的行为应该受到谴责。同时我们也应该注意到，正是相关负责官员，尤其是劳动部门执法人员的妥协、不作为，导致了现在的状况。

The influence of labor laws and regulations of African countries on the investments of China enterprises

Author: Moke Maye

Introduction

A few years ago, we have witnessed an influx of the Chinese investors in Africa in mainland deemed the exclusive domain of the Western countries.

The DRC our country do not have escaped this reality. The latest studies mention over 7 million us dollars invested in the mines, the infrastructure and energy.

Several reasons explain this strong expansion of the Chinese Investments in Africa that are in the process of relegating to the second plan the traditional partners in Africa.

In 90's, the Western assistance in East Africa under tense conditionality by nothing but economic policy.

In the name of those conditionality, the west help the African countries supplying the aforementioned countries get in the way of democracy (view of the West)and good governance(good management).

They must also be collaborating killed when it comes to fighting terrorism not control and immigration.

And these conditionalities on the whole bad perceived and are considered an imposition of the colonial guy.

China though condition does not help to his political and economic orientations. He does not make demands in terms of democracy, transparency in the use of the funds, fight against corruption. Chinese cooperation on non interference in the internal affairs on the African countries.

Job description in the markets, the Chinese too many companies buy the cheap. And finally the Chinese economic operators evolve more comfortable in the most difficult environments prevail. Where preparation abstract and the foreign invest ors are absent. Ultimately, the Chinese help is more efficient and pragmatic.

On the economic plan, the presence of china in Africa is advantageous to a lot of looks. The Chinese wonder drugs the prices of the raw materials and therefore improve the terms of business and the earnings export of the African countries. New relationships the Sino-African contribute to reintroduce Africa in international flows from the formal business of who she was going away for a few decades.

In DRC our country, the Chinese presence is perceptible through the big finish construction works (construction of the roads, the buildings) and (do construction of the second phase of the dam Zongo) and some big project Inga) like in the mining. It is also perceptible in the business.

He should be recognized but Chinese help is double tight.

For one thing, the plans funded by china call mainly on companies and the Chinese work, at the expense of the local.

Besides, the financings of the infrastructure of projects are systematically related to the granting of oil or mining concessions (case of the DRC).

As we said before, the Chinese investors call more on the work of this country to the detriment of the local. This often expresses his displeasure that usually makes a strong tension between the Chinese local population and investors.

In the next lines, we will try to think about the working conditions and the industrial relations in the investments in Africa with a particular accent on the Chinese DRC investments in.

To tell the truth, the working conditions and the industrial relations in the Chinese companies in Africa are the look controversy more Chinese investments in Africa.

We are going to show him trough the hereafter is:

- Working conditions, salary,
- Welfare benefits,
- Relations with the unions,
- Repressions and violations of the rights of the workers,
- Health and safety at work,
- Discrimination and abusive practices man oeuvre,
- Margins of the unions.

1. Working conditions

The work condition was noted in most Chinese companies evolving in DRC the absence of the work contract.

That under article 36 subparagraph 2 of the Labor Code of the DRC (law No.015/2002 of October 16th, 2002), the date of coming into effect and the duration of the contract, the nature and the object of the services of the worker, the places where they must be achieved, remuneration, the perquisites, the refundable expenses and all other conditions are determined by the contract within the framework as of legal tendencies T subject to the observation of the collective agreements, the regulations of companies and the local practice .

And in the absence of the work contracts, the wages and advantages are fixed arbitrary by the employers.

To the problem involved in the absence of the work contracts in the near total of Chinese companies that having milked to the recourse to temporary works.

The relative question is added to the duration of the contract is settled by articles 39 to 43 of the Labor Code.

This code poses the principles hereafter:

- The work contract is at limited duration or unlimited duration
- In the case of commitment from day to day if the worker already achieved twenty-two work days over one two months period, the new commitment concluded before the expiry from two months under penalty famous is concluded for one unlimited duration
- The lasted from the short-term contract cannot exceed two years. This duration is reduced to one year if the worker is married and separated from his family or if it widowed, is separated from body or divorced and separated from his children of which it must assume the guard
- No worker can conclude with the same employer or the same company more than two short-term contracts or to renew more once short-term contract
- When the worker is engaged to occupy an established post in the company or the establishment, the contract must be concluded for one unlimited duration.

In spite of these provisions many Chinese employers their blue-collar workers in the statute of temporary works depriving them of the kind of the advantages maintain to which they legally are entitled.

The article 119 of the code provides that legal working time cannot exceed forty-five hours per week and nine hours per day

It is noted that many employers are unaware of the rules relating to working time and oblige their workers with prester without interruption. Certain workers go until prester during 12 hours without interruption.

2. The wages

The Congolese code of work envisages the rules relating to the wages with title II is articles 86 to 118. The basic principle posed is that remuneration is fixed by the individual contracts freely concluded between workers and employers or by way from collective agreements. Those must take account of the interprofesional minimum wage guaranteed (SMIG).

These principles are often pressed with the feet by the Chinese employers

3. Welfare benefits

In the rare cases where the Chinese companies offer welfare benefits to their workers, those are limited to what appears strictly necessary to them.

In general, these welfare benefits are not recognized with the African workers who are satisfied only with their wages.

The reason in is simple: most these workers are regarded as temporary works, when well even with the eyes of the work contract they are supposed being related to their employer by a permanent contract. So in extremely rare cases, the local workers profit from the transport allowances, the insurance-pension, the housing allowances, the assumption of responsibility of the medical care is ignored.

And yet, the Chinese workers are generally well treated insofar as they profit from the higher wages and much from welfare benefits.

Whereas the Labor Code ensures to the workers the right to an annual leave like with the vacation of circumstances, the near total of the African workers are private. He was denounced even of the cases of deprivation of the right to the maternity leave legally recognized with the women having put at the world or to their spouse.

The accommodation of the workers is also a frequently encountered problem. It relates to primarily the building firms which carry out building sites in distant corners and which must place their teams on the spot. These workers complain about the conditions of accommodation. They are often placed in saturated installations in which the conditions of hygiene are not assured. It even arrives that the employer does not think there, each worker will have to deal with himself.

And yet, all the measures are taken to offer housing to the workers come from China. The building site of the second phase of the dam Zongo in DRC in is an illustration.

4. The relationships to the trade unions

Most Chinese companies do not accept the trade unions in their centre. Some go until setting up true strategies against the union action. Workers were straight forwardly laid off to have only adhered to a trade union. It is made unfortunately that because of economic crisis and of the scarcity of employment, these workers are ready to accept the work conditions close to the exploitation right to preserve their work and their single source of the incomes.

Under these conditions, the persons in charge of the trade unions are known as trouble makers whom it is necessary to keep away. The collective agreements are rare and the employers in the absence of any framework of dialogue with the workers or their representatives determine the wages and the work conditions in a unilateral way. And in the rare cases where the collective bargaining are organized, the wages and working conditions tend to put himself on the national level .

And in the rare case where workers are syndicated, the Chinese employers avoid receiving the trade union officials with the table of the negotiations. And when they do it, they claim that it is impossible for them of official statement effectively in French or in one of the national languages.

The trade unions as for them complain that the negotiations are incredibly slow and tiresome insofar as their Chinese interlocutors advance that they are only agents, true owners remained in China and who have only the power to decide.

All to say, the entry of the Chinese firms on the African job market as a direct threat for the assets as regards rights of the workers whom the trade unions had painfully obtained after the years of the collective bargaining.

5. Repressions and violations of the rights of the workers

Of many conventions of the ILO are frequently violated by the Chinese employers, including the right to affiliate itself with a trade union, the right to the collective agreements, the right to an equitable remuneration and the right of defender against discriminations.

The practice to lock up the workers during the work hours constitutes a particularly serious violation of the workers. It is a question of a practice likely to endanger the workers at the time of the fires of the factories.

It was the case in Nigeria where the fire of a factory had caused 20 deaths and in Kenya with 29 deaths. It was finally report of many cases of forced labor of physical aggressions and verbal.

6. Health and security with work

These questions are not the object of a great concern within the Chinese companies.

In the near total of Chinese companies, there does not exist any measure of precaution taken by the employer.

Local regulations as regards health and with the security with work. There is no formation with health and the security with work. Only a minority of employers provide protective clothing and the adequate equipment to their workers.

In most companies, the toilets are in a deplorable state and present even health risks of the workers.

In certain cases, they also serve as the cloakrooms, and even of canteens.

7. Discrimination and abusive practices

In most Chinese companies, the Chinese workers often enjoy better conditions that the African counterparts for the same tasks.

Certain employers were show to have lain off their workers fallen pregnant. Others were reproached of refusal to grant the right of maternity leave, right however acknowledged by the national legislation.

The rise to power of the Chinese investments in Africa coincides with one difficult period for the African trade unionism, strongly weakened by the reorganization and austerity measures dictated by the International Monetary Fund and the World Bank during the years 1980 and 1990.

These measurements caused to weaken the means of action of the African trade unions. The relevant studies announced the fall of the rate of unionization in sub-Saharan Africa, which does not exceed 10% with the statement of the experts.

In addition, these austerity measures which had a harmful effect on economic fabric increased the computerization of the work world.

This situation effectively compromises the recruitment campaigns of sensitizing aiming at re-examining the rate of unionization upwards.

Weakened for reasons evoked above, the labor movement could not be opposed to the reforms of the industrial legislation pushed by the financial backers of the funds to attract the foreign investors, nor to prevent the general degradation of the work conditions.

The Chinese entrepreneurs benefit from this climate of reconsideration of the rights of the workers and embrittlement of the supposed bodies to guarantee them (Labor inspection, trade unions). One would be even tempted to say that they are ingenient to neutralize all the efforts of reorganization of the structures of collective bargaining.

In spite of these operations, certain African trade unions succeeded in organizing the workers in certain Chinese companies, where they try to make hear the claims of their members.

To cope with the situation created by the Chinese investments in Africa, a base of measurements must be adopted in order to improve legal and social protection of the workers in the Chinese companies.

A. The need for the persons in charge of the African trade unions for learning the Chinese language

The language is one of the factors which prevent the improvement of the industrial relationships within the Chinese companies. The Chinese directors have difficulties in communicating in French, our official language.

In order to reduce the costs of training, CSI Africa and the organization of the African trade-union unit could collaborate with the federation of the trade unions of China (ACFTU) to facilitate the procedure. The legal documents should be translated into Chinese to facilitate the familiarization of the employers with the local legislation.

B. Better aspect of the minimum wage and another industrial legislation of work

The trade unions must put pressure on their governments so that those give essential resources to the labor inspection to prevent that it is at the mercy of wormy investors.

This equipment in sufficient resources will make their presence more visible and what will cause to make it ready to carry out a better control of the work conditions and remunerations. It is also important to sensitize the deputies in this direction.

The trade unions should be firmer in the collective bargaining and bring the Chinese investors to the table of negotiations.

C. Need for an approach coordinated on the levels regional and continental

The African governments in general and that of the DRC in particular, hopelessly try to attract investors in their country. This search for investments results in a crisis downwards as regards respect of the industrial legislation.

The regional trade-union organizations should campaign in favor of the harmonization of the conditions of investments in the African countries.

D. Need to train the trade union leaders negotiation industrial legislation

The trade unions are conscious that their low capacities of negotiation explain their difficulties of treating with their Chinese owners. That is particularly true on the level of the companies.

E. Need for widening the social dialogue

In DRC as in most African countries, there exist mechanisms of consultation between workers, employers and government. The problems which are tackled there are however limited. It matters that the trade unions manage to make widen these spaces of consultation to the problems amongst hours, the social security, the vacation disease, paid vacations, the medical insurances of health and the security at work.

They must be able to document all the violations made by a Chinese campaign and to make available them of the partners (representatives of the employers and the government) and possibly to the International organization of Work.

We could not put an end to our reflections without raising the relative question with the protection of the local labor devoted by the Labor Code and which does not seem to be the concern of several Chinese investors. The protection of the setting of local work is one of the concerns of the Congolese legislator and the executive power through enacted measurements of application.

Article 185 item 8 of the Labor Code indeed limits the manpower of foreign nationality which can work in a company. The ministerial decree No.12 /CAB/MIN/ETPS/ of October 26th, 2005 which was taken pursuant to the legislative measure above concerned, fixed by branch of industry authorized maximum percentage of the foreign workers within the companies.

For the branches of activity of the mining, the percentage applied is of 2% of manpower for the category of the workers concerned with general classification of employment, of 2.5% for the supervisors and frameworks of collaboration and 2% for the managing executives. However because of the specialty related to certain tasks or functions as well as the absence of a local or Congolese qualification, one notes sometimes a going beyond the manpower from abroad in certain companies.

Such is the case in particular drivers of the heavy machines and other special machines, manufacturers and fitters of factory.

The made report is that most Chinese investors do not respect the decisions enacted by the national authorities to ensure the protection of local labor. Apart from the cases justified by the absence of local competences aimed above, it is noted that certain Chinese investors call upon their compatriots to achieve tasks which can easily be assumed by Congolese.

In the same way, it is not observed any will to ensure the formation of the nationals to give to the host country the expert testimony which is lacking in certain fields to him. The impression which emerges is that the Chinese investors make a point of benefiting from this situation to justify the massive presence of the Chinese workers to the detriment of the nationals. It thus belongs to the Congolese public authorities to design suitable policies to prevent that this situation does not continue and does not spread. It is certainly true that as regards texts of the provisions were taken. It is made that the texts cannot alone solve this question.

The DRC has a public agency, the National institute of Professional Preparation in initials INPP which meet the need for formation of local labor. It is however important to reform this institution by taking account of the technological change which causes formerly ignored new technologies and competences. From where need for integrating new sectors in the formation ensured by the INPP.

That is all the more true as the DRC is to date characterized by a shouting deficit of the technical training schools, consequence of the devalorization of the technical education and the absence of the schools of the trades. This state of affair justifies the importance of foreign labor mainly to carry out technical tasks.

In 2011, mining company KCC installed in Kolwezi had called upon hundreds of Indian blue-collar workers specialists in welding in particular the reason advanced by the persons in charge was the absence of Congolese qualified for these tasks. One also found specialists in plumbing there, in cold and masonry because there does not exist with the country of the schools qualified for the formation with these trades. The situation met in company KCC is the same one in the other mining operators. And what is true for the mining ones is also at the building firms or engineering civil.

In a word, China nicked during the twenty-five last years a share of lion in the investments in DRC at the point to become its first economic partner.

The two countries exchange between them development projects of infrastructures and projects of industrial exploitation of the mines.

Today, the Chinese are omnipresent in all the fields of the national life in DRC. They tear off the large markets in the construction and/or the rehabilitation of the road infrastructures and real. Stores, shops and Chinese restaurants flood also the Congolese big cities. And they are already many those which started to exploit the back-country.

Between 2008 and 2014, China invested in ten projects of infrastructures in DRC. The total expenditure on these projects in the course of execution is approximately 459,764,000$. And in 2015, the projects envisaged understand the development of public spaces, the roads, the school projects and more. The total expenditure for these projects planned for 2015 is of 250,000,000$.

At the end of 2014, a total of fourteen mining projects allowed the reinforcement in capacities and the economic development of the country. The entire investment for the mining projects is of 3.72 billion including 320 million $ for the realization of a hydroelectric station (Zongo in the province of Central Kongo).

More recently, the national press mentioned repurchase by the Chinese firm "Clouded Molybdenum" of the shares of the American group Freeport Mc Moran, up to that point majority shareholder in the company Tenke Fungurume Mining (TFM) at the cost of 2.65 billion $. This amount can be in 2018 120 million the American dollars according to the evolution of the courses of copper and 2019. It is to say that whereas one witnesses a major disengagement of certain foreign investors mainly the Westerners of the DRC, the Chinese as for them continue to reinforce their presence in our country. That can only delight Congolese because of more than these investors bring in the development of the DRC.

However, the reaction of the civil society of Fungurume to the announcement of this decision of repurchase is revealing apprehensions raised by the behavior of the Chinese investors in DRC.

The president of the local committee of development of Fungurume, Venance MUMBA, the Chinese do not have the same comprehension of the social activities with Fungurume as American. And inserting the nail, this last affirmed rightly: "one tried a little to traverse the Chinese companies which function in the ex-province of Katanga. It was found that on the social plan, as regards local development, they are not interested in it so much. And that frightens us".

This unhappy report made for the Chinese companies installed in the old province of Katanga is also true for those which are present in other provinces of the DRC.

It should be wished that the Chinese investors who invest in DRC in particular and in Africa endeavor to obey the national law as well as the rights of the workers. By doing this, they will avoid appearing as neo-colonizers which our countries need.

Conclusion

The economic emergence of China in Africa resulted in a recrudescence of the unacceptable practices as regards the industrial relationships and rights of the employees.

Certain Chinese businessmen are wrongly or rightly driven by a good part of their workers and population as of new colonizers who exploit the African workers with same condescension as the former colonizers.

This resulted in to compromise credibility and the legitimacy of the trade-union organizations so much the violations of the rights of the workers in the Chinese companies are systematic.

In spite of the furnished efforts by certain trade unions to improve the things, force is to note that very little progress was carried out in terms of reduction of the violations of the rights of the workers.

This situation mainly results from eagerness that the Chinese employers put to depreciate the trade unions and to threaten the workers who make mine join there.

The African trade unions must impose the development of Africa and the respect of the rights of the workers as two nonnegotiable conditions for any investor It is finally important to develop a dialogue direct and constructive between the labor movements of Africa and China because the practices of the Chinese companies in Africa are the same one as in China.

To understand the environment of the other and its fights to help to fight racism and division in order to open up the way for actions coordinated at the African level.

In the lines which proceed, we tried to paint the painting how much sinks of the work conditions in the Chinese companies in Africa. These conditions are characterized by the ignorance of the even imperative provisions of the Labor Code and the rights of the African workers.

There used to believe that for certain Chinese investors in Africa and particularly in DRC, the workers are reduced to the row of simple production equipments.

Though this behavior is reprehensible, force is to note that it is sometimes supported by the laxism and the compromising of controlling and more particularly of the agents in charge of control and the implementation of the industrial legislation.

关于中非间投资争端解决机制的分析

作者：Angeline Munyeriwa 译者：郭一楠

毋庸置疑，近十年以来，中非之间的贸易和投资飞速发展[①]。自2000年，中非之间贸易额的年均增长率为33.5%。2006年到2008年间，贸易额从550亿美元增至1070亿美元，占到了中国贸易总额的4.5%，超过了2006年中非合作论坛（FOCAC）上制定的2010年达到1000亿美元的目标[②]。据报道，至2012年，中非间贸易额飞跃至2000亿美元。2015年，双边贸易额预期将超过3000亿美元。据标旗银行（Standard Bank）预测，中方在非投资将与2015年超过500亿美元，与2009年相比提高70%[③]。目前，在非洲经营的中国企业约有1600家，分布在约50个国家中。[④]

然而，这两个大洲间的贸易已经不再处于传统进出口贸易的阶段。如今多数贸易是由于双边投资协定（BIT）的存在才得以顺利进行。现阶段，非洲国家大多仍

① Roland Amoussou-Guenou, (2014) *Comparative Regime Of Arbitration In Africa (OHADA) And Selected Asian Countries*, LEGALINK NEWSLETTER, 1(1ST Quarter 2014), http://www.vovan-lawgroup.com/resources/COMPARATIVE%20REGIME%20OF%20ARBITRATION_Legalink%20Global%20Newsletter_1stquarter_2014.Pdf (Last Accessed On September 15, 2014).

② *China And Africa: Friends With Benefits* East Asia Forum, 17 February 2010 Article found at http://www.eastasiaforum.Org/2010/02/17/china-and-africa-friends-with-benefits/.

③ The African Banker (2015) *China targets African support in Western institutions,* Article found at http://africanbusinessmagazine.com/african-banker/china-targets-african-support-in-western-institutions/#sthash.s4JBG8Jw.dpuf.

④ Roland Amoussou-Guenou, (2014) *Comparative Regime Of Arbitration In Africa (OHADA) And Selected Asian Countries*, LEGALINK NEWSLETTER, 1(1ST Quarter 2014), http://www.vovan-lawgroup.com/resources/COMPARATIVE%20REGIME%20OF%20ARBITRATION_Legalink%20Global%20Newsletter_1stquarter_2014.Pdf (Last Accessed On September 15, 2014).

属于发展中国家，它们在寻找能为本国投资的外国投资者，尤其是像中国这样的热切关注非洲投资机会以及非洲经济发展的投资者。这些投资者可能是完全的私有商业主体或半国有制的主体，它们为接受投资国家的各种领域进行投资，包括制造业、电信、基础建设、信息技术产业等[①]。

当然，这些投资的效果是双方互惠共赢。中国经济持续发展需要大量资源和原材料的支持，而非洲国家虽然拥有资源，但并没有开发资源和发展本国经济的资本。双边贸易协定建立了一个双方各取所需的机制。

正如 Dolzer 和 Schreuer 在书中写道的：

> “在过去的 10 年中，双边贸易协定发展的最明显的趋势是与亚洲国家谈判达成协定……1982 年至 2006 年间，与中国达成了 117 项协定。”[②]

尽管双边贸易协定的目标是增加外来投资向非洲国家的流入以及发展受投资国本国经济，协定还起到了保护投资国利益的作用，如中国[③]。这些保护的效果可从如下条款中取得：

公平合理对待

全面保护和安保

征收征用合理补偿

最惠国待遇和国民待遇

投资自由撤回

禁止或歧视性待遇

保护伞条款

行政、立法、司法实质性保护

但是随着外国投资的涌入，法律纠纷的数量也随之增长，包括投资者和国家之

① Nachiketa Mittal (2014) *Arbitration In Africa: 'Chindia' Perspective,* p.3,The Conference On “Enhancing Business Opportunities In Africa: Role, Reality And Future Of Africa Related Arbitration”, November 2-4, 2014, Organised By The Atlanta International Arbitration Society.

② R. Dolzer & C. Schreuer, *Principles Of International Investment Law*, Oxford University Press, p.480 (2nd Ed. 2008).

③ Simon Greenberg Christopher Kee & J. Romesh Weeramantry (2012) *International Commercial Arbitration: An Asia-Pacific Perspective,* Cambridge University Press, p.478.

间的纠纷以及商业贸易各方之间的纠纷①。尤其是在投资协议上这个问题尤为突出，因为投资协议通常有较长的存续期间。尽管商业交易通常只是一次性的货物、服务和资金的交换，但向外国投资的决定的作出却需要投资者和受投资国有长期交往作为基础②。

考虑到通过双边贸易协定产生的数十亿的投资额，争议能够得以及时、高效地以不昂贵的方式解决是双方共同关注的、关乎切身利益的问题，无论是中国和非洲国家之间，还是中国企业和非洲国家之间，因为这样才能避免贸易和投资无谓的停滞③。

由此可以看出，投资争端解决机制在中非贸易关系中有着非常特别的重要地位。合理有效的争端解决机制对于吸引外国投资和发展双方经济增长的重要性是不可能被高估的。本文将简明地分析中非之间现有的争端解决机制，论述哪种机制最为有效，以及如何进一步发展争端解决机制。笔者将主要考虑下列两种机制：

国家法院

仲裁

作出这一区分的原因会在后文的论述中提到。

一、法院

最常见的情况是争端产生在投资者和非洲国家之间，显然这属于一国的国内事务。这是合乎逻辑的，考虑到争端通常发生在非洲国家的领土以内，在缺乏额外约定的情况下，国内法院对这样的争端具有管辖权。

但是毫无疑问，这种方式并非最理想的选择。传统的法院诉讼昂贵、耗时、烦琐并且低效，阻碍了商业纠纷的解决，而非促进④。

---

① This is Africa (2015) *Africa looks to step up its dispute resolution capabilities,* Article found at http://www.thisisafricaonlinc.com/Analysis/Africa-looks-to-step-up-its-dispute-resolution-capabilities?ct=true.

② Nachiketa Mittal (2014) Arbitration In Africa: ‘Chindia’ Perspective,The Conference On “Enhancing Business Opportunities In Africa: Role, Reality And Future Of Africa Related Arbitration”, November 2-4, 2014, Organised By The Atlanta International Arbitration Society, p. 19.

③ Joseph T. Mclaughlin, (1979) *Arbitration And Developing Countries*, The International Lawyer American Bar Association, pp.211-232 (Spring 1979).

④ Joseph T. Mclaughlin, (1979) Arbitration And Developing Countries, The International Lawyer American Bar Association 211, 211-232 (Spring 1979).

不仅如此，诉讼具有的本质特点便是对抗性，这种对抗性对商业关系可能是毁灭性的。显然，这很难有助于投资、贸易或投资关系的平稳发展，因此这种争端解决方式的发展趋势是下行方向。

同时，我们也不能忽视国家法院体系存在诉累繁重的可能性，这意味着纠纷可能在很久之后才可以被呈现到法官面前。这对于贸易流动来说是有害的。贸易不能为了争端解决停滞数月甚至数年，因为这最终会对双方造成巨大打击①。更重要的是，即使争端进入了诉讼程序，仍可能耗费大量时间，并且与之相伴的是结果的不确定性。这些都会打击国际贸易和投资的进行。就这点而言，我们需要一种更加公平、合理的争端解决机制。

最后，复杂的诉讼程序对于诉讼当事人可能较为陌生。更重要的是，外国的判决可能难以执行。非洲这片大陆上有着多种不同的法律体制和法律传统。这里有不同的基于特定信仰的习惯法，比如在西非和北非影响巨大的伊斯兰教和非洲传统宗教；有在东非地区使用的，来自英国殖民时期的普通法；还有南非的来自荷兰殖民时期的荷兰罗马法。

因此，我们需要一个统一的超越国内法的争端解决机制，一种基于国际法的机制，而非国内法怪异的变种。

仲裁已经被证明可以有效的实现这一目标，后文将对此进行论述。

二、仲裁

我们应当注意到，事实上所有双边贸易协定都会包含争端解决条款，并且经常将国际仲裁作为解决双方争议的首选方案。投资者和国家间争端的仲裁通常适用双方国家的双边贸易条约，依据国际贸易争端解决中心制定的规则进行②。这种做法背后的原因非常简单。仲裁降低了腐败，减少了国内法院倾向本国一方的可能性，避免了进展缓慢以及政局不稳的风险，政局不稳的风险已经被证明是对于在非投资具

① Peter D. Ehrenhaft, (1977) *Effective International Commercial Arbitration*, Law & Policy International Business, p.1191 (1977).

② Andrew Tweeddale & Keren Tweeddale, (2010) *Arbitration Of Commercial Disputes: International And English Law And Practice*, Oxford University Press at p.470.

有毁灭性的[①]。

从本质上看，仲裁的目标是为贸易双方提供快速有效、公平并且相对廉价的争端解决机制，这使得仲裁受到投资者和企业家的青睐。毫不意外，仲裁在全球投资争端领域快速发展，毋庸置疑，这是仲裁的适用法律、地点的灵活性以及私密性带来的结果。

不仅如此，仲裁允许当事方选择中立、具有必要的专业知识、来自第三国的仲裁员。另外，他们还可以选择案件适用的法律程序，即使最终执行被判定在他国进行[②]。虽然当事方可以选择仲裁适用的规则，多数时候他们会选择国际通行的规则，如联合国国际贸易法委员会颁布的规则。

与此同时，仲裁还因为其裁判终局性的特点而受到青睐。只有在非常特定的情况下，当事方可以上诉，因此仲裁会成为纠纷的终点。这为仲裁带来了终局性的优势，而诉讼通常并不具有这一特点[③]。尽管这一特点在仲裁裁判不公正、不合乎逻辑时可能成为双刃剑，败诉方可能被禁止通过向法院寻求救济而不得不接受这一裁判。但因为仲裁员通常是该领域的国际贸易纠纷专家，这可以减少错误和不理性裁判产生的机会，进而降低上述风险。

更重要的是，仲裁最大的优势在于，因为《承认及执行外国仲裁裁决公约》（《纽约公约》）的实施，仲裁结果更容易在境外执行。该公约要求成员国的法院认可仲裁协议的效力，在成员国承认并执行仲裁结果。受到广泛推崇的这一国际仲裁基础性的文件，可以适用于在本国领域外作出的仲裁结果，在本国内境内的承认和执行。

53 个非洲国家中的 32 个是这一公约的成员国，这证明了非洲国家对仲裁的认可度，这些国家将仲裁视为最有效的贸易、投资争端解决机制[④]。毫无疑问，正是因为此类纠纷可以通过仲裁解决，仲裁独立于当地政府，并且仲裁结果可以通过上述公

① This is Africa (2015) *Africa looks to step up its dispute resolution capabilities,* Article found at http://www.thisisafricaonline.com/Analysis/Africa-looks-to-step-up-its-dispute-resolution-capabilities?ct=true.

② ISDS Platform 2015, *Africa steps up dispute resolution,* Article found at http://isds.bilaterals.org/?africa-steps-up-dispute-resolution.

③ Allen and Allen (2016) *Arbitration: Advantages and Disadvantages,* Article found at http://www.allenandallen.com/blog/arbitration-advantages-and-disadvantages.html.

④ United Nations Commission on International Trade Law, *Status Convention on the Recognition and Enforcement of Foreign Arbitral Awards (New York, 1958)*, *http://www.uncitral.org/uncitral/en/uncitral_texts/arbitration/NYConvention_status.html.*

约机制得到执行，这大大激励了贸易和投资的进行。

但是，这并不意味着仲裁是解决中非之间投资纠纷的万灵药。这一体系仍有很大的进步空间，并且尚未在全部非洲国家中得以适用。

第一，大多国家已经批准了《承认和执行国际仲裁裁决公约》，但仍有不少国家尚未批准。这本身便对投资纠纷的成功解决形成了阻力，减缓了投资的进展，因为没有投资者会对在一个在得到不利于本国的仲裁结果后并不会执行这一结果的国家投资有信心[①]。

第二，许多非洲南部国家没有现代仲裁法律，只有4个国家设立了根据联合国国际贸易法委员会成立的仲裁机构（马达加斯加、毛里求斯、赞比亚和津巴布韦），以及另外两个将于近期启动颁布与《国际商事仲裁示范法》相一致的法律的立法程序（安哥拉和莫桑比克）。这一地区的6个普通法国家（博茨瓦纳、莱索托、马拉维、纳米比亚、南非和斯威士兰）有根据1950年《英国仲裁法》设立的仲裁立法[②]。

第三，关于“公共利益”的争议。依据1958年《联合国承认及执行外国仲裁裁决公约》第4条规定，当仲裁结果违背成员国本国的公共利益，本国法院可以拒绝执行在另一国作出的仲裁裁判。何为违背成员国本国公共利益的问题尚未被明确定义。当一国法院被要求执行某一裁判，法院要判断执行裁判所要满足的必要条件是否均已达到。为了判断裁判是否违背公共利益，法院可能自行决定或在听取了被告一方的辩护后作出决定[③]。这带来了一个真实的问题，即使当事方胜诉，这一裁判结果最终可能被执行国法院仅以违背公共利益这一难以捉摸的理由拒绝执行，而公共利益原则在非洲不同国家，甚至不同法官之间都有不同的解读。所以在19世纪，公共利益被比作“一匹可能使人远离法律的难以驾驭的马”[④]。

但是，尽管存在这些不足，与国内法院诉讼相比，国际仲裁显然仍可以被视为

① Nachiketa Mittal (2014) Arbitration In Africa: ‘Chindia’ Perspective,The Conference On “Enhancing Business Opportunities In Africa: Role, Reality And Future Of Africa Related Arbitration”, November 2-4, 2014, Organised By The Atlanta International Arbitration Society, p.9.

② M. C. Ogwezzy & S. A. Bello (2014) *Ohada's Common Court Of Justice And Arbitration: Is It A Supranational Institution For The Administration Of Commercial Disputes In Africa?* Open University Law Journal 1, at p.13.

③ Obinna Ozumba, (2012) *Enforcement Of Arbitral Awards: Does The Public Policy Exception Create Inconsistency?* University of Dundee. p.11.

④ Per Burough J in *Richardson V Mellish* (1824) ALL ER 258 at p.266.

更优的投资争端解决方式[①]。即使仲裁在非洲尚不完善，我们有充足的理由对其持乐观的态度。

无疑，非洲国家将逐渐接纳国际仲裁的原则。这一趋势始于1985年《国际商事仲裁示范法》（2006年修订）（《仲裁示范法》），并被《联合国国际贸易法委员会示范法》不断发展。许多非洲国家已经引入了基于《国际商事仲裁示范法》现代仲裁法律，并将其纳入国内立法。以津巴布韦为例，《仲裁示范法》整体已经作为本国《仲裁法》得到批准通过。

可喜可贺的是，17个非洲法语国家组成了OHADA，非洲商法统一组织。1993年10月17日，OHADA在路易士港（毛里求斯）由14个缔约国签署的国际条约设立而成。创立OHADA的理念来源于，为了非洲的发展，必须通过制定一套规制在非商业行为的安全合法的框架，健全非洲的法律体制的政治主张[②]。为了这一点，OHADA鼓励成员国设立共通的现代规则和程序，提倡通过位于科特迪瓦阿比让的普通仲裁法院进行仲裁。冲裁裁决可以在所有成员国内得到执行。

OHADA成员国通过引入《统一仲裁法》实现了法律的标准化。《统一仲裁法》（其主要内容类似于《仲裁示范法》）在各成员国内优于本国国内法。

更重要的是，非洲国家通过建立各自的仲裁中心，展示出了它们对于接纳仲裁作为争端解决方式的决心。1979年，根据1978年亚非法律协商组织多哈会议作出的在亚洲和非洲建立区域性国际商事仲裁中心的决定，埃及成立了由亚非法律协商组织赞助的，独立的非营利国际组织国际商事仲裁开罗中心（CRCICA）。成立这些中心的目的是，通过合理运用有效且经济的方式，帮助解决贸易和投资过程中的纠纷，从而促进亚非国家经济发展[③]。

1998年，在亚非法律协商组织的赞助下，尼日利亚的拉各斯国际商事仲裁区域性中心的成立就是一个进步。这一机构的授权声明如下：

“一个非营利、独立的国际仲裁机构，其目标是为国际商业交易过程中产生的争端提供一个中立的解决平台，通过仲裁以及其他争端解决方式，如调解、斡旋等，

---

① Won Kidane (2014) *China-African Investment Treaties: Old Rules, New Challenges*, FORDHAM INT'L L.J. 1035 (2014).

② Eversheds (2002) *Business Law In Africa – Ohada And The Harmonization Process*, Kogan Page Ltd. (2002).

③ Cairo Regional Centre for International Commercial Arbitration (2014) *About Us*, Article found at http://crcica.org.eg/factsheet.html.

解决争议；为了非洲及非洲以外的贸易、商业和投资中的各方的利益[①]。”

2012 年，卢旺达政府主动成立了基加利国际仲裁中心（KIAC），为了帮助本地区和海外投资者免于法院程序解决纠纷。卢旺达的政治稳定性和良好的政府治理使其成为国际仲裁机构的不二地点[②]。

不仅如此，大多非洲国家是依据《解决国家与他国国民间投资争端公约》（《ICSID 公约》）成立的解决投资争端国际中心的成员，已有 44 个非洲国家对其进行了批准。这是一个被视为领先的国际化的国际投资争端机构。这一公约最核心的条款之一是，缔约国必须自动承认并执行 ICSID 作出的金钱给付决定。非金钱给付决定也应被自动承认，但应通过其他方式保证其有效执行，如通过《纽约公约》[③]。

上述论述表明了非洲国家接纳现代仲裁程序的趋势。无疑，假以时日，仲裁或许真的可以成为非洲国家和中国投资者之间解决投资争议的万灵药。

三、结语

显然，目前中国在非投资不断增长的这一趋势将不可避免地带来更多投资者和受投资国间的争议。更加清楚的一点是，我们越来越需要找寻一套统一的解决国际投资争端的方法。正如上文所提到的，国内法院显然无法胜任这一工作。让西方仲裁中心解决发生在非洲大陆上的争端同样不可取。

因此，目前许多非洲国家已经成为《解决国家与他国国民间投资争端公约》和《国际商事仲裁示范法》等国际争端解决公约的成员国。我们还应看到像是 OHADA 成员国为建立一套统一的仲裁法律，并将这套法律与其他现代国际仲裁法律纳入其国内法的尝试。这一趋势势必将提高中国投资者对于他们在非洲投资的信心，吸引更多对非洲的投资。

---

① Regional Centre for International Commercial Arbitration, (2016) *About RCICAL*, found at http://www.rcicalagos.org/status.html.

② Global Arbitration Review (2016) *The Kigali International Arbitration Centre*, Article found at *http://globalarbitrationreview.com/regional-arbitration/5/category/89/region/20/entry/317/*.

③ Stuart Bruce and Juliette Huard-Bourgois (2016) *Maximising investment protection in Africa: The Role of investment treaties and investment arbitration in Africa*, Article found at *http://www.kwm.com/en/ae/knowledge/insights/role-of-investment-treaties-and-investment-arbitration-in-Africa-20150316*

与此同时，非洲国家在非洲大陆上建立各自的仲裁中心的行为应当得到赞许。无疑，这将在加快仲裁速度的同时大大降低仲裁成本。

但是，除了这些成就，为了真正实现快速有效地解决国际投资争端，避免破坏商业关系的目标，我们还需要一些非洲国家将其国内法与现代仲裁手段相统一，并批准通过国际投资争端解决文件。

不过，我们可以清楚地看到，中非之间的争端解决机制整体上已经得到了很大的进步。有了更多非洲国家的政治意愿，我们没有理由不保持乐观的态度。

The Analysis of Investment Dispute Resolution Mechanism between China and Africa

Author: Angeline Munyeriwa①

There is no question that trade and investment between Africa and China have soared during the last decade.② Since 2000 China-Africa trade has grown at an average annual rate of 33.5 per cent rising from US$55 billion in 2006 to around US$107 billion in 2008, accounting for 4.5 per cent of China's total trade and surpassing the US$100 billion trade target set for 2010 at the 2006 Forum on China- Africa Cooperation (FOCAC).③ By 2012, it had reportedly jumped to just under $200bn. In 2015, bilateral trade was expected to surpass $300 billion. Meanwhile, according to Standard Bank, Chinese investment in Africa was projected to reach $50bn in 2015, a 70% rise on figures from 2009.④ It is estimated that as many as 1600 Chinese companies are operating in Africa at present, in about 50 African countries.⑤

However, this trade between the two continents has moved from the traditional import and export business. Most of the trade is now facilitated through Bilateral Investment Treaties (BIT).

---

① Ms Munyeriwa, is a Corporate Affairs Officer in the Office of the Prosecutor General in Zimbabwe.

② Roland Amoussou-Guenou, (2014) *Comparative Regime Of Arbitration In Africa (OHADA) And Selected Asian Countries*, LEGALINK NEWSLETTER, 1(1ST Quarter 2014), http://www.vovan-lawgroup.com/resources/COMPARATIVE%20REGIME%20OF%20ARBITRATION_Legalink%20Global%20Newsletter_1stquarter_2014.Pdf (Last Accessed On September 15, 2014).

③ *China And Africa: Friends With Benefits* East Asia Forum, 17 February 2010 Article found at http://www.eastasiaforum.Org/2010/02/17/china-and-africa-friends-with-benefits/.

④ The African Banker (2015) *China targets African support in Western institutions,* Article found at http://africanbusinessmagazine.com/african-banker/china-targets-african-support-in-western-institutions/#sthash.s4JBG8Jw.dpuf.

⑤ Roland Amoussou-Guenou, (2014) *Comparative Regime Of Arbitration In Africa (OHADA) And Selected Asian Countries*, LEGALINK NEWSLETTER, 1 (1ST Quarter 2014), http://www.vovan-lawgroup.com/resources/COMPARATIVE%20REGIME%20OF%20ARBITRATION_Legalink%20Global%20Newsletter_1stquarter_2014.Pdf (Last Accessed On September 15, 2014).

African countries, which are largely developing countries, now look for foreign investors to invest in their countries, in particular China which has shown a great keenness to open up investment opportunities in Africa and growing its own economy at the same time. These investors could be an outright private commercial entity or semi-state owned entity which would invest in the host-State in a variety of pursuits. Such areas of investment may include the manufacturing industry, telecommunication sector, infrastructure sector, information-technology industry and so on.①

Of course such investment is mutually beneficial for both parties. China has a growing economy which requires resources and raw materials to support it, while African countries may have the resources, they do not have the capital to exploit them and develop their own economies. Bilateral Investment Treaties provide a bridging mechanism allowing both sides to get what they need from each other.

Indeed and in this regard, the authors Dolzer and Schreuer observe that:

> *"The most significant trends in the evolution of BIT practice in the past decade concerns the negotiation of BITs by Asian states……. China has concluded 117 treaties between 1982 and 2006".*②

While the aim of BITs is to increase inflows of foreign direct investment into African countries, as well as to develop the economy of the State in which the investment is made, they also protect the interests of the State that made the investment into the African country, in this case China.③ Such protection may come in the form of clauses that require :

- Fair and equitable treatment
- Full protection and security
- No expropriation without compensation
- "Most favored nation" and "national" treatment
- Free repatriation of investment and returns
- No arbitrary or discriminatory treatment
- "Umbrella" clause
- Substantive protections reach executive, legislative and judicial actions

---

① Nachiketa Mittal (2014) *Arbitration In Africa: 'Chindia' Perspective,* p.3 The Conference On "Enhancing Business Opportunities In Africa: Role, Reality And Future Of Africa Related Arbitration", November 2-4, 2014, Organised By The Atlanta International Arbitration Society.

② R. Dolzer & C. Schreuer, *Principles Of International Investment Law*, Oxford University Press, p.480 (2nd Ed. 2008).

③ Simon Greenberg Christopher Kee & J. Romesh Weeramantry (2012) *International Commercial Arbitration: An Asia-Pacific Perspective,* Cambridge University Press, p.478.

But, as foreign direct investment flows increase, so too do the number of legal disputes arising in the continent, both between investors and the state, and between parties engaging in commercial transactions.① This is particularly true of investment agreements since they are in the unique position of being largely long term. Whereas a commercial transaction typically consists of a one-time exchange of goods or services and money, the decision to invest in a foreign country initiates a long-term relationship between the investor and the host country.②

Considering the amounts that are involved in investments through BITs, some running into billions, it is important and in the interests of both parties, be it China and the African State, or a Chinese company and the African State, that any disputes be resolved promptly, efficiently, and inexpensively so that the flow of trade and investment is not unduly interrupted. ③

In this light therefore, investment dispute mechanisms have achieved a special importance in the investment relationship between China and Africa. After all, the importance of an appropriate and effective dispute resolution mechanism, to attract foreign investment and foster economic development and growth on both sides cannot be over emphasized. This paper will therefore briefly but concisely consider the available investment dispute resolution mechanisms between Africa and China, to see which one is the most efficient and how the investment dispute mechanism can be improved. In particular it will consider the two main dispute resolution mechanisms:

a) The national Courts

b) Arbitration

The reason for this delimitation will become obvious as this paper progresses.

The National Courts

The first and most obvious scenario is when a dispute arises between the investor and the African State, which is obviously a domestic matter. This is only logical considering that the dispute almost always arises in the territory of the African State, thus making it, in the absence of an ouster clause, to fall within the jurisdiction of the local courts.

---

① This is Africa (2015) *Africa looks to step up its dispute resolution capabilities,* Article found at http://www.thisisafricaonline.com/Analysis/Africa-looks-to-step-up-its-dispute-resolution-capabilities?ct=true.

② Nachiketa Mittal (2014) Arbitration In Africa: 'Chindia' Perspective,The Conference On "Enhancing Business Opportunities In Africa: Role, Reality And Future Of Africa Related Arbitration", November 2-4, 2014, Organised By The Atlanta International Arbitration Society, p.19.

③ Joseph T. Mclaughlin, (1979) *Arbitration And Developing Countries*, The International Lawyer American Bar Association, pp.211-232 (Spring 1979).

However, there is no doubt that this method of dispute resolution is less than ideal. Traditional litigation in a national court can be a costly, time-consuming, cumbersome and inefficient process, which obstructs, rather than facilitates, the resolution of business disputes.①

Added to that, litigation, by its very nature is inherently adversarial and thus can destroy the business relationship. That would of course hardly be conducive for the smooth flow of an investment or trade or investment relationship, thus rendering this method of dispute resolution a slippery slope.

At the same time one cannot discount the possibility of overcrowding in the national courts and a backlog in matters, which means the dispute would be heard after a long time. This would be detrimental for the flow of commerce. Trade cannot be suspended for months or even years pending the hearing of the dispute, that would ultimately prove financially ruinous for both parties involved.② More importantly even if the matter is finally heard, it is likely to take too long and that coupled with the uncertainity of the outcome represents problems which discourage international trade and investment. As such a more equitable and expedient way of dispute resolution is needed.

Finally, the intricacies of the national procedures may be unknown to one or more of the parties. Moreover, foreign judgments may be difficult to enforce. African countries have varied legal systems and traditions operating within the continent. There are various customary laws, laws based on certain faiths for example Islam and African traditional religions which are strong in West and North Africa, while common law which is a legacy of historical and colonial ties to England dominates the East and parts of Southern Africa and Roman Dutch Law, from the Dutch colonialists being dominant in South Africa.

All this calls out for a unified dispute resolution mechanism that can rise above domestic laws. A method that is based on international law, which is not premised on the whims and variances of domestic law.

Arbitration has proved effective at achieving this goal as will be demonstrated.

Arbitration

It is important to note that virtually all BITs will include dispute settlement clauses, frequently by international arbitration as the primary method of resolving any disagreements between the parties. Arbitration of investor-state disputes often follows the terms of bilateral investment treaties between countries, usually according to rules developed by the International Centre for the Settlement of

① Joseph T. Mclaughlin, (1979) Arbitration And Developing Countries, The International Lawyer American Bar Association 211, 211-232 (Spring 1979).

② Peter D. Ehrenhaft, (1977) *Effective International Commercial Arbitration*, Law & Policy International Business, p.1191 (1977).

Investment Disputes.[①] The reason is very simple. Arbitration reduces the possibility of corruption, of local courts favoring the home side, the slowness of proceedings and the risk of political instability, which has often proved destructive for investments in Africa.[②]

Arbitration by its very nature aims to provide commercial parties with efficient, expeditious, fair and relatively inexpensive dispute resolution mechanisms making it an attractive and preferred dispute resolution process for many investors and entrepreneurs. Not surprisingly arbitration is growing as a means of investment dispute resolution growing globally, undoubtedly because of benefits such as, flexibility, choice of rules and venue, privacy and confidentiality.

Furthermore, arbitration allows parties to select neutral arbitrators, with the necessary expertise, from third-party countries. In addition, they may select the 'seat' – the set of legal procedures – against which they want their case to be judged upon, even if the actual proceedings are held in another country.[③] At the same time while the rules of Arbitration and the parties may choose their own, most parties usually opt for the internationally accepted rules, such as those of the United Nations Commission on International Trade Law.

At the same time arbitration is even more attractive due to its final nature. There are very limited opportunities for either side to appeal, so the arbitration will be the end of the dispute. This gives finality to the arbitration award that is not often present with a trial decision.[④] Though this admittedly may prove to be a double edged sword, if the arbitrator's award is unfair or illogical, the losing party may well be stuck with it and barred forever from airing the underlying claim in court. However, this risk is mitigated by the fact that arbitrators in international commercial disputes are usually experts in the field and thus reducing the chances of errors and unreasonable decisions.

More importantly, one of the greatest advantages of arbitration lies in that the arbitration awards are much easier to enforce in other states than those of domestic courts, largely due to the Convention on the Recognition and Enforcement of Foreign Arbitral Awards, also known as the New York Convention. The Convention requires courts of contracting states to give effect to private agreements to arbitrate and to recognize and enforce arbitration awards made in other contracting states. Widely considered the foundational instrument for international arbitration, it applies to arbitrations which are not considered as domestic awards in the state where recognition and enforcement is sought.

---

① Andrew Tweeddale & Keren Tweeddale, (2010) *Arbitration Of Commercial Disputes: International And English Law And Practice*, Oxford University Press at p.470.

② This is Africa (2015) *Africa looks to step up its dispute resolution capabilities,* Article found at http://www.thisisafricaonline.com/Analysis/Africa-looks-to-step-up-its-dispute-resolution-capabilities?ct=true

③ ISDS Platform 2015, *Africa steps up dispute resolution,* Article found at http://isds.bilaterals.org/?africa-steps-up-dispute-resolution.

④ Allen and Allen (2016) *Arbitration: Advantages and Disadvantages,* Article found at http://www.allenandallen.com/blog/arbitration-advantages-and-disadvantages.html

Tellingly about 32 out of 53 African countries are parties to this s convention thus proving the increasing recognition by African States of arbitration as the most effective trade-investment dispute resolution mechanism.① Undoubtedly, it is this knowledge that such disputes can be resolved by mechanisms independent from the local authorities, and that decisions of such mechanisms are enforceable, which incentivizes such trade and investment.

However this not to say, that arbitration is the panacea to all investments disputes between Africa and China. The system is still far from perfect and has not been universally utilized by all African states.

As a starting point, most have ratified the Convention on the Enforcement of Foreign Arbitral Awards (the New York Convention), a significant number have not. This on its own hinders the successful resolution of investment disputes, while at the same time slowing down investment, since no investor would be ultimately confident about investing in a state that would not enforce an arbitral award if it is granted against. ②

Secondly, many of the countries in Southern Africa do not have modern arbitration laws only four have adopted arbitration laws based on the UNCITRAL Model Law (Madagascar, Mauritius, Zambia and Zimbabwe), with two more (Angola and Mozambique) recently having enacted legislation aligned to the Model Law although not strictly adopting the Model Law. The six common law countries in the region (Botswana, Lesotho, Malawi, Namibia, South Africa and Swaziland) have arbitration legislation based primarily on the 1950 English Arbitration Act. ③

Thirdly, there is what can be described as the "public policy" controversy Article V of the UN Convention on the Recognition and Enforcement of Foreign Arbitral Awards 1958 which provides that a domestic Court may refuse to enforce an arbitral award granted in another country, on the basis that the award is contrary to the public policy of the contracting state. The problem then is what constitutes the public policy of the enforcement State has not yet been precisely defined. When a national court is called upon to enforce an award, it has to determine if formal requirements necessary to make it enforceable have been complied with. In the process of doing so, it may determine on its

---

① United Nations Commission on International Trade Law, *Status Convention on the Recognition and Enforcement of Foreign Arbitral Awards (New York, 1958)*, *http://www.uncitral.org/uncitral/en/uncitral_texts/arbitration/NYConvention_status.html.*

② Nachiketa Mittal (2014) Arbitration In Africa: 'Chindia' Perspective,The Conference On "Enhancing Business Opportunities In Africa: Role, Reality And Future Of Africa Related Arbitration", November 2-4, 2014, Organised By The Atlanta International Arbitration Society, p.9.

③ M. C. Ogwezzy & S. A. Bello (2014) *Ohada's Common Court Of Justice And Arbitration: Is It A Supranational Institution For The Administration Of Commercial Disputes In Africa?* Open University Law Journal 1, at p.13.

own motion or upon a defense raised by the respondent, if the award is contrary to public policy.① This raises a real challenge that, while parties may successfully litigate, ultimately their award may not be enforced by the domestic courts simply on the basis of the murky public policy doctrine which may vary from African country to African country, or even from one judge to another. Not surprisingly in the 19th century public policy was compared to an 'unruly horse that may lead one away from sound law' ②

Despite these shortcomings however, saying that international arbitration is a better means of investment dispute settlement is stating the obvious, when the alternative is domestic court litigation.③ While arbitration in Africa may be less than perfect there is a lot of reasons for optimism.

Slowly but surely, African states are looking to embrace the principles of international arbitration. The path that has been taken is through the Model Law on International Commercial Arbitration 1985 (amended in 2006) (the "Model Law"), developed by the United Nations Commission on International Trade Law Model Law. Many of African countries have adopted modern arbitration laws based on the UNCITRAL Model Law and incorporated it as part of their Legislation. In Zimbabwe for example the Model Law as a whole has been enacted as national legislation under the Arbitration Act [Chapter 7:15].

Encouragingly, a group of 17, primarily French-speaking, countries in Africa have banded together to form OHADA, the Organisation for the Harmonisation of Business Law in Africa. OHADA was created by a Treaty signed in Port-Louis (Mauritius) in October 17, 1993 originally by fourteen African States. The idea behind the creation of OHADA sprang from a political will to strengthen the African legal system by enacting a secure and legal framework for the conduct of business in Africa, which is deemed necessary for the development of the Continent.④ In that regard OHADA encourages the adoption of common modern rules and procedures by member States and promotes arbitration through the Common Court of Justice and Arbitration in Abidjan, Côte d'Ivoire. An arbitral award can be enforced in all member states.

OHADA countries have also standardized laws on arbitration through each of their adoption of the Uniform Act on Arbitration. The Uniform Act (which closely resembles the principles enshrined in the Model Law), takes priority over the national laws of OHADA members.

Furthermore, African countries have shown their commitment to embrace arbitration as a method of dispute resolution by creating their own arbitration centres. In 1979 Egypt established

① Obinna Ozumba, (2012) *Enforcement Of Arbitral Awards: Does The Public Policy Exception Create Inconsistency?* University of Dundee. p.11.

② Per Burough J in *Richardson V Mellish* (1824) ALL ER 258 at p.266.

③ Won Kidane (2014) *China-African Investment Treaties: Old Rules, New Challenges*, FORDHAM INT'L L.J. 1035 (2014).

④ Eversheds (2002) *Business Law In Africa – Ohada And The Harmonization Process*, Kogan Page Ltd. (2002).

the Cairo Regional Centre for International Commercial Arbitration (the "CRCICA") which is an independent non-profit international organization, under the auspices of the Asian African Legal Consultative Organization ("AALCO"), in pursuance of AALCO's decision taken at the Doha Session in 1978 to establish regional Centres for international commercial arbitration in Asia and Africa. The purpose of these Centres is to contribute and, and enrich the progress of the economic development scheme in both Asian and African countries by helping settle trade and investment disputes, through fair operations of expeditious and economical procedures. ①

In Nigeria the founding of the Regional Centre for International Commercial Arbitration - Lagos, in 1989, under the auspices of the Asian African Legal Consultative Organization (AALCO), was a positive step. It states its mandate as:

> *"a non profit, independent, international Arbitral Institution, whose purpose is to provide among other things a neutral venue for the resolution of disputes arising out of international commercial transactions by Arbitration and other Alternative Dispute Resolution (ADR) methods such as Conciliation/Mediation; for the benefit of parties engaged in trade, commerce and investments with and* ***within the African region.****" (emphasis)* ②

The year 2012, also saw the opening of the Kigali International Arbitration Centre (KIAC) as an initiative Government of Rwanda in order to help regional and overseas investors to resolve their disputes without need to go to the Courts. Rwanda's political stability and good governance, make it a prime location for carrying out international arbitration. ③

Furthermore most of the African countries are part of the International Centre for Settlement of Investment Disputes (ICSID) which was set up under the Convention on the Settlement of Investment Disputes between States and Nationals of Other Member States (ICSID Convention), which 44 of Africa's states have ratified. It is considered to be the leading international institution for the resolution of international investment disputes. One of the core terms of this treaty is that contracting States must automatically recognize and enforce ICSID monetary awards. Non-monetary awards are also automatically recognized, but they would have to be enforced by other means, such as the New

---

① Cairo Regional Centre for International Commercial Arbitration (2014) *About Us*, Article found at http://crcica.org.eg/factsheet.html.

② Regional Centre for International Commercial Arbitration, (2016) *About RCICAL*, found at http://www.rcicalagos.org/status.html.

③ Global Arbitration Review (2016) *The Kigali International Arbitration Centre,* Article found at *http://globalarbitrationreview.com/regional-arbitration/5/category/89/region/20/entry/317/.*

York Convention. ①

All the above indicate a trend by African countries to adopt modern arbitration procedures. There is no doubt that with time arbitration may indeed prove to be the panacea to investment dispute resolution between the African Continent and Chinese investors.

Conclusion

It is clear that the current trend of increasing Chinese investments in Africa will inevitably lead to more disputes arising between the investor and the State being invested in. What is even clearer is a growing need to find a uniform method of settling international investment disputes. Domestic Courts are obviously unsuited for the job as pointed out above. Neither is it desirable that all investment disputes that arise on the African continent are settled in Western Arbitration Centres.

It is therefore encouraging that many African States are now parties to international dispute resolution treaties like the Convention on the Settlement of Investment Disputes between States and Nationals of Other Member States (ICSID Convention) and the UNCITRAL Model Law. This must also be taken in the context of some countries like the OHADA group of countries, trying to establish uniform arbitration laws in their member states and also incorporating modern international arbitration law as part of their own domestic legislation. This trend will undoubtedly increase Chinese investor confidence, in the security of their investments in African States and incentivise even more investment in Africa.

At the same time, African States must be lauded for establishing their own arbitration centres within the African continent. Undoubtedly this will increase the speed of arbitration while at the same time lessening costs.

However, despite all these achievements there is still a need for some African countries to align their laws with modern arbitration techniques and also ratify international investment dispute instruments if the goal of settling international investments disputes quickly and expeditiously without ruining business relationships is to be achieved.

On the whole however it is clear that dispute resolution mechanisms between Africa and China have advanced. With more political will on the part of African countries, there is no reason why a sense of optimism should not be retained.

① Stuart Bruce and Juliette Huard-Bourgois (2016) *Maximising investment protection in Africa: The Role of investment treaties and investment arbitration in Africa*, Article found at *http://www.kwm.com/en/ae/knowledge/insights/role-of-investment-treaties-and-investment-arbitration-in-africa-20150316*.

中非投资争端解决机制研究

作者：Moza Mussa Kassubi　译者：黄琼慧

一、导言

近些年来，随着科学和技术的飞速发展，经济一体化程度加深。国家间通过双边或多边协定，进行了大量的技术转移与交换。全球化给世界带来了跨国投资的机会。在很多外国投资人眼中，非洲有很多的投资机会。据记录，截至 2013 年，亚洲在非洲已有大量涉及各领域的投资，包括通讯业、制造业、金融服务业、保险业、石油、天然气、开采业和农业。[①]

（一）中国与非洲国家之间的投资

中国经济飞速发展，技术也处于亚洲、世界的领先位置。这让它成为几个通过投资向非洲以及世界其他地区转移技术并且广受欢迎的国家之一。非洲国家普遍对中国直接对外投资持欢迎态度，并且具有大量成功吸引到这些投资的经验。中国在非洲投资的例子包括但不限于：招商局国际有限公司（香港）购得吉布提港口股份有限公司（吉布提）23.5% 的股份、中国海洋石油有限公司购得塔洛石油于乌干达的股份、中国石化（中国）购得阿帕奇公司在埃及业务的 33% 股份。[②] 根据《坦桑尼亚投资法》[Cap. 38 R. E 2002] 第 4、5、6 条的规定，当所有投资活动相互协调配合时，需要设立一个一站式投资中心。这个中心的核心作用是通过协调、鼓励、促进和便捷投资来

① Brian King and Elliot Friedman, International Dispute Resolution in Africa. *Asian International Dispute Resolution Webnar Series*, Freshfields Bruckhaus Deringer, p.2.

② Brian King and Elliot Friedman, International Dispute Resolution in Africa. *Asian International Dispute Resolution Webnar Series*, Freshfields Bruckhaus Deringer, p.2.

创造一个有利于本国和外国投资者的环境，并在投资政策和相关事务上给政府提供建议。

投资法规定了外国投资者可以从国内获取信贷。该法第 25 条规定如下：

（1）第 2 条中所述经营企业的外国投资者可以从国内银行和金融机构获取信贷，其限度将由坦桑尼亚银行和中心协商并考虑经营企业中外国资本数额而定。

（2）根据上述第（1）款获取信贷的外国投资者须在其贷款申请中保证该信贷资金专门用于其投资活动。

（3）根据本条规定提供贷款的银行可指派其官员或代理来验证根据第（1）款中所得到的贷款是否正当使用。

这些努力使得非洲国家和中国以及世界的贸易关系成为可能。另一方面，在商机激增的情况下，很多非洲公司在中国成立。随中非交流而来的是贸易争端的出现，主要是合同、信用证、保函以及劳动方面争端。

（二）外国投资法律保护的概述

为了良好的投资环境，相关国家必须保证有完善的法律制度保护投资者不受风险之害。但是应当注意的是，在大多数情况下，投资受限于投资者和政府之间签订的协议。在协议中，双方都会有自己的规划。双边和多边投资协定也为投资者提供了很多保护，使他们能免受政府行为、立法和司法程序的限制。本论文拟分析国际通用标准和全球双边投资协定下的中非争端解决机制。

关于非洲争端解决法律实践的讨论将以坦桑尼亚的经验为实施不同双边或多边投资协定的法律框架的案例。

二、中非投资争端解决机制

投资争端解决减轻了在运营企业过程中所产生的风险。此处的企业是指每个投资人和政府之间的投资协议中所对应的投资对象。投资争端解决机制很多，可通过投资协定、投资法和国际商事仲裁。中国投机争端解决机制主要是双边投资协定。大多数情况下，条约假定投资者和东道国之间存在关于争端解决的协定。

截至 2011 年 10 月，中国已经和 45 个非洲国家缔结了双边投资协定，并在 49

个非洲国家进行投资。① 这个数字预计会随着油、气等新投资机会的出现和发展而上升。同时，企业的数量也会有所增加。双边投资协定一般会约定在争端所涉及的投资企业所在国的法律框架下解决争端。很多非洲国家的投资法都明确规定，外国投资者和东道国之间的争端须先在东道国的法院或仲裁机构进行审理。这里的东道国常指合同履行地。比如，安哥拉《石油活动法》规定，在安哥拉发生的争端均须依照安哥拉法律仲裁解决。②

在坦桑尼亚联合共和国，投资争端受制于不同法律，但基本法律是《坦桑尼亚投资法》[Cap. 38 R. E 2002] 和《仲裁法》[Cap. 15 R. E 2002]。

适用《坦桑尼亚投资法》的投资争端受制于该法第 23 条的规定。该法第 23 条提供了两种适用于投资者和中心之间争端以及投资者和政府之间争端的不同机制。协商是其中一种，当协商失败时即可采用仲裁的方式。

该条文规定如下：

（1）如果外国投资者和中心或政府在经营企业方面发生争端，则须通过协商努力使争端得以友好解决。

（2）如果外国投资者和中心或政府在经营企业方面发生争端经协商不能解决的话，须按照双方同意的以下方法提交仲裁，就是说：

（a）按照坦桑尼亚关于投资者仲裁法进行；

（b）按照国际中心关于解决投资争端的仲裁程序的规则进行；

（c）在联合共和国政府和投资来源国政府同意的任何双边或多边投资保护协议的框架内解决。

上述法条不意味着任何在普通法院的诉讼。其目的是承认每个投资合同中投资者的权利并维持投资者和政府之间良好的商业关系。该法强调，虽然仲裁和普通法院的诉讼不同，是一种友好解决贸易争端的方式，但在将争端提交仲裁之前仍须尽全力协商解决。该条文第 2 款（b）、（c）项也考虑到被国际投资争端解决中心所普遍接受的程序规则。中非，特别是中国和坦桑尼亚联邦共和国之间的投资争端解决对上述规则的适用可在中心查到。举例来说，原告渣打银行（香港）和被告坦桑尼

① A Brief Analysis of the Dispute Arising from China-African Civil and Commercial Transactions. A Paper submitted at the first China–African Think Tank Forum held in Hangzhou on 27-29 October, 2011.

② A Brief Analysis of the Dispute Arising from China-African Civil and Commercial Transactions. A Paper submitted at the first China–African Think Tank Forum held in Hangzhou on 27-29 October, 2011.

亚供电公司间在国际投资争端解决中心的 ARB/10/20 号案件的仲裁程序。该案件于 2014 年 2 月 12 日送达双方。

《仲裁法》[Cap. 15 R. E 2002]第 4 条规定了争端出现时仲裁程序的开始。

第 4 条　除非另有规定，递交的文件未经法院许可不可撤，并且视为将附表一条款包含在内，在适用于提交文件的引证的限度内。

此处递交的文件不仅包括本国投资和政府之间争端，还包括外国投资者和政府之间的争端。但是，《仲裁法》并没有设立任何独立的仲裁庭，所以争端常诉诸国家建设委员会。顾名思义，国家建设委员会处理的是建设行业相关事宜。

《仲裁法》第 28、29 条以及附表四的条款认可了关于外国裁决执行的国际文书，并规定了登记程序和外国仲裁裁决的执行。法案还认可了双边协定和仲裁裁决的约束力。根据法案，虽然依照其性质，外国仲裁裁决是必然有约束力的，但它依然要受限于《仲裁法》第 30 条的规定。鉴于这三个法条涵盖了许多非洲法律的架构，再现它们是有价值的。

第 28 条　第四章的适用

（1）本章条款适用于所有 1924 年 7 月 28 日后所做的裁决——

（a）按照仲裁协议履行，附表三的议定书适用于前述协议；

（b）发生在受外国仲裁判决执行公约缔约国管辖的主体之间，本法案附件四引用了前述公约；适用本部分条款的裁决属于“外国裁决”。

（2）本部分条款不适用于任何受坦桑尼亚法律管辖的仲裁协议。

第 29 条　外国判决的效力

（1）按照本章规定，外国裁决可以在高等法院凭诉讼或本法案第 16 条的规定执行。

（2）依照本章规定，可执行的外国裁决在任何目的下对裁决所涉当事人都有约束力，并且当事人可以在进行抗辩、债务相抵或其他法律程序时，可依赖该裁决。此外，本章中执行外国裁决的引证均可解释为裁决可依靠的引证。

第 30 条　外国裁决执行的条款

（1）要使外国仲裁在本章规定下可执行，它必须

（a）和仲裁协议相一致，并且依照它受管辖的法律，该协议是合法的；

（b）由约定中所述的仲裁庭或由经双方合意选择的仲裁庭所做；

（c）仲裁程序合法；

（d）在裁决作出的国家为最终裁决；

（e）依照坦桑尼亚法律，裁决所设事由经仲裁解决是合法的，并且该裁决的执行不得违背公共政策和坦桑尼亚法律。

（2）依照本款规定，当法院发现以下事由时，外国裁决不可执行：

（a）该裁决已被仲裁发生国宣告无效；

（b）若裁决执行所针对的对象没有在一定时间内得到仲裁程序的通知，导致他无法参与仲裁，或该对象无民事行为能力，或该对象没能得到恰当的代理；或

（c）该裁决没有解决提出的所有问题，或者在仲裁协议范围外的问题上作出了裁决：如果裁决没有解决提出的所有问题，法院如认为适当，可以暂缓该裁决的执行，或在执行申请人提供了法院认为合适的担保后，执行裁决。

（3）如果外国裁决执行抗议人能以除证明本条第（1）款（a）、（b）、（c）项不存在或本条第（2）款（b）、（c）项规定的事由存在以外的理由对抗裁决的合法性，法院可在它认为合适的情况下拒绝执行裁决，或暂缓听证，直到法院认为抗议人已经享有足够的时间采取必要行动，使有资质的仲裁庭判决该裁决无效。

第 31 条　证据

（1）申请执行的一方必须出示——

（a）裁决原件或在裁决作出国依法获得的真实复印件；

（b）证明裁决是最终裁决的证据；

（c）证明裁决是外国裁决并且符合第（1）款（a）、（b）、（c）项要件的证据；

（2）当按照第（1）款规定需要出示的文件是外文文件时，申请执行的一方有义务出示经其所属国外交或领事官员确认正确无误的翻译或采取依据坦桑尼亚法能确认其翻译正确性的其他措施。

（3）根据本条规定，法院可以依据执行申请方依照本章规定提交的证据来制定规则。

尽管以协商或 / 和仲裁的机制解决投资争端比通过法院解决更为便捷，这两种争端解决机制仍面临不少挑战。

三、中非投资争端解决机制所面临的挑战

（一）本国法院对仲裁程序的介入

前述法条中所规定的要件就是一个典型的阻碍非洲和中国以及其他和非洲有经

济投资关系的国家之间的双边投资协定的实施的例子。投资争端机制面临的主要挑战是本国法院对仲裁的过多干涉。在很多非洲国家，法院被给予了极大的权力介入仲裁程序，甚至在仲裁开始之前就可以介入。比如坦桑尼亚《仲裁法》[Cap. 15 R. E 2002]第 6 条就规定了法院有权介入仲裁程序。法条是这样规定的：

第 6 条　暂缓诉讼程序的权力

当申请方就约定的事项向被申请方提起仲裁时，法律程序参与方可以在提交书状或采取其他行动时或在此之前，向法院申请暂缓诉讼程序；当法院发现没有充分的理由不按照提交的文件解决该事项，并且，在程序开始后至今，原告也有准备并乐意为仲裁的恰当开展做任何有需要的事情时，可以作出暂缓诉讼程序的决定。

法院有权力在仲裁程序开始后控制仲裁程序，包括在仲裁双方对仲裁员的选择有分歧时，最终决定谁来做仲裁员。[①] 其他权力还包括延长仲裁程序开始的时间，[②] 延长作出最终裁决的时间，[③] 决定再审 [④] 以及在发现仲裁员有不当行为或裁决是通过不恰当手段获得的。[⑤]

矛盾的是，法院干涉是为了保证裁决的公正和仲裁程序的恰当和准确，但另一方面，大部分国内法院常因其人员涉及腐败行为、不诚实正直等收到控诉。为了实现有不良动机一方的利益而滥用权力的危险始终存在。

值得注意的是，虽然仲裁的最终裁决等同于法院的可执行判决，[⑥] 但在很多非洲国家，若想仲裁裁决可执行，须先登记裁决，并且被执行的对象必须得到质疑存疑仲裁的机会。[⑦] 对于那些被东道国认可且依据国内法可被执行的外国裁决仍面临严格的条件，这些条件有时被认为是一种拖延战术。有些法院被认为违背了双边或多边协定，甚至违背了缔约国公约的国际义务。

（二）独立仲裁庭和投资争端解决机构的缺失

中非投资争端解决机制的高效实施还面临着另一个挑战，那就是司法外的处理

---

① Sections 8 and 18 of the Arbitration Act, [Cap. 15 R. E 2002].

② Section 7 of the Arbitration Act, [Cap. 15 R. E 2002].

③ Section 14 of the Arbitration Act, [Cap. 15 R. E 2002].

④ Section 15 of the Arbitration Act, [Cap. 15 R. E 2002].

⑤ Section 16 of the Arbitration Act, [Cap. 15 R. E 2002].

⑥ Section 17 of the Arbitration Act, [Cap. 15 R. E 2002].

⑦ Section 12 of the Arbitration Act, [Cap. 15 R. E 2002].

投资争端解决的独立仲裁庭和机构的缺失。只有极少数国家建立了处理投资解决解决的独立仲裁庭，比如乌干达和埃及。独立仲裁庭和其他机构的缺失意味着主要适用诉讼的普通法院对意在以友好方式，通常是双方协定，解决纠纷的仲裁程序起主导作用。

（三）中非司法协助双边协定的缺失

中非投资争端机制的实施面临的另一个挑战是中国和非洲大部分国家之间的司法协助双边协定的缺失。中国和极少数非洲国家签订了司法协助协定，这就给和其他未签订协定的国家之间的合作带来了阻碍。协定的目的是在裁决确定的债权人的住所地或财产所在地执行裁决。[①] 涉外投资争端的裁决一般需要境外服务提供司法文件和证据。双边协定的缺失和违背条约的行为导致了中非投资争端解决实施的不当滞后。比如直至 2011 年 2 月，由埃及向中国提出的 26 项服务请求中，中国相关机构事实上只提供了 14 份司法文件，每份法律文件的平均服务时间是 72.2 天。但中国向香港提出的 5 项服务请求中，埃及当局没有实现任何一项。[②] 此外，国际司法协作是实现涉外案件高效解决的不可或缺的一部分。相应的，世界范围内有很多为实现该目的的多边公约被创设，如 1965 年《关于向国外送达民事或商事和司法文书海牙公约》（以下简称《海牙文书公约》）以及 1970 年《关于从国外调取民事或商事证据的海牙公约》（以下简称《海牙取证公约》）。这些公约的缔约国可在公约提供的机制下在司法层面开展合作。[③] 中国现在加入了两个海牙公约，但在非洲，只有埃及、博茨瓦纳、马拉维和塞舌尔加入了《海牙文书公约》，只有南非和塞舌尔签订了《海牙取证公约》。所以，中非通过多边机制在涉外案子上的合作受到了很大限制。[④]

---

① A Brief Analysis of the Dispute Arising from China-African Civil and Commercial Transactions. A Paper submitted at the first China–African Think Tank Forum held in Hangzhou on 27-29 October, 2011.

② A Brief Analysis of the Dispute Arising from China-African Civil and Commercial Transactions. A Paper submitted at the first China–African Think Tank Forum held in Hangzhou on 27-29 October, 2011.

③ A Brief Analysis of the Dispute Arising from China-African Civil and Commercial Transactions. A Paper submitted at the first China–African Think Tank Forum held in Hangzhou on 27-29 October, 2011.

④ A Brief Analysis of the Dispute Arising from China-African Civil and Commercial Transactions. A Paper submitted at the first China–African Think Tank Forum held in Hangzhou on 27-29 October, 2011.

（四）中非对彼此法律制度认知的缺失

一些非洲国家缺少对中国的法律制度的认识，中国也对很多非洲国家的法律制度没有深入的了解。

知晓双方的法律制度是顺利开展有效的投资争端解决的工具。因为，只有对非洲的法律制度具有充分的认识，中国才可以充满信心在非洲管辖下解决投资争端。同样地，当非洲国家对中国的法律制度有了充分认识后，非洲国家也会有足够的信心在中国管辖下进行投资争端的裁决。相反，如果一方，或双方都对另一方的法律制度没有认识，或只有很少的认识，那么双方间都不会有信心。这是中非投资争端解决机制所面临的重大问题之一。尽管近些年来中非民商事交易往来增速极快，大多数参与交易的中国人不太了解非洲国家的法律制度，甚至对非洲国家的法律和司法系统有一定误解。反之亦然，很多和中国做生意的非洲人也不了解中国的法律制度。在发生争端的情况下，他们不知道该立刻采取什么样的救济。有些时候，他们甚至害怕或担心在对方国家进行诉讼或仲裁。这些都会减慢解决争端的进程。[①]

上述分析显示了中非民商事纠纷中的极大不平衡，即很多争端都是发生在非洲的，只有一部分是发生在中国的。这个事实说明中国一方有必要去了解非洲国家和涉外案件裁决相关的法律制度。

四、结论

中非投资争端解决机制很大程度上依靠的是双方间的了解。机制的目标必须是通过协商或 / 和仲裁，友好、高效地解决投资争端，而非法院的介入。

外国仲裁裁决的执行受限于严格的条件和是否遵从前述条件，否则争端的解决留给本国法院。仲裁裁决的执行，无论本土或外国裁决，都不应该受限于严格的条件。

① A Brief Analysis of the Dispute Arising from China-African Civil and Commercial Transactions. A Paper submitted at the first China–African Think Tank Forum held in Hangzhou on 27-29 October, 2011.

五、建议

在完成上述投资争端解决机制的分析后，笔者建议成立独立的、中立的、专门解决投资争端解决的仲裁庭。建议出台不将投资纠纷限于本国法院审理的国内法，这可以建立信心。

配合上述建议，我们应努力确保中非两国了解对方法律制度，在双方间建立信心。中国和非洲国家应当协商并签订关于送达司法文书以及投资纠纷证据获取的双边协定。尚未签订 1965 年《海牙文书公约》和《海牙取证公约》的非洲国家应当加入这两个公约，促进投资纠纷的解决。

The Analysis of Investment Dispute Resolution Mechanism between China and Africa

Author: Moza Mussa kassubi

1. Introduction

In recent years the world has witnessed tremendous economic integrations simulated by rapid development of science and technology. There is massive exchange and transfer of technology between states through bilateral and multilateral agreements. With globalization the world is now open to investment from one state to another. Africa in particular is an eye of many foreign investors from other continents for having many investment opportunities. It is on record that by 2013 Asian Investment in Africa had huge investments on different sectors including telecommunications, manufacturing, financial services insurance oil and gas, extraction industries and agriculture[①].

1.1 Investment Between China and Africa Countries

Chinese economy fast growing and it is one of countries in Asia and in the world with advancement in technology has become also one the most popular in technology transfer through investment in Africa and the rest parts of the world. African countries have generally favourable attitude toward Chinese foreign direct investment and has had considerable success in attracting it. Examples of Chinese investment in Africa is among others China Merchants Holdings (International) Co. LTD (Hong Kong) which acquires 23.5% stake in Port de Djibout S. A. (Djibout), China National Offshore Oil Corp. acquires stake in Tullow Oil in Uganda, Sinopec (China) which acquires 33%

① Brian King and Elliot Friedman, International Dispute Resolution in Africa. *Asian International Dispute Resolution Webnar Series*, Freshfields Bruckhaus Deringe, p.2.

stake in Apache Corp's operation in Egypt[①]. Under the provisions of Sections 4, 5 and 6 of the Tanzania Investment Act, [Cap. 38 R. E 2002] a one stop centre for investment is established where all investment activities are coordinated. The centre was primarily established to play a pivotal function of creating and promoting a conducive environment for both local and foreign investors by coordinating, encouraging, promoting and facilitating investment and advise the government on investment policies and related matters.

The Act goes further to provide opportunity for obtaining credit from domestic sources by foreign investors under the provisions of section 25 which reads as follows;.

(1) Subject to section 2, a foreign investor may, in relation to the business enterprise which he operates, obtain credit from domestic bank and financial institutions up to the limit established by the Bank of Tanzania in consultation with the Centre having regard to the amount of foreign capital invested in the business enterprise.

(2) A foreign investor who obtains credit in accordance with subsection (1) shall ensure that the proceeds of that credit are used solely for the purpose of carrying out the activities specified in his loan application.

(3) The bank granting the loan may, for the purposes of this section, appoint its officer or agent to verify the due application of the credit obtained under subsection (1).

The above efforts have made possible business relations between African countries with china and the entire world. On the other hand many African enterprises have been established in China following booming business opportunity. These are to mention just a few. Interaction between China and Africa, business disputes emerged which are mainly contractual, dispute arising from the letter of credit or the letter of guarantee and labour disputes.

1. 2 Legal Protection of Foreign Investment in Genaral

In order to have good environment for investment the government involved must ensure investors are protected from investment risk through smooth legal framework. It should be noted however that investment in most cases is governed by agreement between investors and the government in which respective enterprise is to be established. There are also bilateral and multilateral investment treaties which provide for substantive protections to investors against government actions, legislative and judicial process. In this paper it is intended to analyse the mechanism of dispute resolution between China and Africa as provided for in the general international standard and available bilateral investment treaties world wide.

A discussion of legal practice on dispute settlement in Africa will base on the experience of

① Brian King and Elliot Friedman, International Dispute Resolution in Africa. *Asian International Dispute Resolution Webnar Series*, Freshfields Bruckhaus Deringer, p.2.

Tanzania as a case study of legal frame work in implementation of different bilateral and multilateral investment treaties.

2 Investment Dispute Resolution Mechanism Between CHINA and Africa

Investment dispute resolution is a means of mitigating investment risks arising from running of enterprises which are subject of investment between the investor and the government as per investment agreement. There are various mechanisms of resolving investment disputes through investment treaties, investment laws and international commercial arbitration. China investment dispute resolution mechanism mainly depend on Bilateral Investment treaties which in most cases presuppose the existence of mutual agreements on dispute settlement between investors and the host state.

By October 2011 China had concluded Bilateral Investment Treaties with 45 African states while her investment had spread over 49 African countries. [①] The number is presumed to have increased due to development and discovery of new investment opportunities like gas and oil which might have also increase a number of enterprises. The common Bilateral Investment Treaties provide for dispute settlement basing on the legal frame work of the country where the investment enterprise which is subject of dispute situates. In many African countries investment laws provide specifically and expressly that investment dispute between the foreign investor and the host country should first be settled in the courts or arbitral institutions in the host country in most cases where the contract is usually performed. Example the Petroleum Activities Law of Angola provides that in case of any disputes they should be resolved by arbitration taking place in Angola and governed by Angolan Law[②].

In the United Republic of Tanzania investment disputes are governed by different laws but the basic laws are the Tanzania Investment Act, [Cap. 38 R. E 2002] and the Arbitration Act, [Cap. 15 R. E 2002].

Dispute settlement under the Tanzania Investment Act, *Supra* is governed by section 23 of Act which provides for two mechanisms of settling differences between the investor and Centre or the government. The mechanisms are negotiation and in the event it fails arbitration which is the second option of the dispute settlement mechanism.

① A Brief Analysis of the Dispute Arising from China-African Civil and Commercial Transactions. A Paper submitted at the first China–African Think Tank Forum held in Hangzhou on 27-29 October, 2011.

② A Brief Analysis of the Dispute Arising from China-African Civil and Commercial Transactions. A Paper submitted at the first China–African Think Tank Forum held in Hangzhou on 27-29 October, 2011.

The section reads;

23 (1) Where a dispute arises between a foreign investor and the Centre or the Government in respect of a business enterprise, all efforts shall be made to settle the dispute through negotiations for an amicable settlement.

(2) A dispute between a foreign investor and the Centre or the Government in respect of a business enterprise which is not settled through negotiations may be submitted to arbitration in accordance with any of the following methods as may be mutually agreed by the parties, that is to say–

(a) in accordance with arbitration laws of Tanzania for investors;

(b) in accordance with the rules of procedure for arbitration of the International Centre for the Settlement of Investment Disputes;

(c) within the framework of any bilateral or multilateral agreement on investment protection agreed to by the Government of the United Republic and the Government of the country where the investor originates.

The cited above provisions of law do not suggest any litigation in ordinary courts. The intention may be recognition of investor's rights as per the investment agreement and in order to maintain good business relations between investors and the government. The law stresses the use of all efforts to the dispute negotiated in the first place before embarking in arbitration which is also harmonious way of settling trade dispute as opposed to litigations in ordinary courts. Under paragraphs (b) and (c) of subsection 2 the law also takes cognizance of the use of rules of procedure universally accepted for arbitration of the investment disputes in International Centre for Settlement of Investment Disputes. The application of these rules in investment dispute settlement between China and Africa and in particular the United Republic of Tanzania can be learned in many dispute referred to the centre. Example of the dispute is the arbitration proceedings between Standard Chartered Bank (Hong Kong) Limited (Claimant) and Tanzania Electric Supply Company Limited (respondent) ICSID case No. ARB/10/20 dispatched to parties on 12th February, 2014.

The Arbitration Act, [Cap. 15 R. E 2002] does provide under the provision of section 4 commencement of an arbitral proceedings when there is a dispute.

Section 4. Unless a different intention is expressed therein a submission shall be irrevocable, except by leave of the court, and shall be deemed to include the provisions set forth in the First Schedule hereto, in so far as they are applicable to the reference under submission.

The submission referred to herein covers disputes between local investment and the government and also the dispute foreign investors and the government. The Act does not however establish any independent arbitral tribunal instead resort is always made to the National Construction Council which as the name suggests deals with construction industry.

The Arbitration Act of the United Republic of Tanzania under sections 28 and 29 and the fourth schedule thereto gives recognition of international instruments on enforcement of foreign awards and it provides for procedure to register and enforcement of foreign arbitral awards. The Act also provides for binding nature of the bilateral treaties and the foreign arbitral awards. According the Act enforcement of foreign arbitral awards notwithstanding its binding nature is subject to limitations set for under the provisions of Section 30. It is useful to reproduce the three sections as the situation covers many Africans legal frame work.

s. 28. Application of Part IV

(1) The provisions of this Part apply to any award made after 28th July, 1924–

(a) in pursuance of an agreement for arbitration to which the Protocol set out in the Third Schedule applies; and

(b) between persons of who are subject to the jurisdiction of any State which is a party to the Convention on the Execution of Foreign Arbitral Awards which Convention is set out in the Fourth Schedule to this Act; and an award to which the provisions of this Part apply, is in this Part referred to as" a foreign award".

(2) This Part shall not apply to any award made on an arbitration agreement governed by the law of Tanzania.

[s. 27]

s. 29. Effect of foreign awards

(1) A foreign award shall, subject to the provisions of this Part, be enforceable in the High Court either by action or under the provisions of section 16 of this Act.

(2) Any foreign award which would be enforceable under this Part shall be treated as binding for all purposes on the persons as between whom it was made and may accordingly be relied on by any of those persons by way of defence, set-off or otherwise in any legal proceedings; and any reference in this Part to enforcing a foreign award shall be construed as including references to relying on an award.

s. 30. Conditions for enforcement of foreign awards

(1) In order that a foreign award may be enforceable under this Part, it must–

(a) have been made in pursuance of an agreement for arbitration which was valid under the law by which it was governed;

(b) have been made by the tribunal provided for in the agreement or constituted in manner agreed upon by the parties;

(c) have been made in conformity with the law governing the arbitration procedure;

(d) have become final in the country in which it was made; and

(e) have been in respect of a matter which may lawfully be referred to arbitration under the law of Tanzania, and its enforcement must not be contrary to the public policy or the law of Tanzania.

(2) Subject to the provisions of this subsection, a foreign award shall not be enforceable under this Part if the court is satisfied that–

(a) the award has been annulled in the country in which it was made; or

(b) the party against whom it is sought to enforce the award was not given notice of the arbitration proceedings in sufficient time to enable him to present his case or was under some legal incapacity and was not properly represented; or

(c) the award does not deal with all the questions referred or contains decisions on matters beyond the scope of the agreement for arbitration:

Provided that if the award does not deal with all the questions referred the court may, if it thinks fit, either postpone the enforcement of the award or order its enforcement subject to the giving of such security by the person seeking to enforce it as the court may think fit.

(3) If a party seeking to resist the enforcement of a foreign award proves that there is any ground other than the non-existence of the conditions specified in paragraphs (a), (b) and (c) of subsection (1) of this section, or the existence of the conditions specified in paragraphs (b) and (c) of subsection (2) of this section entitling him to contest the validity of the award the court may, if it thinks fit, either refuse to enforce the award or adjourn the hearing until after the expiration of such period as appears to the court to be reasonably sufficient to enable that party to take the necessary steps to have the award annulled by the competent tribunal.

s. 31. Evidence

(1) The party seeking to enforce a foreign award must produce–

(a) the original award or its copy duly authenticated in the manner required by the law of the country in which it was made;

(b) evidence proving that the award has become final; and

(c) such evidence as may be necessary to prove that the award is a foreign award and that the conditions mentioned in paragraphs (a), (b) and (c) of subsection (1) of section 29 are satisfied.

(2) In any case where any document required to be produced under subsection (1) of this section is in a foreign language, it shall be the duty of the party seeking to enforce the award to produce a translation certified as correct by a diplomatic or consular agent of the country to which that party belongs, or certified as correct in such other manner as may be sufficient according to the law of Tanzania.

(3) Subject to the provisions of this section the court may make rules with respect to the evidence which must be furnished by a party seeking to enforce an award under this Part.

Although it may appear more convenient in employing out of court through negotiation and or arbitration as mechanism of investment disputes, yet the said mechanism is not free from challenges.

3 Challenges Facing Investment Dispute Resolution Mechanism Between CHINA and Africa

3.1 Exposure of Arbitral Proceedings to National Courts

The conditions stipulated in the cited provisions are the typical example of legal hurdles on the implementation of Bilateral Investment Treaties between China and Africa and other countries having investment business relations with Africa. One of the major challenge facing investment dispute mechanisms is too much exposure of arbitral process to national courts. In many African jurisdictions courts are given immense power to intervene arbitral proceedings even before they take off. See for example section 6 of the Arbitration Act, [Cap. 15 R. E 2002] of Tanzania where the normal court is empowered to stay arbitral proceedings. It reads;

s.6 Power to stay proceedings where there is a submission

Where a party to a submission to which this Part applies, or a person claiming under him, commences a legal proceedings against any other party to the submission or any person claiming under him in respect of any matter agreed to be referred, a party to the legal proceedings may, at any time after appearance and before filing a written statement or taking any other steps in the proceedings apply to the court to stay the proceedings; and the court, if satisfied that there is no sufficient reason why the matter should not be referred in accordance with the submission and that the applicant was, at the time when the proceedings were commenced, and still remains, ready and willing to do all things necessary for the proper conduct of the arbitration, may make an order staying the proceedings.

Courts have power to control the arbitral proceedings after commencement including having final decision on who should be the arbitrator in the arbitration proceedings in cases of differences in appointing the arbitrator by parties.① Other powers include power to extend time for commencing arbitration proceedings②, power to extend time for making final award③, power to remit award for reconsideration④ and power to set aside award where on the ground either the arbitrator has committed misconduct himself or the award has been improperly procured⑤.

The intervention by court may paradoxically mean ensuring check against impartiality,

① Sections 8 and 18 of the Arbitration Act, [Cap. 15 R. E 2002].

② Section 7 of the Arbitration Act, [Cap. 15 R. E 2002].

③ Section 14 of the Arbitration Act, [Cap. 15 R. E 2002].

④ Section 15 of the Arbitration Act, [Cap. 15 R. E 2002].

⑤ Section 16 of the Arbitration Act, [Cap. 15 R. E 2002].

propriety and or accuracy of the arbitral proceedings, but again most of national courts have in several occasions being accused of its personnel caught up corrupt practices, lack of integrity and so forth. There is always a danger of abusing the powers in fulfilling the interest of ill motive parties.

It is to be noted that a final arbitral award amounts to a decree enforceable in courts of law① but many African jurisdictions for the arbitral award to be enforced it must be registered and the party against whom it is to be enforced must be given opportunity to challenge the award in question.② For the case of foreign award is also recognized by host countries and enforceable under national laws but these awards do face stringent conditions as shown which conditions sometimes are considered as delaying tactics. Some courts have been considered even to be in violation of international obligation on bilateral and multilateral treaties and convention which the respective state is a signatory.

3.2 Lack of Independent Tribunal or Institutions for Investment Disputes Resolution

Another challenge for implementation of China and Africa investment dispute resolution mechanism effectively and efficiently is the lack independent tribunal or institutions outside judicial umbrella to deal with investment dispute resolution. Very few countries that have established independent tribunal for dealing with investment dispute resolution for example Uganda and Egypt. Lack of independent tribunal or other institution paves way to ordinary courts which are primarily meant for litigation, to have a dominant role over arbitration process which aims at amicable dispute settlement in most cases basing on the agreement between parties.

3.3 Lack of Bilateral Judicial Assistance Treaties between China and Africa

Another challenge for implementation of China and Africa investment dispute mechanism is lack of Bilateral judicial assistance treaties between China and most of African countries. China has judicial assistance treaties with very few African countries which hinders cooperation in countries where there are no such treaties. The treaties are aimed at effecting enforcement of award where the judgment debtors reside or where the judgment debtor's property situates.③ The adjudication of investment disputes with foreign element may generally require the service abroad of judicial document and taking of evidence. The absence of bilateral treaties or non compliance of enforcement

① Section 17 of the Arbitration Act, [Cap. 15 R. E 2002].

② Section 12 of the Arbitration Act, [Cap. 15 R. E 2002].

③ A Brief Analysis of the Dispute Arising from China-African Civil and Commercial Transactions. A Paper submitted at the first China–African Think Tank Forum held in Hangzhou on 27-29 October, 2011.

of treaties where it exists causes undue delay in implementing investment disputes resolution between china and Africa. For example out of 26 request for service made by Egypt to China up to February, 2011, only 14 judicial documents were effectively served by the relevant Chinese authority and the average service time for each judicial document was 72.2 days while as to the 5 requirements for service from China to Egypt, no proof of service had ever returned from Egyptian authority.① Additionally, the international judicial cooperation is now indispensable for the effective and efficient adjudication of foreign related cases. Accordingly, many multilateral conventions for such a purpose have been devised worldwide. For example the 1965 Hague Convention on the Service Abroad of Judicial and Extra-judicial Documents in Civil or Commercial Matters and the 1970 Hague Convention on the Taking of Evidence Abroad. The member state of such conventions may cooperate in the administration of justice under the mechanism provided by such conventions.② So far, China has acceded to the two Hague Conventions, but in Africa only Egypt, Botswana, Malawi and Seychelles acceded to the Hague Convention on Service Abroad and only South Africa and Seychelles became parties to the Hague Convention on Taking of Evidence Abroad. Therefore, the cooperation between China and African countries in cases with foreign elements through multilateral mechanism is narrowly limited.③

3.4 Lack of Knowledge of Chinese and African Legal Systems between China and African Countries

There is also lack of or little knowledge of Chinese legal system on the part of African countries and China has lack or little knowledge of the many African countries legal systems.

Understanding each other legal system is a tool to smooth and expeditious investment dispute resolution. China Having sufficient knowledge of African legal systems creates confidence for the investment disputes to be resolved within African jurisdiction. Likewise African countries will have confidence of investment disputes to adjudicated in Chinese jurisdiction if African countries posses sufficient knowledge on Chinese legal system. To the contrary, if one or both of the two parties do not have knowledge or have little knowledge of each other's legal system then there is always lack of confidence between the two parties. This is one of the major obstacles facing China and Africa investment disputes resolution mechanism. Though China-African civil and commercial transactions

① A Brief Analysis of the Dispute Arising from China-African Civil and Commercial Transactions. A Paper submitted at the first China–African Think Tank Forum held in Hangzhou on 27-29 October, 2011.

② A Brief Analysis of the Dispute Arising from China-African Civil and Commercial Transactions. A Paper submitted at the first China–African Think Tank Forum held in Hangzhou on 27-29 October, 2011.

③ A Brief Analysis of the Dispute Arising from China-African Civil and Commercial Transactions. A Paper submitted at the first China–African Think Tank Forum held in Hangzhou on 27-29 October, 2011.

increase so frequently in recent years, most of the Chinese people participating in such transactions do not know much about the legal systems in African countries, or even have some misunderstanding about the laws and judiciaries in African countries. *Vice versa*, Most African people doing business in China know little or nothing about the Chinese legal system. In case of dispute, they do not know what remedy can be resorted to immediately, or sometimes they will fear or worry to litigate or arbitrate in the other party's country, which will lead to the slow settlement process.①

The above analyses manifest a great unbalance in the China-African civil and commercial disputes, namely, most of the disputes originated in Africa, only a few of them occurred in China. This fact signifies the need for the Chinese parties to learn about the legal systems relating to the adjudication of the foreign-related cases in African countries.

4 Conclusion

The investment dispute resolution mechanism between China and Africa depends much on the understanding between the two parties. The mechanism must aim at amicable and expeditious investment disputes settlement through negotiations and or arbitration without too much interference of normal courts. The enforcement of foreign arbitral awards is subjected to stringent conditions and the mandate to determine the compliance or otherwise of the said conditions is left to national courts. Enforcement of arbitral awards is it local or foreign awards should not be subjected to stringent conditions.

5 Recommendations

Following the above analysis of investment disputes resolution mechanism, it is therefore recommended efforts should be made to establish independent and neutral tribunal for dealing specifically with investment disputes settlement. Enactment of national laws which do not subject investment disputes to national courts is also recommended to build confident.

In line with the above recommendation, efforts should be made to ensure China and Africa understands each other legal system to create confidence between the two parties. China and African countries must enter and sign Bilateral Investment Treaties on assistance on service of judicial documents and taking of evidence abroad on investment disputes. African countries which are not signatories of the 1965 Hague Convention on the Service Abroad of Judicial and Extra-judicial

① A Brief Analysis of the Dispute Arising from China-African Civil and Commercial Transactions. A Paper submitted at the first China–African Think Tank Forum held in Hangzhou on 27-29 October, 2011.

Documents in Civil or Commercial Matters (hereinafter referred to as "Hague Convention on the Service Abroad") and the 1970 Hague Convention on the Taking of Evidence Abroad in Civil or Commercial Matters (hereinafter referred to as "Hague Convention on the Taking of Evidence Abroad"), should sign the two Conventions to foster investment dispute resolution.

论非洲国家劳动法律法规对中国企业投资的影响——以赞比亚为视角①

作者：Chenda　译者：吴晶融

一、雇佣关系协商一致的本质和禁止强迫劳动

在赞比亚，雇主和雇员的关系建立在双方自愿、协商一致的基础上，强迫劳动是被赞比亚共和国《宪法》、《反人口贩卖法》和《刑法》所明确禁止的，《宪法》第14条第2款规定：

任何人不得被强迫进行劳动。

《反人口贩卖法》第3条规定强迫劳动的定义为：

通过胁迫、使用武力、恐吓或其他强迫和人身约束的形式获得或维持的劳动服务。

因此，雇员有权随时解除雇佣关系，不得被强迫违反其意愿继续工作。

二、薪酬和工作条件

赞比亚法律规定了最低工资和支付工资的频率。雇佣法案将工资定义为：

为雇员所做的或将要做的工作和服务，雇主应当支付雇员或临时雇员的薪金或报酬。无论如何设定和计算，工资能够以金钱表示，且由劳务合同或外国劳务合同

① 人力资源基础是各投资企业的关键组成部分之一。在本文中，笔者将重点介绍一些相关的赞比亚《劳动法》规定。这些规定对所有在赞比亚投资的中国企业都有影响，但笔者将不会涉及具体投资领域的相关规定。本文为第三届中非法律专业交流项目进修课程成果的一部分。

确定。

根据最低工资和雇佣条件法案，在劳动和社会服务部部长认为没有其他有效调整最低工资或工作条件的方法，尤其是缺乏劳资集体谈判机制时，其有权通过法规命令的形式为赞比亚不同种类的劳动者规定最低工资。

根据上述权力，劳动部出台了法规命令为受保护的特定种类的劳动者规定了最低工资和工作条件，管理人员和已受到劳资集体谈判协议保护的劳动者不属于该法条保护的劳动者。

最低工资法令规定涉及税后工资的基准以及交通费、午餐费、住房补贴等津贴标准的所有事务。该法令也规定了遣散费和工龄福利的计算公式。

根据雇佣法案，雇主应按小时或按日、按十四天、按月支付职工到期工资。在工作任务完成后，雇主有义务支付计件工资的雇员。无论计件工资率如何，如果双方同意，雇主可以在一个月后对按日、按小时计算工资的雇员支付累计工资。《雇佣法案》第 44 条规定：

在所有劳务合同中，雇员的工资将以赞比亚货币支付，且应直接发放给雇员；但如果雇员以书面形式要求，或适用于该雇员的集体协议规定，工资支付可采取以下方法：支付到银行或建房互助协会账户，账户以应得工资人的姓名设立，或以该人与他人共同名义设立；通过邮政汇票支付报酬；通过银行汇票支付报酬；通过支票支付报酬。

当雇员不在时，雇主可以将工资支付给雇员以书面形式授权的其他人。

工资尽可能在工作日并在工作地或较近的地方发放。

本条的任何内容不影响雇主向雇员发放工资外的任何形式的补贴，只要该补贴是根据惯例或与雇员间的协议或集体协议或法律规定发放的；但任何补贴形式的这些发放，应作为雇员个人及其家庭的使用和福利，且不得采用毒品或麻醉剂的形式。

工资的支付不得在商场、商店或食堂或出售烈性酒的场所进行，雇员在这些场所工作的除外。

本条规定受相关外汇管制法律规定约束。

本条规定适用于临时工。

《雇佣法案》第 15 条规定：

（1）在各方达成的待遇不低于本条规定的带薪休假协议书以及依照《最低工资和雇佣条件法案》制定的任何法规基础上，雇员每 6 个月的连续服务后，有权享有全薪假期，假期天数按照每个月的服务享受 2 天，休假时间应由协议各方协议决定；

但对于雇员未满享受上述休假期限前，服务合同非经雇员放弃、辞职或即时解雇而终止，雇员对于每个月完成的服务享有 2 天的全薪。

（2）第 1 款所述的假期不属于公众假日和周末休息日，无论是法定的或是约定俗成的、雇员不需要根据其服务合同被要求工作的假日。

（3）部长可通过法令，将任何一天或几天宣布为《公众假日法案》下的公众假日，且对于任何被宣布为公众假日的日期，每个雇员，如其在改日之前或之后的一天没有在未经雇主应允或无合理理由的情况下旷工，则其有权在该日享受全薪的假日；但如果一雇员或一类雇员在任何被宣布为假日的日期通常约定俗成地工作，则该雇员或该类雇员有权享有通过集体协议或劳务合同下协议的工资水平的工资。

（4）为本条之目的，全薪是指基本工资、可时常提供的食物的等值现金、适用于不超过 1 个月周期的工作或其他补贴，但不包括任何形式的奖金。

（5）不管第 1 款如何规定，雇主经与雇员达成协议，对于雇员在该款累积的任何假期，雇主可通过支付工资代替；且对于合同终止的雇员累积的假期，雇主应向雇员支付这些累积假期的工资。

《雇佣法案》第 54 条规定：

如果任何雇员因为疾病或不可归责于雇员的意外事故而暂时不能工作，雇员有权在提供有效的诊断书后获取该期间的报酬。雇员每年最多享有 26 天带薪病假或事假。如有其他劳动合同、劳资集体谈判协议或其他法律规定更有利于雇员的，从其规定。

雇主可以提供员工超过每年 26 天的带薪病假或事假。

第 15 条 a 款规定：

（1）在对产假待遇作出不低于本条规定的各方任何协议或任何其他法律基础上，女性雇员自入职日期或上次产假日期起完成至少 2 年的连续服务的，经出示注册行医人员签署的与其怀孕相关的医疗证明，享有 12 个星期的全薪产假。

（2）第 1 款中享有的产假不属于女性雇员享有的任何其他假期。

（3）对于孕期并发症导致女性雇员暂时无法履行其工作职责的，该雇员应根据第 54 条享有病假。

（4）任何违反本条规定的雇主构成犯罪。

任何雇员均有权享受带薪公众节假日，除非其在该节假日前一天或后一天未经雇主许可且无合理理由地旷工。带薪公众节假日的工资报酬包括基本工资、餐补以及不超过一个月的津贴，但不包括奖金。职工也有休病假的权利。

赞比亚《宪法》规定公民享有结社自由，在雇佣方面的自由由《工业劳动关系法》规定。因此，赞比亚的工人有权组织、加入或参加工会及其活动和项目。

根据赞比亚《宪法》，工人有权进行合法罢工。《工业劳动关系法》将罢工定义为任何企业雇佣的工人联合起来违反合同约定停止工作或劳动的行为；或者被雇佣提供其劳动的任何数量的工人的一致拒绝工作的行为。

只有在所有其他解决争议的方法失败后，工人们才可以和平罢工。工会多数投票支持罢工后，可以开始10天的罢工行动，之后时间可以无限延长直到争议被解决。工人不得参加未经工会投票授权的非法罢工。

三、健康、安全和补偿

《职业健康与安全法案》规定了赞比亚境内职业健康与安全的相关问题。根据该法案，任何在工作地点有10个以上雇员的雇主必须建立健康与安全委员会：

11. 任何在工作地点有10个以上雇员的雇主必须建立健康与安全委员会。

13.（1）健康与安全委员会的职能是：

① 促进雇主与雇员间的合作以实现和维护健康安全的工作情况；

② 向雇员分享关于职业健康、安全与福利的信息；

③ 调查和解决在工作地点对雇员健康或安全造成威胁的事项；

④ 审查保障雇员健康和安全的措施；

⑤ 制定、审查、向雇员传达在工作地点采取的有关健康与安全的措施。

根据《职业健康与安全法案》，赞比亚内的雇主有以下具体义务：

16.（1）雇主应当：

① 在工作地点，在合理的切实可行范围内保证雇员的健康安全和福祉；

② 将雇员安排到适应其生理和心理能力的工作环境中。

（2）不违反第1条的一般规定前提下，雇主应当：

① 在合理的切实可行范围内，提供和维持安全且不对工人健康造成任何威胁的工厂和工作系统；

② 在合理的切实可行范围内，确保在工作地点提供给雇员使用的装置和物质被安全地使用、处理和储存；

③ 在合理的切实可行范围内，提供保护雇员健康与安全所需的信息、指令和训练；

④ 在合理的切实可行范围内，保持雇主所可以控制的工作场所安全无害的状态；

⑤ 在合理的切实可行范围内，提供并维护工作场所进出口通道的无害和安全；

⑥ 在合理的切实可行范围内，提供充分的设施与安排以创造和保持一个安全无害的工作环境；

⑦ 通知并咨询健康与安全代表：

（i）当得到授权的公职人员检查工作场所时，确保健康安全代表与公职人员的会面机会；

（ii）雇员受伤或疾病的情况以及未来的预防措施；

（iii）提交至工人赔偿基金管理委员会的申请所提及的损伤情况；

（iv）确保雇主和雇员有效合作，改善保障雇员在工作场所健康与安全的措施，并检查这些措施的有效性；

⑧ 提供应对紧急状况和意外事故的措施，包括充分的急救安排；

⑨ 雇主承担费用，向在工作工程中有较大风险受伤的雇员提供适当的保护衣物装置，并充分说明使用方法；

⑩ 免费提供其他所有法律规定的应当由雇主向雇员提供的事物。

除《职业健康与安全法案》之外，《工人赔偿金法案》规定雇主必须向工人赔偿基金管理委员会注册登记。工人赔偿金基金为在工作中由于意外或疾病造成残疾的工人的福祉而设立存在。

根据《工人赔偿金法案》，缴纳工人赔偿金基金为雇主一方的义务，以任何方式扣除雇员报酬以抵扣这一义务将被视为犯罪行为。

56.（1）任何雇主扣留雇员应得的报酬以支付赔偿金或要求、允许工人自行支付赔偿金的，均构成犯罪。

《职业健康与安全法案》和《工人赔偿金法案》互为补充。前者为预防性的，后者为救济性。

四、社会保险，养老金和工龄福利

赞比亚《宪法》规定赞比亚雇员有权获得养老金福利，保护这种福利不被扣留或不被改变为不利于雇员的方式。第 187 条第 1 款：

（1）雇员，包括公务员，有权享有养老金福利。

《宪法》第 266 条规定养老金福利包括：

退休金、补偿金、养老金或类似津贴。

赞比亚《宪法》未规定哪些人是雇员，不过《雇佣法案》将雇员定义为：

为获取报酬，订立劳动合同的全职职工、兼职人员和临时工，但不包括学徒、独立承包人或计件工作人。（第3条）

另外，赞比亚《宪法》规定养老金福利不得被扣留或不得改变为不利于雇员的方式，并且定时强制基于保险精算估值审查养老金福利。

《宪法》同时规定养老金免除收入税，要求养老金福利必须及时支付。

如果即将退休的雇员在最后一个工作日未收到养老金福利，雇主需要继续支付其工资直到其收到养老金福利，此时养老金福利应当基于收到的最后一个月的工资而非退休月的工资。为方便参考，将相关法条列出如下：

187.（1）略。

（2）养老金福利不得以损害雇员的方式扣留或改变。

188.（1）养老金福利应当基于实际评估定期审查。

（2）养老金福利应当免除税收。

189.（1）养老金福利应当及时定期支付。

（2）当雇员在最后一个工作日未收到养老金福利，该雇员应当停止工作但其名字仍然应当保留在工资名单上，直到其收到基于其所实际收到的最后工资计算的养老金福利。

具体的强制养老金福利制度由《全国养老金计划法案》规定，其后在赞比亚税务机关登记过的雇主有义务向全国养老金计划管理局注册登记。

《全国养老金计划法案》第13条规定了上述义务，第12条将雇主定义为：

登记为有雇员的纳税人的自然人、协会、机构或公司；

赞比亚共和国政府、地方政府机构、半国营机构或法定机构。

因此，赞比亚境内所有雇主从税务登记起即需为其雇员缴纳社会保险。雇主也可以设立高于全国养老金计划的养老金标准。

五、终止雇佣的规定及限制

首先，根据赞比亚法律规定，雇主可以在任何时候以任何理由，甚至不需要理由就可以终止书面雇佣合同。

但是，随着《雇佣法案》修改的通过，现在雇主想要终止书面雇佣合同必须给出合理的理由。这些理由必须基于雇员的行为或能力，或者雇主业务操作的要求。

雇主为达到上述要求，雇员有权以非法终止劳动合同或非法解雇为由对雇主提起诉讼。以下为《雇佣法案》规定原文：

第 36 条（1）书面雇佣合同应当以以下方式终止：

（a）略。

（b）略。

（c）雇主以非合同约定或法律规定的方式终止雇佣合同，应当向雇员给出终止雇佣的理由。

（2）略。

（3）除非有关于雇员能力、行为或基于工作业务操作要求的合理理由，雇佣合同不得终止。

现在《雇佣法案》也规定了下列理由不得作为终止雇佣合同的理由。相关的第 36 条第 4 款如下：

（4）不得作为终止雇佣合同的理由包括：

（a）工会成员资格；在工作时间外或经过雇主同意在工作时间内参加工会活动；

（b）作为雇员代表寻求政府机关帮助；

（c）对雇主参与非法活动的情况进行投诉；

（d）种族，肤色，性别，婚姻状况，家庭责任负担情况，怀孕，宗教信仰，政治观点或政党，民族，部落或社会地位；

（e）法律许可的休假。

值得注意的是，第 36 条处于《雇佣法案》只适用于书面合同的第五章规定之下。

关于口头雇佣合同没有相关规定（可能是由于立法者起草时候的疏忽）。

与上述书面雇佣合同相比，口头雇佣合同仍然可以不受严格限制的终止，只需要发给对方一个简单的书面通知。《雇佣法案》第 20 条第 1 款规定：

20.（1）口头合同的任何一方均有权终止雇佣，只需发给另一方书面通知告知其终止雇佣关系的意图，通知期满，雇佣合同即终结。

但是，当法院受理关于口头雇佣合同终止的争议时，总是将适用于书面合同的严格要求同样适用于口头合同。因此，雇主在终止口头或书面雇佣合同时均遵守严格要求更为保险。

六、结论

赞比亚国内《劳动法》规定了投资人力资源基础的各个方面，从禁止强迫劳动到最低雇佣条件，从强制缴纳社保到对雇主终止雇佣关系决定权的限制。因此，中国在赞比亚投资的企业总是要受到这些法律的影响。

因此，作者强烈建议中国投资者就其在赞比亚的投资咨询专业人士，在整个投资过程中也要进行常规的咨询。

遵守赞比亚《劳动法》的代价一定比违反的代价更小，违反相关法律的后果可能包括：法律规定的罚款；面临民事起诉和刑事起诉；负面的公共形象。

限制条件

本文基于文章完成时赞比亚生效的法律，内容的准确性可能不可避免地受到之后法律修改的影响。

作者对赞比亚之外的法律不予考虑，也不发表任何评论。

本文仅限于明确表述的内容，不得做任何暗示的扩大理解。

Paper on the Influence of Labour Laws and Regulations of African Countries on the Investment of Chinese Enterprises – A Zambian Perspective①

Author: Chenda

Consensual Nature of Employment Relationship and Prohibition of Forced Labour

In Zambia, the relationship of employer and employee is founded on mutual consent and forced labour is expressly prohibited under the Republican Constitution, the Anti-Human Trafficking Act and the Penal Code. Article 14(2) of the Constitution provides that:

No person shall be required to perform forced labour.

Forced labour is defined under section 3 of the Anti-Human Trafficking Act as:

Labour or services obtained or maintained through threats, the use of force, intimidation or other forms of coercion or physical restraint.

Employees in Zambia therefore have the right to leave employment at will and cannot be forced to continue working against their wishes.

Remuneration and Conditions of Service

Zambian law prescribes minimum wages to be paid to employees as well as the intervals for

---

① The human resource base is one of the key components of every investment enterprise. In this paper, the author will highlight some of the pertinent Zambian labour law provisions that affect all Chinese Enterprise that invest in Zambia, without any particularity as to the sector of investment.This paper is presented in fulfillment of part of the requirements for the 3rd Course of the China-Africa Legal Professional Exchange Programme.

payment of such wages. The Employment Act defines wages as:

The remuneration or earnings, however designated or calculated, capable of being expressed in terms of money and fixed by a contract of service or a contract of foreign service which are payable by an employer to an employee or a casual employee for work done or to be done or for services rendered or to be rendered.

According to the Minimum Wages and Conditions of Employment Act, the Minister of Labour and Social Services may prescribe wage rates for different categories of workers employed in Zambia and he may do so through a statutory order if he/she is of the opinion that there is no other effective way of regulating the minimum wages or working condition for those groups especially in the absence of collective bargaining.

In pursuance of the said power, the Minister for Labour has issued statutory orders via prescribing the minimum wages and conditions of employment for the categories of protected employees, excluding *inter alia* persons in management and persons who are already protected by a collective agreement bargained with the employer.

The minimum wages orders cover everything from the benchmark take home pay to allowances such as transport, lunch and housing. The minimum wages orders also have a formula for redundancy pay and for long service benefits.

In accordance with the Employment Act, an employer is under the obligation to pay the worker when due and payable on an hourly, daily, fortnightly, or monthly basis. The piece rate employees have to be paid on the completion of their tasks however wages of piece rate, daily/hourly employees can be accumulated and paid after a month, if agreed between the parties. Section 44 of the Employment Act provides that:

In all contracts of service the wages of an employee shall be payable in the currency of the Republic and shall be paid direct to the employee:

Provided that if the employee so requests in writing, or if the provisions of any collective agreement applicable to such employee so provide, payment may be made in any of the following ways:

payment into an account at a bank or building society, being an account standing in the name of the person to whom the payment is due, or an account standing in the name of that person jointly with one or more other persons;

payment by postal order;

payment by money order; and

payment by cheque.

Provided further, that an employer may, in the absence of an employee, pay the wages of such employee to a person other than the employee if such person is duly authorised to receive such wages by the employee in writing.

Wherever possible, wages shall be paid on work days and at or near the place of employment.

Nothing contained in this section shall prevent an employer from paying to an employee, in addition to wages, allowances in kind, where such payment is customary or agreed to by the employee or provided for in a collective agreement or in accordance with any written law:

Provided that any such payment, being an allowance in kind, shall be for the personal use and benefit of the employee, and his family, and shall not be in the form of intoxicating spirits or noxious drugs.

Payment of wages shall not be made in any shop, store or canteen or in places where intoxicating liquor is sold, except in the case of employees employed to work therein.

The provisions of this section shall be subject to any law relating to exchange control.

The provisions of this section shall apply also to a casual employee.

Section 15 of the Employment Act for its part provides that:

Subject to any agreement between the parties providing for holidays with pay on conditions not less favourable to an employee than is provided for in this section, and subject to any statutory determination concerning holidays made in accordance with the Minimum Wages and Conditions of Employment Act, an employee shall, after six months' continuous service, be entitled to a holiday with full pay at the rate of two days in respect of each period of one month's service, to be taken at such time as shall be agreed between the parties.

Provided that where a contract of service is terminated otherwise than by an employee's desertion, resignation or summary dismissal before he has qualified for a holiday as aforesaid, he shall be entitled to be paid two days' full pay for each completed month of service.

The holidays referred to under subsection (1) shall be in addition to any public holiday or weekly rest period, whether fixed by any law, agreement or custom, in respect of which the employee is not required to work under his contract of service.

The Minister may, by statutory order, declare any day or days required to be observed as or declared to be public holidays under the Public Holidays Act to be paid public holidays, and on any day which has been declared to be a paid public holiday every employee shall be entitled to a holiday with full pay if he does not, without the permission of his employer or reasonable excuse, absent himself from duty either on the day immediately preceding or on the day following such public holiday:

Provided that where by virtue of any agreement or custom it is normal for an employee or class of employees to work on any day declared to be a paid public holiday such employee or class of employees shall be entitled to payment of wages at such rate as may be agreed under a collective agreement or contract of service.

For the purpose of this section, the expression "full pay" means basic pay, the cash equivalent of any food which may from time to time be provided, and working or other allowances where applicable for a period not exceeding one month, but does not include payments in respect of any bonus.

Notwithstanding the provisions of subsection (1), an employer may, with the agreement of the employee, pay wages to such employee in lieu of any holiday due to the employee under that subsection and if any leave has been accumulated by an employee whose contract has terminated, the employer shall pay wages to the employee for the period of such accumulated leave.

Section 54 of the Employment Act provides that:

Except as may be provided in any contract of service, collective agreement or other written law more favourable to the employee, if any employee becomes temporarily incapacitated in consequence of sickness or accident not occasioned by his own default, such employee shall, provided he has produced a valid medical certificate, receive pay for the days absent up to a maximum of twenty-six working days in any period of twelve months:Wages while incapacitated

Provided that an employer may continue to pay such employee for any longer period if the employer so agrees.

Furthermore, section 15A provides that:

(1) Subject to any agreement between the parties, or any other written law, providing for maternity leave on conditions not less favourable than are provided for in this section, every female employee who has completed at least two years of continuous service with her employer from the date of first engagement or since the last maternity leave taken, as the case may be, shall, on production of a medical certificate as to her pregnancy signed by a registered medical practitioner, be entitled to maternity leave of twelve weeks with full pay.

(2) The maternity leave granted under subsection (1) shall be exclusive of any other leave to which a female employee may otherwise be entitled.

(3) In case of illness which arises out of pregnancy and results in a female employee becoming temporarily incapable of performing her official duties, such employee shall be entitled to sick leave in accordance with the provisions of section fifty-four.

(4) Any employer who contravenes the provisions of this section shall be guilty of an offence.

From the foregoing provisions, and from the Statutory Instruments on Minimum Wages and Conditions of employment, employees are entitled to several leave days with pay. The workers are entitled to a fully paid public holiday if he/she does not, without the permission of his employer or other reasonable excuse, absent himself from duty either on the day immediately preceding or on the day following such public holiday. Amount of payment received during public holidays is the basic pay, the cash equivalent of any food which may from time to time be provided, and working or other allowances where applicable up to one month, but does not include payments in respect of any bonus. Workers are also entitled to sick leave.

The Constitution of Zambia recognises the human freedom of association and in the employment sector, the said freedom is regulated by the Industrial and Labour Relation Act. Therefore, workers in Zambia have the right to form, join or participate in the activities and programmes of a trade union.

In accordance with the Zambian Constitution, the worker has the right to go on a lawful strike. The Industrial and Labour Relations Act defines strike as the cessation of work or withdrawal of labour contrary to the terms and conditions of a contract by a body of persons employed in any undertaking acting in combination; or a concerted refusal or a refusal under a common understanding of any number of persons who are so employed to continue to work or provide their labour.

Peaceful strike is allowed only after all alternative methods of dispute resolution have failed. Majority members of a union must approve a strike by voting in favour of strike, which may commence ten days following the decision to do so and may continue for an indefinite period during which the dispute remains unresolved. Workers are prohibited from participating in a strike that has not been authorised by a strike ballot taken in the manner provided by the constitution of a trade union under the Industrial and Labour Relations Act.

Health, Safety and Compensation

The Occupational Health and Safety Act deals with the occupational health and safety in Zambia. According to the Act, every employer with 10 or more employees at the workplace must establish a health and safety committee:

11. An employer of ten or more persons at any workplace shall establish a health and safety committee.

13. (1) The functions of a health and safety committee are to-

(a) promote cooperation between the employer and the employees in achieving and maintaining healthy and safe working conditions;

(b) share information about occupational health, safety and welfare with employees;

(c) investigate and resolve any matter that may be a risk to the health and safety of employees at a workplace;

(d) review the measures taken on the health and safety of employees at a workplace; and

(e) formulate, review and disseminate to the employees the standards, rules and procedures relating to health and safety to be carried out at the workplace.

The Occupational Health and Safety Act also imposes the following specific obligations on employers in Zambia:

16. (1) Notwithstanding any other written law, an employer shall -

(a) ensure, so far as is reasonably practicable, the health, safety and welfare of the employees of the employer at a workplace; and

(b) place and maintain an employee in an occupational environment adapted to the employee's physical, physiological and psychological ability.

(2) Without prejudice to the generality of subsection (1), an employer shall-

(a) provide plant and systems of work that are, so far as is reasonably practicable, safe and without any risks to human health and maintain them in that condition;

(b) ensure, so far as is reasonably practicable, that articles, devices, items and substances provided for the use of the employees at a workplace are used, handled, stored and transported in a manner that is safe and without any risk to the health and safety of the employees at the workplace;

(c) provide such information, instruction, training and supervision as is necessary to ensure, so far as is reasonably practicable, the health and safety of the employees at their workplace;

(d) so far as is reasonably practicable, maintain a workplace under the employer's control, in a condition that is safe and without any risk to the health and safety of employees at their workplace;

(e) so far as is reasonably practicable, provide and maintain the means of access to, or exit from, a workplace that are safe and without any risk to the health and safety of the employees using it;

(f) provide and maintain a working environment for the employees that is, so far as is reasonably practicable, safe and without any risks to their health and safety, and which is adequate as regards facilities and arrangements for their welfare at the workplace;

(g) inform and consult a health and safety representative—

(i) where an authorised officer visits the workplace, and give the health and safety representative an opportunity to meet the authorised officer;

(ii) on the circumstances and future prevention of any injury or illness;

(iii) on the circumstances of any injury for which aclaim has been submitted to the Workers' Compensation Fund Control Board; or

(iv) with a view to making and maintaining arrangements to enable the employer and the employees to cooperate effectively in promoting and developing measures to ensure the health and safety of the employees at the workplace, and checking the effectiveness of those measures;

(h) provide for measures to deal with emergencies and accidents, including adequate first-aid arrangements;

(i) provide at the employer's expense all appropriate protective clothing or equipment to be used in the workplace by employees, who in the course of employment, are likely to be exposed to the risk of bodily injuries, and adequate instructions in the use of such protective clothing or equipment; and

(j) do for, or provide to, the employees, free of charge, anything which by law is required to be provided to those employees by the employer.

In addition to the Occupation Health and Safety Act, there is the Workers Compensation Act which makes it mandatory for employers to register with the Workers Compensation Fund Control Board. The Workers Compensation Fund exists for the benefit of workers who get disabled by accident occurring or diseases contracted during in the course of their employment.

The contributions to the Workers Compensation Fund are solely for the account of the employer and according to the Workers Compensation Act, any deduction made by an employee to offset against such contributions is an act that is criminalised.

56. (1) Any employer who withholds any moneys due from employer to any of the workers or any sum which the employer is or may become liable to pay as compensation or assessment under this Act, or who requires or permits any worker to contribute under this Act, commits an offence.

The two pieces of legislation namely the Occupational Health and Safety Act and the Workers Compensation Act are complementary in that the former is preventive whilst the latter is remedial where harm has been suffered by an employee.

Social Security, Pension and Long Service Benefits

The Constitution of Zambia as amended by Act No.2 of 2016 confers a right to pension benefits on employees in Zambia and protects the pension benefits from being withheld or altered to the detriment of an employee. Article 187(1) provides as follows:

(1) An employee, including a public officer and Constitutional office holder, has a right to a pension benefit.

Article 266 of the Constitution defines a pension benefit as including:

A pension, compensation, gratuity or similar allowance in respect of a person's service.

The Constitution of Zambia does not define who is considered to be an ‘employee’, however, the Employment Act defines an employee as:

A person who, in return for wages, enters into a contract of service whether on full time, part time or temporary basis or who is engaged to do casual work, but does not include a person employed under a contract of apprenticeship made in accordance with the Apprenticeship Act, an independent contractor or a person engaged to do piece work. (section 3)

Additionally, the Constitution provides that a pension benefit shall not be withheld or altered to that employee's disadvantage and also makes it mandatory for the periodic review of pension benefits based on actuarial evaluations.

The Constitution also makes the payment of pension benefits exempt from income tax and requires that pension benefits be paid promptly.

If a retiring employee does not receive their pension benefit on their last working day then they have to be kept on the payroll and shall continue to receive a salary until the pension benefit is paid albeit not calculated based on the last salary before retirement but instead on the last salary at time of removal from the payroll. We reproduce the relevant articles as follows for ease of reference:

187 (1) ——

(2) A pension benefit shall not be withheld or altered to that employee's disadvantage.

188. (1) A pension benefit shall be reviewed periodically to take into account actuarial assessments.

(2) A pension benefit shall be exempt from tax.

189. (1) A pension benefit shall be paid promptly and regularly.

(2) Where a pension benefit is not paid on a person's last working day, that person shall stop work but the person's name shall be retained on the payroll, until payment of the pension benefit based on the last salary received by that person while on the payroll.

The actual prescription of the mandatory pension benefits, is done by the National Pension Scheme Act which obligates every employer who is registered for taxation in Zambia to thereafter register with the National Pension Scheme Authority.

Section 13 of the National Pension Scheme Act creates the obligation while Section 12 of the National Pension Scheme Act broadly defines a contributing employer as:

person, association, institution or firm registered as a tax payer with a contract of service with an employee; and the Government of the Republic of Zambia, local authority or parastatal or statutory body.

It is thus mandatory for all employers in Zambia to make social security contributions for their employees from the point at which the employer becomes registered for taxation purposes. This does not however restrict the employers from setting up a private pension scheme to provide for an additional endowment for their employees, over and above what they will receive from the National Pension Scheme.

Restriction and Regulation of Termination of Employment

Previously under Zambian, law a written contract of employment could be terminated by an employer at any time and for any reason or for no reason whatsoever.

However, with the passing of the Employment (Amendment) Act, an employer now has to give valid reasons to justify termination of a written employment contract which reasons must be based on the conduct or capacity of the employee, or the operational requirements of the employer.

Failure to adhere to the said requirements would give rise to a cause of action for wrongful termination and / or dismissal. We reproduce the exact provisions of the Employment Act as follows:

Section 36 (1) A written contract of service shall be terminated-

(a) ——

(b) ——

(c) In any other manner in which a contract of service may be lawfully terminated whether under the provisions of the Act or otherwise except that where the termination is at the initiative of the employer, the employer shall give reasons to the employee for the termination of that employee's employment.

(2) ——

(3) The contract of service of an employee shall not be terminated unless there is a valid reason

for the termination connected with the capacity, conduct of the employee or based on the operational requirements of the undertaking.

The Employment Act also now stipulates what reasons should never be used by an employer for termination of an employee's written contract of service. The relevant provision namely section 36(4) reads:

(4) Reasons that are not valid for termination of contracts include-

(a) union membership or participation in union activities outside working hours or, with the consent of the employer, within working hours;

(b) seeking office as, acting or having acted in the capacity of, an employee's representative;

(c) the filing of a complaint, the participation in proceedings against an employer involving alleged violation of laws or recourse to administrative authorities;

(d) race, colour, sex, marital status, family responsibilities, pregnancy, religion, political opinion or affiliation, ethnicity, tribal affiliation or social status of the employee; or

(e) absence from work during leave or a rest period in accordance with a written law.

It is noteworthy that section 36 of the Employment Act falls under the Part V of the Act that deals with written contracts of service only.

As for oral contracts of employment in Zambia, there was no corresponding amendment to the relevant provisions (possibly on account of legislative drafting oversight).

Oral contracts therefore remain terminable (on paper) by simple notice without the stringent restrictions alluded to above with respect to written contracts of employment. Section 20(1) of the Employment Act reads:

20.(1) Either party to an oral contract may terminate the employment on the expiration of notice given to the other party of his intention to do so, and where the notice expires during the currency of a contract period, the contract shall be thereupon terminated.

However, when faced with a contested termination of an oral contract, the Courts are likely to import the stringent requirements under written contracts and to impute them to oral contracts. It is therefore safer for any employer to adhere to the same requirements when terminating either of a written or oral contract.

Conclusion

Chinese enterprises investing in Zambia are invariably affected by the domestic labour laws which dictate various aspects of the human resource base of the investment ranging from prohibition of forced labour to fixing of minimum conditions of service, mandatory social security contributions and restrictions of the employer discretion to terminate employment.

It is strongly recommended therefore that Chinese investors seek appropriate Counsel from inception and also routinely throughout the lifespan of their investment in Zambia.

The cost of staying compliant with Zambian labour laws would invariably be much less than the cost and consequences of default which could include:

statutory penalties and fines;

litigation in Court (both civil and criminal); and

negative media coverage / publicity.

Limitations and qualifications

This paper is based on Zambian law for the time being in force as at the date of the paper and the accuracy of the contents may invariably be affected by subsequent law reform.

The author expresses no opinion on, and has not taken into account, the laws of any jurisdiction other than Zambia.

The paper is limited to what is expressly stated in this document and it is not to be extended by any implication.

非洲关于中非合作论坛约翰尼斯堡行动计划（2016—2018）制定的支持性法律和政策的解释

作者：Ndimbo 译者：张心诚

一、历史背景

在具有历史意义的“中非合作论坛第一届部长级会议（2000）”期间，中非合作论坛于当年10月正式启动，此次会议确立了中非合作论坛是中国和非洲在平等互利基础上的集体对话框架，谋求和平与发展是中国和非洲国家的共同目标。

二、覆盖领域

中非合作论坛在其首次会议提出了《中非合作论坛北京宣言》的文件。宣言包括了以下领域：

1. 必须尊重《联合国宪章》和《非洲统一组织宪章》的宗旨和原则。所有国家都有平等参与国际事务的权利；任何国家或集团都无权将自己的意志强加于别国或以任何借口干涉别国内政，或单方面对别国实施强制性经济措施。南方和北方之间要加强平等对话与合作。

2. 必须坚持和平解决国际争端原则。国家间的争端不得诉诸武力威胁包括核威胁。努力推动裁军和核不扩散进程，以最终达到全面禁止和彻底销毁核武器和其他大规模杀伤性武器的目标，确保所有国家的安全都得到保证。

3. 尊重和加强联合国安理会在维护世界和平与安全方面的首要作用，积极推动联合国及国际金融机构的改革。发展中国家包括非洲国家在联合国安理会和国际经济及金融组织中的代表性应得到加强，以充分体现国际关系的民主原则。

4. 人权的普遍性原则和基本自由应得到尊重，世界的多样性和求同存异原则必须得到维护和弘扬。每个国家在自己的发展过程中都有权根据本国的国情，选择自己的发展道路、社会制度、历史文化背景和价值观念、发展模式、促进和保护人权的模式和生活方式。

5. 互利合作、共同发展的原则应予倡导。发达国家有责任、有义务在资金、技术等方面向发展中国家包括非洲国家提供援助并制定切实可行的发展计划，同发展中国家在平等互利基础上进行合作，实现南北共同发展。发展中国家包括非洲国家应进一步加强团结协作，趋利避害，共同应对全球化的挑战。

6. 号召非洲国家加强次地区合作、通过建立非洲联盟进一步巩固非洲团结，敦促国际社会和国际组织支持非洲国家为此采取的措施；此举对于加强非洲的团结、和平与发展，妥善解决争端至关重要。

7. 赞赏非洲国家和国际社会与艾滋病、疟疾和其他传染病进行的斗争以及为消除贫困所作出的努力和采取的行动。因此，欢迎设立世界团结基金的倡议，呼吁有关机构大力支持建立该基金。

8. 同意共同努力，在反恐怖主义方面加强合作，以消除各种形式的恐怖主义。

9. 呼吁国际金融机构和发达债权国在减免非洲最不发达国家和中等收入国家债务问题上采取具体措施；欢迎中国作为发展中国家为减免非洲国家债务将采取的切实措施和作出的贡献。

10. 决心进一步巩固和拓展中非在各层次、各领域的合作，在南南合作的框架内建立长期稳定、平等互利的新型伙伴关系。在平等互利、共同发展的原则基础上，大力推动中非在经济、贸易、财政、农业、医疗保健、公共卫生、科技、文化、教育、人力资源开发、交通运输、环境、旅游等领域的合作，促进中非共同发展。

三、成就

从 2000 年 10 月初开始，中非合作论坛已经如宣言中设想取得了下列成就：

1. 在中国的影响下，非洲各国在国际事务中的参与显著提升。不过暂时还没有像《联合国宪章》和《非洲统一宪章》设想的那样处于平等地位。

2. 通过非洲联盟，非洲在国际对话中发出同一个声音。该联盟通过建立执行委员会处理社会经济发展问题，同时建立政府机关，包括行政、立法和司法部门，此举使其得到了显著的权利。

3. 越来越多的国家选择通过和平方式解决国际争端而不是采取如核武器等武力相威胁。例如，肯尼亚、卢旺达、刚果共和国、布隆迪和平谈判，极少涉及恐怖力量。然而，利比亚的非正义武装被北方利用，暴乱并推翻了合法政府。此举引起一些同类非洲国家由于安全问题和国内战争而导致政治动荡社会骚乱。

4. 基于平等互利共同发展的原则，发展中国家和发达国家的合作也日渐增长。发达国家通过免除其责任和义务来为发展中国家（尤其非洲）提供资金、技术和其他帮助。

5. 国际社会和国际组织越来越支持非洲国家加强次地区合作，非洲联盟已经成立并实现了非洲的团结、和平发展、妥善解决争端的目标，在非洲起到了先锋带头作用。

6. 赞赏非洲国家和国际社会与艾滋病、疟疾和其他传染病进行的斗争以及为消除贫困所作出的努力和采取的行动。为此欢迎设立世界团结基金的倡议，呼吁有关机构大力支持建立该基金。

7. 在与恐怖势力作斗争中增加了合作和团结的力量，致力于粉碎非洲的恐怖组织（如西非的博科圣地、索马里的青年党和利比亚的伊斯兰国）。

8. 国际金融机构和发达债权国（尤其是中国）针对非洲国家增加了诸如负债交换和取消债务等债务减免手段。

9. 区域合作显著增多。例如，东非共同体在继续转化为东非政治社会经济共同体。

10. 实现了巩固和拓展中非在各层次、各领域的合作，重视了在南南合作的框架内建立长期稳定、平等互利的新型伙伴关系。在平等互利、共同发展的原则基础上，大力推动了如下领域的发展：经济；贸易；金融；农业；医疗保健和公共卫生；科技；文化，教育；人力资源开发；交通运输；环境；旅游；政治等其他领域。

四、不足

除了已经提到的成就外，完全实现中非合作的既定目标仍然有一些障碍，包括如下问题：

1. 偷猎非洲野生动物和非法贸易野生动物制品仍在增加（尤其是大象和犀牛及其制品）。

2. 不法投资者非法进行森林砍伐，导致了土壤恶化和土地沙漠化。

3. 外来物种的入侵，人类的侵入和国内动荡威胁非洲的生物多样性。

4. 一些非洲国家受到内战和恐怖分子的影响导致国家不稳定性增加。

5. 一些非洲国家受到内战和国家忽视的影响仍时常发生侵犯人权的行为。

6. 缺少外国资本投入。

7. 缺乏教育。

8. 政府官员腐败现象频发导致公共资源的滥用，缺少合适的发展项目。

五、未来前瞻性

中非合作论坛对未来各方面发展的预期在《中非合作论坛——约翰内斯堡行动计划（2016—2018）》作出了如下描述：

政治合作，旨在包括立法机关、政党机关、咨询机关和当地政府各部门交换意见并且互相访问。

经济领域利益如下：贸易；金融；基础设施；农业；投资；能源；医疗保健和公共卫生；文化、教育；人力资源开发；交通运输；环境；旅游。

在社会发展中，相关领域需要各方面的援助，如科学、技术、文化、教育、人力资源开发、医疗卫生、脱贫方案经验的交换以及环境保护。

合作同样放眼于军事安全、政治、反恐怖组织、领事、移民、司法、执法等问题。

六、非洲各国为实现合作尤其是《中非合作论坛——约翰内斯堡行动计划（2016—2018）》所涉及的内容制定了多部法令与政策：以坦桑尼亚案例研究

为了带来社会经济的可持续发展和促进相关部门的转变，我们必须认识到针对社会经济领域的不同部门颁布法令和政策的重要性。当相应的法律和政策具备时，有投资意图的资本家将知道何时进行投资，并且更加确信即使面临征收，他们的投资将会受到法律保护并且后续将归还到其手中。

为了加快实现既定目标、促进中非合作论坛领域更快实现社会经济发展，非洲国家将以前的非洲统一组织转型为非洲联盟（正式成立于 2002 年），并且以南非的约翰内斯堡为基地设立泛非洲议会，在埃塞俄比亚首都亚的斯亚贝巴设立非洲人权

和人民权利委员会，以此来响应非洲国家法令与政策发展计划。

伴随着此次转型，非洲联盟设立了议会制政府，并且命名为非洲联盟政府。该政府包括立法部门、司法部门以及行政部门。根据《非洲联盟组织法》，非洲联盟政府成立了非洲联盟议会，该议会在将非洲经济共同体和非洲联邦重建，为遵守国际公约的非洲起到了重要作用。

非洲联盟议会为了积极实现《中非合作论坛——约翰内斯堡行动计划（2016—2018）》，至今已经颁布了多部有关非洲大陆人类发展的法令与政策。列举如下：

1.《非洲保护自然和自然资源公约》和其相关政策承认大自然赋予非洲的自然环境和自然资源是非洲文化遗产中不可取代的一部分，对于非洲大陆和全体非洲人民非常重要，并且公约进一步呼吁非洲国家坚持《非洲统一组织宪章》。宪章中强调了，每一个非洲国家都有义务将人力物力投入对非洲人民有利的经济、社会、文化和环境建设中。

2. 协议中成立了泛非金融机构，规定该机构为非洲大陆提供充足的资源，以确保非洲大陆 2063 议程发展计划的实现（该议程中的工业任务部分由中国投资赞助）。

3. 关于旅游业与野生动物保护方面，非洲联盟通过非洲委员会执行委员会提出相应的法律政策，呼吁各国确保野生动物和其他具有旅游吸引力的资源受到妥善保护，并且确保使当地包括女性在内的所有民众受益。具体措施包括加强措施来禁止偷猎、非法贸易野生动物制品、生物剽窃。将非洲建设成为非洲人民乃至全国人民的首选旅游目的地，打造强大的非洲旅游品牌。

4.《道路安全宪章议定书》。

5.《非洲宪章老年人人权和人民权利议定书》。

6.《药品管制示范法议定书》。

7.《非洲体育理事会章程议定书》。

8.《非洲矿产开发中心规划议定书》。

9.《非洲联盟人权机关关于设立法律援助基金的议定书》。

10.《非洲科学研究和创新理事会规约议定书》。

11.《非洲科学、技术与创新观察站规约议定书》。

12.《泛非洲知识产权组织章程议定书》。

13.《卫生人口与药物控制专业技术委员会议事规则议定书》。

14.《公共服务、地方政府、城市发展和分权的专业技术委员会议事规则议定书》。

15.《非洲联盟的经济、社会和文化理事会规则议定书》。

16.《社会发展、劳动和就业问题专门技术委员会议事规则议定书》。

17.《文化和体育专业技术委员会议事规则议定书》。

18.《教育、科学和技术专业技术委员会议事规则议定书》。

19.《通信信息和通信技术专业技术委员会议事规则议定书》。

20.《修订后泛非洲大学法律章程议定书》。

21.《非洲反腐败公约》，该公约为非洲联盟和成员或机构的反腐败和治理腐败提供了框架。

然而，我们更要清楚地了解通过非洲联盟委员会颁布的法令政策，只有在得到特定具有管辖权的国家的相关组织调整后才拥有法律力量和可执行力。

因此，为了使这类法律政策适用于每个国家所制定的社会经济计划项目，它们必须得到当地立法和政策的支持。以坦桑尼亚为例，坦桑尼亚重新审视了《中非合作论坛——约翰内斯堡行动计划（2016—2018）》，并且制定了符合该计划范围内的法律和政策。其中包括：

1.《公司法（2002）》以及《商业活动注册登记法（2005）》为坦桑尼亚境内的法人团体登记和进行商业活动提供了法律框架。

2.《所得税法案 (2008)》《东非海关管理法（2004）》《印花税法案（2006）》《坦桑尼亚税务局法案（2006）》《增值税法案（2014）》为包括外国投资者在内的所有人和政府提供了多种多样的税务和税收体系，旨在提高收入和实现社会经济进步。

3.《土地法和农田法（1999 年出台，2008 年修订）》和《国家土地法（1995）》为本国和外国希望在坦桑尼亚进行投资的人提供了框架，详尽解释了取得土地的所有权和使用权。《坦桑尼亚投资法（1997）》进一步讨论了以上问题。

4. 为了促进发展策略，制定了《国家财富增长和减少贫困战略 II（2010）》《国家人口政策（2006）》《国家人居环境发展政策（2000）》《工业可持续发展政策（1996）》和《坦桑尼亚 2025 发展愿景》。坦桑尼亚通过此类政策为社会的可持续发展分析了各种社会经济计划和项目，并且切实缓解了社会面临的严重贫困，包括致力于工业化道路的承诺。

5.《电力法（2008）》《农村能源法（2005）》以及能源政策为私人投资者参与电力生产提供了机会。这不仅对产业化至关重要，而且对于所有的社会经济进步同样至关重要。另外，对包括农村居民在内的所有公民增加电力分配和供给也起到了重要作用。

6.《公私伙伴关系法（2010）》《公私伙伴关系管理法（2011）》和《公私伙伴关系政策（2010）》，这些政策为贯彻公共部门和私营部门公私协议制定了规则、指导方针以及步骤，以此来管理生产和社会经济服务部门公司伙伴关系的形成、发展与落实，包括但不限于以下方面：农业、基础设施、制造业、教育、卫生、自然资源、旅游、能源、采矿、水、土地开发、环境和固体废物管理、适当的国防基础设施、体育、通信、信息和通信技术、贸易、娱乐、休闲、灌溉。

因此，绝大多数坦桑尼亚境内的包括外国投资者（如来自中国的投资商）在内的私营部门在为公私合伙企业提供资源时受到了帮助与保护，其中包括保护其投资资本、管理技能和技术。这些都是实现社会经济的完全转型或进步和减轻贫困所必要的。目前，满足公司合资企业的各级制度安排已经到位。

7.《公共采购法（2011）》《公共采购法规（2013）》也涉及了经济和货币价值的问题，因为过去所有的公共收入直接导致了公私合营企业的社会经济变革。

8. 在矿业领域，坦桑尼亚提出了《新矿产政策（2009）》，废除了旧版的《矿产政策（1997）》，现行法律为《矿产政策（2010）》。

该政策呼吁私人投资者继续投资矿产勘测和开采，强调矿产部门与其他经济体的整合、建立了确保国家利益和保持国际竞争力的财政制度；支持选矿和营销，巩固小规模的矿业发展，促进公众参与采矿活动并为投资商提供旨在坦桑尼亚的矿产资源可持续开发的明确指导，旨在达到《采矿法（2010）》中积极阐述的以双赢的方式实现坦桑尼亚的矿产资源可持续开发的目标。

目前坦桑尼亚丰富的矿物资源（包括黄金、铜、镍、铁矿石、钻石、坦桑石、石灰石、纯碱、石膏、磷、煤、铀和其他未提到的矿物）的开采政策和法律应该有利于国家，从而产生有助于社会经济发展的足够的收入。矿产部门对 GDP 的贡献率从不足 2% 增加到 2025 年的 10%，这有效地缓解了现有的极度贫困状况。

同样，为了矿区及其周边地区的健康、安全和环境管理，政府强调和倡导使用最佳开采方法，如果无法完全消除对健康、安全、环境管理等社会问题的不利影响，政府将采取措施提高和加强矿业的监测和监管措施以降低此不良影响。

9. 关于整体环境控制与保护问题，坦桑尼亚已经提出并实施了多部法律：《环境管理法（2004）》《国家环境政策（1997）》《国家环境行动计划（2013）》，除了描述可持续发展、合理利用环境和利用自然资源的法律和制度框架外，还对任何人类活动土地使用权的许可证书的发行进行管理，包括矿产勘查和开采应附有环境影响评估证书。另外，任何违反该法发布的证书有义务无条件停止，因为所有的投资事宜应当为社会的总体利益考虑，遵守环境保护的措施以合理利用自然资源，以此来应对气候变化的影响。

10.《公共卫生法案（2009）》《国家卫生政策（2007）》《供水和卫生设施法（2009）》《水资源管理法（2009）》《国家水政策（2002）》，上述文件涉及了健康管理、卫生系统、水资源捐助管理等问题。

11.《森林法（2002）》《森林保护区的管理和保护法（1996）》和《养蜂法（2002）》已颁布实施，用以管理森林和蜜蜂以及森林和蜜蜂产品，包括私营部门在内的国家和共同体的合作，以促进和加强林业部门对可持续发展的贡献。立法禁止在森林保护区内进行人类活动，以此来保护和管理当代和未来的自然资源。这些和《国家森林政策（1998）》的指导齐头并进。

12.《旅游法（2008）》管理旅游业和从旅游活动中积累的收入，以此来管理公民的利益，反映了《国家旅游政策（1999）》的重点。

13.《国家公园法案》（CAP.282 RE 2002）、《野生动物政策（2007）》《野生动物保护法（2009）》，用以保护野生动物，管理来自野生动物和野生动物制品的收入，以此来维持旅游业的可持续发展。此类政策旨在为后代保护文化资源，包括《海洋公园和储备法（1994）》中的海洋资源。在坦桑尼亚，包括农作物种植、动物饲养或放牧以及渔业活动在内的农业投资分别受到《植物保护法（1997）》《渔业法（2003）》《国家农业政策（2013）》和《国家畜牧政策（2006）》的保护。

14.《出口加工区法（2002）》和《经济特区法（2005）》为工业部门设立了框架，并且鼓励对其投资，以此达到出口和推进坦桑尼亚社会经济发展的目的。

15.《外汇法（1992）》管理外汇业务和金融机构，尤其是各种可转让票据（如支票）的有效性。

16.《移民法（1995）》和《国家人口流动政策（2010）》为正当管理和控制包括进出坦桑尼亚的移民在内的人口流动提供了准确的、合法的制度框架。同时包括投资者和各类投资企业专家可以获得五个季度的工作许可证。

17. 为了打击危害国家安全和世界安全的刑事犯罪行为，如参与恐怖活动，《恐怖主义法案（2002）》出台。为打击非法致富，例如恐怖活动、非法交易野生动物制品、非法交易毒品、贪污腐败，《洗钱法（2006）》《预防和打击腐败法（2007）》出台。

18. 增加石油和天然气勘测以及切实开始提取天然气迫使坦桑尼亚在2015年提出下列三项立法：

（1）《石油法（2015）》取代了《石油（勘探和生产）法（1980）》（包含上游石油业务）、《石油法（2008）》（包含中下游石油供应业务），为坦桑尼亚的油气勘测与开采作业提供了方案与框架，更好地实现坦桑尼亚共同体的利益。有一点极其重要，即该法案通过国有企业赋予了政府对石油和天然气的所有权。

（2）《采掘业（透明度和问责性）法案（2015）》为所有与采掘业相关的特权、合同和许可的公开性提供了新的道路，而不是像以前那样插入保密条款。尤其体现在矿业发展协议中，目标是遏制石油和天然气行业的腐败和其他渎职行为。

（3）《天然气和石油收入管理法案（2015）》建立了石油和天然气基金，用以维持财政和宏观经济的稳定、加强社会经济的发展、维护后代的资源。开采石油和天然气的预期收入预计将增加 9% ～ 31% 的政府收入，所以，必须指导其如何直接有效地使用这笔收入来满足公民的基本需求。例如，改善并提供优质的医疗保健、教育和其他的社会服务，并且支持长期的经济增长。

七、结论

总之，非洲国家坚信和中国的长期伙伴关系，因此，大多数非洲国家自独立以来制定的法律和政策都注重与中国的合作，尤其是《中非合作论坛——约翰内斯堡行动计划（2016—2018）》，非洲联盟委员会在 63 号决议上予以高度重视并积极响应。

参考文献

［1］The Decision Number EX.CL/Dec.898-918 (XXVIII) of the 28th Ordinary Session of Executive Council of African Union held from 23-28th January 2016, particularly EX.CL/Dec.908 (XXVIII) page 3, retrieved from www.www.au.int.

［2］https://en.wikipedia.org/wiki/Africa. time on line 12:34 pm 2016 May 28.

［3］https://en.wikipedia.org/wiki/Environmental_protection. time on line 8:341 am 2016 May 26.

［4］file:///E:/ How to Invest in Africa_Mutual Funds_Us News.htm time on line 12:13 pm 2016 May 25.

［5］Samwel J. Sitta (2005), "INVESTMENT FOR AFRICAN DEVELOPMENT: Making it happen", NEPAD/OECD INVESTMENT INITIATIVE.

［6］The Combined Draft Version of the Forum on China-Africa Cooperation Johannesburg Action Plan (2016-2018).

［7］http://www.tanzaniaembassy.or.jp/english/Business/investment_in_en.html. time on line 1:39 pm 2016 May 25.

[8] Environment Program, Investing in our Future http://warmheartworldwide.org/biochar-research-environment/gcli. time on line 9:56 am 2016 May 26.

[9] Public-Private Partnerships, http://www.tic.co.tz/menu/314 Tanzania Investment Centre. time on line 4:47 pm 2016 May 27.

[10] http://www.journalism.co.za/blog/topics/categories/china-africa-reporting/Journalism.co.za. time on line 1:04 pm 2016 May 25.

The Interpretation of Supporting Laws and Policies Made by African Counties according to "the Forum on China–Africa Cooperation Johannesburg Action Plan (2016—2018)

Author: Ndimbo

Historical Background

The Forum on China-Africa Cooperation (FOCAC) was officially initiated in October, 2000 during the first and historical gathering of the Forum on China-Africa Cooperation/Relations Ministerial Conference 2000 geared at promulgating a frame work for collective dialogue between China and African Countries on the basis of equality and mutual benefit and seeking peace and development in common objective.

Areas of Coverage

The Forum on China-Africa Cooperation (FOCAC) in its first meeting popularly known as the Beijing declaration of the Forum on China-Africa Cooperation came up with declarations which covered the following areas namely:

- Attainments of right to participate in international affairs for all Countries on equal footing based on recognized principles governing relations among states as enshrined in the UN Charter and the Charter of the Organization of African Unity (OAU) now African Unity (AU) hence preventing Country or group of Countries to interfere under whatever pretext internal affairs in other countries or imposes unilateral coercive economic measures on others as for the case of the North. That is to say the North and the South were required now to strengthen their dialogue and cooperation on the basis of equality.
- Avoiding threat of forces such as use of nuclear weapons in settlement of international disputes

instead peaceful means was required to be encouraged including increased strive to advance the process of disarmament and nuclear non proliferation, with a view of realizing the ultimate goal of complete prohibition and thorough destruction of nuclear weapons and other weapons of mass destruction so as to ensure security to all Countries.

- Requiring all Countries to respect the primary role of the UN Security Council to safeguard world peace and security and increasing efforts geared at reforming United Nations to provide representations to developing countries including African Countries, and International economic and Financial Institutions so as to fully reflect the democratic principles governing international rational relations.
- Respecting and upholding the universality of human rights, fundamental freedom, the diversity of the world and the principle of seeking common ground while reserving differences. That is to say the right of each Country to choose in its course of development, its own social system, historical and cultural background and values, development model, models in protecting and promoting human rights and way of life in light of its national condition.
- Advocating principles of conducting mutually beneficial cooperation and seeking common development among Countries whereby developed Countries were called upon to discharge their responsibility and obligation to provide financial, technological and other assistance to developing countries including African Countries on feasible development programs for cooperation based on equality and mutual benefit with view to achieving common development for both the North and the South. While developing Countries including Africa on their part, were called upon to unite and cooperate with each other more closely, maximizing advantages while minimizing disadvantages and adversities as well as tackle together challenges brought about by globalization.
- Calling upon the international community and international organization acknowledging and supporting African continents efforts in enhancing sub regional cooperation and further consolidating African unity by establishing the African Union which is vital in enhancing solidarity, peace and development of Africa and properly settle conflicts in Africa.
- Appreciating efforts made by African countries and the international community to combat HIV/AIDS, malaria and other infectious/communicable diseases and efforts taken to eradicate poverty. Hence welcoming and called upon institutions initiative geared at establishing a World Solidarity Fund.
- Agreeing working together to improve cooperation in fight against terrorism so as to eliminate the phenomenon in all its forms and manifestation.
- Appealing to international financial institutions and creditor developed countries to adopt more concrete measures aimed at debt relief including debt cancellation measures and reductions for the least developed and middle income African countries and welcoming concrete measures and contribution on the same made by China and a developing country itself.

- Consolidating, expanding and vigorously promoting China-Africa cooperation at all levels and in all fields and to establish within the frame work of south-South cooperation a new-type long-term and stable partnership based on equality and mutual benefit and common developments in aspects of economic, trade, financial, agricultural, medical care and public health, scientific and technological, cultural, educational, human resources development, transportation, environment, tourism and other areas.

Achievements

Since its inception the Forum on China-Africa Cooperation (FOCAC) early in October, 2000 has lead to increased achievements in all aspects as envisaged in the declarations as hereunder illustrated:

- Through the influence of China there has seen a noticeable increases participation of Africans Countries in international affairs though not on equal footing based on recognized principles governing relations among states as enshrined in the UN Charter and the Charter of the Organization of African Unity (OAU) now African Unity (AU).
- Through the African Union which has gained tremendous strength by coming up with an Executive Commission dealing with socio-economic progress issues together with Governmental organs ranging from Executive, legislative and judicial organs Africa now stand as one voice in international dialogue.
- There is increases use of peaceful means in dissolving international disputes instead peaceful means as opposed to threat of forces such as use of nuclear weapons such as Kenya, Rwanda, Democratic republic of Congo, Burundi peace talks to mention few. Though some African Countries such as Libya unjustified forces was invoked by the Northern to suppress and overthrow a legitimate elected Government leading to increased political and social unrest through out of the country due to insecurity and civil uprising/war.
- There has been increased cooperation conducted basing on principles of mutually beneficial and common development where developed countries have seen discharging their responsibility and obligation to provide financial, technological and other assistance to developing countries, Africa particularly.
- Due to increased international community and international organization support to African continents efforts in enhancing sub regional cooperation and consolidation of African unity the African Union has established and acquired active role in spearheading solidarity, peace and development goals in Africa and properly settle conflicts in Africa.
- Appreciating efforts made by African countries and the international community to combat

HIV/AIDS, malaria and other infectious/communicable diseases and efforts taken to eradicate poverty. Hence welcoming and called upon institutions initiative geared at establishing a World Solidarity Fund.

- Increased cooperation and joint efforts in fight against terrorism so as to eliminate terrorist groups in Africa such as Boko haram in West Africa, Al Shabab in Somalia and Islamic State in Libya.
- Increased debt relief such as debt swap or cancellation measures to African countries by international financial institutions and creditor in developed countries, China in particular.
- Increased regional cooperation such as East African Community with the views of continuing transforming the Communities among East African Countries politically, Socially and economically.
- Lead to consolidated, expanded and vigorously promoted China-Africa cooperation at all levels and in all fields emphasized within the frame work of south-South cooperation and stable partnership based on equality and mutual benefit and common developments in aspects of, namely: Economic, Trade, Financial, Agricultural, Medical Care and Public Health, Scientific and Technological, Cultural, Educational, Human Resources Development, Transportation, Environment, Tourism, Political and other areas.

Shortcomings

Apart from the registered achievement but on the contrary there is still some hindrances to successful attainments of intended goals of China-Africa cooperation which includes:

- Increased poaching and illicit trade of Africa wildlife and wildlife product particularly elephants and rhinos.
- Soil degradation and desertification due to deforestation following illegal forest cuttings by unfaithful investors.
- Introduction non-native species, human encroachment and civil unrest threatens biodiversity in Africa.
- Increased insecurity in some of African Countries due internal civil wars and terrorists attaches.
- Human rights abuse still occurs in several parts of Africa due to civil war and some time oversight of state.
- Lack of access to foreign capital.
- Illiteracy.
- Existence of corrupt government hence misuse of public resources and lack of proper development programs.

Future Prospectives

Future prospects of the Forum on China-Africa Cooperation (FOCAC) is enshrined in the Version of the Forum on China-Africa Cooperation Johannesburg Action Plan (2016-2018) which includes the following development aspects:-

5.1 Political cooperation aimed at exchanging experience in legislatures, political Parties, consultative bodies and local government together with encouraging visit.

5.2 Economically areas of interest are as here under: Trade, Finance, infrastructure, Agricultural, Investments, energy, Medical Care and Public Health, Culture and Education, Human Resources Development, Transportation, Environment, Tourism.

5.3 At Social Developments touched areas are assistances, Scientific and Technological, Cultural, Educational and human resources developments, Medical care and public Health, exchanges of experience on poverty eradication strategies and Environmental protections.

5.4 The cooperation also is looking on issues of security like military, police and anti terrorism together with Consular, Immigration, judiciary and Law Enforcement issues.

Various Laws and Policies Made by African Countries to Achieve the Cooperation and Particularly as Envisaged in the Forum on China-Africa Cooperation Johannesburg Action Plan (2016—2018), Tanzania Case Study

Obviously it is pertinent to acknowledge the role and importance of promulgating and formulating laws and policies in different ventures, or sectors of socio-economic arena in any society for the purposes of bringing sustainable socio-economic progress and transformation for the concerned community. Because when there is laws and policies of given aspects those with capital and intention know when to invest and be more certain that there are protected by laws from expropriation by the community concerned for invested property or investments and their money would return once injected therein.

For thc purpose of expedite and achieving goals and making the Forum on China-Africa Cooperation (FOCAC) yield quick and tremendous socio-economic progress in respond to commitment demonstrated by China count part become realistic African Countries started by transforming their unity from the then Organization of African Unity (OAU) to current African Union (AU) officially in 2002 which has established the African Union's Pan-African Parliament (PAP) centered in Johannesburg South Africa for the promulgation of African Countries' development programs legislations and policies and the African Commission on Human and peoples' Rights remain centered in Addis Ababa Ethiopia.

Following such transformations the African Union which now has Parliamentary government, known as the African Union Government, consisting of legislative, judicial and executive organs via its Constitutive Act has formed African Union Commission which play a vital role of transforming African economic community and a federated commonwealth into a state under established international conventions.

The African Union Commission has so far promulgated various Laws and Policies for the formulation of plans and programs which encompassing all walk of human development in African continents most of them are in accordance with Forum on China-Africa Cooperation (FOCAC) as enshrined in the Version of the Forum on China-Africa Cooperation Johannesburg Action Plan (2016-2018) which includes:

- African Convention on the Conservation of Nature and Natural Resources and its policies which acknowledges that the natural environment in Africa and the natural resources with which Africa continent is endowed are irreplaceable part of the African heritage and constitutes a capital of vital importance to the continent and humankind as a whole and goes further to call upon all African Nations to adhere to the Charter of Organization of African Unity which emphasizes to the duty of every African Country to harness the natural and human resources of the continent for economic, social, cultural and environmental advantageous point of view to African peoples
- Protocol establishing the Pan-African financial institutions with the views of providing the continents with adequate resources for the implementation of the continental development Agenda of 2063 including the industrialization mission sponsored and financed by China.
- Concerning Tourism and Wild life Conservation aspects the African union through the Executive Council of African commission has come up with laws and policies which call upon countries to ensure that wild life and other tourist attractive resources in Africa are properly conserved and managed for the purpose of benefiting local communities, including women by increasing measures to ban and combat poaching, illicit trade in wildlife products and bio-piracy and making Africa the preferred tourist destination, of both African and global tourist and building a strong brand Africa.
- Protocol to the road safety charter.
- Protocol to the African Charter on Human and People's Rights on the Rights of older Persons.
- Protocol to Model Law on Medicine Regulation.
- Protocol to the statute of the Africa sports Council.
- Protocol to the statute of the African Minerals Development Centre.
- Protocol to the statute of the Establishment of Legal Aid Fund for the African Union Human Rights Organs.

- Protocol to the statute of the African Science Research and Innovation Council (ASRIC) .
- Protocol to the statute of the African Observatory in Science Technology and Innovation (AOSTI) .
- Protocol to the statute of the Pan-African Intellectual Property Organization (PAIPO) .
- Protocol to the Rules of Procedure of the Specialized Technical Committee on Health Population and Drugs Control .
- Protocol to the Rules of Procedure of the Specialized Technical Committee on Public Service, Local Government, Urban Development and Decentralization.
- Protocol to the Rules of the Economic, Social and Cultural Council of the African Union.
- Protocol to the Rules of Procedure of the Specialized Technical Committee on Social Development, Labour and Employment.
- Protocol to the Rules of Procedure of the Specialized Technical Committee on Culture and Sport
- Protocol to the Rules of Procedure of the Specialized Technical Committee on Education, Science and Technology.
- Protocol to the Rules of Procedure of the Specialized Technical Committee on Communication and ICT.
- Protocol to the amended statute of the Pan-African University.
- African Convention against Corruption provide frameworks for fights against corruption and bad governance both within African Union and member state institutions.

However, it is of paramount important to understand that all promulgated policies and laws by African Countries through African Union Commission can only attain legal forces and become enforceable in a legal jurisdiction of given African Country after being rectified by relevant Authority of such particular Country,

Hence for such policies and law to be applied in formulating socio-economic plans for projects in each Country they must be supported by enactment of local legislations and policy as illustrated in the case study for Tanzania whereby the revisited laws and policies are within the ambit of the Forum on China-Africa Cooperation (FOCAC) as enshrined in the Version of the Forum on China-Africa Cooperation Johannesburg Action Plan (2016—2018) which includes:

· Company Act of 2002 which followed by Business activities Registration Act of 2005 these gives legal frameworks for registration of corporate bodies and business activities wishing to conduct its activities in Tanzania.

· Income Tax Act of 2008, East Africa Customs Management Act of 2004, Stamp Duty Act of 2006, Tanzania Revenue Authority Act of 2006 and the Value Added Tax Act of 2014 provide for schemes of liability of payment of various taxes and duties due to the Government to each person including foreign investors for the purpose of raising Revenues necessary for bringing intended socio-economic progress.

· Land Act and Village Land Acts of 1999 as amended in 2008 together with the National Land

Policy of 1995 in totality narrates and set forth frameworks for acquisition of rights, ownership and uses of land both local and foreign investors who aspires to invest in Tanzania the same is further addressed in the Tanzania Investment Act of 1997.

· To compliments the development strategies there is in place the so called National Strategy for Growth and Reduction of Poverty II of 2010, National Population Policy of 2006, National Human Settlements Development Policy of 2000, Sustainable industrial Development Policy of 1996 and Tanzania Development Vision 2025 through which Tanzania has analyzed various socio-economic plans and projects for sustainable development of the community and indeed alleviation of acute poverty facing the community including the commitment to indulge into industrialization road.

· The Electricity Act, 2008, Rural Energy Act of 2005 and the energy policy open door to private investors to participate in production of electricity which is vital not only for Industrization strive but also in all socio-economic sectors progress and further more addresses increased distribution and availability of electricity to all citizens including village communities.

· The Public Private Partnership Act of 2010, Public Private Partnership Regulation of 2011 and the Public Private Partnership Policy of 2010 these gives institutional frameworks for the implementation of public-private agreements between public sector and private sector entities, set rules, guideline and procedures governing public private procurement, developments and implementation of public private partnership in both productive and socio-economic services sectors including, but not limited to the following Agriculture, Infrastructure, Manufacturing, Education, Health, Natural Resources, tourism, energy, mining, Water, Land development, Environment and solid waste Management, Appropriate defense infrastructure, sports, Communication, Information and Communication Technology (ICT), Trade, Entertainment and Recreation and Irrigation.

Hence, overwhelmingly the private sectors in Tanzania including foreign investor such as from China is now promoted and protected to participate in the provision of resources for Public-Private Partnership enterprises in terms of investment capital, managerial skill and technology necessary for achieving abruptly socio-economic transformation or progresses and alleviation of poverty. Institutional arrangement is now in place at all levels to carter for public-private ventures.

· The Public Procurement Act of 2011 and the Public Procurement Regulation of 2013 it also addresses issues of economy and value of money for all public revenues directed to incur socio-economic transformation ventures on public-private basis for both solicited and unsolicited proposals.

· In Mining industry arena Tanzania came up with New Minerals policy of 2009 which did away with previous Minerals Policy of 1997 and the incumbent Mining Act of 2010 which repealed the previous Mining Act.

The policy call upon private investors continuing investing in exploration and mining of minerals, emphasize integration of the mineral sector with the rest of the economy, establish a fiscal regime which ensures benefits to the country and remain internationally competitive, support mineral beneficiation and marketing, underpin development of small scale miners and promote public participation in mining activities by providing a clear guidance to investors towards sustainable exploitation of mineral resources of Tanzania in a win-win manner as actively articulated in the Mining Act of 2010.

The current policy and Laws on minerals envisage that exploitation of abundant resources of minerals found in Tanzania which includes; gold, nickel, copper, iron ore, Diamond, Tanzanite, Limestone, Soda ash, Gypsum, Phosphate, Coal, Uranium and other no mentioned should be advantageous to the country thereby generating adequate revenue necessary for sustainable socio-economic progress and transformation and alleviating existing acute poverty by increasing contribution of mineral sector to GDP from below two percent to ten percent by 2025.

The same also emphasize and promote best practices for health, safety and environmental management in mining areas and the surrounding by improving and strengthening monitoring and regulation of the mining industry geared at reducing if not eliminating the adverse effects on health and safety, environment and social issues.

· Concerning the question of overall Environmental control and protection in all ventures Tanzania has come up with and enforces the Environmental Management Act of 2004, National Environmental Policy of 1997 and National Environmental Action Plan (2013) which apart of describing legal and institutional framework for sustainable and proper use environment and harness natural resources therein it also requires and direct the issuance process of any license for right of uses of any land for human activities including minerals exploration and mining should be accompanied with certificate of Environmental impact assessment and any certificate issued in contravention to the Act is liable to be cancelled for simple reasons that all investment undertakings should abide to Environmental conservation measures and duty to harness the natural resources for the total advantages of the community concerned so as to carter for impact of climate changes.

· Issue of health managements, sanitation and management of water resources endowments is covered by Public Health Act of 2009, National Health Policy of 2007, Water Supply and Sanitation Act of 2009, Water Resources Management Act of 2009 and National Water Policy of 2002.

· The Forest Act of 2002, Forest Reserve management and Conservation Act (FRMCA) of 1996 Beekeeping Act of 2002 has been promulgated so as to manage forest and bees together with forest and bees products in the country in cooperation of whole community including private sector with the view of promoting and enhancing the contribution of forest sector to the sustainable development. The legislation prohibits human activities to be conducted in the forest reserve and hence, conserve and manage natural resources for the present and future generation. These goes hand in hand with the guidance elaborated in the National Forest Policy of 1998.

· There is also Tourist Act of 2008 manage tourism and revenue accrued from tourist activities so as to be directed to citizens' benefits to reflect the emphasizes in the National Tourism Policy of 1999.

· As to the National park Act (CAP.282 RE 2002), Wildlife Policy 2007 has been and the

Wildlife Conservation Act of 2009 enacted to preserve wild life, manage revenue accrued from wildlife and wildlife product trade for the sustainable development of tourist. The Acts also preserve cultural resources to future generation including marine resources specified in the Marine Parks and Reserves Act of 1994.

Investment in Agriculture which includes crops growing, animals keeping or grazing and fisheries activities in Tanzania the so called Plant protection Act of 1997, Fisheries Act of 2003, National Agriculture Policy of 2013 and National Livestock Policy of 2006 are in place.

· Export processing Zones Act 2002 and Special Economic Zones Act of 2005 set framework and encouraging investment in industry sectors for the purposes in export and boosting economic condition of Tanzanian community.

· Foreign Exchange Act of 1992 it manage business of foreign currency exchanges and financial institution specifically validity of various negotiable instruments such as cheques.

· There is the Immigration Act of 1995 together with the National Irrigational Policy of 2010 which accurately legal and institutional frameworks for proper management and control movement people, including immigrants in and out from the United Republic of Tanzania together with five quarter and working permits issuing to investor and experts of various investment ventures.

· To the involvements in fight against criminal misconduct which jeopardize National and World security such as engaging in terrorist act the Terrorism Act of 2002 is in place. While to the engagements into illicit enrichment in income accrued from illegal activities such as terrorist activities, illicit trade in wildlife products, drugs and corruption the Money Laundering Act of 2006 and Prevention and Combating of Corruption of 2007 is in effects.

· Increased exploration of oil and gas, and indeed commencement of extraction of gas has compelled Tanzania in 2015 to come up with three legislations; namely:

i. The Petroleum Act of 2015 which replaced and repealed the then Petroleum (Exploration and Production) Act of 1980, covering upstream petroleum operations, and the Petroleum Act of 2008, covering mid and downstream petroleum supply operations provides for the scheme and frameworks of operation of gas and oil exploration and extraction in Tanzania for the benefit of Tanzania community. It is important the Act vest title of right of ownership of Oil and Gas to the Government via the National Company.

ii. Extractive Industry (Transparency and Accountability), Act of 2015 which provide for new avenue requiring all concessions, contracts, and licences relating to the extractive industry to be published as opposed to previous stand of inserting confidentiality clauses especially in mining Development agreements aims is to curb corruption and other malpractices in the gas and oil industry.

iii. The Gas and Oil Revenues Management Act, 2015 which establishes oil and Gas Fund responsible for maintaining fiscal and macroeconomic stability, enhancing, social and economic development, and safeguarding resources for future generations. Revenues expected from oil and gas exploitation is projected to add between 9% to 31% to the Government revenue hence guidance must be in place on how to effectively direct and use to provide basic needs for citizens such as improving and strengthening provision of quality healthcare, education and other social services and supporting long-term economic growth.

Conclusion

In concluding we Africans are of firm view that African Countries acknowledges the existing long time cooperation between African Countries and China counterpart and hence most of policies and Laws made by African Countries since Independence and incoming policies and Laws are in accordance with such long time cooperation and specifically the Forum on China-Africa Cooperation (FOCAC) Johannesburg Action Plans (2016-2018), and the same was given positive consideration by the African Union Commission via Resolution Number 63 which in within the Decision Number EX.CL/Dec.899 (XXVIII) of the 28th Ordinary Session of Executive Council of African Union held from 23-28th January 2016.

REFERENCES

[1] The Decision Number EX.CL/Dec.898-918 (XXVIII) of the 28th Ordinary Session of Executive Council of African Union held from 23-28th January 2016, particularly EX.CL/Dec.908 (XXVIII) page 3, retrieved from www.www.au.int.

[2] https://en.wikipedia.org/wiki/Africa. time on line 12:34 pm 2016 May 28.

[3] https://en.wikipedia.org/wiki/Environmental_protection. time on line 8:341 am 2016 May 26.

[4] file:///E:/ How to Invest in Africa_Mutual Funds_Us News.htm time on line 12:13 pm 2016 May 25.

[5] Samwel J. Sitta (2005), "INVESTMENT FOR AFRICAN DEVELOPMENT: Making it happen" NEPAD/ OECD INVESTMENT INITIATIVE.

[6] The Combined Draft Version of the Forum on China-Africa Cooperation Johannesburg Action Plan (2016-2018).

[7] http://www.tanzaniaembassy.or.jp/english/Business/investment_in_en.html. time on line 1:39 pm 2016 May 25.

[8] Environment Program, Investing in our Future http://warmheartworldwide.org/biochar-research-environment/ gcli. time on line 9:56 am 2016 May 26.

[9] Public-Private Partnerships, http://www.tic.co.tz/menu/314 Tanzania Investment Centre. time on line 4:47 pm 2016 May 27.

[10] http://www.journalism.co.za/blog/topics/categories/china-africa-reporting/Journalism.co.za. time on line 1:04 pm 2016 May 25.

中非投资争端解决机制之分析

作者：Rita Chen 译者：贾子东

一、介绍

在过去的十年间，中非贸易额增长了十倍，到2012年，中非贸易额已经达到了1660亿美元。[①] 这些项目主要包括一些基础设施建设，包括道路、桥梁和港口以及水利和电力设施建设。中国在非洲投资的主要国家包括南非、赞比亚、尼日利亚、阿尔及利亚和安哥拉。尽管中国和非洲之间的贸易在过去十年中蓬勃发展，但外国投资者仍然对东道国的风险和不确定性保持敏感。这些风险与东道国的法律环境、监管框架和政治环境有关。

值得注意的是，随着中非贸易和投资的快速发展，大量法律争端也随之涌现。能否确保这种双边关系的持续性，主要取决于能否有效和高效地解决这些争端。此外，中非双方相互间需要复杂且高效的法律和司法系统以制定、规范、仲裁、拓展、执行商事交易规则。中非在投资争端中最近的发展表明，大多数外国投资者不愿意

① *See* H.E. Hu Jintao, President of the People's republic of China, Speech at the Opening Ceremony of the Fifth Ministerial Conference of the Forum on China-Africa Cooperation (July 19, 2012) [hereinafter FOCAC Speech], *available at* http://news.xinhuanet.com/ english/china/2012-07/19/c_131725637.htm; Wang Xiaotian, *Trade between China, Africa Strengthening*, CHINA DAILY (July 19, 2012), http://www.chinadaily.com.cn/business/2012-07/19/content_15599626.htm ("Trade between China and Africa reached $160 billion in 2011, up by 28 percent from the previous year, according to the most recent data released by the Ministry of Commerce. In the past 10 years, bilateral trade has been growing at an average pace of 33.6 percent per year."). According to a report from the Ministry of Commerce, China, the trade volume between China and Africa in 2012 was US$198.5 billion. *See* MINISTRY OF COMMERCE, *China-Africa Trade Volume Reached New Height* (Apr. 18, 2013, 11:31 AM), http://finance.china.com.cn/news/gnjj/20130418/1397454.shtml.

在东道国的地方法院提起争端解决诉讼，因为他们认为地方法院会作出不公平的判决。因此，仲裁被认为是解决中国和非洲公司之间法律争端的优先选择，对这一点，下文会予以更加详细的解释。本文将对中非投资条约（BIT）予以概述，因为该条约包含了解决投资争端的机制。本文还将分析中非贸易和投资中常见的争端类型，以及解决此类争端的方法。

（一）中非投资条约（BIT）概述

在过去几十年中，中国和非洲国家签署了越来越多的双边投资协定，以及上述的重大投资流动协议。1989 年至 2016 年期间，有 33 个非洲国家与中国签署了双边投资条约，其中 16 个双边投资条约已经生效（见下表，该表是对这些双边投资条约的总结）。虽然这些双边投资条约是由中国在一段时间内与不同的非洲国家签署的，但总体来看，这些条约体现了一些共同特点，具体特点如下所述：

1. 所有这些双边投资条约均遵循相同的基本结构，为投资者和解决投资争端的机制提供基本待遇和保护。

2. 最近的双边投资条约在保护水平方面变得更加复杂、全面，扩大了投资者可以提交国际仲裁的范围。

3. 这些双边投资条约中没有包含任何市场准入承诺的规定，它们只保护“进入后”阶段的投资。换句话说，它们不允许缔约国将特定领域开放给外国投资；它们只是在投资正式进入东道国的领土后才予以保护。

这些双边投资条约涉及以下领域：投资的定义和范围、特许和建立、最惠国待遇、公平待遇、在征用或损害投资的情况下的赔偿、资金自由转移的保证和争端解决机制。这些条约既对国家与私人之间的投资进行了规定，也对私人与私人之间的投资进行了规定。因此，批准双边投资条约是衡量某个国家考虑其双边经济和商事关系的认真程度的良好指标。本文旨在分析中非双边投资条约中，与中非投资争端解决机制有关的显著特征。

（二）非洲国家和中国之间的双边投资协定（按签署日期的时间顺序排列）

国家	签署日期	国家	签署日期	国家	签署日期
加纳	12/10/1989	南非	30/12/1997	贝宁 *	18/02/2004

续表

国家	签署日期	国家	签署日期	国家	签署日期
埃及	21/04/1994	佛得角	21/04/1998	乌干达 *	27/05/2004
摩洛哥	27/03/1995	埃塞俄比亚	11/05/1998	突尼斯	21/06/2004
毛里求斯	04/05/1996	刚国共和国 *	20/03/2000	赤道几内亚 *	20/10/2005
津巴布韦	21/05/1996	博茨瓦纳 *	12/06/2000	纳米比亚 *	17/11/2005
赞比亚 *	21/06/1996	塞拉利昂 *	16/05/2001	马达加斯加	21/11/2005
阿尔及利亚	17/10/1996	莫桑比克	10/07/2001	塞舌尔 *	10/02/2007
加蓬	09/05/1997	肯尼亚 *	16/07/2001	马里	12/02/2009
喀麦隆 *	10/05/1997	尼日利亚	27/08/2001	乍得 *	26/04/2010
苏丹	30/05/1997	科特迪瓦 *	30/09/2002	利比亚	04/08/2010
刚果民主共和国 *	18/12/1997	吉布提 *	18/08/2003	坦桑尼亚	24/03/2013

* 这些中非投资条约已经签署，但尚未生效。

（三）投资者——国家争端解决

作为投资保护工具，双边投资协定的一个突出特点是它的独立争端解决机制，也称为“投资者—国家争端解决”（ISDS）。正如该术语所暗示的，它是一个争端解决机制，通过该机制，外国投资者可以有效保护自己免受政府滥用权力所带来的不良后果。ISDS 为解决投资争议提供了独立有效的机制。

与向当地法院寻求救济相比，ISDS 机制有利于保护投资者免受东道国政府在法庭上潜在的政治影响。非洲正在经历快速的经济增长，这使得非洲国家需要法律和司法系统能够更好地发挥功能。并且，不同国家的司法系统的发展水平不同，这意味着东道国政府可能干预国内审判程序的情况不可能完全避免。此外，地方法院适用的法律通常是东道国当地的法律，这些法律可能会出现变化，而这些变化也许不利于投资者。

相比之下，在国际仲裁中，由于投资者可以直接根据条约规定提起诉讼，因此，国际仲裁可以提供更稳定和更高质量的保护。所以，在大多数情况下，当投资争端提交给国际仲裁庭时，投资者可能有更多的成功机会。

1. 国际仲裁的本质与效果

国际投资仲裁对投资条约和合同制度至关重要，因为仲裁法庭解决了国家和投资者之间关于投资措施适用性的争议和问题。鉴于这些项目涉及了一些重要性问题的本质，涉及了与有关东道国管理之间的相互关系，以及本文所讨论的有效解释条约规定所带来的众多挑战，人们开始认识到，在这些争端中，仲裁员所面临任务的严重性①。

尽管投资条约和合同本身存在一些固有的挑战，国际投资仲裁本身也提出了一些重大的问题和争议。通过下面列出的问题清单考虑中非双边投资条约，可以更好地平衡投资者与政府的合法利益。

以下清单中的各项列出了各界主要关切和评论的问题，特别是环境和人权界倡导者提出的主要问题：

（1）排除用尽当地补救办法的初步要求，以避免对投资者不公平的潜在问题，对于发展中国家而言，减少了当地发展和培养更完善的法律机构的机会，减少了当地推动法治进程发展的宝贵机会。②

（2）仲裁员可能会有一些“不正当刺激措施”，以鼓励各方和利益冲突方妥协于仲裁员的裁决、决定。

（3）他们可能会鼓励投资者提起诉讼，例如，对投资者作出支持性的决定或对诉讼管辖权进行扩张解释。

（4）他们在某些案件中作为仲裁员，在某些案件中又以法律顾问的身份参与其中（并且他们的律所是专长于仲裁事务的）。③

（5）参与仲裁的各方通常都会选择一名仲裁员，这对仲裁结果的公正性与独立性提出了挑战。④

---

① See Wallace Perry, “Sustainable Development Law & Policy Volume 12 Issue 3 *Rio+20* Article 6: International Investment Law and Arbitration,Sustainable Development, and Rio+20: Improving Corporate Institutional And State Governance”, pp.27-28.

② Nigel Blackaby and Constantine Partasides, with Alan Rederrn and Martin Hunter, REDERN AND HUNTER ON INTERNATIONAL ARBITRATION 506-08 (Oxford, 5th ed. 2009).

③ Nathalie Bernasconi-Osterwalder et al., Investment Treatment Treaties & Why They Matter to Sustainable Development, International Institute for Sustainable Development (2012), http://www.iisd.org/pdf/2011/investment_treaties_why_they_matter_sd.pdf [hereinafter IISD].

④ Nathalie Bernasconi-Osterwalder et al., Investment Treatment Treaties & Why They Matter to Sustainable Development, International Institute for Sustainable Development (2012), http://www.iisd.org/pdf/2011/investment_treaties_why_they_matter_sd.pdf [hereinafter IISD].

（6）选择仲裁员的机制导致了仲裁员往往限于一些精英或者限于一些狭小的圈子。这些仲裁员无论是在性别、地理位置上，还是在文化、意识形态、种族上，都缺乏多样性。这损害了他们在日益复杂的世界环境中以及在仲裁案件中有越来越多的利益相关者的情况下，作出公正裁决的能力。①

（7）由于对仲裁裁决提出异议的机制有限，因此仲裁中出现的法律或事实错误通常无法纠正；②

（8）仲裁裁决可能非常不一致，并且缺少具有约束力规则的判例或有意义的上诉程序，使仲裁裁决保持一致性；③

（9）对仲裁信息的访问途径通常有限，很多信息不能为公众知悉；④

（10）公众参与仲裁本已十分有限，通常仅限于接受“法庭之友”（译者注：“法庭之友”指非诉讼当事人，因为诉讼的主要事实涉及其重大利益，得请求法院或受法院的请求而于诉讼过程中提出书面意见者）的简报。如果东道国缺乏为公共利益行事的政治意愿，屈服于强大国家“议价能力”或屈服于公司的干涉，抑或屈服于腐败，那么公众参与仲裁的限制将更加严重。⑤

澳大利亚等发达国家表示，传统的双边投资条约模式有缺陷，需要修订。⑥例如，南非政府颁布了《2015 年投资保护法》，该法将取代目前的双边投资条约，将其提供的保护模式编入国内法，以加强和澄清符合《南非宪法》的投资者保护国家法

① Nathalie Bernasconi-Osterwalder et al., Investment Treatment Treaties & Why They Matter to Sustainable Development, International Institute for Sustainable Development (2012), http://www.iisd.org/pdf/2011/investment_treaties_why_they_matter_sd.pdf [hereinafter IISD].

② IISD, supra note 35, at 48.

③ IISD, supra note 35, at 49.

④ IISD, supra note 35, at 50.

⑤ IISD, supra note 35, at 51-52.

⑥ The 2015 World Investment Report presents various policy options for the reform of international investment agreements aimed at synchronising national, bilateral, regional and multilateral levels which include the followings: 1) Safeguarding the right to regulate in the public interest so that limits on state sovereignty imposed by international investments agreements do not constrain public policy making; 2)Reforming investment dispute settlement to address the crisis in legitimacy of the current system; 3) Expanding investment promotion and facilitation in international investment agreements; 4) Ensuring responsible investment to maximise the positive impact on minimising the negative effects of foreign investment; and 5) Enhancing the systemic consistency of the international investment agreement regime to overcome gaps and overlaps, and establish coherent investment relationships.

律框架。

2. 中非投资争端引起的争议类型

根据南非法院的判决，中非商事交易引起的法律争端可分为以下主要类别：①

（1）合同争端

中非商事交易中的主要争端是合同纠纷。合同纠纷分为以下几类：

①合同履行：在收集到的超过30多个案件中，有6个争端是因为合同履行引起的；

②销售合同和投资合同在这其中排名最高，因为中非业务交易主要涉及商品销售和投资。

大多数投资合同纠纷是由于建筑合同引起的，因为中国企业在非洲正在进行大量基础设施项目建设。例如，2009年开罗国际商事仲裁区域中心接受的89个案件以及2010年上半年，销售合同案件和建筑案件占仲裁案件总数的33%；而在89宗个案中，涉及中国当事人的案件数目比例为11%，低于涉及德国当事人的案件数目比例，涉及德国当事人的案件数目比例为12%。②

（2）信用证或保函的争议

信用证和保函或备用信用证被广泛用于商事交易。销售合同中通常规定中非双方之间使用信用证付款，而在双方的项目合同中，非方通常要求中方提供预付款和银行发放的履约担保。因此，偶尔会出现与接受或支付信用证或保函有关的争议。

（3）海洋争端

在非洲有几个重要的国际海运线路和港口，如德班、开普敦、拉各斯和亚历山

① Zhu, W., A Brief Analysis of the Disputes Arising from China-African Civil and Commercial Transactions, Journal of Cambridge Studies, Volume 7, No.3. The paper is also part of the research project sponsored by the China Social Science Research Fund (Project No.08CFX055). This paper was submitted to and read at the First China-African Think Tank Forum held in Hanzhou on 27-29 October 2011.

② CRCICA Annual Report (2009-2010). The Centre accepted 51 international cases in 2009 and 66 in 2010, with an annual increase of 35%. In the first half year of 2011, the Centre accepted another 30 new cases. Among the 66 cases accepted in 2010, the construction contract cases rank at the top, 47% of the total cases. Considering the rapid development of China-African business relations, the Centre is planning to strengthen cooperation with the China Law Society and the China International Economic and Trade Arbitration Commission (CIETAC), to see Report on the AALCO's Regional Arbitration Centre at the 50th annual session of the Asian-African Legal Consultative Organization held in Colombo, Sri Lanka from 27 June to 1st July, 2011, available at: http://www.aalco.int/content/50thannualsession.

大。其他国家的船舶往往在这里停泊，这其中也包括中国的船舶。许多非洲国家有关于海洋管辖权的条款，船舶可能由于各种法律原因而在港口停泊。在过去几年中，几个中国船舶在非洲港口，特别是在南非港口的停泊，引起了许多海洋争端。①

（4）投资者与国家之间的争端解决机制

最后，虽然中国和非洲国家签署的所有双边投资条约都规定了ISDS机制，但是可以提交仲裁的争端类型却因条约而异，如上文第2.1段所述。值得注意的是，根据20世纪80年代后期签署的中国加纳双边投资条约，只有关于"征收补偿金"的争端可提交仲裁庭。②相比之下，中国与南非和尼日利亚在20世纪90年代末以及2000年年初签署的双边投资条约为ISDS机制允许"与投资有关的任何争端"都可以提交仲裁庭。③因此，在对非洲投资时，中国投资者应注意相关的BIT条款，以确保争议在ISDS机制的范围内。

"岔路口"条款

为了确保其可以使用ISDS机制，投资者应密切关注所谓的"岔路口"条款。在所有中非双边投资条约中，均存在要求投资者从国内诉讼或国际仲裁中选择的强制性规定。④换句话说，一旦投资者将争端提交至东道国主管法院，就不再有资格将争端向国际仲裁法庭提交。这样的规定被命名为"岔路口"条款，表明投资者必须在十字路口选择一种或另一种方式。相同地，由于东道国的作为或者违反条约义务的不作为发生之时，从而使投资者遭受损失，投资者可以选择寻求救济的方式。

保证执行

ISDS投资保护机制的另一个优点是保证执行仲裁裁决的机制。无论是哪一家仲裁机构，根据东道国在双边投资条约中的国际义务，一旦裁决作出，东道国就应该执行有利于投资者的裁决。此外，在大多数情况下，裁决可能在东道国以外的国家强制执行。中国与非洲国家签署的20多个双边投资协定中特别提及了国际投资争端

① Great River Shipping v. Sunnyface Marine 1992 (4) SA 313 (C); International Marine Transport SA v. MV "Le Cong", case No.080/05, the Supreme Court of South Africa; another Chinese ship was attached by the Durban Court, South Africa on 26 August 1999, to see http://www.civillaw.com.cn/article/default.asp?id=9896.

② China-Ghana BIT, Art. 10(1).

③ China-South Africa BIT, Article 9(1); China-Nigeria BIT, Article 9(1).

④ For example, Article 9(3) of China- Nigeria BIT and Article 9(2) of China-South Africa BIT.

解决中心（ICSID）作为审理投资仲裁的机构。①

对于根据《ICSID 公约》提交的裁决，《ICSID 公约》的所有缔约国都有承认和执行 ICSID 的裁决的国际义务，这就如同该国际裁决是这些国家地方法院的最终判决一样。换句话说，如果一位中国投资者在国际仲裁中被裁决应获得赔偿，则他不仅可以在他进行投资的那个非洲国家请求执行裁决，他还可以在其他的《ICSID 公约》缔约国请求执行裁决，只要这些缔约国内有那个非洲国家的资产。

更重要的是，ICSID 中的独立审查制度（废止程序）进一步减少了被告国在任何法院企图对裁决结果提出质疑的不确定性。

对于非 ICSID 的裁决，《承认和执行外国仲裁裁决公约》(《纽约公约》) 也可以确保缔约国法院承认并执行那些在其他缔约国作出的仲裁裁决。类似于《ICSID 公约》，根据《纽约公约》，在某个国家作出的仲裁裁决一般可以在任何其他缔约国得到执行。但有一个例外：能否执行须取决于地方法院的审查，在这些地方法院，可能会因为一些特定的缘故从而拒绝执行裁决。②

总之，《ICSID 公约》和《纽约公约》向投资者提供了高度保证，即不利于东道国的仲裁裁决将最终被实施。这也是与投资者向东道国法院诉讼相比的另一个优点。

二、中非商事关系中引发的争端特点

（一）争端通常由非洲仲裁庭或法院解决

非洲国家一般是中国货物和资本的进口国，在大多数情况下，合同在非洲国家制定。因此，当发生争端时，当事各方往往诉诸非洲的法院或仲裁机构。此外，许多非洲国家的投资法明确规定，外国投资者和东道国之间的投资争端应首先在东道

---

① African countries that consent to arbitration in ICSID in BITs with China include: Morocco, Gabon, Cameroon, Ethiopia, Congo Rep., Botswana, Sierra Leone, Mozambique, Kenya, Cote d'Ivoire, Djibouti, Benin, Uganda, Tunisia, Equatorial Guinea, Madagascar, Seychelles, Mali, Chad, Libya, Tanzania.

② Article V of the New York Convention limits the grounds for non-recognition or enforcement to a narrowly-drafted list. The respondent state has to prove one of the following: lack of a valid arbitration agreement, violation of due process, excess of the arbitral tribunal's authority, irregularity in the composition of the arbitral tribunal or arbitral procedure, and the award "has not yet become binding", "has been set aside" or "has been suspended".

国的法院或仲裁机构解决。例如,《安哥拉石油活动法》规定，如果发生任何争端，争端应通过在安哥拉进行的仲裁解决，并由安哥拉法律管辖。

（二）争端涉及了多个非洲国家并且涉及了不同类型的仲裁方

目前，中国与45个非洲国家缔结了双边投资协定，中国的投资已遍布在非洲的49个国家。① 中国在非洲的投资者包括国有企业、非国有企业和个人。这些投资项目主要包括采矿、金融、制造、基础设施、旅游业和林业。投资方式主要是通过兼并或收购，通过股份或与东道国政府的公私伙伴关系。争端无疑会涉及各种不同类型的当事方。例如，许多中国国有企业或非国有企业以自己的名义起诉或起诉，而不是以当地公司的名义起诉。②

（三）缺乏有效的双边或多边司法援助机制

与外国有关的商事纠纷裁决通常需要在国外提供司法文件并提供证据。有时，债权人必须寻求特定的国家执行判决，这些国家须被判定是债务人拥有其居所或财产的国家。这些事项通常在两国之间的双边司法协助条约中被提及。尽管中国和非洲国家之间存在较为频繁的商事纠纷，但截至目前，中国只与摩洛哥、埃及、阿尔及利亚和突尼斯缔结了4项司法协助条约。仅仅根据双边司法条约决定是否进行司法援助是一种低效率的做法，这只会导致审判程序的无理拖延。

此外，国际司法合作对于有效地裁决与外国有关的案件是不可或缺的。③ 因此，在全世界范围内，已经制定了许多用于此类目的的多边公约，如1965年的《关于向国外送达民事或商事司法文书和司法外文书公约》(以下简称《海牙送达公约》)和1970年的《关于从国外调取民事或商事证据的公约》(以下简称《海牙取证公约》)。这些公约的成员国可以根据这些公约提供的机制在司法行政方面进行合作。到目前

---

① The State Council Information Office of the People's Republic of China, White Paper on the China-African Business Cooperation (2010).

② Roosevelt Kgosi v. China Civil Engineering, in the Industrial Court of Botswana, case No. IC. 500/2004; China Henan Internal Economic and Technical Cooperation v. Mwange Contractors Limited (SCZ Judgement No.7 of 2002), [2002] ZMSC 8 (24) January (2002); China Henan International Cooperation Group v. Regasira (civil reference No.22 of 2005) [2006] TZCA 43 (21 March 2006).

③ Richard F. Oppong, Private International Law in Africa, the Past, Present and Future, 55 Am. J. Comp. L. 677, 2007, p.680.

为止，中国已经加入了两个海牙公约。但在非洲，只有埃及、博茨瓦纳、马拉维和塞舌尔加入了《海牙送达公约》，只有南非和塞舌尔加入了《海牙取证公约》。因此，涉及国外机制的中非合作常常受到限制。

（四）中非双方缺乏对彼此司法制度的了解

虽然近年来中国和非洲之间的商事交易增加，但参与这些商事交易的大多数中国人对非洲国家的法律制度知之甚少，有时甚至会对非洲国家的法律和司法制度产生误解。在这种情况下，一旦发生争议，他们不知道可以采取什么直接补救的办法，这往往就会导致解决过程变得十分缓慢。① 因此，中国应该努力了解非洲国家审理涉外案件的有关法律制度，以促进争端的高效解决。

三、中非争端解决

与外商相关商业纠纷的裁决主要通过两种方式解决：诉讼和替代性争议解决，如协商、调解和仲裁。

与外国有关的争端诉讼通常涉及管辖权，法律选择以及承认和执行外国判决。非洲各国的法律制度中存在着诸多的差异性，通过非洲法院的诉讼来解决这些争端是有障碍的，这些障碍可归纳如下：②

首先，很少有非洲国家制订过可以适用于所有法律冲突的系统性和全面性的法典。在 54 个非洲国家中，只有突尼斯在 1998 年通过了一项系统和全面的《国际私法》，这部法律详细地规定了国际管辖权，包括法律选择、承认和执行外国判决。③ 在其他非洲国家，有关国际私法的问题在不同的单一法令中规定，难以归纳和使用。

其次，非洲国家的大多数立法过于落后，不切实际，因为落后的立法程序，造成法律不符合目前的经济状况。大多数非洲国家保留了其殖民国家的法律制度，一

---

① China State Construction Engineering Corporation (Southern Africa) (Pty) Ltd v.Pro Joinery Close Corporation, in the High Court of Namibia, case No. A 230/2007.

② Zhu, W., A Brief Analysis of the Disputes Arising from China-African Civil and Commercial Transactions, Journal of Cambridge Studies, Volume 7, No.3. The paper is also part of the research project sponsored by the China Social Science Research Fund (Project No.08CFX055). This paper was submitted to and read at the First China-African Think Tank Forum held in Hanzhou on 27-29 October 2011.

③ The content of this law is available at http://www.lexadin.nl/wlg/legis/nofr/oeur/lxwetun.htm.

些立法自独立以来仍然保持不变，这些立法已经过时。一些非洲国家重新颁布了其法律，以应对频繁的跨国民事和商事交往，但由于一些技术原因，这些法律是不可操作的。例如，1988 年南非[①]的《外国判决执行法第 32 号法》规定，这一行为只适用于承认和执行南非公报指定的国家判决，而在南非公报中，只有纳米比亚一国被提及。

再次，在一些非洲国家，他们制定的与国际商事诉讼有关的规则与当代的国际法律发展脱节。目前，大多数国家允许诉讼当事人通过协议，选择在与争端没有因果关系的国家提起诉讼，但在南非确立的管辖规则却不同。在诉讼事由未发生在南非的情况下，即使外国原告和外国被告在合同中明确同意，应在南非法院解决争议，南非法院也不能在本国裁决争议。[②]

最后，许多法律冲突问题在非洲仍悬而未决。非洲国际私法学家指出，自 1997 年至 2007 年，在 13 个使用英语的非洲国家所作出的 300 多项判决或报告中，在许多方面存在诸多不确定性，需要立法或判例法在未来加以解决。[③]这些方面包括合同与侵权行为之诉法律适用的选择、互联网活动的管辖权，以及由信托和知识产权引起的国际私法问题。[④]

自 20 世纪 90 年代以来，许多非洲国家根据较为完善的仲裁法律文书，特别是

---

① South African courts will enforce a foreign judgment if certain requirements, based largely on the Roman Dutch common law, are met. A foreign judgment, therefore, is not directly enforceable in South Africa but constitutes a cause of action that will be enforced by South African courts if the following requirements are met (as affirmed in a leading case on the subject, Jones v Krok 1995(1) SA 677(A)):

• the foreign court must have had international competence as determined by South African law;

• the judgment must be final and conclusive and must not have become superannuated;

• the enforcement of the judgment must not be contrary to South African public policy (which includes the rules of natural justice);

• the judgment must not have been obtained by fraudulent means;

• the judgment must not involve the enforcement of a penal or revenue law of the foreign state; and

• enforcement must not be precluded by the Protection of Businesses Act 99 of 1978.

② C F Forsyth, *Private International Law: The Modern Roman-Dutch Law Including the Jurisdiction of the Supreme Courts*, Juta & Co Ltd, 3rd edition, 1996, p.204.

③ Richard F Oppong, A Decade of Private International Law in African Courts (1997-2007) (part I), vol.9, *Yearbook of Private International Law*, 2008, pp.224-225.

④ Richard F. Oppong, Private International Law in Africa, the Past, Present and Future, 55 Am. J. Comp. L. 677, 2007, p.682.

根据 1985 年《贸易法委员会国际商事仲裁示范法》重新颁布其仲裁法，以吸引外国投资，扩大贸易，增强投资者的信心。此外，大多数非洲国家加入了关于仲裁的国际公约，如 1965 年《关于解决国家与其他国家[①]国民之间投资争端的华盛顿公约》、1958 年《关于承认和执行外国仲裁裁决的纽约公约》。[②]另一方面，非洲国家成立了许多仲裁机构、仲裁中心，为非洲有效、高效的仲裁提供了必要的便利。目前，几乎每个非洲国家都有一个仲裁机构或仲裁中心。[③]中非位于约翰内斯堡的联合仲裁中心于 2015 年 8 月启动，并被视为中非双方之间商业争端解决的主要机构，该仲裁中心在中国上海还设置了分支机构。预计在 2016 年年初引入新的国际仲裁法。此举将使南非仲裁法实现现代化，并促进南非作为区域仲裁中心，在包括美国食品安全局和国际商会在内的知名组织的主持下进行仲裁。这些，都会使南非的仲裁法得到进一步发展。

四、结论

从对非洲争端解决机制的简要分析中可以明显地看出，许多非洲国家与外国诉讼有关的法律仍然是非系统性的，与国际发展相脱离的，并且在许多问题上尚未解决。然而，在许多非洲国家目前的法律制度和传统下，通过仲裁而非诉讼解决这些争端是更为合适的办法。

---

① Now 45 African States have signed the 1965 Washington Convention. Ethiopia, Guinea-Bissau, Namibia, Sao Tome and Principe only signed but not ratified the Convention, so 41 African states have been the Contracting States of the Convention. To see http://icsid.worldbank.org/ICSID/FrontServlet.

② Now 30 African countries are parties to the New York Convention, to see http://www.uncitral.org/uncitral/en/uncitral_texts/arbitration/NYConvention_status.html, last visited 18 July.

③ Emilia Onyema, "Regional Approaches to Enforcement: Enforcement of Arbitral Awards in Sub-Sahara Africa", paper presented at the Inaugural Conference of Alumni & Friends of the School of International Arbitration (AFSIA) London, 3 December 2008.

The Analysis of Investment Dispute Resolution Mechanism between China and Africa

Author: Rita Chen

Introduction

In the last decade, trade between China and Africa has increased by tenfold and by 2012 the amount of trade between China and Africa amounted to US$166 billion.① These projects mainly consist of infrastructure construction, including roads, bridges and ports as well as water conservancy and electricity facilities. Major destinations for Chinese investments in Africa include South Africa, Zambia, Nigeria, Algeria and Angola. Despite the fact that trade between China and Africa has been booming over the past decade, foreign investors continue to remain sensitive to risks and uncertainties related to the legal environment, regulatory framework and political climate of the host state.

Notably, numerous legal disputes occurred in Africa as a result of the rapid development of China-African trade and investment and to ensure the continuance of this bilateral relationship it shall depend largely on whether the disputes could be settled effectively and efficiently. Furthermore, both China and Africa require correspondingly sophisticated efficient legal-judicial systems to make,

① *See* H.E. Hu Jintao, President of the People's republic of China, Speech at the Opening Ceremony of the Fifth Ministerial Conference of the Forum on China-Africa Cooperation (July 19, 2012) [hereinafter FOCAC Speech], *available at* http://news.xinhuanet.com/ english/china/2012-07/19/c_131725637.htm; Wang Xiaotian, *Trade between China, Africa Strengthening*, CHINA DAILY (July 19, 2012), http://www.chinadaily.com.cn/ business/2012-07/19/content_15599626.htm ("Trade between China and Africa reached $160 billion in 2011, up by 28 percent from the previous year, according to the most recent data released by the Ministry of Commerce. In the past 10 years, bilateral trade has been growing at an average pace of 33.6 percent per year."). According to a report from the Ministry of Commerce, China, the trade volume between China and Africa in 2012 was US$198.5 billion. *See* MINISTRY OF COMMERCE, *China-Africa Trade Volume Reached New Height* (Apr. 18, 2013, 11:31 AM), http://finance.china.com.cn/news/gnjj/20130418/1397454.shtml.

regulate, arbitrate and expedite and enforce rules governing commercial transactions. The recent developments between China and Africa in the case of investment disputes show that most foreign investors are reluctant to submit a dispute with the host state to local court, because they believe that the local court will make an unfair judgement. Therefore, arbitration is considered as the preferable option for the settlement of disputes between Chinese and African companies which will be explained in more detail below. This paper will provide an overview of China Africa investment treaties (BIT) as it contains mechanisms for resolving investment disputes, analyse the types of disputes arising from China-African trade and investment and the settlement of disputes between China and Africa.

An Overview of China–Africa Bilateral Investment Treaties (BITs)

In the past decades, an increasing number of BITs have been signed between China and African countries along with the significant investment flow noted above. Between 1989 to 2016, 33 African countries have signed BITs with China, among which 16 BITs have entered into effect (see the table below for a summary of these BITs). Although these BITs were signed by China over an extended period of time and with different African treaty partners, an overview shows some common features as follows:

All these BITs follow the same basic structure, providing the basic treatment and protection for investors and mechanisms for resolving investment disputes;

Recent BITs are becoming more sophisticated and comprehensive in terms of protection level by expanding the scope of claims that the investor can submit to international arbitration;

None of these BITs contain any market access commitments, and they only protect investments with respect to the "post-entry" phase. In other words, they do not commit contracting states to open particular sectors to foreign investments; they only protect investments after they have been duly admitted into the territory of the host country.

These BITs cover areas such as definition and scope of investment, admission and establishment, most favored nation, fair and equitable treatments, compensation in the event of expropriation or damage to the investment, guarantees of free transfer of funds and dispute settlement mechanisms, both state to state and to private investors, and between or among private parties. Therefore, ratification of BITs is a good indicator of the seriousness with which the countries involved consider their bilateral economic and business relations. For purpose of this paper, the author will only analyze the salient features relating to mechanisms for resolving investment disputes between China-Africa BITs.

BITs between African countries and China (in chronological sequence of the date of signature)

Country	Signature Date	Country	Signature Date	Country	Signature Date
Ghana	12/10/1989	South Africa	30/12/1997	Benin*	18/02/2004
Egypt	21/04/1994	Cape Verde	21/04/1998	Uganda*	27/05/2004
Morocco	27/03/1995	Ethiopia	11/05/1998	Tunisia	21/06/2004
Mauritius	04/05/1996	Congo Rep.*	20/03/2000	Equatorial Guinea*	20/10/2005
Zimbabwe	21/05/1996	Botswana*	12/06/2000	Namibia*	17/11/2005
Zambia*	21/06/1996	Sierra Leone*	16/05/2001	Madagascar	21/11/2005
Algeria	17/10/1996	Mozambique	10/07/2001	Seychelles*	10/02/2007
Gabon	09/05/1997	Kenya*	16/07/2001	Mali	12/02/2009
Cameroon*	10/05/1997	Nigeria	27/08/2001	Chad*	26/04/2010
Sudan	30/05/1997	Cote d'Ivoire*	30/09/2002	Libya	04/08/2010
Congo D.R.*	18/12/1997	Djibouti*	18/08/2003	Tanzania	24/03/2013

*BITS signed but not yet entered into force

Investor – State Dispute Settlement

A prominent feature of BITs as a tool for investment protection is the independent dispute settlement mechanism, also known as the "Investor – State Dispute Settlement" (ISDS). As the term implies, it is a dispute settlement mechanism through which foreign investors protect themselves against government's abuse of power under an international forum. ISDS provides an independent and effective mechanism for resolving investment disputes.

In comparison to resorting to local courts for remedy, the ISDS mechanism has the benefit of protecting investors from potential political influence by the host state government in court cases. Africa is experiencing rapid economic growth which gives rise to increased demand for a better functioning legal and judicial system., thus there are varying levels of development in judicial systems in different countries which means the possibility that a host state government may interfere in domestic adjudicatory proceedings cannot always be excluded. Furthermore, the applicable law before a local court is usually the local law of the host state, which may be subject to changes unfavorable to investors.

In comparison, under international arbitration, an investor may have a claim directly under the treaty provisions, providing stable and higher quality protection. Therefore, in most cases investors may have a better chance of success when an investment dispute is brought before an international tribunal.

Nature and effect of International Arbitration

International investment arbitration is crucial to investment treaty and contract regimes, as arbitral tribunals resolve disputes and questions between states and investors about the applicability of those investment measures. Given the significant nature of the kinds of projects involved, their interrelation with the governance of the host countries involved, as well as the numerous challenges posed to efficacious interpretation of treaty provisions as discussed herein, one can begin to appreciate the gravity of the tasks placed before the arbitrators in these disputes.[①]

Not with standing the challenges that are inherent in investment treaties and contracts themselves, international investment arbitration itself has given rise to significant questions and controversies. It would be useful to consider the China-Africa BITs in tandem with the list of issues listed below so as to balance the legitimate interest of investors with the interest of the government.

The following list identifies major areas of concern and criticism, particularly as raised by advocates in the environmental and human rights communities:

Exclusion of preliminary requirements to exhaust local remedies, while avoiding potential problems of unfairness to the investor, diminishes valuable opportunities for the development and nurturing of legal institutions and the rule of law, particularly in developing countries;[②]

Arbitrators may have "perverse incentives" to encourage arbitrations and conflicts of interest that compromise their judgments and decisions;

They may be tempted to encourage investor claims, for example, by deciding overwhelmingly in favor of investors or by broadly interpreting their jurisdiction to make claims;

They often serve as arbitrators in some cases and legal counsel in other cases (and their law firms may specialize in arbitration matters);[③]

The parties to the arbitration typically each choose one arbitrator, raising questions about arbitrator impartiality and independence;[④]

---

① See Wallace Perry, " Sustainable Development Law & Policy Volume 12 Issue 3 *Rio+20* Article 6: International Investment Law and Arbitration,Sustainable Development, and Rio+20: Improving Corporate Institutional And State Governance", pp. 27-28.

② Nigel Blackaby and Constantine Partasides, with Alan Rederrn and Martin Hunter, REDERN AND HUNTER ON INTERNATIONAL ARBITRATION 506-08 (Oxford, 5th ed. 2009).

③ Nathalie Bernasconi-Osterwalder et al., Investment Treatment Treaties & Why They Matter to Sustainable Development, International Institute for Sustainable Development (2012), http://www.iisd.org/pdf/2011/investment_treaties_why_they_matter_sd.pdf [hereinafter IISD].

④ Nathalie Bernasconi-Osterwalder et al., Investment Treatment Treaties & Why They Matter to Sustainable Development, International Institute for Sustainable Development (2012), http://www.iisd.org/pdf/2011/investment_treaties_why_they_matter_sd.pdf [hereinafter IISD].

The mechanisms for choosing arbitrators has resulted in an elite and narrow coterie of persons, and the lack of diversity—whether of gender, ethnicity, geography, culture, ideology or race—impairs their ability to decide cases properly and justly in an increasingly complex world with increasingly myriad stakeholders in the outcome of arbitral cases;[①]

There are limited mechanisms for challenging arbitral awards, and often errors of law or fact cannot be corrected;[②]

Arbitral decisions can be highly inconsistent, and there is no binding rule of precedent or meaningful appeals process to lend consistency to them;[③]

Access to information about arbitrations is typically limited, and much information is unavailable to the public;[④]

Public participation in arbitrations is very limited, usually being confined to the acceptance of amicus curiae briefs by outside parties. The limitation is most consequential where a host state lacks the political will to act properly in the public interest, yields to the often-superior "bargaining power" of a more powerful state or company, or is simply corrupt.[⑤]

Developed countries such as Australia indicated that the traditional BIT model is flawed and requires revision.[⑥] The South African government for example, enacted the Protections of investment Act 22 of 2015 which will replace current BIT's by codifying BIT-type protection into domestic law to strengthen and clarify national legal framework for investor protection which is in line with South Africa's Constitution.

---

① Nathalie Bernasconi-Osterwalder et al., Investment Treatment Treaties & Why They Matter to Sustainable Development, International Institute for Sustainable Development (2012), http://www.iisd.org/pdf/2011/investment_treaties_why_they_matter_sd.pdf [hereinafter IISD], supra note 35, at 68.

② IISD, supra note 35, at 48.

③ IISD, supra note 35, at 49.

④ IISD, supra note 35, at 50.

⑤ IISD, supra note 35, at 51-52.

⑥ The 2015 World Investment Report presents various policy options for the reform of international investment agreements aimed at synchronising national, bilateral, regional and multilateral levels which include the followings: 1) Safeguarding the right to regulate in the public interest so that limits on state sovereignty imposed by international investments agreements do not constrain public policy making; 2)Reforming investment dispute settlement to address the crisis in legitimacy of the current system; 3) Expanding investment promotion and facilitation in international investment agreements; 4) Ensuring responsible investment to maximise the positive impact on minimising the negative effects of foreign investment; and 5) Enhancing the systemic consistency of the international investment agreement regime to overcome gaps and overlaps, and establish coherent investment relationships.

Types of disputes arising from China-Africa investment disputes

Based on the judgements rendered by the Southern African courts, the legal disputes arising from China-Africa commercial transactions could be classified into the following main categories:①

Contractual disputes

The main type of disputes in the China-African commercial transactions are contractual disputes. The contractual disputes are broken down into the following categories:

Contract performance - Six disputes arose from the performance of contracts among over 30 cases collected.

Sales contract and investment contract - rank the highest due to the fact that the China-African business transactions involve mainly the sales of goods and investments.

Most of the investment contractual disputes arise out of construction contracts because of the extent of infrastructure projects that the Chinese enterprises are carrying on in Africa. For example: in the 89 cases that the Cairo Regional Centre for International Commercial Arbitration accepted in 2009 and in the first half year of 2010, the sales contractual cases and construction cases covers 33% of the total number; and out of the 89 cases, the number of cases involving Chinese parties amounts to 11% which is just below that involving the German parties at 12%.②

Disputes from the letter of credit or the letter of guarantee

Letter of credit and the letter of guarantee or the standby letter of credit is widely used in commercial transactions. The sales contracts often stipulates payment by letter of credit between the Chinese and the African parties, while in project contracts between both parties, the African party usually obliges the Chinese party to provide the guarantee for the advance payment and for the performance issued by the banks. Therefore, disputes relating to the acceptance or the payment of the letter of credit or letter of guarantee will occasionally arise.

Marine disputes

---

① Zhu, W., A Brief Analysis of the Disputes Arising from China-African Civil and Commercial Transactions, Journal of Cambridge Studies, Volume 7, No.3. The paper is also part of the research project sponsored by the China Social Science Research Fund (Project No.08CFX055). This paper was submitted to and read at the First China-African Think Tank Forum held in Hanzhou on 27-29 October 2011.

② CRCICA Annual Report (2009-2010). The Centre accepted 51 international cases in 2009 and 66 in 2010, with an annual increase of 35%. In the first half year of 2011, the Centre accepted another 30 new cases. Among the 66 cases accepted in 2010, the construction contract cases rank at the top, 47% of the total cases. Considering the rapid development of China-African business relations, the Centre is planning to strengthen cooperation with the China Law Society and the China International Economic and Trade Arbitration Commission (CIETAC), to see Report on the AALCO's Regional Arbitration Centre at the 50th annual session of the Asian-African Legal Consultative Organization held in Colombo, Sri Lanka from 27 June to 1st July, 2011, available at: http://www.aalco.int/content/50thannualsession

There are several important international sea carriage lines and ports in Africa such as Durban, Cape Town, Lagos and Alexandria and the ships from other countries often harbour there, including the ships from China. Many African countries have provisions relating to marine jurisdiction and ships may be attached for various legal reasons. Several Chinese ships have been attached in the past few years in the African ports, especially in South Africa, giving rise to many marine disputes. ①

Investor – State Dispute Settlement mechanism

Finally, while all BITs signed by China and African countries provide for ISDS mechanism, the types of disputes that may be submitted to arbitration vary from treaty to treaty as per paragraph 2.1 above. Notably, according to the China–Ghana BIT signed in the late 1980s, only disputes concerning "the amount of compensation for expropriation" may be submitted to an arbitral tribunal.② In contrast, BITs signed by China with South Africa and Nigeria in late 1990s/early 2000s provide for ISDS mechanism to "any dispute… in connection with an investment" .③ Therefore, when investing in Africa, Chinese investors should be mindful of the relevant BIT provisions to make sure a dispute is covered by the scope of ISDS.

"Fork-in-the-road" provision

In order to secure its access to the ISDS mechanism, an investor should pay close attention to the so-called "fork-in-the-road" provision. In all China–Africa BITs, there is the mandatory requirement on the investor to choose from either domestic proceeding or international arbitration.④ In other words, once the investor has submitted the dispute to the competent court of the host state, it is no longer eligible to bring a treaty claim to an international arbitration tribunal. Such a stipulation is named as the "fork-in-the-road" provision, indicating that the investor has to choose one way or another at the cross-road for ways of remedy in the event that it has suffered loss from a host state's action or inaction which may amount to a violation of a treaty obligation.

Guaranteed Enforcement

Another merit of the ISDS mechanism for investment protection is the mechanism guaranteeing enforcement of arbitral award. Regardless of the forum of arbitration, the host state has an international obligation under the BITs to implement an award in favour of the investor once the award has been rendered. Furthermore, in most cases, the award may be enforced in a country other than the host state. More than 20 BITs signed by China with African countries specifically refer to the International Center for Settlement of Investment Disputes (ICSID) as the forum that may hear an

---

① Great River Shipping v. Sunnyface Marine 1992 (4) SA 313 (C); International Marine Transport SA v. MV "Le Cong", case No.080/05, the Supreme Court of South Africa; another Chinese ship was attached by the Durban Court, South Africa on 26 August 1999, to see http://www.civillaw.com.cn/article/default.asp?id=9896.

② China–Ghana BIT, Art. 10(1).

③ China-South Africa BIT, Article 9(1); China-Nigeria BIT, Article 9(1).

④ For example, Article 9(3) of China-Nigeria BIT and Article 9(2) of China-South Africa BIT.

investment claim. ①

The ICSID Convention is a treaty that establishes the jurisdiction of the ICSID and authorizes arbitration between investors and states. For awards rendered pursuant to the ICSID Convention, all State parties to the ICSID Convention bear an international obligation to recognize and enforce an ICSID award as if the award is a final decision of its local court. In other words, if a Chinese investor has been awarded compensation in an international arbitration, it is not limited to seek enforcement of that award in that African country where its investment is made. Rather, enforcement can be sought in other ICSID Convention contracting states where that African country's asset exists.

More importantly, the independent review system (the annulment proceeding) within ICSID further reduces the uncertainties that may arise from attempts to challenge the awards by the respondent State before any courts.

For non-ICSID awards, the Convention on the Recognition and Enforcement of Foreign Arbitral Awards (the New York Convention) applies to ensure that courts of contracting states will recognize and enforce arbitration awards made in other contracting states. Similar to the ICSID Convention, under the New York Convention, an arbitration award made in any other state can generally be freely enforced in any other contracting state with one exception: enforcement is subject to the review of local courts where such enforcement is sought and could be rejected on certain limited grounds. ②

In summary, the ICSID Convention and the New York Convention provide a high degree of assurances to the investors that an arbitral awarded will eventually be enforced against the host state. This is yet another advantage compared to litigation before a court at the host state.

The features of the investment disputes arising from China–African business relations

Disputes often settled in the courts or arbitral institutions in Africa

African countries are generally the importing countries of Chinese goods and capital and in most

---

① African countries that consent to arbitration in ICSID in BITs with China include: Morocco, Gabon, Cameroon, Ethiopia, Congo Rep., Botswana, Sierra Leone, Mozambique, Kenya, Cote d'Ivoire, Djibouti, Benin, Uganda, Tunisia, Equatorial Guinea, Madagascar, Seychelles, Mali, Chad, Libya, Tanzania.

② Article V of the New York Convention limits the grounds for non-recognition or enforcement to a narrowly-drafted list. The respondent state has to prove one of the following: lack of a valid arbitration agreement, violation of due process, excess of the arbitral tribunal's authority, irregularity in the composition of the arbitral tribunal or arbitral procedure, and the award "has not yet become binding" , "has been set aside" or "has been suspended" .

cases, the contracts were implemented in the African countries. Therefore, when disputes arise, the parties will often resort to the courts or arbitral institutions in Africa.

Furthermore, the investment laws in many African countries expressly provide that the investment disputes between the foreign investor and the host country should first be settled in the courts or arbitral institutions in the host country. For example, the Petroleum Activities Law of Angola provides that in case of any disputes, the disputes should be resolved by arbitration which takes place in Angola and governed by Angolan Law. ①

The disputes cover various African countries and involve different types of parties

At present, China has concluded BITs with 45 African countries and Chinese investments have spread in 49 African countries. ② The investors from China to Africa include state-owned enterprises, non-state-owned enterprises and private individuals. The projects mainly consist of mining, finance, manufacture, infrastructure, tourism and forestry, either through mergers and acquisitions, stock-sharing or through public private partnership with host country governments. The disputes will undoubtedly involve different types of parties which spans across various African countries. For example, numerous Chinese state-owned enterprises or non-state-owned enterprises sue or are sued in their own names rather than the names of their local companies. ③

The lack of effective bilateral or multilateral judicial assistance mechanisms

The adjudication of commercial disputes with foreign elements will generally require the service abroad of the judicial documents and taking evidence abroad. Sometimes the judgment creditor may have to seek the enforcement of the judgments in the country where the judgment debtor has its residence or property. These matters are usually provided in the bilateral judicial assistance treaties between two countries. Despite the frequent commercial disputes between China and African countries, China has only concluded 4 judicial assistance treaties with Morocco, Egypt, Algeria and Tunisia. The inefficiency in implementing the judicial assistance requirements according to the bilateral judicial treaties or non-implementation at all will simply result in the unwarranted delay of

① Oladiran Ajayi, Patricia Rosario, "Investments in Sub Saharan Africa: The Role of International Arbitration in Dispute Settlement". The author thanks Patricia Rosario for sending me a copy of this paper.

② The State Council Information Office of the People's Republic of China, White Paper on the China-African Business Cooperation (2010).

③ Roosevelt Kgosi v. China Civil Engineering, in the Industrial Court of Botswana, case No. IC. 500/2004; China Henan Internal Economic and Technical Cooperation v. Mwange Contractors Limited (SCZ Judgement No.7 of 2002), [2002] ZMSC 8 (24) January (2002); China Henan International Cooperation Group v. Regasira (civil reference No.22 of 2005) [2006] TZCA 43 (21 March 2006).

the trial process.

Additionally, the international judicial cooperation is now indispensable for the effective and efficient adjudication of foreign-related cases. ①Accordingly, many multilateral conventions for such a purpose have been devised worldwide, for example the 1965 Hague Convention on the Service Abroad of Judicial and Extra-judicial Documents in Civil or Commercial Matters (hereinafter referred to as "Hague Convention on the Service Abroad") and the 1970 Hague Convention on the Taking of Evidence Abroad in Civil or Commercial Matters (hereinafter referred to as "Hague Convention on the Taking of Evidence Abroad"). The member states of such conventions may cooperate in the administration of justice under the mechanisms provided by such conventions. So far, China has acceded to the two Hague Conventions, but in Africa only Egypt, Botswana, Malawi and Seychelles acceded to the Hague Convention on the Service Abroad, and only South Africa and Seychelles became parties to the Hague Convention on the Taking of Evidence Abroad. Therefore, the cooperation between China and African countries in cases with foreign elements through the multilateral mechanisms are restricted.

The lack of knowledge of legal system between China and Africa

Although there is an increase in commercial transactions in recent years between China and Africa, most of the Chinese people who are involved in such transactions know very little about the legal systems in African countries and would sometimes misinterpret the laws and judiciaries. In case of disputes, they do not know what the immediate remedy they can resort to which will often lead to slow settlement process.② Therefore, the Chinese should endeavor to understand about the legal systems relating to the adjudication of foreign-related cases in African countries which may result in a more efficient settlement process.

The settlement of disputes between Chinese and African parties

The adjudication of foreign-related commercial disputes are mainly settled through two ways: litigation and alternative dispute resolution such as consultation, mediation and arbitration.

The litigation of foreign-related disputes usually involve the jurisdiction, choice of law and the recognition and enforcement of foreign judgments. Great diversities exists in African legal systems, and there are obstacles to settle such disputes through litigation in African courts, which can be

① Richard F. Oppong, Private International Law in Africa, the Past, Present and Future, 55 Am. J. Comp. L. 677, 2007, p.680.

② China State Construction Engineering Corporation (Southern Africa) (Pty) Ltd v. Pro Joinery Close Corporation, in the High Court of Namibia, case No. A 230/2007.

summarized as follows: ①

Firstly, few African Countries have ever made systematic and comprehensive codes encompassing all aspects of conflict of law issues. Among 54 African countries, only Tunisia adopted a systematic and comprehensive Private International Law Code in 1998, with detailed provisions about the international jurisdiction, choice of law, and the recognition and enforcement of foreign judgments.② In other African countries, the private international law issues are stipulated in different single acts, which are hard to access.

Secondly, most of the legislations in several African countries are too outdated and impractical to suit the current economic situations due to legislative procedures. Most African countries adopted the legal systems from their colonizing countries, but some of the legislations remain intact since their independence, which are outdated. Some African countries re-enacted their laws to respond to the frequent transnational civil and commercial intercourses, but due to some technical reasons, the laws are inoperable. For example, the Enforcement of Foreign Judgments Act 32 of 1988 in South Africa③ provides that this act only applies to the recognition and enforcement of the judgments from the countries designated in South African Gazettes, whereas only Namibia is designated in the Gazette.

Thirdly, the development of the rules in relation to international commercial litigation in some African countries are isolated from the international legal development. Currently, most countries permit the litigants to choose by agreement to litigate their disputes in a country which has no causal links with the dispute, but the jurisdictional rules established in South Africa for example differs. The South African court is incompetent to decide a dispute if the cause of action did not arise in South

① Zhu, W., A Brief Analysis of the Disputes Arising from China-African Civil and Commercial Transactions, Journal of Cambridge Studies, Volume 7, No.3. The paper is also part of the research project sponsored by the China Social Science Research Fund (Project No.08CFX055). This paper was submitted to and read at the First China-African Think Tank Forum held in Hanzhou on 27-29 October 2011.

② The content of this law is available at http://www.lexadin.nl/wlg/legis/nofr/oeur/lxwetun.htm.

③ South African courts will enforce a foreign judgment if certain requirements, based largely on the Roman Dutch common law, are met. A foreign judgment, therefore, is not directly enforceable in South Africa but constitutes a cause of action that will be enforced by South African courts if the following requirements are met (as affirmed in a leading case on the subject, Jones v Krok 1995(1) SA 677(A)):

- the foreign court must have had international competence as determined by South African law;
- the judgment must be final and conclusive and must not have become superannuated;
- the enforcement of the judgment must not be contrary to South African public policy (which includes the rules of natural justice);
- the judgment must not have been obtained by fraudulent means;
- the judgment must not involve the enforcement of a penal or revenue law of the foreign state; and
- enforcement must not be precluded by the Protection of Businesses Act 99 of 1978.

Africa, even if the foreign plaintiff and the foreign defendant have expressly agreed in their contract that the dispute should be settled in the South African court.①

Lastly, many conflict of law issues are still pending in Africa. An African private international law scholar pointed out that over 300 judgments decided or reported in 13 Anglophone African countries from 1997 to 2007, many uncertainties exists in many aspects which needs to be developed by legislation or case law in future.② The aspects include the choice of law in contract and tort, jurisdiction over activities on the Internet, and private international law problems arising from trust and intellectual property.③

Since the 1990s, many African countries re-enacted their arbitration laws based on the advanced arbitration legal instruments, especially the 1985 UNCITRAL Model Law on International Commercial Arbitration in order to attract foreign investment, expand the trade, and enhance the investors' confidence. Furthermore, Most of the African countries acceded to such international conventions on arbitration as the 1965 Washington Convention on the Settlement of Investment Disputes Between States and Nationals of Other States④and the 1958 New York Convention on the Recognition and Enforcement of Foreign Arbitral Awards.⑤ On the other hand, many arbitral institutions or centres have been set up in African countries to provide the necessary facilities for effective and efficient arbitration in Africa. At present, nearly every African country has one arbitral institution or arbitral centre.⑥ The China Africa Joint Arbitration Centre Johannesburg was launched in August 2015 and is briefed to function as the principal forum for commercial dispute resolution between Chinese and African parties, with sister premises to be located in Shanghai. The introduction of a new International Arbitration Act, expected in early 2016, will modernise South African arbitration law and stimulate the development of South Africa as a regional arbitration centre for

---

① C F Forsyth, *Private International Law: The Modern Roman-Dutch Law Including the Jurisdiction of the Supreme Courts*, Juta & Co Ltd, 3rd edition,1996, p.204.

② Richard F Oppong, A Decade of Private International Law in African Courts (1997-2007) (part I), vol.9, *Yearbook of Private International Law*, 2008, pp.224-225.

③ Richard F. Oppong, Private International Law in Africa, the Past, Present and Future, 55 Am. J. Comp. L. 677, 2007, p.682.

④ Now 45 African States have signed the 1965 Washington Convention. Ethiopia, Guinea-Bissau, Namibia, Sao Tome and Principe only signed but not ratified the Convention, so 41 African states have been the Contracting States of the Convention. To see http://icsid.worldbank.org/ICSID/FrontServlet.

⑤ Now 30 African countries are parties to the New York Convention, to see http://www.uncitral.org/uncitral/en/uncitral_texts/arbitration/NYConvention_status.html, last visited 18 July.

⑥ Emilia Onyema, "Regional Approaches to Enforcement: Enforcement of Arbitral Awards in Sub-Sahara Africa", paper presented at the Inaugural Conference of Alumni & Friends of the School of International Arbitration (AFSIA) London, 3 December 2008,

arbitrations held under the auspices of well-known organisations, including AFSA and the ICC.

Conclusion

From the brief analysis of the dispute settlement mechanism in Africa, it is evident that the laws in relation to foreign litigation in many African countries remain unsystematic, isolated from international development, and unresolved in many issues. Nevertheless, under the current legal systems and traditions in many African countries, it is more preferable to settle such disputes through arbitration rather than litigation.

中国企业在非洲蓝色海洋经济发展计划中的机遇和风险

作者：Rita Chen　译者：王钟秀

一、介绍

中国的海上丝绸之路从亚洲延伸到欧洲，全长4000英里。它因在中国的汉朝时期（公元前206年—公元220年）用于运送丝绸而得名。中国国家主席习近平宣布计划建立新的海上丝绸之路。这条新的丝绸之路纪念了古老的丝绸之路，将成为中国两条新的对外贸易路线之一。两条新的对外贸易路线被并称为“一带一路”，既有陆上的丝绸之路经济带，又有海上丝绸之路，它们将中国的资金、专业知识、工业技术以及大量基础设施项目带到沿线地区。海上丝绸之路通过港口和基础设施项目相连接，自中国的东南沿海城市起始，将到达欧洲。在非洲海岸，中国计划在肯尼亚、吉布提、坦桑尼亚、莫桑比克等地建立港口。

在2014年，习近平主席宣布建立一项汇资400亿美元的丝绸之路基金会。[①] 此外，亚洲基础设施投资银行（AIIB）正在建立一项1000亿美元的项目以资助新贸易路线。许多参与新丝绸之路路线上的国家也是中国领导的亚洲基础设施投资银行的成员。[②] 中国计划为参与的国家提供低成本融资，满足基础设施建设的需要。

中国政府从长计议，发展“一带一路”项目。2015年1月，中国外交部部长王毅在肯尼亚奈落比演讲时说：“去年，非洲联盟委员会主席祖马先生在与李克强总理

① The Silk Road Fund Co. Ltd was established in Beijing on 29 December 2014, with investment from the State Administration of Foreign Exchange, China Investment Corporation, Export-Import Bank of China and China Development Bank. See http://www.silkroadfund.com.cn/enwap/27363/index.html.

② For a list of Prospective Founding Members, see http://euweb.aiib.org/html/aboutus/introduction/Membership/?show=0.

会面时说过：‘非洲人民希望有一天所有非洲国家都能有铁路相连接。’作为非洲的好伙伴，中国非常愿意帮助非洲人民实现梦想。这是一个需要综合规划和逐步提升的世纪性项目。”①

中非合作论坛（FOCAC）近期发布了《2016—2018年中国与非洲的合作行动计划》。在海洋经济发展规划中，双方将在海洋经济论坛框架下鼓励建立部长级论坛，中方将加强与非洲国家在海洋方面的交流和技术方面的合作，加强能力建设，积极探索共同建设海洋观测站、实验室和合作中心的可能性。②

非洲拥有丰富的自然生物资源和非生物资源，如水资源；拥有丰富动植物资源，如渔业；以及拥有丰富的矿产资源、碳氢化合物，等等。在45个非洲国家中，38个是沿海国家。

在非洲辖下，海洋经济带有1300万平方千米，包括领海、专属经济区和近650万平方千米的大陆架（各国只对海底有管辖权）③。由此可见，非洲具有非常丰富的海洋资源可供各国的可持续发展。

国际贸易对非洲国家的经济发展非常重要，超过90%的非洲国家通过海洋运输的方式进口和出口。④淡水和海洋渔业资源能够促进超过2亿的非洲人民温饱问题的解决，并且能够提供1000万美元的收入⑤。

本文将提出中国企业在非洲发展蓝色海洋经济的机遇，和与之相伴而来的法律风险。

二、蓝色经济的概念⑥

非洲蓝色经济指水生和海洋空间，包括大洋、大海、海岸、湖泊、河流和地下

---

① “Wang Yi: China Is Ready to Work for Africa’s Dream of Building,” Ministry of Foreign Affairs, the People’s Republic of China, January 11, 2015, accessed March 12, 2015.

② The Forum on China Africa Cooperation Action Plan 2016-2018 paragraph 3.5.2 provides that “the two sides will enhance experience sharing in offshore aquaculture, marine transportation, shipbuilding, construction of ports and port industrial parks, the surveying and exploitation of offshore oil and gas resources, marine environment, marine disaster prevention and reduction, marine scientific research, blue economy development and support mutually beneficial cooperation between Chinese and African enterprises in order to assist Africa to cultivate new economic growth drivers.”

③ GRID-Arendal, 2015. Area coverage of African marine spaces, compiled from unpublished raw data.

④ AU 2050 AIMS.

⑤ FAO, 2014. The Value of African Fisheries, FAO Fisheries and Aquaculture Circular No.1093.

⑥ United Nations Economic Commission for Africa, Africa’s Blue Economy: A policy handbook, March 2016, pp.5-7.

水，它包括一系列生产性行业，如渔业、水产养殖、旅游、运输、造船、能源、生物勘探，水下采矿及相关活动。

蓝色经济的概念包括：认识到健康的淡水资源和海洋生态系统可以使岛屿和其他沿海国家、以及内陆国家从中受益。它还需要在非洲建立一个综合、全面的参与机制，包括可持续利用和管理的蓝色经济资源。因此，蓝色经济框架正在从以往的部门法向一个多部门、多层次、综合性、多方法参与的经济模式转型。

非洲现有的蓝色经济框架是线性的、各国各自为政的，各个参与方（全球，国际和国家）之间的协同作用很弱。而新的蓝色经济框架将会反映一个整体的、系统的、多样的、包容的参与机制，以生态系统为基础、弱化各国政府之间的壁垒，环境、社会和经济各个因素交织在一起，倡导蓝色经济活动。

非盟在发展和完善非洲地区的蓝色经济制度方面发挥着至关重要的作用。在过去的十年里，非洲联盟委员会（AUC）已经建立了一个广泛的共识，扩大非洲蓝色经济将在结构转型中发挥着关键作用。这是非洲联盟发布的第 2050 个非洲的海上综合策略（非洲 2050 目标），它描述了蓝色经济将成为非洲复兴的“新边疆”。此外，蓝色经济是在第 2063 次非洲议程的核心，它被一致认为是“非洲的未来”，是社会经济转型的催化剂。2015 年 7 月，非洲联盟发起“非洲日”（7 月 25 日）和 2015—2025 年非洲海洋经济发展十年计划，大力倡导蓝色经济。[①]

这一议程的核心，是促进非洲的海上运输、物流服务、港口和铁路基础设施的现代化，提高其可靠性和效率，以无缝链接大陆的经济体国家，衔接区域和全球价值链，促进旅游和休闲活动，这与《中非合作论坛—约翰内斯堡行动计划（2016—2018 年）》一致。

三、中国海上丝绸之路之非洲的责任

尽管有些非洲人对中国的大规模介入存在许多批评，特别是一些国际媒体对此喧嚣不已，但是大多数非洲人民对中国的参与仍然持积极态度。因此，我们了解这一重要事实：中国在非洲大陆的影响力与日俱增，这种影响力加强了中国企业海外

① Decision Document (Assembly/AU/16(XXII) Add. 1), 22nd Ordinary Session of AU Heads of State and Governments on the adoption and implementation of the AU 2050 AIMS. See: *http://www.au.int/en/sites/default/files/decisions/9659-assembly_au_dec_490-516_xxii_e.pdf* (accessed 11 May 2016).

可持续发展能力。

不同的国际机构，如皮尤研究中心和非洲民调组织“非洲晴雨表”，根据它们的调查显示，大多数非洲人发现中国的介入对非洲而言是互利的。大多数非洲国家对中国的好感远远大于其不满，其调查比值大约有两倍甚至更多。大约 85% 的尼日利亚人，77% 的塞内加尔人和 75% 的加纳人将中国视为其国家合作伙伴，对于中国人的商业头脑、科学技术水平赞誉甚高。①

在非洲进行的“一带一路”基础设施建设项目的框架包括在沿海城市建设深水港口，如突尼斯的比赛大、塞内加尔的达喀尔、坦桑尼亚的达累斯萨拉姆、加蓬的吉布提和利伯维尔、莫桑比克的马普托以及加纳的特马。这些城市将会成为亚洲非洲沿海上丝绸之路上的货物和必需品中转站。参照中国在新喀麦隆深水港克里比的发展模式，这些港口极可能发展为工业中心。②

2011 年 6 月，中国港湾建设集团开始建设新的港口，其发展计划还包括打造一个 260 平方公里的工业区，以及连接克里比到其他喀麦隆主要城市的公路、铁路，这些项目均由中国企业承担。③ 在肯尼亚，中国正在建设一条连接首都内罗毕和港口城市蒙巴萨的铁路。这条铁路最终将扩展成为肯尼亚地区性的铁路通道——成为一条把乌干达、布隆迪和南苏丹等非洲国家与中国的海上丝绸之路相连的铁路网的一环。④

许多非洲国家并不是十分了解蓝色经济的概念，不过也有非洲国家重新把它们的目光聚焦在蓝色经济的发展上，把发展蓝色经济作为非洲未来发展的一个重要组成部分，并表达了他们自己的海上愿景。例如，南非总统雅各布·祖马最近发表了关于开发和经营国家的海洋资源的“实施行动”计划，旨在开启南非海洋经济的潜力。⑤ 无独有偶，随着非洲东海岸的安全形势好转，塞舌尔政府正在利用印度洋包容性增长的资源支持“蓝色经济”的发展。非盟在《2063 年议程》中概述表示，承

---

① Sakhuja, V., Chan, J., China's Maritime Silk Road and Asia, Vij Books India, 1 February 2016.

② Atul Aneja, "China steps up drive to integrate Africa with Maritime Silk Road," The Hindu, January 21, 2015, accessed 10 May 2016.

③ Shannon Tiezzi, "What's It Like to Have China Build You a Port? Ask Cameroon," The Diplomat, February 27, 2015, accessed 10 May 2016.

④ Cheng Lu, "Return of maritime Silk Road does not forget Africa," Xinhua, February 12, 2015, accessed 10 May 2016.

⑤ Department of Planning, Monitoring and Evaluation - About the Operation Phakisa, see http://www.operationphakisa.gov.za/Pages/Home.aspx.

诺促进和发展蓝色经济的概念是非洲未来发展的一个重要组成部分。[①]

对于非洲来说，十分重要的是建立与邻国合作伙伴关系，通过唤起国际和地区层面的对法律体系和工具的认识，与其他国家共同合作建立资源共享机制，弥补各成员因为海洋环境容量的有限性而造成海洋资源的匮乏。这是理解海洋经济至关重要的一部分。

为了展示非洲市场的重要型，显示其是海上丝绸之路设计中的重要一环，中国和泰国官员同意投资建设 12 个战略性港口，它们将沿着海上丝绸之路排布，对过往货物进行接收、分发和装船。其中 7 个港口位于非洲的海岸线上。

这些港口统称为海上战略配送中心（SMDC），它们主要将为从亚洲来的商业船队提供服务，每个港口都有自己的次级船队可以为它们的次级港口提供服务。这些港口建立在人口密集的地区，与当地或者区域性的市场通过铁路系统紧密相连。例如，加蓬是非洲第四发达的国家，人均 GDP 超过 11000 美元，加蓬的利伯维尔港将作为配送中心，把货物分发到邻近的喀麦隆、刚果、尼日利亚北部。[②]

四、面临的挑战

大多非洲国家的政府能力不足。虽然有些国家的环境法制定得很好，但是执行不畅。在大多数非洲国家，环境法和环境标准远远低于国际通用水平。非洲国家签署了许多国家条约和协议，却没有找到解决环境问题行之有效的方法。因为非洲国家在制定和执行环保措施上存在不足，这为中国企业承担非洲环保实践的责任提供了大量的空间。

尽管蓝色经济坚持绿色发展的原则以促进海洋资源的可持续利用，但发展蓝色经济，我们还需要格外注意其他几个方面的内容，关注国际、区域和各国政策之间

---

① "The Blue Economy": Key to Africa's Vision for the Future, Foreign Affairs Department, Ministry of Foreign Affairs and Transport, The Republic of Seychelles, 30 January 2014. Agenda 63 is both a Vision and an Action Plan. It is a global strategy to optimise use of Africa's resources for the benefits of all Africans and is an approach to how the continent should effectively learn from the lessons of the past, build on the progress now underway and strategically exploit all possible opportunities available in the short, medium and long term, so as to ensure positive socio-economic transformation within the next 50 years.

② China's Maritime Silk Road is all about Africa, November 2014, http://www.eastbysoutheast.com/chinas-maritime-silk-road-africa/ (accessed on 10 May 2016).

的协调和协作。[①]

首先，海洋是人类共有的财富，海洋和海洋资源的利用应当遵守国际规则、权利和义务。解决重大环境问题的国际规则和措施，需要密切的国际合作才能够有效实行。

其次，主要的国家环境问题影响海洋，包括海洋的酸碱度、海平面的高度、海洋变暖和污染情况，这些都对沿海人民和蓝色经济的发展有重要的经济性影响。

再次，海洋内的资源，特别是在管理大量的生物资源上存在极大的挑战。营造良好的海洋投资环境不仅需要国际规则和标准的适用，还需要增加海洋资源权利分配的透明度与稳定性。这是政府良好海洋管理的重要方向。

最后，许多海洋活动在国家管辖之外的公海或者国家 12 海里范围内的领海发生，对于后者而言各国可以适用他们各自的法律。因此海洋企业可以利用一些“蓝洞”规避船旗国、沿海国或者其他国家组织的监督。这些“蓝洞”指的是，打个比方，一艘船或钻井平台可以在一个国家注册，只有二分之一的国家能够提供保险、三分之一的国家能够给被保险人提供安全证书，四分之一的国家可以注册一个公司。正是因为这样的复杂性，如果没有有效的国际合作和规范，对事件的责任或违规行为可能难以确定。

海洋法的机制，特别是 1982 年发布的《联合国海洋法公约（UNCLOS）》，为私营海事安全监管分析提供了起点。虽然它不是现存唯一的相关法律文书，但公约最中肯的是设置了海洋管理的背景，为统一治理提供了最广泛的基础。

《联合国海洋法公约》往往被视为一个框架性公约：它建立一系列机构、以国际群体的利益为基础平衡国家之间的权利和义务。它补充了其他公约和协议。然而，联合国海洋法公约并不是简单地建立广泛的框架，它还详细地划定了专属经济区的海里限制范围，并建立了海洋管理和海上作业的“道路规则”。联合国海洋法公约也包含一个简短但具体的安全措施，应对海上威胁。

在当今的国际安全范式内，《联合国海洋法公约》关于海上安全性的框架常常产生问题。这是为什么呢？因为传统的国家战争形式正在被两个对立的非国家行为体所取代，这既体现了海上安全的威胁，又体现了国际航运贸易保护的重要性。

《联合国海洋法公约》提供了两个具体的机制，它们是海上安全和秩序的基石：连续海洋区域的管辖权、船旗国、沿岸国、港口国三位一体的控制权。事实上，《联

① United Nations Economic Commission for Africa, Africa’s Blue Economy: A policy handbook, 2016.

合国海洋法公约》是唯一规定国家管辖海域框架的国际公约。

从海洋的角度来看,《联合国海洋法公约》于 1982 年通过、1994 年生效，是进行海洋活动公认的一般法律框架。该公约还概述了所有公约涉及的海洋区域国家进行海洋活动的权利和义务，包括与航行、生物和非生物资源，保护和保全海洋环境，海洋科学研究和海洋开发和技术转移。它提供了包括海洋区的划分等多种手段，满足多个领域的法律确定性。

关于海洋区的划分，明确界定和适当公布的海洋区的限制是各国从海洋和海洋资源中获得好处的一个重要基础。这些限制为沿海国家提供了一定程度上的主权或管辖权，从而创造了吸引投资和勘探开发活动的前提条件。

令人鼓舞的是，非洲国家非常积极地参与《联合国海洋法公约》，迈出了非常重要的一步。然而，在实施中仍然存在相当大的困难，包括统一的国家法律与有关规定、统一这些规定的具体运用程序。同时，实施上还要求完善国内法律、政策和制度框架、加强相关部门的相互联系。

《联合国海洋法公约》的框架下考虑到了采用其他协议来促进其规定实施的可能性。因此，公约补充了两个实施协议。《关于执行 1982 年 12 月 10 日联合国海洋法公约第十一部分的协定》，是有关资源的勘探和开发的国际海底地区（被称为该地区）的，国际海底地区被认为是“人类的共同遗产”，换句话说，在该地区的经济收益的好处造福所有人类。该地区由国际海底管理局管理。目前，没有非洲国家在该地区存在活动。1995 年《执行 1982 年 12 月 10 日〈联合国海洋法公约〉有关养护和管理跨界鱼类种群和高度洄游鱼类种群的规定的协定》，它为各国提供了一个框架，即在区域渔业管理组织的合作下，以可持续的方式利用专属经济区和公海的资源。许多非洲国家仍然无法充分利用这些资源，相反，他们通常向其他大陆的舰队颁发许可证。我们还需要注意一些其他的具有约束力的国际公约。包括《关于特别是作为水禽栖息地的国际重要湿地公约》(又称《拉姆萨尔公约》);《生物多样性公约》(CBD) 和“雅加达授权”;《东部非洲地区海洋和沿海环境保护、管理与发展公约》(内罗毕公约);《国际防止船舶造成污染公约》(MARPOL);《非洲海运宪章》;《非洲自然和自然资源保护公约》和《世界遗产公约》。在贸易层面上，世界贸易组织（WTO）的成员国因其经济活动对蓝色经济产生影响而享有权利和义务。

在多样性的背景下，把蓝色经济范式和现存多样性的软法文件结合起来（软法性文件是自愿的、不具约束力的协议或期望)，通过这种方式支持现有的制度安排，也对各国统一和协调的努力提出了挑战。联大最近决定了一个关于区域资源发展和国家管辖权的重要文件“69 / 292 决议（2015 年 6 月 10 日）”，以在《联合国海洋法公约》之下建立一个国际化、具有约束力的国际法律，在国家管辖范围以外区域保护海洋生物多样性的可持续利用。①

筹备委员会将在 2016 开始工作，到 2017 年年底，委员会将对联合国大会作出的草案进行实质性的建议，特别是在“海洋遗传资源，包括共享利益的问题，如基础管理工具方面的措施，包括海洋保护区，环境影响评估能力建设和海洋技术转让”这些方面要尤为注意。②这些谈判在一定程度上将会依赖于资源的可用性，特别是金融资源，非洲国家以协调的方式参与这些谈判是非常重要的。在这个过程中，非洲国家的有效参与也非常值得关注和倡导。

为了追求发展蓝色经济的发展，法律框架和工具的实施和应用也需要谈判技巧，但是，不同国家之间仍然存在技术能力和制度差距。例如，在《气候变化协议》中，非洲利益完全被绿色发展、低碳增长的资金所限制，这些挑战可以证明现行非洲存在的困难。在《京都议定书》下，非洲在清洁发展机制（CDM）和碳交易安排方面的有限参与体现在信息、谈判、技术约束上③。在各方的共同努力下，这些意识上的障碍是可以克服的，各国可以通过促进国际法律文书的制定，建立蓝色经济相关的制度结构、政策过程和监管制度。对于各国来说，另一个主要挑战是缺乏部门间的协调配合、以及中央机构（如部委、委员会或协会）对蓝色经济资源的调配不够。匹配的监管、合适的机构、适当的预算机制都是必不可少的。

许多海上和跨国的水上边界没有正式划定。划定的边界产生的不确定性会导致邻国关系的紧张。此外，这种不确定性可能会阻碍投资，使各国不愿进行与合作或联合开发活动。用合作的方式发展蓝色经济有助于避免潜在的冲突并促进共享。

最后，海上石油和天然气勘探也增加了国际海洋纠纷，对海洋空间的争夺变得越来越多。专属经济区的界限也因此变得更加重要。

五、机遇

国际能源机构估计，海洋可再生能源有足够的潜力，能够提供高达 400% 的全

① http://www.un.org/depts/los/general_assembly/reports/report_70.pdf.

② http://www.un.org/depts/los/general_assembly/reports/report_70.pdf.

③ http://www.unicef.org/esaro/climate_change_in_africa.pdf.

球能源需求。其他估计显示，在 2010 年度海上相关活动的总经济价值达到 1.5 万亿欧元。预计到 2020 年，这一数字将达到每年 2.5 万亿欧元。当然，非洲需要全面和连贯的战略以利用这种潜力。

大多数非洲国家已批准《联合国海洋法公约》。蓝色经济为非洲提供了一个独特的机会，将他们的政治承诺转化为切实有效的实施行为，在公约规定的权利和应尽的职责范围内维护他们的权利。非洲国家最近开始谈判公约的实施，在国家管辖范围以外的海洋生物资源的可持续利用方面，他们提出了另一个践行承诺的机会：遵守国际原则，可持续利用海洋资源保护区，重视海洋生物多样性。事实上，鼓励非洲国家积极参与这一进程，继续合作，践行谈判成果，这将有利于他们实现可持续发展的愿望，确保公平考虑非洲的利益。

蓝色经济提供了一个不同类型的合作和协调的机会，包括公共私人伙伴关系（PPP）。他们强调在测绘、矿产勘探、能源开发、渔业、水产养殖、环境、航空、海上运输和港口安全等领域加强政府与民营资本的合作。他们强调加强科学和技术合作的重要性和联合行动的建议。在这方面，非常需要继续加强能力建设、促进技术的转让、研究和发展，建立新型、创造性、有效的合作伙伴关系。①

蓝色经济国际合作的一个重要组成部分是科学研究。以科学为基础的研究方法对蓝色经济的发展是至关重要的，非洲国家先行安排最初的评估和蓝色资本的估值。这将有助于信息的决策，提供有效的管理途径，为不同的蓝色经济部门的发展提供了依据。它强调技术援助、技术转让和能力建设，以追求可持续发展的重要性。

港口的发展对进一步的经济发展是至关重要的，如渔业和游轮旅游业的发展。许多非洲小岛屿上的发展中国家是十分重要的海上航运枢纽。然而，发展港口或使用港口往往对环境有不利影响，如空气和水的污染、疏浚、野生动物栖息地的损失、水生公害物种数量增加、限制公众访问沿海资源和土地使用冲突的问题。反过来，这可能会影响生物多样性，并对渔业和旅游部门造成影响。往来的船舶对海洋环境也会造成不利的影响，如石油泄漏、噪声和压载水处理等。②

① United Nations Economic Commission for Africa, Africa’s Blue Economy: A policy handbook, 2016, pp.89-90.

② United Nations Economic Commission for Africa, Unlocking full potentials of the blue economy: Are African SIDS ready to embrace the opportunities.

六、结论

不同部门之间的联系越发密切，在经济发展的基础上考虑环境和社会经济后果，加强制度设计以促进非洲国家在不同的蓝色经济部门实现经验、资源的共享，共同追求可持续发展的目标，这是非洲蓝色经济发展计划所带来的机遇。《中非合作论坛—约翰内斯堡行动计划（2016—2018年）》应当要有技术获得的途径，帮助非洲国家和中国共同迎接挑战、协力发展。

Opportunities and Legal Risks for Chinese Enterprises Arising from Blue Marine Economy Development Plan of Africa

Author: Rita Chen

Introduction

China's Maritime Silk Road (MSR) which is a 4000 mile Silk Road stretching from Asia to Europe takes its name from the silk that was carried along it during China's Han dynasty (206 BC – 220 AD). China's President Xi Jinping unveiled plans to establish the MSR, which is one of two new foreign trade routes reminiscent of the ancient Silk Road. The two-part initiative, heralded as "One Belt, One Road" combines the MSR with a land-based counterpart, called the Silk Road Economic Belt which offers Chinese funding, expertise, and industrial technology in the implementation of massive infrastructural projects in the geographical areas. The MSR aims to reach Europe, originating from cities on China's south-eastern coast and using a system of linked ports and infrastructure projects. Along the African coast, China plans to develop ports in Kenya, Djibouti, Tanzania and Mozambique just to name a few.

In 2014, President Xi Jinping announced the creation of a $40 billion Silk Road Fund.① Additionally, the Asian Infrastructure Investment Bank (AIIB) is being established with equity of $100 billion to finance the creation of the new trade routes. Many of the countries involved in the new Silk Road routes are also members of the Chinese-led AIIB.② China plans to offer low-cost financing to participating countries to help enable the infrastructure development required.

The Chinese government takes a long-term view of the "One Belt, One Road" projects. As Foreign Minister Wang Yi mentioned in a speech in Nairobi, Kenya in January 2015:

---

① The Silk Road Fund Co. Ltd was established in Beijing on 29 December 2014, with investment from the State Administration of Foreign Exchange, China Investment Corporation, Export-Import Bank of China and China Development Bank. See http://www.silkroadfund.com.cn/enwap/27363/index.html

② For a list of Prospective Founding Members, see http://euweb.aiib.org/html/aboutus/introduction/Membership/?show=0.

"When Premier Li Keqiang visited the headquarters of African Union last year, Chairperson of African Union Commission Ms. Nkosazana Dlamini Zuma said that African people cherish a dream that one day the capitals of all African countries will be linked by high-speed railways. As a good friend of Africa, China is willing to make efforts to help African friends realize the dream. It is a century project that requires comprehensive planning and gradual advancement."[①]

The Forum on China Africa Cooperation (FOCAC) Action Plan 2016-2018 which was recently adopted includes the development of ocean economy whereby the two sides will encourage the establishment of a Ministerial Forum on marine economy under the framework of FOCAC and the Chinese side will enhance marine exchanges and technology cooperation with African countries, launch capacity building and actively explore the possibility of jointly building marine observation stations, laboratories and cooperation centres.[②]

On the African horizon, Africa is endowed with a variety of natural living and non-living resources, such as water, diverse flora and fauna, including fish stocks, minerals and hydrocarbons. Additionally 38 of the 54 African States are coastal states.

Maritime zones under Africa's jurisdiction total about 13 million square kilometers, including territorial seas and Exclusive Economic Zones (EEZ) and approximately 6.5 million square kilometers for the continental shelf (for which countries have jurisdiction over only the seabed).[③] The continent therefore has a vast ocean resource base that can contribute to sustainable development of African States.

International trade is important to many African economies, with more than 90 percent of Africa's imports and exports conducted by sea.[④] Freshwater and ocean fish make a vital contribution to the food and nutritional security of over 200 million Africans and provide income for over 10 million.[⑤] This paper will identify a number of legal risks for Chinese enterprises arising from blue marine economy development in Africa and the opportunities which may arise pursuant to the identified legal risks.

---

① "Wang Yi: China Is Ready to Work for Africa's Dream of Building," Ministry of Foreign Affairs, the People's Republic of China, January 11, 2015, accessed March 12, 2015.

② The Forum on China Africa Cooperation Action Plan 2016-2018 paragraph 3.5.2 provides that "the two sides will enhance experience sharing in offshore aquaculture, marine transportation, shipbuilding, construction of ports and port industrial parks, the surveying and exploitation of offshore oil and gas resources, marine environment, marine disaster prevention and reduction, marine scientific research, blue economy development and support mutually beneficial cooperation between Chinese and African enterprises in order to assist Africa to cultivate new economic growth drivers."

③ GRID-Arendal, 2015. Area coverage of African marine spaces, compiled from unpublished raw data.

④ AU 2050 AIMS.

⑤ FAO, 2014. The Value of African Fisheries, FAO Fisheries and Aquaculture Circular No.1093.

The blue economy concept[①]

The Blue Economy in Africa covers aquatic and marine spaces, including oceans, seas, coasts, lakes, rivers, and underground water, and it comprises a range of productive sectors, such as fisheries, aquaculture, tourism, transport, shipbuilding, energy, bioprospecting, and underwater mining and related activities.

The Blue Economy concept includes recognition that the productivity of healthy freshwater and ocean ecosystems is a pathway for aquatic and maritime based economies and can ensure that islands and other coastal countries, as well as land-locked States, benefit from their resources. It also requires an integrated, holistic and participatory approach that includes sustainable use and management of Blue Economy resources for societal progress in a diverse Africa. The Blue Economy framework is therefore intended to move from the current sectoral approach to a multi-sectoral, integrated, and participatory approach at multiple levels.

The existing Blue Economy framework in Africa encompasses a linear, compartmentalized, and sectoral approach with weak connections, linkages, and synergies between various scales of intervention (global, international, and national) as well as among the sectors concerned. The new Blue Economy framework should reflect an integrated, systemic, dynamic, inclusive, participatory, and ecosystem-based approach in which sectoral barriers are minimized at the activity and governance level, and environmental, social, and economic dimensions are intertwined and pursued for all Blue Economy activities.

The African Union (AU) plays a crucial role in developing and implementing the Blue Economy policy and strategy in the African region. Over the past decade, the African Union Commission (AUC) has built an enlarged Africa-wide consensus regarding the critical role that the Blue Economy could play in fostering structural transformation in Africa during the next decade. This is encapsulated in the African Union's 2050 Africa's Integrated Maritime Strategy (AU 2050 AIMS), which describes the Blue Economy as the "new frontier of African Renaissance." In addition, the Blue Economy is at the centre of the AU's Agenda 2063, at which it was unanimously declared to be "Africa's future" and recognized as a catalyst for socioeconomic transformation. In July 2015, the African Union launched the African Day (25 July) and Decade of Seas and Oceans 2015–2025 to rally action on the Blue Economy.[②]

Central to this agenda, is the need to modernise Africa's maritime transport and logistics services, its port and railway infrastructure, improve its reliability and efficiency with the view to

① United Nations Economic Commission for Africa, Africa's Blue Economy: A policy handbook, March 2016, pp.5-7.

② Decision Document (Assembly/AU/16(XXII) Add. 1), 22nd Ordinary Session of AU Heads of State and Governments on the adoption and implementation of the AU 2050 AIMS. See: *http://www.au.int/en/sites/default/files/decisions/9659-assembly_au_dec_490-516_xxii_e.pdf* (accessed 11 May 2016).

seamlessly link the continent's economies to national, regional and global value chains as well as facilitate tourism and recreation activities which is in line with the FOCAC Action Plan 2016-2018.

Africa's response to China's Maritime Silk Road

In spite of much criticism about China's large-scale involvement in the African continent, especially in the international press, the overall perception of Africa about China and Chinese engagement remain mostly positive. It is thus important to understand Africa's response to China's growing presence in the continent in general to strengthen overseas sustainable development of Chinese enterprises.

Different researches conducted by international institutions like Pew Research and African counterparts like Afro-barometer shows that most African people find Chinese engagement in Africa to be mutually beneficial. They say that favourable views of China outnumber critical judgements by two-to-one or more in most countries in Africa. About 85% of Nigerians, 77% of Senegalese and 75% of Ghanaians view China as a national partner and have high regard for Chinese business acumen and science and technology.[①]

The infrastructural projects to be undertaken in Africa under the "One Belt, One Road" framework include the development of deep water ports in coastal cities including Bizerte, Tunisia; Dakar, Senegal; Dar es Salaam, Tanzania; Djibouti, Libreville, Gabon; Maputo, Mozambique; Tema and Ghana. These will be key sites of the transcontinental exchange of manufactured goods and commodities between Asian and African economies along the MSR. These ports are also likely to be developed as industrial hubs, following the model of China's development of the new Cameroonian deep water port of Kribi.[②]

While China Harbor Engineering Company started constructing the new port in June 2011, the development plan also includes the creation of a 260 square kilometer industrial zone, as well as roads and railways connecting Kribi to major cities in Cameroon, projects which will be undertaken by other Chinese companies.[③] In Kenya, China is constructing a railway connecting the capital city Nairobi with the port city of Mombasa. This will eventually be expanded into a regional rail corridor connecting Kenya—one of the African gateways to the MSR—with Uganda, Burundi, and South Sudan.[④]

---

① Sakhuja, V., Chan, J., China's Maritime Silk Road and Asia, Vij Books India, 1 February 2016.

② Atul Aneja, "China steps up drive to integrate Africa with Maritime Silk Road," The Hindu, January 21, 2015, accessed 10 May 2016.

③ Shannon Tiezzi, "What's It Like to Have China Build You a Port? Ask Cameroon," The Diplomat, February 27, 2015, accessed 10 May 2016.

④ Cheng Lu, "Return of maritime Silk Road does not forget Africa," Xinhua, February 12, 2015, accessed 10 May 2016.

For many African countries, the blue economy concept is not well known and several African countries of late has renewed their focus on development of blue economy as a significant part of Africa's future development and are coming up with their own maritime visions. For example, the South African President Jacob Zuma recently set out his vision for exploiting the country's maritime resources by launching "Operation Phakisa" which aims at unlocking the economic potential of South Africa's Oceans.① Similarly, as the security situation off the east coast of Africa improves, the Seychelles government is supporting the development of a "blue economy" using the Indian Ocean's resources for inclusive growth. The AU also expressed its commitment to embracing and developing the blue economy concept as a vital part of Africa's future development to be outlined in the AU's agenda 2063.②

It is important for Africa to build up partnerships with its neighbours and pool resources from other players due to its limited maritime capacity by cultivating adequate awareness of existing applicable legal frameworks and instruments at both the international and regional levels is an important part of understanding the blue economy.

To demonstrate the importance of African markets as a key player in the designs for the MSR, Chinese and Thai officials agreed to construct investment vehicles for the development of 12 strategic ports which will receive and distribute cargo shipped along the MSR. Seven of these ports are located on Africa's coastlines.

The idea is that these ports, collectively known as Strategic Maritime Distribution Centers (SMDC) will service the main commercial fleet coming from Asia and each port will have its own secondary fleet of smaller coastal vessels to distribute to secondary ports. The SMDC's are located close to large population centres with reliable road systems for distribution to local and regional markets. For example, the Libreville port in Gabon, Africa's 4th most developed country with a per capita GDP of more than 11,000 USD, will serve as a distribution center to neighboring Cameroon, the Congo, and Nigeria to the north.③

---

① Department of Planning, Monitoring and Evaluation - About the Operation Phakisa, see http://www.operationphakisa.gov.za/Pages/Home.aspx.

② "The Blue Economy": Key to Africa's Vision for the Future, Foreign Affairs Department, Ministry of Foreign Affairs and Transport, The Republic of Seychelles, 30 January 2014. Agenda 63 is both a Vision and an Action Plan. It is a global strategy to optimise use of Africa's resources for the benefits of all Africans and is an approach to how the continent should effectively learn from the lessons of the past, build on the progress now underway and strategically exploit all possible opportunities available in the short, medium and long term, so as to ensure positive socio-economic transformation within the next 50 years.

③ China's Maritime Silk Road is all about Africa, November 2014, http://www.eastbysoutheast.com/chinas-maritime-silk-road-africa/ (accessed on 10 May 2016).

Challenges

Most African states have weak bureaucracies. While their environmental laws are sometimes impressive, implementation is usually lacking. In most African countries, the environmental laws and standards are much lower than accepted international norms. African governments have signed large numbers of treaties and agreements but have largely failed to articulate coherent solutions to their environmental problems. Because of the weakness of African institutions to monitor and enforce environmental protection measures, it will be primarily up to individual Chinese companies to assume responsibility for sound environmental practices.

While the blue economy uses the principles of green growth to pursue the objective of environmentally sustainable use of marine resources, there are several additional aspects of the blue economy that require special attention with regard to coordination and alignment of international, regional and national policies and activities.①

Firstly, the oceans are generally a common property resource and the use of the oceans and ocean resources are subject to international rules, rights and responsibilities. Effective application of the international rules and measures to address major environmental externalities requires close international cooperation.

Secondly, there are major global environmental externalities affecting the oceans, including ocean acidification, sea-level rise, ocean warming and pollution, all of which will have major economic impacts on coastal peoples and the blue economy.

Thirdly, marine tenure, particularly over living resources has proved challenging to design and manage. An attractive 'blue investment climate' not only requires application of international rules and standards, but transparency and stability in allocation of rights and concessions over marine resources – an important dimension of good marine governance.

Fourthly, many marine activities take place in waters either beyond national jurisdiction (high seas) or in waters with limited national jurisdiction - beyond the 12-mile territorial sea, where national legislation may have limited application. Consequently there are numerous legal 'blue holes' where marine enterprises can operate with little supervision either by flag state, coastal state or international authorities. These 'blue holes' mean that, for example, a vessel, or drilling platform may be registered in one country, insured in a second, have a safety certificate from a third, be chartered to a company in a fourth country, operated by a company located in a fifth country and the master may have the nationality and qualifications of a sixth country. With such complexities, responsibility for incidents or violations can be difficult to ascertain without effective international cooperation and norms.

① United Nations Economic Commission for Africa, Africa's Blue Economy: A policy handbook, 2016.

Law of the sea mechanisms, specifically the 1982 United Nations Convention on the Law of the Sea (UNCLOS), provide an engaging starting point for regulatory analysis of private maritime security. Although it is not the only relevant legal instrument in existence, the Convention is the most pertinent, setting the backdrop for oceans management and providing the broadest foundation for uniform governance.

UNCLOS is often regarded as a framework convention: It sets up institutions and balances the rights and obligations of states with the interests of the international community. It is supplemented by other conventions and protocols. Yet UNCLOS does much more than simply set up broad frameworks. It also specifies detailed nautical-mile limits for maritime zones and establishes "rules of the road" for oceans management and operations at sea. UNCLOS also contains a brief, but specific, security component that addresses key tenets of responding to maritime threats.

In today's international security paradigm, the applicability of the UNCLOS framework with regard to maritime security is often called into question. Why? Because traditional state-on-state warfare is being replaced by two opposing groups of non-state actors, embodying threats to both maritime security and the protectors of international shipping commerce.

UNCLOS provides two specific regimes which are fundamental to maritime security and order on the seas: the regime of consecutive maritime zones, and the jurisdictional trinity of flag, coastal and port state control. In fact, UNCLOS is the only international convention which stipulates a framework for state jurisdiction in maritime spaces.

From the oceans perspective, UNCLOS, which was adopted in 1982 and entered into force in 1994 is widely recognized as the general legal framework within which all activities in the oceans and seas must be carried out. This convention also outlines the rights and obligations of States in carrying out these activities, including those relating to navigation, living and non-living resources, protection and preservation of the marine environment, marine scientific research, and development and transfer of marine technology, in all maritime areas provided for in the convention. It provides the means for achieving legal certainty in a number of areas, including the delineation of maritime zones.

With regard to maritime zones delineation, clearly defined and duly publicized limits of maritime zones are an essential basis for States to derive benefits from the oceans and their resources. These limits provide certainty with regard to the extent of the sovereignty or sovereign rights and jurisdiction of coastal States, thereby creating a fundamental precondition to attracting investments for exploration and exploitation activities.

The high rate of ratification of this instrument by African States is encouraging and a valuable step forward. However, there remain considerable challenges with regard to implementation, including harmonization of national laws with relevant provisions and uniform and consistent application of these provisions. Implementation of UNCLOS requires domestic legal, policy, and institutional frameworks, as well as cross-linkages with other sectors.

The framework provided by UNCLOS takes into account the possibility of adopting other agreements to facilitate the implementation of its provisions. The convention is thus complemented by two implementing agreements. The 1994 Agreement Relating to the Implementation of Part XI of the Convention on the Law of the Sea is relevant to the exploration and exploitation of the resources of the international seabed area (known as the Area), which is considered to be the "common heritage of mankind." In other words, the benefits of economic gains from activities in the Area are to benefit all of humanity. The Area is administered by the International Seabed Authority (ISA). At present, no African States are sponsoring any activities in the Area. The 1995 Agreement for the Implementation of the Provisions of the Convention relating to the Conservation and Management of Straddling Fish Stocks and Highly Migratory Fish Stocks (United Nations Fish Stocks Agreement), provides the framework for States, in cooperation with regional fisheries management organizations, to sustainably exploit the resources of their Exclusive Economic Zones (EEZs), as well as those of the high seas. Many African States are as yet unable to fully exploit these resources; instead, they usually issue licenses to fleets from other continents. There are a series of other binding international conventions whose provisions need to be kept in view. An indicative list would include the Convention on Wetlands of International Importance (Ramsar Convention); Convention on Biological Diversity (CBD) and Jakarta Mandate; Convention for the Protection, Management and Development of the Marine and Coastal Environment of the Eastern African Region (Nairobi Convention); International Convention for the Prevention of Pollution from Ships (MARPOL); African Maritime Transport Charter; African Convention on the Conservation of Nature and Natural Resources; and the World Heritage Convention. Member states of the World Trade Organization (WTO) also have obligations and rights with respect to trade that may have implications for economic activities and institutions within the Blue Economy.

Integrating the Blue Economy paradigm into the context of the existing multiplicity of soft law instruments (i.e., voluntary, nonbinding, or aspirational agreements), which were designed to bolster existing institutional arrangements, also poses a challenge with regard to harmonization and coordination efforts. An important development with regard to the resources of areas beyond national jurisdiction is the recent decision by the UNGA (Resolution 69/292 of 19 June 2015) to develop an international, legally binding instrument under UNCLOS on the conservation and sustainable use of marine biodiversity in areas beyond national jurisdiction.①

A preparatory committee will start its work in 2016 and by the end of 2017 shall make substantive recommendations to the UNGA on the elements of a draft text covering, in particular, "marine genetic resources, including questions on the sharing of benefits, measures such as area-based management tools, including marine protected areas, environmental impact assessments and capacity-building and the transfer of marine technology."② The participation of African States in a coordinated

① *http://www.un.org/depts/los/general_assembly/reports/report_70.pdf.*

② *http://www.un.org/depts/los/general_assembly/reports/report_70.pdf.*

manner in these negotiations is important and will depend to some extent on availability of resources, particularly financial resources. The effective participation of African States in this process is also influenced by the need for representatives with a good appreciation of the issues.

The implementation and application of legal frameworks and instruments for pursuing the development of the Blue Economy also require negotiation skills; however, technical capacity and institutional gaps remain at the national level. These challenges can be demonstrated, for example, in the climate change agreements and Africa's limited benefits, which are exclusively limited to funding and investments for green, low-carbon growth. Africa's limited participation to date in the Clean Development Mechanism (CDM) and carbon trading arrangements under the Kyoto Protocol is a demonstration of the prevailing information, negotiation, and technical skill constraints.[①] With concerted effort, these barriers to awareness can be overcome, and leveraging by States of international legal instruments can help shape effective national Blue Economy-related institutional structures, policy processes, and regulatory regimes. Another central challenge at the national level is the insufficient intersectoral coordination combined with the scarcity of central coordinating institutions for the Blue Economy (e.g., ministries, commissions, or units). Matching regulatory and institutional choices with appropriate budget mechanisms is essential.

A number of maritime and transnational aquatic boundaries are not formally delimited. The uncertainty created by demarcated borders can lead to explosive tension between neighbouring countries. Additionally, this uncertainty may discourage investment and leave countries unforthcoming to move forward with cooperation or joint development activities. A collaborative approach to the development of the Blue Economy helps to avoid potential conflicts and facilitates a focus on shared opportunities.

Lastly, offshore oil and gas exploration can also create international maritime disputes as claims to ocean space are becoming increasingly valuable. The boundaries of the EEZ have thus become even more important.

Opportunities

The International Energy Agency estimates that ocean renewable energy has a power potential sufficient to provide up to 400% of global current energy demand. Other estimates indicate that in 2010 the total annual economic value of maritime related activities reached 1.5 trillion euro. It is forecasted that by 2020, this figure will reach 2.5 trillion euro per year. Surely, Africa needs holistic and coherent strategies to harness this potential.

Most African States have ratified UNCLOS. The Blue Economy presents a unique opportunity

① *http://www.unicef.org/esaro/Climate_Change_in_Africa.pdf.*

for Africa to translate their political commitment into tangible and effective implementation and assertion of their rights under the convention as well as the related observation of their duties. The recent agreement by African states to begin a process of negotiations toward an implementing agreement on the conservation and sustainable use of marine biodiversity in areas beyond national jurisdiction presents another opportunity for African States to demonstrate their commitment to agreed international principles for the conservation and sustainable use of marine resources. Indeed, African States are encouraged to actively participate in this process and to continue to cooperate in negotiating outcomes that would favour their sustainable development aspirations and ensure fair consideration of Africa's interests.

The Blue Economy provides an opportunity for different types of cooperation and collaboration, including Public Private Partnerships. They emphasize the value of cooperation in the exchange and strengthening of technical capacities in areas such as mapping, mineral exploration, energy development, fishing, aquaculture, the environment, air and maritime transport, and port security. They underline the importance of enhancing scientific and technical cooperation in areas of interest and proposals for joint actions. In this regard, the continued need for capacity building, technology transfer, and research and development is crucial and would of necessity require the development of integrated, innovative, and effective partnerships.[①]

A key component of international cooperation for the Blue Economy approach is Research. A science-based approach is essential to the development of the Blue Economy; commencing with the initial assessment and critically the valuation of the blue capital at the disposal of the African States. This will provide a basis for informed decision-making and adaptive management and pathways for development of the different blue economy sectors. This underlines the importance of technical assistance, technology transfer and capacity building to the pursuit of sustainable development.

Development of ports are crucial for further economic development in e.g. fisheries but also cruise ship tourism. For African small island developing states a position as a maritime shipping hub is very important. However, development of, or increased use of port often have environmental impacts such as air and water pollution, dredging, loss of wildlife habitat, aquatic nuisance species, restraining public access to coastal resources, and land conflict use issues. This in turn could therefore impact biodiversity and as a result impact the fisheries and tourist sector. Increased shipping through one's ocean also can cause environmental impacts e.g. oil spills as well as noise and ballast water disposal impacts.[②]

① United Nations Economic Commission for Africa, Africa's Blue Economy: A policy handbook, 2016, pp.89-90.

② United Nations Economic Commission for Africa, Unlocking full potentials of the blue economy: Are African SIDS ready to embrace the opportunities.

Conclusion

The interconnectedness of the different sectors has become clear and the development of the different sectors should take the conflicting interest of other sectors into considerations as well as the environmental and socio-economic consequences. Institutional arrangements should be made to facilitate the sharing of experiences, pursuing of mutual goals and sharing resources across the African countries on the different Blue Economy sectors which opportunities are arising from the Blue Economy Development Plan of Africa. Technologies must be made accessible, affordable and adaptable to the needs and particular circumstances of African countries by China as reflected in the FOCAC Action Plan 2016-2018.

非洲各国投资法律规定之介绍

Introduction to Investment laws and Regulations of African Countries

对非投资的市场准入规则与政策

作者：David Furaha　译者：蔡瑶

在开始投资项目之前，投资者需要将市场准入这一重要因素纳入考量范围。投资者必须首先预估其商品将会如何进入市场和创造投资回报。一旦投资者在市场准入方面遇到困难，那么这必定将会成为投资的一大阻碍。

投资者在市场准入方面遇到的困难一方面是由一国国内连通产地与市场之间交通基础设施导致的，另一方面也可能与产品从产地到达国际市场的方式相联系。

这篇文章将会分析国内交通连通程度以及跨境贸易交通所带来的影响。

一、国内市场的连通

在一些非洲国家，不同的地区之间由于缺少道路而无法连通、相互分离。由于投资生产的产品无法深入内部市场，这将会对投资带来巨大的挑战，而投资者也可能会遭受重大损失。

因此，对于正在制定投资政策的国家而言，建立一个便利投资者进入市场的政策是十分重要的，这样的政策保证一旦投资项目启动，商品将可以进入市场，并为投资者创造投资回报。

完善的道路和基础设施建设可以多方面促进经济增长并减少贫困。道路的完善将会减少交通运输的成本，从而进一步减少商品服务的生产和消费成本（BIDS 2004）。完善的道路让生产者更易于进入市场和获取技术，增加可能的相关生产要素投入、降低生产成本，促进农业和非农业生产（Binswanger, Khandker 和 Rosenzweig, 1993; BIDS, 2004; Levy, 1996）以及乡镇企业的发展（Lokshin 和 Yemtsov, 2005）。①

① Shahidur R. Khandker et al, The Poverty Impact of Rural Roads: Evidence from Bangladesh, http://web.worldbank.org/archive/website01021/WEB/IMAGES/WPS38750.PDF, Accessed on 06th May 2016.

落后不便的道路交通促使交通运输成本居高不下，同时使得生产者更不易于获取高质量的生产要素投入，生产产品的销售范围也只能限于本地市场，这种道路交通的缺陷也为人们购买日用消费品造成不便，并使得非农就业的机会降低。①

比如，实证研究表明，落后的基础设施特别是落后的道路设施是造成老挝国内贫困的重要原因。过往的一些研究也指出，道路设施的提升会或多或少地帮助减少贫困。例如，van de Walle（2001）阐述了道路设施投资对发展中国家减少贫困的重要作用；Peter Warr（2005）提出，道路系统的提升促进了老挝国内贫困的减少；Tim Purcell（2005）指出了老挝农村地区连通农场和市场的道路的重要性，这些道路促进了农民经济活动的繁荣，使他们能够得到更好的生产要素投入和生产技术，并最终提高了他们的收入，减少了贫困状况。②

老挝政府强调，道路交通业对支持市场体系和国家发展具有关键性作用。自1986年启动“新经济体制”之后，老挝国内建设了许多道路基础设施项目。从表面上看，道路交通的建设能够提高人们在本地市场和邻国的地区市场的参与度，从而带来有利的结果，但是，现在人们普遍认为，仅仅去除其他的阻碍市场运作的障碍，带来的积极作用可能微乎其微，因为落后的交通仍然会使得边远地区的人们无法参与市场活动（Peter Warr, 2005）。在实施了新经济体制后，老挝的贫困率显著下降，从1992—1993年的46%下降到了1997—1997年的39%。最新估计显示，老挝国内（2002—2003年）的贫困率大概是32%。老挝国内的贫困人口主要集中在边远地区，根据估计，1992—1993年，46%的边远地区人口生活在国家贫困线下，1997—1998年为39%，而2002—2003年，这个数据为33%。③

由于道路交通业对支持国家市场体系的作用得到广泛认可，老挝政府一直强调道路基础设施的建设是国家发展中的关键环节。1995年，道路交通业的公共投资占经济部门投资的64%，占总公共投资的47%。2000年，道路交通业的公共投资占经济部门投资的76.4%，占总公共投资的59.1%。④

---

① Institute of Developing Economies, Infrastructure (Rural Road) Development and Poverty Alleviation in Lao PDR http://www.ide.go.jp/English/Publish/Download/Dp/pdf/151.pdf, Accessed on 12th May 2016.

② Institute of Developing Economies, Infrastructure (Rural Road) Development and Poverty Alleviation in Lao PDR http://www.ide.go.jp/English/Publish/Download/Dp/pdf/151.pdf, Accessed on 12th May 2016.

③ Institute of Developing Economies, Infrastructure (Rural Road) Development and Poverty Alleviation in Lao PDR http://www.ide.go.jp/English/Publish/Download/Dp/pdf/151.pdf, Accessed on 12th May 2016.

④ Institute of Developing Economies, Infrastructure (Rural Road) Development and Poverty Alleviation in Lao PDR http://www.ide.go.jp/English/Publish/Download/Dp/pdf/151.pdf, Accessed on 12th May 2016.

与老挝相同，在许多非洲国家，为了便利生产要素投入和连通市场以促进发展，道路网的建设被置于首要地位。但从这一点而言，在过去的几十年间，撒哈拉以南非洲地区的道路发展十分迅速。

在国际层面，比如，东非地区的首要目标就是促进跨国道路网的快速发展。2013 年非洲开发银行（AfDB）的研究表明，东非地区重要的交通走廊总长达约 2900 公里，连接东非共同体五国（坦桑尼亚、肯尼亚、卢旺达、布隆迪和乌干达）。这些交通走廊具有重要的价值，因为它们使得农产品可以在一国国内重要的城市间流动，同时也能实现跨境流动。①

在乌干达国内，道路交通已经成为发展规划的一部分，特别是在过去的几十年中。乌干达国家道路局（UNRA）在 2008 年启动了一个项目，目的是要促进国内道路网的扩张。乌干达在这一项目上的投入占 2013—2014 财政年度国家预算的 15%。乌干达政府同时明确表示，道路交通对其经济十分重要，且重点是发展农业生产地区的道路、连通出口渠道的道路，以及贯穿南部北部走廊连通海洋的道路（UNRA, 2012）。由于边远地区的道路对于该地区居民前往当地市场、学校、医院以及获取其他服务十分重要，因此乌干达政府也同样十分重视边远地区道路的维护工作。②

东非共同体 2020 年基础设施发展规划的首要目标包括修缮主要交通走廊、扩大铁路网和促进港口运营。然而，对这些发展项目的持续跟进与评估也应当得到重视。③

为了展现道路连通对非洲发展的重要性，这些国家设立了不同的机构，以具体解决道路交通问题和道路网发展与维护费用的筹集。出于这种考虑，卢旺达建立了专门负责交通发展的“卢旺达交通发展局”以及专门负责筹集道路维护费的“道路维护基金”。

总的来说，忽视道路连通性而只谈投资发展是不可能的，因为交通运输是投资

① Yuki Tanaka, Road infrastructure and rural development in sub-saharan Africa, http://www3.grips.ac.jp/~esp/en/event/group_a-event/road-infrastructure-and-rural-development-in-sub-saharan-africa/, Accessed on 11th May 2016.

② Yuki Tanaka, Road infrastructure and rural development in sub-saharan Africa, http://www3.grips.ac.jp/~esp/en/event/group_a-event/road-infrastructure-and-rural-development-in-sub-saharan-africa/, Accessed on 11th May 2016.

③ Yuki Tanaka, Road infrastructure and rural development in sub-saharan Africa, http://www3.grips.ac.jp/~esp/en/event/group_a-event/road-infrastructure-and-rural-development-in-sub-saharan-africa/, Accessed on 11th May 2016.

项目获得成功的关键因素。因此，每一个希望吸引外国投资的国家都必须制定相应的政策，便利投资者进入市场。

二、跨境市场准入

自由贸易通过增加消费选择和降低价格，为消费者带来了好处，但是由于全球经济的不稳定性，许多国家的政府都选择征收关税和构筑其他的贸易壁垒来保护本国产业。在追求经济贸易效率与政府保障低失业率之间，存在着微妙的平衡关系。

在对这一点的讨论中，我们将会看到一些关税和非关税措施，以及国家规定的特殊商品的禁运。我们也会分析投资者将其产品投入外国市场过程中可能面临的其他挑战。我们也会讨论其他问题，包括贸易保护主义、进口方面的挑战（如海关、腐败），以及国际交通运输的成本。最后，我们也会分析世界贸易组织对待外国投资者如何进入市场方面的一些措施。

贸易保护主义是指政府采取限制国际贸易的措施或政策，通常为了保护本国产业和就业岗位不受外国竞争者的冲击。典型的贸易保护主义措施包括进口关税、配额、对本国企业的补贴或税收减免，以及直接的政府干预。任何时候一国政府采取了上述的任意措施，该国政府即在实施贸易保护主义。关于贸易保护主义，人们对其优劣产生了较大的争论。批评者认为，从长期看，贸易保护主义通常反倒会伤害其本欲保护的人民，这些批评者也提倡将自由贸易置于较贸易保护主义而言更为优越的地位。①

尽管许多人支持自由贸易和贸易开放度的提高，在现实中贸易保护主义仍然被广泛应用，以下是支持贸易保护主义的观点：

（1）保护朝阳产业

贸易壁垒可以被用于保护朝阳产业，也称新兴产业，比如那些发展高新技术的产业。这种贸易保护主义可以使得新生的企业获得发展空间，成为具有国际竞争力企业。

对国内产业的保护会使得国内产业相对于外国企业获得优势。比如，当国内企业受到保护，免于外国竞争的冲击，其可以扩张并从规模经济中获利。企业在发展过程中，可能会对实物和人力资本进行投资，发展出新的竞争能力和优势。一旦这些能力和优势得到充分发展，国家对贸易保护主义的需求会降低，贸易壁垒最终也

---

① X, Protectionism, http://www.investopedia.com/terms/p/protectionism.asp, accessed on 08th May 2016.

会被消除。①

（2）保护夕阳产业

天平的另一端是夕阳产业，也被称为逐渐没落的产业，这类产业需要一定的支持使其免于逐渐衰落以及逐渐衰落带来的负面影响。在英国，每一代都产生了属于该时期的夕阳产业，比如20世纪50年代的造船业、20世纪70年代的汽车业以及20世纪90年代的钢铁制造业。②

（3）保护战略性产业

为了保护能源、水资源、钢铁、军备、粮食等战略性产业，国家也可能实行贸易壁垒对其进行保护。欧盟共同粮食政策的隐含目标就是构筑粮食安全的防线，以保护欧盟国家的粮食产业。③

（4）保护不可再生能源

包括石油在内的不可再生能源被认为是不适用自由贸易规则的例外。对于希望长期依赖石油出口的国家，如具有丰富石油储量的中东地区国家，可以通过配额制度在短期内限制出口量，以达到保护能源的目的。

（5）防止不公平竞争

贸易壁垒可以用于防止不公平竞争，如用于针对外国企业的倾销行为。

（6）挽救就业岗位

保护产业可能会在短期内挽救国内民众的就业岗位，虽然从长期看不可能永久地保护这些岗位不流失。④

（7）保护环境

一些国家可能通过保护贸易以减少对环境造成的破坏，如减少因为产量和交通运输增长而导致的二氧化碳排放。⑤

① X, Trade Protectionism, http://www.economicsonline.co.uk/Global_economics/Trade_protectionism.html, Accessed on 08th May 2016.

② X, Trade Protectionism, http://www.economicsonline.co.uk/Global_economics/Trade_protectionism.html, Accessed on 08th May 2016.

③ X, Trade Protectionism, http://www.economicsonline.co.uk/Global_economics/Trade_protectionism.html, Accessed on 08th May 2016.

④ X, Trade Protectionism, http://www.economicsonline.co.uk/Global_economics/Trade_protectionism.html, Accessed on 08th May 2016.

⑤ X, Trade Protectionism, http://www.economicsonline.co.uk/Global_economics/Trade_protectionism.html, Accessed on 08th May 2016.

（8）限制过度专业化

许多经济学家指出，过于强调比较优势可能会带来过度专业化的危害。在全球经济下行和过度依赖国际的背景下，保证一定的自给自足被认为是理智的经济战略。

不同国家通过关税、配额、非关税壁垒等形式实施贸易保护主义，这些措施都会对市场准入带来影响，并会直接影响投资。

1. 关税作为贸易保护主义的手段

这是对进口商品征收的关税。通过提高商品价格，关税抑制了消费者对进口商品的需求。关税同时改变了商品的相对价格，可以保护竞争力不强的国内企业和它们定价过高的商品。①

关税通常是为了保护新型产业和发展中经济体，但是也会被发达经济体运用于对发达产业的保护。以下是政府可以采取的集中关税和壁垒：从量税；从价税；许可证；进口配额；自动出口限制；当地成分要求。②

（1）从量税

从量税是按照对每单位进口货物征收的固定费用。这种关税会由于进口货物类型的不同而有所差别。比如，对于每双进口的鞋子，进口国可能会征收每双 15 美元的关税，而对于进口的电脑产品，则是每台征收 300 美元的关税。

（2）从价税

Ad valorem 是一个拉丁短语，意为“按照价值”，这种关税是基于一定比例的商品价值所征收的。例如，日本对美国进口的汽车征收 15% 的关税，这里 15% 的税率是进口汽车完税后增加的价格比例，因此，日本消费者现在需要支付 11500 美元去购买一辆价值一万美元的进口美国汽车。进口汽车价格的上涨，不仅能够保护国内厂商免受冲击，同时也人为地降低了进口汽车对于日本消费者价格上的吸引力。③

总的来说，他国对本国商品征收的关税对一国经济会造成损害。他国征收的关税会提高国内生产者的生产成本，导致他们在外国市场上的销量下降。在软木材争端中，由于美国近期的关税，加拿大软木木材生产商可能会遭受 15 亿加元的损失。

---

① Tejvan Pettinger, Protectionism, https://www.economicshelp.org/blog/6911/alevel/examples-of-protectionism/, Accessed on 08th May 2016.

② Brent Radcliffe, http://www.investopedia.com/articles/economics/08/tariff-trade-barrier-basics.asp, accessed on 10th May 2016.

③ Brent Radcliffe, http://www.investopedia.com/articles/economics/08/tariff-trade-barrier-basics.asp, accessed on 10th May 2016.

由于需求的减少，生产商们降低了产量，导致工作机会流失。这些流失的工作岗位会对其他产业造成冲击，因为就业率降低将会导致对消费品的需求降低。① 这也就是说，关税构成了一种贸易壁垒，并且会对外商投资带来负面的影响。

2. 配额

配额是对进口商品数量的限制。根据各个国家规定的不同，配额可能是对某种特定商品销售量比例的限制，也可能是对商品数量的限制。美国纺织产业的一些领域就受到了配额制度的保护。②

配额经常会被用于保护新型产业和降低国内生产者进入市场的成本。通常在这个产业成熟发展之后，配额制度仍会存在。配额也会被用来保护如军备和农业等战略性产业。在一个进口不断增长的国家，配额制度是比关税更能达到保护国内产业目的的措施。当一个国家实施配额制度，它的贸易伙伴也会照搬实施，并且对其行为进行同样的解释。这种现象最终会减少所有生产者的出口机会，对消费者而言，商品的价格也会提高。对于国家而言，配额制度实施起来也是十分麻烦的。政府需要准备大量的文件，为每个配额实施对象国提供允许进口的商品数量。同样，配额制度对国内产业的保护程度也很难确定。③

配额同样也是自由贸易中的壁垒，阻碍投资的增长，也使得投资无法发挥促进国家发展的作用。

3. 非关税贸易壁垒

非关税措施（NTMs）是政府采取的影响国际贸易的非关税政策和具体措施。非关税措施包括许多不同的具体措施，这些措施与贸易有着直接或间接的关系，由于在后续的 WTO 谈判回合中关税税率降低，这些措施被更多地运用。在许多案子中，非关税措施被界定为阻碍贸易的非关税壁垒（NTBs）。一些非关税措施受到具体 WTO 协议的规范，其中具有代表性的是实施卫生与植物检疫措施的协定、技术性贸易壁垒协定、反倾销协定、补贴与反补贴措施协定以及保障措施协定。WTO 成员不断寻求通过常规的 WTO 工作计划和诸如 2001 年 11 月的多哈部长级会议等谈判方式

① Mike Moffatt, The Economic Effect of Tariffs, http://economics.about.com/cs/taxpolicy/a/tariffs.htm, accessed on 10th May 2016.

② *Monica Sanders*, The Disadvantages of Tarrifs & Quotas, http://smallbusiness.chron.com/disadvantages-tarrifs-quotas-20726.html, aceesed on 10th May 2016.

③ *Monica Sanders*, The Disadvantages of Tarrifs & Quotas, http://smallbusiness.chron.com/disadvantages-tarrifs-quotas-20726.html, aceesed on 10th May 2016.

便利市场准入。

（1）许可证

许可证是政府发放给企业的允许其进口特定类型商品的证明。比如，国家限制奶酪的进口，那么许可证可能会被发放给特定企业，允许其作为进口商进口奶酪。许可证制度限制了市场竞争，同时对于消费者而言，商品的价格也会提高。①

（2）进口配额

进口配额是对特定商品实施的进口数量的限制。这种贸易壁垒通常会与许可证一起实施。比如，一个国家可能设定一个允许一定数量的柑橘进口的配额。②

（3）自动出口限制

这种贸易壁垒被称为“自动”是因为其是由出口国而非进口国设置的。自动出口限制通常会在进口国发出请求的情形下适用，通常进口国也会设置对应的自动出口限制。比如，在加拿大的请求下，巴西可以对其向加拿大出口的白糖进行自动出口限制。加拿大同样地也会在其对巴西出口的煤炭上设置一个相应的自动出口限制。两国的行为会导致煤炭和白糖的价格上升，但也保护了两国相应的国内产业。③

（4）当地成分要求

与其对进口商品数量设置配额，政府可能会规定特定比例的商品在进口国国内生产。这个限制可以是对商品数量的限制，也可以是对商品价值数目的限制。比如，对于进口电脑的限制可能会规定电脑 25% 的零部件应当是在进口国国内生产的，或者也可能会规定该商品 15% 的价值必须是来自进口国生产的零部件。④

4. 行政壁垒

对国际贸易设置的行政壁垒是非关税壁垒中的一种特殊类型，这种壁垒主要表现为限制国际贸易的行政政策和程序。学者列举的行政壁垒包括在征收关税、实施卫生检疫和其他规则过程中的行政措施。然而，更为全面的定义认为这些措施都是

---

① *Monica Sanders*, The Disadvantages of Tarrifs & Quotas, http://smallbusiness.chron.com/disadvantages-tarrifs-quotas-20726.html, aceesed on 10th May 2016.

② *Monica Sanders*, The Disadvantages of Tarrifs & Quotas, http://smallbusiness.chron.com/disadvantages-tarrifs-quotas-20726.html, aceesed on 10th May 2016.

③ *Monica Sanders*, The Disadvantages of Tarrifs & Quotas, http://smallbusiness.chron.com/disadvantages-tarrifs-quotas-20726.html, aceesed on 10th May 2016.

④ Brent Radcliffe, http://www.investopedia.com/articles/economics/08/tariff-trade-barrier-basics.asp, accessed on 10th May 2016.

对国际贸易的阻碍，且它们都产生于国家法律法规与行政程序之间的不同，而这推动国内商品走向外国市场的行政程序则是必要的。①

全球各地的出口商和进口商都会面临许多行政壁垒。他们需要适应各地复杂的政策规定、准备大量的文件，他们的商品也需要经受频繁的检验检疫，而且需要花费大量时间完成清关手续。对于发达国家和发展中国家的政策制定者而言，最大限度地减少这些冗繁的程序，实现“贸易便利化”一直以来都是他们的首要目标。2013 年 12 月，世界贸易组织全体成员达成了巴黎一揽子协定，这是多哈回合谈判达成的第一个全面协定。巴黎一揽子协定的重点在于贸易便利化，它要求世界贸易组织成员采取大量简化通关手续的措施，包括对货物的预裁定、电子文件和电子化支付，以及在最终关税确定前的货物提前放行，这些措施是为了最大程度地降低货物进口、出口、过境手续的复杂性，同时减少货物进口、出口、过境所需要的文件。②

三、自由贸易的好处

自由贸易是指国家能够在没有任何关税和非关税贸易壁垒的情况下进口和出口货物。实质上，自由贸易能够降低商品的价格并增加出口，使得消费者从规模经济和更多的商品选择中获益。更具体而言，自由贸易的好处包括以下几点：

比较优势理论阐述的是各国通过专门生产对其而言成本较低的商品，最终可以使得所有国家都获得更大的经济利益。自由贸易使得国家可以集中生产具有比较优势的商品。

1. 降低关税能够促进贸易创造

当产品从生产成本较高的国家转向成本较低的国家生产时，就产生了贸易创造。

2. 增加出口

在英国具有比较优势的产业中，如同消费者从商品进口中受益一样，出口商同样也能获得更多的经济利益。对英国出口货物征收的较低关税能够增加出口货物的

① Predrag Bjelić, Administrative Trade Barriers And Trade Facilitation, http://www.academia.edu/191614/Administrative_Barriers_and_Trade_Facilitation, accessed on 10th May 2016.

② Cecília Hornok[b], Miklós KorenJournal of International Economics: Administrative barriers to trade, http://www.sciencedirect.com/science/article/pii/S0022199615000033, Accessed on 11th May 2016.

数量，促进英国就业和经济增长。

3. 规模经济

如果一国能够实现专业化生产，其将可以从规模经济和较低的平均成本中获利，这一点在固定成本较高或者需要大量投资的产业中尤其明显。规模经济最终可以为消费者带去更低廉的商品，也可以提高出口商的经济效率。

4. 促进竞争发展

在国际贸易繁荣的情况下，国内企业将会面临更多来自外国企业的竞争，这将会导致它们有更大的动力去降低成本和提高效率。这将会防止在国内的垄断企业肆意大幅度抬高价格。

5. 贸易是经济发展的引擎

自 1945 年以来，世界贸易量平均增长了 7%，这也成为了推动世界经济发展的重要因素之一。

6. 促进过剩原材料的利用

卡塔尔等中东地区国家拥有丰富的石油资源，但如果没有石油贸易，拥有这么大量的石油资源并不会为这些国家带来什么好处。相反，日本是一个资源贫瘠的国家，如果没有国际贸易，这个国家可能会十分落后。

7. 关税可能会导致效率低下

如果一国通过提升关税来保护国内产业，那么其国内产业可能会缺乏降低生产成本的积极性。①

四、世界贸易组织在保障市场准入中的角色

世界贸易组织是唯一一个提供解决国家间贸易问题规则的国际性组织。WTO 协议是世界贸易组织的核心，这些协议都是由世界上大多数贸易国谈判、签署和批准的。世界贸易组织的宗旨是帮助商品和服务的生产者、提供者、出口商和进口商的发展。②

① Tejvan Pettinger, Protectionism, https://www.economicshelp.org/blog/6911/alevel/examples-of-protectionism/, accessed on 08th May 2016.

② WTO, Role of WTO, https://www.wto.org/english/thewto_e/whatis_e/whatis_e.htm, Accessed on 11th May 2016.

除了其他事项，世界贸易组织的工作包括确保国家间的贸易谈判能够进展顺利，并保证国际贸易的规则能够被正确适用和执行。

世界贸易组织协议涵盖了货物、服务和知识产权。这些协议清楚地展示了自由主义的原则，并提供了一些可被允许的例外情形。这些协议的内容包括国家对降低关税、减少其他贸易壁垒、打开服务市场的承诺。这些协议还规定了争端解决的程序。WTO 协议并不是僵化的，而是经历反复的重新谈判，并不断有新的协议被纳入这个框架。WTO 协议要求政府为 WTO 提供其现行有效的法律和措施并制定透明的贸易政策。不同的 WTO 理事会和委员会积极寻求保证这些要求和 WTO 协议能够被遵守和正确执行。所有的 WTO 成员必须经历周期性的审查，这种审查针对的是成员的贸易政策和行为，每次审查都要求相关国家和 WTO 秘书处提供相应报告。①

WTO 协议内包含了针对发展中国家的特殊规定，这些规定包括给予它们更长时间履行协议和承诺、提供增加其贸易机会的措施，以及帮助其提高贸易能力、解决争端和提高技术性标准。WTO 每年针对发展中国家会开展上百次的技术合作项目。同时 WTO 每年在日内瓦也举办针对政府官员的各类培训课程。贸易援助项目的开展是为了帮助发展中国家提高增加贸易必需的技术和基础设施。

WTO 的谈判成果包括关税与贸易总协定、服务贸易总协定和与贸易有关的知识产权协定。

关税与贸易总协定由一系列多边贸易协定组成，其目的是为了在缔约国中消灭配额制度、降低关税。该协定中最重要的原则是非歧视原则，非歧视原则是指各成员国都应当将市场平等地对其他国家开放。这一原则在无条件最惠国待遇条款中得到体现，这一条款是指，当一国与其最大贸易伙伴一旦达成协议降低关税，那么降低后的关税也自动适用于其他 GATT 成员。②GATT 中另外一个重要的原则是国民待遇原则，在这一原则下，成员不能够对进口商品和国内商品进行歧视性的区别对待。③

和关税与贸易总协定为货物贸易提供多边贸易体系一样，服务贸易总协定的制

① WTO, Role of WTO, https://www.wto.org/english/thewto_e/whatis_e/whatis_e.htm, Accessed on 11th May 2016.

② X, General Agreement on Tariffs and Trade (GATT), http://www.britannica.com/topic/General-Agreement-on-Tariffs-and-Trade, Accessed on 12th May 2016.

③ X, National Treatment Clause, http://www.meti.go.jp/english/report/downloadfiles/gCT0213e.pdf, Accessed on 12th May 2016.

订是为了将该多边贸易体系延伸至服务领域。①

与贸易有关的知识产权协定是在 1986 年至 1994 年的乌拉圭回合达成的，该协定首次将知识产权规则带入多边贸易领域。②

通过以上的协定和其他各种不同的协定，WTO 积极寻求建立一个贸易服务自由流动的自由市场，而这也将会对不同成员国的投资带来积极的影响。

五、结语

市场准入是任何一个国家在促进投资时不能忽视的一个重要因素。因此，各国都需要尽快建立一个相关体制，保证交通运输网的建设并便利投资者进入国内和国际市场。

一旦市场准入得到保证，这将会成为增加对该国投资吸引力的重要一步。非洲国家需要在这一点上特别注意，它们中的一些国家缺少健全的国内交通网，而且其产品在进入发达国家市场时受到了阻碍。

---

① X, GATS, https://en.wikipedia.org/wiki/General_Agreement_on_Trade_in_Services, Accessed on 12th May 2016.

② WTO, TRIPS, https://www.wto.org/english/thewto_e/whatis_e/tif_e/agrm7_e.htm, Accessed on 12th May 2016.

Market Access Rules and Policies on Investment in Africa

Author: David Furaha

Market access in an important element to be considered before starting an investment project. The investor must first assess how his products will reach the market and provide the investor with investment returns. Whenever there are challenges in market access certainly they become an impedment to investment.

Challenges in market access may be related to internal connectivity or transport infrastructures from the production site to the market but also relate to how products may leave the country from where they were manufactured and reach the international market.

This paper will analyse impact of internal connectivity on one hand and the access to cross border markets.

Internal Connectivity

In some of African countries, regions are disconnected from others by lack access roads. This cause a great challenge in investment because the products from investment can not read the internal market and the investor is likely to suffer serious losses.

It is therefore important for a country that is developping investment policies to consider putting in place a market access policy as a way of assuring investors that once they start projects there products will be able to get to the market and bring returns to them.

Improved roads and infrastructure can create opportunities for economic growth and poverty reduction through a range of mechanisms. Roads reduce transportation costs and the costs of consumption and production of goods and services (BIDS 2004). With easier access to markets and technology, improved roads expand farm and nonfarm production through increased availability of relevant inputs and lower input costs (Binswanger, Khandker, and Rosenzweig 1993; BIDS 2004; Levy 1996) as well as growth in rural enterprises (Lokshin and Yemtsov 2005)①.

The inadequate roads and poor road access put the high cost of transportation; reduce ability to use access high quality inputs; limit the uses of local markets to the sales of their produces, the purchase of consumer goods and opportunities for off-farm employment②.

For instance, empirical reviews evident that inadequate infrastructure particularly poor and absent of road infrastructure is a significant cause of poverty in Lao PDR. Previous studies have also pointed out that improvement of road infrastructure would more or less help reduce poverty. For example, van de Walle (2001) explained the significant of rural road investment helps reduce poverty in developing countries; Peter Warr (2005) suggested that the improvement of seasonal road access contributes to poverty reduction in Lao DR; Tim Purcell (2005) pictured out the significant of Farm-To-Market road in rural areas of Lao PDR helps improve farmer livelihood activities, access to better inputs and technology, raise income and reduce poverty③.

The government of Lao PDR emphasizes road/transportation sector as the key sector to support market system and development of the country. After launching the New Economic Mechanism (NEM) in 1986, number of road infrastructure projects have been introduced and constructed. This has seemingly contributed to favorable outcomes by permitting greater participation in both local and regional markets in neighboring countries. However, it is recognized that removal of obstacles to the functioning of markets maybe little or no assistance to rural people if very poor roads prevent them from participating in these markets (Peter Warr 2005). As a result of socio-economic performance after implementing NEM, poverty rate in Lao PDR has significantly declined from 46 per cent of total population at a national level in 1992/93 to 39 per cent in 1997/98. The recent estimation of poverty level in Lao PDR (2002/03) is about 32 per cent. Poverty in Lao PDR is concentrated in rural areas as the estimation of rural population with consumption expenditures below national poverty line were 46 per cent in 1992/93; 39 per cent in 1997/98; and 33 per cent in 2002/03④.

Due to recognition of the significant of road/transport sector as an important means to shore up market system of the country, the government of Lao PDR always emphasizes the development of road infrastructure as a key for country development. In 1995, public investment in road/transport

① Shahidur R. Khandker et al, The Poverty Impact of Rural Roads: Evidence from Bangladesh, http://web.worldbank.org/archive/website01021/WEB/IMAGES/WPS38750.PDF, Accessed on 06th May 2016.

② Institute of Developing Economies, Infrastructure (Rural Road) Development and Poverty Alleviation in Lao PDR http://www.ide.go.jp/English/Publish/Download/Dp/pdf/151.pdf, Accessed on 12th May 2016.

③ Institute of Developing Economies, Infrastructure (Rural Road) Development and Poverty Alleviation in Lao PDR http://www.ide.go.jp/English/Publish/Download/Dp/pdf/151.pdf, Accessed on 12th May 2016.

④ Institute of Developing Economies, Infrastructure (Rural Road) Development and Poverty Alleviation in Lao PDR http://www.ide.go.jp/English/Publish/Download/Dp/pdf/151.pdf, Accessed on 12th May 2016.

sector accounted for almost 64 per cent in economic sector and 47 per cent in total public investment. It accounted at 76.4 per cent for total investment in economic sector and 59.1 per cent for total public investment in 2000①.

In the same line as LAO, the development of Road network has been taken to be a priority in order to boost the development through provision of access to input and to the markets in different African countries. In this regard, Development of roads in Sub-Saharan Africa has been significant over the past decade.

On the international level, the East Africa region, for example, the priority is fast developing the trans-national road networks. According to a study carried out by African Development Bank (AfDB) in 2013, the key transportation corridors in the East Africa region totals around 2,900km connecting all five countries in the East African Community (Tanzania, Kenya, Rwanda, Burundi, Uganda). These are valuable corridors that enable agricultural goods to be transported to major cities within a country and across the borders②.

In Uganda, road has been an important part of development effort, especially so in the last few decades. Uganda National Road Agency (UNRA) started operation in 2008 to accelerate the expansion of national road network. It was allocated 15% of the total national budget in FY 2013/14. The Uganda government also clearly states how roads are important for its economy and that priority is given to "roads in agricultural areas, the export routes and the accesses to the sea through the southern and northern corridors" (UNRA, 2012). Furthermore, the maintenance of rural roads by the local governments have also been put in the fore for it is crucial for rural community who mainly foot their ways to local markets and services including schools, health centers and extension services③.

East African Community's priority areas in infrastructural development to year 2020 include rehabilitation of major transportation corridors in addition to expanding rail networks and ports operations. However, continuous efforts should also be given to following-up the assessment of such development efforts④.

---

① Institute of Developing Economies, Infrastructure (Rural Road) Development and Poverty Alleviation in Lao PDR http://www.ide.go.jp/English/Publish/Download/Dp/pdf/151.pdf, Accessed on 12th May 2016.

② Yuki Tanaka, Road infrastructure and rural development in sub-saharan Africa, http://www3.grips.ac.jp/~esp/en/event/group_a-event/road-infrastructure-and-rural-development-in-sub-saharan-africa/, Accessed on 11th May 2016.

③ Yuki Tanaka, Road infrastructure and rural development in sub-saharan Africa, http://www3.grips.ac.jp/~esp/en/event/group_a-event/road-infrastructure-and-rural-development-in-sub-saharan-africa/, Accessed on 11th May 2016.

④ Yuki Tanaka, Road infrastructure and rural development in sub-saharan Africa, http://www3.grips.ac.jp/~esp/en/event/group_a-event/road-infrastructure-and-rural-development-in-sub-saharan-africa/, Accessed on 11th May 2016.

To indicate the priority that road connectivity has in Africa's development, different organs have been put in place to specifically consider the problem of roads and transport as well as putting in place funding mechanisms for all activities related to road network development and maintenance. It is in this regard that Rwanda has put in place the Agency for transport development called "Rwanda Transport Development Agency" and other one to fund the activities regarding road maintenance under the name of "Road Maintenance Fund" .

Briefly, it is impossible to think of investment development and leave behind the issue of road connectivity as transport is a key factor to a successful investment project. Therefore every country that aspires to increase investment activities must put in place policies that aim to ease market access to investors.

Cross Boarder Market Access

Free trade benefits consumers through increased choice and reduced prices, but because the global economy brings with it uncertainty, many governments impose tariffs and other trade barriers to protect industry. There is a delicate balance between the pursuit of efficiencies and the government's need to ensure low unemployment.

Under this point we looked at the conditions, tariff and Non-tariff measures (NTMs), embargoes set by countries for the entry of specific goods into their markets. We also looked at other challenges that investors may face while striving to take their products at cross boarder markets. Among other issues we looked at protectionism, export challenges (customs, corruption), cost of international transport. We finally looked at the measures of World Trade organization to deal with market access issues.

Protectionism refers to government actions and policies that restrict or restrain international trade, often done with the intent of protecting local businesses and jobs from foreign competition. Typical methods of protectionism are import tariffs, quotas, subsidies or tax cuts to local businesses and direct state intervention. Any time a government undertakes any of these actions, they are engaging in protectionism. There is significant debate surrounding the merits of protectionism. Critics argue that, over the long term, protectionism often ends up hurting the people it is intended to protect and often promotes free trade as a superior alternative to protectionism[①].

Despite the arguments in favour of free trade and increasing trade openness, protectionism is still widely practiced and the following are the arguments that are usually made in its favour:

a. Protect sunrise industries

Barriers to trade can be used to protect *sunrise industries*, also known as *infant industries*, such

① X, Protectionism, http://www.investopedia.com/terms/p/protectionism.asp, accessed on 08th May 2016.

as those involving new technologies. This gives new firms the chance to develop, grow, and become globally competitive.

Protection of domestic industries may allow them to develop a comparative advantage. For example, domestic firms may expand when protected from competition and benefit from economies of scale. As firms grow they may invest in real and human capital and develop new capabilities and skills. Once these skills and capabilities are developed there is less need for trade protection, and barriers may be eventually removed①.

b. Protect sunset industries

At the other end of scale are *sunset industries*, also known as *declining industries*, which might need some support to enable them to decline slowly, and avoid some of the negative effects of such decline. For the UK, each generation throws up its own declining industries, such as ship building in the 1950s, car production in the 1970s, and steel production in the 1990s②.

c. Protect strategic industries

Barriers may also be erected to protect *strategic industries*, such as energy, water, steel, armaments, and food. The implicit aim of the EUs Common Agricultural Policy is to create *food security* for Europe by protecting its agricultural sector③.

d. Protect non-renewable resources

Non-renewable resources, including oil, are regarded as a special case where the normal rules of free trade are often abandoned. For countries aiming to rely on oil exports lasting into the long term, such as the oil-rich Middle Eastern economies, limiting output in the short term through production quotas is one method employed to conserve resources.

e. Deter unfair competition

Barriers may be erected to deter *unfair competition*, such as *dumping* by foreign firms at prices below cost.

f. Save jobs

Protecting an industry may, in the short run, protect jobs, though in the long run it is unlikely that jobs can be protected indefinitely④.

g. Help the environment

---

① X, Trade Protectionism, http://www.economicsonline.co.uk/Global_economics/Trade_protectionism.html, Accessed on 08th May 2016.

② X, Trade Protectionism, http://www.economicsonline.co.uk/Global_economics/Trade_protectionism.html, Accessed on 08th May 2016.

③ X, Trade Protectionism, http://www.economicsonline.co.uk/Global_economics/Trade_protectionism.html, Accessed on 08th May 2016.

④ X, Trade Protectionism, http://www.economicsonline.co.uk/Global_economics/Trade_protectionism.html, Accessed on 08th May 2016.

Some countries may protect themselves from trade to help limit damage to their environment, such as that arising from CO_2 emissions caused by increased production and transportation①.

h. Limit over-specialization

Many economists point to the dangers of over-specialization, which might occur as a result of taking the theory of *comparative advantage* to its extreme. Retaining some self-sufficiency is seen as a sensible economic strategy given the risks of global downturns, and an over-reliance on international trade.

Protectionism is practiced by different countries through Tariffs, Quotas and non tarrif barriers and all these have repercussions on market access and indirectly have impact on investment.

1. Tariffs as tool for Protectionism

This is a tax on imports. By making products more expensive to consumers, tariffs hamper demand for imports. They also alter the relative prices of products, and can protect uncompetitive companies and their overpriced products②.

Tariffs are often created to protect infant industries and developing economies, but are also used by more advanced economies with developed industries. There are several types of tariffs and barriers that a government can employ:

- Specific tariffs
- Ad valorem tariffs
- Licenses
- Import quotas
- Voluntary export restraints
- Local content requirements③

a. Specific Tariffs

A fixed fee levied on one unit of an imported good is referred to as a specific tariff. This tariff can vary according to the type of good imported. For example, a country could levy a $15 tariff on each pair of shoes imported, but levy a $300 tariff on each computer imported.

b. Ad Valorem Tariffs

---

① X, Trade Protectionism, http://www.economicsonline.co.uk/Global_economics/Trade_protectionism.html, Accessed on 08th May 2016.

② Tejvan Pettinger, Protectionism, https://www.economicshelp.org/blog/6911/alevel/examples-of-protectionism/, Accessed on 08th May 2016.

③ Brent Radcliffe, http://www.investopedia.com/articles/economics/08/tariff-trade-barrier-basics.asp, accessed on 10th May 2016.

The phrase ad valorem is Latin for "according to value" , and this type of tariff is levied on a good based on a percentage of that good's value. An example of an ad valorem tariff would be a 15% tariff levied by Japan on U.S. automobiles. The 15% is a price increase on the value of the automobile, so a $10,000 vehicle now costs $11,500 to Japanese consumers. This price increase protects domestic producers from being undercut, but also keeps prices artificially high for Japanese car shoppers.①

In Brief, a foreign tariff hurts the economy of a country. A foreign tariff raises the costs of domestic producers which causes them to sell less in those foreign markets. In the case of the softwood lumber dispute, it is estimated that recent American tariffs have cost Canadian lumber producers 1.5 billion Canadian dollars. Producers cut production due to this reduction in demand which causes jobs to be lost. These job losses impact other industries as the demand for consumer products decreases because of the reduced employment level②. In other words, Tariffs constitute trade barriers and have a negative impact on investment.

2. Quotas

A quota is a limit on volume of imported products. Depending on the country, this limit may be expressed as a percentage of sales of certain products or a limit on the number of units sold. Some parts of the textile sector are protected by quotas in the United States③.

Quotas are usually employed to protect infant industries and keep market entry costs low for domestic producers. Often the quotas last long after the industry has matured. Other uses for quotas are to protect strategic industries such as defense and agriculture. In market environments where imports are on the rise, quotas are more protective than tariffs. When one country uses quotas, its trading partners do the same and cite the same reasons. The end result is less exporting opportunity for all producers and higher prices for all consumers. Quotas are also cumbersome for the country using them. They require a lot of paperwork indicating exact amounts of products for each country facing a quota. It is also difficult to measure the precise degree of protection quotas offer④.

Quotas are also a barrier to free trade and hence hinder investment from growing and contribute

---

① Brent Radcliffe, http://www.investopedia.com/articles/economics/08/tariff-trade-barrier-basics.asp, accessed on 10th May 2016.

② Mike Moffatt, The Economic Effect of Tariffs, http://economics.about.com/cs/taxpolicy/a/tariffs.htm, accessed on 10th May 2016.

③ *Monica Sanders*, The Disadvantages of Tarrifs & Quotas http://smallbusiness.chron.com/disadvantages-tarrifs-quotas-20726.html, aceesed on 10th May 2016.

④ *Monica Sanders*, The Disadvantages of Tarrifs & Quotas http://smallbusiness.chron.com/disadvantages-tarrifs-quotas-20726.html, aceesed on 10th May 2016.

to the growth of the nation.

3. *None Tariff Barriers*

Non-tariff measures (NTMs) are non-tariff policy measures that affect international trade. NTMs cover a broad range of measures both directly and indirectly related to trade, and their use has risen as tariff rates have fallen under subsequent WTO negotiation rounds. In many cases, NTMs can be classified as non-tariff barriers to trade (NTBs). Some areas of NTMs are dealt with under specific WTO agreements, notably the Agreement on the Application of Sanitary and Phytosanitary Measures, the Agreement on Technical Barriers to Trade, the Anti-dumping agreement, the Agreement on Subsidies and Countervailing Measures and the Agreement on Safeguards. WTO Members seek to continually improve market access through the regular WTO work programme and through negotiations such as those launched at the Doha Ministerial Conference in November 2001.

a. Licenses

A license is granted to a business by the government, and allows the business to import a certain type of good into the country. For example, there could be a restriction on imported cheese, and licenses would be granted to certain companies allowing them to act as importers. This creates a restriction on competition, and increases prices faced by consumers[①].

b. Import Quotas

An import quota is a restriction placed on the amount of a particular good that can be imported. This sort of barrier is often associated with the issuance of licenses. For example, a country may place a quota on the volume of imported citrus fruit that is allowed[②].

c. Voluntary Export Restraints (VER)

This type of trade barrier is "voluntary" in that it is created by the exporting country rather than the importing one. A voluntary export restraint is usually levied at the behest of the importing country, and could be accompanied by a reciprocal VER. For example, Brazil could place a VER on the exportation of sugar to Canada, based on a request by Canada. Canada could then place a VER on the exportation of coal to Brazil. This increases the price of both coal and sugar, but protects the domestic industries[③].

---

① *Monica Sanders*, The Disadvantages of Tarrifs & Quotas http://smallbusiness.chron.com/disadvantages-tarrifs-quotas-20726.html, aceesed on 10th May 2016.

② *Monica Sanders*, The Disadvantages of Tarrifs & Quotas http://smallbusiness.chron.com/disadvantages-tarrifs-quotas-20726.html, aceesed on 10th May 2016.

③ *Monica Sanders*, The Disadvantages of Tarrifs & Quotas http://smallbusiness.chron.com/disadvantages-tarrifs-quotas-20726.html, aceesed on 10th May 2016.

d. Local Content Requirement

Instead of placing a quota on the number of goods that can be imported, the government can require that a certain percentage of a good be made domestically. The restriction can be a percentage of the good itself, or a percentage of the value of the good. For example, a restriction on the import of computers might say that 25% of the pieces used to make the computer are made domestically, or can say that 15% of the value of the good must come from domestically produced components.①

4. Administrative Barriers

Administrative barriers to trade are a special category of non-tariff barriers and their main source are administrative regulations and procedures that have a restrictive effect on international trade. Some authors specify that administrative barriers are administrative measures in the process of levying customs, applying health regulations and other regulations. But the most comprehensive definition of administrative barriers to trade defines these measures as obstacles to international trade derived from differences in national legal and administrative regulations and administrative procedures that exporter had to carry out in order to put its product on a foreign market②.

Exporters and importers around the globe face many administrative barriers. They have to comply with complex regulations, deal with a large amount of paperwork, subject their cargo to frequent inspections, and wait for lengthy customs clearance. Minimizing the burden of these procedures, "trade facilitation" has been a priority for policymakers from developed and developing countries alike. In December of 2013, all members of the World Trade Organization (WTO) have agreed to the Bali Package, the first comprehensive agreement of the Doha round of negotiations. The main component of the Bali Package is an agreement on trade facilitation, requiring WTO members to adopt a host of measures streamlining the customs process, such as pre-arrival processing of shipments, electronic documentation and payment, and the release of goods prior to the final determination of customs duties, with a view to minimizing the incidence and complexity of import, export, and transit formalities and to decreasing and simplifying import, export, and transit documentation requirements③

---

① Brent Radcliffe, http://www.investopedia.com/articles/economics/08/tariff-trade-barrier-basics.asp, accessed on 10th May 2016.

② Predrag Bjelić, Administrative Trade Barriers And Trade Facilitation, http://www.academia.edu/191614/Administrative_Barriers_and_Trade_Facilitation, accessed on 10th May 2016.

③ Cecília Hornok[b], Miklós KorenJournal of International Economics: Administrative barriers to trade, http://www.sciencedirect.com/science/article/pii/S0022199615000033, Accessed on 11th May 2016.

Benefits of Free Trade

Free trade means that countries can import and export goods without any tariff barriers or other non-tariff barriers to trade. Essentially, free trade enables lower prices for consumers, increased exports, benefits from economies of scale and a greater choice of goods. In more details, the benefits of free trade include:

a. The theory of comparative advantage

This explains that by specialising in goods where countries have a lower opportunity cost, there can be an increase in economic welfare for all countries. Free trade enables countries to specialise in those goods where they have a comparative advantage.

b. Reducing tariff barriers leads to trade creation

Trade creation occurs when consumption switches from high cost producers to low cost producers.

c. Increased exports

As well as benefits for consumers importing goods, firms exporting goods where the UK has a comparative advantage will also see a big improvement in economic welfare. Lower tariffs on UK exports will enable a higher quantity of exports boosting UK jobs and economic growth.

d. Economies of scale

If countries can specialise in certain goods they can benefit from economies of scale and lower average costs, this is especially true in industries with high fixed costs or that require high levels of investment. The benefits of economies of scale will ultimately lead to lower prices for consumers and greater efficiency for exporting firms.

e. Increased competition

With more trade, domestic firms will face more competition from abroad therefore there will be more incentives to cut costs and increase efficiency. It may prevent domestic monopolies from charging too high prices.

f. Trade is an engine of growth.

World trade has increased by an average of 7% since the 1945, causing this to be one of the big contributors to economic growth.

g. Make use of surplus raw materials

Middle Eastern counties such as Qatar are very rich in reserves of oil but without trade there would be not much benefit in having so much oil.

Japan on the other hand has very few raw material without trade it would be very poor.

h. Tariffs may encourage inefficiency

If an economy protects its domestic industry by increasing tariffs industries may not have any incentives to cut costs①.

The Role of World Trade Organization in ensuring Market Access

The World Trade Organization (WTO) is the only global international organization dealing with the rules of trade between nations. At its heart are the WTO agreements, negotiated and signed by the bulk of the world's trading nations and ratified in their parliaments. The goal is to help producers of goods and services, exporters, and importers conduct their business②.

WTO ensures, among other things, that trade negotiations among States progress smoothly and that the rules of international trade are correctly applied and enforced.

The WTO agreements cover goods, services and intellectual property. They spell out the principles of liberalization, and the permitted exceptions. They include individual countries' commitments to lower customs tariffs and other trade barriers, and to open and keep open services markets. They set procedures for settling disputes. These agreements are not static; they are renegotiated from time to time and new agreements can be added to the package. WTO agreements require governments to make their trade policies transparent by notifying the WTO about laws in force and measures adopted. Various WTO councils and committees seek to ensure that these requirements are being followed and that WTO agreements are being properly implemented. All WTO members must undergo periodic scrutiny of their trade policies and practices, each review containing reports by the country concerned and the WTO Secretariat③.

WTO agreements contain special provision for developing countries, including longer time periods to implement agreements and commitments, measures to increase their trading opportunities, and support to help them build their trade capacity, to handle disputes and to implement technical standards. The WTO organizes hundreds of technical cooperation missions to developing countries annually. It also holds numerous courses each year in Geneva for government officials. Aid for Trade aims to help developing countries develop the skills and infrastructure needed to expand their trade.

Among the negotiated agreement, include the General Agreement on Tariffs and Trade (GATT) and the General Agreement on Trade in Services (GATS) as well as Trade-Related Aspects of Intellectual Property Rights (TRIPS).

---

① Tejvan Pettinger, Protectionism, https://www.economicshelp.org/blog/6911/alevel/examples-of-protectionism/, accessed on 08th May 2016.

② WTO, Role of WTO, https://www.wto.org/english/thewto_e/whatis_e/whatis_e.htm, Accessed on 11th May 2016.

③ WTO, Role of WTO, https://www.wto.org/english/thewto_e/whatis_e/whatis_e.htm, Accessed on 11th May 2016.

The General Agreement on Tariffs and Trade is a set of multilateral trade agreements aimed at the abolition of quotas and the reduction of tariff duties among the contracting nations. Its most important principle was that of trade without discrimination, in which each member nation opened its markets equally to every other. As embodied in unconditional most-favoured nation clauses (MFN), this meant that once a country and its largest trading partners had agreed to reduce a tariff, that tariff cut was automatically extended to every other GATT member①. Another important Principle provided for in GATT is the National Treatment Clause by which members must not accord discriminatory treatment between imports and "like" domestic products②.

In the same way as GATT, GATS was created to extend the multilateral trading system to service sector, in the same way the General Agreement on Tariffs and Trade (GATT) provides such a system for merchandise trade③.

Agreement on Trade-Related Aspects of Intellectual Property Rights (TRIPS), negotiated in the 1986-94 Uruguay Round, introduced intellectual property rules into the multilateral trading system for the first time④.

By the above agreements and different others, the WTO seeks to ensure that they is free movement of goods and services through a liberalized market which in return positively impacts on investment in different member states.

Conclusion

Market Access is an important factor in the promotion of investment in any country. It is therefore imperative for every country to put in place mechanisms that with ensure that there is sufficient transportation network to facilitate investors to access the markets at domestic and international level.

When market access is guaranteed, it is an important step that is made which may encourage investment initiative in the country. A special attention should be paid by African countries some of which do not have sufficient internal connectivity networks but whose products are tended to be discouraged from entering the market of developed countries.

① X, General Agreement on Tariffs and Trade (GATT) http://www.britannica.com/topic/General-Agreement-on-Tariffs-and-Trade, Accessed on 12th May 2016.

② X, National Treatment Clause, http://www.meti.go.jp/english/report/downloadfiles/gCT0213e.pdf, Accessed on 12th May 2016.

③ X, GATS, https://en.wikipedia.org/wiki/General_Agreement_on_Trade_in_Services, Accessed on 12th May 2016.

④ WTO, TRIPS, https://www.wto.org/english/thewto_e/whatis_e/tif_e/agrm7_e.htm, Accessed on 12th May 2016.

埃及税收政策对外国直接投资的影响

作者：Ahmed Hamouda　译者：陈晨

概　述

包括埃及在内的大多数发展中国家都面临着经济发展水平偏低的问题，这是因为埃及的收入水平较低，这种偏低的经济发展水平又反过来使居民的收入和积蓄难以增长，同时难以吸引外来投资。

由于国家未能提供发展所需的资金来源，这些经济问题变得更加严重；因此，发展中国家不得不转而从国外寻找资金来源，包括从外部借款、接受国际援助和外国直接和间接投资等方式。

许多国际经济学家和组织认为，外国投资尤其是直接投资是解决目前发展中国家面临所这些问题的最合适的方法。因此，国家需要做的是提供稳定、高效和服务导向环境，以吸引投资者进行投资。

一些人可能会认为，外国投资问题仍是当前最值得讨论的话题，实际上在埃及经济领域已经出现了一些致力于打造本国良好投资环境的新思路（本文将会提及这些新的建设思路）。因此，本文将对这些新的建设思路进行讨论，以评定这种新环境能否吸引到新的投资。此外，如何利用新环境也是本文将要讨论的问题。

一、外国直接投资（FDI）是外国资金的主要来源之一①

当今世界，很多国家为了推动改革和经济的发展，正在向自由市场经济转变，这使得现在大多数发达国家和发展中国家在吸引外国直接投资方面展开竞争。外国直接投资在促进世界各国一体化方面发挥着关键作用，在全球化发展的今天，这样的投资显得尤为重要。

外国直接投资有以下几种定义：

（1）外国资本可以以现金或实物的形式进行转移，其目的是从事商业活动并赚取盈利。投资国通常会转移在被投资国获取的利益，并通过为被投资国提供资源、技术和人才来获得更多经济收益。

（2）外国投资者在购买被投资国公司后，可以对该公司从事的商业活动进行管理；外国投资者可以是个人、组织或公司分支（此分支不得属于被投资国的公司）。

（3）外国资本被应用于进行特定商业行为，投资者能够拥有全部投资或者投资的一部分，并与当地投资者共同管理这些投资。投资者可以对被投资国包括资金、技术、管理经验、市场营销和财务技能在内的所有领域进行投资（通常包括参与管理、合资经营、引进先进技术和经验）。

（4）在其他经济领域内成立的企业，当地投资者应享有固定的份额。

二、外国直接投资的形式

以下是外国直接投资的三种主要形式：

---

① (1) National Bank of Egypt, “An Analysis on the trends of the Foreign Direct Investment during the period from 2003 till 2004”, NBE Economic Bulletin, vol. 57 No.4, Cairo, p.84.

(2) Basiouny, Mohamed, (1986). The role of the Economic Policy on the Foreign Direct Investment. Thesis (PhD). Faculty of Commerce, Ain Shams University (The economic advantages of foreign investments, Arab Institute for researches and Studies, Studies on guarantees of investments under the legislation of the Arab Countries, Cairo, 1978).

(3) Al Athiem, Ahmed, 2005. Foreign Direct Investment in the Arab Region.

(4) Shakyier, Farouk, 1999. The global Trade System and effects on the foreign trade to the Islamic States, initial conclusions, The Conference of the Islamic States under globalization, Saleh Kamel Center for Islamic Economy, Al Azhar University, 1999 .

（1）私人投资

私人外国直接投资通常发生在第一产业，特别是石油部门，外国投资者通过这些产业能够获得巨额利润，但这也导致发展中国家的自然资源以很低的价格被消费掉。

（2）双边投资

民族主义和独立运动的兴起，萌生了双边投资，这种形式主要表现为本地和外国投资者共同出资成立公司，双方建立合作伙伴关系。在这种形式投资中，外国投资者能够获得更多的保护。

（3）跨国公司

这种类型的投资控制着全世界近80%的外国直接投资；它完全控制着一些高科技产业，如电子工业和一些机械工业。同时，跨国公司也出现在发展中国家的基础产业当中，如银行、保险、旅游、快餐、软饮料产业等。

三、埃及的外国直接投资

这一部分将主要讨论埃及外国直接投资的问题，将探讨埃及所处的新经济环境的特点以及外国直接投资对埃及经济的重要性。这里将会提出以下三个问题：

问题一：外国直接投资对埃及经济具有怎样的重要性？此处，外国直接投资将被视为筹集所需投资的主要方法之一。

问题二：埃及新经济环境中有利于吸引外国直接投资的要素有哪些？

问题三：考察1980年至2005年期间埃及的外国投资数额，选取这个特别的时期是为了比较在新经济环境前后埃及国内的情况，以检验这些新因素是否有助于外国投资的流动？

（一）外国直接投资为什么对埃及这么重要？

外国直接投资对埃及经济至关重要的原因有很多，其中包括这几项：国内储蓄无法满足当时的投资需求，而就像上文中提到的，外国直接投资能够发挥贷款、财政拨款和外国援助的作用。外国直接投资还可以提高埃及产品在国内外的竞争力，成为出口的关键推动力。

本文将从以下两个方面分析外国直接投资在埃及很重要的原因：

（1）国内储蓄与国内投资的资金需求[①]

虽然有政府和企业储蓄支持，但由于居民收入水平过低，包括埃及在内的大多数发展中国家仍面临着国内储蓄水平较低的问题。

人均收入还不是储蓄下降的唯一原因，财产和实际利率也对国内储蓄有所影响。

虽然说内部因素尤其是人均收入是影响国内储蓄的最重要的因素，但一些外部因素也会导致国内储蓄减少，这些外部因素包括通货膨胀、税收和出口、外国资金、人口特点及社会政治等。

（2）埃及的出口[②]

外国直接投资的倡导者认为这种投资能够推动出口，提升竞争力。这也就是为什么外国直接投资对发展中国家尤其是埃及的市场如此重要的主要原因之一。

国内储蓄主要来源的两种类型：

① 主要来源：家庭存款，企业存款，政府存款；

② 次要来源：银行，证券交易市场，贷款，外部投资，保险行业，税收，投资信托。

（二）有利于埃及经济的新环境对外国直接投资流入的影响

鉴于外国直接投资对推动发展的作用日益重要，埃及政府正在努力通过制定和修改若干法律来创造一个有利于促进投资的环境，以便为投资者铺平道路。埃及已经完成了对《投资法》的修订，为鼓励投资者进行投资，在新修改的《投资法》中规定了一些新的激励措施，这项法律的修订为吸引外国直接投资创造了有利的环境。

为了创造有利投资的环境，埃及政府在政府经济改革方案中推行私有化方案，鼓励当地和外国私营企业在埃及投资。

1974 年，埃及着眼于制定一项投资法，同年埃及开始推行经济开放政策，并通过了关于阿拉伯和外国基金以及自由区第 43 号法令，经过 1977 年第 32 号法令修正，埃及开始为当地投资者提供与阿拉伯和外国投资者同样的待遇。

投资环境中同时存在着经济和非经济因素；其中既有积极的经济因素，也有消

---

① (1) Nagaa, Abdel Wahab Ibrahim, (1995). The Foreign Direct Investments and its impacts on the Economic Development in Egypt (Master Degree) Faculty of Alexandria;

(2) Abdel Ghafar, Mohamed, 1997. The Savings problem in Egypt: Causes and solutions.

② Eissawy, Ibrahim, (1998). Determinants of the saving policy in Egypt,

极的经济因素，积极的经济因素包括国内生产总值发展水平高，总预算中工资比例低，能够利用高素质劳动力。消极的经济因素包括国际收支赤字较高，通货膨胀率较高。

这种投资环境能够吸引外国直接投资也离不开非经济因素，这些非经济因素包括国内政治格局稳定，建立了能够有效保护投资者的法律体系。在此情形下，埃及于 1971 年颁布了第 65 号法案。

有利于投资的环境意味着国内的社会状况、政策和经济制度能够吸引并确保外国投资者将其资金投入本国。立法框架是创造有利于外国直接投资环境的主要影响因素之一，因此，埃及对新《投资法》进行了更新修正。以下是对这个问题的探讨：

1974 年第 43 号法令仅吸引了不超过总投资 32% 的外国投资，由于这项法令并未达到预期目标，埃及政府于 1989 年颁布了新法令，即第 203 号法令，其中规定了几项鼓励外国投资者进行投资的新措施，随后这项法律又被新颁布的《投资保障与鼓励法》)（1997 年第 8 号）所替代。新法旨在促进生产和国内外投资，并为投资者提供了以下几种潜在的激励措施：

1. 制造业可以免受价格控制或利润限制。

2. 对根据《投资法》和由其他私营部门设立的企业实行平等的财政对待。

3. 根据本法建设的住房建筑物可以免受由其他租赁法律规定的统一租赁费率。

4. 可以不受第 97/1976 号（原文为 97/19976 号，译者校对为 97/1976 号）关于规范外汇业务法律的制约。

5. 可以不受第 159/1981 号法律若干规定的制约，投资者投资可以享受以下特权。

（1）公司成立规则的例外；

（2）董事会数量的例外；

（3）工人参与管理制度的例外；

（4）董事会中大多数成员必须为埃及公民的例外；

（5）禁止董事会成员担任多家股份公司总经理的规定的例外；

（6）除非经政府的同意，否则不得主张任何投资公司违反海关法、外汇和消费税；

（7）为投资行为设定专门的进出口制度。

保证[①]：

投资法还为投资者提供了如下几个保证：（1）以任何合法形式成立的投资项目都应该被视为私人投资项目，而不论其中来自埃及的资金的法律性质；（2）禁止国有化、没收和冻结投资财产；（3）在执行投资法规定时发生的任何争议，都应与投资方协商解决；（4）投资方享有收回其资本及其利润的权利。

免税：

以下是埃及投资法中几种对投资者的免税规定：（1）项目利润和股息免征所得税；（2）在新工业区、新城市社区和偏远地区建设的项目，10 年之内免征所得税；（3）住房项目 15 年之内免税；（4）免除不动产和遗产税；（5）免除财政印花及认证费用；（6）免税期结束之后无需缴纳一般性所得税。

为了吸引更多的外国投资，埃及立法者颁布了 2004 年第 13 号法令，随后又对其进行了许多修正，以扫除投资过程中的障碍。特别是在看到外国投资价值从 1997—1998 年的 11 亿美元下降至 2002—2003 年的 7000 万美元时之后，埃及立法者又进行了修法。

新修订的《投资法》提出了以下措施：（1）简化投资者的投资程序；（2）鼓励投资并扫除投资障碍；（3）提供一系列的激励和保证措施，以创造更有利于吸引更多投资的环境；（4）为投资者提供窗口服务，简化投资程序。

至于对法律的修订，内容如下：[②]

1. 受本法管辖的公司，其资本可以是任何可自由兑换的货币，其财务报表应以和资本相同的货币为单位编制出版，对其资本的认购也必须是此种货币，公司应当在缴足其发行资本后将其存入指定银行的外币账户中。这是为了增加埃及市场中的外汇，同时避免由于埃及镑的贬值导致的外国投资者流失的不利后果。

2. 投资和自由贸易区的管理总局，应无例外地适用本法的规定，管理局的董事会应发布与其财务、行政和技术事项有关的内部条例和执行决议，应建立其组织结构，并应采取一切必要程序来管理和组织管理局的工作。管理局的董事会可在国内或国外设立管理局的办事处。

---

① (1) The annual report of the General Authority for Investment.

(2) Hassb Allah M., Amira. 2005. The determinants of the foreign direct and indirect investment in the Arab economic environment, Ain Shams.

② The Economic bulletins of The Ministry of Foreign Trade, several series.

3. 根据本法，管理局被授予较为广泛的权利，政府应向管理局董事会提交与投资问题有关的法律、条例、决定的草案，供其审议。

4. 所有与投资者打交道的政府机构、经济和服务机构都应当在管理局及其每一个分支机构设立办事处，只有这个办事处有权接受申请、完成交易、起草合同并授予必要的许可证以建立投资项目并开展活动。

5. 管理局主席或其代表有权向享有税务和关税以及其他事项豁免的公司和机构颁发必要证书，这一证书具有终局性，且无须经其他机构批准即可生效，所有机构应当按照所述证书行事，并应与其中的数据保持一致。

6. 根据法律，本管理局将收集与投资有关的数据信息，公布并随时更新信息，并通过其当地分支机构、互联网网站和国外办事处进行定期传播。

7. 法律允许投资者通过管理局的办公室及其分支，签订实施投资项目所需的必要公共设施，并由主管机构授权实施；管理局应当建立一个数据库，其中应包含与投资项目所需的公共事业和服务有关的信息，并将其提供给投资者。

8. 本法规定，管理局有权通过其分支机构设立的办事处，根据行政法律，将国家拥有的土地承包给投资者；同时，办事处应当建立一个关于可用于承包的土地数据库，其中应包含土地面积、地理位置、价格和处置条件。

9. 根据本法，管理局有义务根据每项活动的性质为投资申请准备标准表格；应包括活动所需的所有数据和文件，特别是记录活动类型的清单、项目投资成本及关于其服务、能源来源的要求，以及各机构要求的有关成立投资项目、开展经营活动和清算的许可证。

10. 一家以综合发展为目而成立的公司，在其创建并运营所有业务的申请得到批准后，此公司的每项业务均可以享有从活动开始之日起设立投资担保和优惠政策。

11. 管理局根据其董事会制定的规则，可以向外国公司发放在自由区设立代表处和分支机构的许可证。这些办事处和分支机构享有与管理局在这些区域设立许可的项目相同的地位。

12. 根据本法规定，授予成立项目、开展经营活动许可证的机构有权按照其规定检查被许可项目，以确保这些项目和经营活动与许可条件相符；授予许可证的机构应以合理适当的方式进行检查，检查不应影响经营项目的顺利运行。

13. 如果某一经营项目违反法律、条例和法令的任何规定，行政机构应通知投资者，并连同该通知的副本一并呈递至管理局。根据违约的程度和性质，投资者应在通知中规定的时间内矫正该经营项目。如果在规定的期限内违法行为未得到矫正，管理局应发出终止经营项目的活动的决定。投资者可以在管理局及其分支机构成立委员会或部长级委员会以解决其与行政机构的纠纷之前进行投诉。

14. 免税区出口或为进行其活动而进口的货物不应被缴纳海关税、一般销售税和其他税款及关税，这包括各种工具、必需品、机械设备以及各种运输工具等为使免税区经营活动正常进行的货物，但不包括过路的汽车。

在实施《投资保障与鼓励法》修正案时，政府通过了若干法令，包括：

（1）投资总管理局应发布统一表格，其内容包括在商业登记处注册时所需的所有信息、文件和所享受的免税措施。这有利于简化与缺乏经验的外国投资者进行交易时的程序，并将官僚主义的阻碍最小化；

（2）发布公告，展示企业颁发许可证所需的所有程序，包括所需的文件、应缴费用以及发放许可证所需的时间；

（3）绘制地图，展示用以投资的土地，并附上每块土地的价格、划拨土地所需的条件以及合同的格式，为土地的挑选提供便利；

（4）为投资者安排合适的地区，以便他们能够获得所需要的服务。

为创造一个更有利于投资的环境，埃及政府制定了以下鼓励措施：

（1）建立一个新的投资部门，旨在改善投资环境并消除一切投资障碍；

（2）降低关税并取消进口限制；

（3）埃及镑实行浮动汇率制；

（4）达成更多的经济协定；

（5）发展大型基础设施项目。

《投资法》的修正案和政府施行这些修正案的决定旨在简化投资流程，消除投资障碍，同时为投资者提供更有利的投资环境以吸引更多的外国直接投资。

The Impact of Taxation Policies in Egypt on Foreign Direct Investment

Author: Ahmed Hamouda

Introduction

Most of developing states, including Egypt, are suffering from several economic challenges to include low development index which is as a result of the low income; that results in low savings and poor investments opportunities.

Failure of state(s) to provide needed funding sources increases the severity of the problem; as a result, developing states are forced to look for alternative foreign funding sources to include the external borrowing, international aid and foreign direct and indirect investment;

Many international economists and organizations see that the foreign investment especially the direct investment is the most proper to the circumstances under which the developing states are living if only states provide stable, efficient, and service-oriented environment that welcomes investors

Some may believe that the issue of foreign investment is a very much-discussed topic though there are new updates have been introduced to the Egyptian economic that made Egypt an appropriate environment for investment; that what will be addressed herein. That is why this paper will go through such new updates to assess if such new environment has attracted new investments or not; and to identify the best ways to utilize the new environment.

Section I: Foreign Direct Investment (FDI) is as one of the main foreign funding resources①

Attracting foreign direct investment constitutes now an area of competition among most of the developed and developing states alike since many states are turning into free- market economy to attain reform and economic growth. Foreign direct investment plays an crucial role in promoting the integration among the world states in a way that gives that kind of investment a particular importance especially in the age of globalization;

There are several definitions to the foreign direct investment including:

(1) The foreign capital transfers, which may be either in cash or in kind, with a purpose to do businesses and generate profits. Investor States usually ensure the transfer of the profits gained at the host countries abroad and achieve further economic gains that is in return of the contributions paid at the host countries of sources, technology and expertise;

(2) The business owned and managed by investor from another country for which the foreign investor has control over the company purchased; foreign investor might be an individual, association or a branch of multi-branch company; (in an enterprise operating in an economy other than that of the investor)

(3) The capital transferred from another state used for certain purpose(s) under which investor owns the whole or part of the investment and shares the management thereof with the local investor in that investor transfers money, technology, expertise, and managerial, marketing and financial skills in all areas to the host state; (usually involves participation in management, joint-venture, transfer of technology and expertise)

(4) The fixed share to the resident investor in an enterprise set up in another economy.

① (1) National Bank of Egypt, "An Analysis on the trends of the Foreign Direct Investment during the period from 2003 till 2004", NBE Economic Bulletin, vol. 57 No.4) Cairo, p.84.

(2) Basiouny, Mohamed, (1986). The role of the Economic Policy on the Foreign Direct Investment. Thesis (PhD). Faculty of Commerce, Ain Shams University [The economic advantages of foreign investments, Arab Institute for researches and Studies, Studies on guarantees of investments under the legislation of the Arab Countries, Cairo, 1978].

(3) Al Athiem, Ahmed, 2005. Foreign Direct Investment in the Arab Region.

(4) Shakyier, Farouk, 1999. The global Trade System and effects on the foreign trade to the Islamic States, initial conclusions, The Conference of the Islamic States under globalization, Saleh Kamel Center for Islamic Economy, Al Azhar University, 1999.

Section II: Forms of Direct Foreign Investment

There are three main forms of the Foreign Direct Investment that are as follow:

(1) Private Investment

Private Direct Foreign Investment usually goes for the primary industry especially the oil sector through which foreign investor(s) makes huge profits though resulted in the depletion of the natural resources of the developing states at lowest prices;

(2) Bilateral investment

As a result of the movements of nationalism and independence this type of direct foreign investment emerged; it means that both local and foreign investors are partners in the enterprises that set up with joint capital; this form is mostly designed to protect the foreign investors;

(3) Multinational corporations

This type of investment controls almost 80% of the foreign direct investment in the whole world; it has complete control over some high-technology industries such as the industry of electronics, and some machinery. It also goes for the investments in primary industries in the developing countries, as well as the banking, insurance, tourism, fast food, soft drinks industries… Etc.

Section III – Foreign Direct Investment in Egypt

This section deals with the main issue of the research which is the direct investment in Egypt; it will identify the features of the new economic environment under which Egypt lives and the importance of the direct foreign investment to the Egyptian economy. Three questions will be raised herein.

- Question I: what is the importance of the direct foreign investment to the Egyptian economy? Herein the importance of the foreign direct investment will be addressed as one of the main methods for financing needed investments;
- Question II: the elements of the new economic environment in Egypt that are favorably attract direct foreign investment;
- Question III: The volume of the foreign investment in Egypt between 1980 to 2005; that special period is chosen to identify the status in Egypt post and prior to the new economic environment created and if such new introduced factors assisted in increasing the flow of the foreign investment or not?

Question I: Why does foreign direct investment matter for Egypt?

There are many reasons why foreign direct investment is important for the Egyptian economy including the low domestic savings compared to the volume of the investment required from here the importance of foreign direct investment appears as an alternative to loans, grants and foreign aid, as showed above. It also constitutes a key driver for the success of the exports through increasing the competitive ability of Egyptian products internally and externally;

Herein two main reasons why foreign direct investment matters for the Egyptian economy will be addressed as follow:

(1) Drop in the domestic savings in relative to the volume of investments that needed fund①

Most of developing states, including Egypt, suffer from low domestic savings which is the result of low incomes though it is not the sole determinant since there are the Government saving and Business Sector Savings;

Though per capita income is not the sole cause for the drop in the savings, other determinants assisted in such drop, since wealth and the real interest rate are found to have influence over domestic savings;

External determinants represent the inflation; tax and exports revenue; foreign funds and population characteristics as well as social and political elements also cause a decline in domestic savings. Though it could be argued that the internal determinants are the most important especially the per capita income.

(2) Drop in the Egyptian Exports②

The supporters of the foreign direct investments see that it causes an increase in the exports and the competitive ability; and such in fact one of the main causes of the importance of the direct foreign investment to economics of the developing countries in general and to the Egyptian market in particular;

The Main Sources for domestic savings are of two main types:

1) Main channels are: Family savings; the business sector savings; and government savings;

2) Sub-channels are: banks; stock exchange market; loans; external financing, insurance sector, tax revenue, and investment trust.

Question II: New Favorable Economic Egyptian Environment for the inflows of Foreign Direct Investment

To cope the increasing importance of the direct foreign investment as gate for attain development, the Egyptian authorities worked to create an environment conducive to thriving investment through passing and amending several laws with the aim of smoothing the way for investors. Among the amended law is the Investment Law through which new number of incentives was introduced for foreign investors; such a law provides a favorable climate for FDI;

In pursue to create a much favorable climate; Egyptian government went for the privatization

① (1) Nagaa, Abdel Wahab Ibrahim, (1995). The Foreign Direct Investments and its impacts on the Economic Development in Egypt (Master Degree) Faculty of Alexandria;

(2) Abdel Ghafar, Mohamed, 1997. The Savings problem in Egypt: Causes and solutions.

② Eissawy, Ibrahim, (1998). Determinants of the saving policy in Egypt,

program within the Government Economic Reform Program to encourage the local and foreign private sectors to invest in Egypt;

Egypt started paying attention to develop an investment law in 1974 while adopting open economic policy evidenced in giving the Law No.43 of 1974 concerning the investment of Arab and foreign funds and the free zones, as amended by Law No.32 of 1977 that gives to the local investor the same benefits granted to the Arab and foreign investor(s);

The investment climate consists of number of economic and non-economic elements; economic elements are positive and negative; the positive economic elements are the high level of gross domestic products, low wages in the general budget, and availability of skillful labor power. The negative economic elements are in high deficit of the balance of payments, and high inflation rate;

This type is the one that encourages foreign direct investment; the non-economic factors are the security and political stability and the effective legal system that protects the investor. In that effect, the law (65) of year 1971 was issued.

The favorable investment climate means package of circumstances, policies and economic institutions that attract and assure foreign investors to invest his funds in another country; The legislative framework is one of the main factors that create a favorable FDI environment; therefore new amendments have been introduced to the new investment law that will be addressed hereunder:

The issuance of law 43 of 1974 succeeded only to attract foreign investment of no more than 32% of the total investment which shows that such a law failed to attract much foreign investments as expected that calls for introduction of a new law namely law 230 of 1989 that provided new incentives for foreign investor(s) that was replaced by the Egypt's new Investment Incentives and Guarantees Law (Law No.8/1997). The new law aims to boost production and foreign and domestic investment and offers potentially good incentives for investors, including:

- The exemption the manufacturing projects from price controls or profit limitations;
- Equal fiscal treatment to the businesses established under the investment law and other private sector businesses
- Housing buildings established under this law are exempted from the unified rental rate system provided for other rental laws;
- Not subjected to the provisions of law 97/19976 on regulating foreign-exchange operations

Exemption from some of the provisions of law 159/1981 through which the investments granted the following privileges:

Exception to the rules governing the establishment of companies;

Exception of having a certain number at the board of directors;

Exception of the provisions on the participation of workers in management;

Exception of the must of having the majority in the Board of Directors of Egyptians;

Exception of the provision that prohibit the members of the Board of Directors to be managing director to more than one company of joint-stock companies;

The inadmissibility of bring criminal action against any investment firm on violation of the laws of customs, foreign exchange and consumption tax unless after having the opinion of the Authority;

Investment projects enjoying special system for import and export;

Guarantees①:

The investment law provides as well several guarantees for investors are as follow:

(1) projects incorporated under any legal structure shall be deemed of the private sector projects regardless to the legal nature of the Egyptian funds shared therein;

(2) The prohibition of nationalization, confiscation, and freezing of assets;

(3) The settlement of any disputes concerning the implementation of the provisions of the Investment Law shall be in the manner to be agreed upon with the investor;

(4) The right to repatriate capital and profits;

Tax Exemptions:

The Egyptian Investment law ensures number of tax exemptions for investors that are as follow:

(1) Exemption from income taxes for project profits and dividends;

(2) Ten year income tax exemption for ten years for projects established in new industrial zones, new urban communities, and remote area

(3) Fifteen year tax exemption for housing projects;

(4) Exemption from Estate and inheritance tax;

(5) Exemption from the fiscal stamps and authentication fees;

(6) Exemption from the general income tax after the end of the exemption period.

With a view to attract more foreign investment, Egyptian legislators passed the law 13 of 2004 and later many amendments have introduced thereto to smooth the process of investment especially under the drop of the foreign investment to which Egypt witnessed in year 2002/2003 that valued $700 million compared to $1.1 billion on year 1997/1998

The New amendments introduced the following facilities:

(1) Simplify and facilitate procedures for investors;

(2) Encourage investment and smoothing its challenges;

(3) Providing package of incentives and guarantees to create a more favorable climate to attract

---

① (1) The annual report of the General Authority for Investment.

(2) Hassb Allah M., Amira. 2005. The determinants of the foreign direct and indirect investment in the Arab economic environment, Ain Shams.

more investments;

(4) Provide one window service and simplified procedures for investor;

As to the Amendments introduced to the law, it is as the follow[①]:

1. The capital of companies that are governed by this Law may be determined in any convertible currency, and their financial statements prepared and published in same currency, provided that subscription to its capital must be in that same currency, and the entire amount of the issued capital shall be paid, and shall be deposited at any one of the recognized banks in foreign currency accounts. that with a view to increase the foreign currency in the Egyptian market and to avoid the negative consequences for any drop in the value of the Egyptian pound to attract more foreign investors;

2. The General Authority for Investment and Free Zones is the competent Authority, which exclusively apply the provisions of this Law, and the Authority's Board of Directors shall issue the Internal Regulations and Executive Resolutions pertaining to the Authority's financial, administrative and technical matters, and shall set up its organizational structure, and shall take all necessary procedures to manage the Authority and organize its work. The Authority's Board of Directors may establish offices for the Authority in the country or abroad.

3. The Authority is given vast competence, under this law, where the government shall submit to the Authority's Board of Directors, the drafts of laws, regulations and decisions related to investment issues for consideration thereon.

4. All Government bodies, economic and service authorities dealing with investors are requested to establish offices at the Authority and at every one of its branches and it is only this office that shall receive applications, conclude transactions, draw up contracts and grant the necessary licenses for establishing projects and conducting activity.

5. The Chairman of the Authority or his representative is the one authorized to issue the necessary certificates to the companies and establishments, which enjoy tax and customs exemptions, and any other exemptions applicable to companies, Such certificates are final and effective without the need for any approvals from other bodies, and all bodies are acting in accordance with said certificates and comply with the data mentioned therein.

6. This Authority according to the law is the body competent to collect; provide and update investment data and information and to regularly disseminate same through various means of dissemination via its local branches, internet websites, and offices abroad.

7. The law permits investors to contract for the necessary utilities for implementation of the projects through the Authority's offices and branches, authorized by the competent bodies to effect same; obliges The Authority to establish a database to comprise information pertaining to the utilities and services necessary for the projects or to be provided to investors.

8. This law permits the competent Authorities to assume the appropriation of lands owned by

---

① The Economic bulletins of The Ministry of Foreign Trade, several series.

the State to investors according to the governing legislations through the offices established at the Authority and its branches; and such offices are obliged to establish a database on the lands available for appropriation, its areas, location, prices, and the conditions of its disposal.

9. The Authority is obliged, under this law, to prepare standard forms for the investment applications according to the nature of each activity; and shall incorporate all data necessary for the activity, and the required documents, in particular, the list of the type of activity, project investment cost and requirements thereof concerning services, energy sources, and all licenses, approvals and documents required from various bodies to establish the project, conduct activity and liquidation thereof.

10. Companies, which are incorporated for the purpose of integrated development is granted a single approval for establishing and operating all of their projects, and each of the company's projects is enjoying the investment guarantees and incentives established from date of startup of the activity;

11. The Authority, pursuant to the rules set by its Board of Directors, may issue licenses to foreign companies to establish their representatives' offices and branches in the free zones. These offices and branches receive the same status as projects licensed by the Authority to be established in such zones

12. Bodies entrusted with granting licenses for establishment of projects and conducting activities, in accordance to the provisions of this Law, have the right to inspect the licensed projects in compliance with its provisions, in order to ensure adherence to the licensing conditions; provided that inspection to be taken place in accordance with programs duly prepared and implemented in a manner that does not affect the smooth operation of the projects

13. The administrative bodies, in case the project is in breach of any provision of the laws, regulations and decrees, shall notify the investor together with a copy of such notice to the Authority, to rectify the causes of the breach within a period to be defined in the notice in light of the extent and nature of such breach. In case such period lapses without rectification of the breach, the Authority shall issue a causative decision to terminate the activity of the project. The investor may file a grievance before one of the committees to be formed at the Authority and branches thereof, or before the Ministerial Committee to settle investors' disputes with administrative bodies;

14. Goods exported abroad by the free zone projects or imported for the pursue of their activity shall not be subject to customs taxes, the general sales tax and other taxes and duties, to include all types of tools, supplies, machinery and all different means of transportation, necessary for pursuing the activity licensed for all kinds of projects existing inside the free zones, with exception to passengers' cars;

In implementation to the amendments introduced to the Law on Investment Guarantees and Incentives, the government passed number of decrees to include:

- The issuance of a unified form by the General Authority for Investment includes all needed information for the registration into the Commercial Registry, the needed documents and the tax exemptions provided. Such facilitates the procedures for doing business for young and foreign investors and minimize the bureaucratic challenges;

- issuance of a bulletin showing all procedures required to have licenses for businesses including documents needed, fees and the duration required for having needed licenses;
- Developing of a map showing the plots of land that are put for sale for the purpose of investment attached to the price allocated for each, the needed requirements for allocation thereof, and format of the contracts in a view to facilitate the process of selection;
- Allocating special proper place for investors where they can have the services needed;

In pursue for more welcoming investment climate, the Egyptian Authorities introduced the following incentives:

- The development of a new ministry for investment aimed at improving the investment climate and remove any challenges
- Reducing the tariffs and removal of restrictions on imports;
- the Floating of the Egyptian pound against foreign currencies;
- Activate more economic agreements;
- The development of giant infrastructure projects

The amendments to the investment law as well as government decisions aimed at activating these amendments are made to facilitate procedures and remove obstacles. It also made in a view to provide more favorable climate for investors and attract more foreign direct investments.

埃及银行业的发展趋势以及银行设立中存在的法律问题

作者：Ahmed Hamouda 译者：陈晨

一、概述

如今，技术的普遍发展使国际金融市场的效率得以提高，在了解到这一重要性之后，为了提高本国市场的效率、吸引投资和资本，埃及正在推动银行业的改革和发展，使银行能够在埃及国民经济的发展中发挥更加重要的作用。

埃及政府通过采取多项政策和措施，以期提升银行系统在投资方面的作用，使银行能够更有效地满足市场的需求。由此，政府制定了措施对银行业进行改革和发展，同时将小型企业合并，并且在确保有效应用金融监管规则的同时提高信贷的利率。

埃及中央银行制订了银行业发展和重组计划，通过提高银行业的竞争能力，使银行高效地发挥其在经济活动中的作用，从而提高经济增长率。此外，埃及中央银行批准了一项计划，包括对银行的兼并、私有化、回收合资银行中社会资金、公共银行风险管理等问题，同时为解决银行的坏账问题提供了解决方案；

埃及中央银行认识到信息和通信技术在提升银行业效率和竞争力中的重要性，开始着力于发展支付系统和信息技术，以期提升金融系统的安全性和稳定性，最小化信用风险的同时提高支付速度，实现支付结算的可信性和保密性；

埃及中央银行还致力于发展和评估电子银行服务，通过互联网提供传统的和新兴的银行服务，以实现与技术发展的同步。中央银行于2002年通过了对于银行相关服务行为的规定，随后于2010年发布了关于移动电话支付的规定，并正在修订与在线服务相关的控制措施，以尽量减少银行可能面临的风险。

二、银行的发展阶段[①]

（一）开放政策（1974—1982）

这一时期的埃及正在实施对外开放政策，积极吸收阿拉伯国家和其他国家的投资，取消了1971年关于银行业的有关决定；开放政策在很多方面影响着银行的体系结构，其中最重要的一点是设立了投资银行和投资企业，为投资主体提供所需资金；政策还允许银行用户在埃及和其他阿拉伯国家同时设立两个账户，从而提供资金推动贸易的发展。在这一政策下，银行可以不受中央银行的监督，私人也被允许注册并成立银行，如阿拉伯国际银行和伊斯兰银行。

随后银行之间的竞争级别不断提升，以及在另一方面，经济开放政策使越来越多的资金从银行系统流向私营企业，这些因素都影响了此阶段银行的政策及其运作机制。

在这一阶段，1971年法令被废除，同时投资银行被引入埃及市场，并且允许进行银行兼并和估值。允许建立不受埃及中央银行控制的银行，并且为之设特别的规定，如阿拉伯国际银行和伊斯兰银行。于是从这之后，在银行的业绩和竞争力得到提升的同时，银行业对私人投资融资的贡献越来越大。

（二）对若干银行违规行为的治理（1982/1983—1990）

这一阶段，某些银行为了尽可能多地吸引客户而采取了一些违规手段进行激烈竞争，随即埃及通过一系列措施控制这些违规行为，包括修改银行和信贷法，进一步授权中央银行加强对这些银行的控制，在授予信用额度方面进行新的监控，同时对外汇交易进行了几项修正，最终建立起了银行间的外汇市场（1987年5月）。

（三）银行业的全面改革（1990—1995）

这一时期被视为自由阶段和实体经济改革的开端；在这一时期，利率和汇率实现自由化，同时，国库券开始为预算赤字提供资金。此时，埃及中央银行的新任务是进行改革的一个重要步骤，它要为任何处于困境中的银行提供帮助。

---

① http://www.sis.gov.eg 2016.

这一阶段，银行业在自身持续蓬勃发展的同时，通过投资信托、国库券以及购买公司股份的方式在股票市场的发展过程中扮演了重要的角色。这是真实的、活跃的市场的首次转变，在这种市场环境下，银行成为设定利率的主体，利率真正实现了自由化。

（四）当前阶段（1997 年至今）

这一阶段，埃及采取了若干政策和措施以增加银行系统在投资中的作用，使银行能够满足市场的需求。同时也制订了旨在重组银行、合并小型企业、确保金融监管有效实施的执行计划。

具体采取了以下措施：

（1）构建合理的银行监管结构（或称为合理的银行治理机构），以确保责任认定和绩效评估、控制的准确性，同时还要有具备良好职业素养的职员。

（2）协调好各银行的资产负债管理政策，对风险投资组合进行分配，确保银行信贷组合的质量，达到更高的利润率，推动零售银行业务的发展。

（3）发展银行系统中的信息系统，使用现代技术，将所有的银行单位及其分支机构连接到银行中心，以提供准确的信息。

（4）通过专业公司评估客户的信誉。

（5）通过提供多种新型银行服务提高投资资金的盈利能力，通过后续提高最低资本充足率标准压力来改善银行的财务状况。

（6）通过鼓励银行合并和收购重组银行系统。

（7）通过重新实施合资银行社会公共资金退出计划（包括对合资银行的公共捐款）来扩大所有权基础。

2007 年，在超过 32 家银行的参与下，埃及第一家信贷信息公司开始运营，其第一笔债券是用埃及镑发行的，并且在全球资本市场率达到 250%，这可以反映出外国投资群体对埃及经济的信任。

即使在 2011 年、2012 年，由于其政治和社会的变动，埃及的经济形势有所变化，但埃及银行的业绩仍然展现出积极、均衡的一面，能够保障好客户的储蓄，减少货币的投机行为，遵循中央银行的指示，在最糟糕的形势下维持住了银行的工作。

三、影响电子银行服务发展的因素[①]

（一）银行业的发展和重组

埃及中央银行制订了四项精简计划以发展银行系统，这四种主要精简计划以合并和私有化为代表，同时通过财政和行政的方法重组公共银行，以解决坏账问题，并且增强了中央银行的控制和监管职能。

银行的大量合并使得在埃及营业的银行数量减少；同时很多银行也已经进行了重组，公共银行对其所有部门都进行了发展规划，在风险管理、信息技术、人力资源等方面建立了新的部门。

关于坏账，银行采用了新的手段进行结算，同时还设置了数据库，收集统计不按期还款的用户的信息数据，并且每月更新、分析这些数据，银行采用世界上先进的方法来监管和控制其各个部门。

银行现在具有水平优良的职员以及配有精良设备的信息技术部门，这些职员和信息技术部门能够在最短的时间内使银行获取准确的信息。

为取得进一步的成果，埃及中央银行制订了第二阶段的发展方案，旨在提高银行的运作效率，并提升其竞争能力和风险管理能力。

（二）银行的合并与收购

埃及政府曾经在20世纪60年代初期通过国有化的方式对银行业进行控制，随后通过合并的方式推动银行的发展。

随着银行合并的推行，巨大的银行机构也随之建立起来，这样的银行机构能够提供足够的资金来提供合理的信贷措施，同时能够利用高科技和行政经验来以较低的费用提供更高质量的服务。

20世纪90年代，埃及政府在银行领域采取的改革措施使其银行体系具有了更高的自由度。

---

① Rasha Abdelrahman-FEPS, August 2011.

（三）电子银行服务的发展

为了与国际性银行相竞争，并试图吸引更多的潜在客户、资本和外国投资，埃及银行从 1997 年以来一直致力于电子银行服务的发展。埃及银行在移动电话、互联网等平台上提供电子服务，包括对信用卡进行开发和发展，扩展更多的自动提款机和销售终端。

（四）支付手段

由于支付系统对于财务结算的稳定至关重要，埃及中央银行正在努力发展支付系统的基础设施，并采取了以下几项措施：

（1）加入环球银行金融电信协会（SWIFT），以保证银行间网络的稳定和金融机构间信息的流通；

（2）提高银行系统的实际运作效率，将国家应缴费用的支付时间从三周缩短到最多两天；

（3）提高银行系统的实际运作效率，使政府部门之间的资金流转在当天或者次日内完成；

（4）提高即时支付结算系统实际运作效率，以使高价值电子支付、信贷和流动性管理的风险达到最小；

（5）与财政部合作，使用电子信用卡支付公职人员的薪金和养老金；

（6）通过自动清算系统和直接付款服务进行直接支付；

（7）促进银行信息技术的发展。

1. 银行职员、人事制度的建设和发展

为了使埃及中央银行与银行业的普遍发展同步，在各方关注下，银行很重视对银行职员的培训，还组织了一些专门的培训班培训各领域银行的职员。

2. 埃及中央银行对电子银行服务的控制和监管

埃及中央银行为控制和监管电子银行服务，采取了以下措施：

（1）只有在埃及中央银行注册的银行才可被授予许可证；

（2）银行应当在其对资本充足率、贷款分类和供应标准的承诺范围内接受央行的所有监督和控制行为；

（3）银行应当遵守审慎的标准，管理与电子银行服务相关的风险，对此类风险进行评估、管理和控制；

（4）银行应在申请许可证之时确定其通过网络提供的服务类型；

（5）银行应当确定提供电子服务方的责任；

（6）银行应当确定接受电子服务方的责任。

3. 对被授权提供电子银行服务的银行的要求

（1）银行应满足银行服务条款的所有要求；

（2）银行进行直接扣款时须经客户同意；

（3）埃及中央银行允许进行移动支付，同时也在寻求制定一系列对银行网络的控制措施，以使电子银行服务的风险最小化。除此之外，埃及与 Fawry 银行支付技术服务公司合作，通过自动提款机完成账单的支付。

4. 埃及信息技术的发展

在埃及加入《服务贸易总协定》（GATS）和世贸组织《基础电信协议》后，埃及正在致力于通过立法和行政渠道使各个地区与现代技术的发展水平保持一致；于是在 1999 年，埃及设立了通信和信息技术部。自那时以来，埃及提出了一些倡议和发展项目，并组织了培训和讲习班，在公共和私营部门之间建立伙伴关系，以期发展电信基础设施。

5. 互联网中的电子银行服务

埃及中央银行在授权银行提供电子银行服务的同时，也使这些提供服务的银行具有较高的可靠性和良好的信誉。所有银行都需要通过 SSL 协议来提供各种信息保护手段，SSL 协议是一种被用于在服务器和客户端之间建立加密链接的标准安全技术，诸如信用卡号，社会保险号和登录凭证之类的敏感信息都可以通过 SSL 协议进行安全传输；

电子银行服务分为金融性服务和非金融性服务，具体包括以下几种：接收来自不同账户的转账；通过互联网支付票据；获得银行账户及签证卡账户；获得银行存款；存取储蓄证书；提供下载财务报表服务；检查支票簿以及托收的支票。

6. 银行电话服务

1999 年之后，埃及出现银行电话服务，埃及银行的电话服务使银行客户能够随时随地享受银行的各种服务；

银行提供的电话服务包括：不同账户之间的汇款；支付账单；查询信用卡余额；查询银行对账单；查询当前账户的对账单；查询银行提供的银行服务；查询外国银行的利率和利率。

7. 手机银行服务

手机银行是一种很方便的临时管理账户的方法，它采用最先进的信息技术方法使信息能够十分安全地传播；

手机银行包括以下几种服务：在多个银行账户之间转移资金；通过手机进行购买和卖出；查询信用卡余额；在宽限期结束前支付最低的限额；查询支付期限；查询卡上最新的交易和购买；访问账单。

它还提供一些短信服务，包括：访问当前银行账户；通知信用卡的续订时间；当货币汇率改变时通知客户；当交易完成时进行通知客户。

8. 埃及市场中的支付卡

埃及开发出取款机器并将其推广普及埃及大部分省份，大多数使用智能卡片的机器已经投入使用。埃及中央银行注意到这些情况后，为银行工作人员组织了几次培训讲习班，加深他们关于各种保护支付卡方法的了解，关于支付卡伪造和诈骗行为以及不同类型支付卡的信息也在讲习班中有所涉及。

（1）信用卡

现在埃及银行正准备发行一些可以在国际上使用的信用卡，并使这种信用卡可以在一些著名的国际信用卡组织中使用，如 VISA 和万事达卡。除此之外，一少部分银行还发行一些信用卡，它们类似于联合银行发行的大来卡以及奥迪银行发行的美国运通卡。

（2）借记卡

这种卡片与储蓄账户相连接，它有着标准 ATM 卡的所用功能——能够提取现金，也能够与其他银行进行交易。借记卡通常可以像 ATM 卡一样进行即时取现。

（3）互联网卡

一些埃及银行与 Visa 或万事达合作签发互联网卡，为用户提供更高的安全性。这些卡易于使用，客户可以在有效期内进行多次存款。但它不能用于直接购买和现金提取。

（4）智能卡

这种卡是一种具有嵌入式集成电路的袖珍卡，它具有很高的灵活性，可以用作借记或存款卡，并允许持有人在支付时收到现金。它内设若干安全措施，如对卡片的使用次数设置某些限制，在某一时间段内限制可兑现的金额以及一些其他的措施。

9. 自动取款机

埃及银行在 20 世纪 80 年代开始提供自动取款机的服务，在当时只能在有存款账户的银行实现这一服务，但现在它与银行之间的网络相连，使人们可以在不同机器上取款和存款；

根据其所在地区，自动取款机可以分为以下几种类型：

（1）独立的自动取款机，这是一种会经常在角落商店 / 酒吧和购物中心看到的自动取款机；

（2）在墙壁外的自动取款机，这种机器多出现在各种金融分支机构的墙外或者一些商家的墙外；

（3）机器多见于各种金融分支机构的大厅的一种 ATM，有些银行会专门为一定数量的自动取款机开设一个房间，以方便其客户的使用；

（4）设置在银行或任何对现金提取有高需求的地方（如商业市场和购物中心）的自动取款机；

（5）移动 ATM，可以临时放置在人们需要的地方，用完之后再将其移走，我们通常在节日时或者工厂发放薪水时使用。

10. 经济改革方案时期的货币政策

埃及的经济改革着力于满足国内市场价格指数的需求，同时为了尽量减少政府在经济活动中的参与度，埃及的经济改革还广泛地推动私有化进程，改善公共财政资源，并且为解决国家总的财政赤字提供资金支持。

为了实现这些目标，埃及正在寻求实现金融市场自由化，并将私营部门参与各种经济领域的大门持续敞开。

11. 现金和信贷市场

埃及市场中推行的主要改革措施如下：

（1）由于存款和放款利率的自由化受到限制，埃及政府颁布了针对银行和信贷法中关于银行设定自由利率条款的立法修正案，所有银行服务的价格都由银行自由确定，埃及中央银行将不会对此直接干预。

（2）提高各种信贷增长率的一切贷款限额，同时寻求通过使用间接货币政策工具来控制信贷的增长。

（3）为国家预算提供资金而拍卖公共国库券的期限设定为 91 天以上，1 年以下。

（4）将中央银行的折现率与国库券利率联系起来，以期提升与市场趋势相关的贴现率的活跃性。

（5）以银行作为货币和信贷市场的主要参与者，使银行达到巴塞尔委员会所规定的偿付能力标准。

12. 对发展的信息技术的利用

一项对埃及经济改革方案中头十年货币政策的研究表明，对货币政策决策者来说，金融、货币和非货币信息是迫切需要的。众所周知，信息和指示的任何延误都会对决策的质量造成显著影响。因此，埃及中央银行开始发展基础设施，并通过以下方式提高其运营水平：

（1）2002 年 7 月，建立起埃及中央银行的信息技术网络，并将其作为埃及银行和中央银行之间的直接通信渠道。

（2）建立电子结算所，于 2002 年 6 月启用，并准备向实施实时全额结算系统的方向迈出第一步。

（3）决定将银行分行连接到其主银行，然后再连接到 CBE 网络。

（4）向 CBE 引入入门级电子系统，以实现非物质化交易，同时加速在开放市场的交易。2002 年 6 月，在埃及经营的 57 家银行的分行的注册数量为 2544 个。

（5）使各个银行了解其在埃及中央银行的账户数量，以便他们改善流动性管理技术并最大限度地提高利润率。

13. 2003 年第 88 号中央银行、银行业和货币体系法对银行注册事项的规定

任何在埃及经营的银行及其在海外的子公司均受本法规定的约束；任何未按照本法规定注册的银行机构，不得进行任何与银行业务有关的工作，其名称、地址或者宣传内容中不得出现银行或者与银行具有相同含义的用语。

计划从事银行业务的主体在埃及中央银行完成登记前，需要满足以下条件：

（1）埃及股份公司应以公共法人的名义发行其所有股份，并应将开展银行业务作为其营业目的。

（2）总行国籍明确的外国银行的支行，应受其总行所在国金融管理局的监管。

（3）埃及银行发起时应缴资本的数额不得少于 5 亿埃及镑，在阿拉伯埃及共和国开设的外国银行分行，其发起资本不得少于 5000 万美元或与其等价的其他自由流通货币。

（4）中央银行行长经董事会同意后，应批准通过银行章程，并与任何委托其进行管理的主体订立管理合同。任何对法条和管理合同的修订都应根据本条款进行。

持牌银行的分行及代理机构须记录在上述登记册内。在获得中央银行董事会的批准之后，银行才可建立其分行或代理机构并开始营业。

如果该银行违反本法有关条款及其执行条例，或对该银行、银行分行及其代理机构的成立授权不符合当地总体经济利益和状况，中央银行董事会应当拒绝银行的

注册申请。

中央银行行长在获得董事会批准后，可以授权在阿拉伯埃及共和国境内没有分支机构的外国银行开设代表处，其总部应接受这些代表处所在地相关部门的监督；该代表处的活动仅限于研究埃及市场和投资潜力，从而与国外的总部进行沟通。它们应当帮助其在埃及境内的代理银行解决潜在问题，走出困难处境。

14. 银行的登记

每家银行在阿拉伯埃及共和国境内拥有的资金应与其债务和应付款项相当，且不少于其发起时应缴的资本。

每家银行都有权根据交易性质决定其交易时的利率。它们还可以确定其银行服务的收费标准，且不受任何其他法律规定的限制。

在任何情形下，银行都应根据本法执行条例所确定的公开规则，向客户公开利息的利率和银行的服务费用。

在满足本委员会确定的条件和程序后，任何银行都可以根据中央银行董事会的事先授权并入另一家银行，但在合并时应当合理考虑被合并银行工作人员的权益。

合并的法律后果是撤销被合并银行的注册，在宣布合并决定之日起 10 日内应当在《埃及日报》上发布对其除名的决定。

任命银行董事会主席和成员，任命负责信贷、投资、投资组合管理以及外部交易（包括互换交易）和内部检查的执行董事时，应咨询中央银行行长。针对各方提出的候选人名单，应当在征求中央银行行长的意见后将其提交中央银行董事会。

如果通过对银行的内部检查，发现负责信贷、投资、投资组合管理以及外部交易（包括互换交易）和内部检查的执行董事违反了存款人和银行资产的安全规则，那么中央银行行长有权要求撤销这些执行董事的职位。

银行协会的设立应当遵循本法规定，有关其章程的决定由中央银行董事会发布。银行协会享有独立法人资格，并在中央银行的特别登记册上进行登记。关于成立协会及其章程的决定应在《 埃及日报》上公布，并由协会承担相关费用。

中央银行行长应委派一名代表参加银行协会。代表有权参加协会的会议并参与讨论，但无权对决议进行投票。

银行研究所位于开罗市，由中央银行建立同时隶属于中央银行。它具有法人人格以及独立的预算。银行研究所关注银行、金融、货币经济、打击洗钱等领域的业务水平的发展，致力于提升中央银行、地方银行和本领域内其他机构从业人员的业务能力，以期与世界发展水平保持一致，同时建立健全稳固的专业规则。研究所的董事会负责制定并贯彻落实总的发展政策，其资源包括中央银行的专项拨款，政府的补助金以及银行和各种金融机构为培训其工作人员而支付的费用。

The Development Trends of Egypt's Banking Sector and Legal Issues on the establishment of banks

Author: Ahmed Hamouda

Introduction

The Universal Technology development resulted into an increase in the efficiency of the world financial market; being aware of its importance; to increase the efficiency of the Egyptian market, and in a view to attract investment and capital, Egypt is witnessing ongoing process of reform and development to the banking sector in order to improve its performance and promote its role in the national economy.

In that number of policies and measures were adopted to increase the role of the banking system in funding the investment and enable banks to be more capable of dealing with the demands of the market. Therefore, an executive program was set to reform and develop banks and merge small entities together, ensure an efficient application of the rules of financial regulation and supervision while increasing credit rates.

The Central Bank of Egypt developed plan for the development and restructuring of the banking sector, to promote and create banking sector able to compete, perform its role in the economic activity efficiently and increase the economic growth rate. Central Bank of Egypt approved a plan to mergers, privatization and the exit of public funds from the joint venture banks, and risk management of public banks, while provide solutions to the problem of bad debts;

The Central Bank of Egypt realized the importance of the role of information and communication technology in the development of the efficiency and competitively in banking sector, thus it worked in the development of payment systems and information technology in order to enhance the safety and stability of the financial system, minimize the credit risk and increase the speed, and achieve credibility and confidentiality of payments settlement;

The Central Bank of Egypt also worked in developing and evaluating the e-banking services to keep pace with technological advances, which include provision of traditional and innovative services through internet. The central bank approved in 2002 the controls for the practice of banks of those services, also issued in 2010 the rules governing the mobile phone payments and is updating the controls that are associated to the online services to minimize the risks to which banks might be exposed;

Banks Development Stages①

The Open Policy (1974—1982)

This period witnessed the application of the opening-up policy to encourage Arab and foreign investment, which was canceled career customization banks Resolution of 1971, also affected the banking system structure in many ways the most important .. the establishment of investment banks and business to provide funding to serve the investment, also allowed the presence of two banks subscribers between Egypt and Arab countries to finance trade and development. As well as the existence of banks are not subject to the supervision of the Central Bank and is registered and has organized a private, such as Arab International Bank and the Islamic banking laws.

Consequently banking policy and the mechanism of performance and handling at this stage has been affected, with increased degree of competition between banks, on the other hand, increased funding for the banking system to the private sector in line with the policy of economic openness.

The Law 1971 was repealed and investment banks were introduced to the Egyptian market; merger in banks and the assessments of the banks were allowed. Establishing banks that are not subjected to the control of the Central banks of Egypt is allowed that enjoy special rules such as the international Arab bank and the Islamic banks. Accordingly the performance and competitively of banks have increased as well as the contribution of the banking sector into financing the private investments have increased since then.

Having control over series of undisciplined actions of banks (82/1983 1990)

Series of measures were taken to series of undisciplined actions by some banks which embarked on rash competition to attract the biggest number of clients that included the amendment of the banking and credit law, and further mandates were given to the Central Bank to tighten its control over the banks, new regulatory controls were introduced on granting credits, and several amendments

① http://www.sis.gov.eg 2016.

were made on the foreign exchange dealings, which ended with the establishment of interbank foreign exchange market (May 1987)

Comprehensive banking reform (1990—1995)

This period is seen as the beginning of the liberation stage and the real economic reform; under this period, the interest and exchange rate was set free, and the method of funding the budget deficit was changed to be through treasury bills. One of the important procedures that were taken at that period was the new mandates for the Central Bank of Egypt namely the mandate of the Central bank to assist any bank in distress;

This stage witnessed positive and ongoing developments to the banking sector as it played an important role in promoting the stock market through investment trusts, treasury bills, and the purchase of shares in sector companies; It was the first shift in a real active market under which the interest rates were liberalized and banks are the one who shall set it.

The current stage (from 1997 until now)

Number of policies and measures are adopted increase the role of the banking system in the investment and enable banks to meet the demands of the market. Executive program were developed that are aiming at restructuring the banks, merge small entities, and ensure the effective application of financial regulation.

In that the following actions were taken:

-The existence of proper regulatory framework for bank or the so-called the good governance of banks, which ensures accuracy in identifying responsibilities, control and performance evaluation, as well as having skillful cadres;

-The coordination of asset/liabilities management policies of each bank, the distribution of risk portfolio, ensuring the quality of credit portfolios of banks, achieving higher profitability rates, and the development of retail banking activity.

-Developing the information systems in the banking system, the use of modern technology and connect all banking units to the oversight on banks and branches to the main centers to provide accurate information.

-Assess the creditworthiness of customers through specialized companies.

-Providing new and various banking services to increase the profitability of the invested funds, and strengthen the financial positions of banks through the follow-up and the pressure to raise the minimum capital adequacy standard;

-Restructuring the banking system through encouraging banks on mergers and acquisitions.

-Broaden the ownership base through the revival of the exit of public funds from joint ventures program, which includes public contributions to the joint venture banks.

Year 2007 saw the run of the first Credit Information Company with the participation of more than 32 banks, also the issuance of the first bond in Egyptian pounds as the volume of coverage reached 250% in the global capital markets which reflected the trust of foreign investment community in the Egyptian economy.

Though the changes to which the Egyptian economy witnessed in years 2011 and 2012 as a result of the political and social transformation, the performance of the Egyptian banks showed a positively balanced performance through securing of its clients' savings, reducing the operations of currency speculation, comply to the Central Bank's instructions, and maintaining the work in the banking sector under the most improper circumstances;

Factors for the Development of E-Banking Services①

I. The development and restructuring the banking sector

The Central bank of Egypt developed four-axe plan for the development of the banking system of four main axes represented in mergers and privatization, restructuring public banks financially and administratively, solve the problem of bad debts, and develop the controls and supervision of the Central Bank;

Many mergers have occurred that resulted into lowering the numbers of banks operating in Egypt; and banks have been restructured; Public banks undergone development plan to all departments, new departments are introduced on risk management, IT, and human resources.

As to the bad debt, settlements were occurred through the introduction of new means; a data base was set up of defaulting clients; and such data are updated and analyzed on a monthly base; and best global practices on the banking regulatory and control sector, were adopted;

New skillful cadres and highly equipped IT department are present through which accurate information is obtained in very short time;

In continuation to the success accomplished, the Central Bank of Egypt developed a second phase of the development program that is aiming at raising the efficiency of the performance of the banks, and increase its competitively and ability on risks monument

① Rasha Abdelrahman- FEPS, August 2011.

II. Merger & Acquisition of Banks

The Egyptian government had control over the banking sector at the early of the 1960s through the nationalization of banks, and then it promoted the banks through the merger of Egyptian banks;

Under the merger occurred, huge banking institutions established that having the ability to contribute in financing the development plan as of the provision of proper credit facilities and having access to high technical and administrative experiences and capabilities that offer better quality services at lower costs;

The Egyptian authorities undertook major banking reforms in the 1990s towards a more liberal system.

III. The development of e-banking services

In competing the international banks, and in attempt to attract further potential clients, capitals, and foreign investments, the Egyptian banks pursued the development of the e-banking services since 1997. in that the numbers of the banks that implement the e-services over mobiles phone and internet to include the development of credit cards and the expansion of teller *machines* (*ATM*) and *Point* of *Sale* (POS) terminals

IV. Payment methods

Egypt's central bank is pursuing the development of the infrastructure for payment systems due to its importance to maintain the financial settlements in that the following measures were taken:

- Being member in the Society for Worldwide Interbank Financial Telecommunication (SWIFT) in an attempt to secure reliable network for transmitting messages between financial institutions;
- The actual operation of banking system through which the state dues can be paid in that the time consumed has been cut from three-week to two days maximum;
- the actual operation of banking system through which checks drawn from government units in favor of other government units are settled on the same day or at most on the following day;
- the actual operation of the RTGS to minimize risk in high-value electronic payment, credit and liquidity management;
- Payment of the salaries and pensions of the public civil servants through the electronic credit cards in cooperation with the Ministry of Finance;
- The direct payment through the automated clearing house and the direct debit service;
- The promotion of the means of the information technology in the banking sector

The Development of Human cadres in banking sector

Under the framework of the mutual concern of Egypt's Central Bank to be in line with the universal updates in the banking sector, it gives a great attention to trainings and the specialized workshops in all areas of the banks;

The Egyptian Central bank regulatory and supervisory control over e-banking services

Set of regulatory and supervisory control over e-banking services were adopted by the Central Bank of Egypt, to include:

-Granting licenses are limited to the banks that are registered under the Central Bank of Egypt

-Bank shall satisfy all supervisory controls on the extent of its commitment to Capital Adequacy and standards of Loan Classification and Provisioning.

-The observance of bank(s) to the prudent standards for the management of risks associated to the e-banking services; that to include assessing, managing and controlling such risks;

-Bank shall identify at the application for a license the type(s) of services that will be performed over networks.

-Bank shall identify the responsibilities for granting e-services;

-Bank shall identify the responsibilities of the clients for receiving e-services.

The requirements for granting the banks the access to provide the e-banking services shall include:

-Bank shall satisfy all requirements for the provisions of banking services;

-Bank shall have the consent of the client on the direct debit mandate;

-The Central Bank of Egypt gave consent over the operation of mobile payment; and is pursuing now the identification of the set of controls of banking internet to minimize the e-banking services risk. Moreover, Egypt adopted the payment of bills through the ATMs in cooperation with Fawry Banking & Payment Technology Services

The Development of the IT in Egypt

Within the framework of Egypt's accession to the General Agreement on Trade in Services (GATS): THE WTO Agreement on Basic Telecommunications, Egypt is seeking hard through legislative and executive channels to go in line with modern technology in all areas; in that Egypt established the Ministry of Communications and information technology in 1999. Since then, many initiative and projects established, training and workshops are being provided, and partnership between the public and private sector have been effected to develop the telecommunications infrastructure;

E-banking services through internet

Egyptian banks offer e-banking services under authorization from the Central Bank of Egypt that give it the reliability and trust; all banks provide all means of protection through the effect of the SSL protocol which is a standard security technology for establishing an encrypted link between a server and a client that allows sensitive information such as credit card numbers, social security numbers, and login credentials to be transmitted securely;

The e-banking services are of financial and non-financial services that include:

-Money transfers from different accounts;

-Payment of bills through internet;

-Access to bank account(s) and visa card account(s);

-Access to banking deposits;

-Access to saving certificates;

-Accessibility of downloading the financial statement;

-Requesting checkbook and follow the checks under collection;

Phone banking services

Phone banking service appeared in Egypt since 1999, service appeared in the Egyptian bank where at anytime from anywhere bank-client(s) can have full access to many services.

Phone banking services include:

-Money transfers between different accounts;

-payment of bills

-Check Credit Card Balance

-Check the bank statement(s)

-Check current account statement

-Making inquiries on the banking services provided by the bank;

-Making inquiries on the rates of the foreign currieries and the benefit rates.

Mobile Phone Banking Service

Mobile phone banking is a convenient way to manage occasional administrative tasks on the go through the use of the most modern IT methods through which information are sent in a highly secured manner;

Mobile phone banking service includes:

-transferring funds between accounts;

-Purchasing and sales through the mobile phone;

-Checking credit cards balances.;

-The Payment of the minimum before the end of the grace period.

-Check the permitted ceil of payments;

-Check the last transactions and purchases made to the card.

-Access to statement of account.

It also give access Short Message Service to include:

-Access to current accounts.

-Being informed of the renewal time of credit cards.

-Being informed when the currency exchange rates are changed;

-Being informed if any deals made.

Payment cards in the Egyptian market

Teller Machines have been developed and been expanded to cover most of the governorates of Egypt, and most developed machines that are operated with smart cards are being used. Such gain the concern of the Central Bank of Egypt in that several training workshops were made for bankers to raise awareness of the various cards and means of protection, forgery, fraud, and other information about the various types of payment cards.

Credit cards

The Egyptian banks are now issuing credit cards that are operated internationally with prominent international card organizations such as VISA and MasterCard. Few banks, in addition, issue similar cards such as Diners Club by the United Bank and American Express by Audi Bank;

Debit Cards

It is a payment card linked to current or saving-account; it combines all the uses of standard ATM card allowing getting cash and performing other banking transactions. Debit cards usually also allow for instant withdrawal of cash, acting as the ATM card for withdrawing cash.

Internet cards

Some Egyptian banks issued in cooperation with Visa or Master cards the internet cards to give greater security to users. These cards are easy to use, client may make several deposits through the validity period. It cannot be used for direct purchases; as well as cash withdrawals.

Smart Cards

Card is any pocket-sized card that has embedded integrated circuits; it is characterized of flexibility, It can be used as debits or deposit cards and allows the holder to receive cash at paying off purchases. It include several means of security such as setting certain limits on the number of times of using the card, the ceil of amounts that can be cashed during a certain period of time or other means

Automated Teller Machines

The Egyptian banks started to offer ATM service in the 1980s, its use was limited to the bank where the account is deposited but now it is connected to interbank networks, enabling people to withdraw and deposit money from different machines;

ATMs are mainly divided in terms of their places to:

-Stand Alone ATM are the lobby style ATM's you see at most corner stores/pubs and shopping centres.

-Through The wall ATM that exist outside the wall of branches of various financial institutions and machines that are through the walls of the shops.

-ATMs Lobby that exists in the branches of financial institutions machines and some banks made a chamber for number of machines to facilitate use by customers.

-Machines that are fixed outside banks or in any place where there is high demand on the cash withdrawal, such as the commercial markets and shopping malls machines.

-Mobile ATM that can be placed in places temporarily when needed and then moved, it is what we use for festivals, or factories at the salary time;

Monetary policy under the economic reform program

The economic reform bases on the need to satisfy domestic demand in the light of the price indices that are based on market forces, while working to reduce the degree of the involvement of government in the economic activity through applying extensive program of privatization, improving public financial management, and financing the deficit of the general budget of the state.

To achieve this, seeking the liberalization of financial markets is being pursued and the door is being opened to private sector participation in various economic areas;

Cash and credit market

Main reforms that have been introduced to Egyptian market are as follows:

1. The liberalization of the interest rate on the deposit and lending from any restrictions, thus legislative amendments have been issued to the Banking and credit Law of the text on the freedom of banks in setting interest rate, and the freedom to identify the prices of all banking services without direct intervention from the Central Bank of Egypt;

2. Lift all the credit ceilings that were prevalent on all types of credit growth rates, and seeking to control the credit growth through the use of the indirect monetary policy tools.

3. Financing the deficit in the state budget through auctions on the public treasury bills for deadlines ranging from a minimum of 91 days and a maximum of a year;

4. Linking the discount rate at the central bank to the interest rates on treasury bills to reduce the degree of inertia that was suffered by the discount rate and linked to market trends.

5. Looking at banks as the main player in the money and credit market, banks have been required to solvency standards according to the rules of the Basel Committee.

The utilization of the development of the information Technology

The researched made on the monetary policy in the first ten years of the economic reform program experienced in Egypt showed the urgent need for the flow of financial and monetary and in-kind information to the decision makers of the monetary policy. It is known that any delay in the availability of information and indicators significantly affect the quality of the decision. As a result the Central Bank of Egypt started in the development of the infrastructure to improve its performance through the follow:

1. The Establishment of the IT network of the Central Bank of Egypt in July 2002 to be direct communication channel between the Egyptian banks and the Central Bank.

2. Create Electronic Clearing House, which opened in June 2002, and considered the first step in the direction towards the implementation of the RTGS;

3. Conclude the operation of linking bank branches to its main bank and then to the network of the CBE.

4. The introduction of the entry book electronic System to the CBE which led to the

dematerializing transactions and accelerate dealing in the open market. In June 2002 the number of registered branches of banks operating in Egypt was 2544 owned to about 57 banks.

5. Complete the requirements needed to give access to banks to know the volume of its accounts with the Central Bank of Egypt so that they can improve liquidity management techniques and maximize profitability.

How banks are registered according to the law No.88 of 2003 on Central Bank, Banking Sector and Monetary System

All banks operate in Egypt and its subsidiaries abroad are subject to the provisions of this Law; Any person or entity or establishment not registered in accordance with the provisions of this law are banned to proceed with any work of bank business, or use the word bank or any term equivalent in any language in its title, address or propaganda;

Any entity willing to engage in banking business shall be registered under of the Central Bank of Egypt after being satisfied the following requirements:

-to be an Egyptian joint stock company, all shares thereof being nominal a public legal person, comprising within its purposes the exercise of bank business

-to be a branch of a foreign bank, the head office of which enjoys a defined nationality, and is subject to supervision by a monetary authority in the country where its head office is situated

-The issued and fully paid-up capital shall not be less than five hundred million Egyptian pounds, and the capital appropriated for the activities of the branches of foreign banks in the Arab Republic of Egypt shall not be less than fifty million US dollars or their equivalent in free currencies.

-The Governor of the Central Bank, following consent of the Board of Directors, shall approve the statute of the bank, and the management contracts to be concluded with any party entrusted with its management. This provision shall apply to any renewal or modification of the statutes or management contracts.

The branches and agencies of the licensed bank shall be recorded in the above mentioned register. The approval of the Board of Directors of the Central Bank shall be obtained before starting the establishment of the branch or agency, and before opening it for dealing.

The registration application shall be rejected by a substantiated decision from the Board of Directors of the Central Bank upon violation of any of the provisions stipulated in this Law, or its Executive Regulations, or the decrees issued for its enforcement or if licensing to the bank, the branch, or the agency does not comply with the general economic interest or the conditions of the region where the bank, the branch or the agency is required to be established.

The Governor of the Central Bank, following approval of the Board of Directors, may authorize foreign banks to open representative offices for them in the Arab Republic of Egypt, if they have no branches in the Arab Republic of Egypt; and their head offices shall be subject to supervision by the authority concerned in the countries where these offices are situated; and the activity of the representative offices shall be restricted to studying the markets and investment potentials, and they shall act as a liaison with the head offices abroad. They shall contribute to overcoming the problems and difficulties that may face their correspondent banks in the Arab Republic of Egypt.

Registration of Banks

The bank shall have funds in the Arab Republic of Egypt equivalent to its obligations and payable therefor, in addition to an amount of not less than the minimum issued and paid-up capital

Each bank shall have the power to determine the interest rates on banking transactions it carries out, according to the nature of these transactions. It may also determine the fees it applies for the banking services, without being restricted by the limits and the provisions prescribed in any other law.

In all cases, the bank shall disclose to the customer the rates of the interest, and the fees on banking services according to the rules of disclosure as determined in the Executive Regulations of this Law.

Any bank may merge into another bank by virtue of a prior authorization from the Board of Directors of the Central Bank, after fulfilling the conditions and procedures to be issued by a decision of this Board, with due regard to guaranteeing the rights of the staff in the merged bank.

The merger shall result in delisting the registration of the merged bank, and in publishing the decision for its delisting in the Egyptian Journal within ten days from the date of issuing the merger decision.

The Governor of the Central Bank shall be consulted on the appointment of the chairmen and members of banks' boards of directors, as well as the executive directors in charge of credit, investment, portfolio management, and external transactions including swaps; and internal inspection. The Governor shall be consulted on a list of candidates presented by the parties concerned, for submission to the Board of Directors of the Central Bank.

Governor of the Central Bank may ask for the removal of one or more of banks' boards of directors, executive directors in charge of credit, investment, portfolio management, and external transactions including swaps; and internal inspection if, through inspection on the banks, it is established that they have violated safety rules of depositors' funds and the bank's assets.

An Association shall be established among the banks subject to this Law, and a decision concerning its statute shall be issued by the Board of Directors of the Central Bank. The Association shall enjoy the status of independent legal personality, and be recorded in a special register at the Central Bank. The decision concerning the establishment of the Association and its statute shall be published in the Egyptian Journal at the expense of the Association.

The Governor of the Central Bank shall appoint a delegate to the Association. The delegate shall have the right to attend the sessions of the Association and participate in its discussions, without having a counted vote in its deliberations.

Banking Institute is established and affiliated to the Central Bank. It has legal personality and an independent budget. It is located in the city of Cairo. The Banking Institute is concerned with the development of skills in the fields of banking, financial, and monetary business, and combating of money laundering, for staff of the Central Bank, banks and other parties operating in these fields, with the aim of keeping abreast of world developments and firmly establishing sound professional rules. The Board of Directors of the Institute shall be responsible for setting its general policy and following up its implementation. The resources of the Institute are comprised of the appropriations to be earmarked therefor by the Central Bank., subventions contributed to the Institute and amounts paid by banks and different parties for training their staff therein.

非洲国家财政政策对外国直接投资的影响

作者：Moke Maye 译者：雷宇

乍听起来，讨论非洲国家的财政政策对外国直接投资的影响，这一说法有些自负。但这是事实，非洲国家有独特的现实，为了应对现实问题，我们应当处理它的财政政策和吸引外国直接投资问题。

但仔细来看，想看清上述问题，我们要了解，所有非洲国家的经济都有一个特点——受外部习惯的强烈影响。他们本质上是外向型经济，外来资助大量来自剥削的收益贡献。

另外，几十年来，70 个非洲国家计划了一个发展项目，它最终将给它们的人民提供更好的生活条件。为了实现这个目标，国家的管理者们必须要满足两种需求：了解国内收入的增长和对外国投资的吸引力。按着上述观点的逻辑看，明确财政政策定义和净化司法环境，是经济发展项目中基本的两步。

税收在非洲国家的作用至关重要。在为物质基础设施等发展目标提供经费时，税收提供了一项稳定的收益来源。由于能刺激经济活动的增长，公共政策对整合经济活动进行正式治理，税收横跨了其中许多领域。

财政政策中，描述的所有贸易和投资的相关事项都是真实的。非洲国家面临的主要挑战是找到一种最佳平衡，可以既有利于社会的税收制度，又能促进地方经济发展活动的投资。

大部分非洲国家都对外国直接投资特别重视，因为他们认为外国直接投资会对他们国家的发展有决定性影响。在非洲，特别是在刚果民主共和国，外国投资被视为是拉动经济增长的引擎，它们为投资提供所需资本，并增加东道国的工业竞争力。外国资本能帮助支持本地企业，应鼓励它们更多投入人力资本中。外国直接投资是一项创造就业岗位的资本来源，并且能为当地企业打开海外市场、引入新技术。

为了管理和制定最理想的财政政策，非洲的政府官员们必须面对挑战，在以下

的 优先事项目中保持一种平衡:（1）调动资源，扩大收税基础，确保落后的发展融资有收入，确保税收多样化，尤其是在海关关税自由化严重压榨税收的情况下。（2）打击避税逃税现象，打击缺乏可行规则造成的逃税现象和某些公司的逃税行为。（3）清理高度依赖重税的投资发展环境。（4）促进基于有效税收的良好监管，重申政府和投资界的责任。

税收有利于帮助全体非洲国家的政府完成他们的千禧年目标。非洲各国政府将税收用于:（1）资助他们在社会和基础设施方面的需求。（2）营造一个稳定可预测的环境，推动经济增长和投资。（3）通过调整政府与行政相对人的关系结构，支持政府的良好治理，配合政府职责。（4）确保公平分享发展成果，分担发展代价。

要着重注意的是，一个国家的经济增长和投资活力最终都要受到税收的影响。引入新科技、新技能和资本的外国投资者们在增加新的就业岗位中作用重大。因此他们需要一个明确的税收政策，以顺利实现他们的交易和更好地发展。

然而，许多非洲国家信赖经济发展与合作组织的相关研究，使其税收结构极为复杂，而该结构成为减缓那些有增长潜力公司的商业活动的原因之一。

应当注意，健康的财政政策能提升公司运营的环境，鼓励国际贸易和投资。它允许对经济增长的刺激。外国直接投资对东道国的税收改革的态度可能取决于该国中最普遍的条件情况如何，这是投资者们竭力想了解的。

总体来说，几乎所有非洲国家采纳的财政政策包含旨在拓宽税种降低税率的措施。在已实施的税收改革中，我们可以明确看到以下趋势：引入增值税；降低自然人和公司的所得税税率；增加应纳税额；降低出口关税，简化税率结构；废除出口税；限制偏向投资者的特殊奖励措施。

由此，非洲国家得以建立一套透明可靠的税收制度并在税收的资助下提供公共服务。

（一）刚果民主共和国财政政策

1. 刚果（金）税收简述

刚果（金）的税收制度是申报所得税和财产税，需要了解的有五种税：非个人所得税；所得税；针对本国侨民特别所得税；针对侨民的最低税；增值税。

2. 非个人所得税

（1）与是否修建不动产有关的土地税。修建与否的依据是不动产类型与城镇道路规划。

（2）针对水陆空等使用发动机的交通工具税。该项税的税率根据每种交通工具的重量和耗能设定。

（3）租金所得税。针对在刚果民主共和国国内土地和建筑物的租金所得。

（4）针对采矿业和烃类物开采的税。其合理性在于，是专有开采或科研的特许。该项税的税率设定依据是每公顷的开采量和开采物种类（矿物或烃类物）。

（5）动产税。其来源有：① 利息收入或股份收入。② 债务所得。③利用从专业人员借入的资本产生的所得。④ 利润分成。⑤ 版税净值。⑥ 按部门进行的分配，其来源有减价拍卖或使社会资本降低的其他事项。⑦ 所得税收益：A. 所有商业交易、家庭小工商业、农场或现实中的施舍优惠带来的收益。B. 自由职业者、劳工、办公室人员或其他任何职业的收入利润。C. 存在风险的商业带来的利益。

（6）分期缴税：在 8 月 1 日前预交第二财政年度的第一笔税款，并于 12 月 1 日评估前年度业绩。在纳税人为财政年度应缴税额的平衡做打算时，分期税款已经从那时的税款报表中减去了。

（7）针对支出的特别税：

A. 海关关税，享有进口权者要缴纳关税，以保护国内生产，让它们能与外国相竞争。提供财政补助资源，旨在打击出口原材料。

B. 交通运输税和消费税，它们针对一切支出和与奢侈品、快速消费品、污染性或有害的化学物质有关的产品。

C. 转让税的支付和注册费：在资金流转中要负担这些税费。

D. 增值税：在经济术语中，增值额被理解为公司生产的商品或提供的服务的价值与为中间消费而产出的商品服务价值的差额。

我们很快在每个阶段的生产分配找到了方法。每家公司都本应当按其最终阶段生产的增值比例纳税，这部分可由负债最少的卖家来支持。合理的销售税额是基于最终价格而非商品标签来征收的，这使得生产和为渡口上可征税的货物服务提供买家成为可能，渡口是相应征税领域的运营商，这是因为其运营事业的本质，或出于对法律的选择或社会的选择。

在渡口的运营管理下，整合出了以下三点须知标准：有形动产的交付，经济和服务活动的执行，支付与交税。

（二）刚果民主共和国的财政状况

参考刚果民主共和国 2003 年 3 月 13 日的 2003 年第 4 号法律。

税收改革的明显特征有：① 有关税收程序的法律条文的统一，使之成为刚果民主共和国征税程序的第一部法典。② 取代原有角色，改掉试图预先掌控发布材料并预警的观点。③ 折扣力度从 5% ～ 10% 到惯例中的 15% ～ 30%，以此建立税收，恢复剩余部分的管理实施，要根据法律经济的可控参数，鼓励国税局迅速执行任务。④ 广泛的支付程序机制要考虑偏见带来的麻烦，善意纳税人不应面对针对财富权利的偏见。⑤ 在流失大量税收时，处罚相关税收的活动主体。

2003 年第 4 号法律解释了 2003 年 3 月 13 日税收改革的程序，共围绕总体经济的五方面：

1. 明确规定的义务

债券是必不可少的。

活动之初：使纳税人了解国税局的税额计算方法是强制义务，这部分将会在地址注册后报给纳税人。

在活动实施中:（1）汇报会影响税收因素或解散公司的事件的义务。（2）签认清理超期申报的车辆所有权的义务，这些车辆的减价销售是每笔税收债务的必要附加项。

2. 管理与控制

行政机关享有在现场准确检查所有含借款人签名（借款情况）的专有权力，在某些情况下可行使任意检查权。

当涉及商业方法时，我们需要谨记：

（1）对房屋保证的管控不一定要拘泥于当场进行，除非纳税人请求在他建议的场所或在行政机关服务期间进行权。

（2）在发出第一次警告前的至少 8 天内，国税局机构要向纳税人明确税收内容和宽限期，以帮助其决策。

（3）某种税或规定的时间不能在欺诈调查已预先存在的情况下再次检验。

（4）减少了 5 年到 10 年的行政记录。

（5）在双方矛盾的程序纠正中，举证责任在行政机关。

（6）政府可以采用合适方法检验纳税人的材料，最终经电脑统算。

3. 涵盖项目

在减价拍卖车辆时，相关的税首先转让给债主。当人们在按次序缴纳不同种类的税时，上述税额也一并缴纳。

按计划收取的分期付款包含了按其他手续雇佣的所得税和由用人单位培训产生的所得税。

4. 处罚

法律中有以下处罚：

（1）在法律存在滞后、不准确、不完整或虚假的表述时，为削弱表述缺陷的影响而缴纳的罚款。

（2）对当晚延迟缴纳税款或其他应付款的制裁而缴纳的罚金。

（3）税收核算和手段，以及纳税人、债权人和其他将会失去财产的权利人的行为，都是罚金要压制的对象。

（4）债券中针对有产阶层的那部分作为财务制裁。

（5）与违反税收规定相关的刑事处罚。

5. 主张和求助

认为其缴纳税款没有法律依据或超额的纳税人，可将他的主张交至征税负责部门的管理者或政府官员。

行政机关必须对这一决定做出回复。管理者或政府官员应在税款支付或收到意见的 6 个月内回复。此处的有争议不需要实际证明是真实的。对反馈决议可以表示反对，之后才可以上诉。法院在收到决定通知的 6 个月内审理案件。在此期间，政府部门不出庭视为不同意该诉讼请求。

总体来说，过去的十年被认为是刚果民主共和国税收改革发展迅速的十年，刚果税收制度曾繁重、无效、复杂、碎片化。税收种类都相近，税额重复累加。

（三）税收与外国投资

任何当代国家都希望实现其社会、经济和政治发展。我们知道，在生产领域投资能创造财富，实现上述突破。

刚果民主共和国不会在此规则下受损。它的目标是在发展投资中经济繁荣且具有竞争力。它将通过与投资有关的税收策略来专门刺激几项改革。

为了确保经济管理，提升司法案件条件，要检查这些税收策略。投资能刺激经济发展并延长就业。

在全球或区域框架下，税收使得对存款的处理成为一项挑战。

刚果民主共和国的税收制度是提升司法案件条件和引导经济政策的工具。这来源于它独特的吸引和鼓励投资的多种方法。

1969 年 6 月 26 日，第一部投资法—惯例法 64/032 号颁布。这部法律后来被 1979 年 9 月 27 日惯例法 79/027 号取代。在它之后颁布了 1986 年 3 月 12 日 86-033

号惯例法。

大量的（现行）法律出自 2002 年 2 月 21 日 004/2002 号法律。

现行法律追求以下目标：（1）对创办负责建筑施工的土木工程公司进行支持，并与和水陆空的乘运货运相关的道路或高速公路（建设公司）商讨合作。（2）对发展机械化的农业和农用工业的投资进行支持，以确保国内粮食自足，减少主要产品的问题。同时，允许增长乡下公社的收入，提高食品加工业的原材料供给。最终侧面上丰富消费物品。（3）对能稳定物价和国内自然资源价格的投资进行支持，同时增加可出口量和附加税。

所有人都可接受的投资受一系列有条件的法律的管控：

（1）随后将成为刚果（金）经济体的权利；（2）最少要达到 200000 美元；（3）在责任感和总体框架正常运作下减少其国内员工培训；（4）尊重环境和自然保护规则；（5）确保附加值率不少于 35%。

法律通过后，各类投资的收益期间与其刺激领域有关：（1）在经济领域 A 的投资为 3 年；（2）在经济领域 B 的投资为 4 年；（3）在经济领域 C 的投资为 5 年。

法律还设置了一系列有利条件：

1. 海关关税优惠

除了行政专有投资，用于公众领域的投资享受免进口新机器、工具、设备和一流备件的进口税和免进口权责的优待。将对上述设备的需求上报投资促进署并获得通过后，海关税不超过到岸价格的 10%。

除了行政专有的海关税，官方批准进口的设施 5% 的到岸价格。创办新公司或已创办社团必需的设备中，不超过 10% 到岸价的机器、工具和备件免除出口权责和出口税。二手重型机器、船、飞机可以获得免税。

免除进口税和进口权责要服从以下条件：（1）刚果民主共和国国内不生产的相关产品。（2）经全国监管的互联网公司产品的税收，和进口产品相比，价格超过 10%。

计划将其终端产品全部或部分出口的投资，经批准，在有利于支出平衡的条件下运转，可免除出口权限和出口税。初次出口要上交海关文件方能免除税费。

2. 税收刺激和参与税

批准通过的新投资可以享受所得税全额免税。在新投资成立或投资的社会资本有所增长时，有限责任联合股份公司（即现在的有限公司）被批准免除相应比例的权利，参考针对上市公司的 1887 年 2 月 27 日法令第 13 款的设置。

公共基础设施包括学校、医院、体育器材和与上述地点相通的道路等，对应的社会经济投资，根据贬值减值的相关规则可获得偿还。获批准的公司免除地税、财产特许和根据投资计划建设的部分。

此外，那些购买当地生产设备的资本并在刚果民主共和国工业化中获得或要求获得房地产工程服务的人，可免除这些产品和服务的营业税。应当注意的是，这些海关关税、税收优惠和参与税计划是曾经在投资法律中规定的。

3. 对中小企业的特别措施

根据总体规定的设置，中小企业可免税。符合第 2 条 h 款所写条件的计划投资人将免除下列进口税和相关义务，包括机器、设备和工具，不超过上述设备 10% 到岸价的设备、审批通过的工业生产投资。否则，他们可以获得应税利润消息信息，改善承包商和他的工作人员，保护和自然保护，除了根据减少的份额计算其折旧。最后，对合伙企业、公司以及个人财产的商业和贷款登记的注册费的免除，能使他们获益。

4. 投资者安全与保证

外国自然人与刚果（金）本国自然人获得同等待遇，适用国内同一平等保护原则，即国家对遭遇危险的自然人有责任。刚果民主共和国致力于确保国际法原则下对投资者、领土内的投资行为的公平待遇，除非其权利行使是虚假错误的。投资者筹集分配的私人财产受宪法保护。投资不能直接或间接完成部分或完全国有化，或通过新法律和地方当局的决定部分或完全国有化，除了出于公共服务、实现公平支付和平等补偿津贴的原因。

刚果（金）保证外国公司向国外转账的自由。这与根据中央控制的投资运作和其股利的转移相关，就如同再投资于公司的股息产生的收入一样。它保证刚果（金）公司收到特许权使用费的主要及相关利益的转让，在投资法律下，这些公司以债务的名义签订合同来为投资募资。付给第三方的津贴不允许转移。

刚果民主共和国的外国直接投资事务。

法律定义了：

（1）外国指导的投资：用于建立维系新公司的投资；针对货物服务生产能力，用于机器化生产，提高公司生产力的投资；用于提高货物服务质量的投资。

（2）外国直接投资：外国参与投资至少达到 10%的投资。

（3）外国投资者：居住在国外的非刚果（金）籍自然人，在刚果（金）领土外没有注册的公 / 私法人，并在刚果民主共和国内进行直接投资。

刚果民主共和国是一个发展中国家，其生存环境的现状是，国家间的竞争增加，国家间吸引力越来越大，吸引了大量的直接外国投资。

由于在 1974 年扎伊尔时期刚果（金）国内的许多错误会议的影响，刚果民主共和国仍然是在一个外国投资者记忆中有非常残酷的回忆的国家。但从那之后，刚果（金）采取了一系列改革措施：

（1）支持面向国际市场开放。

（2）增加面向国外的股票推广，尝试让有资质能力的管理者向投资者解释，说服他们在刚果当地开展业务，但只有少量外国直接投资流入刚果（金）。

对政府当局首脑来说，关键是要成功说服外国投资者。实现这一假设，要努力采取一系列特别措施：

（1）提高国家对经济政策的了解水平。

（2）改善与接受外国直接投资有关的制度设置，实施相关战略，促进刚果成为一片欢迎外国直接投资的大陆的形象。

（3）积极的经济外交的姿态，以发展刚果和外国的公司之间、广播之间和经济及法律信息出版社之间的伙伴关系等，以便了解刚果民主共和国的资产和投资机会；

（4）解决土地和行政问题对投资造成的所有常见障碍。

（5）为外国投资提供赠款和其他财政援助。

（6）软化选择条款，使项目许可程序合理化，并加快批准程序。

应该承认的是，刚果民主共和国是一个具有巨大经济潜力，应该吸引许多外国直接投资的国家。几项研究致力于分析外国直接投资在刚果（金）的演变问题，这些研究显示，进入刚果（金）的外国直接投资与进入世界的投资相比，是微不足道的。

根据 2007 年世界投资报告，0.028% 的世界外国直接投资进入刚果（金）。

外国对刚果直接投资起初不平衡地开展于四个主要经济活动领域：交通和通信；碳氢化合物；服务；工业。

阻碍刚果吸引外国直接投资主要体现在三方面：腐败；政治不稳定；国家的风险状况。

我们要看到，目前大量改革正在进行。它们将改善商业环境以吸引大量外国投资者。我们要不懈努力。因为只要能根除上述三个阻碍，再多的努力也是值得的。

Impact of the fiscal policies of the African countries on the foreign direct investment

Author: Moke Maye

At first sight sounds pretentious to release the impact of the fiscal policies of the African countries on the foreign direct investment as well he is real as very African country has a separate reality and who has supposed to tackle it matters of the fiscal policies and the attraction of the direct foreign investments.

But seen closely that fear is only apparent when we know all the African savings are characterized by several important what their strong habit from the outside. It is the savings essentially extroverts and largely financed y the contributions outside and proceeds of exploitation.

On the other hand in the several decades 70, African countries designed a program development is finality to offer them the more people living conditions. To achieve this goal the states users must answer two demands to know the increase of internal revenue and the attraction of foreign investments.

In that order of ideas the definition of a clear fiscal policy so that the cleansing of the climate of the case is two basic steps on the economic development program.

The taxation plays a crucial role in the African countries. It is that it provides a steady flow of the proceeds to finance the development goals such as the pose of material infrastructure.

He is riding in many their areas of public policy things from the governance of the integration of the economic activity in the formal through the stimulation of the growth.

All things considered the fiscal policy states part which trade and the investments are true.

The main challenge for the African countries is in finding optimum balance between a tax system that is in favor of society and the investments who contribute to local development and economic activity.

Besides most African countries tie a particular importance of foreign direct investment (IDE) whose role is considered to be determining for their development.

In Africa, in general as a Democratic Republic of Congo in particular, foreign investments are considered a growth engine insofar as they provide the necessary capital for the investment and increase competition in industries of the host country.

They contribute to the kind of support local businesses encouraging them to become more productive y investing in human capital.

The direct foreign investments are a source of capital of job creation and bear the access to the overseas markets and bring new technologies for local businesses.

To manage, to make an optimal fiscal policy, the African agents must face the challenge to maintain a balance between the next priority lists:

- To mobilize the resources and to widen the taxability to ensure the recipes for stale funding from the development and diversify the taxability especially in the context of the liberalization of customs tariffs that deteriorates the revenues from taxes heavily
- To fight against the tax evasion fed by the tax havens insufficiencies the rules of practical and some of the companies
- To clean up the climate of the investment and development that depends largely on the tax diet
- To promote the good governance that is based on an effective taxation reaffirming responsibility for governments and the community of the investments.

The taxation contributes in total helping African countries to wait for their goals of the millennium for the government.

The African governments can use the taxation for:

- To finance their needs in the social domain and equipment for the infrastructure
- To setup a stale and predicable environment, to promote economic growth and investment
- To support the good governance and the responsibility for the leaders through the structure of the relationship between you and the controlled surfaces.
- To make sure that the cost and advantages of development are shared in a fair way.

It is important to note that ultimately economic growth and the dynamics of the investment of a country are subject to have the influence of the taxation.

Foreign investors who bring new technologies, a new skill and capital play an important role in the growth, job and the new.

So they need a policy clear duty to carry out their transactions and to develop.

However most African countries, to believe to the relevant studying OECD, of them are characterized by a tax complex structure which exerts an element of braking on the activity of the company close by the growth possibilities.

It should be noted that a healthy fiscal policy improves the environment in which companies are on their activities and encourages the international trade and the investment. It allows promoting economic growth.

A probable response from direct foreign investment in the tax reform adopted by the host country depends costs a large measure on the condition that prevail in this country.

On the whole, the fiscal policies adopted by almost all of the African countries consist of adoption measurement of aiming at widening the taxable amount as narrow the rates. We can clearly see the next tendencies operated in the tax reform:

- Introduction of the tax on added-value,
- Lowering on the income tax rates on the income from the natural people and benefit of the corporation,
- Widening the taxable of the dosage,
- The discount of rights to the imports and simplification of the structure of rates,
- Abolish the export taxes
- Limitation of the resort to specific incentives in favor of investors.

It is that of the African countries to setup a transparent and reliable tax system and be able to offer public services funded by the revenues taxes.

The fiscal policy in DRC

The Congolese tax system is declaratory income-tax and belonging. He has four kinds of taxes to know:

- Non-personal set taxes,
- Taxes on the income,
- The special tax on remunerations of expatriates
- The tax minimum for expatriate
- The tax on the added-value.

Non-personal taxes:

- Tax on the land which is about the properties built and not built according to the nature of buildings and the line of the towns.
- The tax on the vehicles that hit the engine machines used as air transport, earth and marine. The rate of this tax is set according to the weight and the power of every kind of vehicle.
- Income tax rental: hits the income from the rental su-renting or from the buildings and land DRC located in.
- The tax on the surface of the claim mining and hydrocarbons shoots the surfaces of the concessions answered either for the exploitation or for research in exclusive title. His tax rate is set according to the surface a hectare of claim according to whether it is the exploitation of mines or hydrocarbons.
- The movable tax which is taken from:

1. Income from the interest or shares.
2. Income from obligations,
3. Income from the capital borrowed from professionals ends.
4. Percentages
5. Net value of the royalties.
6. They are distributed in case of division to have her social in consequence of fire sale or

different causes made deduction of the social capital really free rest my money back.

7. The income tax benefits and sitting on:

a. The benefit of all the businesses, industrial and commercial homemade, farm or real including any liberalities and benefits.

b. Profits that either the denomination of the liberal professions, load, offices or any other occupation.

c. Profits whatever the nature of business at stake here-high.

- Tax installments: are versed before August 1st(deposit first) and before December 1st deposit of the year of achievement assessed the income and I represent 10% of the tax reported in the name of the increased previous exercise of the possible complete set by theirs. These installments are to be deduced from tax that had by the taxpayer for the fiscal year considered the balance had to be paid at the time of related the statement.
- Special tax on expenses:

  Customs duties: the rights to the imports do that to protect the domestic production against foreign competition and in second place to provide to the condition of the complementary fiscal resources.

The export homework that hit the exported raw materials consumer.

The tax traffic and excise homework that constitute a tax on expenses and what about: luxury products, fast-moving consumer goods, polluting chemicals or harmful.

The transfer tax payment and lead registration fee: they are loaded in the circulation of capital,

The tax on the added-value: in economic terms, the added-value is understood the difference between the value of the goods and services produced by a company and the goods and services for the production that is the intermediate consumptions.

We get way in a crack at every stage of a tour of production distribution, every company was supposed to contribute to the proportionately added-value he produced the final charge is supported by the last not indebted buyer of the ferry. The fine sale of tax is executed on the final price but stay independent of the economic tags made it possible to produce and put a buyer for the goods and services involved are taxable on the ferry, the operators who in the field of application of tax and it is because of the nature of the operation or by a quick shopping of the law or because of an option of society.

Subjugated these operations at the ferry to round up the next three criteria to know: delivery of the movable tangible property and performance of service activities, economic and lead payment, led taxable by a person.

Condition of the fiscal in DRC

With the law No.004/2003 March 13th, 2003 DRC.

The initiated a tax reform vast the characteristic features is:

1. Unification of all the procedures in a text, so that will be the first book of tax procedures in

the DRC.

2. The replacement of the role and climbed out of warning part y the opinion to cover (AMR).

3. The discount of the time remember from 10 to 5 and prescription from 30 to 15 and give the establishment of the tax and the manager of remains to be recovered are carried out according to the legal and economic controllable parameters and to encourage the IRS (Internal revenue service) to exercise his missions promptly.

4. Institution of the procedure of spreading out of payment to consider about the trouble with prejudice that taxpayers in good faith are faced and without prejudice to the value of the rights for the treasure.

5. Sanction by the end of the exercise of an activity subject to the tax without getting a number of tax.

The law number 004/2003 of the bearing march 13th 2003 tax reform procedures articulated is around five stocks for which it is general economy:

Titrate I: Declaratory obligations

Those bonds are indispensable so much on the beginning of the activity than in the exercise of the activities.

At the beginning of activities: it is the obligation to make himself known by formulating for tax number with the irs will deliver it to them after the certification of location.

In the exercise of activities: 1. Obligation to report any event that influence the taxable elements or puts an end to the business.

2. Obligation to sign to clean the deadline the declaration car belonging to fire sale could may annexes necessary by for every tax debt.

Titrate II: Control

The administration has the exclusive right check all parts on it at the scene of the accuracy of the signed by the debtors and executes in some cases the arbitrary checkup.

When it comes to the methods of business we need to write down the hereafter is projecting:

1. Control on the scene can proceed with the house of the undertaking unless the taxpayer solicits to happen in the buildings of his advice or the administration and during the hours from service

2. It can be realized only the agent for the irs equipped with an order of worm who must at least eight days before the first surgery warn the taxpayer using an opinion of checking in particular specifying the nature of the taxes and the time to be controlled straight from the taxpayer to assist the advice of his choice

3. A tax or an already ruled time cannot be checked out again in case of denunciation of the fraud investigation which have to establish the existence beforehand

4. That reduced remember the administration of ten to five years

5. In the contradictory procedures rectification the burden of proof is on the administration

6. The government can take appropriate tests on the material of the taxpayer when that last has computer accounting.

Titrate III: Covering

Taxes are implanted in priority by the debtors themselves in their statements car belonging to fire sale. They are paid at the time of people at the line attached to different kinds of taxes.

Statements and the thoughts to cover not followed by installment on schedule are subject to the charges in covering hired right by the income tax of no other formalities and trained by the users.

The rights of the treasure so determines statements in autoliquidatives or opinions to cover beneficent of a number of guarantees to knowing the right, the mortgage, solidarity in case of a multitude of the taxpayers.

Titrate IV: The penalties

The law has the penalty hereafter:

- The penalties of dish suppress the defects of statements taking into consideration legal delay, in accurate, in complete or false statements.
- The penalties of sanctioning covering the delay in the payment of the tax and other nights due.
- The fines to suppress a respect for the tax accounting and formalities as well as the behavior of the tax payer, the debtor or any other person tending to lose with the treasure had rights.
- The bonds that are financial penalties who hit the formal people though.
- Criminal penalties attached to the tax offenses.

Titrate V: Claims and resort

The taxpayer thinks who paid the fee required or do not have no legal basis or extra duties the address written his claim to the Director or the guy in charge of the service is at the bottom of the impositions argued.

The administration must answer this are decision of the Director or the guy in charge of the service is at the bottom of the impositions fought with 6 months from the payment or receiving the opinion to cover.

It is the contentious pretend here. The decisions of refection or do not fine satisfaction can be attacked before the appellate.

Court within 6 months from the notification of the decision. The absence of the decision of the administration within the time is equivalent to a denial.

On the whole, the present decade known at the acceleration of the tax reform DRC in the Congolese taxation is heavy, in effective, complex and fragmented. The taxes next to each other, there are a multitude tax Para taxes.

Taxation and foreign investments

Any modern State aspires to his social, economic development and politics. This breakthrough we know passes it especially for the creation of wealth from the productive investment.

The DRC does not derogate from this rule motivated by the problem of building a competitive and prosperous economy in the development of the investments, It will locked several reform inciting through tax devices with the investments.

Check these devices to ensure the regulation of the economy, to improve the climate of the case, the investment impel and perennialize job to his economic development.

The taxation became a challenge of positioning of the savings as well on an international frame as under-regional.

The DRC taxation is an instrument of improvement of the climate of the case and orientation of the economic policy. She got from her independence with a diversity measures likely to attract and encourage the investments.

The first code of the investments was sanctioned by the prescription-law No.64/032 June 26th, 1969. This code will be replaced by this set by the prescription-law No.79/027 September 27th, 1979. It will be followed by that sanctioned by the prescription-law No.86-033 March 12th, 1986.

The code in strength is part of that law No.004/2002 February 21st, 2002.

The current code pursues the goal hereafter:

- To support the establishment of the companies civil engineering in charge with construction and talk with the roads and highway like these of carrying the people and the goods that is the river, the transportation or air.
- To support the investments that develop agriculture and agro-industry by mechanization, to ensure self sufficiency food reducing the matters of the main products and at the same time allow the increase of the income in rural communes, the improvement of the supply the raw material industries food and finally in side deal enlargement of the consumer goods.
- To support the investments valorization of national natural resources at the scene to increase the added-value exportable and volume of it.

His investments acceptable to everyone have set of the code of the investments in conditions:

- later to be an economic entity of Congolese right,
- To have a minimum amount is equivalent to 200,000$,
- To kill himself national staff training with the functions of framing and responsibility,
- To kill you respecting the rules when it comes to environmental protection and nature conservation,
- To ensure an added-value rate of equal or greater than 35%.

The investments approved at the code will benefit from the related perks there for a length of:

- 3 years when they are executed in the economic area A,
- 4 when they are executed in the economic area B,
- 5 when they are executed in the economic area C.

The code is planning a number of advantages to know:

1. Customs benefits

Benefits other than the administrative royalty investments the use of public benefit from the total exoneration of the rights and import tax for the new machines, tools and equipment; the spare parts in first gear not exceeding 10% CIF price of the aforesaid equipment after presentation of their demands approved by the ANAPI.

Other than the administrative royalty from customs officials set at 5% CIF of imported facility approved the companies has the total exoneration of the rights and exports tax for the machines, the tools and the spare parts in first gear not exceeding 10% CIF price of the aforesaid necessary equipment to the installation of a new company or an existing society. The heavy machinery, the ships, the plane of second hand is accepted in total exoneration.

The exemption of rights and import tax is subject to the conditions hereafter:

- The thing concerned cannot be made in DRC,
- The price tax internet company came back from national superior product is of more than 10% compared to the price of the imported stuff.

The approved investments that plan the whole export or part of their end products, worked or e-worked under the favorable conditions for balance of payments have the exemption from the rights and exports tax. This exemption is from the first export, the customs documents getting caught

2. Tax incentives and Para tax

The benefit led by approved the new investments are completely exonerated of the contribution on the income.

At the time of their constitution or increase in their social capital, the joint stock company with limited responsibility (now limited companies) exonerated are approved from the right proportional planned to article 13 of the order of February 27th, 1887 on the marketing companies so far as altered.

The socio-economic investments in infrastructure as schools, hospitals, sports equipment and roads led by the way of projects are approved redeemable according to the rules of depreciation of diminishing values.

The companies are approved exonerated of the contribution on the surface of the land and the concessions properties and built it for the surface only related to the investment plan.

Besides, those of the ones who buy the local producers capital equipment and intrans made in industrial DRC or of request the services on real estate works are exonerated of the contribution to the turnover in on these products and services. It should be noted that these customs, tax benefits and Para tax plan in the code of the investments are given once.

3. Specific measures in PME and PMI

PME or PMI receive the exemptions planned with the general set. People who lead an investment plan under the conditions in article 2 subparagraph h benefit from the total exoneration of the rights and import tax for the machines and the equipment, the tools of second gear not exceeding 10% CIF price of the aforesaid facilities, industrial intrans to production of the approved investment.

Otherwise they are allowed to take their taxable profit are spent in formation, improvement of the contractor and his staff, the protection and nature conservation and in addition to calculate their depreciation according to a decreasing diet. Finally they profit from the exemption of rights on the deeds of corporate partnership or cooperative and the registration fee to the registry of business and loan on personal property.

4. Guarantees and safety of the investor

Foreign natural moral people and receive treatment identical to that of the Congolese natural people or moral subject to the application of the same principle of equal treatment by the State that the natural person or morals at stake in amenable.

The DRC is committed to ensure a fair and treatment according to the principles of international law, the investors and investments ran over his territory and doing the exercise of the right so confessed is neither right nor in fact.

The rights of the personal properties collective and granted by an investor are guaranteed by the constitution.

An investment cannot right or indirectly in his whole or partially nationalized expropriated or by a new law and or a decision of a local authority having the same effect except for the reasons of public service and realizing the payment of fair and equitable compensatory allowance.

The State guarantees the freedom of transfer abroad, is connected to the operations of investments according to central control and the transfer of their dividends just like that of the income generated by the dividends reinvested in the company.

He guarantees the transfer of the royalties' main interest and the related to change to be accepted by a Congolese company on a diet plan by the code of the investments in the name of the debt contracted abroad for the funding for the investment. No allowance due to a stranger is transferable.

Matter of direct foreign investments in DRC

The code defines:

- The investment foreign direct: investment like any under consideration by a new company to exist or putting target a production capacity of the goods or services of the service through the thing done in or manufactured goods, increasing production of the company or at improving the quality of goods *or* services.
- The foreign direct investment: any investment whose foreign participation in the investment executed at least is equal to 10%.
- Foreign investor: very natural person not nationality and Congolese residing abroad and no public or private legal person having his seat outside the Congolese territory and who takes a direct investment in DRC.

The DRC is a developed country under a rule that grew more and more competition and a passion between the countries to attract much the direct foreign investments in the country.

The DRC is still a country where the foreign investors have very cruel memories in their memory because of many misdeeds meetings in the country at the time of cups zairianisation 1974.

Yet the DRC with undertaken since then to setup a series of reform aiming in

Supporting has opening on the international market.

Multiply that stock promotion abroad and trying to get a performance out of the executives capable qualified to explain and convince the investors to locate their activities on the Congolese ground. But there is little influx of IDE in DRC.

It is essential to the head of the political authority to succeed in convincing the foreign investors.

Assume this effort a series of special measures:

- To improve the sight of the State on the level of the economic policy;
- To improve the institutional setting relating to the reception of the IDE, the implementation of a strategy to promote the image of the DRC as a land of welcome IDE;
- The pose of an active economic diplomacy to develop the partnership between the Congolese and foreign companies and the broadcast and the publication of economic and legal information to make known the assets of the DRC and investments opportunities.
- Lifting of all the usual obstacles to the investment in this land and administrative problems,
- To give grants and other financial aid to the foreign investments,
- To soften the terms of selection and to rationalize the procedures of approval or the acceleration of the permits from the projects.

He should be acknowledged that the DRC is a country with the huge economic potentialities and who should have attract many direct foreign investments.

Several studies devoted to the question of the evolution of IDE in DRC to show that they are insignificant compared to the flow of IDE which enter in the world.

According to the world report on the investment in 2007, IDE entering in DRC does not mean that 0,028% of flow enters in the world IDE.

In additional the IDE to the DRC is unequally starting in four main areas of the economic activity to know:

- Transportation and communication,
- The hydrocarbons and the services
- And finally industry

The attractively IDE of the DRC is in stop by three main obstacles:

- Corruption,
- Political instability
- And the situation of country at risk.

You must know a lot of reform was undertaken to improve the climate of business and to attract a lot of foreign investors.

This effort is worthy to be insufficient as long as these three plagues are not eradicated.

非洲国家有关境外直接投资之税收政策概述

作者：Stephen 译者：朱萸

一、简介

在驱动全球化的进程中，私人投资属于主导力量之一。仅跨境投资流量就在过去的十年间增长了二倍，外资股总量目前已为全球国民生产总值（GDP）的二倍。私人投资是经济增长的强效催化剂；就从亚洲到北美的新兴经济体而言，私人投资也是稳步解决贫困难题的攻坚力量。然而，要想收获私人投资的上述红利就必须以审慎的态度制定引导私人投资的政策。①

税收刺激并不能弥补被投资国投资环境的固有缺陷，亦无法激发原本期待的外部效应。但当如基础设施、交通费用、政治经济环境稳定性等其他因素相差无几的情况下，意向投资地的税收状况在投资者的决策中就会占据重要分量。但由于税收分配、跨国公司性质，以及投资国和被投资国间税收系统的关系等变量的影响，前述分量在具体被投资国间不尽相同。

20 世纪 90 年代，随着越来越多的政府争相吸引跨国公司进驻，财政刺激手段逐渐在全球流行开来。贫穷的非洲国家依赖免税期和进口关税豁免吸引外资，而发达的西欧国家则采取投资津贴鼓励和加速折旧等不同手段。值得深思的是，当前政府是否为吸引外资而采取了过于宽松的激励政策？

本文旨在综述当前税收外国直接投资（FDI）的基本学说，并拓展深化本领域研究的可能性。

① Schekulin M. Investing for development: The Policy Framework for Investment, OECD Observer No 251, September 2005 retrieved from http://www.oecdobserver.org/news/archivestory.php/aid/1673/ on 23-05-2016.

墨瑞斯特（Morisset）和皮尼亚（Pirnia）认为，税收优惠既无法弥补被投资国投资环境的固有缺陷，亦不能激发原本期待的外部效应。提高人力资源和基础设施建设、并在必要时优化政府决策和行政程序的长期策略相较于税收优惠而言更能吸引到优质的长期投资。但最近的情况表明，在其他因素如基础设施、交通费用、政治经济环境稳定性等相差无几的情况下，意向投资地的税收状况在投资者的决策中就会占据重要分量。[①]

然而，这种影响并非直接。它可能取决于当局运用的税收工具、跨国公司性质，以及投资国和被投资国间税收系统的关系等变量。举例来说，对移动通信公司、在多类市场占有份额的公司，及对住所地免除外国所得税（如加拿大、法国）的公司而言，退税更为重要；而住所地采取税收优惠制度（如日本、英国及美国）的公司可能并不会将是否退税作为核心条件进行考量。

即使税收优惠在提高投资流方面的效果立竿见影，其政策成本很可能远高于收益。税收优惠不仅可能对财政收入造成消极影响，亦有极大的概率增加海关和公司的不法行为。上述成本在新兴经济体中更为瞩目，因为他们相较于发达国家而言面临更严重的财政限制和官僚腐败。墨瑞斯特和皮尼亚建议在如下五个方面进行深入研究：

（1）税率对跨国公司投资决策的最终非线性影响。

（2）税收政策对外国直接投资分布的影响（如未开发地区，再投资收益及企业兼并与收购）。

（3）税收优惠敏感型的新兴科技和跨国公司的发展。

（4）跨国公司税收标准全球化的需求。

（5）税收优惠是否仅当提供给符合被投资国价值观（如生产环保产品）的（外国）投资者，或广泛地向提供工作、技术转移、市场营销技巧等的投资者倾斜。

二、税收政策之基线

政策分析必须建立在一个或多个经济模型之上，并模拟多种可能的情况，以便更好地指导有关外国直接投资的税收政策。模型包括：（1）国际生产折中理论（OLI）；（2）经济合作与发展组织（OECD）有关投资的模型；（3）新古典主义投资

① Jacques Morisset, Neda Pirnia How Tax Policy and Incentives Affect Foreign Direct Investment: A Review.

模型;(4)新地缘经济模型。本文将着重解构 OLI 和 OECD 模型。

(一)OLI 模型

本折中主义模型建立于经济学理论的基础上,由约翰·H. 邓宁(John H. Dunning)于 1979 年从内部化理论发展而来,又名 OLI 经济框架。① 内部化理论本身建立在交易成本理论的基础上。交易成本理论认为,当在自由市场的交易成本高于内部交易时,交易通常会倾向于在内部进行。这种过程被称作内部化。

折中主义模型试图将几个鼓励的国际经济理论通过该模型联成一体。公司的国际化行为可以归纳为以下三种分类:出口,外国直接投资和许可贸易。OLI 因素则为以下三种类型的优势:所有权优势,区位优势以及内部化优势。②

一个公司国际活动的前提是其拥有净所有权优势。这些优势既可以是实体的,也可以是非实体的。净所有权优势指一公司在外国和未知市场所占有的优势。邓宁认为,除公司结构之外的其他三个因素亦非常重要:③

1. 所有权优势(商标、生产技术、管理策略、规模收益):所有权实际转化为收益要求参与外国直接投资行为的企业拥有比较优势。参与投资的企业的比较优势越大,他们参与外国实际生产环节的概率也越大。

2. 区位优势(原材料、低薪、特种营业税或关税):区位吸引力指相较于其他潜在投资国家或地区而言,本地区对跨国公司的比较优势。本地区拥有越多的固定的、自然的或人为的资源,并且这些资源与跨国公司自身的比较优势结合的越紧密、利用越容易,就越可能吸引外商直接投资。

3. 内部化优势(优势并非来源于借助如许可证或联合经营等合作关系的经营,而是来源于企业自身):企业倾向于创造并利用核心竞争力。内部化跨国生产中间产品的净利润越大,公司就越有可能亲自参与外包的生产过程,而非仅仅止步于取得营业许可。

邓宁认为外国直接投资可以分为如下两种:

---

① Twomey, Michael J. (2000). A Century of Foreign Investment in the Third World (Book). Routledge. p.8. ISBN 0-415-23360-7.

② Hagen, Antje (1997). Deutsche Direktinvestitionen in Grossbritannien, 1871-1918 (Dissertation) (in German). Jena: Franz Steiner Verlag. p.32. ISBN 3-515-07152-0.

③ Dunning, John H. (2000-4). "The eclectic paradigm as an envelope for economic and business theories of MNE activity".

1. 资源寻求型投资：旨在获得基础生产资料，如原材料。

2. 市场寻求型投资：旨在进入某个既存市场，或开拓一新市场。

邓宁继而用效率寻求型投资，策略寻求型投资以及支持型投资细化了上述分类。①

在 OLI 框架下，包括外国生产产品在内的水平外国直接投资在 OLI 条件符合的情况下可以获得经营许可。首先，跨国公司必须拥有所有权优势（即专利、专有技术、商标），以及与本地公司相比在外国市场拥有利润优势。其次，外国直接投资必须拥有区位优势（廉价劳动力，交易、能源和税负），这些区位优势需使得本地生产较进口产品相比更有利润空间。最后，外国直接投资必须拥有国际优势，这些国际优势能使在外国市场上通过外国直接投资的生产经营较许可其他公司合作经营有比较优势。比如，公司可以对知识资本进行保值。垂直外国直接投资则是将生产过程中的特定阶段转移至外国，其考量因素与水平投资相似，均围绕所有权、区位和内部化优势。（OECD，2007 年）②

（二）OECD 主张的投资政策性架构

经济合作与发展组织（OECD）成立于 1961 年，拥有 34 个成员国，旨在促进经济进步和全球贸易。OECD 宣称，他们致力于民主和市场经济，提供一个比较治理经验的平台，为共性问题寻求解决方案，推广行之有效的经济实践，并协调其成员的国内国际政策。

OECD 投资政策构架（PFI）最早提出于 2006 年，旨在为发展中国家及转轨经济体的决策者们提供包括税收在内的十个领域的指导，使经济政策既重点突出又运转高效。其税收部分大部分来源于实地调查，意在比较公司税收优惠和其他替代税收政策的利弊及核心问题，制定切实吸引外资的政策，同时利用外资收益加强本国的基础设施投入。

首先，针对 PFI 的讨论需要在一定背景下进行。引进外资并不意味着万事大吉。相反地，外资只是保证经济发展的一种手段。发展中国家亦需要认识到，任何减少

① Twomey, Michael J. (2000). A Century of Foreign Investment in the Third World (Book). Routledge. p.8. ISBN 0-415-23360-7.

② OECD, 2007, Tax Effects on Foreign Direct Investment – Recent Evidence and Policy Analysis ISBN 978-64-03837-0.

贫困的政策都离不开私人企业的参与。前述共识促使182个国家和地区于2002年达成了蒙特雷共识（the United Nations Monterrey Consensus）。今年9月，联合国峰会进一步深化该共识，表示将以国内外私人资本流动化为手段，促进经济发展，最终实现联合国千年发展宣言的目标。

除此之外，PFI也是通过整体性政府深化蒙特雷共识的手段。狭义的投资政策并不能有效地吸引外资。相似地，考虑不周的招商引资策略可能使商业政策背离原定目标，甚至使私人投资者望而却步。比如提供税收减免的同时对外资企业征收其他名目的新税或利用外资去投资教育，对刺激外资的效果就较为有限，甚至会破坏原本良好的商业氛围。

OECD发布并持续更新税收协议的模型，该模型适用于有关税收协调和合作的双边谈判。OECD还对模型进行了一系列的评注，解决了OECD对模型实际应用中遇到的一系列问题。整体而言，该模型并非将掌控税收的话语权分配给被投资国（东道主国或来源国），而是将其归属于投资国（居住国或归属地国）。因而该模型在两个有互惠投资流的国家（如OECD的成员国们）之间更为有效，但若交易一方的经济实力明显弱于对方（如OECD成员国与非OECD成员国间）则有可能造成税负不公的后果。

自1998年起OECD就致力于整顿与税赋相关的不法行为，并着重打击避税天堂（然而，与此同时OECD也不顾潜在的税负竞争风险接受了其成员国的一系列税负政策）。这些举措自然也激发了不同的应对措施：最主要的反对声音认为，税赋事关一国主权完整，应少由他国置喙。[①]OECD曾有“不合作的避税天堂名册”，上面详细列出了据其考量在促进税赋公开及信息披露方面拒绝合作的国家。但2009年5月，OECD移除了所有榜上有名的国家。

2008年，在OECD的一次巴黎峰会上，以德国和法国为首的17个国家决定另起一份避税天堂的黑名单并要求OECD调查超过40个疑似为新避税天堂的国家。他们被指控隐瞒收益并包庇大量在2008年金融危机下监管外的对冲基金。德国、法国以及其他国家特别提请OECD将瑞士列入鼓励税收欺诈的黑名单中。

2014年10月29日，在柏林召开的全球税赋透明度和信息公开论坛上，所有OECD及G20成员国偕同时间主要国际金融机构签署了《多边主管当局协议》

① “Sanctions threat to ‘tax havens’”. BBC News. 2000-06-26. Retrieved 2016-05-20 http://news.bbc.co.uk/2/hi/business/806236.stm.

（multilateral competent authority agreement）。该协议旨在促进有关税赋的财政数据的自动共享。在《外国账户税收遵从法》（the Foreign Account Tax Compliance Act）下，美国将于2015年起和其他国家自动共享有关信息。2017年，英国、西班牙、法国、葡萄牙、塞浦路斯、马耳他、德国、意大利、英属马恩岛、泽西岛、根西岛、直布罗陀、百慕大、开曼群岛、英属维京群岛、爱尔兰、冰岛、列支敦士登、卢森堡、圣马力诺、塞舌尔、阿根廷以及南非等58个“元老级”签署者将启动信息自动共享进程。2018年，澳大利亚、奥地利、巴哈马、巴西、文莱、加拿大、中国、中国香港、中国澳门、卡塔尔、俄罗斯、新加坡、阿联酋及瑞士亦将加入这一进程。

三、税赋对FDI的影响分析

潜在投资者在投资的决策过程中，一个重要考量就是被投资国与投资国间是否拥有关税条约。关税条约的订立旨在避免重复征税。贝纳希（Bénassy-Quéré）、冯塔涅（Fontagné）和拉赫谢（Lahrèche-Révil）是税赋对外国直接投资重要考量理论的忠心拥护者。前述理论激起了巨大争议，主要因为许多有关外国直接投资的弹性的研究建立在纯经验主义的基础之上，并过于侧重税赋的影响。（贝纳希、冯塔涅和拉赫谢，2001年）[①]

究竟何种被投资国加以何种税赋才能实现双边共赢，其核心问题在于外资如何应对税赋。理解这一问题，被投资国需要认识到如何向外资施加合适的税赋压力。与此同时，进行免税条件下的投资成本/收益评估，及预估公司税赋政策对财政的影响也至关重要。(OECD，2008)

有关跨国资本流动的研究表明，平均而言，针对外资的税赋每增长1%，外资投入便减少3.7%。不过更大基数的研究与估值表明，外资投入减少的区间在0%至5%之间。区间的浮动鲜明地反映了样本行业和国家之间，及取样时间之间的差异。近期的研究则表明外资对税赋的敏感度正逐步走高，这也正反映了对于外资而言，资本的流动性所造成的阻碍不再。该类研究可供探求公司税赋对外资的长期影响之参考。(OECD，2008)

在预测外资如何应对税赋方面，税赋会对投资决策造成何种影响，以及投资者

① Rădulescua* Magdalena & Elena Druicab, The impact of fiscal policy on foreign direct investments. Empiric evidence from Romania DOI:10.1080/1331677X.2014.947133, pp.86-106.

对何种程度的税赋敏感均为其中的不确定因素。有研究将成文法规定的公司所得税（CIT，标题利率）为主要考量，有研究则着重于有效税率 (AETRs)，还有研究则认为边际有效税率 (METRs) 更好地反映了可被税利润的百分比。有效税率考虑投资项目的平均税负，而边际有效税率考察边际（被投资项目的最后一组资本，利润几乎为零）税负。成文法规定的税率可能和实际有效的税率相差甚远，以至于可被税利润与实际利润不成比例。①

近期研究表明，外资对税赋的敏感度取决于被投资国别及税赋下经营活动的自主性。该种自主性尤其体现在跨国公司从本地生产中减少的生产成本的比重。生产成本包括了交通运输费用，它直接被公司的区位选择所决定。投资国从经营活动中收益，并在被投资国投入了一定比重的固定生产资料。这一事实很好地证明了适当对外资企业征税不会打击外资积极性。

OECD 经济体中，拥有大体量出口市场和外资流的国家（如美国、日本和德国），其国内对公司营业征税相对较高。这一发现与前述结论是一致的。最新的研究模型也表明，理想的税赋能刺激交易成本下降，资本流动性增强，同时抑制外资过热。实践中，许多国家倾向于对流动性更强的行业（如造船业、电影业）减轻税赋。

四、肯尼亚税赋概述

肯尼亚各行业的营业税均为 37.5%。联合国贸易与发展会议 2005 年指出，自 1985 年起资本利得税便停滞不前，然而 2015 年肯尼亚政府重新开始征收资本利得税。联合国贸易与发展会议认为，肯尼亚的税收系统相较于其他发展中国家而言更为有效和公平，在财政收入占 GDP 百分比方面较非洲其他国家而言也有较大优势。

肯尼亚政府的财政刺激政策针对法人团体，出口加工区内的企业和在内罗毕股票交易所上市的公司。法人团体可享受多至 30% 的税收减免。出口加工区内的企业入驻前十年免于税赋，十年之后营业税率为 25%，其他税率参照同期立法标准。在内罗毕股票交易所上市的公司亦享受税收优惠：新上市的公司若保持 30% 至 20% 的浮动资本，则前五年可享受 25% 到 27% 的税率。

以制造业为代表的第二产业亦从针对建筑和其他资本支出的税收优惠中获益，而酒店业则仅从对建筑的优惠中获利。投资抵扣是企业第一年享受的折旧优惠。在

① OECD 2008, Tax Effects on Foreign Direct Investment, Policy Brief, February 2008.

2004年至2008年间，投资抵扣的折旧率达到了100%。然而2008年以后，折旧率处于持续震荡的状态。

肯尼亚已签署了八个双边税赋条约，其中包括引英国、加拿大和德国的外资进入肯尼亚的条约。投资国还包括丹麦、印度、挪威、瑞典及赞比亚，值得一提的是赞比亚是唯一与肯尼亚签署该类条约的非洲国家。1999年起东非国家间就有签署该类条约的尝试，然而尽管东非国家殷切地期盼着东非共同市场的建立，至今他们仍未签署双边税赋条约。

与澳大利亚近30%的营业税相比，肯尼亚的营业税相当之高。然而，肯尼亚的税率总体低于加拿大的综合税率（28%营业税+14%地方税）。

五、坦桑尼亚的税收政策

坦桑尼亚的营业税为公司所得的30%。农业、矿业、旅游业及制造业公司可享受税收优惠。购置生产设备的支出在37.5%的基础税率上根据具体生产设备种类享受25%或12.5%的不同程度的优惠或冲销。如特殊生产设备、渔业和酒店业营业第一年享受50%的津贴，第二年起按正常税率征税。

农业生产设备的购置享受免税待遇；厂房的支出享受5%的无条件折旧免税额；无形资产则享受使用周期内的免税待遇。农业企业亦享受上述优惠政策。用于农业、牲畜或渔业的建筑、水坝、水库、藩篱及类似生产资料享受5年内的无条件免税。矿业企业在采掘和技术研发方面享受100%的资本免税额。

坦桑尼亚拥有内陆加工出口区及桑给巴尔岛的经济特区。内陆加工出口区并非由政府主导建立，政府仅提供土地和利好政策，其成长有赖于私人资本扶植。有潜力将80%以上的产品出口的公司有资格获得内陆加工出口区的土地。桑给巴尔岛的经济特区则享受10年的免税期，免税期不覆盖股利、利息和其他交易所得、税后盈利汇返、25%的投资津贴及100%的所有权保留、生产及出口目的的免征进出口税，以及政府持有地的49年期低价地租，该地租租期可延长至98年。

与加拿大、丹麦、芬兰、印度、意大利、挪威、南非、瑞典和赞比亚的双边免税条约目前已生效，包括与乌干达订立的许多其他双边免税条约已经签订但尚未生效。坦桑尼亚企业税率与澳大利亚的税率相同，均为30%；较低于加拿大综合税率（国家28%税率加上地方征收14%的税率）。

OECD认为针对外资的税赋减免已成全球性共识。投资者与决策者均定期对税赋进行全球视野下的比较，比较的对象通常为区位相近或市场容量相当的国家。通常认为，税赋在被投资国经济水平相当及其他条件差别不大的情况下对投资者的投资决定有更大的影响。

国际税赋竞争日趋激烈，一被投资国当前看似优惠的税收政策也许与其他国家的其他时期相比优势不再。然而，税收减免并非吸引外资的充分条件。一国虽有相对较高的税赋，但在基础设施、公共服务上占优势；一国虽市场容量大，但政策优惠力度强，这样的两国在吸引外资方面并无明显差别。事实上，OECD 中有着较高有效税负的大国通常对外资更具吸引力，这体现了市场容量和他国认可对吸引外资的重要性，亦提示政府可利用财政杠杆打造区位特色。

六、结论

随着决策者逐渐减轻对内投资税负，被投资国进一步发展，国际经济新秩序的逐步建立，税赋竞争的影响应当放在更深远的语境下考量。

非洲国家应当警惕目前对农业企业过分的政策倾斜，及该政策可能对国际税收系统造成的失衡影响。各国亦应当采取适合国情的对内和对外投资税赋。决策者针对本国税收系统治理经验的信息共享也无疑是行之有效的解决策略。

非洲政府应当通过增加税收决策透明度及税收政策确定性来提高财政机构的威信；非洲政府还应当引进针对特定投资问题的提前应对机制。税收双边条约和约定则是保证双边投资的稳定性和确定性的关键所在。

The Impact of Taxation Policies of African Countries on Foreign Direct Investment

Author: Stephen

Introduction

Private investment is a dominant force driving globalization. Cross-border investment flows have tripled over the last decade alone and foreign capital stocks are now twice the size of global GDP. Private investment is acting as a powerful catalyst for growth and, as emerging economies from Asia to South America have shown, is one of the surest ways to sustained poverty reduction. But this requires having the right policies in place.①

Tax incentives neither make up for serious deficiencies in a country's investment environment nor generate the desired externalities. But when other factors—such as infrastructure, transport costs, and political and economic stability—are more or less equal, the taxes in one location may have a significant effect on investors' choices. This effect varies, however, depending on the tax instrument used, the characteristics of the multinational company, and the relationship between the tax systems of the home and recipient countries.

With an increasing number of governments competing to attract multinational companies, fiscal incentives have become a global trend that has grown considerably in the 1990s. Poor African countries rely on tax holidays and import duty exemptions, while industrial Western European countries allow investment allowances or accelerated depreciation. Have governments offered unreasonably large incentives to entice firms to invest in their countries?

The objective of this paper is to review the existing literature on tax policy and Foreign Direct Investment (FDI) as well as to explore the possibilities of further research.

Morisset and Pirnia observe that tax incentives neither make up for serious deficiencies in

---

① Schekulin M. Investing for development: The Policy Framework for Investment, OECD Observer No 251, September 2005 retrieved from http://www.oecdobserver.org/news/archivestory.php/aid/1673/ on 23-05-2016.

a country's investment environment nor generate the desired externalities. Long-term strategies to improve human and physical infrastructure—and, where necessary, to streamline government policies and procedures—are more likely than incentives to attract genuine long-term investment. But more recent evidence has shown that when other factors—such as infrastructure, transport costs, and political and economic stability—are more or less equal, the taxes in one location may have a significant effect on investors' choices.①

This effect is not straightforward, however. It may depend on the tax instrument used by the authorities, the characteristics of the multinational company, and the relationships between the tax systems in the home and recipient countries. For example, tax rebates are more important for mobile firms, for firms that operate in multiple markets, and for firms whose home country exempts any profit earned abroad (Canada, France) rather than using tax credit systems (Japan, the United Kingdom, the United States).

Even if tax incentives were quite effective in increasing investment flows, the costs might well outweigh the benefits. Tax incentives are not only likely to have a negative direct effect on fiscal revenues but also frequently create significant opportunities for illicit behavior by tax administrators and companies. This issue has become crucial in emerging economies, which face more severe budgetary constraints and corruption than industrial countries do. Morisset and Pirnia suggest research in five areas:

- The eventual nonlinear impact of tax rates on the investment decisions of multinational companies.
- The effect of tax policy on the composition of FDI (for example, greenfield, reinvested earnings, and mergers and acquisitions).
- The development of new technologies and global companies that are likely to be more sensitive to, and able to exploit, incentives.
- The need for a global approach to the taxation of multinational companies.
- The question of whether tax incentives should be directed only at (foreign) investors that make the "right things" (such as environmentally safe products) or more broadly at those that bring jobs, technology transfers, and marketing skills.

Taxation Policy Underpinings

To guide tax policy in relation to FDI, policy analysts may rely on one or more economic models or frameworks to examine possible channels of influence. These include:

a. the OLI framework;

① Jacques Morisset, Neda Pirnia How Tax Policy and Incentives Affect Foreign Direct Investment: A Review

b. the OECD policy framework for investment;

c. the neo-classical investment model;

d. models derived from the new economic geography literature.

This paper will briefly examine the OLI and OECD models.

1. The OLI model

The eclectic paradigm is a theory in economics and is also known as the OLI-Model or OLI-Framework,[①] which was derived from the internalization theory developed by John H. Dunning in 1979. Internalization theory itself is based on the transaction cost theory. This theory says that transactions are made within an institution if the transaction costs on the free market are higher than the internal costs. This process is called internalization.

The idea behind the Eclectic Paradigm is to merge several isolated theories of international economics in one approach. Three basic forms of international activities of companies can be distinguished: Export, FDI and Licensing. The so-called OLI-factors are three categories of advantages, namely the ownership advantages, locational advantages and internalization advantages.[②]

The precondition for international activities of a company is the availability of net ownership advantages. These advantages can both be material and immaterial. The term net ownership advantages is used to express the advantages that a company has in foreign and unknown markets. For Dunning, not only the structure of organization is important. He added 3 more factors to the theory[③]:

1. Ownership advantages (trademark, production technique, entrepreneurial skills, returns to scale) Ownership specific advantages refer to the competitive advantages of the enterprises seeking to engage in FDI (FDI). The greater the competitive advantages of the investing firms, the more they are likely to engage in their foreign production.

2. Location advantages (existence of raw materials, low wages, special taxes or tariffs) Locational attractions refer to the alternative countries or regions, for undertaking the value adding activities of MNEs. The more the immobile, natural or created resources, which firms need to use jointly with their own competitive advantages, favor a presence in a foreign location, the more firms will choose to augment or exploit their specific advantages by engaging in FDI.[④]

---

① Twomey, Michael J. (2000). A Century of Foreign Investment in the Third World (Book). Routledge. p.8. ISBN 0-415-23360-7.

② Hagen, Antje (1997). Deutsche Direktinvestitionen in Grossbritannien, 1871-1918 (Dissertation) (in German). Jena: Franz Steiner Verlag. p.32. ISBN 3-515-07152-0.

③ Dunning, John H. (2000-4). "The eclectic paradigm as an envelope for economic and business theories of MNE activity".

④ Twomey, Michael J. (2000). A Century of Foreign Investment in the Third World (Book). Routledge. p.8. ISBN 0-415-23360-7.

3. Internalization advantages (advantages by own production rather than producing through a partnership arrangement such as licensing or a joint venture) Firms may organize the creation and exploitation of their core competencies. The greater the net benefits of internalizing cross-border intermediate product markets, the more likely a firm will prefer to engage in foreign production itself rather than license the right to do so.

Dunning distinguishes between two different types of FDI. He stipulates that:

a. *resource seeking investments* are made in order to establish access to basic material like raw materials or other input factors,

b. *market seeking investments* are made to enter an existing market or establish a new market.

A closer distinction is made by Dunning with the terms efficiency seeking investments, strategic seeking investments and support investments.①

Under the OLI framework horizontal FDI involving production abroad can be expected in place of exports or licensing where OLI conditions are met. Firstly, a multinational enterprise must possess ownership advantages (that is patents, know-how, trademark) conferring profit advantage over local firms in foreign markets. Secondly, FDI must offer location advantages (low labor, trade, energy and taxation burden) that make local production more profitable than exporting. Thirdly, FDI must offer internalization advantages that make undertaking a business activity directly through FDI more profitable than licensing to other firms in foreign markets the right to use assets conferring ownership advantages, for example by safeguarding knowledge capital. Vertical decisions over locating or outsourcing certain stages of production to a foreign location similarly center on ownership, location and internalization advantages (OECD, 2007).②

2. OECD policy framework for investment

The Organization for Economic Cooperation and Development (OECD) is a 34-member organization founded in 1961 to stimulate economic progress and world trade. It is a forum of countries describing themselves as committed to democracy and the market economy, providing a platform to compare policy experiences, seeking answers to common problems, identify good practices and coordinate domestic and international policies of its members.

The OECD's Policy Framework for Investment (PFI) was first adopted in 2006. It is targeted at policy makers in developing and transition economies, and proposes guidance in ten policy fields including tax, in an effort to identify priorities and help develop effective policies. The tax chapter draws largely on survey studies to identify key issues in weighing the pros and cons of corporate tax

① Twomey, Michael J. (2000). A Century of Foreign Investment in the Third World (Book). Routledge. p.8. ISBN 0-415-23360-7.

② OECD, 2007, Tax Effects on Foreign Direct Investment – Recent Evidence and Policy Analysis ISBN 978-64-03837-0

incentives and alternative tax policies and design options to attract FDI, while also raising revenue from FDI to help finance infrastructure development.

First it is necessary to place PFI into context. Attracting investment is not an end in itself, but rather a means to sustain growth and development. The development community too has recognized the crucial role of private enterprise within any strategy aimed at reducing poverty. This common ground led to 182 governments adopting the United Nations Monterrey Consensus in 2002, and this September, the UN World Summit renewed its commitment to mobilizing private investment, both domestic and foreign, for advancing economic development and as a way to achieve the goals of the Millennium Declaration.

Against this background, the PFI is an initiative designed to advance implementation of the Monterrey Consensus through a whole-of-government approach. Just as a narrowly defined investment policy is not the best way to attract business investment, a poorly conceived investment attraction strategy may create incentives which distort business decisions, and in some cases even deter private investors. Providing tax concessions, for instance, will have a limited impact, or indeed do more harm to the business climate, if these are compensated by other new taxes, or draw funds away from education.

The OECD publishes and updates a model tax convention that serves as a template for bilateral negotiations regarding tax coordination and cooperation. This model is accompanied by a set of commentaries that reflect OECD-level interpretation of the content of the model convention provisions. In general, this model allocates the primary right to tax to the country from which capital investment originates (i.e., the home, or resident country) rather than the country in which the investment is made (the host, or source country). As a result, it is most effective as between two countries with reciprocal investment flows (such as among the OECD member countries), but can be very unbalanced when one of the signatory countries is economically weaker than the other (such as between OECD and non-OECD pairings).

Since 1998, the OECD has led a charge against harmful tax practices, principally targeting the activities of tax havens (while principally accepting the policies of its member countries, which would tend to encourage tax competition). These efforts have been met with mixed reaction: The primary objection is the sanctity of tax policy as a matter of sovereign entitlement.[①] The OECD used to maintains a "blacklist" of countries it considered uncooperative in the drive for transparency of tax affairs and the effective exchange of information, which was officially referred to as the "The List of Uncooperative Tax Havens" .[②] In May 2009, all remaining countries were removed from the list.

① Christians, Allison (August 29, 2008). "Sovereignty, Taxation and Social Contract" . Minnesota Journal of International Law 18.

② "Sanctions threat to 'tax havens'". BBC News. 2000-06-26. Retrieved 2016-05-20 http://news.bbc.co.uk/2/hi/business/806236.stm.

At an OECD meeting in Paris in the year 2008, 17 countries led by France and Germany decided to draw up a new blacklist of tax havens. The OECD was asked to investigate around 40 new tax havens in the world where undeclared revenue is hidden and that host many of the non-regulated hedge funds that came under scrutiny during the 2008 financial crisis. Germany, France, and other countries called on the OECD to specifically add Switzerland to a blacklist of countries that encourage tax fraud.

On October 29, 2014, in Berlin, during the Global Forum on Transparency and Exchange of Information for Tax Purposes, all OECD and G20 countries, as well as most major international financial centers, signed a "multilateral competent authority agreement" that will activate the automatic sharing of financial data for tax purposes. Under the Foreign Account Tax Compliance Act (FATCA), the United States will automatically exchange information with other countries beginning in 2015. In 2017, 58 jurisdictions of the "early adopters" —the UK, Spain, France, Portugal, Cyprus, Malta, Germany, Italy, Isle of Man, Jersey, Guernsey, Gibraltar, Bermuda, Cayman Islands, British Virgin Islands, Ireland, Iceland, Liechtenstein, Luxembourg, San Marino, Seychelles, Argentina, and South Africa—start to share information automatically. In 2018, another 35 jurisdictions, including Australia, Austria, Bahamas, Brazil, Brunei, Canada, China, Hong Kong, Monaco, Qatar, Russia, Singapore, United Arab Emirates, and Switzerland begin sharing information.

How Responsive is FDI to Taxation

It would appear that one of the important questions that potential investors ask themselves is whether there exists a tax treaty between their home country and the potential host country. Tax treaties are used to avoid double taxation. Bénassy-Quéré, Fontagné, and Lahrèche-Révil are categorical that tax rates play a significant role in investment location for FDIs. Disputes about the importance of corporate taxation on FDIs location are lit, especially because many empirical studies regarding the elasticity of FDI to corporate taxation have focused most often on the issue of taxation (Bénassy-Quéré, Fontagné, and Lahrèche-Révil 2001).①

At the center of debate over what is the appropriate level of a host country's corporate tax burden is the difficult question of how FDI reacts to taxation. Addressing this issue is crucial to assessing how to address pressures for internationally competitive tax treatment of FDI. It is also essential for carrying out cost/benefit assessments of tax relief provided for such investments, and for estimating the impact on tax revenues of any reform of corporate tax policy (OECD, 2008).

Studies examining cross-border flows suggest that on average, FDI decreases by 3.7% following

① Rădulescua* Magdalena & Elena Druicab, The impact of fiscal policy on foreign direct investments. Empiric evidence from Romania DOI:10.1080/1331677X.2014.947133, pp.86-106.

a 1% point increase in the tax rate on FDI. But there is a wide range of estimates, with most studies finding decreases in the range of 0% to 5%. This variation partly reflects differences between the industries and countries being examined, or the time periods concerned. Some recent studies find, for example, that FDI is becoming increasingly sensitive to taxation, reflecting the increasing mobility of capital as non-tax barriers to FDI are removed. Such estimates may be used to estimate the long-run impact on FDI of corporate tax reform (OECD, 2008).

In gauging how FDI responds to tax reform, one uncertainty is how tax factors into FDI decisions, and what tax rate(s) are considered by investors. Comparisons may focus on statutory "headline" corporate income tax (CIT) rates; or it may be that average effective tax rates (AETRs); or marginal effective tax rates (METRs) matter more than headline rates, as they incorporate rules determining the percentage of profits that are taxable. AETRs consider the average tax burden on investment projects, while METRs consider the tax burden at the margin (on the last unit of capital invested in a given project, where profits are exhausted). Statutory tax rates may differ significantly from effective tax rates, to the extent that taxable profits differ from true (economic) profits.[①]

Recent analysis supports the view that the sensitivity of FDI to tax depends on the host country and the mobility of business activities underlying the tax base. In particular, where firms benefit from locating production in large markets to reduce the costs of trade, such as transportation costs, a certain degree of inertia is predicted in the location choice of firms. Host country benefits and some fixity of capital mean that profits may be taxed up to some point without discouraging investment.

This view is consistent with the observation that a number of OECD economies with large domestic output markets and strong FDI inflows (e.g. US, Japan and Germany) have relatively high corporate tax rates. New explanatory models also suggest that the optimal tax rate on business falls as trade costs fall and capital is more mobile. This view is consistent with the observation that a number of countries impose a lower tax burden on more mobile business activities such as shipping, film production or head-office activities.

The Tax Regime in Kenya

The corporate tax rate in Kenya is 37.5%, this rate counts for all the sectors. Tax on capital gains had been suspended since 1985(UNCTAD, 2005), however in the 2015 budget the Kenyan government reinstated capital gains tax but has yet to bring it into operation. According to UNCTAD the overall tax regime in Kenya is efficient and fair relative to other developing countries. Kenya compares favorably with other countries in the region and elsewhere in terms of revenue collection as a percent of GDP (UNCTAD, 2005).

① OECD 2008, Tax Effects on Foreign Direct Investment, Policy Brief, February 2008.

The incentives that the Kenyan government uses are for resident corporations, EPZs and companies listed on the Nairobi stock exchange. Resident corporations have a reduced corporate tax rate of 30 percent. In EPZs there is an exemption of tax for the first ten years. After the ten year period corporate tax is pegged at the rate of 25 percent and the standard rate thereafter. Corporations that are listed at the Nairobi stock exchange have an incentive too. Newly enlisted corporations are taxed at either 25 percent or 27 percent for five years from the year of listing if they float a minimum of 30 percent or 20 percent of their capital, respectively (UNCTAD, 2005).

The manufacturing, secondary, sector also benefits from an 'investment deduction' for expenditure on buildings and other capital spending, while hotels benefit from the investment deduction on buildings only. The investment deduction is an accelerated rate of depreciation in the first year. Between 2004 and 2008, the investment deduction allowed a 100 percent rate of depreciation in the first year, however since then, the rate has fluctuated widely (UNCTAD, 2005).

Kenya has signed eight DTTs, including the major sources of FDI towards Kenya: United Kingdom, Canada and Germany. The other countries are: Denmark, India, Norway, Sweden and Zambia. Thus the only African country that has signed a double taxation treaty with Kenya is Zambia. Since 1999 there are talks with the East African Community members to sign a treaty. Although the East African Community is ambitious, with creating a common market in East Africa, to date they have not ratified a double taxation treaty.

Compared with the corporate tax rate of Australia (30 percent) is the corporate tax rate of Kenya quite high however the Kenyan tax rate is lower than the Canadian corporate tax rate plus the provincial tax rate (28 percent plus 14 percent).

Tax policy in Tanzania

The corporate tax rate in Tanzania is set on 30 percent of the corporate income. For agricultural, mining, tourism and manufacturing companies there are incentives. Expenditure on plant machinery is generally written off on a reducing balance basis at rates of 37.5 percent, 25 percent or 12.5 percent depending on the category of the asset, such as specified plant and machinery for manufacturing, fish farming and tourist hotels benefits from a 50 percent allowance in the first year, with the normal rates applying to the remaining balance in subsequent years.

There is an immediate write-off of expenditure on plant and machinery used in agriculture. Expenditure on buildings qualifies for a depreciation allowance of 5 percent straight-line. For intangible assets, the write off is over the useful life of the asset. Agricultural businesses also benefit from the immediate write off of plant, machinery and agricultural improvement expenditure. Buildings, structures, dams, water reservoirs, fences and similar works of a permanent nature used in agriculture, livestock or fish farming are written off on a straight-line basis over 5 years. Mining companies are entitled to a 100 percent capital deduction in respect of capital expenditure on exploration and development (Price Waterhouse Coopers, 2009).

Tanzania has EPZs on the mainland and special economic zones on Zanzibar. The EPZs on the mainland are not developed by the government. The private sector has to develop the zones; the government provides land and attractive legislation. EPZ status is to be given to individual factories with the potential to export 80 percent or more of their production. The special economic zones on Zanzibar included a 10 year tax holiday, no withholding tax on dividends, interest and any other income accrued from business transactions during the tax holiday period, free repatriation of dividends after taxation, 25 percent investment allowance and 100 percent ownership retention, several exemptions from customs and import duties used for manufacturing and export purposes and a generous term of government land lease for 49 years, which can be extended to 98 years (UNCTAD, 2002).

Double taxation treaties are in force with Canada, Denmark, Finland, India, Italy, Norway, South-Africa, Sweden and Zambia. Certain other DTTs (including an East African double tax treaty with Kenya and Uganda) have been signed but not yet ratified (Price Waterhouse Coopers, 2009). The Tanzanian corporate tax rate is the same as the Australian corporate tax rate (30 percent) and lower than the Canadian corporate tax rate plus the provincial tax rate (28 percent plus 14 percent).

The OECD states that tax competition for FDI is a reality in today's global environment. Investors routinely compare tax burdens in different locations, as do policy makers, with comparisons typically made across countries that are similar in terms of location and market size. A widely-held view is that taxes are likely to matter more in choosing an investment location as non-tax barriers are removed and as national economies converge.

There is broad recognition that international tax competition is increasing, and that what may have been regarded as a competitive tax burden on business in a given host country at one point in time may no longer be so after rounds of tax rate reductions in other countries. However, it is not always clear that a tax reduction is required (or is able) to attract FDI. Where a higher corporate tax burden is matched by well-developed infrastructure, public services and other host country attributes attractive to business, including market size, tax competition from relatively low-tax countries not offering similar advantages may not seriously affect location choice. Indeed, a number of large OECD countries with relatively high effective tax rates are very successful in attracting FDI. This points to the importance of market size and other host country attributes in attracting FDI and the presence of location-specific profits that governments are able to tax.

Conclusion

It has been postulated that the limits of tax competition are expected to be further tested, with further reductions in corporate tax burdens on inbound investment resisted where viewed by policy-makers as unnecessary to attract investment, owing to host country attributes, and raising equity concerns (OECD 2008).

Increased vigilance by African countries may also be exercised to limit artificial shifting of tax base to no/low tax havens, to avoid imbalances in the global tax system. Different approaches in the treatment of inbound and outbound investment can be expected across countries, reflecting different country circumstances. The sharing of experiences in addressing these challenges will no doubt be increasingly helpful, as policy makers refine the scope of their national tax systems (OECD 2008).

African Governments should try to improve the business friendliness of their tax administration by improving the transparency and certainty of tax treatment. African countries should introduced advance ruling procedures where tax authorities respond in advance to questions about the tax status of a particular type of investment. Tax treaties and mutual agreement procedures have also been identified as key to certainty and stability in the treatment of cross-border investment.

非洲投资市场准入规则及政策

作者：Abdoul Khadir DIOP　译者：徐伟刚

非洲是一块有着丰富自然资源的大陆。然而矛盾的是，它又被认为是地球上最贫穷的一块大陆。因此，非洲需要大量的投资来发展经济。但是想要获得投资，非洲国家就必须制定能够吸引投资者的政策。

非洲由 54 个国家组成，这些国家的政治、经济以及文化状况各不相同。因此本文不会深入对整个非洲情况的研究层面，因为这需要大量的研究以及时间，一方面它反映了非洲各国政策不一致的现实，另一方面反映了非洲各国和谐共处、相互联合的需要。

因此我们将把视角集中在其中一个国家——塞内加尔。

塞内加尔是一个位于非洲大陆西部的国家，它是前法国殖民点，1960 年和平取得独立。塞内加尔位于大西洋西岸，东北部毗邻毛里塔尼亚，东部接壤马里，南部则是几内亚与几内亚比索共和国。冈比亚共和国为一狭长平原嵌入塞内加尔共和国境内。

塞内加尔领土面积 196722 平方公里，总人口大约 14354690 人（根据国家统计与人口部门 2015 年数据）。

塞内加尔总统由民选产生，国会由单一内阁组成，并且有着被认为是非洲最有效之一的司法系统。塞内加尔是国际上公认的民主共和国，自由选举定期举行，即使有着一些争议需要由国家法院裁决，但是始终没有大的冲突。塞内加尔 2012 年经历了第三次国家中枢的民主转变，Macky Sall 是塞内加尔的现总统。

塞内加尔在很长一段时间里都被认为自然资源并不丰富，然而在陆地领土外却发现了越来越多的石油及天然气田①。塞内加尔的东南部 Sabadola 以及 Kedougou 地

① see http://www.cairnenergy.com/index.asp?pageid=27&newsid=484, retrieved on May 12, 2016.

区也有着金矿、铁矿以及磷酸盐。

农业在塞内加尔的国内经济中占据着十分重要的位置。国内大概 50% 的人从事农业生产，14% 的 GDP 来自农业。① 主要农作物包括棉花、花生、甘蔗、小米等。

塞内加尔有着漫长的海岸线以及丰富的渔业资源。畜牧业也有着一定程度的发展。塞内加尔致力于 2035 年成为新兴国家，为达到这一目标，“新兴塞内加尔计划②”制定并实施了。这一计划尤其强调了经济发展及出口的多样化，旨在增加塞内加尔公共及私人领域各方面的经济产出。

由于能源的消耗，行政的僵化，资源的非最佳使用，塞内加尔在很长一段时间内没有太多的投资吸引力③。塞内加尔正努力通过改善商业环境，简化市场及投资准入程序以及提供投资优待等方式改变现有状况以吸引尤其是外商直接投资的各种投资从而促进企业发展、提高就业。

因此，塞内加尔发布一系列规定以建立简化程序、吸引投资、加强投资保护的法律架构。

然而，需要强调的是这些规定并非歧视性的，国内以及外国投资者都可以从规定中受益。与外国的协议有的已经签署，有的正在商讨当中。与中国方面，投资促进及互惠保护协定以及双重税收协定正在协商之中。④

本文中，笔者将论述：保障投资的制度框架、市场准入规则、对投资者的保障以及最终结论。我们将会用一份简单的报告来显示出本文主题所涉及的塞内加尔的有关情况。

一、保障投资的制度框架

下面笔者将会论述新兴塞内加尔计划对商业环境的改善以及保障投资者的制度结构，尤其是“APIX”。

---

① presentation Document of the World Bank, accessed may 7, 2016 at the address http://www.banquemondiale.org/fr/country/senegal/overview retrieved on May 12, 2016.

② http://www.gouv.sn/IMG/pdf/PSE.pdf retrieved on May 12, 2016.

③ The 2015 Doing Business report classes Senegal 161 with a score of 49.37 a step since it ranked 171 in 2014 with a score of 46.09.

④ See http://investinsenegal.com/IMG/pdf/accords_de_conventions_internationales_du_senegal.pdf, retrieved on May 12, 2016.

（一）新兴塞内加尔计划（ESP）

新兴塞内加尔计划是一个气势磅礴的经济复苏计划，由塞内加尔政府及其伙伴关系方于 2012 年 11 月制订。该计划旨在到 2035 年实现经济振兴并且反对“优先措施计划（PAP）”。

优先措施计划首先规划了 2014 年至 2018 年这一时期，是所有相关方（国家、技术及金融伙伴、公私合伙）的交涉以及公民广泛参与的中期参考。

新兴塞内加尔计划的成功以塞内加尔政府规定的先决条件为基础，包括解决能源问题，建立现代基础设施以保障生产，强化人力资本以及公共行政现代化。

2016 年的改革已经开始，旨在持续改善商业环境，行政程序自动化、税收制度的建立、优待法律体系的简化、生产竞争力因素的提升以及投资促进等方面尤为显著。

新兴塞内加尔计划 2014—2018 年建立在 96857 亿西非法郎的资金基础之上，与世界银行塞内加尔咨询小组 2014 年 2 月在巴黎进行的会议帮助塞内加尔从其技术及金融伙伴那里筹得了 37290 亿非洲法郎[①] 作为项目资金，因此 57376 亿即 59.2% 的资金[②] 已经有了保证。

这份计划带来了希望，但是投资的实现要求对投资者提供法律上和物质上的支持。这便是 APIX 部门的职责所在。

（二）APIX

因为投资者设立公司、进入特定经济领域的程序十分复杂，塞内加尔政府注意到简化相关规则以及为潜在投资者提供支持的需要。因此，2000 年 APIX——国家投资及主要公共项目促进部（以下简称国投部）这个特殊部门成立了，该部门旨在为投资者提供一切相关信息。

国投部的职责包括提供经济、贸易以及技术的相关有效信息，接待各方投资者，提供办理登记手续、取得行政许可的帮助以及对资金及研究伙伴的引导。国投部同时还掌管投资项目的批准。

① See http://www.gcsenegal.gouv.sn/, retrieved on May 12, 2016.

② See http://www.finances.gouv.sn/index.php/finances/136-resume-du-plan-senegal-emergent retrieved on May 12, 2016.

这个部门还是承担一切相关职能的唯一窗口①。这个窗口促进了设置、实施相关活动所需手续的完成，缩短了发布某些文件及许可的等待时间。因此投资法规定的海关手续免除的批准可在10日内完成，许可在21日内完成，行政登记手续［国家企业行政机构代码（NINEA），IPRES（Pensions），（CSS）社会保障基金］可以在本部门以一份手续在48小时内完成。

国投部还可以提出关于调整投资促进相关的行政结构的建议从而使其更加高效，其还负责解决行政问题。

二、市场准入规则

满足塞内加尔关于准入、住所以及开展活动规定②的一切主体都可以在塞内加尔境内参与经济活动。塞内加尔是尊重个人权利并保障私有财产的法治国。因此，自然人及法人都可以自由开展经济活动，但医疗、律师等特定行业除外。因此，对于市场准入没有国籍的限制。相反，以投资法及自由出口企业法为代表的法律旨在根据同样的要求鼓励一切适格的投资者，既包括本国的，也包括外国的。自由出口企业法明确规定自由出口企业的资金可以全部或部分由塞内加尔或外国投资者出资。投资法规定，符合法律规定的自然人以及经过许可的法人，无论国籍如何均享有本法规定的、塞内加尔立法机关赋予的关于开展经济活动的同等权利与义务。因此，个人以及外国企业与塞内加尔公民及法人享受同等对待，这一保障是由于互惠原则、对一切外国国民的非歧视措施以及塞内加尔共和国签订的条约义务实现的。

关于获得塞内加尔市场准入资格的步骤与手续，投资者有两种选择：按照开展经济活动的一般规定或者以吸引外资而制定的有更多优待的特别条款。

（一）获得市场准入资格的一般规定

对于一般规定来说，多部法律及特别法规提供了个人及企业参加经济活动的规定，这取决于参加者是自然人还是法人，但主要标准在于合同签订方的资质，尤其是其是否属于商业交易方。

交易方的认定适用特别法规，该特别法规可以促进经济活动的开展并以程序高

① Single location for the completion of all the formalities necessary for business acces.

② Law No.71-10 of 25 January 1971 on the conditions of admission, residence and establishment of foreigners.

效为特征。特别法规必须在交易登记部门（RCCM）登记。

根据统一法典关于一般《贸易法》第 2 条规定，“以实施贸易行为为本职的一切主体视为交易方”。

上述贸易行为包括购买动产或不动产，重新出售，运营银行，股票交易，外汇，行纪业，保险业，以及交易方合同中介业，工业矿石开采，开采任何自然资源，融资租赁，制造、运输、电讯经营，委托、行纪、居间服务，购买中介，收购，出售或出租建筑物，股票、商事企业股份、不动产交易以及商事企业实施的其他活动。

对于需要大量投资的活动，通常采用公司形式。投资者可以根据其是否意图对公司债务按出资承担有限责任有较广泛的选择，或是成立有限责任公司（SARL），或是有限公司（SA），或是简化股份公司（SAS）。

简化股份公司是非洲商事法律协调组织（OHADA）新近规定的公司形式，该类公司的设立没有最低股本要求，股东既可以是自然人也可以是法人。它为股东及操作提供了更多灵活性，在外资进入非洲之前有限公司（SA）一直是主要形式。简化股份公司不同于有限责任公司及有限公司，没有最低注册资本要求。资本可以由成员续缴、新成员认缴，也可以由股东全部或部分撤回。资本的多样化使得投资者易于在企业存续期间注入资本。

公司的设立要求订立章程，章程由公证人起草或由公证人封存。章程应当规定民事股东或商事企业与企业及企业之外第三人的关系。章程或由当事人过半数同意在设立公司的当事人之间产生合同关系，或是特定股东的单方当事人的意思表示，章程条款应当符合法律规定[①]。

（二）特殊情形

除了上述通过对商事领域的干预赋予投资者的机会之外，塞内加尔政府为促进投资，规定了特殊规则以赋予投资者各种优待。

1. 投资优待

一系列旨在促进一般或特殊领域投资的法律对投资进行调整，包括矿法[②]以及石

① See art. 13 AUSGIE.

② Law No.2003-36 of 24 November 2003 on the Mining Code, amended by Law No.2012-32 of December 31, 2012.

油法[①]，它们提供了大量优待。笔者将重点论述投资法及自由出口企业法。

（1）投资法[②]

塞内加尔投资法以促进中小企业（SMEs）发展，权力分散，地方资源发展，鼓励创新及研究多样性为第一目标。要实现这一目标就需要海关、税收及社会福利为加强私人投资创造条件。投资法的目标拓展至鼓励创造就业，为投资者提供便利，包括港口基础设施建设、铁路建造及管理等方面。

投资法适用于本法规定的领域，但重售交易活动以及非企业的产品购买除外。[③]

法律规定的适格活动[④]可根据最低投资分为两类：

①适格活动：最低1500万西非法郎（23000欧元）

这些活动包括农业，渔业，种植业，地方生产的作物、牲畜、鱼类单品的仓储、包装、加工活动，农业食品工业，保健，教育，设备安装、建造、维护以及电信业务。

②适格活动：最低1亿西非法郎（15万欧元）

这些活动包括制造、生产、运输工业，矿物开采冶炼，旅馆业及旅游业，其他酒店业，文化产业（图书，唱片，发表中心，音像制品中心等），港口、机场及铁路基础设施，贸易实现，工业园区，名胜区，网络村庄以及技能中心。

（2）自由出口企业法

1995年12月29日第95-34号法令，由2004年2月6日第2004-11号法令修正，规定了自由出口企业（FEE），替代了自由贸易区以及自由贸易市场。

其目的是将所有产品出口的工业、农业以及电信企业为适格主体，包括所有工业（加工），农业（园艺、林业、畜牧业、渔业、水产业）以及在线服务。

取得准入资格需要得到财政部长的批准，投资者需要提交包括市场目标、本地销售及出口收入分配、达到其目标的投资细则、与消费者订立合同的副本、订单、电信企业购买意向书在内等信息的申请。

自由投资企业的资本可以由塞内加尔或外国投资者[⑤]持有。

---

① Law 98-05 of January 8, 1998 on oil Code.

② Law No.2004-06 of February 6, 2004 Code investments, amended by Law No.2012-32 of December 31, 2012.

③ S. 1 Investment Code.

④ S. 1 Law No.2004-06 of February 6, 2004 Investment Code and art. 250 law No.2012-31 of December 31, 2012 on the Tax Code.

⑤ S. 1 Law 95 - 34, of December 29, 1995.

本法规定的自由出口企业[①]自申请之日起25年内有效，期满后可续期。

2. 赋予投资者的优势

优待包括海关、财政以及社会等方面，包括税收免除、雇主与同一雇员可签订的固定期限劳动合同的限制等。

这些优待是暂时性的而非永久性的，其持续期间根据具体情况确定。

（1）投资法规定的优待

包括新项目入关免除3年，增值税免除3年[②]，项目实施期间相关农业方面的免除[③]。

实施期间，雇主须缴纳的与工资总额3%相等的固定数额（CFCE）可以免除，如果雇主能够增设200个工作岗位的，免除期间为5年；如果90%的工作岗位是在达卡区域[④]之外的，免除期间为8年。此外，投资者还享有订立5年期合同[⑤]（CDD）的优待。

项目延期的，如获得批准的投资项目，现存企业发起的增加25%生产力的或固定资产收购价值的或对生产设备投资至少1亿西非法郎的投资项目，投资者可以获得相应优待，获得免除须增加的工作岗位要求缩减至至少100个。

（2）自由出口企业法规定的优待

①劳动法规定的优待

出口加工企业可自由雇佣塞内加尔国内或外国职工。

对于因包括硬件故障，机器停摆，自然灾害，天气条件，稀有资源、工具、交通工具意外短缺等短期或以外情况需要停工的，雇主与职工代表协商后可以决定全部或部分职工全体停工[⑥]。

②税收及入关优待

出口加工企业可享受下列税收政策：因公司发放红利而征收的股利税免除；企业应缴纳的薪资税及雇主应承担的固定数额免除；所有登记税、印花税以及公司章程及补充协议规定的税务的免除；所有职业税、土地建设税、不动产税以及执照费

① S. 2 Law.

② S. 11 Law No.2012-32 of December 31, 2012 amending various legislative provisions relating to tax scheme.

③ S. 373 Law No.2012-31 of December 31, 2012 on Tax Code.

④ Art 263 Law No.2012-31 of December 31, 2012 on Tax Code.

⑤ Art 19 - b Law No.2004-06 of February 26, 2004 Investment Code.

⑥ S. 6 Act.

用免除；应交税率为 15%。①

但是，自由出口企业仍需缴纳地质、矿产、海洋及森林的使用费。

自由出口企业进出口的办公用品、稀有材料、成品以及半成品免除关税及印花税。上述物品经海关部门许可后可以向其他自由出口企业转让、出售或出租。

自由出口企业制造的产品出口海外免税②。

例外的是，自由出口企业经许可后可根据法律③规定的比例及方式在当地市场出售其全年产品的一部分。

三、对投资者的保障

（一）法律保障

政府对投资者的保障包括：

（1）保证自由出口企业向法郎区外转让经营满足对贸易、金融经营投资的全部数额；

（2）保证自由出口企业职工、合作者、股东以及经许可的外国债权人根据外汇法规④向法郎区外转让；

（3）保证自由出口企业不受与其他企业相比的任何歧视措施⑤；

（4）在自由出口地位存续期间不得适用加重其义务的法律法规⑥。

自由出口企业违反出口义务的，行政机关可取消其一定优待，情节严重的，可通过决定中止或撤销其自由出口地位⑦。

（二）司法保障

自由出口企业与塞内加尔行政机关之间的对于自由出口企业法解释或实施的争

---

① S. 7 Law 95 - 34, December 29, 1995.

② S. 9 Law 95 - 34, December 29, 1995.

③ S. 14 Law 95 - 34, December 29, 1995.

④ S. 4 Law 95 - 34, December 29, 1995.

⑤ S. 5 Law 95 - 34, December 29, 1995.

⑥ S. 8 Law 95 - 34, December 29, 1995.

⑦ S. 17 Law 95 - 34, December 29, 1995.

议由塞内加尔法院裁判。

国家与个体或组织之间对于自由出口地位法律适用的争议由仲裁机构裁决或调解机构调解：

（1）根据世界银行附属机构——国际投资争议解决中心（ICSID）关于国家间投资争议解决的规定；

（2）根据塞内加尔与相关自然人或法人的国籍国签订的投资协定或条约；

（3）根据当事双方合意选择的仲裁规则。[①]

四、结论

非洲因其优质、充足的自然资源而具有极大的经济潜力。经济环境的改善对其吸引投资，尤其是外资而言至关重要。然而要想实现这一目标，非洲国家必须进行深入的改革以使他们的规则符合商业世界的要求。从这方面来讲，不仅需要和平稳定以保障投资者的安全，还需要法律及海关规则适用的协调。塞内加尔明确地显示出通过开展项目、制定促进本土有效投资的规则以吸引投资的决心。

① S. 18 Law 95 - 34, December 29, 1995.

The Market Access Rules and Policies on Investing in Africa

Author: Abdoul Khadir DIOP

Africa is a continent renowned rich in natural resources. It is also, paradoxically, regarded as the poorest continent of the planet. Therefore, it needs massive investments to develop its economy. But to receive those investments, African countries have to create the conditions to attract investors.

Africa is made up of 54 States which are as different they are various both politically, economically, culturally, and in the social level. Therefore, this study which aim to scrutinize "The Market Access Rules and Policies on Investing in Africa" , will not be extended to the whole African continent, and include all African States, which would require a lot of research and time and would reflect, at most, one the one hand, the disparities and the non-homogeneous nature of African policies in this matter, and, on the other hand, the need for harmonization and greater integration (see the study conducted in 2009 by Anthony Yaw Baah and Herbert Jauch *Chinese Investments in Africa: A Labour Perspective*).

Consequently, we will restrict our remarks to one particular African country: Senegal.

Senegal is a country located in the western part of the African continent. It is a former French colony, which gained independence in 1960 peacefully. It is bordered by the Atlantic Ocean on its West side and by the Republics of Mauritania to the North and the East, Mali to the East, Guinea and Guinea-Bissau to the South. The Republic of Gambia forms a quasi-enclave inside Senegal, penetrating its territory over a distance of 300 km.

Senegal's territory covers an area of 196 722 km². The country's population is estimated at 14 354 690 (Statistics of the National Agency of Statistics and Demography, 2015).

Senegal is a Republic with a President elected by the population, a Parliament composed of a single Chamber and a judicial system considered as one the most efficient in Africa. The country is recognized and respected internationally as a major democracy, in which free elections are regularly held, without major tension even though disputes, decided by national courts are noted sometimes. Senegal has experienced its third democratic change of head of state in 2012 with the election of Mr. Macky SALL as President of the Republic.

For a long time Senegal has been regarded as not being gifted with many natural resources, but is becoming increasingly attractive with the discovery of large oil and natural gas fields offshore see http://www.cairnenergy.com/index.asp?pageid=27&newsid=484, retrieved on May 12, 2016.① The country has also gold and iron deposits in the Southeast of the country, precisely in Sabadola in the region of Kedougou. It has phosphate as well, among others.

Agriculture occupies a very important place in the economy of the country. It is approximately 50% of the active population and contributes 14% to GDP.② The main crops include cotton, groundnut, sugarcane, millet etc.

The country has a long coastline and a sea abounding in fish. Livestock also is relatively developed. Senegal aspires to become an emerging country by the year 2035. To achieve that goal, a plan called "Emerging Senegal Plan" ③ was designed and is being implemented. This plan, specifically, emphasizes the diversification of the economy and the exportations. It aims to increase the productivity of the Senegalese economy, both in the public and the private sector.

For a long time regarded as being not very attractive for investments because of the costs of energy, administrative delays, non-optimal use of resources④, Senegal aims to improve its image by improving the business climate, by simplifying procedures to get access to the market and for investment, and by introducing incentives intended to attract investment, particularly foreign direct investment, in order to encourage the creation of enterprises and employment.

Therefore, several texts were adopted in order to create or develop a legal framework to help simplify the rules, attract investment and strengthen the protection of investment.

However, it is important to note that these policies did not introduce a discriminatory regime. Both national and foreigners can benefit from the advantages they offer. Nonetheless, agreements with foreign countries have been signed or are under discussion. With regard particularly to China an Agreement on Promotion and Reciprocal Protection of Investment and a Double Taxation Agreement are being negotiated⑤.

In this paper, we will examine the Institutional Framework Sustaining the Investment (I), the Market Access Rules (II), the Advantages and Benefits (III) and the Guarantees Granted to Investors (IV) before making a few concluding remarks, which, in our view, will allow a simplified presentation

① see http://www.cairnenergy.com/index.asp?pageid=27&newsid=484, retrieved on May 12, 2016.

② presentation Document of the World Bank, accessed may 7, 2016 at the address http://www.banquemondiale.org/fr/country/senegal/overview retrieved on May 12, 2016.

③ http://www.gouv.sn/IMG/pdf/PSE.pdf retrieved on May 12, 2016.

④ The 2015 Doing Business report classes Senegal 161 with a score of 49.37 a step since it ranked 171 in 2014 with a score of 46.09.

⑤ See http://investinsenegal.com/IMG/pdf/accords_de_conventions_internationales_du_senegal.pdf, retrieved on May 12, 2016.

of the particular situation in Senegal, with regard to the topic.

The Institutional Framework Sustaining Investment

We will discuss here the improvement of the business environment through the Senegal Emerging Plan and the structures implemented for the accompaniment of investors, in particular "APIX" .

A-The Emerging Senegal Plan (ESP)

The "Emerging Senegal Plan" is an ambitious economic recovery program adopted by the Senegalese Government and its partners in November 2012. It targets the economic emergence by the year 2035 and is declined in "Priority Action Plans" (PAP).

The PAP, the first covering the 2014-2018 period, is the reference document of as well the interventions of all the parties involved (the State, the technical and financial partners, the public-private partnership) as the citizen participation, in the medium term.

The success of the ESP is based on prerequisites, towards which the Government of Senegal is committed, including fixing the question of energy, the establishment of modern infrastructure to sustain the production, the improvement of the business environment, the strengthening of human capital, the modernization of Public Administration.

Reforms have been initiated for the term of 2016 to substantially improve the business environment, notably on the automation of administrative procedures, the establishment of a tax and legal system simplified with incentives and, the improvement of factors production competitiveness as well as the promotion of investment in high-impact.

The PAP 2014-2018 is built on the basis of a program estimated at 9685.7 billion FCFA. In this regard, a meeting of the World Bank Consultative Group for Senegal, held in Paris in February 2014, has helped the State gather from its technical and financial partners new commitments amounting to 3729 billion CFA francs① for the funding of the program, so that 5737.6 billion CFA, or 59.2% are already granted②.

This plan arouses much hope, but the realization of investments requires legal and material assistance to investors. It is in this regard that an Agency called APIX operates.

---

① See http://www.gcsenegal.gouv.sn/, retrieved on May 12, 2016.

② See http://www.finances.gouv.sn/index.php/finances/136-resume-du-plan-senegal-emergent retrieved on May 12, 2016.

B-APIX

Because of the complexity of the procedures investors have to go through to create companies and access to the specific sectors of the economy, Senegalese Government became conscious that it needed to simplify the rules and provide assistance to those wishing to invest on its soil. Therefore, it established in 2000 a specialized agency, referred to as APIX (National Agency for the Promotion of Investment and Major Public Projects) whose mission is to provide all information needed by the investors.

APIX's mission includes giving and making permanently available information on economic, commercial and technological matter, welcoming and accompanying investors in all stages of investment, providing assistance for the accomplishment of registration formalities and obtainment of administrative authorizations, orientation towards the funding and research partners. APIX also keeps track of approved investment projects.

This Agency is also devolved all the functions of the single window①. This window facilitates the accomplishment of some formalities needed for the installation or the exercise of a proposed activity. It allows shortening the deadlines for issuance of some documents or authorizations. Thus, the approval to the Investment Code with delivery of the Title of Exemption for Customs Formalities can be obtained in 10 days, the Free Export Enterprise Status Approval, in 21 days, and execution of the administrative registration formalities (Companies and Administrations National Identification Number (NINEA), IPRES (Pensions), (CSS) Social Security Fund), at the same place, on a single sheet, in 48 hours.

APIX can also make proposals for the redeployment of administrative structures related to the promotion of investments for greater efficiency. Its mission includes the resolution of administrative problems as well.

The Market Access Rules

Subject to comply with the regulations on the entry, residence and exercise of an activity in Senegal②, anyone can engage in an economic activity in the territory. Senegal is a Rule-of-Law State which respects individual's rights and guarantees private property. Consequently, both natural persons and legal entities may undertake economic activities freely, except certain occupations that are regulated like medicine, bar, etc. Therefore, there is no discrimination for access to sectors of

---

① Single location for the completion of all the formalities necessary for business acces.

② Law No.71-10 of 25 January 1971 on the conditions of admission, residence and establishment of foreigners.

activities in favour of nationals. Instead, the law, especially in the Investment Code and the law on the Free Export Enterprise, intends the incentive provisions to be for all investors, nationals as well as foreigners, subject to the same eligibility requirements. The latter Act expressly provides that the capital of a Free Export Enterprise may be held wholly or partly by Senegalese or foreign investors. The Investment Code stresses that, individuals or approved Legal Entities, subject to comply with the regulations, regardless of their nationality, receive the same treatment with regard to rights and obligations arising from the Senegalese legislation relating to the exercise of activities defined by the code. Accordingly, individuals or foreign companies receive the same treatment than Senegalese natural persons or legal entities, subject to reciprocity and without prejudice to measures that may apply to all foreign nationals or result from the provisions of treaties and agreements to which the Republic of Senegal is a party.

To get access to the Senegalese Market, regarding the steps and formalities to accomplish, two options are available to investors: they can either apply the general rules for economic activity creation or the more incentive ones established by special provisions to attract investment.

A-The General Rules Implemented to Get Access to the Market

Regarding the General rules, various codes and specific laws govern the participation of individuals and corporations to economic activities, depending on whether the entrepreneur is a natural or legal person. But the main issue is the quality of the contractor, especially if they are regarded as a commercial trader or not.

The trader is subject to special rules designed to identify them but also to facilitate the exercise of their activity, characterized by the rapidity. They must be registered in a the Trade Register (RCCM).

According to article 2 of the Uniform Act relating to General Commercial Law, is deemed a trader anyone whose profession is to perform acts of trade by nature.

These acts are the purchase of property, movable or immovable, for resale; bank operations, stock exchange, Exchange, brokerage, insurance and transit contracts between traders for the purpose of their business, industrial exploitation of mines, quarries and any deposits of natural resources, furniture rental operations, manufacture, transport and telecommunications operations, commercial operations such as commission, brokerage, agency intermediates, as well as the operations of intermediary for the purchase, the acquisition, sale or rental of buildings, of stock actions or shares of commercial companies or real estate, the acts carried out by commercial companies.

For activities requiring heavy investment, the corporate form is normally used. In this regard, a relatively wide selection is available for investors who can, depending on whether they intend to limit their liability with regard to the company debts or are concerned about the volume of social capital, opt for the Limited Liability Company (SARL), the Limited Company (SA), or the Simplified Stock

Company (SAS).

The Simplified Stock Company was recently introduced among existing companies in the area of the OHADA (Organization for the Harmonization of Business Law in Africa). It is a company which can be created without a minimum share capital and its shareholders can be legal persons as well as natural persons. It is seen as offering much more flexibility to shareholders and executives that the Limited Company (SA), which was the main vehicle used until then in connection to foreign investment in Africa. No minimum capital is required unlike the SARL and the SA. The capital, when it exists, can be either increased by successive subscriptions by members or admission of new partners or reduced by the withdrawal of a shareholder wholly or partially. Variability of the capital makes easy the entry of investors to the capital during the company's life.

The creation of a company requires the establishment of the statutes which is a document drawn up by a notary or under private seal and kept by a notary. The statutes are the document which sets out the treaty provisions which regulate, on the one hand, the relationships between shareholders of civil or commercial companies and the relationships between the company and the third parties who are not part of the Corporation. The statutes constitute either the contract between partners creating the company, in case of plurality of shareholders, or the act of will of a single person, in the case of a unique shareholder. Their provisions are defined by law[①].

B-The Specific Cases

In addition to these above opportunities given to investors to intervene in the business field, the Senegalese Government has, in light of promoting investment, elaborated incentives by introducing special rules which grant a bunch of benefits to investors.

1-The Incentives

Several Legislative Acts intended to promote investment in general or in specific sectors exist. For instance, the Mining Code[②] and the Oil Code[③] which provide a number of benefits. However, we will focus on the Investment Code and the Law on the Status of Free Export Enterprise.

a) The Investment Code[④]

Senegal has an Investment Code whose first objective was the promotion of Small and Medium-sized Enterprises (SMEs), the decentralization, the development of local resources, the encouragement of innovation and the valorization of research. This goal was accompanied by customs, tax and

---

① See art. 13 AUSGIE.

② Law No.2003-36 of 24 November 2003 on the Mining Code, amended by Law No.2012-32 of December 31, 2012.

③ Law 98-05 of January 8, 1998 on oil Code.

④ LawNo.2004-06 of February 6, 2004 Code investments, amended by LawNo.2012-32 of December 31, 2012.

social benefits with a view to creating the conditions for the enhancement of private investment. The purpose of this law was extended by other texts to encourage job creation, make it easier for investors and include other areas such as Ports' infrastructure, installations and the management of railways.

This code applies to companies that operate in the sectors defined by the Act. However, the trading activities defined as resale activity as such of products purchased outside the company are expressly excluded from its scope①.

Eligible activities are specified by the law② and can be split in two groups according to the minimum amount of investment.

-Eligible Activities: Minimum 15 million francs Cfa (23,000 euros)

It's about activities such as agriculture, fishing, farming, or storage, packaging and processing activities of products locally produced from plant, animal or fish, as well as agro food industry, health, education and training, installation, assembly and maintenance of equipment, and Teleservices.

-Eligible Activities: Minimum 100 million francs Cfa (150,000 euros)

Are referred here manufacturing, production or transformation industries such as extraction or processing of minerals, accommodation and tourism activities, other hotel activities, cultural industries (Books, disk, documentation centers, audiovisual production center, etc.), port, airport and railway infrastructure, commercial complexes realization, industrial parks, touristic areas, cyber villages and craft centers.

b) The Law on the status of Free Export Enterprise

The Law No.95-34 of December 29, 1995, amended by Law No.2004-11 of February 6, 2004 established the status of the Free Export Enterprise (FEE), which replaces the Free Trade Zones and Free Trade Points.

May be eligible to this status industrial, agricultural and teleservice companies whose destine their whole production to export.

All industrial sectors (processing) agricultural (primary sector heard in the broad sense: horticulture, forestry, livestock, fishery, aquaculture), and online services are included.

The access to this status is subject to obtaining an approval which is granted by the Minister of Finance after submission of an application indicating needed information such as the markets targeted, the repartition of the revenue from local sales and exports, as well as details on the investments required to achieve these objectives, accompanied by copies of the contracts signed with customers, purchase orders and/or letters of intent, for teleservice companies.

The share capital of a Free Export Enterprise may be held wholly or partly by Senegalese and

① S. 1 Investment Code.

② S. 1 Law No.2004-06 of February 6, 2004 Investment Code and art. 250 law No.2012-31 of December 31, 2012 on the Tax Code.

foreign investors[①].

The status of the Free Export Enterprise is granted for a renewable term of 25 years from the date of application of the Act[②].

2-The advantages granted to investors

The benefits are of customs, fiscal or social nature. They consist of tax and duty exemptions. They may also consist of derogation to the limitation of the number of limited term contracts that may sign an employer with the same worker.

These benefits are not perpetual but temporary. Their duration varies depending on the case.

a) Benefits Under the Investment Code

Benefits include for instance for new projects in phase of implementation customs exemptions for 3 years, suspension of VAT for 3 years[③] and exemption for the agricultural sector during the phase of the project[④].

In the operating phase, the benefits may include exemption of the Fixed Contribution paid by Employers (CFCE), which is equal to 3% of the payroll, for 5 years and 8 years if there are at least 200 jobs created or if 90 % of the jobs created are out of the Dakar region[⑤]. Furthermore, the possibility to conclude contracts (CDD) term for a period limited to 5 years[⑥] is offered.

If there is an extension project, i.e. any authorized investment program, initiated by an existing enterprise which results in an increase of at least 25% of the production capacity or the acquisition value of fixed assets or an investment in equipment for the production of at least 100 million CFA, the same benefits as listed above may be granted, the number of jobs created for the exemption of the CFCE being reduced to 100 at least.

b) Benefits Under the Law on the status of Free Export Enterprise

Benefits related to Labor law

Export processing companies can freely recruit their staff, be them Senegalese or expatriate.

In case of necessity of a work stoppage, resulting from short-term or accidental causes such as hardware failures, stoppage of machines, natural disaster, and weather conditions, accidental scarcity of raw materials, or tooling, or means of transportation, the employer may, after consultation with the workers representatives, decide a collective interruption of work of all or part of the staff[⑦].

Tax and customs incentives

---

① S. 1 Law 95 - 34, of December 29, 1995.

② S. 2 Law.

③ S. 11 Law No.2012-32 of December 31, 2012 amending various legislative provisions relating to tax scheme.

④ S. 373 Law No.2012-31 of December 31, 2012 on Tax Code.

⑤ Art 263 Law No.2012-31 of December 31, 2012 on Tax Code.

⑥ Art 19 - b Law No.2004-06 of February 26, 2004 Investment Code.

⑦ S. 6 Act.

Export processing companies are subject to the following tax regime:

-Exemption from the tax on income from stocks levied by the company on distributed dividends;

-Exemption from any tax based on wages paid by companies and supported by them and in particular the fixed contribution borne by employers;

-Exemption from all registration and stamp duties, particularly those collected at the constitution and the amendment of companies statutes;

-Exemption from the contribution of the professional tax, the land tax on the built-up properties, the real estate tax on non-built-up properties, the contribution of licenses;

-Collection of the tax at the rate of 15%①.

However, Free Export Enterprises which have received concessions remain subject to fees charged for the use of geological, mining, and maritime domain or forest.

Furniture goods, raw materials and finished or semi-finished products are imported or exported by Free Export Enterprises in exemption from duties and taxes and the Customs stamp. They can be transferred, sold or rented to other Free Export Enterprises with the approval of the customs service.

The products manufactured by these companies are exported abroad free of duties and taxes②.

Exceptionally, Free Export Enterprises may be authorized to sell on the local market part of their annual production in proportions and in a manner laid down by Decree③.

The Guarantees Granted to Investors

A-The Legal Guarantees

The Government guarantees to investors:

The commitment to grant Free Export Enterprises, permissions allowing them, as part of their operation, to transfer to countries outside the Franc zone, all the sums necessary for the fulfillment of investment and their commercial and financial operations.

The commitment to grant Free Export Enterprises employees, collaborators, shareholders and foreign lenders of authorizations to transfer to countries outside the Franc zone in accordance with the regulation of foreign exchange④.

Free Export Enterprises are guaranteed from being subject to any discriminatory action

① S. 7 Law 95 - 34, December 29, 1995.

② S. 9 Law 95 - 34, December 29, 1995.

③ S. 14 Law 95 - 34, December 29, 1995.

④ S. 4 Law 95 - 34, December 29, 1995.

compared with those applied to enterprise not approved to this status①.

For the duration of the status, it cannot be applied to Free Export Enterprises laws, regulations aggravating the regulations and texts applicable to them at their date of approval to the status②.

However, failure to comply with their export obligations, the administration may withdraw one or several benefits. In cases of serious fraud, the approval to the status may be suspended or revoked by Decree③.

B-Judicial Guarantees

Disputes between a Free Export Enterprises and the Senegalese Administration arising on the interpretation or enforcement of the Law on the Status of Free Export Enterprises are decided by the Senegalese courts.

However, disputes between the State and the individuals or entities arising on the application of the law on the status are settled by arbitration and conciliation:

-either by the rules established by the Convention for the Settlement of Disputes Related to investments between States and other States developed by the International Centre for the Settlement of Disputes in the Investments (ICSID), which is an institution affiliated with the World Bank.

-either by agreements and treaties for the protection of investments signed between Senegal and the State of which the natural or legal person is a national.

-or any other arbitration rule adopted by mutual agreement between the two parties④.

Conclusion

Africa has considerable economic potential with good quality and abundant natural resources. The betterment of its economic environment is more than a necessity if it wants to attract investments, especially those from abroad. But to attain this goal, African countries, will have to go through in-depth reforms to adapt their procedures to the requirements of the business world. In this regard, not only must be established peace and stability, guarantee of security for investors, but an harmonization of the laws and customs procedures must be carried out. Senegal shows a clear desire to make its territory attractive by initiating programs and developing rules aimed to facilitate the cost-effective investment on its soil.

① S. 5 Law 95 - 34, December 29, 1995.

② S. 8 Law 95 - 34, December 29, 1995.

③ S. 17 Law 95 - 34, December 29, 1995.

④ S. 18 Law 95 - 34, December 29, 1995.

在非洲投资的市场准入规则和政策

作者：Mashaba Bookholane① 译者：符佳慧

一、介绍

2008 年金融危机以后，非洲越来越受外国投资者的欢迎。依照 Cheadle（2016）的观点，主要有以下原因:（1）与大多数工业化国家的日益下滑的经济增长率相比，非洲有着较高的经济增长率。（2）人口的迅速增长。（3）中产阶级的日益壮大。（4）非洲大陆政治和经济环境的改善。（5）丰富的矿产资源和大量的可耕地。

尽管在 2008 年金融危机后，非洲对投资者有着强大的吸引力。但其自身也没能够免除金融危机的影响，这样使得世界各地愿意去冒险的人减少了，而且由于人们将非洲看成投资风险最高的地区，投资者的信心有所下降。市场中有很多的案例可以证明这一点，比如说，国际银行向非洲出口商削减信用证的程度要远远大于其他地区（Collier，2010）。但是尽管受到全球金融危机的影响，非洲在尼日利亚和南非两个最大的国家的带领下，仍然“毫发无伤”。

数统计据显示，2009 年至 2014 年年底，非洲的外商直接投资流入量大约比之前增长了 20%。而且在这五年期间，非洲南部地区的外商直接投资流入取得显著上升，紧随其后的是中非和东非地区。与此同时，北非地区和西非地区的外商直接投资的流入从 2010 年开始一直在下降（Cheadle，2016）。即使是像卢旺达这样的居于内陆并且人口过剩的国家，尽管它并没有丰富的自然资源，但是其政府在证明了自己致力于经济转型后，已经能够维持 10% 的经济增长率（Collier，2010）。

① Masechaba Bookholane, Senior Legal Advisor at Transnet Freight Rail, a division of Transnet SOC Limited, a state-owned country established under the laws of the Republic of South Africa.

McGowan（2004）认为，在一般情况下，外商直接投资对跨国公司越来越重要。研究表明，美国的跨国公司在美国本土之外的外商直接投资以及非美国的跨国公司在美国本土进行的外商直接投资显著增加。外商直接投资的重要性上升，与之相联系的是对政治和金融 / 经济风险分析需求的增加。作为一个外国投资者，为了成功地制定出一个在非洲投资的策略，重要的是在做出走进非洲市场的投资决策时，了解需要考虑和评估的因素。

一方面，人们必须考虑非洲大陆上有哪些地区拥有足够丰富的自然资源，能够使其在一个显著时期内维持有意义的经济增长。另一方面，这一地区的政治、经济和安全方面的因素，将会影响商业环境和总体投资经验。Blancheton and Opara-Opimba（2010）认为，外商直接投资的流入与发展中经济体，特别是非洲国家的之间关系是十分复杂的，并且国际上的竞争力和全球化的深远影响使外国企业必须在其投资决定中考虑除了传统因素（如自然资源、廉价劳动力和市场规模）外其他新的因素。此外，人力资本的活力，基础设施和资本主义的发展，政府机构和司法部门的稳健性，以及接受外国直接投资流入国家的邻近环境或商业环境，这些都是需要探究的问题。

本文试图探索矿产资源丰富的非洲地区对投资吸引力如何与市场准入规则、政策、治理以及这些地区的商业环境之间相互作用，以及这种投资吸引力如何影响外商直接投资流入该地区。经验数据表明，由于非洲大陆不成比例的矿产资源的分布，造成了外商直接投资在非洲大陆不均匀的分布。数据还显示，24 个主要靠石油和其他矿产资源带来总收入的国家，在过去的二十年几乎每年都获得了四分之三的流入非洲的外商直接投资（Blancheton Opara-Opimba, 2010）。

本文力图论述即使未必拥有丰富的矿产资源，非洲国家是否能够利用对投资者友好的市场准入规则和政策来吸引外商直接投资。此外，本文还深入研究了某些非洲国家在选择某些市场准入规则和政策时与其他国家的差异，以及这与流入该国的外商直接投资的关系。Blancheton and Opara-Opimba 观察到，从整体来看，非洲大陆，尤其是撒哈拉以南的地区，十分注重调整和重新定位它的制度和监管框架，以加强其在潜在外国投资者的国际信誉。通过这个现象，本文旨在探索市场准入规则和政策和外商直接投资流入的相关性。

二、市场准入政策对外商投资的影响

从历史上看，最成功的吸引外商直接投资的非洲国家是有着丰富的矿产资源和自然资源的国家，以及被誉为拥有最大国内市场的国家（Morisset, 2001）。实证研究证实，在 1996 年至 1997 年间流入非洲大陆的外商直接总投资中，大约有百分之六十五的外商直接投资主要流入了南非、尼日利亚、科特瓦迪。这一流入也可归因于同一时期大陆三分之二的国内生产总值。（Morisset, 2001）

Morisset（2001）认为，通过优先进行政策改革，非洲国家也有能力吸引外国直接投资，这种外国直接投资不仅仅建立在该国拥有的自然资源之上，或者只针对当地市场，反之，这种投资是针对区域和全球市场的。他还进一步指出，一国如能采取积极主动的政策并且拥有以改革为导向的政府，在吸引外商直接投资上更有利。该政策对一个国家吸引外商直接投资的能力有更重要的影响。

根据 Morisset（2001）研究，当涉及外商直接投资流入大陆时，更有用的方法是当这些非洲国家无法依靠自然资源和国内市场吸引外商直接投资的时候，再去确定哪个非洲国家有最强的吸引外商直接投资的能力。因为传统上，已经有大量的研究证实了许多非洲国家对矿产资源和市场规模的大量依赖，以及这与他们吸引外商直接投资能力的联系。

Morisset（2001）承认，即使用于上述研究的指标反映的是现存的而不是潜在的数据，这也不会因此是一个未来外商直接投资流入可靠的预测。在这些非洲国家需要依靠除了自然资源和市场规模以外的其他因素的时候，该指标确实能够证实他们吸引外商直接投资的能力，因此，它不仅反映了政策和政治的变量，还反映出了一系列的结构性因素，如基础设施、运输和人力资本的成本。

Morisset（2001）研究了 29 个非洲国家的商业环境变化对外商直接投资的吸引力。研究表明，总的来说，29 个国家的排名在所选期间保持相对稳定，这与确定是否有良好的声誉是要经过一段时间的结论是一致的。

随着时间的推移，对 29 个非洲国家关于外商直接投资的商业环境的比较研究显示，在十年期间，一些国家的商业环境出现了显著的变化，并且外国投资者对这种变化做出了反应，比如马里（从 1986—1990 年排名第二十六，到 1995—1997 年的排名第五），乌干达（从排名二十四到排名十三），莫桑比克（从排名十三到排名第三），他们的外商直接投资流入在 1994—1995 年与 1995—1997 年间分别增加了

600%，100% 和 90%。(Morisset, 2001)

Morisset (2001) 总结道，他认为尽管这个任务本身就是有难度的，但是马里和莫桑比克的做法是正确的，因为建立具有吸引力的外商直接投资商业环境是一个多维的任务。这两个国家的一些主要行为被确定为如下：这两个国家在一段时间内给各自所管辖的区域建立了相对稳定的宏观经济环境；他们通过动态的贸易自由化和私有化吸引外国投资者；两国政府批准了立法的关键内容，包括在马里和莫桑比克的一个新工业自由区政权的新矿业 (1991) 和投资法 (1995)；订立关于外国直接投资的国际条约提高了这些国家政府在国际商业界的地位和信誉，并为潜在的外国投资者提供了额外的保险。(Morisset, 2001)

还有其他数据证实莫里赛特的发现，即外商直接投资与经济增长和发展之间存在正相关关系，并且，采取相对更开放和透明的政治和经济系统的国家往往能吸引更多的外商直接投资。(McGowan, 2004)

世界上的一些地区已经做出一致的努力，通过政策和市场准入规则减少外商直接投资的阻碍。然而，在世界上某些地区，人们却是更加敌视外商直接投资 (McGowan, 2004)。Bonaglia 等从质和定量的角度解释非洲国家的结构和体制改革，研究表明 1985 年至 1997 年期间改革措施最多的国家是非洲大陆南部的那些国家，它们包括：博茨瓦纳、毛里求斯、南非和坦桑尼亚，改革不太显著的国家有赞比亚和津巴布韦。实证研究表明，当经济政策环境是开放和透明的时候，跨国公司会倾向于外商直接投资到其他国家；否则，他们会限制对他国进行外商直接投资，与此同时，他们将有能力为特定交易谈判以及执行对他们有利的条款。此外，跨国公司更有可能使外商直接投资进入那些为所有公司提供长远保护的国家，或者是保护特定企业、特定经济部门或特定投资的国家。(McGowan, 2004)

Stoever 对一个机制和方式做出了讨论，这个机制和方式中国家经济环境自由化的具体行动会影响外国直接投资和经济发展。他解释说，随着东道国政府对经济环境的开放，跨国公司被允许更大范围和更灵活地在东道国从事他们的业务活动。在经济自由化的环境下，跨国公司受到的限制将会减少。

McGowan's (2004) 分析道，对跨国公司的外商投资减少了限制，降低了跨国公司的成本和风险，同时，跨国公司将因为风险的减少而要求更低的投资回报率。对于东道国而言，这将会使其获得更大利益。他接着得出结论，一个国家，如果要制定关于外商直接投资的政策的话，应当注意消除矛盾，优先考虑清晰的经济优先权，逐步推进政策，以确保放松管制的速度与经济增长的速度保持一致，使其在公共领域的语言表达与其行为一致。实施有意义的改革，最重要的是避免过多干预经济的自由化的过程。

三、金融市场对外商直接投资的影响

除了政策和外商直接投资的流入之间存在明显的正相关关系，正如上面所探讨的，尊重金融市场管辖权的市场准入规则与外商直接投资的水平之间也有类似的正相关关系。任何时候，当跨国公司将他们的业务转移到国外管辖之下，他们必须利用国内的金融市场。因为他们要开一个本地银行账户，这是一个基本的例子。Agbloyor et al.（2013）建议，当外国企业决定在另一个司法管辖区做生意，对国家风险的分析是他们对跨国资本预算的一部分。外国企业更倾向于在银行制度较为完善的国家进行投资，理由很简单，因为这使得他们使用自己的资金更加容易。一个发展不完善的银行制度会对公司保持其业务效率带来不好的影响，并且，从效率低下中产生的任何成本必然要转嫁到最终消费者身上。

除了利用金融市场的基本功能以外，在外国司法管辖区经营的一些跨国公司选择在当地证券交易所上市。最近，矿业公司 Golden Star Resources 以及 Tullow Oil 在加纳证券交易所上市，这些上市公司已将加纳证券交易所变成非洲撒哈拉以南地区的第三大证券交易所（Agbloyor et al., 2013）。这种外国企业上市的重大影响是，他们增加了市场总值和股市的有效流动性，以及吸引其他外国企业考虑在当地证券交易所上市。（Agbloyor et al., 2013）

Agbloyor et al.（2013）指出，一个地方管辖的金融市场，尤其是国内的股票市场，如果效率很低的话，外国投资者将不愿意在此上市，因为他们投资的价值不太可能以客观公正的方式来确定。言外之意是，这些外国公司希望筹集新股本，但是由于他们认为市场低估了他们股票的价值，这将导致他们获得的价值低于他们发行股票的本质价值，所以他们筹集新股本的能力可能会受到阻碍。

Adam and Tweneboah（2009）推断，股票市场的发展与外商直接投资之间有着显著地联系。更确切地说，统计上数据表明，加纳的外商直接投资与股票市场的发展之间有着显著的关系。在某种程度上，一个百分比的外商直接投资的增长可以最终使得市场总值增长 1.5%。如果规则和政策得到改进和发展，使得市场准入对于外国投资者来说不仅是一个可行的，而且也是一个有吸引力的主张，那么上述发现会是衡量市场准入规则和政策能对投资产生何种积极影响的一个重要指标。

四、非洲南部对投资者提供的保障

为了说明市场准入规则和政策对投资者经验和最终流入该地区的外商直接投资的影响，南部非洲提供了一个特别有趣的案例研究。联合国贸易和发展会议 (UNCTAD) 做出的 2014 年世界投资报告显示，2013 年非洲获得的外商直接投资，增长了 4%，这很大一部分流入了南部非洲。在南部非洲地区，外商直接投资流入是 2013 年的两倍。南部非洲地区在为投资者提供投资保障方面的特殊机制上做出了一个很好的示范：签订双边投资条约（BIT），为投资者提供在南部非洲发展共同体（SADC）中均能够享受的保护程序，以及提供非洲东部和南部共同市场（COMESA）。

大量的双边投资条约包括了 SADC 国家为投资者提供各种保障，如公平公正待遇以及避免被国有化和征收（包含于 2010 年 4 月生效的涵盖在南部非洲发展共同体内的关于金融和投资的协议，“金融和投资协议”），而且大多数双边投资条约包含投资保障机制，允许投资者在 BITs 中的权利被侵害以后，提请国际仲裁，一般是在国际投资争端解决中心（ICSID）的管辖下，而不必依赖国内法庭。(Pierce and Scekic, 2015)

有趣的是，人们注意到，涉及非洲国家的 ICSID 仲裁结果与在世界其他地方已经做出的投资争端判决没有本质上的差别，这表明，当涉及国外投资时，非洲不一定比世界上任何其他地区更加不稳定。（Pierce and Scekic, 2015）

金融和投资协议的一个显著特征是，投资者的定义并不局限于向另一方境内投资的那一方，也就是说，金融和投资协议规定所有的投资者（无论是来自 SADC 还是其他任何地区）能够在国际仲裁要求任何 SADC 国家（包括他们自己的国家）赔偿（Pierce and Scekic, 2015）。这对于那些在 SADC 间接投资的投资者来说是很重要的，因为尽管他们是间接投资，也能够得到一些保护，比如说他们能够获得的国际仲裁等保护机制。

最近的一次市场回落，已经引起了评论家和投资者们的担忧，这样的担忧已经导致了南部非洲共同体法庭暂停的结果。南部非洲共同体法庭是建立在金融和投资协议的三个通道之一，它能够被用于投资者和当事国就双方当事人间的纠纷提请国际仲裁。Pierce and Scekic（2015）表明，对该法庭的暂停是对大量反对津巴布韦的言论所做出来的反应，津巴布韦对投资和人权的保护在整个南部非洲地区都有着深远的影响。南共同体领导人决定在 2010 年南共同体国家元首和政府首脑峰会支持南共同体法庭暂停，并且通过选举进入关于南共同体法庭新的协议的谈判，这新的协议通过限制成员国之间纠纷的管辖权，以减少南共同体法庭的管辖，因此彻底剥夺南共同体法庭决定涉及人权和投资者与当事国纠纷案件的能力。（Pierce and Scekic, 2015）

尽管南共同体法庭的工作方式受到了较大的限制，但是仍然还有其他两个可用的纠纷解决渠道被用来保护投资者利益，一个是 ICSID 仲裁，另一个是特别仲裁。只要投资者能够证明他们已经用尽了当地一切补救措施，他们就能够根据联合国国际贸易法委员会规则（UNCITRAL），在通知相应的南共同体国家六个月后提起上述两种仲裁。（Pierce and Scekic, 2015）

还有其他一些非洲南部国家，如刚果民主共和国、马达加斯加、塞舌尔、斯威士兰、赞比亚和津巴布韦，他们除了是南共同体的成员以外，也是东南非共同市场的成员。东南非共同市场是一个有 19 个非洲成员国组成的团体，为了开发他们的自然和人力资源，在本区域内促进和保护投资，他们之间形成了合作关系。（Pierce and Scekic, 2015）

就像南共同体投资保护制度一样，东南非共同市场是在东南非共同市场条约（根据其要求，除其他事项外，成员国需要保障私人投资者得到公平和公正的待遇，为私人投资创建一个稳定、透明和具有吸引力的投资环境，禁止私人投资的国有化和征收）和东南非共同市场共同投资区投资协议（CCIA 协议）下建立起来的。它是一个涉及内容广泛的机制，能够保存一个安全的投资环境，促进跨国投资和保护外商直接投资，但是由于还没有得到其中六个成员国的批准，所以它还尚未生效。（Pierce and Scekic, 2015）

与南共同体金融和投资协议不一样的是，CCIA 协议可在双方同意的基础上为投资者提供可供选择的争端解决机制。投资者能够向投资所在的成员国的法院提请诉讼，也能向在东南非共同市场协议约束下的东南非共同市场法院提起，或者是向国际仲裁庭提起，国际仲裁庭受到 ICSID 条约、ICSID 附加贷款规则、联合国贸易法委员会仲裁规则或者其他任何仲裁规则的约束。（Pierce and Scekic, 2015）

Pierce and Scekic（2015）得出结论，尽管在南部非洲地区已经采取并实施了一些措施，这些措施向投资者表明，在该地区已经为外国投资者形成了一个稳定、透明和东平的投资环境，但是仍然还存在着巨大的挑战，如事实上，大多数南部非洲国家签订的 BITs 还没有获得批准或者已经失效了，由于成员国仍未解决批准问题而导致 ICSID 公约的未生效；而且，南共同体此时的暂停则被认为是保护人权的一个重要工具。如果不加以制止的话，这些挑战很可能会削弱该地区投资者的信心。

五、总结

非洲国家所采用的市场准入规则和政策具有很显著的影响，增加了他们对外商直接投资流入本国的吸引力。而且这些国家有能力通过创建一个良好管理的、稳定的商业环境以及制定对投资者友好的市场准入规则和政策，使人们认识到他们除了丰富的矿产资源以外，还有其他的吸引力。一些非洲国家对特定的市场准入规则和政策的选择与流入他们国家的外商直接投资总量似乎存在正相关关系。

跨国公司和工业化国家对在非洲投资产生了新的兴趣，这在很大程度上可以归因于非洲国家在受惠于外商直接投资流入非洲大陆的热潮所采取的关键市场准入规则和政策。此外，非洲国家政府作出一致努力制定政策和立法，以促进吸引外国直接投资进入其国家所得到的报酬，这已成为他们能够在进程中确保可持续经济增长和发展并使其国家公民受益的保障。

参考文献

[1] Adam, A. and Tweneboah, G., (2009), Foreign direct investment and stock market development: Ghana's evidence, International Research Journal of Finance and Economics Volume 26, pp. 178-185.

[2] Agbloyor, E., Abor, J., Adjasi, C. and Yawson, A., (2013), Exploring the causality links between financial markets and foreign direct investment in Africa, Research in International Business and Finance Volume 28, pp. 118-134.

[3] Amoah, G., (2014), Foreign direct investment: attracting foreign direct investment to Ghana: lessons from the Republic of Korea, SSRN Electronic Journal, available at http://ssrn.com/abstract=2390141.

[4] Blancheton, B. and Opara-Opimba, L., (2010), Foreign direct investment in Africa: what are the key factors of attraction aside from natural resources?, Working Papers of GRETHA, No.2010-14, accessed at http://ideas.repec.org/p/grt/wpegrt/2010-14.html.

[5] Bonaglia, F., Goldstein, A. and Richard, C., (2002), Measuring reform, Study from the OECD Development Centre.

[6] Cheadle, R. (2016, 7 January), What influences foreign direct investment into Africa?, How We Made It In Africa, accessed at http://www.howwemadeitinafrica.com/53018-2/53018/.

[7] Collier, P. (2010, June), The case for investing in Africa, accessed at http://www.mckinsey.com/global-themes/middle-east-and-africa/the-case-for-investing-in-africa.

[8] McGowan, C., (2004), The relationship between political and economic openness and foreign direct investment, Southwestern Economic Review, Volume 31, Issue 1, pp.177-188.

[9] Morisset, J., (2001), Foreign direct investment in Africa: policies also matter, accessed at file:///D:/Users/0150336/Downloads/SSRN-id632551.pdf.

[10] Pierce, J. and Scekic, M., (May-June 2015), Investment protection in southern Africa, accessed at www.cdr-news.com.

[11] Tapera J. (2016), African industrial revolution and strategies for attracting foreign direct investment for sustainable economic growth & development in African countries: The Zimbabwean case, International Journal of Economics, Commerce and Management, Volume IV, Issue 4, pp.956-972.

The Market Access Rules and Policies on Investing in Africa

Author: Mashaba Bookholane①

Introduction

After the 2008 financial crisis, Africa became increasingly attractive to foreign investors and according to Cheadle (2016), this is because of Africa's (i) high growth rate as compared to the declining growth rates of most industrialised nations, (ii) rapidly increasing population, (iii) flourishing middle class, (iv) deemed improvements in the general political and economic climate across the continent and (v) abundant mineral resources and vast quantities of cultivatable land.

Despite its post-2008 financial crisis attractiveness to investors, Africa was not exempted from the consequences of the financial crisis itself, the effects of which saw the appetite for risk world-wide depleted, and as a result of Africa's perception as the riskiest region in which to invest, investor confidence in Africa declined, which was evidenced in the market by examples of international banks cutting back on letters of credit to African exporters far more significantly than to those in other regions (Collier, 2010). But despite the effects of the global financial crisis, Africa emerged intact, led by its two largest economies, Nigeria and South Africa.

Statistics have shown that between 2009 and the end of 2014, the estimated inflows of FDI to Africa have increased by 20% from the previous period, and that the Southern African region showed the most significant rise in FDI inflows over this five year period, followed by the Central African region and East Africa, whilst on the corollary, FDI inflows into the North African region and West Africa have declined since 2010 (Cheadle, 2016). Even in a landlocked and over-populated country like Rwanda, which is not rich in natural resources, its government, which has proved itself committed to economic transformation, has been able to sustain a growth rate of 10% (Collier, 2010).

---

① Masechaba Bookholane, Senior Legal Advisor at Transnet Freight Rail, a division of Transnet SOC Limited, a state-owned country established under the laws of the Republic of South Africa.

McGowan (2004) contends that in general, FDI has become increasingly important for MNEs, and research shows that the level of FDI by US MNEs outside of the United Sates and by non-US MNEs into the United States has increased, and this rise in the importance of FDI is now coupled with the increased need for political and financial/economic risk analysis. In order to successfully map out a strategy for investing in Africa as a foreign investor, it is important to understand what factors one must consider and evaluate in making the investment decision to enter the African market.

On the one hand, one must consider which regions on the African continent have significantly high enough natural resources to sustain meaningful growth over a notable period of time, and on the other hand, the political, economic and security considerations in that region that will influence the business environment and overall investor experience. Blancheton and Opara-Opimba (2010) contend that the correlation between FDI inflows and developing economies, especially African economies, is complex and that competitiveness on the international plain and the far-reaching effects of globalisation are necessitating that MNEs adopt new factors into their investment decisions in addition to the traditional factors (such as natural resources, cheap labour and market size) and that data reveals that additional parameters such as the dynamism of human capital, infrastructural and capitalistic development, the robustness of institutional and judicial arms of government, and the effects of proximity or the business environment in the country receiving the FDI inflows have all been integrated into the inquiry.

This paper sets out to explore how the investment attractiveness of mineral rich African regions interplays with the market access rules, policies, governance and business environments of those regions and how that influences the FDI inflows into that region. Empirical data shows that the disproportionate distribution of mineral resources across the African continent has resulted in an uneven breakdown of FDI across the continent, and that the 24 African countries whose revenues are mostly all generated by oil and other mineral resources have over the past two decades secured on average virtually three-quarters of the FDI inflows into Africa (Blancheton and Opara-Opimba, 2010).

This paper seeks to establish whether African countries that do not necessarily have an abundance of mineral resources can still attract FDI inflows into their country by using investor friendly market access rules and policies to attract foreign investment. In addition, the paper delves into the difference that is made in certain African countries as a consequence of choosing certain market access rules and policies over others and the correlation it then has to the inflows of FDI in that country. Blancheton and Opara-Opimba (2010) observe that on the whole, the African continent, especially the sub-Saharan region, is mindful of the indisputable necessity to restructure and re-position its institutional and regulatory framework to strengthen its international credibility in respect of potential foreign investors, and it is through this lens that this paper seeks to explore this correlation between market access rules and policies and the inflows of FDI.

The effect of policies on FDI

Historically, the African countries that have been the most successful in attracting FDI have been those countries that have an abundance of mineral wealth and natural resources and those countries that have been hailed as having the largest domestic markets (Morisset, 2001). Empirical research confirms that approximately 65 percent of the total FDI that flowed to the African continent in 1996/1997 was mostly focussed in South Africa, Nigeria, and Côte d'Ivoire, and that this inflow was also attributable to about two-thirds of the sub-continent's GDP during the same period (Morisset, 2001).

Morisset (2001) asserts that African countries are also capable of attracting FDI that is not solely based on the natural resources that the country possesses, or attracting FDI that is aimed at the local market, but rather FDI that is aimed at the regional and global markets, by making policy reform a priority. He further makes the point that countries that adopt pro-active policies and are led by reform-oriented governments are better positioned to attract FDI, and that policies can make a more significant impact on the ability of a country to attract FDI.

The more helpful approach, according to Morisset (2001), when it comes to the study of FDI inflows into the continent, would be to examine which African countries have shown the strongest ability to attract FDI when they were not able to rely on natural resources and the size of their domestic market, because traditionally, there has already been a plethora of research confirming the significant reliance by many African countries on their mineral wealth and market size and the relation that has to their ability to attract FDI.

Morisset (2001) conceded that even though the indicator used in the above study reflects existing rather than potential data, and consequently wouldn't be a reliable predictor of future FDI inflows, the indicator does capture the ability of these African countries to attract FDI when they are required to rely on everything except for their natural resources and market size, therefore it reflects not only policy and political variables, but also a series of structural factors such as infrastructure, the costs of transportation and human capital.

Morisset's (2001) study examined 29 African countries and looked at the changes in the business climate as a source of attraction for FDI. The study showed that in general, the rankings of the 29 countries remained relatively stable over the chosen period, which is consistent with the conclusion that establishing a positive or poor reputation is something that happens over an extended period of time.

The study comparison over time of the business climates for FDI in the 29 African countries revealed that a number of countries exhibited noteworthy variations in their business climate over a ten year period and foreign investors reacted to the result-yielding changes implemented by countries such as Mali (from a ranking of 26th in 1986-1990 to a ranking of 5th in 1995-1997), Uganda (from a ranking of 24th to a ranking of 13th) and Mozambique (from a ranking of 13th to a ranking of 3rd) where FDI inflows increased about 600 percent, 100 percent and 90 percent, respectively, between 1993-1994 and 1995-1997 (Morisset, 2001).

Morisset (2001) summarises what he thinks Mali and Mozambique managed to do correctly, despite the difficulty inherent in this task, because establishing an attractive business climate for FDI is a multi-dimensional task. A few of the major actions of these two countries were identified as follows: these two countries established comparatively stable macroeconomic environments over an extended period of time, given their respective regional locations; both these countries attracted foreign investors through the use of dynamic trade liberalisation and privatisation programmes; the governments of both countries approved key pieces of legislation, including new Mining (1991) and Investment (1995) Codes in Mali and a new Industrial Free Zone regime in Mozambique (1994); the adoption of international treaties dealing with FDI raised the profile and the credibility of both these governments in the international business community, as well as gave additional insurance to potential foreign investors (Morisset, 2001).

There is also other data that corroborates Morisset's finding that there is a positive correlation between FDI and economic growth and development, and that countries that have comparatively more open and transparent political and economic systems tend to attract the most FDI (McGowan, 2004).

Whilst some regions of the world have made a concerted effort to minimise barriers to FDI through policy and market access rules, there are, however, other regions in the world that have instead become notably more hostile to FDI (McGowan, 2004). A study conducted by Bonaglia et al. (2002) which sought to explain structural and institutional reforms in African countries from a qualitative and quantitative perspective revealed that countries that adopted the highest number of reformative measures between 1985 and 1997 were those in the south of the continent, and they included: Botswana, Mauritius, South Africa and Tanzania, and to a less significant extent, Zambia and Zimbabwe.

Empirical research suggests that MNEs would be inclined to make FDI into countries where the economic policy environment is open and transparent, failing which, MNEs would likely limit FDI to countries where they would have the ability to negotiate and enforce advantageous contract terms for specific transactions (McGowan, 2004). Further, MNEs are shown to be more likely to make FDI into countries that provide far-reaching protections for all firms, or protections for particular firms, particular sectors of the economy or particular investments (McGowan, 2004).

The mechanism and manner in which specific acts of liberalising a country's economic environment leads to FDI and economic development is discussed by Stoever (2002a), who explains that with the advent of a host country government opening up the economic environment of the country, the result is that MNEs are allowed more scope and flexibility for their business activities in the host country, meaning that fewer constraints on the activities of MNEs follows from economic liberalisation.

McGowan's (2004) analysis is that these reduced restrictions lower the costs and risks to MNEs that make FDI into a foreign country, and with lower risks, the MNEs will as a result require a lower rate of return on their investment, which will translate into a larger benefit to the host country. He goes on to conclude that a country that develops economic policies for FDI should be mindful of eliminating inconsistencies, prioritise the development of its well-articulated economic priorities, gradually advance policies, ensure that the rate at which deregulation occurs matches the speed at which the economy is growing, maintain consistency between its utterances that are in the public domain and its actions, implement meaningful reforms and most importantly avoid excessive interference in the process of the liberalisation of the economy.

The effect of financial markets and FDI

In addition to the apparent positive correlation between policies and the inflows of FDI, as explored above, there seems to be a similarly positive correlation between the market access rules in respect of the financial markets of a jurisdiction and the levels of FDI inflows. Anytime that MNEs move their operations to a foreign jurisdiction, they have to make use of the domestic financial markets, as they are going to need to open a local bank account, as a basic example. Agbloyor et al. (2013) suggest that when foreign enterprises make the decision to do business in another jurisdiction, part of the exercise of doing their multi-national capital budgeting involves analysing country risk, and foreign enterprises will tend to choose to invest in countries where the banking system is more sophisticated, for the simple reason that it will make access to their funds easier, as an under-developed banking system will have implications for the firm's ability to keep their operations efficient, and any costs arising out of inefficiencies will inevitably have to be passed onto the end consumer.

In addition to making use of the most basic functions of any country's financial markets, some MNEs operating in foreign jurisdictions elect to list their enterprises on the local stock exchange. Recent examples in Ghana of such listings are the listing of mining company Golden Star Resources on the Ghana Stock Exchange, as well as Tullow Oil, and these listings, amongst others, have moved the Ghana Stock Exchange to the third largest stock exchange in sub-Saharan Africa (Agbloyor et al., 2013). The effect of such significant listings by foreign enterprises is that they increase the market capitalisation and the liquidity of the stock exchange concerned in an impactful manner, as well as attract other foreign enterprises to consider listing on the local stock exchange (Agbloyor et al., 2013).

Agbloyor et al. (2013) make the point that if the financial market of a local jurisdiction, especially the domestic stock market, is inefficient, foreign investors will be reluctant to list on it because the value of their investment is unlikely to be priced in an objectively fair manner, and the implication is that should these foreign firms want to raise new equity, their ability to do so may be hindered because of their perception that the market has under-priced the value of their shares, which will then result in them receiving less value than the intrinsic value of the equity that they issued.

Adam and Tweneboah (2009) have concluded that there is a notable correlation between FDI and the development of the stock market in Ghana, and that more specifically, there is a statistically remarkable relationship between FDI and the development of the stock market in Ghana, to the extent that the data has shown that a single percentage increase in FDI can eventually lead to a 1.5 percent rise in market capitalisation. This finding is an important indicator of the positive effects that market access rules and policies can have on investment, if such rules and policies are improved and developed in a manner that makes market access for foreign investors not only possible, but also an attractive proposition.

Investor protection offered in southern Africa

Southern Africa offers a particularly interesting case study for illustrating the effects of market access rules and policies on the investor experience and ultimately the inflow of FDI into the region. The World Investment Report 2014, which is published by the United Nations Conference on Trade and Development ("UNCTAD"), showed that the FDI inflows into Africa in 2013, which increased by 4 percent, were largely driven by FDI inflows into southern Africa, a region in which FDI inflows doubled in 2013. This region provides examples of particular mechanisms that offer investment protection to investors into the southern African region: bilateral investment treaties ("BITs") as well as the protection procedures offered to investors available within the Southern African Development Community ("SADC") and the Common Market for East and Southern Africa ("COMESA").

A number of the BITs concluded by the SADC countries offer investors various guarantees, such as fair and equitable treatment and protection from nationalisation and expropriation (as contained in the SADC Protocol on Finance and Investment, which entered into force in April 2010, the "Finance and Investment Protocol"), and the large majority of these BITs contain investment protection mechanisms that allow investors, whose rights under the BITs have been encroached upon, to make claims to international arbitration, commonly under the authority of the International Centre for the Settlement of Investment Disputes ("ISID"), rather than having to rely on the domestic courts (Pierce and Scekic, 2015).

Interestingly, it has been noted that the outcomes of the ISID arbitrations involving African countries have not been significantly different in substance from the outcomes of investment disputes that have been adjudicated upon in other parts of the world, which suggests that Africa may not necessarily be more volatile than any other region in the world when it comes to foreign investment (Pierce and Scekic, 2015).

A noteworthy feature of the Finance and Investment Protocol is that the definition of investor is not confined to a party that has made an investment in the territory of the other party, therefore the implication of this is then that the Finance and Investment Protocol makes provision for all investors (whether from a SADC country or from any other territory) to launch claims against any SADC country (including their own country) in an international arbitration (Pierce and Scekic, 2015). This is significant for those investors whose interests in investments made into the SADC may be indirect, as there appears to be some assurance that despite their indirect investment, a protection mechanism such as international arbitration is available to them.

A recent clawback that has raised concern amongst commentators and investors alike has been the suspension of the SADC Tribunal, which tribunal was established under the Finance and Investment Protocol as one of the three channels that could be utilised by an investor and a state party for the submission of international arbitrations. Pierce and Scekic (2015) suggest that this suspension was implemented in response to a number of judgements against Zimbabwe, which had far-reaching implications for the protection of investments and human rights in southern Africa. The leaders of the SADC took a decision at the 2010 SADC Summit of Heads of State and Government to uphold the suspension of the SADC Tribunal and elected to enter into negotiations for a new protocol in respect of the SADC Tribunal which would serve to curtail the jurisdiction of the SADC Tribunal by limiting its jurisdiction to disputes arising between member states, consequently completely removing the SADC Tribunal's ability to decide upon cases involving human rights matters and investor-state disputes (Pierce and Scekic, 2015).

Despite this significant limitation of the workings of the SADC Tribunal, investor protection is still guaranteed by the other two available channels for dispute resolution under the Finance and Investment Protocol, namely ICSID arbitration and ad hoc arbitration which can be brought under the United National Commission on International Trade Law ("UNCITRAL") Arbitration Rules provided that investors are able to demonstrate that they have exhausted all local remedies, as required of them, and that a six month period has elapsed since the SADC country was notified of the dispute (Pierce and Scekic, 2015).

There are a number of other southern African countries such as the Democratic Republic of Congo, Madagascar, Seychelles, Swaziland, Zambia and Zimbabwe that in addition to their SADC membership belong to the COMESA, an organisation comprising of 19 African member states that have entered into a cooperative relationship for purposes of developing their natural and human resources, and pursuing the objective of the promotion and protection of investments in their region (Pierce and Scekic, 2015).

Much like the SADC investment protection regime, the COMESA is organised under the COMESA Treaty (in terms of which member countries are required, amongst other things, to assure private investors of their fair and equitable treatment, to create an investment environment that is stable, unambiguous and inviting, and to outlaw the nationalisation or expropriation of private investments) and the Investment Agreement for the COMESA Common Investment Area ("CCIA Agreement"), which is an all-inclusive instrument that is concerned with the preservation of a secure investment climate, the promotion of cross-border investments and the protection of FDI, but that has not yet entered into force on account of being short of ratifications from six member states (Pierce and Scekic, 2015).

The CCIA Agreement, not unlike the SADC Finance and Investment Protocol, offers investors a choice of dispute mechanisms ranging from the ability to submit a claim to a competent court of the member country in whose jurisdiction the investment has been made, to the COMESA Court of Justice under the COMESA Treaty, or to international arbitration under the ICSID Convention, the ICSID Additional Facility Rules, the UNCITRAL Arbitration Rules or any other arbitration rules, on condition that both parties to the dispute are agreeable thereto (Pierce and Scekic, 2015).

Pierce and Scekic (2015) conclude that although measures already adopted and put into place in the southern African region have given investors an indication that the investment environment being fostered in the region is one of stability, transparency and fairness in respect of foreign investors, significant challenges remain, such as: the fact that the majority of BITs signed by southern African countries are yet to be ratified or have already expired; the inoperative status of the ICSID Convention owing to ratifications by member states that remain outstanding; and the suspension of the SADC Tribunal just at the point that it was being recognised as an important tool for the protection of individual rights, and these challenges are likely to erode investor confidence in the region should they continue unchecked.

Conclusion

The type of market access rules and policies adopted by African countries have been shown to make a noteworthy difference to their attractiveness as destinations for FDI inflows and that these countries have the ability, through the creation of a business environment that is driven by good governance, stability and market access rules and policies that are investor friendly, to be recognised for more than just their mineral richness. There appears to be a positive correlation between some African countries choosing certain market access rules and policies over others and the inflows of FDI into that country.

Some of the renewed interest of MNEs and industrialised nations in investing in Africa can also be shown in large part to be attributable to the key market access rules and policies that have been adopted by the African countries that seem to have benefited the most from this upsurge of FDI inflows into the continent. In addition, the reward of the governments of the African countries that have made a concerted effort to put in place policies and legislation that fosters an environment for attracting FDI into their respective countries, has been that they have been able in the process to safeguard their country's ability to secure sustainable economic growth and development and benefit for the citizens of their country.

REFERENCES

[1] Adam, A. and Tweneboah, G., (2009), Foreign direct investment and stock market development: Ghana's evidence, International Research Journal of Finance and Economics Volume 26, pp. 178-185.

[2] Agbloyor, E., Abor, J., Adjasi, C. and Yawson, A., (2013), Exploring the causality links between financial markets and foreign direct investment in Africa, Research in International Business and Finance Volume 28, pp. 118-134.

[3] Amoah, G., (2014), Foreign direct investment: attracting foreign direct investment to Ghana: lessons from the Republic of Korea, SSRN Electronic Journal, available at http://ssrn.com/abstract=2390141.

[4] Blancheton, B. and Opara-Opimba, L., (2010), Foreign direct investment in Africa: what are the key factors of attraction aside from natural resources?, Working Papers of GRETHA, No.2010-14, accessed at http://ideas.repec.org/p/grt/wpegrt/2010-14.html.

[5] Bonaglia, F., Goldstein, A. and Richard, C., (2002), Measuring reform, Study from the OECD Development Centre.

[6] Cheadle, R. (2016, 7 January), What influences foreign direct investment into Africa?, How We Made It In Africa, accessed at http://www.howwemadeitinafrica.com/53018-2/53018/.

[7] Collier, P. (2010, June), The case for investing in Africa, accessed at http://www.mckinsey.com/global-themes/middle-east-and-africa/the-case-for-investing-in-africa.

[8] McGowan, C., (2004), The relationship between political and economic openness and foreign direct investment, Southwestern Economic Review, Volume 31, Issue 1, pp. 177-188.

[9] Morisset, J., (2001), Foreign direct investment in Africa: policies also matter, accessed at file:///D:/Users/0150336/Downloads/SSRN-id632551.pdf.

[10] Pierce, J. and Scekic, M., (May-June 2015), Investment protection in southern Africa, accessed at www.cdr-news.com.

[11] Tapera J. (2016), African industrial revolution and strategies for attracting foreign direct investment for sustainable economic growth & development in African countries: The Zimbabwean case, International Journal of Economics, Commerce and Management, Volume IV, Issue 4, pp.956-972.

非洲国家税收政策对外商直接投资的影响

作者：Angeline Munyeriwa 译者：郭一楠

过去的几十年中，外商直接投资（FDI）已经在世界范围的资金、技术分配中成为一股强大的动力，它甚至超过了中非间贸易额的增速。对于非洲国家来说，随着FDI的增加，将其用于发展的重要性同样大幅增长[①]。

本文中，外商直接投资（FDI）是指，具有对尚未进入的一国进行投资的潜力和能力的多国公司（MNCs）或跨国公司（TNCs），在这些国家进行长期投资，或个别情况下短期投资的行为[②]。

FDI对于非洲国家的吸引力非常明显。FDI促进发展的增长和可持续性，激励国家竞争力，促进就业，并且缩小社会收入差距。更重要的是，在面对危机时FDI显得更有弹性，因为在投资时，投资者通常具备长远眼光，并且FDI具有在接受国和投资者间分担风险的特质。所以，FDI在经济增长方面提供了比其他形式资金流动更强大的激励。更不用说FDI可以让从发展中国家获得资源的发达国家受益，并向世界传播知识。这无疑会带来更大的科技进步，因为知识是创新和新思想产生的平台。

随着越来越多非洲政府竞相吸引跨国公司，大多数非洲国家采取不同种类的税收政策，意图鼓励投资，并将投资引导至政府认为应优先发展的领域。这样的税收政策大多以财政激励的形式存在，比如已经成为世界趋势的自由税收政策。中国近些年已经成为非洲大陆最大的投资者，且大多数非洲国家正是通过免税期、进口关

① Neumayer, Eric (2007) *Do double taxation treaties increase foreign direct investment to developing countries?* Journal of Development Studies, 43 (8), p.5.

② Nduga Rayray (2016)*Taxation System in Kenya; Foreign Direct Investment*, Article Found at https://raymonduga.wordpress.com/2016/02/20/taxation-system-in-kenya-foreign-direct-investment-nduga-rayray/ (accessed 27/05/2016).

税减免和其他专门为中国投资者设计的税收政策来吸引投资[①]。

必须说明的是，为了吸引 FDI，非洲国家的税收政策几乎全部以某种激励的形式存在。几乎从未有一个非洲国家为吸引 FDI，向外国投资者增加或收紧税收政策。这是本文的基本假定，同时本文将在这一假定下论述非洲国家的税收政策。

一、税收激励

为了全面了解非洲国家税收政策和 FDI 之间的关系，最重要的是首先要了解税收激励本身。根据 Easson 的观点，税收激励可以被定义为：

> "根据法条，税收激励可以被定义为一种为适格投资项目制定的特殊税收条款，其代表了一种受到法律认可的，与适用于普通投资项目（如没有获得特殊税收条款的项目）的税收政策相偏离的条款。这一定义暗示了任何对一切投资项目均适用的税收条款不构成税收激励……"[②]

正如上述定义，税收激励是一种根据税法，向特定合格投资者颁布的税收制度。与没有获得税收激励的投资者相比，达标者将获得更多优惠[③]。

非洲国家为吸引 FDI 提供了多种税收激励政策。这些激励措施可以通过它们的原理和其如何影响预期投资者投资的收益和成本进行分类。主要的税收激励类型可以被归纳为下列几类[④]：

（1）免税期：免税期是一种众所周知的税收激励措施，专门针对新成立的公司施行。在这种激励措施下，新投资者将在一定期限内被免除任何种类的所得税（通常

---

① Morisset, J., & Pirnia, N. (2000). *How tax policy and incentives affect foreign direct investment. A review.* The World Bank and International Finance Corporation Foreign Investment Advisory Service. Policy Research Working Paper, no.2509, pp.1–34.

② Easson, A., (2004) *Tax Incentives for Foreign Direct Investment.* Netherlands: Kluwer Law international.

③ Muhammad Reza Fahmi (2012) *Analyzing The Relationship Between Tax Holiday And Foreign Direct Investment In Indonesia,* Unpublished Thesis, Graduate School Of Asia Pacific Studies Ritsumeikanasia Pacific University Japan, p.31.

④ Muhammad Reza Fahmi (2012) *Analyzing The Relationship Between Tax Holiday And Foreign Direct Investment In Indonesia,* Unpublished Thesis, Graduate School Of Asia Pacific Studies Ritsumeikanasia Pacific University Japan, p.31.

是 3 年到 5 年）。除免除所得税，政府通常还将其和关税、消费税、货物 / 服务税等的免除相结合。

（2）投资税额优惠：在某些国家，投资税优惠是一定比例的合格投资可以被减免税赋。这类税收激励措施减少企业纳税后购买新的固定设备的成本。

（3）减少对海外支付的股息利润征税：对海外利润或股息征税是十分常见的。随着股息税率的增长，投资者不再愿意拓展他们的投资。因此，这类税收的减免可以保持投资者的信心。

（4）长期资本利得的优惠：这种税收激励的目的是刺激投资者保护投资，并在可能的情况下长期扩大投资。特别待遇可以以降低长期投资所得税税率的形式存在。

（5）零关税或降低关税：这是为了促进投资，尤其是在进口固定设备，包括进口备用配件或更换老旧机械方面。这类激励会减少投资者承担的投资成本。所以，它会鼓励投资者更换老旧设备或升级过时的设备。

（6）基于雇佣关系的减免：在拥有大量劳动力的国家，失业率是一项难题。政府可以制定税收激励政策，促使投资者在生产过程中雇佣更多员工。所以，劳动密集型产业比自动化机械程度高的行业更受欢迎。

（7）避免双重征税：当一家跨国企业（MNC）为一项在外国的经济活动产生的同一笔公司收益支付了两次税赋，这便是双重征税：一次是向外国政府缴纳，也就是经济活动所在国，另一次是向母国政府所缴纳，也就是公司所在地。比如一家中国企业向津巴布韦政府纳税，并且向中国政府因其在津巴布韦的投资行为纳税①。因此一些非洲国家制定了限制属地主义课税的协议，这意味着发展中国家只能在一定限度内向外来投资者征税。

以上并未穷尽所有税收激励政策。非洲政府正在制定更多创新税收政策吸引投资者。上面这一列举只是为了展示非洲最常见的用于激励 FDI 所采取的税收激励政策。

然而，最重要的问题仍是，投资者驱动的非洲国家税收政策是否对吸引外来投资有效。这个问题的答案其实并不明确。税收政策在吸引 FDI 方面的效果在税收专家当中有着激烈的争论。即使在适用税收政策吸引 FDI 的非洲国家当中也并未形成针对税收政策对 FDI 影响的共识。我们甚至可以说，学界在这一问题上分为了两派。因此，本文将从正反两面分析这两派观点，并表达笔者对于非洲国家税收政策在吸

① Neumayer, Eric (2007) *Do double taxation treaties increase foreign direct investment to developing countries?* Journal of Development Studies, 2007 43 (8), p.1.

引 FDI 方面效果的见解。

二、税收政策对吸引外商直接投资有很大影响

理论上，非洲国家的税收政策会影响投资决策，因为对税赋的评估影响投资者的利润和成本。这一方的逻辑非常简单：高税自然导致了人工成本和生产成本上升，所以会进而影响投资者向更低、更友好的税收政策国家投资[①]。按照这种推理，很显然拥有更好的税收政策的国家会比相反政策的国家吸引更多投资。

的确，Gastanaga，Nugent 和 Pashamova（1998）学者在他们对 FDI 向发展中国家转移的分析中提到，税收对投资有着显著的负面影响[②]。

税收和 FDI 的相互影响体现在当外国投资者单纯因为税收因素成功设立公司或未成功设立公司上。比如，2004 年 8 月，一家计算机装配销售公司在肯尼亚的出口加工区（EPZ）成功设立，但是最终停业并搬至南非，并称肯尼亚的高税赋是它们转移的原因[③]。

不仅如此，税收毫无疑问对某类投资者尤为重要。出口驱动型投资对成本因素更加敏感，因为国际市场本身竞争非常激烈。所以不同税率会很大程度影响投资决策。

在考虑非洲国家通过避免双重征税来激励企业时，税收政策的影响就更加明确。当投资者有多个选择时，避免双重征税的政策显然会使一国对外来投资者更有吸引力[④]。

能够避免双重征税的税收政策可以保证外国投资者的投资收益不会因为在母国和东道国的双倍税收而减少，进而使得非洲国家对外来投资更有吸引力，且进一步

---

① Easson, A., (2004) *Tax Incentives for Foreign Direct Investment.* Netherlands: Kluwer Law international.

② Gastanaga, V.M., Nugent, J.B. and B. Pashamova, (1998) *Host Country Reforms and FDI Inflows: How Much Difference Do They Make?* World Development, 26 (7), pp.1299-1314.

③ Ngowi, H. P. J. (2000).*"FDI Determinants: Can sub-Sahara Africa Increase its Global FDI share?"* Morogoro: IDM Mzumbe.

④ Egger, P., M. Larch, M. Pfaffermayer and H. Winner, 2004. The Impact of Endogenous Tax Treaties on Foreign Direct Investment: Theory and Empirical Evidence. Working Paper. University of Innsbruck, Department of Economics and Statistics, p.1.

带来更多的外商直接投资[①]。

显然，就这一点而言，Hines（1998）预计拥有税收减免协议的发展中国家的FDI，会比没有这类协议的情况下高出1.4倍至2.4倍[②]。

由于上述原因，可以说非洲政府的税收政策对FDI投资者有直接影响。的确，税收政策与外来投资者明显对立，或者只为其提供与本地投资者相同待遇，这对潜在外来投资者都是一种打击。反之亦然。对投资者友好的政策，即倾向于外来投资者的政策，或甚至给予由于本地投资者的待遇的国家当然会吸引更多的外来投资者以及FDI。

但是现实并没有这么简单。税收政策和FDI之间的相互影响更加复杂，并且会受到更多外来因素的影响。

三、税收政策对吸引外商直接投资没有影响

但是，学界仍对税收政策是否会影响FDI存在争议。的确一些学者已经开始论证，只将税收政策作为吸引FDI的因素是谬误，税收政策并不一定会吸引投资，因为投资者还会考虑其他更重要的有利投资环境的因素。

世界银行数据银行称（WBI，2002），尽管税收政策也许对外来投资者选择向哪里投资有一定的影响，但与下列因素相比，这只是第二位因素[③]：（1）一贯稳定的宏观财政政策；（2）充足的物理、金融、法律和制度基础；（3）高效、透明并且负责的行政管理；（4）高技术的劳动力和灵活的雇佣劳动政策；（5）多种可采取的争端解决机制；（6）语言文化状况；（7）生产要素市场和产品市场——规模和效率。

这一观点受到其他学者的青睐。Ngowi（2000）称，FDI的流向很大程度取决于一些FDI决定因素的临界最小值在一国的存在状况。这些决定因素给予MNC向外国市场大量投资昂贵资本的信心和兴趣。他列出了税收政策以外的决定因素：经济、政治和社会的稳定性；商业准入和运行的规则。

---

① United Nations, 2001, *United Nations Model Double Taxation Convention between Developed and Developing Countries*. New York: United Nations.

② Hines, J.R. Jr., 1998, "Tax Sparing" and Direct Investment in Developing Countries, Working Paper 6728. Cambridge, MA: National Bureau of Economic Research.

③ World Bank Institute. 2002. *Tax Incentives*. Available: http://siteresources.worldbank.org/INTTPA/Resources/EassonZoltPaper.pdf.

Ngowi（2000）进一步指出对待外国机构的标准：除去投资激励的商业促进、市场规模、增速，结构和获取度，原材料，低廉高效的劳动力和物理基础设施，包括港口、公路、能源、通信等要比单独的税收政策对投资者更为重要 ①。

毫不意外，在布隆迪、卢旺达、坦桑尼亚的投资者调查显示，多数投资者在作出投资决策时，并没有明显受到税收激励或免除的影响。这些决策很大程度上是基于市场潜力、融资渠道、可靠的电力供应和良好的基础设施而作出的。三个国家中仅有 7.9% 的受访者表示，如果没有税收财政激励是不会投资的。对于投资者来说，矿产资源的质量和良好的经济政治环境比一国的税收制度更为重要 ②。

显然，Akinboade，Siebrits 和 Roussot（2006）指出，东道国经济不稳定可能成为 FDI 流入的巨大阻力。任何形式的不稳定带来的不确定性都歪曲了投资者对在该国未来收益状况的预期 ③。比如，津巴布韦 2008 年政局不稳，投资者信心大幅下降 ④。同时，本土化法案颁布，企图强迫所有外国公司将其 51% 的股份交于本土居民，这使投资者感到不安，政府为了吸引新投资者不得不作出让步 ⑤。

传统来讲，政府不得不使用税收激励制度吸引投资，尤其是与外来直接投资相权衡。包括联合国、世界银行、国际货币基金组织、经济合作与发展组织和欧盟在内的国际组织共同抵制使用税收激励制度吸引投资，它们称发展一国政治、经济政策和基础设施建设，并解决其他阻碍投资的问题优于试图通过税收激励来弥补这些不足 ⑥。但是，考虑到没有资金投入基础设施建设的国家才需要吸引 FDI，这一倡导的可行性有待商榷。

必须明确一点是，尽管证明税收政策和长期增长的投资之间关系的证据非常模

① Ngowi, H. P. J. (2000). *"FDI Determinants: Can sub-Sahara Africa Increase its Global FDI share?"* Morogoro: IDM Mzumbe.

② Organization for Economic Co-operation and Development (2012) Investor Motivation Surveys in East Africa, Global Tax Simplification Team, World Bank Group, Bogota, Colombia, p.7.

③ Akinboade, O. A., Siebrits, F. K., & Roussot, E. N. (2006). *Foreign direct investments in South-Africa. In Ajayi (Ed.), Foreign direct investments in Sub-Sahara Africa – Origin, targets, impacts and potential* Nairobi: African Economic Research Consortium. pp.177–209.

④ Zimbabwe (2014) *Scoping Report, British Expertise* Foreign Commonwealth Office.

⑤ *Indigenisation Regulations Suspended For New Investors*, Zimbabwe Daily 19 July 2012.

⑥ *The Determinants Of Foreign Direct Investment: A Survey Of The Evidence,* U.N. Doc. ST/CTC/121, U.N. Sales No. E.92.II.A.2 (1992); *Tax Incentives And Foreign Direct Investment: A Global Survey,* U.N. Doc. CTAD/ITE/IPC/Misc.3, U.N. Sales No. E.01.II.D.5 (2000).

糊，税收政策只在个别情况下影响了投资地点的决策，有更多的证据表明外来投资者将对基础设施质量、劳动力是否受到良好教育和当地市场状况以及其他上述所提及因素的考虑放在了更优先的位置[①]。

按照逻辑，投资者不可能仅仅因为免税期和其他税收激励政策，向处于内战状态的国家或受到动荡政局困扰的国家投资。同样，没有投资者会因为偏向的税收政策，向没有用于矿产运输的公路等基础设施的国家，或向没有高技术的劳动力的国家投资。根本来说，高税率并不一定会阻止 FDI，正如低税率并不一定会吸引 FDI。税率不足只能弥补落后的基础设施、落后的公共服务、有限的市场和其他可能的落后的投资条件。非洲政府应当关注为自身创造有助于外来投资者投资的环境，因为不管税收激励政策多么有吸引力，单凭这一点，不足以弥补落后的首要投资影响因素[②]。

可以说，除了一些不确切的好处，投资者税收政策对非洲国家的弊大于利。

即使税收激励对 FDI 有效，最终一段时间之后，它的弊端仍会大于优势。最直接的代价与东道国政府潜在的税收损失相关。这种情况很可能对东道国国库和财政预算产生负面、甚至灾难性的影响[③]。考虑到目前大多非洲国家面临的预算和财政限制，这个问题显得格外重要。税收减少和随之而来的税收受限无疑会使发展中国家付出巨大的代价[④]。简单来说，这样的税收政策会增加投资国收入，但并不会为非洲国家带来太多收益。

使用税收激励制度要求国家依赖其他财政来源，但大多非洲国家并没有理想财政的来源。为了提高公民生活水平，非洲国家需要一种可行的税收制度，为公共服务和良好的公共设施提供资金支持。

就此而论，近期对非洲的研究表明，税收激励制度导致国家收入减少，削弱政

① Andrew Mold(2004) *A proposal for unitary taxes on the profits of transnational corporations*, CEPAL Review 82, April 2004.

② Garbarino, C. (2012) Comparative Analysis of Tax Incentives: Circulation of Models and Tax Policy Alternatives. Available: https://www.yumpu.com/en/document/view/16202981/1-comparativeanalysis-of-tax-incentives-intrweborg.

③ Morisset, J., & Pirnia, N. (2000). How tax policy and incentives affect foreign direct investment.
A review. The World Bank and International Finance Corporation Foreign Investment Advisory.
Service. Policy Research Working Paper, no.2509, pp.1–34.

④ Neumayer, Eric (2007) Do double taxation treaties increase foreign direct investment to developing countries? Journal of Development Studies, 43 (8), p.10.

府治理能力和发展中国家对抗贫困的能力。在坦桑尼亚，国内的税收激励导致税收方面流失相当于约 3% 的 GDP①。相似的是，税收正义联盟和国际行动救援组织预计肯尼亚每年从税收激励政策和税收免除当中损失大约 1000 亿肯尼亚元（11 亿美元）。

与此同时，在非洲国家看上去受到追捧的倾向于投资者的税收政策，如果吸引来的是“不合适”的投资者，则达不到预期效果。比如掠夺东道国矿产资源但并未建造基础设施或永久设施，在矿产资源枯竭后便离开的投资者。此外，这样的税收政策被证明是腐败的根源，对形成有竞争力的市场和合理的政策造成阻碍②。

与此同时，我们也不能忽视这对本地企业造成的不利影响。非洲国家用以吸引投资者的税收政策通常被认为以牺牲本地企业为代价，偏向外来投资者的。为外来投资者削减税赋意味着给本地企业增大负担，因为政府需要通过增加本地企业税收弥补潜在的国库收入损失。税收政策带来的不公平竞争环境不能被忽视。当外国公司可以免税进口它们的机械时，显然本地企业必须负担沉重的税赋。

总而言之，非洲政府用来吸引投资的税收政策更像是非洲政府用过于沉重的代价换取了不成比例的回报。

四、结论

即使非洲国家的大部分税收政策倾向于投资者，这也很难成为吸引 FDI 来到这片大陆的动力。税收政策并不独立运作，而是大大受到外部和内部的经济因素，包括基础设施、宏观经济环境、国家政治稳定性等的影响。

就这一点而论，在评价非洲国家税收政策对 FDI 的影响时，更保守的评判应该是介于两极之间。总体来说，国家的税收政策和其他决定性因素，比如基础设施、运输成本和政治经济稳定性是互补的存在。

如果非洲国家继续以带有倾向性的税收政策吸引 FDI，毫无疑问，长此以往这将是一把双刃剑。非洲国家需要实行平衡税收目标和 FDI 的政策。Ngowi（2004）认为，税收激励措施只有在投资收益中获得回报的这种情况下才会起作用，也就是说，

① Yolanda Vamusse (2012) Tax incentives and exemptions not necessary to attract investment, Institute of Development Studies www.ids.ac.uk/news/tax-incentives-and-exemptions-not-necessary-to-attract-investment.

② Morisset, J., & Pirnia, N. (2000). How tax policy and incentives affect foreign direct investment.
A review. The World Bank and International Finance Corporation Foreign Investment Advisory.
Service. Policy Research Working Paper, no.2509, pp.1–34.

税收如果可以增加就业机会、增加出口或降低进口、换取技术、提高竞争力等与经济发展其他方面建立联系，那么[①]这些收益大于付出的成本，即因税收激励政策损失的国库收入。

总而言之，政治稳定性、合理的财政政策、具有技术的劳动力和良好的基础设施建设比偏向性的税收政策更具拉动效果。

① Ngowi, H. P. J. (2000). *"FDI Determinants: Can sub-Sahara Africa Increase its Global FDI share?"* Morogoro: IDM Mzumbe.

The Impact of Taxation Policies of African Countries on Foreign Direct Investment

Author: Angeline Munyeriwa

Foreign Direct investment (FDI) has in the past several decades become a major force in the worldwide allocation of funds and technology, even outpacing the volume of trade between Africa and China. With increasing FDI, its importance to African countries as a source of funds for development has also dramatically increased. ①

For the purposes of this paper, Foreign Direct Investment (FDI) refers to when multi-national corporations (MNCs) or transnational corporations (TNCs) that have the potential and capability to invest in another country in which they do not already have a presence, do so, for usually a long term return, though in rare cases in can be a short term.②

The attraction of FDI to African countries is obvious. FDI promotes growth and sustainable development, boosting countries' competitiveness, generating employment, and reducing social and income disparities. Moreover, FDI is considered to be more resilient toward crisis, since investors commonly have a long-term perspective when investing in a country and it has the nature of risk sharing between recipient countries and investor. Therefore, FDI provides a stronger stimulus to economic growth than other types of capital flows. This is not to mention that FDI also benefits the developed country, which receives resources from the developing country, while also at the same time spreading knowledge and sharing it with the world population, which inevitably leads to greater technological progress, since knowledge serves as a platform for the generation of new ideas and innovations.

With an increasing number of African governments competing to attract multinational

① Neumayer, Eric (2007) *Do double taxation treaties increase foreign direct investment to developing countries?* Journal of Development Studies, 43 (8), p.5.

② Nduga Rayray (2016)*Taxation System in Kenya; Foreign Direct Investment*, Article Found at https://raymonduga.wordpress.com/2016/02/20/taxation-system-in-kenya-foreign-direct-investment-nduga-rayray/ (accessed 27/05/2016).

companies, most African countries use a variety of tax policies in an attempt to encourage investment and to channel this investment into areas that are considered national priorities. Such tax policies largely in the form of fiscal incentives, like liberal tax policies have become a global trend. Most African countries rely on incentives like tax holidays, and import duty exemptions and other tax policies that are designed to attract investors from China, which in recent years has become the largest investor on the African continent.①

It must be stated from the onset, that the tax policies of African countries, in seeking to attract FDI, have almost all been in the form of an incentive, one way or the other. There has hardly been, if any, an instance, where an African country actually increased or tightened tax regulations against foreign investors in order to attract FDI. This is the basic assumption of this paper and the tax policies of African countries will be examined in this light

Understanding Tax Incentives

In order to be able to fully appreciate the relationship between the taxation policies of African countries and FDI, it is important firstly to understand tax incentives themselves. According to (Easson, 2004), tax incentives can be defined as:

> *"In statutory terms, a tax incentive can be defined as a special tax provision granted to qualified investment projects (however determined) that represents a statutory favorable deviation from a corresponding provision applicable to investment projects in general (i.e. projects that receive no special tax provision). An implication of this definition is that any tax provision that is applicable to all investment projects does not constitute a tax incentive...."*②

As it has been defined above, according to statutory regulation, a tax incentive is a tax facility granted to specific investors that meet certain criteria as stipulated in tax law. Those who are eligible will benefit more than those who do not receive tax incentives.③

---

① Morisset, J., & Pirnia, N. (2000). *How tax policy and incentives affect foreign direct investment. A review.* The World Bank and International Finance Corporation Foreign Investment Advisory Service. Policy Research Working Paper, no.2509, pp.1–34.

② Easson, A., (2004) *Tax Incentives for Foreign Direct Investment.* Netherlands: Kluwer Law international.

③ Muhammad Reza Fahmi (2012) *Analyzing The Relationship Between Tax Holiday And Foreign Direct Investment In Indonesia,* Unpublished Thesis, Graduate School Of Asia Pacific Studies Ritsumeikanasia Pacific University Japan p.31.

There are many types of tax incentives that may be offered by African countries in order to attract FDI. The incentives offered can be categorized according to the mechanism or channel through which they influence the benefits and costs of investment by a prospective investor. The main types of tax incentives may be summarized as follows:①

(a) Tax holiday - Tax holiday is a well-known tax incentive specified for newly established companies. Under this incentive, new investors will be exempted from any form of income tax during a specified period (commonly three to five years). In addition of income tax exemption, governments usually combine it with duty and excise, goods and / or services tax exemption.

(b) Investment tax credits - In some countries, investment tax credits will be regarded as a proportion of qualified investment which will be deducted in tax liability. This type of incentive reduces the after-tax cost to businesses for purchasing new capital equipment.

(c) Reduced taxes on dividends and interest paid abroad - It is common to levy tax on repatriated profit or dividends. As dividend tax rate increases, investors will be less attracted to expand their investment. Therefore, this tax can be discounted to maintain investor's confidence.

(d) Preferential treatment of long-term capital gains-The intention of this incentive is to stimulate investors to preserve investment and if possible to expand it for a longer period. Special treatment will be granted in the form of a reduced income tax rate for a longer period of investment.

(e) Zero or reduced tariffs - In order to promote investment particularly in imported capital equipment including its spare parts, or the replacement of old and obsolete machinery. This incentive will reduce the cost of investment borne by investors. Therefore, it will encourage investors to replace its obsolete machine or upgrade the outdated plants.

(f) Employment-based deductions - In many countries with an abundant labor force, the unemployment rate is an inherent condition which is troublesome. Government may formulate tax incentive to motivate investors for hiring more employees in their productions. Therefore, labor intensive industry is preferable than fully automatic machine industry

(g) Prevention of double taxation- Double taxation occurs if a multinational company (MNC) pays tax on the same corporate income earned from economic activity in a foreign country twice: once to the tax authorities of the foreign country, which is host to the economic activity, and also to the tax authorities of the home country, in which the company is domiciled. For example a Chinese company pays tax to the government of Zimbabwe and also to the government of China on any income that is a result of their investment in Zimbabwe.② Some African countries have therefore

① Muhammad Reza Fahmi (2012) *Analyzing The Relationship Between Tax Holiday And Foreign Direct Investment In Indonesia,* Unpublished Thesis, Graduate School Of Asia Pacific Studies Ritsumeikanasia Pacific University Japan p.31.

② Neumayer, Eric (2007) *Do double taxation treaties increase foreign direct investment to developing countries?* Journal of Development Studies, 2007 43 (8), p.1.

entered into agreements that limit source-based taxation, which means that developing countries can only collect tax revenues from foreign investors to a limited extent.

The list is not exhaustive. African governments are coming up with new and more innovative tax policies to attract investors. The list is therefore mainly to demonstrate the most common type of tax incentives that are offered by African governments to boost FDI.

However, the ultimate question remains, whether the investor oriented tax policies of African countries are effective in attracting foreign direct investment. In truth the answer is not so clear. The effectiveness of tax policies in attracting FDI is widely debated among tax professionals. Even as African countries use tax policies to attract FDI, there is no consensus in empirical work on the actual effect of taxation on FDI. It can even be argued that the scholarship on the subject is split right in the middle. This paper, will therefore present both sides of the coin and express the author's view on the effectiveness of tax policies by African countries, in attracting FDI.

One side: Tax policies have a major effect in attracting FDI

It can be argued that, theoretically, the taxation policies of African countries affect investment decisions because tax assessment influences the amount of investors' benefits and costs. The logic for such a position is very simple: a high level of taxes contributes in raising labor costs and naturally production, and may thus influence an investor to invest its production and capital in a country with a lower or more investor friendly tax regime.[①] Following such reasoning, it would be patently obvious that countries with better investor tax policies would induce companies to invest in them, more than countries with opposite policies.

Indeed, scholars Gastanaga, Nugent and Pashamova (1998) in their analysis of FDI flows to developing countries find that taxes have a noticeable and statistically significantly negative impact on investment.[②]

The interplay between taxation and FDI is demonstrated by cases where a foreign investor either sets up an operation, or fails to do so purely because of a tax consideration. For example, in August 2004, a computer assembling and sales company that had set up under the Export Processing Zone (EPZ) enterprise scheme in Kenya, closed shop and moved to South Africa, citing heavy taxation in Kenya as the cause for its relocation.[③]

---

① Easson, A., (2004) *Tax Incentives for Foreign Direct Investment.* Netherlands: Kluwer Law international.

② Gastanaga, V.M., Nugent, J.B. and B. Pashamova, (1998) *Host Country Reforms and FDI Inflows: How Much Difference Do They Make?*World Development, 26 (7), pp.1299-1314.

③ Ngowi, H. P. J. (2000)." *FDI Determinants: Can sub-Sahara Africa Increase its Global FDI share?* " Morogoro: IDM Mzumbe.

Furthermore, there is no question that taxes are very important for some types of investors. For example export oriented investments are relatively more sensitive to cost factors, since international markets are inherently highly competitive. Therefore, difference in tax rates will significantly influence investment decision.

The influence of tax policies becomes even clearer when one considers the above discussed incentive by African countries of doing away with double taxation. Certainly the avoidance of double taxation can make a country more attractive to foreign investors, who often have a choice among multiple locations.①

A tax policy that avoids double taxation can re-assure foreign investors that profits from their investment are not doubly reduced by taxation in both host and residence country, thus making the African country more attractive to the foreign investor and by extension bringing in much needed foreign direct investment. ②

Tellingly, in this regard Hines (1998) estimates that FDI in developing countries with whom a "tax sparing" agreement exists is 1.4 to 2.4 times higher than what it would have been otherwise.③

For the above reasons it can be argued that African governments' tax policies have a direct impact on the flow of FDI to their respective foreign investors. Indeed, where a country has tax policies that are clearly hostile to foreign investors, or at least treats them like the local investor, taxing both equally, may discourage potential foreign investors. The opposite is also equally true. Investor friendly policies, which favour the foreign investor, even granting him or her, more favourable tax terms than the local investor would certainly attract foreign investors and naturally also FDI

However things are not as simple as they appear on paper. The interplay between tax policies and FDI is more complex and subject to other external factors as will be shown.

On the other side: Tax policies have no impact in attracting FDI

However, as pointed out above, the scholars are still divided on whether tax policies have an effect On FDI. Indeed some scholars have gone on to argue that considering tax policies as being

---

① Egger, P., M. Larch, M. Pfaffermayer and H. Winner, 2004. The Impact of Endogenous Tax Treaties on Foreign Direct Investment: Theory and Empirical Evidence. Working Paper. University of Innsbruck, Department of Economics and Statistics, p.1.

② United Nations, 2001, *United Nations Model Double Taxation Convention between Developed and Developing Countries*. New York: United Nations.

③ Hines, J.R. Jr., 1998, "Tax Sparing" and Direct Investment in Developing Countries, Working Paper 6728. Cambridge, MA: National Bureau of Economic Research.

the only factor in attracting FDI is clearly fallacious, and tax policies are not necessary for attracting investment as investors will generally consider other factors that improve a country's investment climate as more important.

According to the World Bank Institute (WBI, 2002), while taxation policies may play a role in the decision of where foreign investors choose to invest, it is recognized as being secondary to other factors such as:[①]

- Consistent and stable macroeconomic and fiscal policy;
- Political stability;
- Adequate physical, financial, legal and institutional infrastructure;
- Effective, transparent and accountable public administration;
- Skilled labour force and flexible labour code governing employer and employee Relations;
- Availability of adequate dispute resolution mechanisms;
- Foreign exchange rules and the ability to repatriate profits;
- Language and cultural conditions;
- Factor and product markets — size and efficiency.

This position has found favour with other scholars. According to Ngowi (2000) FDI inflows to a country depend largely on the presence in that country, of a certain critical minimum of FDI determinants. The determinants are among the factors that give MNCs the confidence and interest to invest their massive and expensive capital in foreign markets. He lists these determinants as being inter alia: economic, political and social stability; and rules regulating entry and operations of businesses.

Ngowi (2000) further points out that standards of treatment of the foreign affiliates; business facilitation including, inter-alia, investment incentives; market size, growth, structure and accessibility, raw materials, low cost but efficient labor force and physical infrastructure in form of ports, roads, power and telecommunication are more important to investors than tax policies alone. [②]

Not surprisingly an investor survey conducted in Burundi, Rwanda, Tanzania shows that the majority of investors were not highly motivated by tax incentives or exemptions when making investment decisions. Those decisions were largely based on market potential, access to finance, reliable electricity supply and good infrastructure. Only 7.9% of all respondents in all three countries said they would not have invested without the tax and fiscal incentives they received. To the investors the quality of the mineral resource and favourable economic and political conditions were more

① World Bank Institute. 2002. *Tax Incentives*. Available: http://siteresources.worldbank.org/INTTPA/Resources/EassonZoltPaper.pdf.

② Ngowi, H. P. J. (2000). "*FDI Determinants: Can sub-Sahara Africa Increase its Global FDI share?*" Morogoro: IDM Mzumbe.

important than the taxation policies of the countries.[①]

Tellingly, Akinboade, Siebrits, and Roussot (2006) point out, a host country's economic instability can be a major deterrent to FDIs inflow. Any form of instability introduces a form of uncertainty that distorts investors' perceptions on the future profitability in that country.[②] For example Zimbabwe's political instability in 2008 saw a significant drop in investor confidence. [③]At the same time the country's promulgation of the Indigenization Act, which sought to compel all foreign owned companies to hand over 51% of their shareholding to indigenous citizens unsettled investors and the government had to make some concessions for new foreign investors.[④]

Conventional wisdom therefore weighs against using tax incentives to attract investment in general and foreign direct investment in particular. International organizations including the United Nations, World Bank, IMF, OECD and the EU have unanimously opposed the use of tax incentives to attract investments, arguing that it is better for developing countries to deal with the political, economic policy and infrastructural considerations and all the other problems that make developing countries less attractive for investments, instead of trying to compensate for the disadvantages by offering tax incentives. [⑤] However, the practicality of such a recommendation may be questionable considering that the same countries have no funds and would need FDI, in order to develop the infrastructure that would make them more attractive to foreign investors.

What is clear is that despite the evidence linking tax policies to increased long term investment being at best ambiguous and tax policies having worked in rare individual cases to sway locational decisions, there is more evidence that foreign investors rank quality of infrastructure, well-educated workforce and a local dynamic market and other factors mentioned above, far higher on their list of priorities.[⑥]

Logically, it would make no economic sense for an investor to go and invest in a country that is in the middle of a civil war or suffering some form of political instability, merely because that

---

① Organization for Economic Co-operation and Development (2012) Investor Motivation Surveys in East Africa, Global Tax Simplification Team, World Bank Group, Bogota, Colombia, p.7.

② Akinboade, O. A., Siebrits, F. K., & Roussot, E. N. (2006). *Foreign direct investments in South-Africa. In Ajayi (Ed.), Foreign direct investments in Sub-Sahara Africa – Origin, targets, impacts and potential* Nairobi: African Economic Research Consortium. pp.177–209.

③ Zimbabwe (2014) *Scoping Report, British Expertise* Foreign Commonwealth Office.

④ *Indigenisation Regulations Suspended For New Investors*, Zimbabwe Daily 19 July 2012.

⑤ *The Determinants Of Foreign Direct Investment: A Survey Of The Evidence,* U.N. Doc. ST/CTC/121, U.N. Sales No. E.92.II.A.2 (1992); *Tax Incentives And Foreign Direct Investment: A Global Survey,* U.N. Doc. CTAD/ITE/IPC/Misc.3, U.N. Sales No. E.01.II.D.5 (2000).

⑥ Andrew Mold (2004) *A proposal for unitary taxes on the profits of transnational corporations*, CEPAL Review 82,April 2004.

country offers tax holidays or some other such tax incentive. In the same vein no investor would sensibly invest in a country that had no infrastructure like roads to facilitate movement of minerals for example, or a skilled workforce to employ as labour in its operations merely because that country had an investor biased tax policy.

Ultimately, high taxation rates are not necessarily a deterrent of FDI as are low taxation rates not necessarily an attractor of FDI. Taxation rates are not able to make up for a lack of poor infrastructure, poor public services, limited access to markets, or other possible poor investment conditions. African governments ought to concern themselves with creating environments which are conducive for foreign investors investment, as no matter how attractive the taxation incentives are, that alone, cannot make up for poor primary investment factors[①].

Indeed it can actually be argued that aside from their dubious benefits, that pro investor tax policies are actually doing more harm than good for African countries.

For a start even if tax incentives were effective in FDI, ultimately, in the long run their disadvantages may well outweigh the benefits. The first and most direct costs are those associated with the potential loss of revenues for the host government. Such a situation is very likely to have a negative if not disastrous impact on the national treasury and the fiscal budget of the host country.[②] This issue becomes even more important when one considers the budgetary and financial constraints most African countries are under. The reduction in tax revenue following limits on source-based taxation clearly represents a huge cost to developing countries.[③] In short such tax policies may grow the treasury of the investing country while not bringing much into the coffers of the African state.

Using tax incentives requires that a country rely on alternative revenue sources, which most African countries do not have at least in ideal quantities. To improve the living standards of their citizens, African countries need a viable tax base to fund public services and good institutions.

In this light, recent studies in Africa have found that tax incentives result in revenue losses, undermine governance processes and the efforts of developing countries in their attempts to fight poverty. In Tanzania tax incentives in that country have led to a loss of around 3% of GDP in tax

① Garbarino, C. (2012) Comparative Analysis of Tax Incentives: Circulation of Models and Tax Policy Alternatives. Available: https://www.yumpu.com/en/document/view/16202981/1-comparativeanalysis-of-tax-incentives-intrweborg.

② Morisset, J., & Pirnia, N. (2000). How tax policy and incentives affect foreign direct investment.
Areview. The World Bank and International Finance Corporation Foreign Investment Advisory.
Service. Policy Research Working Paper, no.2509, p.1–34.

③ Neumayer, Eric (2007) Do double taxation treaties increase foreign direct investment to developing countries? Journal of Development Studies, 43 (8). p.10.

revenues.① Similarly, Tax Justice Network and Action Aid estimate Kenya's revenue loss at KES 100 billion (USD 1.1 billion) a year from all tax incentives and exemptions.

At the same time investor biased tax policies that seem to be the rave among African countries can prove counter-productive if they contribute to attracting more investors of the 'wrong kind', for example the type of investor who can loot the mineral resources of the host country without building any infrastructure or permanent structures and pack up and leave as soon as the mineral is exhausted. Furthermore such tax policies have also proved to be significant sources of corruption, effectively screening out desirable investment, and detrimental to the processes of developing competitive markets and sound policymaking.②

At the same time one cannot ignore the disadvantage to local companies. Tax policies to attract investors in African countries are usually designed to give preferential treatment to foreign investors at the expense of local companies. Offering tax cuts to foreign investors would ultimately place a heavier burden on the local companies as the government seeks to make up for the potential revenue lost through tax incentives by taxing the local companies even more. Neither can the uneven playing field that is created by such tax policies be disregarded. When foreign companies can import their machinery duty free while local companies pay heavy duty the disadvantage becomes obvious.

All in all, it can be argued that the tax policies of African governments in attracting investment are more of a case of African governments having conceded too much in exchange for too little

Conclusion

It is clear that the tax policies of African countries which are largely pro investor can hardly be said to have been the greatest driver of FDI into the continent. Taxation policies do not operate in isolation and are highly affected by both external and internal economic factors, including infrastructure, the macroeconomic environment the political stability of the country among others.

As such, in assessing the effect of taxation policies by African countries on FDI, it is probably safer to say that the truth lies in between. For most part, the tax policies of the country and other determinant factors like infrastructure, transport costs, and political and economic stability are a complementary set.

If African countries continue to rely on favorable tax policies to attract FDI, there is no doubt

① Yolanda Vamusse (2012) Tax incentives and exemptions not necessary to attract investment, Institute of Development Studies www.ids.ac.uk/news/tax-incentives-and-exemptions-not-necessary-to-attract-investment.

② Morisset, J., & Pirnia, N. (2000). How tax policy and incentives affect foreign direct investment.
Areview. The World Bank and International Finance Corporation Foreign Investment Advisory.
Service. Policy Research Working Paper, no.2509, p.1–34.

that the long term effects will prove a double edged sword. African countries need to adopt policies that strike a balance between tax revenue targets and FDI. Ngowi (2004) argues that tax incentives could work only if availed in situations where the return to be realized from a benefiting investment, say by way of taxation, leads to employment opportunities being created, increased exports and/or reducing imports, technology transfer, increased competitiveness, and increased linkage with the rest of the economy, as this will outweigh the cost, in this case, the lost revenue due to availing the tax incentives.[①]

However, ultimately, political stability, sensible fiscal policies, a skilled workforce and where possible infrastructural development may prove to be more of a pull factor than investor biased tax policies.

① Ngowi, H. P. J. (2000). *"FDI Determinants: Can sub-Sahara Africa Increase its Global FDI share?"* Morogoro: IDM Mzumbe.

非洲投资背景下的环境法

作者：Ndimbo　译者：邱颖通

一、介绍

涉及投资方面的问题纷繁复杂，关键问题是如何决定投资方向。非洲大陆面积为3030万平方公里（包含邻近岛屿，相当于1170平方英里），占全球面积的6%、总陆地面积的20.4%，是世界第二大洲。同时，非洲也是世界人口第二大洲，截至2013年，非洲人口大约11亿，占全球总人口的15%。非洲北至地中海，东北至西奈半岛临苏伊士运河及红海，东濒印度洋，西临大西洋。除大陆外，非洲还包括马达加斯加岛以及其他许多群岛。

非洲民族是所有大洲民族中最年轻、最富有活力的民族。阿尔及利亚是非洲面积最大的国家，而尼日利亚是人口最多的国家。赤道横跨非洲大陆，因此非洲各地气候不同；地跨北温带至南温带，最严重时，温度相当于热带与亚北极区的区别。非洲北部是沙漠以及干旱地区，而其中部、南部地区则是大草原和密集的热带雨林。在这两者交汇处被荒原沙漠以及干草原所覆盖。

可以说，非洲是世界上野生动物分布密度最大、数量最多、族群最丰富的地方。大型食肉动物种群（例如狮子、土狼和猎豹）以及食草动物（例如野牛、大象、骆驼以及长颈鹿）在公有平原上自由地漫步。同时，非洲也是蛇、灵长类动物、水生动物、鳄鱼、两栖动物等丛林动物的家园。另外，相对于其他大洲，非洲是受更新世巨型动物群灭绝影响最小的大洲，因此非洲拥有世界上数量最多的巨型动物种群。

虽然曾两次遭受森林资源退化，但由于固有的生态环境以及生物多样性，非洲仍然保有3000多个保护区，其中有198个海洋资源保护区，50个生态保护区以及80个湿地保护区。

非洲拥有大量的自然资源，其中包括钻石、盐、黄金、铁、钴、铀、铜、铝土矿、银、石油、可可豆、木材以及热带水果。这些资源当中，许多还未被发现或者未能充分利用。因为在很长一段时间里，非洲的人口密度保持在低位。于是，更有精力的民族便来到非洲建立殖民地，并借此剥削非洲的资源。非洲人民生活在巨大压力之下，被驱使开采这些稀有原材料。这导致非洲本土地区时常爆发战争，阻碍了地区发展。

值得注意的是，虽然非洲天然拥有大量丰富的自然资源，但这些资源经常被美国、加拿大、法国、德国、英国等西方国家以及一些日渐发展的经济强国所剥削。与中非合作论坛（FOCAC）所强调的平等互利、共同发展的理念截然不同，与这些国家开展的所谓合作使得大部分因自然资源而产生的价值流向西方以及其他剥削国家，而不是非洲国家。这加剧了非洲国家的贫困程度。

2003 年的石油危机以及近年新油田的发现令非洲原油的重要性日益增加。苏丹和尼日利亚是非洲主要的产油国。石油来源于大陆和海洋开采两方面。尼日利亚、利比亚、阿尔及利亚、埃及和安哥拉（顺序按石油产量由大到小）五国在非洲上游油气产量中占支配地位，共占非洲油气产量的 85%。其他石油生产国有加蓬、刚果、喀麦隆、突尼斯、赤道几内亚、刚果民主共和国（刚果金）以及科特迪瓦。另外，石油勘探也在许多国家里紧锣密鼓地进行着，这些国家包括乍得、苏丹、纳米比亚、南非、马达加斯加以及乌干达，他们志在加大石油出口量或成为第一生产商。而莫桑比克、肯尼亚和坦桑尼亚则是潜在的石油生产国。

在坦桑尼亚和莫桑比克新发现了丰富的油气资源，这一消息加大了各国对石油的勘探和提炼活动的力度，并因此增加了各国的外汇收入。

非洲还有丰富的矿石资源，其优势因为近年来其他大陆面临的资源损耗问题而日益凸显。

赞比亚的加丹加省是闻名于世的“铜带”，塞拉利昂、安哥拉、博茨瓦纳拥有丰饶的钻石矿，加纳、南非、坦桑尼亚的黄金储备因其产量巨大在公共财政收入中扮演着举足轻重的角色。

这些都是非洲大陆聚焦的环境问题。

二、与环境相关的问题

如今，人们常会提及“环境”一词，人人都在关注环境的保护问题。为建立讨论环境问题的平台，国际社会定期召开国际峰会。2015 年，联合国在法国召开巴黎气候峰会上，各国代表们为抑制全球变暖、旱灾等严重的气候问题提出了许多解决环境问题的措施。

英语中“environment（环境）”源自法语中的“environia”，意为“周围”。它同时指向生物以及非生物环境。环境的本义是生物体生活的地方。环境与生物体是自然界的两个动态且复杂的组成部分。环境调节包括人类在内等生物体的生命。与其他生物相比，人类与环境的互动更为积极。通常，环境是指围绕着生物的物质和外界作用。

环境是在特定的时间和空间围绕着我们的所有条件的总和。它由相互间具有内在联系的物理、生物和文化元素单独以及相互作用的系统所组成。因此，环境是有机体生存、维持其生命过程的条件总和。它影响着生存形式的进化和发展。

换句话说，环境指的是围绕着生物体方方面面并在总体上影响着他们的生存的周遭条件。它包括大气、水圈、岩石圈和生物圈。它的主要组成部分是土壤、水、空气、生物体以及太阳能。它为地球上所有的栖息者提供了舒适生活所需要的一切资源。

总体来说，非洲大陆的环境拥有丰饶程度令人惊讶的自然资源包括：黄金、镍、铜、铁矿、钻石、坦桑黝帘石、石灰岩、苏打灰、石膏、磷酸盐、煤、铀等，包括上文提到的石油、天然气以及在栖息于平原的食肉动物（例如狮子、土狼和猎豹）、食草动物（例如野牛、大象、骆驼以及长颈鹿），蛇、灵长目动物以及鳄鱼、水生动物、两栖动物，当然还有栖息在森林里的动物和各科各目的植物。这些自然资源吸引了全球各地的投资者，尤其是来自中国的投资者。

三、在非洲的投资

非洲大陆丰饶程度令人惊讶的自然资源包括：黄金、镍、铜、铁矿、钻石、坦桑黝帘石、石灰岩、苏打灰、石膏、磷酸盐、煤、铀等，包括上文提到的石油、天然气以及在栖息于平原的食肉动物（例如狮子、土狼和猎豹）、食草动物（例如野牛、大象、骆驼以及长颈鹿），蛇、灵长目动物以及鳄鱼、水生动物、两栖动物，当然还有栖息在森林里的动物和各科各目的植物，正如先前所提到的那样，吸引了国内外投资者。

非洲是世界上工业化程度最低的大洲，世界各地的投资者们，尤其是那些来自西方的德国、加拿大、美国、英国、法国和意大利的投资者，以及来自亚洲的中国和印度的投资者都希望能够利用这里丰富的自然资源：黄金、镍、铜、铁矿、钻石、坦桑黝帘石、石灰岩、苏打灰、石膏、磷酸盐、煤、铀等，包括上文提到的石油、天然气以及在栖息于平原的食肉动物（例如狮子、土狼和猎豹）、食草动物（例如野牛、大象、骆驼以及长颈鹿），蛇、灵长目动物以及鳄鱼、水生动物、两栖动物，还有森林和各科各目的植物，在下面会具体提到。

1. 投资范围包括对南非、尼日利亚、利比亚、阿尔及利亚、埃及、安哥拉、加蓬、刚果、喀麦隆、突尼斯、赤道几内亚、刚果民主共和国、科特迪瓦、乍得、苏丹、纳米比亚、马达加斯加、乌干达、莫桑比克、肯尼亚和坦桑尼亚的石油、天然气的勘探和提炼。

2. 投资进行的勘探和开采的矿业的包括：赞比亚的加丹加省的铜，塞拉利昂、安哥拉、博茨瓦纳的钻石，加纳、南非、刚果民主共和国、坦桑尼亚的黄金，刚果民主共和国的钶钽，坦桑尼亚及其他各国的铀，几内亚的铝土，铬、铂、钽铁、锰、银、镍、铁矿、坦桑黝帘石、石灰岩、苏打灰、石膏、磷酸盐、煤等。

3. 对为利用自然资源而建造的道路交通基础设施进行投资，如标准铁路、港口、机场、公路、桥梁等。

4. 对自然森林保护区、林木种植园的木材产业以及植树造林的投资。

5. 对制造业和加工行业，如食品加工和生产等行业所进行的投资。

6. 对旅游业中非洲各天然公园中为充分展现自然风光与人文元素的旅游景点所进行的投资。

7. 对在广大可耕地上进行的粮食种植以及牧场上的动物畜养，包括对粮食加工产业开展的投资。

8. 对信息通信产业进行投资，如移动通信。

9. 对交通产业进行投资，如航空、铁路、公路以及海运系统。

10. 对河流、湖泊以及更广阔的海域的水产业开展投资。

11. 对能源板块开展投资，其中包括氢能、核能、水能、煤、天然气、石油。

12. 对包括学校以及技术院校建设的教育板块投资。

13. 对旨在发现新的自然资源的科学研究，如种子和矿产研究实验室，开展投资。

14. 对为自然资源开采行业起到辅助作用的贸易以及组装生产行业进行投资。

15. 对非洲广泛的甘蔗种植园以及制糖工业投资。

16. 对油料生产以及加工业，如棕榈油。

四、非洲环境法以及坦桑尼亚案例

1. 开展上文提到的各种投资，适当地、可持续地勘探、开采以及利用非洲得天独厚的自然资源（黄金、镍、铜、铁矿、钻石、坦桑黝帘石、石灰岩、苏打灰、石膏、磷酸盐、煤、铀等，包括上文提到的石油、天然气以及在栖息于平原的食肉动物（例如狮子、土狼和猎豹）、食草动物（例如野牛、大象、骆驼以及长颈鹿），蛇、灵长目动物以及鳄鱼、水生动物、两栖动物，还有森林和各科各目的植物），对这些投资的管理制度框架必须落到实处。

因此，只有通过颁布有效的法律和政策以界定如何利用自然资源，才能达到可持续发展以及消除社会贫困问题的目标。这些法律和政策则被称为环境法和环境政策。

根据国际环境守法与执法网络（INECE），干旱、洪涝、空气污染、森林砍伐、生物多样性流失、淡水可利用度、土壤和植被退化，加之普遍的贫困是如今非洲地区主要的环境问题。

美国环境保护署（EPA）中肯地提出，非洲的主要环境问题对气候变化起到负面作用。非洲各国已经通过统一而有力的非洲联盟，在《养护自然和自然资源非洲公约》的基础上建立了法律框架。

该公约指出，非洲大陆的自然环境与其固有的自然资源是不可替代的，它们是非洲古老的自然遗产，且对这片大陆乃至全人类来说都具有举足轻重的重要性。公约还号召所有非洲民族牢牢遵守《非洲统一组织宪章》，该宪章强调每一个非洲国家应从造福非洲经济、社会、文化以及环境的角度出发，利用非洲大陆上的自然与人力资源。

在旅游业和野生动植物保护方面，非洲联盟通过非洲委员会下设的执行委员会号召确保非洲的野生动植物以及其他具有吸引力的旅游自然资源受到切实的保护，包括增加禁止和打击偷猎、非法贸易以及生物剽窃行为的措施，同时其管理也应以利于当地社会为准则和限度。

除了在法律方面掌握主动权建立非洲保护环境和自然资源的统一水平外，一些成员国出于地区考虑相互开展合作，如东非共同体通过签订协议建立了维多利亚湖流域委员会，以此来进行维多利亚湖流域环境治理及保护项目。这个项目旨在减轻维多利亚湖持续下降的水平面危机和解决日益严重的污染问题。

另外，东非共同体为保证东非运输航道的各国立法协调性，于2004年修订了内河航道运输三方协议，保障和加强航道运输安全。

2. 坦桑尼亚的案例。

为了促使与环境相关的政策与法律获得足够的法律地位、适用效力且最终能够造福非洲社会，非洲各国都应当在批准、给予它们足够的适用效力后，在当地颁布与之相应进行具体实施的配套法律。

作为非洲联盟的创建国之一，坦桑尼亚为造福当地社区，除批准通过《非洲自然和自然资源保护公约》之外，还出台了一系列保护自然资源合理、安全、可持续利用的法规条例。这些自然资源包括：黄金、镍、铜、铁矿、钻石、坦桑黝帘石、石灰岩、苏打灰、石膏、磷酸盐、煤、铀等，包括上文提到的石油、天然气以及在栖息于平原的食肉动物（例如狮子、土狼和猎豹）、食草动物（例如野牛、大象、骆驼以及长颈鹿），蛇、灵长目动物以及鳄鱼、水生动物、两栖动物，还有森林和各科各目的植物。这些在下文中会详细提到：

（1）《2008年所得税法》《2004年东非海关管理法》《2006年印花税法》《2006年坦桑尼亚税收管理局法》以及《2014年增值税法》为从自然及其他资源获取的所有收入阶层建立了承责机制，包括向坦桑尼亚境内的外国投资者征收相关税赋以合理增加国家财政收入，开展环境治理及保护项目，从而促进社会经济可持续发展。

（2）为了保证自然资源的合理利用，在坦桑尼亚进行投资的外国投资者与本国投资者在授权使用土地和权利取得的程序中，都同样受到土地法、于2008年修订的《1999年农村土地法》以及《1995年国家土地政策》的约束。《1997年坦桑尼亚投资法》就此进行了详细阐述。

（3）《2008年电力法》《2005年农村能源法》和其他强调为工业使用及其他各类活动，如农村社区的照明、烹饪，提供足量可靠电力的能源政策在环境保护进程中起到了积极作用。

（4）《2010年公私合作伙伴关系法》《2011年公私合作伙伴关系规则》和《2010年公私合作伙伴关系政策》为利用自然资源的公私协议中确保遵守环境保护措施建立了制度框架。

（5）坦桑尼亚在矿业领域方面出台了《2009年新矿产政策》以及现在的《2010年采矿法》，它们的颁布分别废除了《1997年矿产政策》和之前的《采矿法》。

（6）政策呼吁私人投资者继续对勘探和开采矿产业投资，强调矿产部门与其余经济部门的整合，建立确保国家利益并保持国际竞争力的财政制度，支持矿产业和销售业，支持小规模采矿业者，通过投资者对国家矿产资源的可持续利用提供明确指导的方式，促进采矿活动中的公众参与，奠定双赢的基础。

（7）现行关于矿产资源的政策和法律提出了设想：对在坦桑尼亚境内发现的丰富的包括黄金、镍、铜、铁矿、钻石、坦桑黝帘石、石灰岩、苏打灰、石膏、磷酸盐、煤、铀以及其他未提及的矿产资源的开采将作为国家的巨大优势，以获得充足的财政收入进行社会经济可持续发展与转型，同时通过矿产业对 GDP（国内生产总值）的贡献减轻现存的严重贫困问题。预计到 2025 年，矿产业对 GDP 的贡献将增加 2% 到 10%。

（8）同样，为了最大限度减少采矿对人类健康、安全的危害和对社会、环境造成的负面影响，现行政策还强调通过提升并加强监管和规制以促进矿区及其周围的环境管理，保障人民的健康与安全。

（9）考虑到总体环境以及该国自然资源的管控问题，坦桑尼亚出台并实施了《2004 年环境管理法》《1997 年国家环境政策》以及《国家环境行动计划（2013）》。该行动计划除了详细给出合理可持续利用自然资源的制度性框架外，还对石油、天然气、矿物的勘探与开采、农业种植园、旅游业等土地使用权利签发流程做出了要求。这些土地使用权利签发流程应当附环境影响评估证书，违反法律而发出的评估证书将被依法取消。

（10）环境保护措施同时遵守《2009 年公共卫生法》《2007 年国家卫生政策》《2009 年水供应和水质卫生法》《2009 年水资源管理法》以及 2002 年国家水资源政策中健康管理、卫生管理和水资源管理的相关议题。

（11）《2002 年森林法》《1996 年森林保护区管理与保护法（FRMCA）》与《2002 年养蜂法》的出台是为了管理包括私营部门在内的森林、蜜蜂及其衍生产品，以促进和提高林业板块对可持续发展的贡献。这些立法禁止在森林保护区里从事任何对其有害的人类活动，从而对目前以及将来的自然资源起到保护与管控作用。这些立法都是在国家林业政策的指导下协同作用的。

（12）《2008 年旅游法》规制了旅游业和旅游活动的收入，以此造福群众，呼应了《1999 年国际旅游政策》的核心要求。

（13）为了保护野生动物，管理来自野生动物和野生动物产品贸易的收入，保障旅游业的可持续发展，国家颁布了《国家公园法》，并出台了《2007 年野生动物保护政策》和《2009 年野生动物保护政策》。

（14）对农业的投资包括在坦桑尼亚境内种植粮食、饲养动物或进行放牧、渔业活动。国家为保障在相关土地上自然资源的合理利用，颁布了《1997 年植物保护法》《2003 年渔业法》《2010 年国家水利政策》《2013 年国家农业政策》以及《2006 年国家畜牧业政策》。

（15）因参与恐怖活动、涉及野生动物产品的非法贸易、毒品交易以及贪污行为等非法致富的不法活动而造成自然资源损害的，由《2006 年洗钱法》和《2007 年预防及打击腐败法》规制。

（16）日益增加的对石油、天然气的勘探以及天然气开采，驱使坦桑尼亚于 2015 年颁布了三项立法，它们包括：

①《2015 年石油法》：该法废除并取代了内容涵盖上游石油业务的《1980 年石油（勘探与生产）法》以及内容包括中下游石油供应业务《2008 年石油法》，以造福坦桑尼亚社会为目标，提供石油、天然气勘探和开采的方案及框架。重要的是，该法将石油和天然气的所有权通过国有企业授予政府。

②《2015 年采掘业（透明度与问责制）法》要求与采掘业相关的特许权、合同以及执照公开化。这说明，先前允许矿业开发协议中插入保密条款的立场发生了转变。该法旨在遏制石油和天然气行业的腐败和其他营私舞弊行为。

③《2015 年天然气石油收入管理法》建立了石油和天然气基金，以达到保持财政和宏观经济稳定、提高社会经济发展以及保护后代的自然资源的作用。从石油和天然气开采中获得收入预计将增加 9% 到 31% 的政府收入。因此，有必要出台相关规定以规范有效使用这些收入，将它们投入民众的基本需求当中，如改善、增加优质医疗保健、教育和其他社会服务的规定，并支持环境保护措施和自然资源保护事业以促进经济长期增长。

五、总结

总的来说，非洲人民与国家尤其是非洲联盟的成员国认识到非洲大陆的自然环境与其固有的自然资源不可替代，它们是非洲古老的自然遗产，且对这片大陆乃至全人类来说都具有举足轻重的重要性。抱着这样的共识，非洲各国动员起来并号召所有非洲民族牢牢遵守《非洲统一组织宪章》，该宪章强调每一个非洲国家应从造福非洲经济、社会、文化以及环境的角度出发，利用非洲大陆上的自然与人力资源。

此外，我们呼吁国际社会，尤其是中国，与非洲国家携手持续采取措施对非洲的自然资源和人力资源进行可持续利用。

考虑到对非洲自然资源和人力资源的投资日益增加，在产业化措施中遵守环境法与环境政策是至关重要的。因此，在非投资者应当对这些法律多加注意。

参考文献

[1] The Decision Number EX.CL/Dec.898-918 (XXVIII) of the 28th Ordinary Session of Executive Council of African Union held from 23-28th January 2016, particularly EX.CL/Dec.908 (XXVIII) page 3, retrieved from www.www.au.int.

[2] https://en.wikipedia.org/wiki/Africa. time on line 12:34 pm 2016 May 28.

[3] https://en.wikipedia.org/wiki/Environmental_protection. Time on line 8:341 am 2016 May 26.

[4] file:///E:/ How to Invest in Africa_Mutual Funds_Us News.htm time on line 12:13 pm 2016 May 25.

[5] Samwel J. Sitta (2005), "Investment for African development: Making it happen" NEPAD/OECD INVESTMENT INITIATIVE.

[6] The Combined Draft Version of the Forum on China-Africa Cooperation Johannesburg Action Plan (2016-2018).

[7] http://www.tanzaniaembassy.or.jp/english/Business/investment_in_en.html. time on line 1:39 pm 2016 May 25.

[8] Environment Program, Investing in our Future, http://warmheartworldwide.org/biochar-research-environment/gcli. time on line 9:56 am 2016 May 26.

[9] Public-Private Partnerships, http://www.tic.co.tz/menu/314 Tanzania Investment Centre. time on line 4:47 pm 2016 May 27.

[10] http://www.journalism.co.za/blog/topics/categories/china-africa-reporting/Journalism.co.za. time on line 1:04 pm 2016 May 25.

[11] www2.hull.ac.uk/hubs/pdf/memorandum58.pfd retrieved at 1:53pm on 2016 May 30.

The Environment Laws in the Context of Investing in Africa

Author: Ndimbo

Introduction

One among controversial questions to decide in reaching to the conclusion pertaining to investment issues is decide where to invest. African countries are within Africa continent which is known as world's second largest and second most populous continent covering areas of about 30.3 million km^2 which is equivalent to 11.7 million Square miles including adjacent islands, it covers six percent of earth's total surface area and 20.4 percent of its total land areas with 1.1 billion people as of 2013, it account about 15% of the world's human population. The continent is surrounded by the Mediterranean sea to the north, both the Suez canal and the red Sea along the Sinai Peninsula to the northeast, the Indian Ocean to the southeast, and the Atlantic Ocean to the West. The continent includes Madagascar and various archipelagos.

Africa's population is the youngest amongst all the continents with Algeria being the Africa's largest country by area and Nigeria by population. Africa straddles the equator and encompasses numerous climate areas; it is the only continent to stretch from the northern temperate to southern temperate zones ranging from tropical to subarctic on its highest peaks. Its northern half is desert or arid, while its central and southern area contains both savannah plains and very dense jungle (rainforest) region. In between there is a convergence, where vegetation patterns such as Sahel and steppe dominate.

Africa boosts perhaps the world's largest combination of density and range of freedom of wild animals populations and diversity, with population of large carnivores (such as lions, hyenas and cheetah) and herbivores (such as buffalo, elephants, camel and giraffes) ranging freely on primarily non private plains. It is also home of jungle animals including snakes and primates and aquatic life such as crocodile and amphibians. In addition Africa has the largest number of mega fauna species, as it was least affected by the extinction of the Pleistocene mega fauna.

Concerning ecology and biodiversity Africa has been affected twice by deforestation though still has over 3,000 protected areas with 198 marine protected areas, 50 biosphere reserves, and 80 wetlands reserves.

Africa has large quantity of natural resources including diamonds, salt, gold, iron, cobalt, uranium, copper, bauxite, silver, petroleum and coco beans, but also woods and tropical fruits. Much of its resources are undiscovered or barely harnessed. Having a low human density, for a long period of time Africa has been colonized by more dynamic groups, exploiting African resources. These large quantities of rare raw materials put Africa under heavy pressures and tensions leading to sometimes war and slow development.

It is pertinent to note that despite existences of the endowed abundant natural resources it has been experienced that many Western nations like United State, Canada, France, German and United Kingdom as well as emerging some economic powerhouse's nations who often exploiting African's natural resources not on the basis of equal benefit and common development as emphasized by the Forum on China-Africa cooperation (FOCAC) but rather they cause most of value and money from the natural resources to go to the West or rather to the exploiting countries rather than Africa, further causing poverty to shrine in Africa.

African oil takes growing importance, mainly after the 2003 oil crisis and recent oil reserves discoveries. Sudan and Nigeria are of the main oil producers. Oil is provided by both continental and offshore productions. But five countries dominate Africa's upstream oil production together they account for 85% of the continent's oil production and are, in order of decreasing output, Nigeria, Libya, Algeria, Egypt, and Angola. Other oil producing countries are Gabon, Congo, Cameroon, Tunisia, Equatorial Guinea, the Democratic Republic of Congo and Cote d'Ivore. However exploration of oil is taking place in a number of countries that aim to increase their output of oil production or become first time producers. Included in this list are Chad, Sudan, Namibia, South Africa, Madagascar and Uganda while Mozambique, Kenya and Tanzania are potential future oil producers.

Recent information reveals abundant discoveries of gas reserves in Tanzania and Mozambique which also has increased exploration and extraction of gas activities hence leading to increased foreign earning in the countries.

There are also abundant ores resources in Africa and more extremely so nowadays as other continents are beginning to face depletion of resources. The copper belt of Katanga Zambia, the diamond mines in Sierra Leone, Angola and Botswana are well known for their abundance and rich produce, without forgetting the abundance reserves of Gold in Ghana, South Africa and Tanzania which plays a considerable d ay today production output and public revenue collection. These what about Environmental issues is concern in Africa continents.

What is all about Environment

Now a day the word environment is often being used by almost all people around us every one is speaking about the protection and preservations of environment. Global summits are being held regularly to discuss environmental issues including the recent world Summit held by UN in France which came up more measures for preservation of environment so as to curb the impact of acute climate change such as Global warming and droughts.

The term environment has been derived from a French word "Environia" means the surrounding. It refers to both a biotic (physical or non-living) and biotic (living) environment. The word environment means surroundings in which organisms' lives. Environment and the organisms are two dynamic and complex component of nature. Environment regulates the life of organisms including human beings. Human beings interact with the environment more vigorously than other living beings. Ordinarily environment refers to the materials and forces that surround the living organism.

Environment is the sum total of conditions that surrounds us at a given point of time and space. it is comprised of the interacting system of physical, biological and cultural elements which are interlinked both individually and collectively. Hence, environment is the sum total of conditions in which an organism has to survive or maintain its life process. It influences the growth and development of living forms.

In other words environments refer to those surroundings that surround living beings from all sides and affect their life in Toto. It consists of atmosphere, hydrosphere, lithosphere and biosphere. Its chief components are soil, water, air, organisms and solar energy. It provides the world inhabitants all the resources all the resources for leading a comfortable life.

That is to say the environment of Africa continent that provides the amazing and abundant natural resources ranging from minerals which includes; gold, nickel, copper, iron ore, Diamond, Tanzanite, Limestone, Soda ash, Gypsum, Phosphate, Coal, Uranium and other no mentioned, oil and gas mentioned above, wild animals covering carnivores (such as lions, hyenas and cheetah) and herbivores (such as buffalo, elephants, camel and giraffes) ranging freely on primarily non private plains and jungle animals including snakes and primates and aquatic life such as crocodile and amphibians and indeed extending to forest and various species of plants attracting investors from all over the World, China in particular.

Investimenting in Africa

Abundant and amazing endowment of natural resources in Africa continent ranging from minerals which includes; gold, nickel, copper, iron ore, Diamond, Tanzanite, Limestone, Soda ash, Gypsum, Phosphate, Coal, Uranium and other no mentioned, oil and gas mentioned above, wild animals covering carnivores (such as lions, hyenas and cheetah) and herbivores (such as buffalo, elephants, camel and giraffes) ranging freely on primarily non private plains and jungle animals including snakes and primates and aquatic life such as crocodile and amphibians and indeed extending to forest and various species of plants as afore noted attract both internal and external (foreign) investors in African Continent.

Since Africa is least industrialized continent in the world investors all over the world particular from industrialized countries from Western such as German, Canada, United States, United Kingdom, France and Italy and from Asian countries like China and India harnessing the natural resources like minerals which includes; gold, nickel, copper, iron ore, Diamond, Tanzanite, Limestone, Soda ash, Gypsum, Phosphate, Coal, Uranium and other no mentioned, oil and gas, wild animals covering carnivores (such as lions, hyenas and cheetah) and herbivores (such as buffalo, elephants, camel and giraffes) and jungle animals including snakes and primates and aquatic life such as crocodile and amphibians and indeed forest and plants of various species as illustrated here under.

3.1 Investment in oil and gas exploration and extraction in South Africa, Nigeria, Libya, Algeria, Egypt, Angola, Gabon, Congo, Cameroon, Tunisia, Equatorial Guinea, the Democratic Republic of Congo and Cote d'Ivore, Chad, Sudan, Namibia, Madagascar, Uganda, Mozambique, Kenya and Tanzania

3.2 Investment in exploration and mining of mineral including:

- Copper in Katanga Zambia,
- Diamond in Sierra Leone, Angola and Botswana,
- Gold in Ghana, South Africa the Democratic Republic of Congo and Tanzania,
- Coltan in the Democratic Republic of Congo,
- Uranium in Tanzania,
- Bauxite in Guinea,
- Chromium, Platinum, Tantalite, Manganese, Silver, nickel, iron ore, Tanzanite, Limestone, Soda ash, Gypsum, Phosphate, Coal and etc.

3.3 Investment in infrastructure construction such standard railways, ports, airports, road and bridges for transportation of harnesses natural resources.

3.4 Investment in timber industries in natural forest reserve and forest plantations together with forest or tree planting.

3.5 Investment in constructions and processing industries such as food processing and production industry.

3.6 Investment in Tourism sectors for harnessing both cultural and natural tourist attraction in various parks in Africa.

3.7 Investment in crop cultivation and animal keeping in the vast arable land and green pasture including crop processing industry.

3.8 Information and communication industry such as mobile telecommunication.

3.9 Investment in transportation industry such as aviation, rail, roads and marine.

3.10 Investment in fisheries industry in the vast rivers and lake together with broader ocean.

3.11 Investment in energy sector generated from hydro, nuclear, water, coal, gas and oil.

3.12 Investment in education which include construction of school and college for training.

3.13 Investment in science and research geared at discovering new natural resource such as seed and mineral research laboratories.

3.14 Investment in trade and assembly industry as supportive to natural resources extraction industry.

3.15 Investments in sugarcane plantation and sugar processing industry in vast basis in Africa.

3.16 Investment in oil seed production and processing industry such as palm oil, cash nut, grand nuts.

Environmental Laws in Africa with Further Tanzania Case Study

4.1 Exploration, extracting and indeed harnessing of abundant natural resources endowed in African ranging from minerals which includes; gold, nickel, copper, iron ore, Diamond, Tanzanite, Limestone, Soda ash, Gypsum, Phosphate, Coal, Uranium and other no mentioned, oil and gas mentioned above, wild animals covering carnivores (such as lions, hyenas and cheetah) and herbivores (such as buffalo, elephants, camel and giraffes) ranging freely on primarily non private plains and jungle animals including snakes and primates and aquatic life such as crocodile and amphibians and indeed extending to forest and various species of plants through injecting various investment in different ventures as afore noted cannot be properly and sustainably without putting in place institutional framework for its managements.

Therefore the institutional frame works for harnessing natural resources found in environmental demarcations of Africa continent for the sustainable development and alleviation of poverty within the community can only be installed by promulgation of effective laws and policies and such Laws and policies are called environment laws and policies.

According to the International Networks for Environmental Compliances and enforcement (INECE) addresses drought flooding, air pollution, deforestation, loss of biodiversity, freshwater availability, degradation of soil and vegetation and hence widespread poverty to be the major environmental issue in Africa.

In views to the extent of impact of major Environmental issues in Africa which also are adequately addressed by the US Environmental protection Agency (CPA) which has adverse result to climate change African countries via the strong and united African Union has come up with legal framework which is established by promulgation African Convention on the Conservation of Nature and Natural Resources.

The Convention in Toto acknowledges that the natural environment in Africa and the natural resources with which Africa continent is endowed are irreplaceable part of the African heritage and constitutes a capital of vital importance to the continent and humankind as a whole and goes further to call upon all African Nations to adhere to the Charter of Organization of African Unity which emphasizes to the duty of every African Country to harness the natural and human resources of the continent for economic, social, cultural and environmental advantageous point of view to African peoples.

Concerning Tourism and Wild life Conservation aspects the African union through the Executive council of African commission is called to ensure that wild life and other tourist attractive resources in Africa are properly conserved and managed for the purpose of benefiting local communities, including women by increasing measures to ban and combat poaching, illicit trade in wildlife products and bio-piracy.

Apart from Africa level's legal initiative to protecting Environments and natural resource found therein there in also regional initiative launched by some of members states of the relevant regional undertaking cooperation such as the East African Community has come up with a protocol which establishing Lake Victoria Basis Commission so as to implement the Lake Victoria basis Environmental Management and protection Program which is sanctioned or geared to alleviate the crises of persistent decline of water level in lake Victoria and increasing pollution level.

There is also the so called Tripartite Agreement on Inland Waterways Transport which was rectified by East African Community in 2004 with the views of harmonizing legislations pertaining waterways transport in the East Africa aimed at enhancing transport and safety in the lakes.

4.2 A case study in Tanzania. For policies and Laws concerning environment to acquire legal status and force and ultimately to be applied for the benefit of African community must first be rectified and given applicable power by member state of African continents an act which is followed by promulgating local legislation for enforcements of the same.

Likewise Tanzania being one of founder member of African Union apart from rectifying the African Convention on the Conservation of Nature and Natural Resources has enacted number of local legislation which preserve natural resources ranging from minerals such as gold, nickel, copper, iron ore, Diamond, Tanzanite, Limestone, Soda ash, Gypsum, Phosphate, Coal, Uranium and other not mentioned, oil and gas, wild animals covering carnivores (such as lions, hyenas and cheetah) and herbivores (such as buffalo, elephants, camel and giraffes), and jungle animals including snakes and primates and aquatic life such as crocodile and amphibians and extending to forest and various species of plants for the proper, safe and sustainable use for the benefit of local communities as illustrated here under:

- Income Tax Act of 2008, East Africa Customs Management Act of 2004, Stamp Duty Act of 2006, Tanzania Revenue Authority Act of 2006 and the Value Added Tax Act of 2014 provide for schemes and liability of every income earners from both natural and non natural resources, including foreign investors in Tanzania to pay relevant taxes and duties due to the Government for enabling raising of Revenues necessary for socio-economic sustainable progress, including Environmental management and protection programs.
- For the proper use of natural resources found in the granted land and procedure of acquisition of rights, ownership and uses of land to both local and foreign investors who aspires to invest in Tanzania the same Land Act and Village Land Acts of 1999 as amended in 2008 together with the National Land Policy of 1995 is further addressed in the Tanzania Investment Act of 1997.
- The Electricity Act, 2008, Rural Energy Act of 2005 and the energy policy which emphasizes production of reliable and adequate electricity not only for Industrial uses but also as source of energy to all activities, including lights and cooking energy in village communities plays an active role in Environmental preservation.
- The Public Private Partnership Act of 2010, Public Private Partnership Regulation of 2011 and the Public Private Partnership Policy of 2010 these gives institutional frameworks for public-private agreements to extent into activities for harnessing natural resources by observing environmental protective measures.
- In mining industry arena Tanzania came up with New Minerals policy of 2009 and the incumbent Mining Act of 2010 which did away with previous Minerals Policy of 1997 and repealed the previous Mining Act.
- The policy call upon private investors continuing investing in exploration and mining of minerals, emphasize integration of the mineral sector with the rest of the economy, establish a fiscal regime which ensures benefits to the country and remain internationally competitive, support mineral beneficiation and marketing, underpin development of small scale miners and promote public participation in mining activities by providing a clear guidance to investors towards sustainable exploitation of mineral resources in the country basing in a win-win situation.
- The current policy and Laws on minerals envisage that exploitation of abundant resources of minerals found in Tanzania which includes; gold, nickel, copper, iron ore, Diamond, Tanzanite, Limestone, Soda ash, Gypsum, Phosphate, Coal, Uranium and other no mentioned should be advantageous to the country thereby generating adequate revenue necessary for sustainable socio-economic progress and transformation and alleviating existing acute poverty by increasing contribution of mineral sector to GDP from below two percent to ten percent by 2025.
- The same also emphasize and promote best practices for health, safety and environmental management in mining areas and the surrounding by improving and strengthening monitoring and regulation of the mining industry geared at reducing if not eliminating the adverse effects

on health and safety, environment and social issues.

- Concerning the question of overall Environmental control and the natural resources found therein Tanzania has come up with and enforces the Environmental Management Act of 2004, National Environmental Policy of 1997 and National Environmental Action Plan (2013) which apart from describing legal and institutional framework for sustainable and proper use environment and harness natural resources therein it also requires and direct the issuance process of any license for right of using any land for human activities such as oil, gas and minerals exploration and extraction, agricultural plantations, tourism and others should be accompanied with certificate of Environmental impact assessment, such certificates issued in contravention to the Act is liable to be cancelled.
- Environment protection measures also observed on issues concerning health managements, sanitation and hence management of water resources endowments by Public Health Act of 2009, National Health Policy of 2007, Water Supply and Sanitation Act of 2009, Water Resources Management Act of 2009 and National Water Policy of 2002.
- The Forest Act of 2002, Forest Reserve management and Conservation Act (FRMCA) of 1996 Beekeeping Act of 2002 these has been promulgated so as to manage forest and bees together with forest and bees products in the country in cooperation of whole community including private sector with the view of promoting and enhancing the contribution of forest sector to the sustainable development. The legislation prohibits human activities to be conducted in the forest reserve and hence, conserve and manage natural resources for the present and future generation. These goes hand in hand with the guidance elaborated in the National Forest Policy of 1998.
- There is also Tourist Act of 2008 manage tourism and revenue accrued from tourist activities so as to be directed to citizens' benefits to reflect the emphasizes in the National Tourism Policy of 1999.
- As to the National park Act (*CAP.282 RE 2002*), Wildlife Policy 2007 and the Wildlife Conservation Act of 2009 has been enacted to preserve wildlife, manage revenue accrued from wildlife and wildlife products trade for the sustainable development of tourism.
- Investment in Agriculture which includes crops growing, animals keeping or grazing and fisheries activities in Tanzania the so called Plant protection Act of 1997, Fisheries Act of 2003, National Irrigational Policy of 2010, National Agriculture Policy of 2013 and National Livestock Policy of 2006 are in place to manage use of natural resources found in the concerned land.
- To the involvements in fight against criminal misconduct which jeopardize natural resources through engagements into illicit enrichment in income accrued from illegal activities such as terrorist activities, illicit trade in wildlife products, drugs and corruption the Money Laundering Act of 2006 and Prevention and Combating of Corruption of 2007 is in effects.
- Increased exploration of oil and gas, and indeed commencement of extraction of gas has

compelled Tanzania in 2015 to come up with three legislations; namely:

i. The Petroleum Act of 2015 which replaced and repealed the then Petroleum (Exploration and Production) Act of 1980, covering upstream petroleum operations, and the Petroleum Act of 2008, covering mid and downstream petroleum supply operations provides for the scheme and frameworks of operation of gas and oil exploration and extraction in Tanzania for the benefit of Tanzania community. It is important the Act vest title of right of ownership of Oil and Gas to the Government via the National Company.

ii. Extractive Industry (Transparency and Accountability), Act of 2015 which provide for new avenue requiring all concessions, contracts, and licenses relating to the extractive industry to be published as opposed to previous stand of inserting confidentiality clauses especially in mining Development agreements aims is to curb corruption and other malpractices in the gas and oil industry.

iii. The Gas and Oil Revenue s Management Act, 2015 which establishes oil and Gas Fund responsible for maintaining fiscal and macroeconomic stability, enhancing, social and economic development, and safeguarding resources for future generations. Revenues expected from oil and gas exploitation is projected to add between 9% to 31% to the Government revenue hence guidance must be in place on how to effectively direct and use the earnings for incurring basic needs for citizens such as improving and strengthening provision of quality healthcare, education and other social services and supporting long-term economic growth such environmental conservation initiatives and natural resources protection undertakings.

Conclusion

In concluding we Africans believe that, African Countries specifically members of African Union strongly or rather firmly acknowledges that the natural environment in Africa and the natural resources with which Africa continent is endowed are irreplaceable part of the African heritage and constitutes a capital of vital importance to the continent and humankind as a whole. With such understanding in mind the continent itself has mobilized and goes further to call upon all African Nations to adhere to the Charter of Organization of African Unity which emphasizes to the duty of every African Country to harness the natural and human resources of the continent for economic, social, cultural and environmental advantageous point of view to African peoples.

However we call upon the international community, China in particular to join hand with African Countries to the initiative taken and continued to be taken for the sustainable harnessing and uses of natural and human resources found in Africa.

Concerning increased and promoted investments in harvesting both natural and human resources in Africa including through the industrialization initiatives adherence to laws and policies in Environment is of paramount important. Hence those who are aspiring to invest in Africa should be aware with such laws.

REFERENCES

[1] The Decision Number EX.CL/Dec.898-918 (XXVIII) of the 28th Ordinary Session of Executive Council of African Union held from 23-28th January 2016, particularly EX.CL/Dec.908 (XXVIII) page 3, retrieved from www.www.au.int.

[2] https://en.wikipedia.org/wiki/Africa. time on line 12:34 pm 2016 May 28.

[3] https://en.wikipedia.org/wiki/Environmental_protection. Time on line 8:341 am 2016 May 26.

[4] file:///E:/ How to Invest in Africa_Mutual Funds_Us News.htm time on line 12:13 pm 2016 May 25.

[5] Samwel J. Sitta (2005), "Investment for African development: Making it happen" NEPAD/OECD INVESTMENT INITIATIVE.

[6] The Combined Draft Version of the Forum on China-Africa Cooperation Johannesburg Action Plan (2016-2018).

[7] http://www.tanzaniaembassy.or.jp/english/Business/investment_in_en.html. time on line 1:39 pm 2016 May 25.

[8] Environment Program, Investing in our Future, http://warmheartworldwide.org/biochar-research-environment/gcli. time on line 9:56 am 2016 May 26.

[9] Public-Private Partnerships, http://www.tic.co.tz/menu/314 Tanzania Investment Centre. time on line 4:47 pm 2016 May 27.

[10] http://www.journalism.co.za/blog/topics/categories/china-africa-reporting/Journalism.co.za. time on line 1:04 pm 2016 May 25.

[11] www2.hull.ac.uk/hubs/pdf/memorandum58.pfd retrieved at 1:53pm on 2016 May 30.

非洲的市场准入规则和投资政策

作者：Stephen 译者：张韵

一、引言

市场准入是指由各国为准许特定商品进入本国市场而设立的条件、关税及非关税措施（NTMs）。在世界贸易组织中，货物的关税承诺是商定的，并在每个成员国的商品减让表中列出。减让表中的税率具有约束性，即当关税高于表中标准时，该关税不适用于成员国。在世界贸易组织的规则下，若受侵害成员国未得到补偿，约束税率不得提高。市场准入由“乌拉圭回合农业协作”所管控，该协定调整国家减让表中关于关税约束力、削减关税以及最低限度的进口承诺等。

由于非洲的贪污腐败状况、有限的法制水平及不力的合同执行等管理缺位，国内外的投资者望而却步，以法治精神治理国家是转变这一趋势的关键。非洲各国政府必须采取有效的措施，如有效打击贪腐、强化法院职能等行动改变现状。其他重要措施包括减少寻求经济租金的机会——比如免除即席税、鼓励投资、采取交易配额和双重税率制等。

本文旨在回顾非洲投资市场准入管理规则的现有文献并探索进一步调查研究的可能性；本文亦将探求可降低非洲投资风险的金融机制。

现存的风险导致实际流入非洲的资本偏少，但事实上非洲蕴藏着巨大的市场。虽然资本在全球其他地区，尤其是亚洲获得了巨大的收益，非洲却未因此获利。尽管其拥有巨大的潜力、廉价的劳动力和丰富的自然资源，投资者仍持谨慎态度。他们害怕将资金投入非洲，这个在太多人眼中（姑且不论真假）被战争、饥荒、艾滋和腐败蹂躏的大陆。（泰勒，2003 年）

在 WTO 的 142 个成员国中，超过三分之二的国家是自行定义的发展中国家。虽然世界贸易组织协定中大量提及了发展中国家的特别条款及权利义务，但事实上并没有一个关于发展中国家的官方定义。在现今的协定下，一些发展中国家应享有更优惠的待遇，这些国家包括食品净进口国、最不发达国家以及人均年收入低于1000美元的国家。

总的来说，在WTO体系下，发展中国家可从145项特别待遇及差别待遇条款中受益。这些规定涉及贸易机会、保护发展中国家利益、承诺的灵活性、过渡时期和技术援助等问题。

在多哈回合谈判中，部长们同意启动谈判以进一步开放非农产品贸易。为此，市场准入谈判小组（NGMA）于2002年年初在贸易谈判委员会第一次会议上成立。

二、市场准入规则

大多数发展中国家视扩大出口及增加出口多样性为难题，许多依赖出口的初级产品面临着需求不足和价格不稳定的困境。发展中国家在农业、纺织品和服装等劳动集中性制造业具有巨大的比较优势，然而这些产业在发达国家和发展中国家均受到严格的保护。（兰克斯，2002年）

自从乌拉圭回合贸易谈判后，多数定额贸易与其他非关税壁垒已经转变为关税，此举提高了贸易管理体制的透明度。事实上，贸易保护主义在某些情况下有所抬头，发展中国家产品面临的贸易壁垒仍比发达国家的坚实。部分原因在于发展中国家在乌拉圭回合前鲜有机会参与多边贸易会谈，部分原因在于农业自由化和劳动集中型制造业是政治敏感性话题。发展中国家自身高额的关税也使得跨国贸易受限。发展中国家的平均关税是14%，最不发达国家是17.9%，然而发达国家仅为5.2%。服务贸易通常面临更严格的限制，但其自由化为发展中国家提供更多的、甚至大于商品贸易所能提供的机会（比如对工人流动性有所要求的劳动集中型服务业）。（世界银行，2002年）

各国根据服务贸易总协定（GATS）提供市场准入（第16条），在减让表中列出其承诺向其他成员国减免的项目，未被列入减让表的事项则没有市场准入承诺。除在减让表中另有规定外，五种被禁止的限制性行为包括：（1）对服务供应商数量的限制；（2）对服务交易或资产的总数的限制；（3）对服务操作的总数和对服务输出的总量的限制；（4）对特定服务部门或服务供应商可能雇佣的自然人总量的限制；（5）对

在外资股权最大比例限制方面的限制以及对外资总额的限制。（帕那加利亚，2014）[①]

关税及贸易总协定（GATT）中，国内税和国内法规方面的国民待遇是一般义务。但在服务贸易总协定中，作为实现贸易自由化的重要工具，国民待遇是具体承诺（第 17 条）。国民待遇仅仅适用于成员国的减让表中包含的服务，但即使如此它也受制于特别条款。例如，相较于国内提供的同一服务，进口服务受制于更高的税费。（帕那加利亚，2014 年）

承诺的过程（第 20 条）是负面清单和正面清单的结合。成员国必须首先在减让单中确定其希望作出承诺的项目。根据正面清单，该国仅对列出的项目作出承诺。但是根据负面清单，除明确的条件及已被列出的限制外，该国被推定同意完全准入和国民待遇。

减让表有水平和垂直两方面部分。前者是常规部分，适用于在垂直部分列出的所有领域。后者则说明了适用具体项目的资格。水平部分以及每一具体垂直部门必须分别在各支付模式下列明其限制，同时还需列出有关市场准入和国民待遇的限制。四种供应方式在水平方向分散至八部分中，垂直方向则均匀分布于各个部分。

设计减让表的水平部分旨在避免重复，同时将适用于所有计划项目的市场准入及国民待遇的限制纳入其中。市场准入和对特定交付模式的国民待遇的条目显示“无”时意味着完全没有限制和条件。另外，如果条目显示“不负有义务”，那么则不存在在特定交付模式下作出的承诺。

三、保护模式

不论是工业化国家还是发展中国家，都为保护主义付出了沉重的代价。资料（世界银行，2002）显示，由于商品贸易壁垒的消除，年度社会静态福利由 2500 亿美元上涨到 6200 亿美元，其中三分之一到二分之一会使发展中国家获益。对更自由的国际贸易体制，投资和技术的回应会产生额外的动态收益。（兰克斯，2002）

然而，贸易保护仍然存在，并在多方面、在更大程度上比通常提及的平均最惠国待遇（MFN）关税所揭示的程度更严重。这些不将从量关税和关税配额，反倾销税等贸易救济措施，以及原产地规则和环境和技术标准作为考量因素。平均最惠国待遇既不能反映关税高峰、关税升级和优惠计划，也不能解决市场准入不确定性的

① Core WTO Agreements: Trade in Goods and Services and Intellectual Property, Arvind Panagariya 2014.

影响，从而阻碍出口扩张。（兰克斯，2002）

四、在非投资的挑战

风险和机会矩阵强调了利益相关者的四个主要群体，以合理评估不同非洲市场的利弊。较低的风险、较高的报酬显然是最有吸引力的，因为它们提供了稳定的商业环境和较高的增长潜力。尽管最近发生了一系列不利事件，南非仍然脱颖而出，不仅是因为风险评级较高，还因为经济和整体市场规模，以及其固定资本投资持续增长。

由于加纳的高经济增长率（受近期石油生产的推动）、稳定的政治环境和友好的贸易环境，其贸易表现也很突出。

政治不稳定仍然是对非投资的巨大风险。尽管最近存在政治动乱和动荡，北非国家表现相对较好，尤其是突尼斯和摩洛哥，并继续吸引外商直接投资项目。赞比亚也正在成为这一类别中日益具有吸引力的市场，而整个东非地区（包括东非共同体中的肯尼亚、乌干达和坦桑尼亚以及与之接壤的埃塞俄比亚和莫桑比克）正在迅速向这个方向发展。

有一些国家正在变得越来越有吸引力，它们以一贯增长的高利率，稳定的政治且进步的社会为特点，并且普遍创造越来越有利于经商的环境。这些国家包括尼日利亚和几个东非经济体。而其他国家在资源方面表现出了强劲的增长特征，其中以安哥拉和刚果民主共和国最为突出，然而他们的商业环境仍然更具挑战性。

对许多考虑在非洲投资的人而言，政治不稳定和腐败是他们主要的顾虑，因此必须采取进一步措施改善治理。商业和政府之间更密切和更有成效的合作也将有助于进一步鼓励对非洲大陆的外国直接投资（FDI）。

然而，非洲的投资环境仍然十分复杂。对许多公司来说，至少在短期内很少有市场可能提供经济上可行的投资条件，这也使得投资环境更为复杂化。因此，增长和风险管理都是由跨越多个运营和领域有效“连接点”的挑战构成的。除了规模问题，不发达还意味着需要寻找更多解决方案以克服种种困难与挑战，如在物流、通信、运输和能源等基础设施方面的差距，而这些因素在其他地区可能甚至不需要考虑。

在非洲起步或处于增长早期阶段的公司应该考虑一些成功的关键因素。也许其中最重要的是对非洲增长的坚定信念——非洲有利于商业和投资，商业和投资有利于非洲。

对扩大世贸组织职权范围的反对声音不绝于耳。证据表明，减少发展中国家政策空间和保证工业化国家跨国公司市场准入的新规则将产生发展成本而不是收益。世贸组织是否能够制定对发展中国家公平的规则和协定，还有待观察。（哈德斯塔夫、赖斯，2003 年）

每次达成的新协议，都倾向于惠及富国及其公司。一旦达成这样的协议（例如关于与贸易有关的知识产权和与贸易有关的投资措施），根据国际实践它们几乎不可能变更。虽然该决定将根据发展中国家政府和民间团体提供的证据仔细审查，但世贸谈判的现实世界更多是基于强权政治、权衡和政治交易。（哈德斯塔夫、赖斯，2003 年）

我们能越来越清楚地看到，“新问题”的主要支持者 —— 欧盟 —— 追逐着农业改革的“胡萝卜”（或更少改革的“大棒”），在所有领域的谈判中交替使用。正如 2002 年 6 月欧盟贸易专员帕斯卡尔 · 拉米所说的：“欧盟显然会进一步对农业、工业部门、关税升级等开放其市场。我们将这样做，以换取发展中国家的开放……如果我们的合作伙伴在一定的规则制定领域同意我们的规则的话。”①

某贸易杂志中的一份报告证实了这一点，指出：“欧盟认为，关于投资和其他‘新’问题的谈判对于确保欧盟经济利益是至关重要的，以平衡预期将在农业领域的让步。”②

从量关税，是不论价格如何，平均单位进口的货币绝对金额。与从价税相比，从量税一般被认为是不透明且扭曲的。随着关税配额浮动，关税高于或低于进口物品的具体数量或价值。根据乌拉圭回合建立的关税率配额最初旨在确保敏感产品的最低市场准入，然而，超额配额关税可能过高，甚至配额关税往往也很高。（兰克斯，2002 年）

尽管平均工业关税下降在四国集团（Quad）（根据世界贸易组织的说法，即加拿大、欧盟、日本和美国）6% 至 14% 的关税线受“关税峰值”（关税高于或等于 15%）制约。在加拿大和美国，关税高峰集中在纺织品和服装业，欧盟和日本则集中在农

① Lamy, P. (2002). The EU Trade and Development Agenda – From Doha via Johannesburg to Cancun. Speech by EU Trade Commissioner to All Party group on Overseas Development, London, House of Commons, 27th June 2002.

② Pruzin, D. (2003). EU Sets out Modalities Options for Discussing “Singapore Issues”. WTO Reporter, March 3 2003, Washington, Bureau of International Affairs.

业、食品和鞋类。关税高峰在发展中国家更为常见。据估计，如果所有关税上限为15%，那么从大多数国家进口到美国的纺织品和服装将下降20%，从中国进口的话则下降59%，而欧盟由中国进口农产品和食品将下降40到60%（兰克斯，2002年）。这将使非洲和发展中国家的商品有更大的市场准入。

另一个需要考虑的因素是相机保护措施，包括世贸组织所允许的对付不正当贸易做法或管理进口突然增加的贸易救济。大多数经济学家都认为，最广泛使用的反倾销措施被滥用于保护主义目的。自1995年以来开展了1800多次反倾销调查。传统上主要使用这种措施的一直是工业国家，但近年来发展中国家更加积极；在1994年至2001年期间，发展中国家几乎开展了三分之二的调查。发展中国家也成为近60%调查的目标，其中大多数调查是由其他发展中国家发起的。（兰克斯，2002年）

大多数反倾销行动主要集中在少数行业，特别是钢铁、化工、纺织行业，以及往往在产品范围的低技术末端的消费类电子产品。反倾销调查，甚至只是反倾销调查的可能性，都对出口的潜在投资者造成了很大的不确定性，并阻碍出口商传递其效率增益，从而迫使进口国的消费者和下游工业支付更高的价格。（兰克斯，2002年）

大多数发展中国家都有优先进入工业国家市场的机会。这种偏离“关贸总协定”的传统非歧视原则的做法已经在普遍优惠制（GSP）下得到批准。在2001年，大约有15个这样的计划生效。然而，许多普惠制方案的好处是有限的。虽然它们降低了许多低收入国家出口的关税，但它们也使同样贫困的国家失去贸易。此外，对于享受最大保护的敏感产品，优惠幅度通常较小，而且大多数受益于优惠计划的国家，降低了这些计划可能带来的任何竞争优势，这些通常具有类似的出口结构。（欧盟优惠贸易目前覆盖除九个国家之外的所有国家，但这些国家占欧盟进口的40%以上）优惠关税对其受益者可能是昂贵的，因为它们取决于对原产地规则或社会和环境条件的加强和监督。此外有证据表明，普惠制方案可能会削弱参与贸易自由化的动力，从而使反倾销行为永久化。（兰克斯，2002年）

然而，尽管有上述证据，兰克斯（Lankes）仍然相信，最近的倡议似乎在贸易多样化方面具有以相当低的成本提供额外收益的可能，如欧盟的“除武器之外的一切”倡议。这一倡议为最不发达国家（LDC）除武器和弹药（香蕉、大米和糖将逐渐实现自由化）以外的所有产品免税并开放无配额市场准入，因为最不发达国家仅占世界贸易的0.5%（前提是原产地规则是自由的，它确定了多少附加值来自出口国）。模拟结果表明，如果四国集团（Quad）所有的国家都提供这种条件，那么最不发达国家的出口可能增加25亿美元，增幅约11%（霍克曼等，2001年）。随着2000年《非洲增长和机遇方案》（AGOA）的出台，美国已朝着这一方向迈出了一步，但此法案仍然存在一些限制，如严格的原产地规则和其他资格条件，而这些条件是许多非洲最不发达国家难以达到的。

偏好方案不是长期解决方案。它们存在着风险，即它们可能被看作更广泛自由化的替代品，或甚至会通过在现状中创造既得利益而成为障碍。因此，应在迅速的多边自由化的背景下牢牢地确定这些标准。（兰克斯，2002年）

五、建议

尽管非洲富有极具吸引力的投资机会，但在非从事商业交易仍然存在着陷阱。在作出决定之前，公司应实施足够的内部控制和合规计划，以减少腐败。无论是现有实体、合资企业还是从头开始建立管理模式，尽职调查可能不仅是简单地评估操作本身的管理和控制。它还可能需要查看与供应商的关系，如顾问和中间人，他们可能代表公司与政府打交道。一旦公司开始在一个国家开展生意，确保有足够且有效的内部控制是非常重要的。这可能不仅仅需要适当的内部政策和控制程序，管理层还可能需要确定基调并制定适当的员工培训计划。因为一旦进行投资，对这些计划的持续监测和审查可能有助于进一步降低风险。

各组织应密切监测该区域的政治发展情况，因为政府的变化可能影响在某一特定国家开展业务的可行性。在某些情况下，新政府可能会更稳定、更透明并且对经济基础设施实施问责制。然而，反腐败法律可能无法完全消除风险。据国际透明组织研究，经合组织公约（OECD）关于反贿赂建议的执行有限。在38个成员国中，超过一半（21个）的成员国很少或甚至没有执行其规定。

跨国公司在非面临着巨大机会，然而，与政治和经济基础设施腐败有关的风险和不确定性也为其造成挑战。寻求在该地区投资的公司应该注意这些风险，并考虑积极开发一个可以消除这些风险的控制环境。目前，在全球范围内对反贿赂法律加强监管的大背景下，一个新的执法时代即将来临，上述考量的现实化也指日可待。

改变贸易规则并给予更多的援助，以帮助非洲国家贸易的承诺并没有实现。尤其八国集团（G8）承诺在2005年“让贸易推动非洲”，并在2007年再次进行此项目，但其最强大的成员国仍然坚持补贴和原产地规则，这使得非洲贸易十分艰难。

与此同时，非洲内部贸易也面临着基础设施缺乏和一体化程度低下的困境。（非政府组织 ONE，2007 年）

将贸易特权扩大到非最不发达国家的较大经济体，以使它们成为整个非洲大陆增长的推动力同样是必须之举。必须对原产地规则进行改革。“原产地规则”用于定义产品是否符合贸易优惠计划。为了符合免税待遇的条件，出口产品必须包含指定比例的原产地非洲的产品。原产地规则的复杂性和严格性，使得这些方案难以取得进展，并且平均增加 10%的出口成本，在欧盟情况更为严重。这些方案所需的非洲投入品的数量也各不相同，这使非洲生产者向不同市场出口变得复杂。非洲委员会和世界银行都建议采用起点为 10%的低附加值规则，这将使非洲国家能够进口低成本产品，为最终产品贡献价值，并仍然有资格获得免关税的待遇。这种调整将使发达经济体付出很少，使非洲产品更具竞争力。①（非政府组织 ONE，2007 年）

增加区域贸易对非洲经济也将是好兆头。他们不再是向西方寻找非洲制造的商品市场，而是要在非洲大陆上大量增加贸易，发现新的或未充分利用的市场，旨在充分利用制造能力，改进合作，促进相互理解。

为了制定和执行加强个别国家减贫战略的贸易政策，必须使非洲国家的多边协定、区域协定和双边协定具有适当的灵活性。这将确保非洲国家具有足够使八国集团国家受益的灵活性，就像他们在追求自己的经济增长时从中收获的一样。确定这些优先事项的援助可以由捐助者和私营者赞助的国内独立智库提供，确保这些援助侧重于特定国家或地区的需要。（非政府组织 ONE，2007 年）

政策空间是多边协定、区域协定和双边协定的重要组成部分。特别规定必须有的放矢，并与贸易政策和减贫战略相协调，以产生真正的影响。尤其是欧盟和非洲国家之间的经济伙伴关系协定（EPAs），不能要求高水平的相互快速开放市场。非洲贸易政策必须由非洲政府独立设计，而不是由欧盟或美国确定。（非政府组织 ONE，2007 年）

非洲各国政府必须从世贸组织中独立采取主动行动，以解决扭曲的贸易补贴，即对与非洲产品市场相竞争或扭曲市场的产品提供补贴的影响。在政治上，发达国家的补贴计划改革必须在世贸组织谈判内进行，而且不能不涉及影响非洲农民的具体部门。因此，提供这些补贴的发达国家应该设法减轻国内补贴对非洲产品的影响。

---

① Making Trade Work for Africa November 20 2007, accessed at www.one.org/us/policy/making-trade-work-for-africa/.

（非政府组织 ONE，2007 年）

在短期内取消补贴之前，捐助者应通过提供相当于收入的援助来补偿这些补贴对非洲生产者的影响。例如，欧盟可以将相当于向他们自己的番茄生产商每年提供补贴的金额投向生产番茄的非洲国家以发展产业，以及改进农业加工业的技术、能力和基础设施。（非政府组织 ONE，2007 年）

应追求能力建设以满足质量和营销标准，如扩大美国标准联盟倡议（USTDA），这是美国国际开发署和美国国家标准协会之间的公私伙伴关系，以帮助非洲生产者达到美国质量标准和营销要求。目前非洲贸易办事处下的东非共同体以及南非发展共同体正在开展工作。美国标准联盟倡议将与美国电气制造商协会就美国非洲能源部门标准合作计划展开合作，举行一系列技术研讨会，旨在促进美国和撒哈拉以南非洲国家公私部门之间的广泛参与，意在标准和法规上加强网型和离网型能源基础设施上的合作。①（白宫新闻秘书办公室，2014 年）

参考文献

[1] AlixPartners,(2016). Investing in Africa New Opportunities, But Risks Remain accessed at http://www.alixpartners.com/en/Publications/AllArticles/tabid/635/articleType/ArticleView/articleId/351/Investing-in-Africa.aspx#sthash.9rui9lVF.dpuf.

[2] EY Press, (2012).Increasing investment opportunities across Africa but challenges remain accessed at http://www.ey.com/GL/en/Newsroom/News-releases/News_Increasing-investment-opportunities-across-Africa-but-challenges-remain.

[3] Hardstaff, P., and T. Rice., (2003). More Market Access for Less Policy Space – a Bad Deal for Development A Joint policy briefing by the World Development Movement and ActionAid, May 2003.

[4] Lankes, H. P., (2002. Market Access for Developing Countries, Finance and Development A quarterly magazine of the IMF, September 2002, Volume 39, Number 3.

[5] Office of the White House Press Secretary, (2014). Fact Sheet: Investing in African Trade for our Common Future, Office of the Press Secretary White House, Aug 2014.

[6] ONE, (2007). Making Trade Work for Africa November 20 2007 accessed at https://www.one.org/us/policy/making-trade-work-for-africa/.

[7] Panagariya, A., (2014). Core WTO Agreements: Trade in Goods and Services and Intellectual Property.

① FACT SHEET: Investing in African Trade for our Common Future, Office of the Press Secretary White House, Aug 2014.

The Market Access Rules and Policies on Investing in Africa

Author: Stephen

Introduction

Market access means the conditions, tariff and Non-tariff measures (NTMs), set by countries for the entry of specific goods into their markets. In the WTO, tariff commitments for goods are agreed upon and set out in each member's schedules of concessions on goods. The schedules represent commitments not to apply tariffs above the listed rates—these rates are "bound". Under WTO rules, bound rates may not be raised without compensating the affected members. Market access is governed by provisions of the Uruguay Round Agreement on Agriculture which refer to concessions contained in the country schedules with respect to bindings and reductions of tariffs and to other minimum import commitments.

In Africa, poor governance – including corruption, limited rule of law, and lack of enforcement of contracts—scares off domestic and foreign investors. Ruling justly is critical to reversing that trend. Actions African governments must take include effective anti-corruption initiatives, and strengthening of the courts. Another important step is to reduce opportunities for rent-seeking—such as ad hoc tax exemptions and investment incentives, trade quotas, and dual exchange rates.

The objective of this paper is to review the existing literature on the rules governing market access to investing in Africa as well as to explore the possibilities of further research. This paper discusses the financial mechanisms that might be able to mitigate some of the risks of doing business in Africa.

Risk—both real and perceived—is the primary reason why less capital is flowing to Africa. Africa represents incredible potential. While capital flows have occurred quite successfully elsewhere, most notably in Asia, Africa has been left behind. Despite Africa's enormous potential, low cost labor, and vast natural resources, investors, quite frankly, remain wary. They are afraid of putting their money in a place which all too often is perceived (however true or not) as a continent wracked by war, famine, AIDS, and corruption (Taylor, 2003).

More than two-thirds of the WTO's 142 members are considered to be developing countries by virtue of their self-designation to that status. While WTO agreements make extensive references to special provisions, rights and obligations for developing countries, there is no official definition of what constitutes such a country. Certain groups of developing countries qualify for more generous treatment under some of the existing provisions. These include net food importing countries, least developed countries and countries with a per capita income of less than US$1 000 per year.

Overall, the developing countries could potentially benefit from 145 special and differential treatment provisions operating within the WTO system. These provisions deal with such issues as: trade opportunities; safeguarding developing country interests; flexibility of commitments; transitional time periods; and technical assistance.

At the Doha Round of talks, Ministers agreed to initiate negotiations to further liberalize trade on non-agricultural goods. To this end, the Negotiating Group on Market Access (NGMA) was created at the first meeting of the Trade Negotiations Committee, in early 2002.

Market Access Rules

Most developing countries are unable to overcome the obstacles to expanding and diversifying their exports. The primary commodities on which many rely for export earnings have faced stagnant demand and been battered by volatile prices, and the two sectors in which developing countries have a strong comparative advantage—agriculture and labor-intensive manufactures, like textiles and clothing—are heavily protected not only in the industrial countries but in developing countries as well (Lankes, 2002).

Most quantitative restrictions and other nontariff barriers have been converted into tariffs since the Uruguay Round of trade talks, improving the transparency of trade regimes. Protectionism has actually increased in some cases, however, and trade barriers are still higher for the products typically exported by developing countries than for those from industrial countries. This is partly because developing countries made little effort to participate in multilateral trade talks before the Uruguay Round and partly because of the political sensitivity of liberalizing agriculture and labor-intensive manufactures. Developing countries themselves have high tariffs that limit trade among them. The average tariff in developing countries is 14 percent, and in the least developed countries, 17.9 percent, compared with 5.2 percent in the industrial countries. The liberalization of trade in services, which is generally subject to far greater restrictions, offers opportunities for developing countries that, according to some estimates, are even greater than in merchandise trade (for instance, in labor-intensive services that require the temporary movement of workers (World Bank, 2002)).

Each country gives market access (Article XVI) under GATS through a schedule that lists the sectors in which it commits to giving concessions to other members. No market access commitment is presumed to exist in a sector not listed in the schedule. Six types of restrictive actions are prohibited unless otherwise specified in the schedule. These are: (i) limitations on the number of service suppliers, (ii) limitations on the total number of service transactions or assets, (iii) limitations on the total number of service operations or total quantity of service output, (iv) limitations on the total number of natural persons that may be employed in a particular service sector or by a service supplier, (v) measures which restrict or require specific types of legal entity joint venture, and (vi) limitations on the participation of foreign capital in terms of maximum percentage limit of foreign shareholding or the total value of investment (Panagariya, 2014).①

In GATT, national treatment on internal taxation and regulation is a general obligation. But in GATS, being an important instrument of liberalization, it is a specific commitment (Article XVII). National treatment applies only to those services included in the schedule of the member and even then it can be subject to specific conditions. For instance, it may subject the imported services to a higher tax than identical domestically supplied services (Panagariya, 2014).

The process of scheduling sector-specific commitments (Article XX) is a hybrid between negative- and positive-list approaches. A Member must first identify in its schedule the sectors in which it wishes to make commitments. Following the positive-list approach, the country makes commitments with respect to the listed sectors only. But following the negative-list approach, it is presumed that complete access and national treatment are granted except to the extent that explicit qualifications and limitations are listed.

The schedule has a horizontal and a vertical section. The former is a general section applying to all sectors listed in the vertical section. The latter spells out qualifications applying to specific sectors. In the horizontal section and for each specific sector in the vertical section, qualifications to commitments must be listed separately for each mode of delivery and with respect to market access and national treatment. Given four modes of supply, this leads to eight entries in the horizontal section and for each specific sector in the vertical section.

The schedule's horizontal section is designed to avoid repetition and contains market access and national treatment limitations that apply to all scheduled sectors. When the entry in the market access or national treatment column for a given mode of delivery says "none," it implies a complete absence of limitations and conditions. On the other hand, if the entry says "unbound," no commitment under the particular mode of delivery has been made.

① Core WTO Agreements: Trade in Goods and Services and Intellectual Property, Arvind Panagariya 2014.

Patterns of Protection

Developing and industrial countries both pay dearly for protectionism. Estimates from a variety of sources (in particular, World Bank, 2002) of annual static welfare gains from eliminating barriers to merchandise trade range from $250 billion to $620 billion, of which one-third to one-half would accrue to developing countries. The response of investment and technology to a freer international trade regime would generate additional dynamic gains (Lankes, 2002).

And yet protection persists, in many guises and to a greater extent than is revealed by the customary references to average most-favored-nation (MFN) tariffs. These do not reflect specific tariffs and tariff-rate quotas, trade remedies such as antidumping duties, and the effects of rules of origin and environmental and technical standards. Nor do the averages capture the impact of tariff peaks and escalation, preference schemes, or measures that contribute to the uncertainty of market access and therefore discourage export expansion (Lankes, 2002).

Challenges to Investing in Africa

The risk and opportunity matrix highlights four main groups for key stakeholders to rationally assess the pros and cons of different African markets. That is, *the lower risk, higher reward quadrant* is clearly the most attractive, *offering a stable business environment* and *high potential for growth*. Despite recent events, South Africa stands out not only for its positive risk rating, but also because of the size of the economy and overall market, as well as ongoing investments being made in fixed capital assets.

Ghana is also prominent in this category, with its high economic growth rates (boosted by recent oil production), political stability and an environment that is generally conducive to doing business.

Political instability remains a huge risk to investment in Africa. Despite the recent political unrest and turmoil, the North African countries, particularly Tunisia and Morocco, performed relatively well and continue to attract FDI projects. Zambia is also emerging as an increasingly attractive market in this category, while the entire East African region (including the East African Community countries of Kenya, Uganda and Tanzania, and the bordering countries of Ethiopia and Mozambique) is moving rapidly towards this quadrant.

There are a number of countries that are becoming increasingly attractive, growing at consistently high rates, making steady political and social progress and generally creating environments that are increasingly conducive to doing business. These include Nigeria and several of the East African economies. Others, perhaps most notably Angola and the Democratic Republic of Congo, display strong growth characteristics in terms of resources, however, their business environments remain more challenging.

Perceptions of political instability and corruption are dominant themes for many of those considering investing in Africa therefore further measures must be made to improve governance. Closer and more productive collaboration between business and government will also help to further encourage FDI into the continent.

Africa remains, however, a complex environment in which to do business. This complexity is compounded by the fact that for many companies very few individual markets are likely to provide the kind of scale — in the shorter term at least — that makes them economically viable. Both growth and risk management are therefore framed by the challenge of effectively "connecting the dots" across multiple operations and territories. Besides the issue of scale, underdevelopment also means that solutions for challenges need to be found that may not even need to be considered in other regions; the infrastructure gap – in logistics, communications, transport and energy – being among the most significant.

For companies beginning or in the early stages of their African growth journey there are critical success factors that should be considered. Perhaps most important is a strong belief in the African growth story—that Africa is good for business and investment, and that business and investment is good for Africa.

There has been continued opposition to the expansion of the WTO's remit because the evidence demonstrates that new rules to reduce developing country policy space and guarantee market access for industrialized country multinationals will create development costs not benefits. It is also yet to be seen whether the WTO is capable of producing rules and agreements that are fair for developing countries (Hardstaff & Rice, 2003).

Every time a new agreement is reached, it is skewed to benefit rich countries and their companies. And once such agreements are reached (e.g. on Trade Related Intellectual Property Rights and Trade-Related Investment Measures) it becomes virtually impossible to change them in light of experience. Though it may be presumed that that decisions will be based on a careful examination of the evidence presented by developing country governments and civil society, the real world of WTO negotiations is based more on power politics, trade-offs and political deal-making (Hardstaff & Rice, 2003).

It is also becoming clear that the principal proponent of 'new issues' – the European Union – will dangle the 'carrot' of agricultural reform (or the 'stick' of less reform) as a trade-off for negotiations in all these areas. As Pascal Lamy, EU Trade Commissioner stated in June 2002, "European Commission has obviously to further open its markets to agriculture, peak industrial sectors, tariff escalation and so on. We will do so, in return for some improvements in openness from developing countries··· and if our partners sign on to some rule making areas." ①

① Lamy, P. (2002). The EU Trade and Development Agenda – From Doha via Johannesburg to Cancun. Speech by EU Trade Commissioner to All Party group on Overseas Development, London, House of Commons, 27th June 2002.

A report in a trade journal confirmed this, stating, "The EU views the talks [on investment and other 'new' issues] as essential for securing gains in areas of economic interest to Brussels in order to balance off the concession it is expected to make in the area of agriculture." ①

Specific tariffs and tariff-rate quotas account for a significant share of the AVEs shown in Table 1. A specific tariff, an absolute amount of money charged per unit of imports regardless of the price, is generally regarded as less transparent and more distortionary than an ad valorem tariff. With tariff-rate quotas, the tariff is different above or below a specific quantity or value of imported items. Tariff-rate quotas, established under the Uruguay Round, were originally intended to ensure minimum market access for sensitive products. However, out-of-quota tariffs can be prohibitive, and even in-quota tariffs are often high (Lankes, 2002).

Although average industrial tariffs have dropped, between 6 and 14 percent of Quad (Canada, the EU, Japan, and the United States, in World Trade Organization (WTO) parlance) tariff lines are subject to "tariff peaks" (tariffs at or over 15 percent). In Canada and the United States, tariff peaks are concentrated in textiles and clothing, in the EU and Japan, in agriculture, food products, and footwear. Tariff peaks are even more common in developing countries. It has been estimated that if all tariffs were capped at 15 percent, AVEs on textiles and clothing would drop 20 percent for imports from most countries into the United States and 59 percent for imports from China, while AVEs on agricultural and food products imported by the EU would drop 40-60 percent (Lankes, 2002). This would grant greater market access to commodities from African and developing countries.

Tariff escalation, which is seen in both industrial and developing countries, is designed to protect a processing or manufacturing industry in the importing country, which sets low tariffs on imported materials used by its industry and higher tariffs on imported finished products that would compete with the domestic industry's own products. This creates hurdles for countries trying to move up the technology ladder, discouraging them from expanding their processing industries and diversifying exports, and therefore leaving them dependent on commodities, whose prices are often volatile (Lankes, 2002).

Another factor to be considered is contingent protection which includes trade remedies permitted by the WTO to counter unfair trade practices or manage sudden surges in imports. Most economists agree that antidumping measures, the most widely used, have been abused for protectionist purposes. Over 1,800 antidumping investigations have been initiated since 1995. While industrial countries have traditionally been the main users of such measures, developing countries have been more active in recent years; between 1994 and 2001, they initiated almost two-thirds of all investigations. Developing countries have also been the target of nearly 60 percent of investigations—most of which have been initiated by other developing countries(Lankes, 2002).

① Pruzin, D. (2003). EU Sets out Modalities Options for Discussing 'Singapore Issues'. WTO Reporter, March 3 2003, Washington, Bureau of International Affairs.

Most antidumping actions have been concentrated in a small number of sectors, especially steel, chemicals, textiles, and consumer electronics, often at the low-technology end of the product range. Antidumping investigations—or even the mere possibility of them—create a great deal of uncertainty for potential investors in export sectors and discourage exporters from passing on their efficiency gains, thus forcing consumers and downstream industries in importing countries to pay higher prices (Lankes, 2002).

Standards and regulations play an important role in trade by ensuring the quality, safety, and technical compatibility of products and production processes, but they may at times be more stringent than is appropriate and abused by those seeking to raise the costs of potential competitors. Annual notifications of new technical barriers to the WTO and its predecessor, the General Agreement on Tariffs and Trade (GATT), increased from about 10-20 in the early 1980s to over 400 in 1999. Low- and middle-income countries reported that, from 1996 to 1999, they were unable to meet sanitary and phytosanitary requirements on more than 50 percent of their potential exports of fresh and processed fish, meat, fruit, and vegetables into the EU (OECD, 2001a). In fact, these measures were viewed as more important barriers than tariffs and quotas. The WTO Agreement on Technical Barriers to Trade and Agreement on the Application of Sanitary and Phytosanitary Measures are intended to strengthen international rules governing product standards to minimize their abuse, but they entail substantial costs (Lankes, 2002).

Most developing countries have preferential access to industrial country markets. This departure from the traditional nondiscrimination principle of the GATT has been sanctioned under the Generalized System of Preferences (GSP). In 2001, some 15 such schemes were in effect. The benefits of many GSP schemes have been limited, however. Although they lower tariffs for exports from many low-income countries, they also divert trade from other countries that are often just as poor. In addition, preference margins are usually smaller for sensitive products, which enjoy the greatest protection, and the fact that a large number of countries—often with similar export structures—benefit from preference schemes reduces any competitive advantage the schemes might convey. (EU preferential trade now covers all but nine countries, though these account for over 40 percent of EU imports.) Preferential tariffs may be costly for their beneficiaries because they are contingent on the imposition and monitoring of rules of origin or of social and environmental conditions. Moreover, evidence suggests that GSP schemes may undermine incentives to engage in trade liberalization and thus perpetuate antiexport biases (Lankes, 2002).

Despite the evidence as postulated herein above, Lankes is however convinced that recent initiatives like the EU's Everything But Arms initiative—which grants duty-and quota-free market access to LDCs for all products except arms and ammunition (bananas, rice, and sugar will be liberalized gradually)—seem to offer the prospect of additional benefit at a fairly low cost in terms of trade diversion, because LDCs account for a mere 0.5 percent of world trade (provided that the rules of origin, which determine how much value added has to come from the exporting country, are liberal). Simulation results suggest that, if such conditions were offered by all Quad countries, exports from LDCs might increase by $2.5 billion, or about 11 percent (Hoekman et al, 2001). The United States has taken one step in this direction with the African Growth and Opportunity Act (AGOA) of 2000, which nonetheless maintains a number of restrictions, such as tight rules of origin and other conditions for eligibility that many African LDCs have found difficult to meet.

Preference schemes are not a long-term solution. There is a danger they may be seen as a substitute for broader liberalization or even turn into an obstacle to it by creating vested interests in the status quo. They should therefore be set firmly within a context of rapid multilateral liberalization (Lankes, 2002).

Recommendations

Despite the attractive investment opportunities, there remain pitfalls associated with doing business in Africa. Before making a decision to do so, companies should implement adequate internal controls and compliance programs that can help reduce the risk of corruption. Whether acquiring an existing entity, entering a joint venture, or building an operation from scratch, due diligence may require more than simply evaluating management and controls within the operation itself. It may also be necessary to look at relationships with vendors such as consultants and brokers, who may deal with governments on the company's behalf. And once companies have begun to do business in a country, it is important to make sure that adequate internal controls are in place and are effective. This may require more than proper internal polices and control procedures. It may be necessary for management to set the tone and develop appropriate employee training programs. Once an investment has been made, ongoing monitoring and reviews of these programs may help to further reduce risk.

Organizations should closely monitor political developments in the region, as governmental changes may impact the viability of doing business in a particular country. In some cases, a new government could represent an opportunity for greater stability and increased transparency and accountability into economic infrastructures. Yet, anti-corruption laws may not eliminate the risks completely. According to Transparency International, enforcement of the OECD Convention's recommendations on anti-bribery has been limited. Of the 38 member countries more than half (21) were perceived as having little or no enforcement of its provisions.

Multinationals have before them great opportunities in this region, however the risks and uncertainties associated with corruption in political and economic infrastructures may pose challenges. Companies seeking to invest in the region should be mindful of these risks and consider proactively developing a control environ-ment that can account for them. This is particularly true as the heightened policing of anti-bribery laws on a global scale ushers in a new era in enforcement.

Promises to change trade rules and boost aid that helps African countries trade are not being met. The G8 in particular promised to "make trade work for Africa" in 2005 and again in 2007, but its most powerful members maintain subsidies and rules of origin that strangle African business. At the same time intra-African trade suffers from a lack of infrastructure and poor integration (ONE, 2007).

It is also essential that trade privileges are extended to the larger economies which are not LDCs so that they become drivers for growth across the continent. There has to be a reform of the Rules of origin. "Rules of origin" are used to define whether a product qualifies for a trade preference programme. In order to qualify for duty-free treatment, the exported product must contain a specified percentage of African inputs. The complexity and strictness of the rules of origin requirements, especially in the EU, make these programmes extremely difficult to access and add an average of 10% to export costs. The amount of African content required by these programmes also varies, making it complicated for African producers to export to different markets. Both the Commission for Africa and the World Bank recommend a low value-added rule of origin of 10% which would allow African countries to import low-cost inputs, contribute value to the final product and still qualify for duty-free access. These types of adjustments would cost developed economies very little and make African products much more competitive (ONE, 2007).[①]

Increased regional trade would also auger well for African economies. Instead of looking west for markets for commodities made in Africa, there has to be an upsurge of trade within the continent and the discovery of new or underutilized markets in order that not only are manufacturing capabilities utilized but also cooperation and mutual understanding improved.

In order to develop and implement trade policies that enhance individual countries' poverty alleviation strategies, there must be an appropriate level of flexibility in multilateral, regional, and bilateral agreements for African countries. This will ensure that African countries have access to the same flexibilities that G8 countries benefited from as they pursued their own economic growth. Assistance in determining these priorities could be provided by in-country independent think tanks that are funded by donors and the private sector and are focused on the needs of specific countries or regions (ONE, 2007).

Policy space is an essential component of multilateral, regional, and bilateral agreements. Special provisions must be effectively sequenced and coordinated with trade policy and poverty alleviation strategies so as to have a real impact. EPAs between the EU and African countries in particular must not require high levels of rapid reciprocal market liberalization. African trade policies must be designed by African governments not determined in Brussels or Washington (ONE, 2007).

African governments must spearhead separate initiatives from the WTO that would be geared towards addressing the impact of trade-distorting subsidies on products that compete with or distort the market for African products. Politically, reform of subsidy programmes in developed countries

① Making Trade Work for Africa November 20 2007, accessed at www.one.org/us/policy/making-trade-work-for-africa/.

may be impossible to undertake outside the WTO negotiations and also may not address specific sectors that impact African farmers. Therefore, developed countries that provide these subsidies should find ways to mitigate the impact of domestic subsidies on African products (ONE, 2007).

In the near term, before their own subsidies are abolished, donors should compensate for the impact of these subsidies on African producers by providing assistance equivalent to the revenue lost to Africa. For example, the EU could direct the amount equivalent to annual subsidies to their own tomato producers to the development of a value-added industry in tomato-producing African countries and improvements to the technology, capacity, and infrastructure of the agricultural processing industry (ONE, 2007).

Capacity building to meet quality and marketing standards should be pursued such as the expansion of the United States Standards Alliance initiative(USTDA), a public-private partnership between USAID and the American National Standards Institute, to help African producers meet U.S. quality standards and marketing requirements. Work is currently underway with the EAC, under the Trade Africa umbrella, and with the Southern Africa Development Community. USTDA will also partner with the National Electrical Manufacturers Association on the U.S.-Africa Energy Sector Standards Cooperation Program, a series of technical workshops to facilitate greater engagement between the public and private sector in the United States and sub-Saharan African countries to increase cooperation on standards and regulations for grid and off-grid energy infrastructure (Office of White House Press Secretary, 2014)①.

REFERENCES

[1] AlixPartners,(2016). Investing in Africa New Opportunities, But Risks Remain accessed at http://www.alixpartners.com/en/Publications/AllArticles/tabid/635/articleType/ArticleView/articleId/351/Investing-in-Africa.aspx#sthash.9rui9lVF.dpuf.

[2] EY Press, (2012).Increasing investment opportunities across Africa but challenges remain accessed at http://www.ey.com/GL/en/Newsroom/News-releases/News_Increasing-investment-opportunities-across-Africa-but-challenges-remain.

[3] Hardstaff, P., and T. Rice., (2003). More Market Access for Less Policy Space – a Bad Deal for Development A Joint policy briefing by the World Development Movement and ActionAid, May 2003.

[4] Lankes, H. P., (2002. Market Access for Developing Countries, Finance and Development A quarterly magazine of the IMF, September 2002, Volume 39, Number 3.

[5] Office of the White House Press Secretary, (2014). Fact Sheet: Investing in African Trade for our Common Future, Office of the Press Secretary White House, Aug 2014.

① FACT SHEET: Investing in African Trade for our Common Future, Office of the Press Secretary White House, Aug 2014.

[6] ONE, (2007). Making Trade Work for Africa November 20 2007 accessed at https://www.one.org/us/policy/making-trade-work-for-africa/.

[7] Panagariya, A., (2014). Core WTO Agreements: Trade in Goods and Services and Intellectual Property.

在非投资的法律风险

Legal risks of Foreign Investment in African Countries

非洲农业投资的法律风险

作者：Mashaba Bookholane[①] 译者：陈乐

一、简介

在2009年期间，媒体针对非洲、拉丁美洲、中亚和东南亚的大规模农田收购做了许多报道（Cotula等人，2009年）。Cotula等人指出，尽管国际媒体披露了土地交易情况，但这只是在这些地区发生的土地交易的一小部分。他还指出，尽管有越来越多的报告和研究发表，但对于这些交易造成的影响，人们仍然没有适当的理解。

Cotula等人指出，通常在土地收购中可得到的初级和次级数据，在非洲却很难获得，而且即使获得了，其可靠性往往有限。尽管收购的数据很少，但有迹象表明，非洲的土地收购程度非常高。2004年以来，埃塞俄比亚、加纳、马达加斯加、马里和苏丹（以下称"被研究国家"）五国，总共有2492684公顷的土地被批准分配（不包括1000公顷以下的土地分配）（Cotula等，2009年）。

一般来说，农业投资者可以分为公共或私人投资者、外国或国内投资者。大量的国内私人投资者是农民，他们无疑是中低收入国家农业投资最重要的来源（Lowder，Carisma和Skoet，2012年）。第二大农业投资主体来自国内公共投资者，主要是国家政府。外国公共投资者如发展合作伙伴，以及外国私人投资者如公司都被第二大投资主体远远甩在后面（Lowder，Carisma和Skoet，2012年）。

Cotula等人在2009年调查得到的数据的结果表明，从2004年年初到2009年年初，所有被研究的五个国家涉及土地收购的项目数量和土地分配面积都呈上升趋势，

① Masechaba Bookholane, Senior Legal Advisor at Transnet Freight Rail, a division of Transnet SOC Limited, a state-owned country established under the laws of the Republic of South Africa.

数据还显示未来为了投资而进行的土地收购很有可能会增加。此外，数据表明，私营部门往往是土地收购交易的主要对手，虽然也有迹象显示，这些私营部门行为人从政府获得了重要的财政和其他支持。数据也表明，政府本身在土地收购投资中扮演了所有者和参与者的角色。

Cotula 等人表明，对大规模土地收购日益增长的兴趣归因于以下几个因素，包括但不限于:（1）收购主体特别是投资国对粮食安全日益关注，这很大程度解释了政府支持投资的增长原因;（2）由政府支持的土地收购投资交易所提供的投资机会；现有的土地投资驱动模式，如全球对生物燃料和其他非粮食农产品的需求增加；对农业和土地价格更高回报率的预测；本国和东道国采用的土地政策。土地需求的激增让许多发展中国家农业部门重拾希望，这些国家在历史上严重欠发达，而激增的需求给予他们将受益于新利益的希望。（Nolte 和 Väth，2013 年）

Liu 认为，粮食安全是土地收购高潮的一个关键驱动因素。他主张发展中国家农业投资数量的增长是减轻贫困、实现粮食安全和为数百万人提供营养的需求。他还指出，在世界上贫困人口众多的农村地区，消除贫困最有影响力和最重要的战略是开始农业投资。

Liu 声称，重新提起对提高发展中国家初级农业生产的投资额是一个急需的发展趋势，因为过去 30 年对农业部门和小农场的低水平投资，已导致生产量的下降和生产效率下降。此外，Liu 警告说，农业部门面临着艰巨的任务，那就是必须满足到 2050 年估计有 90 亿人口的食物需求，这比目前农业产业所满足的人口还多 25 亿人。

虽然人们承认，增加对农业产业投资的水平是一个积极的发展方向，这个发展是人们将开始应对粮食安全等的挑战，因为国内和外国投资者的农业投资可以刺激生产力，促使粮食产量、技术创造力、扶贫水平、技术转让以及获得资本和市场的机会提高，然而这些利益不能自动实现。（Liu，2014 年）

利益也可能伴随不利的后果，其对东道国的影响在短期内可能不会特别明显。Nolte 和 Väth 在 2013 年写道，虽然我们仍然缺失一些关于造成影响的关键证据，但证据数量正在增加。可能对东道国和国内人口产生的潜在负面影响，已经引起了民间社会组织的担忧，这些影响包括社区的迁移、当地人的生存困难、逃税和在劳动合同形成的不受制约的依赖。 Cotula 等人回应了这种观点并写道，由于政府或市场使潜在投资者获得土地，大规模土地收购实际上可能导致当地的人们无法得到他们赖以获得粮食安全的资源，特别是许多接受国本身正在应对粮食不安全而造成的问题。

Cotula 和 Blakemore 声称，为了适当地了解和获得发展中国家增加的农业投资案例的主要内容，人们必须理解他们所谓的“投资链”的概念，它囊括了任何一个项目中无数参与者和其相互关系，还有价值流动在这些角色扮演者之间共享的方式。他们继续解释道，每个投资链在决策、资源分配和运营建模上都有不同的侧重点，这些侧重点通常会跨越不同的管辖范围。

本文将对非洲土地征用的行为者和驱动因素进行挖掘，讨论对这些征用的法律规定和合同协议的性质，评估国家征用农村土地的影响，探讨非洲农业投资的法律风险。本文还将针对非洲撒哈拉以南的土地交易分析研究。

二、农业投资交易的参与者

在大多数大规模土地收购的投资链中，参与者可以被大致归类为三个组成部分：第一类是获得土地权利的企业（通常是公司）；第二类是东道国政府，即土地所在国的政府；第三类是受土地交易影响的当地社区。（Cotula 和 Blakemore，2014 年）任何数量的中间人都可以在整个交易过程中促进这三类参与者之间的关系，我们也可以观察到每个参与者（甚至在相同利益群体中的参与者）所追逐的利益差异性及其相应的议价能力。（Cotula 和 Blakemore，2014 年）

Cotula 和 Blakemore 解释说，在任何一个投资链中的参与者数量可能有很大的差异，因为在最终资金来源和实施项目的实体之间的投资链中可能有多个参与者。他们进一步解释道，投资链也可能在其整合程度上有所不同，这体现在投资链中某个环节的参与者能否有通过高度一体化来控制投资链中其他参与者的能力，高度一体化是由投资者通过多层级的全资或多数控股子公司实现的，并由遍布投资链实体的全部和直接所有权证明的。

农民的国内私人投资有以下几种：涉及实现土地数量、质量或生产力重大改善的土地开发；牲畜，包括固定资产（种用家禽）、（用于屠宰的年幼家畜和牲畜）中的牛和水牛、骆驼、马、骡、驴、猪、山羊、绵羊和家禽等存储资产；机器和设备，包括拖拉机（及其配套配件）、收割机和打谷机、挤奶机和手持工具；种植园作物，即那些可重复使用作物（包括藤和灌木）的树木，这些树木用于培育果实和坚果、生产汁液和树脂以及生产树皮和树叶产品；家畜用建筑物，包括为牛、水牛、马、骆驼和家禽鸟建造的棚屋。（Lowder，Carisma 和 Skoet，2012 年）

国内公共投资者的投资可以通过国际食物政策研究所（“IFPRI”）生成的两个数

据库来衡量。一个是经济发展公共支出统计（“SPEED”）数据库（IFPRI，2012a），它提供政府在农业领域支出的数据；另一个是农业科技指标（“ASTI”）数据库（IFPRI，2012b），它提供农业研发公共支出的数据。SPEED 数据库包括如下分类：农业事务的管理；耕地的服务、保护、开垦或扩展；对农民在农业活动的补偿、赠款、贷款或补贴。（Lowder，Carisma 和 Skoet，2012 年）

外国公共投资指标由经合组织（2012 年）收集的关于农业官方发展援助（“ODA”）的数据来计算，指标所涉及的部分包括但不限于土地改革、农业政策和行政管理以及财政服务。（Lowder，Carisma 和 Skoet，2012 年）农业和其他相关部门的私人外来投资的实施方法可以从联合国贸易和发展会议编制的关于外国直接投资的数据（2011 年）中收集，这些方法包括对作物、园艺以及农业和畜牧业服务的投资措施。（Lowder，Carisma 和 Skoet，2012 年）

政府越来越多地选择通过国内公司对投资进行援助，而不是直接投资于发展中国家的农业用地，这部分是因为他们希望降低风险和曝光率，包括负面覆盖后的金融风险和声誉风险。（Liu，2014 年）这种援助可以采取公私合作伙伴关系的形式，政府可以提供担保贷款、退税和技术援助或其他形式的帮助。（Liu，2014 年）

三、大规模土地收购交易对东道国的影响

大规模的土地收购产生了跨文化、经济、环境、伦理、法律和社会学科的复杂问题。研究表明，外国参与者对土地的投资往往通过购买或长期租赁来进行。Liu 在 2014 年指出，对于外国投资者，农业土地的长期租赁比直接购买土地更常见，这因为许多国家具有向外国人出售土地的立法限制。他进一步指出，尽管存在这种差别，但由于租赁合同通常是长期的，一般为 50 年，有时甚至长达 99 年，所以产生的经济和社会效果在一般情况下往往相似。

The Land Matrix 是伯尔尼大学发展与环境中心（“CDE”）、国际农业发展合作中心（“CIRAD”）、德国全球和区域研究所（“GIGA”）、德国国际合作署（“GIZ”）和国际土地联盟（“ILC”）之间形成的合作伙伴关系的名称，它整合并寻求证实有关大规模土地收购的信息。这一实验式的数据来自媒体报道、国际和非政府组织、学术界，以及关于发展中国家农业土地交易的 1217 份报告，这些报告囊括了 2000—2012 年期间超过 8300 万公顷的土地面积。（Anseeuw 等，2012 年）Liu 提醒说，the Land Matrix 估计，通过与其他可用来源进行交叉比对，可以判断为“可靠”的交易

相关区域仅占该区域（3270万公顷）的39.3%，并且这一数字应该被有所保留地接受，因为可用的关键数据质量普遍较差。

根据Liu 2014年的研究，the Land Matrix的实证研究揭示了一个趋势，这个趋势是投资者把最贫困国家以及那些在世界食品交易中参与程度较低的国家作为投资目标。Liu进一步指出，投资者关注的国家是最贫穷的国家，它们融入全球经济的程度很低，饥饿率高，土地制度薄弱，并且在the Land Matrix发现的土地交易中，约66%发生在饥饿率高的国家。

The Land Matrix数据库记录的大约45%的土地收购涉及农田或作物植被，这与投资者获得的土地须为肥沃且具有灌溉能力的观察一致。（Liu，2014年）因此，这意味着地方群体与投资者竞争的可能性上升。Liu在2014年补充说，这一发现令人质疑土地投资主要集中在未利用土地之上，并将其投入生产的假设。

Liu认为，大规模获取农业土地可能会产生其他不利影响，特别是在良治和法治不健全，以及有关土地权属立法不容易确定和不透明的国家。Liu还进一步指出，不利影响包括农民从小农地中流失，小农户获得牧场的机会减少，农村的人们不再具备谋生和赚取收入的能力，生产资源的耗尽。另外一般来说，由于资源的获取受到限制而对当地社区人民的生活产生的负面影响，很可能导致社会的分裂。

Liu得出的结论是，研究表明，对于在土地所有权不明确且不可靠的国家进行大规模土地收购的投资，交易的缺点往往超过了对当地社区有限的利益，特别是在短期内。

四、农业投资中土地权属的挑战

根据Feder，Roth与Haase的观点，拥有支持维护土地权属的措施能增加对农业投资的需求，这些农业相关投资反过来又导致农业产量上升和农民收入增加，并因此减少贫困个体的数量。Liu认为，基于农业的投资最重要的增长需要来自私营部门，特别是农民自己的投资，因为最近的一项研究表明，农民是农业领域最大的投资者。（Lowder，Carisma和Skoet，2012年）

根据Liu的研究，各种研究表明，投资者瞄准那些土地权属安全性较弱的国家，尽管他们也在寻求给投资者提供相对较高水平保护的国家。Domeher和Abdulai（2012）接着指出，有人认为，与低于平均水平的农业相关投资，和由此形成的非洲高贫困率，应被归因于让人有隙可乘的土地所有权制度。

因此，土地登记机制被认定为改变许多发展中国家土地所有权普遍存在的不稳定性质的工具。因此，许多发展中国家政府已经在国际捐助者的支持下，采取了土地登记的方案，这可以被为了实施这些方案而花费大量资金的现象所证明，开支范围从加纳的 2051 万美元，马拉维的 2700 万美元，玻利维亚的 1.06 亿美元，多米尼加共和国的 1.40 亿美元，到乌克兰的 1.95 亿美元。（Griffith-Charles，2004 年）

关于土地登记与土地权属安全之间的联系有两个派别的说法，一个学派认为土地登记是解决土地所有权不安全问题的方案，但缺少获得资本的渠道和投资增长的能力（Feder 和 Nishio，1999 年；MacGee，2006 年；World Bank，2007 年）。另一个学派认为土地登记机制本身不能保证所有权的安全性（Deininger，2003 年；Durand-Lasserve 和 Payne，2006 年；Abdulai，2010 年）。

根据 Domeher 和 Abdulai，来自包括布基纳法索、喀麦隆、加纳、肯尼亚、卢旺达、塞内加尔、索马里和乌干达在内的大多数发展中国家的数据没有表明土地登记与获得资本和投资水平之间有任何明显的联系。他们进一步表明，在其他地方，实证研究也没有找到土地登记和获取信用之间的直接因果关系（Angel 等人，2006 年），吉尔伯特（2002 年）在波哥大的研究也表明，获得登记的所有权和通过正式流程获得信贷仅有一点点或没有差别。

Domeher 和 Abdulai 解释说，许多国家正在明确国内实施土地登记方案的方向，因为出于对土地登记能够促进土地权属安全的信任，土地登记制度可以有助于改善农业生产，提高收入水平和减轻贫困。然而他们认为，虽然土地登记可能有能力为农业投资创造激励机制，但关于土地登记能促进土地权属安全，因而有可能刺激农业投资水平的说法，没有充分地说明为促进这种农业投资激励机制所需的土地权利安全水平或确定程度。

Domeher 和 Abdulai 认为，既然安全主要基于认知，因此，更有关联性的调查是要知道农民在农业土地上投资的确定程度。所以问题应该是土地登记本身是否给了农民这种安全感。然而，他们也承认，尽管土地登记方案出台后土地争议在一些非洲国家仍然存在，但是相关法律往往不被执行，并不足以说明土地登记制度是不成功的。

Fiadzigbey（2000）指出，加纳的某些例子说明，在冲突期间，可靠的土地所有权被法院认定为无效，因为有时这些权利是不被认为在现行的宪法法律规定下获得的。Domeher 和 Abdulai 的结论是，这意味着两件事，第一，注册过程可能有一些问题；第二，问题可能在于为保障注册土地所有权的立法可执行性。

Domeher 和 Abdulai 进一步指出，官员和法院无法充分执行法律，事实上可能影响人们对注册制度的信任，甚至导致诉讼的增加。他们认为，在加纳实行土地登记之后，土地权属不安全状况的增加可能是由于不恰当的土地登记立法和无法充分执行的法律。由于缺乏计划和土地登记文件中缺少附带地图，在同一土地上会进行多重登记，这个事实可以用来证明上述理论。而这种情况会不可避免地导致争端。

虽然土地安全被一个学派认为是投资决策过程中一个重要的因素，Domeher 和 Abdulai 却认为它可能不是最重要的影响因素。他们断言，在非洲和其他发展中国家，筹集进行农业投资所需资本的过程很可能是最难克服的障碍，因为许多农民生活在一个非常贫困的状态。Domeher 和 Abdulai 认为，即使土地登记可能提供刺激投资所需的担保，许多农民的低水平收入可能会削弱投资的规模和质量。然而，鉴于许多非洲国家的经济正在以前所未有的速度增长，Domeher 和 Abdulai 相信，随着收入水平的提高，土地安全将更有效地促进农业投资和发展。

Domeher 和 Abdulai 探讨了另一个支持作为增加农业投资机制的土地安全制度的说法，其中心内容是土地登记通过其安全性增强的能力，能够改善抵押制度和提高土地的价值，使土地成为一种更好、更安全和对资本更有吸引力的抵押形式（De Soto，2000 年）。因此，这意味着土地登记最大限度地减少了未设担保抵押获得信贷的障碍，这个障碍被认为是获得投资过程中受到限制的最大原因之一。（De Soto，2000 年）

Domeher 和 Abdulai 认为这种说法是有问题的，原因如下：第一，注册不改变土地的位置，而位置已被证明是贷方在决定土地本身是否符合抵押目的的重要驱动因素；第二，登记不一定能提高农村土地的价值，因此，如果在被认为具有固定价值的陆上抵押品基础上做出有利的信贷决定，这可能令人望而却步；第三，土地登记不太可能影响正现金流量和提高农业投资的盈利能力，因此贫困农民将无法从无利可图的农业活动里产生足够的现金流动，以吸引贷款人的信贷。

Domeher 和 Abdulai 得出结论，即使土地登记被认定为是促进土地权属安全的最有效方法，并能反过来刺激土地市场的运作，降低获得信贷的门槛，促进农业投资和通过提高收入水平来减轻贫困，实验式数据却未能最终证明土地登记一定是解决非洲农业投资问题的灵丹妙药。

五、总结

虽然大规模土地收购给予了人们一些希望，希望这些交易可以刺激生产和长期增长，但实验式数据似乎对此却不太乐观。在土地管理机构不完善和不能够独立运作的国家，当地社群更有可能成为这些土地收购交易的失败者。

参考资料

[1] Abdulai, R. T., (2010), *Traditional landholding institutions in sub-Saharan Africa – the operation of traditional landholding institutions in sub-Saharan Africa: A case study of Ghana*, LAP Lambert Academic Publishing, Saarbrücken.

[2] Angel, S., Brown, E., Dimitrova, D., Ehrenberg, D., Heyes, J., Kusek, P., Marchesi, G., Orozco, V., Smith, L. and Ernesto, V., (2006), *Secure tenure in Latin America and the Caribbean: regularisation of informal urban settlements in Peru, Mexico and Brazil*, Woodrow Wilson School of Public and International Affairs, Princeton University Princeton, NJ.

[3] Anseeuw, W., Boche, M., Breu, T., Giger, M., Lay, J., Messerli, P. and Nolte, K., (2012), *The state of large-scale land acquisitions in the" Global South" Analytical Report based on the Land Matrix database*, The Land Matrix Partnership, ILC, CDE, CIRAD, GIGA, GIZ.

[4] Cotula, L. and Blackmore, E., (2014), *Understanding agricultural investment chains: lessons to improve governance*, Rome and London: FAO and IIED.

[5] Cotula, L., Vermeulen, S., Leonard, R. and Keeley, J., (2009), *Land grab or development opportunity? Agricultural investment and international land deals in Africa*, IIED/FAO/IFAD, London/Rome.

[6] Deininger, K., (2003), *Land policies for growth and poverty reduction*, World Bank, Washington, DC.

[7] De Soto, H., (2000), *The mystery of capital: why capitalism triumphs in the west and fails everywhere else*, Bantam Press, London.

[8] Domeher, D. and Abdulai, R., (2012), *Land registration, credit and agricultural investment in Africa*, Agricultural Finance Review, Volume 72 Issue 1, pp.87-103.

[9] Durand-Lasserve, A. and Payne, G., (2006), *Evaluating impacts of urban land titling: results and implications: preliminary findings*, Draft Report for Geoffrey Payne and Associates, London.

[10] Feder, G. and Nishio, A., (1999), *The benefits of land registration and titling: economics and social perspectives*, Land Use Policy, Volume 15, No.1, pp.25-43.

[11] Feder, G., Onchan, Y., Chalamwong, F. and Hangladoran, C., (1986), *Land policies and farm productivity in Thailand*, John Hopkins University Press, Baltimore, MD.

[12] Fiadzigbey, M., (2000), *The impact of title registration on stool land administration*, in Asiama, S. O., (Ed.), *Land title registration as an effective tool of land delivery and administration*, Report of Seminar, Centre for

National Culture, Kumasi, 16-17 February.

[13] Gilbert, A., (2002), *On the mystery of capital and the myths of Hernando De Soto: what difference does legal title make?*, International Development Planning Review, Volume 24, No.1, pp.1-19.

[14] Grifith-Charles, C., (2004), *The impact of land titling on land transaction activity and registration system sustainability: a case study of St Lucia*, University of Florida, Gainesville, FL.

[15] International Food Policy Research Institute (IFPRI), (2012a), Statistics of Public Expenditure for Economic Development (SPEED) database, available at https://www.ifpri.org/publication/statistics-public-expenditures-economic-development-speed.

[16] IFPRI, (2012b), Agricultural Science and Technology Indicators (ASTI) database, available at http://www.asti.cgiar.org/data/.

[17] Liu, P., (2014), *Impacts of foreign agricultural investment on developing countries: evidence from case studies*, FAO Commodity and Trade Policy Research Working Paper No.47, Rome.

[18] Lowder, S., Carisma, B. and Skoet, J., (2012), Who invests in agriculture and how much?, Working Paper No.12-09, Rome, FAO.

[19] MacGee, J. C., (2006), *Land titles, credit markets and wealth*, Research Paper No.2006/150, UNU-WIDER, World Institute for Development Economic Research, Helsinki.

[20] Nolte, K. and Väth, S. J., (2013), *Interplay of land governance and large-scale agricultural investment: evidence from Ghana and Kenya*, Joint Discussion Paper Series in Economics by the Universities of Aachen, Gie β en, Göttinggen, Kassel, Marburg and Siegen, accessed at http://www.uni-marburg.de/fb02/makro/forschung/magkspapers/index_html%28magks%29.

[21] Organisation for Economic Co-operation and Development (OECD), (2012), Credit Reporting System Aid Activities (CRS) database, available at https://stats.oecd.org/Index.aspx?DataSetCode=CRS1.

[22] Roth, M. and Haase, D., (1998), *Land tenure security and agricultural performance in southern Africa*, LTC Paper, land Tenure Centre, University of Wisconsin, Madison, WI.

[23] The World Bank, (2007), *World Bank assistance to Agriculture in sub-Saharan Africa: an IEG review*, The World Bank, Washington, DC.

[24] United Nations Conference on Trade and Development (UNCTAD), (2011), (internal data not publicly available at the country level).

Legal Risks of Agricultural Investment in Africa

Author: Mashaba Bookholane①

Introduction

During the course of 2009, there were an increasing number of reports in the media concerning significantly sized farmland acquisitions in Africa, Latin America, Central Asia and Southeast Asa (Cotula *et al.* 2009). Cotula *et al.* 2009 assert that despite this increase flurry of international media reporting regarding this international land deals, this transactions are only a fraction of the land deals that were taking place in those regions, and that despite the upsurge in the reporting of these acquisitions and the related published research, there is still relatively little that is properly understood about the impact that these international deals have.

According to Cotula *et al.* 2009, much of the primary and secondary data that is available on land acquisitions in Africa is difficult to find and often its reliability is limited. Despite the scarcity of data in respect of these acquisitions, there are indications that there are significant levels of acquisition activity, with an overall total of 2,492,684 ha of approved land allocations (excluding land allocations that were below 1000 ha) being documented since 2004 in five study countries, being Ethiopia, Ghana, Madagascar, Mali and Sudan (the "study countries") (Cotula *et al.* 2009).

In general, investors in agriculture can be grouped as public or private and foreign and domestic. The vast number of private domestic investors are farmers and they are undoubtedly the most significant source of investment in agriculture in low- and middle-income countries (Lowder, Carisma and Skoet, 2012). The second largest investor in agriculture is from domestic public investors, being mainly national governments, followed a long way behind by foreign public investors such as development partners and by foreign private investors, such as corporations (Lowder, Carisma and

① Masechaba Bookholane, Senior Legal Advisor at Transnet Freight Rail, a division of Transnet SOC Limited, a state-owned country established under the laws of the Republic of South Africa.

Skoet, 2012).

The data that Cotula *et al.* 2009 examined indicated that stretching over the period from the beginning of 2004 to the beginning of 2009, there has been an upward swing in the number of projects involving land acquisitions as well as a rise in the allocated areas of land in all of the study countries, and there is a strong suggestion that there will be an increase in the levels of land acquisitions for investment purposes in the future. In addition, the data showed, firstly, that the private sector tended to be the dominant counterparty in land acquisition deals, although there was also an indication that these private sector actors received significant financial and other backing from government and secondly, the data also showed that the governments themselves were owners and participants in land acquisition investments.

Cotula *et al.* 2009 suggest that this increasing interest in large-scale land acquisitions is attributable to several factors, including, but not limited to, (i) growing concerns regarding food security, especially in investor countries, which largely explains the growth in government-supported investment and (ii) the investment opportunity presented by government-backed land acquisition investment deals, given driving patterns for land investment such as an increasing global demand for bio-fuels and other non-food agricultural commodities, predictions of higher rates of return in agriculture and land prices and the adoption of land policies in home and host countries. The upsurge in the demand for land has awakened hopes that the agricultural sectors of many developing countries, which have been historically grossly under-developed, will benefit from the renewed interest (Nolte and Väth, 2013).

Liu (2014) shares the sentiment that food security is a key driving factor in the observed upsurge in land acquisition through his assertion that growth in the number of agricultural investments in developing countries is required in order to alleviate poverty and attain food security and the nourishment of millions of people, and he points out that the most impactful and significant strategy for combatting poverty in rural areas, which is where a vast number of the world's most impoverished people live, is to embark on agricultural investment.

According to Liu (2014), the renewed interest in improving the amount of investment poured into primary agricultural production in developing countries is a much-needed developmental trend, because the low levels of investment into the agricultural sector and into smallholder farms over the past 30 years has caused decreased productivity and slowing rates of production. In addition, Liu (2014) cautions that the agricultural sector is faced with the enormous task of having to cater for the food requirements of an estimated 9 billion people by 2050, which is approximately 2.5 billion more people than are presently being catered for by the agricultural industry.

Although there is an acknowledgment that increased levels in investments into the agricultural industry are a positive development that will begin to address challenges such as food security, because agricultural investments by domestic and foreign investors can stimulate an increase in productivity, higher availability of food, job creation, poverty alleviation, technology transfer and access to capital and markets, these benefits are not capable of attainment automatically (Liu, 2014).

The benefits may also be accompanied unfavourable consequences, the impact of which on host countries may not always be identifiable in the short-term. Nolte and Väth (2013) write that even though the evidence in respect of impacts is still largely unavailable, evidence on impacts is growing, and civil society organisations have raised concerns about the potential negative impact impacts for host countries and the domestic population, ranging from displacement of communities, the eradication of the livelihoods of the locals, tax evasion and unchecked dependency through labour contracts. Cotula *et al.* (2009) echo this sentiment and write that as governments or markets give prospective investors access to land, significantly-sized land acquisitions can in fact result in people in the local communities being denied access to the resources on which they depend for their food security, especially since many of these recipient countries are themselves battling the scourge of food insecurity.

Cotula and Blakemore (2014) assert that in order to properly appreciate and capture the landscape of the case for increased agricultural investment in developing countries, one must understand a notion they term "investment chains" , which captures the myriad of role players and relations associated with any one project, and the manner in which value flows and is shared among those role players. They go on to explain that every investment chain will have a number of different points for decision-making, resource allocation and operation modelling and these points will often extend across various jurisdictions.

This paper seeks to examine the legal risks of agricultural investment in Africa by exploring the actors and drivers in land acquisitions in Africa, the legal arrangements upon which these acquisitions rest and the nature of the negotiations underpinning these contractual agreements, as well as assessing the effect of these land acquisitions on those that inhabit the rural lands in the countries that are the subject of these acquisitions. In particular, this paper will make use of research that examines land deals that are situated in sub-Saharan Africa.

Role players in agricultural investment deals

The role players in the investment chain of most large-scale land acquisitions can loosely be categorised as being comprised of three components: firstly, the enterprise (often corporate) that is the acquirer of the land rights; secondly, the host government, being the government of the country in which the land is situated and; lastly, the local communities that are affected by the land transaction (Cotula and Blakemore, 2014). The relationship between these three actors will be facilitated by any number of intermediaries throughout the transaction process, and one may observe varying disparities in the driving interests of each role player (and even within the same stakeholder group) and their corresponding bargaining power (Cotula and Blakemore, 2014).

Cotula and Blakemore (2014) explain that the number of role players that can be found in any one investment chain can vary significantly in length, as there may be number of role players along the investment chain between the ultimate source of funds and the entity that implements the project. They further explain that investment chains may also vary in their degree of integration, which is denoted by the degree to which role players in one fragment of the investment chain have the ability to exercise control over role players in other fragments of the investment chain, with a high level of integration being evidenced by an investor's full and direct ownership of the entities along the investment chain through layers of wholly- or majority-owned subsidiaries.

The domestic private investment from farmers is indicated by investments into the following: land development, which involves effecting major improvements in the quantity, quality or productivity of land; livestock, which comprises fixed assets (breeding stock) and inventories (young livestock and livestock kept for slaughtering) of cattle and buffalo, camels, horses, mules, asses, pigs, goats, sheep and poultry; machinery and equipment, which includes tractors (with accompanying accessories), harvesters and thrashers, milking machines and hand-held tools; plantation crops, which is a reference to trees that are capable of bearing repeated products (including vines and shrubs) cultivated for fruits and nuts, for sap and resin and for bark and leaf products; and structures for livestock, including sheds constructed for housing cows, buffalo, horses, camel and poultry birds (Lowder, Carisma and Skoet, 2012).

Investment by domestic public investors is measured by two databases produced by the International Food Policy Research Institute ("IFPRI") (i) government expenditures in and for agriculture from the Statistics of Public Expenditure for Economic Development ("SPEED") database (IFPRI, 2012a) and (ii) public expenditures on agricultural R&D from the Agricultural Science and Technology Indicators ("ASTI") database (IFPRI, 2012b). The SPEED database includes categories such as administration of agricultural affairs and services, conservation, reclamation or expansion of arable land and compensation, grants, loans or subsidies to farmers in connection with agricultural activities (Lowder, Carisma and Skoet, 2012).

Indicators of foreign public investment are captured by data on Official Development Assistance ("ODA") to agriculture collected by the OECD (2012), and the sectors covered include, but are not limited to, agrarian reform, agricultural policy and administrative management and financial services (Lowder, Carisma and Skoet, 2012). Measures for private foreign investment in agriculture and other related sectors is collected from data on Foreign Direct Investment compiled by UNCTAD (2011), and these measures include investments in crops, gardening and horticulture as well as agricultural and animal husbandry services (Lowder, Carisma and Skoet, 2012).

Increasingly, governments, are electing to assistance to investment by their domestic companies as opposed to investing directly into agricultural land in developing countries, and this is a consequence partly from a desire to reduce their risk and exposure, including financial risks and reputational risk in the wake of negative coverage (Liu, 2014). This assistance can take the form of public private partnerships whereby the government extends or guarantees loans and offers tax rebates, technical assistance or other forms of assistance (Liu, 2014).

The impact of large-scale land acquisition transactions on host countries

Large-scale land acquisitions introduce complicated issues across a number of disciplines: cultural, economic, environmental, ethical, legal and social. Research has revealed that investment in land by foreign actors often occurs through purchase or long-term leases. Liu (2014) notes that long-term lease of agricultural land is a more common occurrence than the outright purchase of land in respect of foreign investors, in part attributable to the fact that many countries have legislation that restricts the sale of land to foreigners. He notes further that despite this difference, the economic and social effects are in any event often similar owing to lease contracts generally being for long periods of time, generally 50 years and sometimes up to 99 years.

The Land Matrix is a partnership between the Centre for Development and Environment ("CDE") at the University of Bern, the Centre de cooperation Internationale en Recherche Agronomique pour le Développement ("CIRAD"), the German Institute of Global and Area Studies ("GIGA"), the German Agency for International Cooperation ("GIZ") and the International Land Coalition ("ILC"), and it methodically combines and seeks to corroborate information on large-scale land acquisitions. This empirical data is gathered from media reports, international and non-governmental organisations and academics, and 1217 reports have been collected in respect of agricultural land deals in developing countries, which accounts for in excess of 83 million hectares of land over the period 2000-2012 (Anseeuw *et al.*, 2012). Liu (2014) cautions that the Land Matrix estimated that the area concerned by transactions that it judged as "reliable" on account of having being cross-checked with other available sources, accounted for only 39.3 percent of this area (32.7 million hectares), and that even this reduced figure should be accepted with reservations because of the generally poor quality of the available primary data.

According to Liu (2014), the empirical research from the Land Matrix reveals a trend for investors to target the poorest countries, and those countries that are also involved to a lesser degree in world food exchanges. Liu (2014) notes further that the countries on which the investors focussed were among the poorest, were poorly integrated into the world economy, had a high incidence of hunger, and had weak land institutions, with some 66 percent of land transactions captured in the Land Matrix being in countries with a high prevalence of hunger.

Roughly 45 percent of the land acquisitions recorded by the Land Matrix database involved cropland or crop-vegetation, which is consistent with the observation that the land acquired by investors was good quality land, which is fertile and has irrigation capabilities (Liu, 2014). The implication, therefore, is that the likelihood of local communities having to compete with investors rises. Liu (2014) adds that this finding calls into question the assumption that land investments are primarily focussed on non-utilised land and serves to bring it into production.

Liu (2014) contends that large-scale acquisition of agricultural land can have other unfavourable impacts, particularly in countries where good governance and the rule of law are not robust and the legislation in respect of land tenure rights is not easily ascertainable and transparent. Liu contends further that the adverse effects include the displacement of farmers on small holdings, diminished access to grazing land for pastoralists, rural people no longer having the ability to make a living and earn an income, the exhaustion of productive resources, and in general, negative impacts on the lives of the people in the local communities due to restricted access to resources, which will in all likelihood lead to social splintering.

Liu (2014) concludes that studies suggest that for investment involving large-scale land acquisitions in countries where land tenure rights are unclear and not unassailable the disadvantages of these transactions often outweigh the limited benefits to local communities, especially in the short term.

Land tenure as a challenge to agricultural investment

According to Feder *et al.* (1986) and Roth and Haase (1998) having structures that support secure land tenure increases the demand for agro-based investments, and these agriculture-related investments are then in turn projected to cause an upswing in agricultural output, the income earned by farmers and consequently decrease the number of impoverished individuals. Liu (2014) contends that the most important rise in agro-based investment needs to come from the private sector, and in particular, investments made by the farmers themselves because a recent study showed that farmers are by far the largest investors in agriculture (Lowder, Carisma and Skoet, 2012).

According to Liu (2014), a variety of studies have demonstrated that investors are targeting countries with weak land tenure security, although they also seek countries that offer comparatively higher levels of investor protection. Domeher and Abdulai (2012) then make the assertion that it has thus been argued that the absence of or the below average level of agriculture-related investments and consequently the high rate of poverty in Africa has been imputed to the assailable nature of land tenure.

The mechanism of land registration has therefore been identified as the tool for altering the prevailing insecure nature of land tenure in many developing countries. Consequently, the governments of many developing countries have taken to adopting land registration programmes, with the support of international donors, as evidenced by the large amounts of money spent for purposes of putting these programmes in place, which expenditure ranged from US$20.51m in Ghana, US$27m in

Malawi, US$106m in Bolivia, US$140m in the Dominican Republic to US195 in Ukraine (Griffith-Charles, 2004).

The notion of the link between land registration and security of land tenure is divided between two schools of thought, namely the one school of thought that holds that land registration is the solution to the issues of the insecure nature of land tenure, lack of access to capital and the ability to grow investments (Feder and Nishio, 1999; MacGee, 2006; World Bank, 2007), whist the other school of thought asserts that the mechanism of land registration on its own is not able to guarantee ownership security (Deininger, 2003; Durand-Lasserve and Payne, 2006; Abdulai, 2010).

According to Domeher and Abdulai (2012), data from most developing countries including Burkina Faso, Cameroon, Ghana, Kenya, Rwanda, Senegal, Somalia and Uganda has not demonstrated that there is any noteworthy correlation between land registration on the one hand and access to capital and the levels of investments on the other hand. They show further that elsewhere, other empirical research has also failed to find a direct causal nexus between land registration and credit access (Angel *at al.*, 2006), and research by Gilbert (2002) in Bogotá also illustrated that having registered title either made a marginal or no difference to the availability of credit through formal structures.

Domeher and Abdulai (2012) explain that many countries are being pointed in the direction of implementing land registration programmes domestically based on the reasoning that land registration can aid in improving agricultural production, increase income levels and alleviate poverty because of the belief that land registration promotes land tenure security. They argue, however, that even though land registration may have the ability to create incentives for agricultural investments, the assertion that land registration promotes land tenure security, which in turn has the potential to stimulate increased levels of agricultural investment, does not adequately outline the level of security or degree of certainty in land rights that would be needed in order to stimulate such agricultural investment incentives.

Domeher and Abdulai (2012) assert instead that the more pertinent enquiry would be to know the level at which farmers will feel certain enough to invest in agricultural land, since security is largely based on perception, and the question should therefore rather be whether land registration itself gives farmers such a sense of security. They do go on to acknowledge, however, that despite the fact that land disputes have persisted in several African countries even with the advent of land registration programmes, this may not be a sufficient indicator to conclude land registration has not been successful in that the related laws are often not enforced.

Fiadzigbey (2000) points out that in Ghana, there are examples where supposedly unassailable titles to land have been invalidated by the courts during times of conflicts as such titles are issued sometimes without cognisance having been taken of certain prevailing constitutional law provisions, and Domeher and Abdulai (2012) conclude that this implies two things, the first of which being that there may be aspects of the registration process which are problematic, and the second of which being that the problem may lie with the enforceability of the legislation in place for purposes of safeguarding registered land ownership.

Domeher and Abdulai (2012) go further by suggesting that the inability of officials and the courts of law to adequately enforce the law may in fact have a bearing on people's trust in the registration system and even result in an increase in litigious actions and applications. They contend that it's possible that the rise in the insecurity of land tenure experienced after the introduction of land registration in Ghana, may be partly attributable to the fact that land registration legislation is improperly and inadequately enforced, evidenced by instances of multiple registrations of the same land, due to a lack of plans and maps accompanying land registration documentation, and such instances inevitably result in disputes.

Although land security is held out by one school of thought as being a significant persuasive factor in the investment decision-making process, Domeher and Abdulai (2012) argue that it may not be the most important influencing factor. They assert that it is common cause that in Africa and the rest of the developing world, the process of raising the capital needed to make an agro-based investment is likely to be the most difficult hurdle to surmount, as many farmers are living in a state of far-reaching impoverishment. Domeher and Abdulai (2012) maintain that even though land registration may provide the security required to spur investment, the low levels of income of many farmers will likely curtail the size and quality of the investment that is made. However, given that that economies of many African countries are improving and growing at an unprecedented rate, Domeher and Abdulai (2012) believe that as income levels rise, land security will be better placed to more effectively facilitate agricultural investment in order to sustain development.

Domeher and Abdulai (2012) explore an alternative supporting argument for land security as a mechanism for increasing agro-based investment, the key tenant of which is that land registration through its security enhancing ability, is able to improve on the collateral properties and value of land, making the land a better, more secure and attractive form of collateral for purposes of accessing capital (De Soto, 2000). The implication therefore is that land registration minimises the hurdle of the absence of collateral for securing credit, which is viewed as one of the biggest reasons why access to investment can be limited (De Soto, 2000).

This alternative argument is shown to be problematic by Domeher and Abdulai (2012) for the following reasons: firstly, registration does not change the location of land, and location has been shown to be a key driver for lenders when it comes to deciding whether or not the land itself is suitable for purposes of collateral; secondly, registration may not necessarily improve the value of rural land, so this may be prohibitive given that a favourable credit decision will be decided upon on the back of the land-based collateral being regarded as having a solid value; and thirdly, land registration is unlikely to influence positive cash flows and raise the profitability of agricultural investments, therefore impoverished farmers will be unable to produce sufficient cash flows from unprofitable farming activities to attract credit from lenders.

Domeher and Abdulai (2012) conclude that even though land registration has been pin-pointed as the most capable method for promoting land tenure security, and in turn stimulate land market operation, lower the hurdles to access to credit, promote agro-based investment and alleviate poverty through raising income levels, the empirical data has failed to demonstrate conclusively that land registration is indeed the panacea for the agricultural investment question in Africa.

Conclusion

Whilst the upswing in large-scale land acquisitions has ignited some hope that these transactions can stimulate an increase in production and long term growth, the empirical data appears to paint a less optimistic picture. In countries where institutions governing land are not well entrenched and independently functional, then local communities are more likely to be the losers in these land acquisition deals.

REFERENCES

[1] Abdulai, R. T., (2010), *Traditional landholding institutions in sub-Saharan Africa – the operation of traditional landholding institutions in sub-Saharan Africa: A case study of Ghana*, LAP Lambert Academic Publishing, Saarbrücken.

[2] Angel, S., Brown, E., Dimitrova, D., Ehrenberg, D., Heyes, J., Kusek, P., Marchesi, G., Orozco, V., Smith, L. and Ernesto, V., (2006), *Secure tenure in Latin America and the Caribbean: regularisation of informal urban settlements in Peru, Mexico and Brazil*, Woodrow Wilson School of Public and International Affairs, Princeton University Princeton, NJ.

[3] Anseeuw, W., Boche, M., Breu, T., Giger, M., Lay, J., Messerli, P. and Nolte, K., (2012), *The state of large-scale land acquisitions in the" Global South" Analytical Report based on the Land Matrix database*, The Land Matrix Partnership, ILC, CDE, CIRAD, GIGA, GIZ.

[4] Cotula, L. and Blackmore, E., (2014), *Understanding agricultural investment chains: lessons to improve governance*, Rome and London: FAO and IIED.

[5] Cotula, L., Vermeulen, S., Leonard, R. and Keeley, J., (2009), *Land grab or development opportunity? Agricultural investment and international land deals in Africa*, IIED/FAO/IFAD, London/Rome.

[6] Deininger, K., (2003), *Land policies for growth and poverty reduction*, World Bank, Washington, DC.

[7] De Soto, H., (2000), *The mystery of capital: why capitalism triumphs in the west and fails everywhere else*, Bantam Press, London.

[8] Domeher, D. and Abdulai, R., (2012), *Land registration, credit and agricultural investment in Africa*, Agricultural Finance Review, Volume 72 Issue 1, pp.87-103.

[9] Durand-Lasserve, A. and Payne, G., (2006), *Evaluating impacts of urban land titling: results and implications: preliminary findings*, Draft Report for Geoffrey Payne and Associates, London.

[10] Feder, G. and Nishio, A., (1999), *The benefits of land registration and titling: economics and social perspectives*, Land Use Policy, Volume 15, No.1, pp.25-43.

[11] Feder, G., Onchan, Y., Chalamwong, F. and Hangladoran, C., (1986), *Land policies and farm productivity in Thailand*, John Hopkins University Press, Baltimore, MD.

[12] Fiadzigbey, M., (2000), *The impact of title registration on stool land administration*, in Asiama, S. O., (Ed.), *Land title registration as an effective tool of land delivery and administration*, Report of Seminar, Centre for National Culture, Kumasi, 16-17 February.

[13] Gilbert, A., (2002), *On the mystery of capital and the myths of Hernando De Soto: what difference does legal title make?*, International Development Planning Review, Volume 24, No.1, pp.1-19.

[14] Grifith-Charles, C., (2004), *The impact of land titling on land transaction activity and registration system sustainability: a case study of St Lucia*, University of Florida, Gainesville, FL.

[15] International Food Policy Research Institute (IFPRI), (2012a), Statistics of Public Expenditure for Economic Development (SPEED) database, available at https://www.ifpri.org/publication/statistics-public-expenditures-economic-development-speed.

[16] IFPRI, (2012b), Agricultural Science and Technology Indicators (ASTI) database, available at http://www.asti.cgiar.org/data/.

[17] Liu, P., (2014), *Impacts of foreign agricultural investment on developing countries: evidence from case studies*, FAO Commodity and Trade Policy Research Working Paper No.47, Rome.

[18] Lowder, S., Carisma, B. and Skoet, J., (2012), Who invests in agriculture and how much?, Working Paper No.12-09, Rome, FAO.

[19] MacGee, J. C., (2006), *Land titles, credit markets and wealth*, Research Paper No.2006/150, UNU-WIDER, World Institute for Development Economic Research, Helsinki.

[20] Nolte, K. and Väth, S. J., (2013), *Interplay of land governance and large-scale agricultural investment: evidence from Ghana and Kenya*, Joint Discussion Paper Series in Economics by the Universities of Aachen, Gie β en, Göttinggen, Kassel, Marburg and Siegen, accessed at http://www.uni-marburg.de/fb02/makro/forschung/magkspapers/index_html%28magks%29.

[21] Organisation for Economic Co-operation and Development (OECD), (2012), Credit Reporting System Aid Activities (CRS) database, available at https://stats.oecd.org/Index.aspx?DataSetCode=CRS1.

[22] Roth, M. and Haase, D., (1998), *Land tenure security and agricultural performance in southern Africa*, LTC Paper, land Tenure Centre, University of Wisconsin, Madison, WI.

[23] The World Bank, (2007), *World Bank assistance to Agriculture in sub-Saharan Africa: an IEG review*, The World Bank, Washington, DC.

[24] United Nations Conference on Trade and Development (UNCTAD), (2011), (internal data not publicly available at the country level).

非洲外国投资的法律风险

作者：Moza　译者：黄江硕

一、概述

（一）历史背景

农业是种植庄稼及饲养牲畜的科学和实践。① 投资是以获得利益为目的而对金钱、时间等其他任何资源进行的分配。② 在经济领域，投资获得的未来累计利益被称为收益。收益包括资本累积或如股息、利息、租金等投资收入。③ 投资的最终结果是财产的取得。财产也被称为一种投资。如果在值得投资的价位获得财产，通常认为该财产可以创造收入或升值，因它可以被卖到一个更好的价钱。④

根据投资者的说法，投资风险是指某项投资的实际收益因为市场指向的不确定性而在某种程度上产生风险的可能性。⑤

因此，农业投资是对于包括种植作物及饲养牲畜的投资。

在非洲，农业投资是地区性控制贫困和保障食物安全的重要手段。这是在大部分人属于世界上最贫困人群的偏远地区用来消除贫困的一种策略。

外商直接投资（FDI）是其他国家的公司或实体进行的投资。⑥

---

① Concise Oxford Dictionary, 10th Edition.

② Wikipedia, Retrieved in 9th May, 2016.

③ Wikipedia, Retrieved in 9th May, 2016.

④ Wikipedia, Retrieved in 9th May, 2016.

⑤ www.investorwords.com, Retrieved in 9th May, 2016.

⑥ www.investipedia.com, Retrieved in 9th May, 2016.

无论怎么说，进行直接投资的实体对其投资的公司具有影响力和控制力。投资公司可以通过各种形式在境外建立附属公司进行境外投资。它可以通过取得境外公司股份、并购或合伙来实现。法律规定境外投资者必须拥有被投资公司不少于10%的普通股。外商直接投资与间接投资不同的地方在于，外商直接投资的对象是国家证券交易所注册的股本。良好的投资环境，如具备熟练工人和良好增势的开放型经济，比封闭的高度管制的经济更能吸引外商直接投资。①

外商直接投资发生在以下情况，外国投资者成为某国公司的所有人或共有人，直接影响着公司的管理。

无论怎样，外商直接投资可以被解释为资本跨国境的流动。这种流动可通过购买现存公司或设立新公司来实现。

外商直接投资运行的方式就像外国公司向被投资国兄弟公司提供借款一样。

另一种方式是境外投资者在被投资国建立新工厂。

美国公司在中国拥有大部分股份就是境外投资控制的例子。

根据维基百科，外商直接投资是指一个国家的实体在另一国企业中拥有治理权。②

外商直接投资通常包括在管理、合伙、技术和专业转让中的参与。

一般情况下，外商直接投资在生产成本较低的地方更加常见，因为较低的生产成本可以让境外的投资者获得更大规模的利益空间。这些地方通常是非洲一些不太发达的国家。

在进行外商直接投资之前，境外投资者会考虑诸多因素，比如竞争力因素和投资风险。

像其他的欠发达国家一样，非洲国家大力吸引外商直接投资，因为这些投资会给它们带来许多好处，比如新技术的引进和新工作岗位的产生。通过投资，被投资国可以从外国人身上学到如何更好地组织工作和管理，外国人也可以从这些国家获得低价的商品和服务。

由于世界上大部分贫困人民都生活在偏远的欠发达国家，而这些国家农业是它们维持生计的唯一办法，引进农业投资对于更好地发展农业具有十分重要的意义。

---

① *Ibid.* The Organization of Economic Cooperation and Development (OECD) defines control as owning 10% or more of the business.

② www.wikipedia com, Retrieved in 10th May, 2016.

这是因为如果只是小规模发展农业，农业发展在这些国家只能处于停滞状态，因为贫穷让他们只能使用一些最基础的设备，如使用长柄锄带来的低收成甚至不足以维持当地人温饱。

由于上述原因，仅依靠公共部门投资是不足以在非洲国家解决温饱问题的，因此，我们强烈需要私人投资。

然而，非洲农业投资面临着许多挑战，包括不能满足需求的低产量作物和牲畜。

不断增长的非洲农业投资将促进粮食产量的大幅增长，就业岗位的大幅增加，技术的转移，资本市场的更多参与和贫困的减少。[①]

非洲国家要想从外商投资中获得上述好处，就必须建立完备的投资合同和商业模型分类，并加强小股东与东道国制度框架的联系。

（二）境外投资的地位

尽管在非洲有大量的农业可耕地，但是囿于较弱的经济能力，非洲大部分商业银行只能提供小额贷款，很多非洲人没有足够的资本进行农业投资，所以非洲的农业投资发展仍然十分有限。

除此之外，很多非洲人因为贫穷无法借到足够的钱进行农业投资。研究表明，在非洲撒哈拉以南，商业银行的农业借款只占不到 10%。[②]

外商直接投资可以填补非洲农业投资的空缺。

另一方面，对于农产品的外商直接投资出现于 2000 年，出现的原因是在包括非洲的很多发展中国家，农业部分的投资一直处于空缺状态。另外，2007—2008 年，粮食价格居高不下导致了大量需求。受此影响，高度依赖粮食进口的国家开始对那些拥有良好耕地、充足水源、适宜发展农业的国家进行农业投资，外商直接投资迅速发展。

此外，国际投资者在农业中引入大量外商直接投资，是由于高能源价格和原材料需求导致对生物燃料原料作物生产的高需求。[③]

① Pascal Liu, "Impacts of Foreign Agricultural Investment on Developing Countries: Evidence from Case Studies." Food and Agriculture Organization of the United Nations, Rome, 2014. Retrieved on 09/05/2016.

② Da Silva and Mhlanga, 2009, cited in the Pascal Liu Paper "Impacts of Foreign Agricultural Investment on Developing Countries: Evidence from Case Studies." FAO (2014).

③ Pascal Liu, "Impacts of Foreign Agricultural Investment on Developing Countries: Evidence from Case Studies." Food and Agriculture Organization of the United Nations, Rome, 2014. Retrieved on 09/05/2016.

（三）外商直接投资的重要性

结合上述，外商直接投资带来的经济增长是由于资本的流入和被投资国的税收收入增加。

除此之外，外商直接投资还通过培训转让技能、创造就业以及向国内市场转让先进技术和获得研究与开发资源等途径。① 当地社会因为这些新经济创造的就业岗位而获得好处。②

外商直接投资的另一个重要性在于境外投资公司将他们的老机器转移到被投资国，因东道国发展落后，在这里老机器起到了良好作用。另外，境外投资者进行机器转让，以避免东道国与其自己的产品竞争。

无论如何，在发展中国家，外商投资大大促进了当地生产的增长。③ 中国是一个很好的例子，中国通过外商直接投资取得了巨大的利益，在 2012 年前 6 个月的投资额就已高达 191 亿美元，这使得中国成为超越美国的外商直接投资的最大接受者，美国拥有 174 亿美元的外商直接投资。④

然而，对流入农业的外商直接外资的定量分析却缺乏可靠的详细数据。

数据表明，自 2007—2008 年以来，发展中国家农业食品部门的外商直接投资有所增加。

（四）发展中国家外商直接投资的流量

虽然农业外商直接投资流量在 2009 年高峰之后收缩，但 2010—2011 年之间的水平高于 2003—2007 年的平均水平。⑤ 这些流量受区域因素影响，区域内流动大于区域外流动，但非洲除外。在 2000—2005 年和 2006—2008 年，进入农业食品部门

---

① UNCTAD "Foreign Direct Investment, the Transfer and Diffusion of Technology and Sustainable Economy Development." (2010).

② Slaughter and May "Legal Regimes Governing Foreign Direct Investment (FDI) In Host Countries" . (2012), cited by Pascal Liu, *Op cit*.

③ Thomas Hauranek and Zuzana Irsova, "Which Foreigners are worth wooing? A meta- analysis of Vertical Spillovers from FDI." (30th April 2011).), cited by Pascal Liu, *Op cit*.

④ China tops US as Investment Target in first half of 2012. Reuters, cited from ww.wikipedia.com, Retrieved in 12th May, 2016.

⑤ Pascal Liu, "Impacts of Foreign Agricultural Investment on Developing Countries: Evidence from Case Studies." Food and Agriculture Organization of the United Nations, Rome, 2014. Retrieved on 09/05/2016.

的外商直接投资所占份额翻了一番，但与其他经济部门相比仍然很低，在2006—2008年期间只占总量的不到5%。

大量农业外商直接投资流量流向粮食制造部门，而2006—2008年期间农业生产不足10%。研究表明，在初级农业部门的外商直接投资方面没有任何最新数据。①

二、非洲农业外商投资的影响

（一）扶贫

非洲外商直接投资的一个重要影响是扶贫。农业投资是消除贫困的重要关键所在，特别是在大多数穷人生活的偏远地区。②

这是因为高效农业为商品和服务提供了农村市场，从而为提供者创造了就业和收入。

因此，利益从村庄扩大到整个经济体。

（二）减少饥饿

减少饥饿是农业投资的另一个重要好处。增加粮食产量使其降低市场价格，从而使城市和农村消费者可以获得粮食。③

然而在非洲，农业投资的缺乏导致粮食低产量，从而导致饥饿。同时，非洲人口将在饥饿和自然资源退化广泛蔓延的地区增长。

为解决这个问题，增加农业投资是不可避免的。在发展中国家，公共部门的参与是必要的。据报道，公共部门在非洲农业方面的支出下降近7%。④较高的粮食价格警示政策制定者们重视农业投资的重要性。因此，政府公共投资对于为农民生存创造有利条件至关重要。然而，仅凭公共部门投资是不足以消除饥饿的，私人投资也是非常需要的。

尽管如此，各种境外组织一直担心东道国在一些新形式的外商直接投资方面受

① Pascal Liu, "Impacts of Foreign Agricultural Investment on Developing Countries: Evidence from Case Studies." Food and Agriculture Organization of the United Nations, Rome, 2014. Retrieved on 09/05/2016.

② World Bank, 2008, Food and Agriculture Organization, 2012.

③ Alston et. Al, 2000, cited by Pascal Liu, *Op cit*.

④ Hallam, 2011cited by Pascal Liu, Op Cit.

到影响，特别是在大规模土地收购问题上，而这有可能带来复杂的环境问题。

三、土地投资和外商直接投资

境外资本向农业产业进行投资，如土地。因此，国际上对外商投资向大规模农业土地的控制问题非常关注，并进行了许多辩论和研究。这都是因为土地本身的性质。除了经济价值，土地在许多国家包括非洲具有社会、文化和宗教价值。大规模的土地获得在道德和文化层面都引起了复杂的法律、经济、社会和环境问题。

通常来说，土地上的外商投资是通过长期租赁实现的。农业土地的长期租赁比购买更可取，因为许多国家禁止向外国人出售土地。以坦桑尼亚为例，《土地法》第20条［Cap. 113 R. E］禁止土地为外国人所有。

尽管经济和社会影响是相同的，但租赁合同一般要花50年到99年，时间更长。外商投资者一直遭到地方反对，因为他们中的很多人只使用土地的一部分而空置剩余的大片土地。

外商投资也导致了一些关于国家主权和独立的问题，由于许多国家曾遭殖民统治，这些问题显得非常敏感。

与本地投资者相比，外商投资主要涉及投资1万公顷至50万公顷。①

然而，世界银行（2011年）规定，当地投资者参与80%的土地交易。研究表明，尼日利亚的97%的土地为国家参与投资，这一数据在莫桑比克、苏丹和埃塞俄比亚为53%。②

四、外商直接投资土地的目的地

非洲是外商直接投资土地的首要目的地。矩阵数据显示，在754项交易中，有5620万公顷位于非洲，1770万公顷在拉丁美洲。外商投资者在大量国家（84个）进行投资，其中11个国家占了总公顷数的70%。这些国家中有7个来自非洲，分别是苏丹、埃塞俄比亚、莫桑比克、坦桑尼亚联合共和国、马达加斯加、赞比亚和刚果

① Hallam, 2011cited by Pascal Liu, Op Cit.

② Pascal Liu, “Impacts of Foreign Agricultural Investment on Developing Countries: Evidence from Case Studies.” Food and Agriculture Organization of the United Nations, Rome, 2014. Retrieved on 09/05/2016.

民主共和国。①

五、非洲农业投资的法律风险

如上所述，农业投资涉及收购 1 万公顷至 50 万公顷的大规模土地，如果缺乏良好管理、法律制度、透明度和明确的权属权利，就会产生负面影响。如上所述，许多非洲国家法律禁止外国人拥有土地。因此，投资者在没有完全财产权的土地上投资，缺失保障。另外，资源有限导致有关地区社会分化和生产资源减少，令当地农民流离失所，失去了放牧土地也失去了生计。土地、水资源和森林也在面临退化。②

这些影响引起了当地人的反对，他们可能会对公司的财产造成损害，投资者开始参与诉讼，回报投资也在减少。以下讨论的是非洲农业投资的法律风险。

（一）缺失良好的争议解决机制

在许多非洲国家，没有明确地机制解决投资者与被投资国和当地人之间的争端。这就导致了对投资风险的一种疑虑，即如果投资合同引起争议，将没有足够的保护。没有明确的投资争议解决机制也是缺乏双边投资条约造成的。

（二）良好管理的缺失

东道国的管理制度是投资的一个重要因素。然而，大多数非洲国家都面临法律和政策不一致的问题。缺乏良好管理会导致不遵守现行法律和不尊重人权的现象发生，从而造成腐败和侵犯人权。

（三）腐败

腐败是非洲法治的一个大问题，由于非洲外商投资的历史背景，腐败问题被给予了更多的关注。非洲自独立以来一直参与温饱型农业和大规模采掘业，这些行业使用的都是像石油、矿物和树木这样的公共资产，因为在非洲，由于缺乏明显的所

① Pascal Liu, “Impacts of Foreign Agricultural Investment on Developing Countries: Evidence from Case Studies.” Food and Agriculture Organization of the United Nations, Rome, 2014. Retrieved on 09/05/2016.

② Pascal Liu, “Impacts of Foreign Agricultural Investment on Developing Countries: Evidence from Case Studies.” Food and Agriculture Organization of the United Nations, Rome, 2014. Retrieved on 09/05/2016.

有者，这些财产权都被国家直接控制。[1]

因此，这些资产需要国家正式的许可证才能开放，所以行贿受贿一直存在。大多数政府官员都参与了游戏。即使需要引进良好的资本，境外投资者也会被索贿的官员逼走。

为了遏制这一腐败现象，非洲各国政府应通过实施公务员制度改革保护流入的资本，改革措施包括提高工资，及严厉惩罚从事腐败行为或交易的人。此外，外商直接投资可以通过拒绝贿赂和向有关政府报告来发挥其抑制腐败的作用[2]。

法治的存在是影响境外投资的一个重要因素。土地制度、法律法规和明确的财产权制度保证了境外和本地投资者的土地安全。对投资农业、水资源，使用自然资源制定适当的法规及有效的措施是非常重要的。

具备良好的管理制度、法制制度、问责制度、透明度、和平稳定和消除腐败的非洲，将成为有利于投资项目可持续发展的环境。[3]

除此之外，还应当有效建立有能力审查投资建议、设计提案、规范当地利益相关者和执法的国家机构。[4]

为监督和执行投资合同，提高国家机构纠错的能力和建立调解和解决冲突机制是必要的。

六、协商程序的构想

投资项目的协商、设计和规划，对后续投资的透明度、包容性、参与性、民主性的重要影响是不言而喻的。

投资合同的条件和条款涉及项目合作伙伴之间的关系、责任分担、决策制定、利益和风险。[5]

---

① Peter C. Hansen "Legal Consideration for investing Africa". Retrieved on 9/5/2016.

② Peter C. Hansen "Legal Consideration for investing Africa". Retrieved on 9/5/2016.

③ Pascal Liu, "Impacts of Foreign Agricultural Investment on Developing Countries: Evidence from Case Studies." Food and Agriculture Organization of the United Nations, Rome, 2014. Retrieved on 09/05/2016.

④ Pascal Liu, "Impacts of Foreign Agricultural Investment on Developing Countries: Evidence from Case Studies." Food and Agriculture Organization of the United Nations, Rome, 2014. Retrieved on 09/05/2016.

⑤ Pascal Liu, "Impacts of Foreign Agricultural Investment on Developing Countries: Evidence from Case Studies." Food and Agriculture Organization of the United Nations, Rome, 2014. Retrieved on 09/05/2016.

由于投资合同内容不清，我们需要具体的可执行条款。也就是说，合同必须规定当地能从投资者手中获得的利益，如投资创造的工作岗位、建造的基础设施和提供的培训。

七、结论

非洲已经认识到农业企业对农业投资的贡献以及他们在与农民可持续和互惠关系方面的责任。

此外，我们承认，农业投资的成功在很大程度上是建立在公平、良好的监督机制和健全的评价程序以及争端解决机制的法律框架上。

同时，较高的透明度是良好管理的必然结果，我们应加强管理以增强土地投资的透明度。

投资是农民和私人投资者之间的关系，通过给予土地完全控制权的方式，这对当地经济和社会发展产生了积极的影响。

大规模征地的损害超过了对当地的利益。在治理不善的地方大规模征地会导致自然资源的减少和生计的丧失，使当地面临高风险，投资变得非常困难。

通过自然法促进对农业和粮食系统可持续和负责任的投资是非常重要的。 此外，东道国应采取措施降低农业投资风险，同时最大限度地提高经济和社会效益。

适当地影响评估监测和执行的需要也应被纳入考虑。

提高国家和地区法规透明度，并制定一项关于土地交易透明度的示范法，对于促进境外投资至关重要。被投资国必须协调关于土地治理的立法和法律框架。

国际投资法、国际公司法、反腐败法的立法和实践，迎合了境外投资风险管理的需要，为境外投资提供了有利环境。

基于非洲农业投资现存风险，我提出以下建议。

八、建议

（一）加强农业投资的国内立法

如果能降低农业投资的风险，非洲将受益于外商直接投资。如果与土地和农业投资相关的政策、法律和规范能够得到改进，风险就有可能降低。颁布的法律要彼此一致，且应得到良好的实施，这样才能不留下漏洞。

除此之外，必须根据投资项目的类型清晰界定土地使用权。加强土地权属和土地财产权，认可小规模农民的政策非常重要，因为它们不仅能保障境外投资，而且还能增强对当地生产者在土地问题上的信心。① 人权也必须得到充分尊重，公民不应在工作中被忽视，也不应在新岗位中被隔离。

此外，投资者获得的土地应根据特定项目所需的规模进行。这将避免农村地区人民和长期持有未使用土地的境外投资者之间的冲突。

我们应建立一个使投资者出让多年未使用土地的机制。② 这会帮助降低农业投资的相关风险。

（二）加强土地交易方面国家法律的透明度

根据维基百科，透明度意味着开放、沟通和有效问责。它通常以其他人易于监督的方式操作。③

为了避免法律风险，应公开土地分配合同，这样有利于确保处理土地交易的政府机构的透明度和责任。公众可以知道投资者被分配的土地和时长，东道国将实现良好的治理，农业投资的风险也可以最小化。

（三）东道国的能力建设

成功的农业投资依赖于东道国良好的投资环境。我们可以通过提高中央和地方政府的行政管理质量来确保这一点。目前，非洲的国家法律体系较为混乱，政府能力较弱。境外投资者需要通过加强关于土地问题的教育和信息交流来为东道国做出贡献。研究认为，国际组织必须支持非洲政府官员和农民，关注国家和地方政府的能力建设、政策和技术支持等方面的需求，促进良好的管理。④ 这些可以通过训练政府官员在理解投资提案和与投资者谈判的能力来实现。农村人民不应被忽略，因为正是这些地方的土地投资才是最多的。也就是说，必须向基层社区提供关于投资合

① Jasper Karlsson, "Challenges and Opportunities of Foreign Investment in Developing Country Agriculture for Sustainable Development," FAO (2014).

② Jasper Karlsson, "Challenges and Opportunities of Foreign Investment in Developing Country Agriculture for Sustainable Development," FAO (2014).

③ www.wikipedia.com, retrieved in 12th May, 2016.

④ Jasper Karlsson, "Challenges and Opportunities of Foreign Investment in Developing Country Agriculture for Sustainable Development", FAO (2014).

同和法律框架以及政府机构的信息。

政府应当为降低小规模农业组织机构的农业投资风险制订计划。地方组织应通过提供加强利益方伙伴关系的方案实施风险管理战略，这将有利于可持续发展。为实施农业投资的成功战略，政府、投资者和农民应当各司其职，加强合作。

（四）国际指导

本文中已经讨论过，非洲的主要特点是法律体系不完善、政府行政能力弱，这些特点导致了外商投资的风险。

不合理的土地保有体系、对权利的忽视、农村人民因为投资者长期空置土地的抗议，都对境外农业投资产生了负面影响。

为了消除这些风险因素，必须呼吁国际指导，以便使非洲农业经济得到可持续发展的保证。

接受国际公约对降低治理风险来说是不可避免的。2012 年 5 月，世界粮食安全委员会及粮食和农业组织通过了《国家粮食安全范围内土地、渔业及森林权属负责任治理自愿准则》（VGGT）。根据 Liu 的观点，VGGT 提供了确保实现粮食安全为目的的改善土地治理、渔业和森林权属的指导方针。①

通过以上方式，非洲农业投资的法律风险将会有效降低，投资项目也会更好地在非洲展开。

“在非洲，不成功的投资者是那些不仔细计划就开始投资业务的人。”②

Moza Mussa Kassubi，坦桑尼亚预防和打击腐败局法律检控组首席研究员。

① Pascal Liu, “Impacts of Foreign Agricultural Investment on Developing Countries: Evidence from Case Studies.” Food and Agriculture Organization of the United Nations, Rome, 2014. Retrieved on 09/05/2016.

② Peter C. Hansen “Legal Consideration for investing Africa”. Retrieved on 9/5/2016.

Prepared by Moza Mussa Kassubi, Principal Investigator, Legal and Prosecution Section. Prevention and Combating of Corruption Bureau, Tanzania. 15th May, 2016.

Legal Risks of Foreign Investment in Africa

Author: Moza

Introduction

1. Historical Background

Agriculture is the science or practice of farming including the rearing of crops and animals.① Investment is the act of allocating money or any other source such as time for the purpose of gaining benefits in future.② However in the financial aspect the accrued future benefit from the investment is termed as a return. The return may consist of capital gain and or investment income including dividends, interest and rental income and the like.③ The end result of investment is acquiring of asset. Asset is also called as an investment. If the asset is available at a price worth investing it is normally expected either to generate income or to appreciate in value, so that it can be sold at a higher price or both.④

According to investor words investment risk is a probability that an actual return on an investment has some level of risk associated with unpredictability of the market direction.⑤

Therefore Agricultural investment is the investment in agriculture of farming including rearing of crops and animals.

An agricultural investment in Africa is highly as the means of curbing poverty in the Region and establishing food security. It is the strategy for poverty eradication in rural areas where majority of poorest people in the world live.

---

① Concise Oxford Dictionary, 10th Edition.

② Wikipedia, Retrieved in 9th May, 2016.

③ Wikipedia, Retrieved in 9th May, 2016.

④ Wikipedia, Retrieved in 9th May, 2016.

⑤ www.investorwords.com, Retrieved in 9th May, 2016.

Foreign Direct Investment (FDI) is an investment made by a company or entity based in another country.①

However it is said that entities making direct investments have influence and control over the company into which the investment is made. The investing company may make its overseas investment by making a subsidiary associate company in the foreign country in various ways. Firstly it may make it by acquiring shares of an overseas company or secondly through a merger or a joint venture. It is established that the foreign investor must own not less than 10% of ordinary shares of the investee company. FDI's differ from indirect investment in which the foreign investment is done in equities listed on a nation's stock exchange. Conducive environment such as open economies accompanied by skilled labour together with good growth attract lager amounts of FDI's than closed highly regulated economies.②

Foreign Direct Investments is taking place where the foreign investor becomes the owner or co owner of a company which is found in another country and its operation directly influences its management.

However the Foreign Direct Investment can be explained as the capital flow across the national boarder. This may be done through purchasing the existing business or creating a new business right from the beginning.

Ways in which FDI's operate is like when founder company in the foreign country gives loan to the sister company in the host country.

Another way is when foreign investors construct new plants in host countries.

An example of foreign direct investment control is American Company taking a majority stake at China.

According to Wikipedia, A Foreign Direct Investment is a controlling ownership in a business enterprise in one country by an entity based in another country.③

FDI usually involves participation in management, joint-venture, transfer of technology and expertise.

Normally the Foreign Direct Investments are plunged in places where the production costs are lowest so as to enable the foreign investors retrieving large scale profit margins. These places are found in the least developing countries Africa being amongst.

However the foreign investors always take into consideration various factors before selecting where to inject their FDI's. These are competitiveness factor and the investment risks.

However African countries like many other least developing countries always attract Foreign

① www.investipedia.com, Retrieved in 9th May, 2016.

② *Ibid.* The Organization of Economic Cooperation and Development (OECD) defines control as owning 10% or more of the business.

③ www.wikipedia com, Retrieved in 10th May, 2016.

Direct Investments due to the fact that they bring so many advantages including introduction of new technology and jobs creation. Apart from that host countries obtain advantages by attaining knowledge in better organization of work and management from foreigners who in turn provides low prices of goods and services produced.

Since the majority of the poorest in the world live in rural areas of the low developed countries where agriculture is their only means to strive their livelihoods introduction of agricultural investment is very important for the better growth of agriculture. That is because with the small scale farmers, agriculture in those countries remains stagnant due to the fact that poverty makes them low equipped agricultural instruments such as the use of hand hoe which in turn provides lowest production which cannot sustain hunger in those countries.

Due to the reasons explained above Public Sector Investment alone is not enough to eradicate hunger in African countries and therefore Private Sector Investment is highly needed.

However Agricultural investment in Africa faces a lot of challenges; these include low production of crop and livestock to meet the demand.

Increasing Agricultural investment in Africa will lead to high increase of food production and creation of employment, technology transfer, access to capital market and poverty reduction.[①]

However for African countries to obtain all such above mentioned benefits from foreign investment there must be well established investment contracts, types of business model and linkage with small holders and institutional frame work in the host countries.

2. The Role of Foreign Investments

In spite of the good arable land for agriculture in Africa still there is no capacity to build good agricultural investment due to low financial capacity given a situation that most commercial banks in Africa provide small loans so that many Africans cannot have enough capital for agricultural investment.

Apart from that many Africans are unable to borrow enough money for agricultural investment because of poverty. The study indicates that commercial bank lending to agriculture is less than 10% in sub Saharan Africa.[②]

Foreign Direct Investment can take charge in bridging the investment gap in Africa's agriculture.

On the other hand it has been seen that Foreign Direct Investment in agricultural production has

① Pascal Liu, "Impacts of Foreign Agricultural Investment on Developing Countries: Evidence from Case Studies." Food and Agriculture Organization of the United Nations, Rome, 2014. Retrieved on 09/05/2016.

② Da Silva and Mhlanga, 2009, cited in the Pascal Liu Paper "Impacts of Foreign Agricultural Investment on Developing Countries: Evidence from Case Studies". FAO (2014).

been emerging from the year 2000 due to couple of years of under-investment in agricultural sector in developing countries including Africa. In addition to that there was occurrence of high prices of food commodities in between the year 2007-2008 As a result of that there was a great demand of food products which led countries which highly depend on importation of food to start investment in agriculture especially in countries where there is good arable land plenty of water of which are favourable in agriculture and thus plunge of FDI's in agriculture.

Furthermore introduction of vast FDI's in agriculture by international investors was backed up by the high need of production of feedstock crops for biofuels which arose due to high energy prices as well as need for raw materials.①

3. *The Importance of Foreign Direct Investments*

As it is narrated above the FDI's increase growth of economy due to capital influx and tax revenues to the host countries.

In addition to that FDI leads to transfer of skills through training and creates employment as well as transfer of advanced technology for domestic markets and access to research and development resources.② The local communities therefore benefit from job created by new business created.③

Another importance of FDI's is that the foreign investing companies transfer their older machine to the host countries of which become more advantageous to them due to underdevelopment they are found to be very useful. On the other side the foreign investors do that transfer of machineries in order to avoid competition against its own products by the host country.

However it is suggested that in the developing world Foreign Investment strongly increases growth of local production.④ China is a very good example whereby FDI has made tremendous benefits as for the first 6 months of the year 2012 it had been reached up to$ 19. 1 Billion, which made China to be the largest recipient of FDI above USA which had $ 17.4 Billion of FDI.⑤

Nevertheless quantitative analysis of FDI flows into agriculture is backed up by the lack of

① Pascal Liu, "Impacts of Foreign Agricultural Investment on Developing Countries: Evidence from Case Studies." Food and Agriculture Organization of the United Nations, Rome, 2014. Retrieved on 09/05/2016.

② UNCTAD "Foreign Direct Investment, the Transfer and Diffusion of Technology and Sustainable Economy Development." (2010).

③ Slaughter and May "Legal Regimes Governing Foreign Direct Investment (FDI) In Host Countries". (2012), cited by Pascal Liu, *Op cit.*

④ Thomas Hauranek and Zuzana Irsova, "Which Foreigners are worth wooing? A meta- analysis of Vertical Spillovers from FDI." (30th April 2011).), cited by Pascal Liu, *Op cit.*

⑤ China tops US as Investment Target in first half of 2012. Reuters, cited from www.wikipedia.com, Retrieved in 12th May, 2016.

reliable detailed data.

There is a data which indicates that there is a rise in FDI into the agri-food sector of developing countries since 2007-8.

4. The Flow of Agricultural FDI's In Developing Countries

Though Agricultural FDI flows contracted after their peak in the year 2009, their level between the year 2010-2011 was higher than the average for the year 2003-2007.① The flows are manned by the regional patterns whereby intra regional flows are greater than inter-regional flows except for Africa. The share of FDI that goes to agri-food sector is doubled between 2000-2005 and 2006-2008 though it is still low as compared to other economic sectors, accounting for less than 5% over the period of 2006-2008.

The bulk agricultural FDI flows is directed to food manufacturing sector while agriculture production is less than 10% over the period of 2006-2008.②

The study shows that there is no any recent data in FDI in the primary agricultural sector.③

Impacts of Foreign Investment of Agriculture in Africa

1. Poverty Reduction

One great impact of FDI's in Africa is poverty reduction. Agricultural investment is the important key for poverty eradication especially in remote areas where majority of poor people live.④

This is due to the fact that effective agriculture provides rural market for goods and services therefore creating employment and income for the providers.

Due to that, benefit is generated from the village to the broad economy at large.

① Pascal Liu, "Impacts of Foreign Agricultural Investment on Developing Countries: Evidence from Case Studies." Food and Agriculture Organization of the United Nations, Rome, 2014. Retrieved on 09/05/2016.

② Pascal Liu, "Impacts of Foreign Agricultural Investment on Developing Countries: Evidence from Case Studies." Food and Agriculture Organization of the United Nations, Rome, 2014. Retrieved on 09/05/2016.

③ Pascal Liu, "Impacts of Foreign Agricultural Investment on Developing Countries: Evidence from Case Studies." Food and Agriculture Organization of the United Nations, Rome, 2014. Retrieved on 09/05/2016.

④ World Bank, 2008, Food and Agriculture Organization, 2012.

2. Reduction of Hunger

Reduction of hunger is another essential benefit of Agricultural Investment. Increase food productions make it lower prices in the market thus making it accessible to urban and rural consumers.①

However lack of Agricultural Investment in Africa leads to low production and thus hunger. Growth of population in Africa will be on areas where hunger and natural resource degradation is wide spread.

In overcoming that situation increase of Agricultural investment is inevitable. Involvement of public sector in developing countries is necessary. It is reported that Public Sector spending show on agriculture in Africa is dropping up to less than 7%.②Higher food prices has rang bell to policy makers who see the importance of Agriculture investment. Thus Government public investment is essential in creating favourable conditions whereby farmers can thrive. However Public Sector investment alone is not enough to eradicate hunger. Private Sector Investment is highly needed.

Nevertheless, it has been a concern in various foreign organizations that host countries face impacts in some new forms of Foreign Direct Investment (FDI) especially in the issue of large scale land acquisitions hence bringing complex and environmental issues.

Land Investment and FDI's

Foreign Capital is invested in a wide range of agricultural assets such as land. Due to that International debate and research are focused on foreign investments for the control of agricultural land on a large scale. That is due to characteristics of land. Despite its economic value land has social, cultural and religious value in many countries, Africa being among them. Large scale acquisition of land raises complex issues in legal, economic, social and environmental ethical and cultural dimensions.

Commonly foreign investment in land is done through purchase on longer term leases, though long term lease of agricultural land is more preferable than purchase since many countries prohibit sale of land to foreigners. In Tanzania for example, section 20 of the Land Act, [Cap. 113 R. E] prohibits land to be owned by the foreigners.

In spite that the economic and social impacts are the same since lease agreements take longer from about 50 years up to 99 years. Foreign investors have been experiencing local opposition due

① Alston et. Al, 2000, cited by Pascal Liu, *Op cit.*

② Hallam, 2011cited by Pascal Liu, Op Cit.

to that since many of them utilize only part of the while holding the remaining large pieces of land without utilization.

Foreign investments lead to issues regarding to national sovereignty and independence which are sensitive due to colonial history of many countries.

Foreign investment mainly involves between 10,000 hectares and 500,000 hectares as compared to local investors.①

However the World Bank (2011) provides that local investors engage themselves in 80% of the land transactions. Studies indicate that surveyed 97% of land in Nigeria is engaged by national 53% in Mozambique and around Sudan and Ethiopia.②

Destination of FDI in Land

Africa is the basic destination of FDI in land. The matrix figures show that 754 deals covering 56.2 million hectares are located in Africa (fn), 17.7 million hectares in Latin America. Foreign investors have tangled large number of countries (84) though only 11 of them concentrate 70% of the area. Those countries include 7 countries from Africa which are Sudan, Ethiopia, Mozambique, United Republic of Tanzania, Madagascar, Zambia and Democratic Republic of Congo.③

Legal Risks of Agricultural Investment in Africa

As it has been explained above agricultural investment involves large scale acquisition of land between 10,000 hectares to 500,000 hectares that brings negative impacts where there is a lack of good governance, rule of law, transparency and absence of clear tenure rights. As stated above, ownership of land by foreigners is legally prohibited in many African countries. Investors are therefore less secured by investing on land which they have no full property rights. On the other hand there is displacement of local farmers, lost of grazing land, loss of livelihood due to limited access to resources resulting to social fragmentation in the area concerned and decrease of productive

① Hallam, 2011, *Loc Cit.*

② Pascal Liu, "Impacts of Foreign Agricultural Investment on Developing Countries: Evidence from Case Studies." Food and Agriculture Organization of the United Nations, Rome, 2014. Retrieved on 09/05/2016.

③ Pascal Liu, "Impacts of Foreign Agricultural Investment on Developing Countries: Evidence from Case Studies." Food and Agriculture Organization of the United Nations, Rome, 2014. Retrieved on 09/05/2016.

resources. There is also degradation of land, water and forest.①

All these impacts lead to opposition by local people whom their reaction may lead to damage the company's property as a result the investor's starts to involve themselves in litigation and law suits. By so doing return to investment is reduced. The following discussed below are the legal risks for Agricultural Investment in Africa.

1. Lack of Good Dispute Resolution Mechanism

In many African countries there is no clear mechanism for resolving disputes between investors and the host state and or indigenous. This leads to investment risk on suspicion that in case of dispute arising from investment contract there would be enough protection. The absence of clear investment disputes resolution is also caused by lack of Bilateral Investment Treaties make investment insecure.

2. Lack of Good Governance

The quality of good governance in the host country is an important factor for investment. However, most African countries are covered up with inconsistent laws and policies.

Lack of good governance leads to non adherence of the existing laws and human rights which results to corruption and human rights abuse.

3. Corruption

Corruption is the big issue in the rule of law in Africa, so that more attention is given due to historical background of foreign investment in Africa. The reason is that Africa since independence has been involved in substance agriculture and large scale extractive industries which were using public assets like oil, minerals and trees. Since Africa property rights were handed to direct control of state ownership for lack of obvious owner.②

Therefore the removal of those assets to the State required formal licenses for their release, thus, bribe for investors was a long time behavior. Most government officials involved themselves in the game. As a result the foreign investors are driven away by officials who needed payments even when there is a need for introduction of good capital inflow.

To end this corruption it is suggested that African Governments should protect capital inflows by enacting civil service reforms which raise wages and impose severe penalties for anyone engaging

① Pascal Liu, "Impacts of Foreign Agricultural Investment on Developing Countries: Evidence from Case Studies." Food and Agriculture Organization of the United Nations, Rome, 2014. Retrieved on 09/05/2016.

② Peter C. Hansen "Legal Consideration for investing Africa". Retrieved on 9/5/2016.

in corrupt practices or transactions. [①] In addition to that foreign direct investment can play their role to suppress corruption by refusing paying bribes and reporting the officials to relevant government authorities.

Existence of rule of law is an important factor in foreign investment. The land tenure system, laws and regulations and clear property rights promotes land security for foreign and local investors. What is important is to have adequate regulations on investment, agriculture, water, the use of natural resources and their effective implementation.

If Africa has good governance, the rule of law, accountability, transparency, peace, stability and absence of corruption there would be a sustainable environment for investment projects.[②]

In addition to that effective national institutions with ability to review investment proposals, designing the proposal, involve local stake holders and enforcing regulations essential.[③]

Monitoring and enforcing investment contracts, ability of national institutions to correct failures and creating a mechanism of mediation and conflict resolution are necessary.

Formulation of Negotiation Process

How investment project is negotiated designed and planned are important for a successive investment outcomes transparency, inclusion, participatory, democratic and documented processes are inevitable.

The conditions and terms of investment contracts entails the relationship between the project partners, the sharing of responsibilities, decision making, benefits and risks.[④]

Since investment contracts are vague there is a need for specific enforceable terms. That is to say the contract must specify the benefits the local community would obtain from the investor. Theses are for example number of jobs created, types of infrastructures built and the training provided.

Conclusion

African recognizes contribution of agricultural enterprises in support of agricultural investment

① Peter C. Hansen “Legal Consideration for investing Africa”. Retrieved on 9/5/2016.

② Pascal Liu, “Impacts of Foreign Agricultural Investment on Developing Countries: Evidence from Case Studies.” Food and Agriculture Organization of the United Nations, Rome, 2014. Retrieved on 09/05/2016.

③ Pascal Liu, “Impacts of Foreign Agricultural Investment on Developing Countries: Evidence from Case Studies.” Food and Agriculture Organization of the United Nations, Rome, 2014. Retrieved on 09/05/2016.

④ Pascal Liu, “Impacts of Foreign Agricultural Investment on Developing Countries: Evidence from Case Studies.” Food and Agriculture Organization of the United Nations, Rome, 2014. Retrieved on 09/05/2016.

and their responsibility in the implementation of sustainable and mutual beneficial relationships with farmers.

In addition to that it acknowledges that the success of agricultural investment is based on largely on the implementation of legal framework that is fair, well monitored and with sound evaluation procedures and disputes resolution mechanisms.

It affirms also that transparency is a corollary of good governance and should be applied to land investments.

It is suggested that investment is involving relationship between local farmers and private investors by giving them full control of their land results in positive impacts to local economy and social development.

Where large scale land acquisition occurs, the disadvantages outweigh few benefits to the local community. In place where there is poor governance large scale land acquisition leads to high risks for the local community concerned due to decrease of access to natural resources and loss of livelihoods. All these results to resistance to the investment.

Promotion through natural laws sustainable and responsible investment in agriculture and food systems is of great importance. Further, host countries should develop tools to reduce risks associated with agricultural investment while maximizing the economic and social benefit.

Consideration should also be taken to the need for appropriate impact assessment monitoring and implementation.

Strengthen national and regional regulations on transparency and develop a model law on transparency in land transactions is essential in promoting foreign investment. Host countries have to harmonize legislation and legal framework on land governance.

International Investment Law, international corporate law, anti corruption law and rule of law implementation promotes conducive environment for foreign investment due to the fact that they entail investment risk management.

Following the observed risks of the agricultural investment in Africa the following are recommendations.

Recommendations

1. Enhancing national laws relating to agriculture investment

Africa could benefit from FDI if the risks for agriculture investment are reduced .That is possible if there are improvement policies, laws and regulation associated with land tenure and agricultural investment. The enacted laws must be consistent and well implemented so as not to leave any gap.

Apart from that the land tenure must be well expressed and provided according to the type of investment projects. Strengthened tenure and property rights in land and other policies which acknowledge small scale farmers are of great importance as they not only assure success to foreign investment but also promote confidence to local producers especially in issues of dispossession of land.① Human rights must also be well observed citzens should not be neglected in the project jobs and never should they be segregated in the kinds of jobs created.

Furthermore acquisition of land by investors should be applied according to the size required by a particular project. This would avoid the conflicts between the people in rural areas and foreign investors who hold land which is unused for a long period of time.

It is suggested that there should be a mechanism to with draw land from investors who hold land they do not utilize for many years.②That is the tool to reduce the risks associated with agricultural investment.

2. Strengthening National Regulations on Transparency in Land Transactions

According to wikipedia transparency implies to openness, communication and accountability. It is usually operated in the manner that it is easy for others to see what actions are performed.③

In order to avoid legal risks land allocation contracts are supposed to be publicized so as to ensure transparency and accountability by the government institutions dealing with land transactions. By so doing it could be easy for public to have a chance to scrutinize who investor has been allocated what in which location and for how long. Through that practice good governance will be assured in host countries and the risks of agricultural investment could be minimized.

3. Capacity building in host countries

Successiful agricultural investment depends on conducive environment in host countries. That can be ensured by the quality of governance nationally and locally. African countries are suffered with inconsistent laws and policies together with poor institutional capacity. Foreign investors have to make sure that they contribute to give knowledge by strengthening education, information and communications regarding land issues to the African governments. Studies insist that the international organizations have to support African government officials and small scale farmers so as to foster good governance at national and local level by looking at their needs particularly in capacity building, policy and technical support.④ That could be done through training government officials

---

① Jasper Karlsson, "Challenges and Opportunities of Foreign Investment in Developing Country Agriculture for Sustainable Development," FAO (2014).

② Jasper Karlsson, "Challenges and Opportunities of Foreign Investment in Developing Country Agriculture for Sustainable Development," FAO (2014).

③ www.wikipedia.com, retrieved in 12th May, 2016.

④ Jasper Karlsson, "Challenges and Opportunities of Foreign Investment in Developing Country Agriculture for Sustainable Development", FAO (2014).

in understanding investment proposals and negotiating contracts with investors. Rural people should not be left aside where knowledge regarding land matters and investment is concerned. That is to say there has to be a literacy to the grassroots communities on investment contracts and legal framework and the government institutions as well.

The governments should plan tools for reduction of foreign agricultural risks for small scale farmers organizations. The local organizations should implement the risks management strategy by providing programs which will enhance multi-stake holder partnerships. That will lead to the sustainable development. To have a successful strategy for agricultural investment there has to be a partnership between governments, donors and farmers of whom everyone will be performing his own responsibility.

4. International Guidance

As it has been discussed above in this study Africa is characterized by inconsistent laws and policies together with law institutional capacity. All these bring risks to the foreign investment.

Land tenure systems which are not working properly, neglect of rights and time to time claims of land by the rural people due to holding of un utilized land by investors for so many years bring negative impacts to agricultural foreign investment.

To avoid all those risk factors there must be a need for a call for international guidance so as to obtain assurance of sustainable agricultural development in the African economy.

Adoption of international agreements is inevitable so as to suppress the tenure risks. There are the Voluntary Guidelines on the Responsible Governance of Tenure of Land, Fisheries and Forests (VGGT) adopted in May, 2012 by the Committee on World Food Security (CFS) together with Food and Agriculture Organization (FAO) Voluntary Guidelines on the Right to Food. According to Liu the VGGT provides guidelines on how to improve tenure of land governance, fisheries and forests with the aim of assuring achievement on food security for all is attained.①

By observing all the above mentioned recommendations legal risks on agricultural investment in Africa could be under taken that investment projects would be in the good place to succeed.

"Unsuccessful investors in Africa are those who jump to start investment business without carefully mapping out the investment." ②

① Pascal Liu, "Impacts of Foreign Agricultural Investment on Developing Countries: Evidence from Case Studies." Food and Agriculture Organization of the United Nations, Rome, 2014. Retrieved on 09/05/2016.

② Peter C. Hansen "Legal Consideration for investing Africa". Retrieved on 9/5/2016.

Prepared by Moza Mussa Kassubi, Principal Investigator, Legal and Prosecution Section. Prevention and Combating of Corruption Bureau, Tanzania. 15th May, 2016.

在非洲投资农业的法律风险

作者：Oni Oluyemisi Oyinkansola 译者：王璐瑶

一、简介

农业被认为是非洲经济最重要的支柱和组成部分。非洲大陆因其拥有全球60%的荒地而成为“全世界超过一半的被荒废的农业用地的家园”。① 在大多数非洲国家，农业经济不仅是其国内生产总值（GDP）的主要贡献者，也是其外汇的最大来源。

以尼日利亚为例，2016年的第一季度，农业占到其国内生产总值的19.17%。② 由于尼日利亚“气候条件多样，土壤肥沃，水资源丰富，具有大量人口来种植农作物、饲养动物和鱼类、种植树木”，农业在尼日利亚的郊区一直处于主导地位。③

目前，尼日利亚政府的政策方向是使其经济更加多元化，并摆脱对石油经济的依赖。在这种趋势下，对农业领域的投资变得十分关键。“东南亚繁荣的市场使经营农业综合企业变得拥挤、昂贵而又充满竞争，而非洲得以获得更多机会。”④ 的确是这样，这对于非洲来说就是最好的时机。尤其对于尼日利亚来说可以利用好这次投资机遇。

然而，对农业综合业的投资同时伴随着各种风险，包括币值波动、基础设施风险、技术风险以及法律风险。其中，法律风险（也是本文意图解决的）十分巨大，

① Where to Invest in Africa, A Guide to Corporate Investment, (2015-2016 edition).

② National Bureau of Statistics, GDP Q4 2015.

③ V.M. Manyong et al. *Agriculture in Nigeria: Identifying Opportunities for Increased Commercialization and Investment*, (2005); International Institute of Tropical Agriculture.

④ Where to Invest in Africa, A Guide to Corporate Investment, (2015-2016 edition).

种类多样。因此，本文将关注尼日利亚现有的法律体系。在分析投资农业经济固有的法律风险的同时，本文将阐述尼日利亚农业领域的投资机会。此外，本文还将提出一些风险降低机制，无论是公有企业还是潜在的地方和外国投资者都必须在投资之前对此有所认识。

二、尼日利亚农业领域现有的投资机会

由于尼日利亚具有农业投资所需要的富饶环境，许多外国和当地投资者一直以来都想在某些重要领域进行投资，包括："生产投入和供给部门、畜产部门、渔业、林业以及商品加工和存储部门。""其他还有商品销售、农业加工、农产品出口以及农业支持服务等。"①

目前在非洲，尤其是在尼日利亚，农业投资的机会越来越多，而以下八个要素是吸引投资的关键：

1. 用于栽培主要作物和生产生物燃料的大量耕地；
2. 全球可用土地的不足；
3. 可利用廉价劳动力；
4. 可利用灌溉用水；
5. 尼日利亚不断增长的人口带动了消费需求；
6. 生物燃料在全球使用的增加；
7. 全球食品安全问题；
8. 政府对农业的重视②。

在上述要素存在的同时，下列领域作为未来农业投资的主要部门已经被开发：③

1. 畜牧业、农作物和蔬菜如大米和土豆的生产，以解决现存的供应短缺问题；
2. 油棕榈产业，因为油棕榈一直主导全球食用油类的生产；
3. 依赖原材料的农业配套产业，如橡胶业；
4. 机器与设备的生产和制造，因联邦政府正鼓励农业工业化来实现大规模生产；

① Where to Invest in Africa, A Guide to Corporate Investment, (2015-2016 edition).

② Where to Invest in Africa, A Guide to Corporate Investment, (2015-2016 edition).

③ Investing in Nigeria's Agricultural Sector, http://www.abrahamandco.com/wp-content/uploads/2016/03/April-Newsletterwebsite-version.pdf April, 2016.

5. 农业的研究与开发，因为这会增加“在农产品培育、仓储、加工和保存方面开发新技术的专业领域的投资者的机会”。[①].

三、投资农业领域的法律风险

对于发展农业来说，公私企业的成员和利益相关者的投资是不可或缺的一部分。这与政府想要促进尼日利亚经济多元化的目标是相适应的，因为投资最终会转化成有利于促进出口贸易达到更高水平的商品化和集约生产。

然而，在认识到目前投资农业领域的机会之后，就应该强调和分析伴随着投资的法律风险。这是十分重要的。以下是我们要强调的法律风险的分类：

（一）立法和管理规定的模糊

我们已经注意到，“除了影响农业和其他任何部门的一般经济政策（比如税款、利息、汇率等等）以外，对农业的规制还包括一个复杂的政府干预和调整的系统。这会给农业投资带来风险”[②]。尤其是当政治和政策方向致力于通过推进农业领域的贸易实现经济多元化时，政府干预的存在就更加明显。例如，尼日利亚众议院已经开始依据其立法日程展开农业方面的辩论。这些辩论的内容是如何推进新政策和政府管制以促进农业的发展，最终促进尼日利亚的经济发展。为了与政府工作日程相一致，这些辩论之后必然会起草并颁布新法以及对现存法律的修正案。因此，这些努力虽然值得赞赏，却为不确定性和不可预见性留下了空间。

对于尼日利亚这样经济发展迅速的国家来说，法律的动态性固然很重要。但是，我们同样要认识到，如果出现下面这些问题，农业政策就会无效：“政策不稳定、政策不一致、政策形成的基点狭窄、政策执行不力，以及政策协调的体制框架薄弱。”[③]因此，鉴于私营企业在农业领域的投资有赖于一个清晰合理的监管结构，有必要在动态和可预见的立法框架间找到一个平衡点。

---

① Investing in Nigeria’s Agricultural Sector, http://www.abrahamandco.com/wp-content/uploads/2016/03/April-Newsletterwebsite-version.pdf April, 2016.

② Managing Risk in Agriculture: A holistic Approach (OECD, 2009).

③ V.M. Manyong et al. *Agriculture in Nigeria: Identifying Opportunities for Increased Commercialization and Investment*, (2005); International Institute of Tropical Agriculture.

（二）政府投资不足

在之前，政府在农业领域的投资一直不足，尤其是在从自给农业到农产品加工业的转化方面。[①] 这是因为每年的财政拨款多集中于经常性支出，而不是对某个部门基本建设项目的投资。这种忽视造成了尼日利亚基础设施的不足。因此，尼日利亚目前面临基础设施方面的诸多挑战，如道路交通网络十分糟糕，存储设备和仓库不足，铁路运输系统薄弱以及加工设备的缺乏等。

这些基础设施如果健全的话，可以缓和农业经营的相关风险，如商品的损坏和消耗，收割期后的损失，以及商品输出的不安全性。如果政府没有在这些相关基础设施上投资，私营企业在农业领域的投资会更加冒险。此外，“适当的基础设施，尤其是在郊区，可以将投资者与他们的消费者、供应商联系起来，使他们研究并利用好新技术，从而增加产量、提高收入”[②]。

值得庆幸的是，尼日利亚政府似乎想要改变现状。在 2016 年的财政拨款中，农业与农村发展部的经常性支出为 296.3 亿奈拉，而其基础建设费用为 461.7 亿奈拉。政府似乎也热衷于投资那些可以促进农业投资的战略性领域，如农村道路的复原，向农民提供补贴，战略性畜牧保护区的发展，稳定价格，担保机制等。

（三）腐败和透明度风险

腐败一直是尼日利亚投资领域的毒药。这是因为，在很多时候，缔约程序、监管许可的适用和恢复等对于潜在的投资者来说是非竞争且不透明的。这可能是由于存在大量的法律规制和过度的繁文缛节导致投资者花费增多，时间上也发生了拖延。

税务活动中的贿赂和腐败行为无疑“增加了交易成本，扭曲了竞争环境，因此阻碍了投资”[③]。“腐败行为削减了私营企业的投资利益，或者通过增加获取资源的成本和冲突发生的可能性而阻碍了私营企业的投资。”[④] 腐败也可能影响政府补贴贷款的分配，而这些贷款本应该促进该领域投资并增加投资收益。

---

① Where to Invest in Africa, A Guide to Corporate Investment, (2015-2016 edition) .

② Managing Risk in Agriculture: A holistic Approach (OECD, 2009).

③ Managing Risk in Agriculture: A holistic Approach (OECD, 2009).

④ Managing Risk in Agriculture: A holistic Approach (OECD, 2009).

（四）贷款人的贷款风险

金融服务业的利益相关者在农业领域的投资经常被视为高风险的投资。这是因为农业经营会被一些很难预测到或不可能预测到的事情影响。这些不可预测的事情包括但不限于季节性波动、价格波动，以及可购得的产品及其供应质量的不确定性。如果借贷者未能偿付用于农业经营项目的贷款，银行和金融机构就会预见到很高的违约风险。因此，他们在调查该领域的投资和出资时会更加谨慎。

在这种情况下，大量充分的抵押条款本应该鼓励贷款者投资农业经营，然而“由于财产权和土地使用权的模糊，登记程序费时费钱以及社会制约的存在，可用的抵押品或替代品十分缺乏”①。而尼日利亚有关抵押品登记和强制执行的法律规制又加剧了现有的法律风险。

（五）地方的法律规范

尼日利亚的地方政策旨在通过使用当地原材料、产品和服务促进当地自主能力的提高，从而促进尼日利亚增值。②这种地方政策赋予了农业投资者各种义务，如培养本土的参与者、促进能力和技术转让，以及使用本土的原材料和设备。这些地方政策希望通过这种方式提高全国在农业领域的参与水平。

目前，有关尼日利亚农业的地方立法和管理机制还很不健全（与石油和油气相比）。但是在未来，地方法律规范将会扩展到包括农业在内的其他领域。这与政府促进经济多元化和减少石油依赖的目标相一致。而潜在的投资者就要因此意识到，为了履行地方法规赋予的义务，农业投资的成本就有增加的风险。同样需要指出的是，地方法律不能与其他法规相抵触，而法律的实施也要与相关监管部门的行为相一致。

（六）税收风险

税收通常是政府用来增加国家收入的手段，为政府的发展提供资金。③税率和税收水平会极大地影响农业投资。农业领域的普通税包括“农业投入的进口关税、农

① Calvin Miller, *Risk Management for Agricultural Investment: Investment and Resource Mobilization*(2008); Food and Agricultural Organisation of the United Nations.

② S.C. Rapu, et al; *Fiscal Incentives in Nigeria: Lessons of Experience, Central Bank of Nigeria (Fiscal Sector Division* (September, 2013).

③ Managing Risk in Agriculture: A holistic Approach (OECD, 2009).

产品的出口关税、所得税和增值税”。①

值得注意的是，尼日利亚是存在税收优惠的，其目的是促进农业领域的投资。先驱产业政策（有资格的或符合条件的产业享有的免税政策）的出台使相关产业在其成长期可以获得可观的利润。如果该先驱产业位于经济欠发达地区，还可以享受7年的免税期和额外的5%资本折旧限额。

下表列出的是受益于尼日利亚的先驱产业免税政策的农业领域的产业和产品：

产业、产品	产业	产品
1.	粮食和水果的种植、加工和保存	腌制的罐装食品和水果、茶、咖啡、精制糖等
2.	完整的乳业生产	黄油、奶酪、牛奶和奶粉、冰淇淋（副产品，家畜和可食用产品）
3.	深海拖网和加工	罐装海鲜、鱼、虾米和鱼粉
4.	本地小麦粉材料加工	面粉和动物内脏
5.	橡胶种植和加工	橡胶
6.	阿拉伯树胶种植和加工	阿拉伯树胶
7.	氨、尿素等化肥的制造	过磷酸钙和氮肥
8.	油棕榈种植和加工	棕榈油、棕仁和动物内脏
9.	大规模机械化农业	小麦、玉米、稻米和高粱
10.	拥有至少500头牛和猪的养牛场和猪舍	不低于500头的牛和猪
11.	大规模的内陆鱼塘	鱼和小虾米
12.	农业机器和设备制造	犁、收割机、打谷机、种植机等

虽然税收优惠可以鼓励农业领域的投资，但是该优惠政策的权限和范围却可能发生改变（经常取决于现任政府）。同样地，农业经营项目启动时的投资计划可能会突然发生改变。

例如，2004年产业发展（所得税减免）法案为先锋地位的产业提供了一些申请指南。之后颁布的2014年先锋地位优惠条例又在之前法案的基础上增加了额外的条

① Managing Risk in Agriculture: A holistic Approach (OECD, 2009).

件。特别是该条例规定，投资者应按照 2% 的租金节约额向尼日利亚投资促进委员会（NIPC）缴纳服务费。这笔服务费来源于五年财政计划，增加了获取先锋资格的成本。而投资者在产业发展（所得税减免）法案颁布时很可能没有想到这一点。[①] 然而，在原油价格崩溃和联邦政府现金流出现问题之后，先驱产业的范围被重新审视。目前，尼日利亚投资促进委员会（NIPC）仅给予先驱企业三年的期限。

（七）纠纷解决

合同的履行对于取得投资者的信任十分关键。“法律必须确保合同得到履行、财产权受到保护，纠纷得到公正的解决。这些都是一个高效的市场的标志。”[②] 因此，尼日利亚投资促进中心法案（NIPC Act）为自由开放的投资框架确立了一个法律基础。这项跨部门的立法包含了一个纠纷解决条款，用来解决尼日利亚政府部门和国内外投资者之间的纠纷。根据尼日利亚投资促进中心法案（NIPC Act），投资者有权通过调解和仲裁解决任何与尼日利亚政府部门之间的投资纠纷。

然而，大多数投资项目的纠纷通常由法庭裁决解决。在尼日利亚，通过司法系统解决纠纷十分缓慢，同时还有案件积压过多、休庭期长、司法人员负担过重等问题。[③] 尼日利亚司法制度的形势使得纠纷解决进程十分缓慢，从而导致过去许多投资者在这方面花费了很多时间、金钱和资源。而这使一些潜在的投资者打消了在尼日利亚投资农业的念头。

近日，“一些国际机构如世界银行认为，只有所有经济领域共同发展才能实现全面发展”[④]。因此，为了降低农业投资的风险，尼日利亚应当开展有关商业纠纷裁决的司法改革。

四、风险降低机制

尼日利亚的农业已经做好准备接受国内外的投资。但是，联邦政府和潜在的投资者都应当意识到下面这些能够促进投资的长期的风险降低机制。

---

① Pioneer Status and the Return of the 3-year Rule; Deloitte.

② Policy Framework for Investment in Agriculture; OECD.

③ The Courts and Commercial Disputes Resolution in Nigeria: The Need for Specialization.

④ The Courts and Commercial Disputes Resolution in Nigeria: The Need for Specialization.

（一）与投资农产品的特定需求相关的政策法规的颁布

有关优先农产品的特别政策将会增加高产量的优先产品的投资。这种特别政策还可以解决很多问题，如采取什么样的评分标准有利于相关产品的使用。①

尼日利亚似乎在这方面做得不错。尼日利亚中央银行（CBN）、银行家委员会和联邦农业和农村发展部共同成立了尼日利亚激励型农业贷款风险分担系统（NIRSAL）。这一公有性质的有限责任公司主要管理一项风险分担基金，用于鉴定、重新定义、计算、重新定价以及发展策略从而增加农业产业价值链的贷款并降低其风险。因此，该公司有权向农业产业价值链的参与者发放贷款，并与利益相关者共同修补断裂的农业产业价值链。从 2012 年开始至今，尼日利亚激励型农业贷款风险分担系统（NIRSAL）已经担保了 454 个总计价值 611.61 亿奈拉的项目。

尽管相关政策在降低法律风险方面有所成就，“投资者拥有透明高效的反馈渠道向政策制定者表达他们的特殊需求”仍然是十分重要的。② 这将使得动态的法律规范与投资者的需求保持一致，从而促进农业领域的投资。

（二）改善农业及其他部门的基础设施

之前已经提到，农业领域配套基础设施的缺乏是由于之前政府在农业及与农业相关的经济领域投资不足。为了扭转这一局面，完善农业和非农业领域的基础设施，我们需要“在农业部门和负责基础设施的部门之间建立一个协调机制，完成政策的制定和实施”③。例如，权力部和工程与住房部可以和农业与农村发展部合作，从全盘考虑，共同完善农业和非农业领域相关的基础设施。

下面是一些可以在短期内缓释农业领域投资风险的措施：④

1. 与政府保持透明的投资关系；

2. 与政府的投资和商业利益保持一致；

3. 鼓励政府直接参与投资；

4. 潜在投资者的投标过程应开放透明并具有竞争性（避免安排“快速通道”）；

---

① Calvin Miller, *Risk Management for Agricultural Investment: Investment and Resource Mobilization*(2008); Food and Agricultural Organisation of the United Nations.

② Managing Risk in Agriculture: A holistic Approach (OECD, 2009).

③ Managing Risk in Agriculture: A holistic Approach (OECD, 2009).

④ Conrad Marais, *Investing in African Infrastructure Projects: Risk and Risk Mitigation* (September, 2013).

5. 遵守法律规范。

五、结论

本文以尼日利亚农业投资中的法律风险为主题，简要叙述了农业投资中的机会，深入研究了以下法律风险：立法和管理规定的模糊、政府投资不足、腐败和透明度风险、贷款人的贷款风险、税收风险、地方法律法规的实施以及投资过程中的纠纷解决。本文还提出了长期和中短期的风险缓释机制，其中的两大关键是制定与农业投资相关的特别政策法规和完善农业与非农业领域的相关基础设施。而短期的风险缓释机制则包括与政府的投资和商业利益保持一致，以及遵守法律法规等。

Legal Risks of Agricultural Investment in Africa

Author: Oni Oluyemisi Oyinkansola

Introduction

Agriculture is termed as the most important sector and backbone of the African economy. The continent is often described as "home to more than half of the worlds agriculturally suitable yet unused land" ① as Africa holds 60% of global uncultivated land. In most countries in Africa, the agro-economy is the biggest source of foreign exchange as well as a major contributor to Gross Domestic Product (GDP).

In Nigeria in particular, agriculture contributed 19.17% to nominal GDP during the first quarter of 2016.② This economic sector remains dominant in the rural areas of Nigeria due to "the diversity of climatic conditions, the richness of soil types and water resources, and the high population density which provides great potentials for crop, animal, fish and tree production" ③.

Given the particular indication of the current Nigerian government's policy direction to diversify the economy and step away from the current dependency on the petro-economy, investment in the agricultural space has become critical. The time is right as the "booming market in Southeast Asia has become crowded, competitive and expensive for doing agribusiness, making way for growing opportunities in Africa." ④ Indeed, the time is right for Africa, and in particular Nigeria to leverage on this fantastic investment opportunity.

Investment in agribusiness is however linked to diverse risks including currency fluctuation, infrastructural risks, technology risks and legal risks. The legal risks in particular (which this article intends to address), of agricultural investment in Africa remain vast and diverse; therefore this article

① Where to Invest in Africa, A Guide to Corporate Investment, (2015-2016 edition).

② National Bureau of Statistics, GDP Q4 2015.

③ V.M. Manyong et al. *Agriculture in Nigeria: Identifying Opportunities for Increased Commercialization and Investment*, (2005); International Institute of Tropical Agriculture.

④ Where to Invest in Africa, A Guide to Corporate Investment, (2015-2016 edition).

will focus on what is obtainable under Nigerian jurisprudence. The article will explore the current opportunities for investment in the Nigerian agricultural sector, while assessing the legal risks inherent in investment in the agro-economy. The article will proffer risk mitigation mechanisms that both public sector and potential local and foreign investors must be cognizant of prior to agricultural investment in Nigeria.

Current Opportunities for Investment in the Nigerian Agricultural Sector

Given the fertile environment for agricultural investment in Nigeria, there are certain important areas in which both foreign and local investors have been willing to divest funds and invest in the past. These are "input production and supply enterprises, livestock production, fisheries, forestry, and commodity processing and storage enterprises. Others are commodity marketing, agro industry manufacturing, agricultural commodity export, and agricultural support services." ①

The current opportunities available in Africa, and in particular, Nigeria, with regards to agricultural investment are expanding especially in view of the following eight key factors which have been identified as key to attracting future investment in the agro economy:

a. Large areas of arable land for staple crop cultivation and biofuel production;

b. Lack of available land globally;

c. Availability of low –cost labour;

d. Availability of water for irrigation;

e. Growing population in Nigeria, which has translated to growing consumer demand;

f. Increased biofuel use globally;

g. Global food security concerns; and

h. Government placing importance on agriculture.②

With the existence of a combination of the above listed factors, the following agricultural businesses have been tapped as key subsectors for future agricultural investment:③

a. Livestock farming, crop and vegetable production such as rice and tomatoes since a huge supply gap currently exists that needs to be addressed;

b. Oil palm industry because palm oil continues to dominate global edible oils production;

c. Support for agro-allied industries that are dependent on agriculture for feed stock, for example

① Where to Invest in Africa, A Guide to Corporate Investment, (2015-2016 edition).

② Where to Invest in Africa, A Guide to Corporate Investment, (2015-2016 edition).

③ Investing in Nigeria's Agricultural Sector, http://www.abrahamandco.com/wp-content/uploads/2016/03/April-Newsletterwebsite-version.pdf April, 2016.

the rubber industry;

d. Manufacture and fabrication of plant and machinery as the Federal Government is encouraging the utilization of industrialised agriculture for large scale production; and

e. Agricultural research and development as this opens up "opportunities for investors whose area of expertise involve developing new techniques for the cultivation, storage, processing and preservation of agricultural produce." ①

Legal Risks of Investment in the Agricultural Sector

Investment in the agricultural sector of the economy by both public and private sector participants and stakeholders is integral to growing the agricultural sector. This will fit in with the government's stated aim of diversification of the Nigerian economy as investment ultimately translates to a higher level of commercialization and intensive production which will promote and foster export trade.

However, having identified the current investment opportunities in the agricultural sector, it is important to highlight and analyse the legal risks attendant with investment in this sector of the economy as categorised and highlighted below:

1. Legislative and Regulatory Uncertainty

It has been noted that "besides the general economic policies that affect agriculture as any other sector (example taxes, interest rates, exchange rates, etc.), agriculture is typically characterised by an intricate system of government interventions and changes which may create risk for agricultural investment." ② Government intervention especially occurs where polity and policy direction are geared towards economic diversification by boosting trade and commerce within the agro economy. The Nigerian House of Representatives for example has begun sectoral debates on agriculture, pursuant to its legislative agenda. These sectoral debates will focus on driving new policies and government regulation that will propel growth in the agricultural sector and foster development of the Nigerian economy. These efforts although laudable, leave room for uncertainty and unpredictability as such sectoral debates will inevitably lead to the crafting and enactment of new laws or the amendment to existing legislation in order to align with the Government of the day's agenda.

---

① Investing in Nigeria's Agricultural Sector, http://www.abrahamandco.com/wp-content/uploads/2016/03/April-Newsletterwebsite-version.pdf April, 2016.

② Managing Risk in Agriculture: A holistic Approach (OECD, 2009).

Although dynamism of laws is important for a fast paced economy such as Nigeria, it is also important to note that the ineffectiveness of agricultural policy also lies on the recurrence of the following factors: "policy instability, policy inconsistencies, narrow base of policy formulation, poor policy implementation and weak institutional framework of policy coordination." ① Consequently, there is need for a balance between dynamism and predictability of the legislative framework as private sector participation in the agricultural sector relies on clear and sound regulatory structure.

2. Government Investment is not Forthcoming

It has unfortunately been the case in the past that Government has underinvested in the sector, especially in terms of shifting subsistence farming to agro-processing.② This is as a result of the fact that the yearly budgetary allocation, more often than not focusses on recurrent expenditure as opposed to investment in capital projects in the sector. The oversight or neglect, as the case may be, has created a dearth in infrastructural capacity as currently Nigeria is faced with infrastructural challenges such as pitiful road transport network, inadequate storage facilities and warehouses, poor rail transportation system and inadequate processing machinery.

Without government investment in core infrastructure in this regard, investment in the agricultural sector by private participants is riskier as such infrastructure, if existent, should ordinarily mitigate associated risks of agribusiness such as spoilage and wastage of commodities, post-harvest losses and insecurity of available commodity output. Furthermore, "adequate agriculture-related infrastructure, in particular in rural areas, can connect investors to their customers and suppliers and enable them to specialise and take advantage of new technologies, thereby increasing productivity and improving incomes." ③

The Nigerian government thankfully appears to be taking a diversion from the status quo. The 2016 budget allocates 29.63 billion Naira recurrent expenditure to the Ministry of Agriculture and Rural Development while 46.17 Billion Naira has been allocated for capital expenditure. The government also appears keen on investing in strategic areas that would improve agricultural investment such as the rehabilitation of rural roads, providing subsidies to rural farmers, development of strategic grazing reserves and price stabilization and guarantee schemes.

---

① V.M. Manyong et al. *Agriculture in Nigeria: Identifying Opportunities for Increased Commercialization and Investment*, (2005); International Institute of Tropical Agriculture.

② Where to Invest in Africa, A Guide to Corporate Investment, (2015-2016 edition).

③ Managing Risk in Agriculture: A holistic Approach (OECD, 2009).

3. Corruption and Transparency Risks

Corruption has been continually described as the bane of Nigerian investment. This is as a result of the fact that most often than not, contracting processes, applications and renewal of regulatory permits and licences, etc., are not perceived by intending investors as competitive or transparent. This may be due to the state of affairs of heavy statutory regulations and excessive red tape which increases costs and foster delays for investors.

Bribery and corrupt tax practices inevitably "increase transactions costs and distorts competitive conditions, thus hindering investment." ① "Corruption can reduce the benefits of private agricultural investments or prevent them from being realised by augmenting the cost of accessing resources and increasing the potential for conflict." ② Corruption may also affect the allocation of government-subsidised credit which ordinarily should foster investment returns and encourage investment in the sector.

4. Credit Risk for Intending Lenders

Investment in the agro economy by stakeholders in the financial services sector is often termed as high risk investment because agribusiness can be affected by eventualities that are difficult and almost impossible to predict. Such eventualities include and are not limited to seasonal variations, price volatility and uncertainty in available production and supply quantity. Subsequently, banks and financial institutions are more cautious about delving into investment and funding of the sector because of the preconceived notion of high risk of default as a result of borrower's failure to make required payments on monies borrowed for agricultural projects.

Although the provision of adequate and substantial collateral in this instance should ordinarily encourage lenders in investing in agribusinesses, there is a "lack of usable collateral or substitutes (especially in rural finance) due to often ill-defined property and land use rights, costly or lengthy registration procedures, and social constraints." ③ The Nigerian legal terrain on registration and enforcement of collateral as such appears to exacerbate already existing legal risks in this instance.

---

① Managing Risk in Agriculture: A holistic Approach (OECD, 2009).

② Managing Risk in Agriculture: A holistic Approach (OECD, 2009).

③ Calvin Miller, *Risk Management for Agricultural Investment: Investment and Resource Mobilization*(2008); Food and Agricultural Organisation of the United Nations.

5. *Local Content Laws and Regulations*

Nigerian local content policy is aimed at the promotion of value addition in Nigeria through the utilization of local raw materials, products and services in order to stimulate the growth of indigenous capacity.[①] Local content policies as such seek to increase level of national participation in an industry by imposing obligations on sector participants and investors alike to amongst other things, train indigenous participants, foster skill and technology transfer and utilise locally sourced feedstock and machinery.

While at present, local content legislation and mechanisms are less established in the Nigerian agricultural sector (as opposed to the oil and gas sector), it is the case that local content regulations, legislations and requirements will be extended to other sectors of the economy, including the agro economy. This is especially in line with government objectives to diversify the economy and reduce the dependency on the petro economy. Once this occurs, intending investors must be aware of the risk of increased cost of funding of agricultural investment in order to comply adequately with obligations imposed by local content requirements. It is also important to note that such enactment and enforcement of local content laws will create an added layer of bureaucratic and regulatory compliance and interface with the relevant regulatory body.

6. *Taxation Risk*

Taxation is more often than not, utilised by governments for the flow of domestic revenue which may be utilised to finance the developmental objectives of the government.[②] Agricultural investment is heavily influenced by the rates and level of taxation. Common taxes in the agricultural sector include "import duties on agricultural inputs and export taxes on agricultural commodities, income tax, and value added tax." [③]

In Nigeria, it is important to note that tax incentives aimed at promoting investment in the agricultural sector are in place. Pioneer Status (which is a tax holiday granted to qualified or eligible industries) is granted to enable the industry concerned to make a reasonable level of profit within its formative years. A pioneer industry also sited in economically disadvantaged Local Government Area is also entitled to 100% tax holiday for seven years and an additional 5% capital depreciation allowance over and above the initial capital depreciation allowance.

① S.C. Rapu, et al; *Fiscal Incentives in Nigeria: Lessons of Experience, Central Bank of Nigeria (Fiscal Sector Division* (September, 2013).

② Managing Risk in Agriculture: A holistic Approach (OECD, 2009).

③ Managing Risk in Agriculture: A holistic Approach (OECD, 2009).

Below is a table that highlights the industries and products within the Nigerian agricultural sector that benefit from this form of tax holiday by virtue of Pioneer Status:

S/N	INDUSTRIES	PRODUCTS
1	Cultivation, processing and preservation of food crops and fruits	Preserved canned foodstuff and fruits, tea, coffee, refined sugar, tomato puree/ juice, etc.
2	Integrated diary production	Butter, cheese, fluid milk and powder, ice cream (by products, livestock, minor edible products)
3	Deep sea trawling and processing Coastal fishing and shrimping	Preserved sea foods, fish and shrimps and fishmeal
4	The processing of local wheat flour materials	Flour and offal
5	Rubber plantation and processing	Rubber
6	Gum/Arabic plantation and processing	Gum Arabic
7	Manufacture of fertilizers Ammonia, Urea	Superphosphate and nitrogenous fertilizers
8	Oil palm plantation and processing	Palm oil, palm kennel and offals
9	Large scale mechanized farming	Wheat, maize, rice and sorghum
10	Cattle ranching and piggery of not less than 500 herds	Cattle and pigs of not less than 500 herds
11	Large scale inland fishing farms	Fish and shrimps
12	Manufacture of agricultural machinery and equipment	Ploughs, harvesters, threshers, planters, etc.

Although tax incentives may encourage investment in the agro sector, it is important to note that the purview and scope of such tax incentives are subject to change (often depending on the government of the day). As such, investment projections may suddenly differ from what was obtainable at inception of the agricultural project.

For example in Nigeria, while the Industrial Development (Income Tax Relief) Act 2004 provided for application guidelines for Pioneer Status, further Pioneer Status Incentive Regulations 2014 were enacted and additional conditions were included to those contained in the Income Tax

Relief Act. More prominent in the Regulation was an inclusion of a 2% service charge based on estimated tax savings to be paid to the Nigerian Investment Promotion Commission (NIPC). The service charge is derived from five-year financial projections. The service charge effectively results in additional costs for obtaining a pioneer certificate most likely not envisaged by an investor at inception of the Industrial Development (Income Tax Relief) Act.

Furthermore, while the Income Tax Relief Act provided that pioneer status be granted for an initial period of three years, with a possibility of extension for another two year period, in practice, the NIPC had for fourteen years, granted pioneer status to successful applicants for a straight period of five years. This was in "consideration of the need to eliminate a renewal/extension process that had become a maze of bureaucratic bottlenecks and constraints.① However, after the crash in crude oil prices and the resulting cash flow challenge of the Federal Government, the purview of Pioneer Status was reviewed and the NIPC now grants Pioneer Status to companies for an initial period of three years.

7. Dispute Resolution

It has been noted that contract enforcement is critical "to gain investors' trust… The legal framework must ensure contract enforcement, property rights' protection and fair dispute resolution – all hallmarks of an efficient market." ② In view of this reality, the Nigerian Investment Promotion Commission Act (NIPC Act) which is the cross-sectoral legislation that establishes the legal foundation for a very liberal and open investment framework, contains a dispute settlement clause that governs disputes arising between Nigerian authorities and both domestic and foreign investors. By virtue of Section 25 of the NIPC Act, investors have the right to resort to conciliation and arbitration to settle any investment dispute against the Nigerian authorities.

It is however the case, that more often than not, disputes often arise in investment projects that lead to court adjudication. In Nigeria, dispute resolution via the court system is slow paced and riddled with over-congested court lists, long adjournments and over-burdened judicial personnel.③ The state of affairs of the Nigerian judiciary has resulted in very slow resolution of disputes, which in turn has led to loss of time, money and resources for some investors in the past. This in turn has deterred intending investors from delving into agricultural investment in Nigeria.

Recently, "international institutions such as the world bank have identified that development can only take place in a comprehensive manner if all sectors of the economy are borne along." ④ As such,

---

① Pioneer Status and the Return of the 3-year Rule; Deloitte.

② Policy Framework for Investment in Agriculture; OECD.

③ The Courts and Commercial Disputes Resolution in Nigeria: The Need for Specialization.

④ The Courts and Commercial Disputes Resolution in Nigeria: The Need for Specialization.

to reduce the legal risk of investment in the agricultural sector, it is imperative that judicial reform in the area of commercial dispute adjudication occurs.

Risk Mitigation Mechanism

While it has been noted that the Nigerian agricultural sector is ready and open for investment on both the international and domestic levels, it is important for both the Federal Government and intending investors to be cognizant of the following long-term risk mitigation mechanisms that can improve investment prospects in the sector.

1. Enactment of Policies and Regulations Tailored to the Specific Needs of Investments Agriculture Commodities

It is suggested that sectoral specific policies aimed at priority agricultural commodities would help attract investment towards such high-priority and high-yielding commodities. Such sector specific policies would also address issues such as the design and adoption of grades and standards that favour the utilization of the commodity in question.①

Nigeria appears to be doing something right in this area with the employment of the Nigeria Incentive-Based Risk Sharing System for Agricultural Lending (NIRSAL), which is an initiative of the Central Bank of Nigeria (CBN), THE Banker's Committee and the Federal Ministry of Agriculture and Rural Development. NIRSAL, which is a public limited liability company, essentially administers a Risk Sharing Fund designed to identify, redefine, measure, re-price and evolve strategies to de-risk and catalyse lending to the Nigerian agriculture value chain. As such, the company has the mandate of facilitating the flow of credit to agribusiness value chain players and collaborating with stakeholders to fix broken agriculture value chains in Nigeria. It is worthy to note that from inception in 2012 to date, NIRSAL has guaranteed 454 projects valued at 61.161 billion Naira.

Regardless of the strides being achieved in mitigation of legal risks through well-tailored policy initiatives, it is also important that "investors have access to clear and efficient commination channels to indicate their specific needs to policy makers" ②. This will enable dynamic legislations and regulations are relevant to investor needs and subsequently able to promote investment in the sector.

① Calvin Miller, *Risk Management for Agricultural Investment: Investment and Resource Mobilization*(2008); Food and Agricultural Organisation of the United Nations.

② Managing Risk in Agriculture: A holistic Approach (OECD, 2009).

2. Improvement of Sector-Specific and Non-Sector Specific Infrastructure

As previously highlighted, the deficiency of relevant infrastructure in the agriculture economic space is partly as a result of previous government under-investment in not only the agro economy, but other sectors of the economy that work in tangent with the agro sector,

In order to reverse the dearth of infrastructure and improve both sector specific and non-sector specific infrastructure in this regard, it is important that "co-ordination mechanisms are established across the various government agencies responsible for infrastructure and agriculture throughout the policy design and implementation stages." ① For instance the Ministry of Power, Works and Housing for instance will work hand-in-hand with the Ministry of Agriculture and Rural Development towards ensuring a holistic approach to improving both sector and non-sector specific infrastructure in this regard.

The following have also been identified as short-term, quick mitigants to already identified legal risks of investment in the agricultural sector:②

a. Investment in transparent relationships with the Government;

b. Alignment of investment and business interests with the Government;

c. Encouragement of direct government participation in the investment;

d. Open, competitive bidding by intending investors (avoiding 'fast track' arrangements; and

e. Compliance with regulatory and legislative requirements.

Conclusion

This article has concentrated on the legal risks of agricultural investment in Nigeria. It has explored briefly the inherent opportunities in the sector and has delved into the following particular legal risks: legislative and regulatory uncertainty, lack of government investment in the sector, corruption and transparency risks, credit risks for intending lenders, taxation risks, implementation of local content laws and regulations and dispute resolution. Long term and short-medium term risk mitigation mechanisms have also been proffered in the article. It has been suggested that the enactment of policies and regulations tailored to the specific needs of agro investment and the improvement of both sector and non-sector specific infrastructure are key to mitigating the legal risks already identified. Short-term mitigants such as investment and alignment of business interests with the government and compliance with regulatory and legislative requirements, have also been noted in the article.

① Managing Risk in Agriculture: A holistic Approach (OECD, 2009).

② Conrad Marais, *Investing in African Infrastructure Projects: Risk and Risk Mitigation* (September, 2013).

在非洲进行农业投资方面的法律风险

作者：David Furaha　译者：赵瀚杰

一、引言

农产品是公民生活中的必需品，同样也为工业提供原材料。正因如此，农业部门对每个国家而言都是不可或缺的部门领域。

农业部门在大部分非洲国家的长期发展中扮演着关键角色。对于许多非洲国家来说，就业、收入、全民健康的保障来源于农业。农业为国家收入做着最大的贡献：既是外汇的最大来源，同样也是储蓄投资的主要来源。[①]

非洲农业仍然主要集中于生存基础层面，人们为了生存努力抗争。尽管许多尝试都用以将农业从生存层面调动到工业层面，但必要条件是需要以低休耕比例和资本、劳动力在单位土地上的高投入为特征的充足投资。[②]

在农业领域进行投资会带来一定的风险，且大部分同样影响着其他领域，包括环境风险、市场风险、法律风险等。我们在这篇文章中主要论述农业投资领域中的法律风险。

① Walter Odhiambo, Financing African Agriculture: Issues and Challenges, http://www.afdb.org/fileadmin/uploads/afdb/Documents/Knowledge/25120395-EN-ISSUES-AND-CHALLENGES-IN-FINANCIN-FINAL.PDF, Accessed on 27th April 2016.

② X, Industrial Agriculture, https://en.wikipedia.org/wiki/Intensive_farming, Accessed on 26th April 2016.

二、农业投资中的法律风险

法律风险这个术语涵盖两方面，分别为商业风险带来的法律上的后果以及具有法律因素的商业风险（因不确定的法律或不合适的法律文件等带来的风险[①]）。

在我们所讨论的风险范畴下，与其相关的内容涉及移民法律和政策、投资政策、银行法规、土地收购和管理政策，以及双边投资协议、控制资本货物相关规则、征用和特许法规等对投资者友好的内容缺失。

（一）移民法律及政策

在某些非洲国家进行农业投资，需要用到该国可能并不具备的商业手段，而这种困难能够通过允许外国投资者启动项目得以解决。为了促成这一目标，一个国家需要弹性的移民规则，如避免在获得工作许可和入境文件上设置烦琐的程序和过大代价。我们留意到若是一个国家期望外国投资者在其领地上工作，那么他们的移民法律和政策必须灵活到一定程度以吸引投资者。

以美国为例，基于投资的移民法律中为外国投资者提供各种途径以获取投资，以提供相关签证或是基于投资的绿卡作为交换，使其来到美国建立、领导、管理、提供核心技术或是投资某项具体行业。[②]

作为一个鼓励引入外商的国家，卢旺达同样基于投资制定其移民法律，而这也为欢迎投资者进入国家包括农业领域在内的部门提供了极大的帮助。相应地，国家欢迎投资者参与到咖啡豆与茶种植、加工和出口以及农产品工业中。

（二）有关土地管理和取得的法律风险

必须指出的是，一旦谈及农业上的投资便不可避免地涉及国家的土地法规，因为农业和土地是紧密相关的。正由于农业投资需要大量的土地，投资者可能需要通过购买或是从政府手中取得租赁权和特许权以得到大片土地。

---

① Professor Richard Moorhead and Dr. Steven Vaughan, Legal Risk, https://www.ucl.ac.uk/laws/law-ethics/research/papers/erc-executive-report-legal-risk-definition-management-ethics.pdf, Accessed on 27th April 2016.

② Ritter HALLIDAY LLP, Investment Based Immigration, http://ritterhalliday.com/services/investment-based-immigration, accessed on 27/04/2016.

出于以上原因，让每个国家拥有明确的关于土地取得和土地管理的法规显得至关重要。后者的缺失可能成为危及投资者利益的争端来源。一旦投资者通过其对管理土地法规的评估感应到了潜在的风险，那么他一定会抑制投资。简单地说，基础设施、气候以及环境等因素同样会给非洲的农业带来风险，因此国家的领导层应尽量避免这一法律风险。

以卢旺达为例，几年前未经注册的土地会产生许多争议，并且没有人能将这部分土地担保给银行以换取贷款。如果所有的土地都被注册并署上所有者，那么一切问题都将得到解决。但这并不足够，还需要制定不同法律法规，明确规定取得及管理土地的简明程序。

就目前中国的情况来看，为了促进投资，改善土地管理的法律已经实行。相应地，1998 年制定的一项法律与其实施细则已经生效。①

这一法律将城镇和农村的土地所有权赋予集体。这些土地必须经过县级以上人民政府的登记和记录。国有土地可以被个人或单位使用，并且记录在地方人民政府。政府使用一种土地调查和统计系统。各级人民政府负责制订土地使用计划，并且城镇土地的使用计划必须同整体的土地使用计划一致。在河流和水域部分，使用方式必须同河流发展的综合方案一致。各级人民政府必须采取保护耕地、保持灌溉和排水、改善土质、防止沙漠化、控制土壤盐度和侵蚀等措施。任何人造成土壤沙漠化或侵蚀都将承担损害赔偿责任。②

相关的管理办法包括《江苏省外商投资企业土地使用管理办法》。现有的法规是为了加强股份制、非股份制联合企业、外资企业在投资上对于土地的管理利用以及鼓励省内的外商投资。外资企业选择的地点和范围将由地方计划当局进行确认和批准。③

取得土地分配的程序将经由外资主体提交申请而发起。申请一经批准，申请人将签署一份土地使用合同。在那之后，申请人将获得土地使用凭证以及土地使用权。土地使用权不包括所有权且不能转让。土地使用者要保护使用权范围内土地下层的

① FAO, http://faolex.fao.org/cgi-bin/faolex.exe?rec_id=002201&database=faolex&search_type=link&table=result&lang=eng&format_name=@ERALL, accessed on 27th April 2016.

② FAO, http://faolex.fao.org/cgi-bin/faolex.exe?rec_id=002201&database=faolex&search_type=link&table=result&lang=eng&format_name=@ERALL, accessed on 27th April 2016.

③ FAO, http://faolex.fao.org/cgi-bin/faolex.exe?rec_id=002201&database=faolex&search_type=link&table=result&lang=eng&format_name=@ERALL, accessed on 27th April 2016.

水、矿产资源等资源，避免其遭受一切污染和破坏。其余的条款则规定了转让的期间、费用（农业、林业、畜牧业以及渔业的发展项目都将受益于优惠）以及争议解决方案。[①]

（三）征用的法律风险

无论是否投资农业领域，每个投资者都应当评估征收和征用所带来的法律风险。

征用是指，国家出于公共或其他目的而取得财产。征用可以分为直接或间接两类。

直接征用是指国家通过行使其主权获得项目，无论出于个体原因或是作为更大规模国有化工程中的一部分。总的来说，直接征用是国家的明确行为，将冠有投资者头衔的项目转让于国家名下。作为被征用对象，投资者可以此为理由寻求国家赔偿。

间接征用则没有那么具体。在某些情况下，国家会通过干预和妨碍的手段征用财产；尽管其明确否定存在干扰的意愿，并且声称不会介入财产权的行使，但仍然会通过某些具体行为致使财产所有权效力近乎无效从而推定为征用。

评论往往将间接征用形容为掩饰的、渐进的以及结果的征用，如拒绝更新或撤销许可（*Tecmed v Mexico*），破坏合同效力（*CME v Czech Republic*），以及出于不相关的原因终止合同 (*Azinan v Mexico*)。

在一个征用法规不明确的国家里，问题的关键在于国家的任何行为以及从中应该产生的赔偿都缺乏相应的定义。投资者很可能陷入一种不明朗的局面，即是否应当继续经营此类不盈利的项目，或者放弃并声称国家的间接干预已经实质上构成征用行为。[②]

值得一提的是，国家修订的某些法律法规会致使项目受到损害，但并不是所有此类行为都应视为征用行为。国家依法实施的非差别措施，包括规定配额、改变税收、环境保护、劳动法等都会在不同情况下使得投资者和贷方遭受损失且鲜有补偿甚至没有补偿，但这些都不应视为征用行为。这些非差别措施无论如何都必须同国

---

① FAO, http://faolex.fao.org/cgi-bin/faolex.exe?rec_id=017262&database=faolex&search_type=link&table=result&lang=eng&format_name=@ER.

② Norton Rose Fulbright, Expropriation, http://www.nortonrosefulbright.com/knowledge/publications/30459/expropriation-investment-protection-and-mitigating-the-risks.

际法一致并且不能具备剥夺投资者权利的效力（*Eureko v Poland*）。

因此，每一个期望吸引大量投资的国家必须拥有足够清晰的征用法规，明确表明国有化、征用等都是基于超越个体私人利益的公共利用、公共安全及国家利益等目的，无论对于国内或国外人员。在此类情况下，所有者将得到相应的征用赔偿；国家行使此种主权时，必须同国内施行的法律和国际法上的规定一致。①

当以上条件都满足时，投资者便会感觉在投资时拥有更大保障并准备投资到包括农业在内的不同领域。

（四）资本收回以及投资回报

资本收回指的是资本从国外回到其原始国家，将投资在国外的资本以及获得的利润转回国内，或是将商品买卖和服务中换取的外汇转移回国。②

投资收回的可能性以及附带的回报是影响外国投资流入经济的主要因素。每一个外国投资者都想确保随时能将自己的财产转移回母国。

以印度为例，在完成一定的正式手续后，资本投入和利润方可全部收回。所有想要在印度收回投资价值的外国投资者必须首先将其在印度公司的份额出售给当地人。为了达到这个目的，外国投资者必须向诸如印度储备银行的主管总经理、外汇管制司、中央办公室、对外投资和运营司提交 TSI 形式（印度储备银行手册中规定）的申请以获得银行的允许。当申请被印度储备银行批准后，投资可通过一位授权交易人在满足一定正式手续后收回，如从印度的收入税收机构获得非异议凭证和完税凭单。③

许多非洲国家没有足够的国内投资来源，因此需要国外投资进入包括农业在内等领域。为了吸引投资者，国家就需要避免在资本收回上设置严格限制。

以卢旺达为例，这个国家在过去的几年里一直在努力研究并完善其投资政策和银行业法规，为的就是营造一个良好的投资氛围。基于以上原因，一部涵盖了为投资者提供诸多便利的投资法典制定出台，同时还有确保投资者能够收回投资的银行业法规。这一系列举措所带来的大量投资者极大地提升了国家的经济，使得卢旺达

① August Reinisch, Expropriation in international investment Law, http://ils.univie.ac.at/fileadmin/user.

② Repatriation of Capital Investment and Return on Investment http://it4b.icsti.su/1000ventures_e/countries/india/india_reg_caprepatr.html, Accessed on 24th April 2016.

③ Repatriation of Capital Investment and Return on Investment http://it4b.icsti.su/1000ventures_e/countries/india/india_reg_caprepatr.html, Accessed on 24th April 2016.

的经济发展领先于其他非洲国家。

（五）双边投资协议的缺失

双边投资协议是推进和保护外商直接投资的文件。[①]协议旨在促成两个国家之间的互惠，推进和保护各自领域所属公司的投资。双边投资协议对全球外商直接投资的流动管理来说是至关重要的法律文件，并且有众多研究表明此类协议和外商直接投资都对发展具有正面作用。

只有当国家加入双边投资协议中，两方国家才可能同意为对方国家的外商投资提供保护。双边投资协议对外商投资十分有利，其中包括了国民待遇，公平与公正待遇，保护投资免于征用且为其提供必要条件，以及中立的争端解决机制。

以中美之间的双边投资协议为例，中国在美国的投资早已置于美国法律的框架下并被赋予了大部分以上提及的权利，其中包括正当程序和保护其免于征用，同时还给予中国投资者一些附加的利益，如可以获得具有中立性质的投资者与东道国间的争端解决方式。

双边投资协议确保外国政府同等对待投资者和国内公司。这一项权利被称为“国民待遇”。双边投资协议同时还保证缔约国在其市场中给予外商投资的优待不低于现时或将来任何第三国，也被成为“最惠国待遇”。比如，在一个强有力的双边投资协议的制约下，中国政府给予美国公司的待遇与新西兰、德国、韩国的公司一样；这些都属于同中国有投资协议的国家。

说到公平待遇的保证，这对双边投资协议效力形成之前市场中的原有投资和之后新加入的投资同样适用。这意味着双边投资协议禁止外国政府使用，如所有权限制等妨碍外国投资进入本国市场的投资管制。这在目前的中国显得尤为重要，原因在于从制造业、服务业再到农业等一百多个工业部门中都设置了投资管制；反观美国，仅有五个领域完全管制外商投资，同时还有二十四个部门设置了次要条件和管制。一旦中国市场给予美国同等优惠，这些次要管制将被移除。

在双边投资协议下，政府还保证在对待投资者时采取同国际法一致的“公平和公正待遇”。美国已经将这些利益给予外国投资者，因此双边投资协议的主要用处在

---

① Valentin Jentsch, the role of Bilateral investment treaties, http://papers.ssrn.com/sol3/papers.cfm?abstract_id=1400747, Accessed on 22nd April 2016.

于美国投资者在中国得到更好的保护。[①]

双边投资协议确保公司不会遭受非公正的投资要求，如要求当地公司无须提供的许可证等。双边投资协议还在其他方面保护投资者。比如，协议限制国外政府在自己国内控制资本。一旦此类征用发生，协议将确保投资者公平地、适时地获得补偿。协议同样限制政府给美国投资者在其国内市场运营时施加种种繁重的条件。例如，政府不能制定强制要求公司在其产品中使用当地原材料以及将技术授予国内公司作为投资条件的法规。最终，协议确保美国投资者能够将投入的资本自由地转移出入境，正如像在美国本土一样。

总体而言，任何投资者在选择投资地点时一定会偏向于同本国有双边投资协议的国家，因为那样才能使其感到安全，投资得到保障。

就非洲国家而言，许多双边投资协议的商讨及签署旨在认为这一举措会吸引投资者并促进本国内的经济发展，但反对的声音同样存在，部分认为签订这些协议主要维护的是另一方的利益。首先，大多双边投资协议包含了对于投资者保护的详细条款但却在投资者义务上保持沉默。进一步讲，诸多协议集中在东道国义务的规定上，而少许提及东道国的权利。其次，许多人担心这些协议将赋予外商投资者以高于本国投资者的权利；他们或许还会主张东道国政府执行损害本国投资者或是使其难以同自身进行面对面竞争的政策。最后，有的人担心协议还会限制东道国政府的规则权限。

南非的贸易与工业部门指出，发展中国家关于主要问题的担心并未在商讨双边投资协议的过程中提及。协议甚至延伸到了发展中国家的政策层面，强加损害性的、带给可持续发展深远影响的投资规则。协议中的新投资规则防止发展中国家的政府提出让国外公司转让技术，培训当地工人，或是将资源输入本地的要求。在这些条件下，将无法促进或加强投资的可持续发展。

除去这些事关双边投资协议实质内容的担心，发展中国家还对国际上的投资争端如何解决感到忧心忡忡。协议通常采用一种投资者对国家提起诉讼的争端解决机制（ISDS），其结果就是这种机制使得投资者越过国内法庭并直接向国际仲裁机构提起对于东道国的诉讼。在过去的二十年里，这类诉讼的数量呈现猛增的态势，这都要归因于ISDS条款。发展中国家和民间社会组织担心大型公司可能会滥用这种权利

① The US-China Business Council, https://www.uschina.org/reports/bilateral-investment-treaties-what-they-are-and-why-they-matter, Accessed on 25th April 2016.

并借此搞垮东道国的经济。①

总结一点，双边投资协议对非洲国家从外商投资中受益来说至关重要，尽管存在对于此类协议的种种批评。

（六）同税法相关的风险

每一位投资者在投入资金之前都会考虑一个极其重要的方面，即税收政策。了解税收法规和政策是十分必要的；上交给税务部门的税额事关投资者对于投资回报的预期。

这是因为一个人所缴纳的税额将减少其实际投资带来的收益。举个例子，如果一个人从投资股票当中获得了 15% 的利润，那么他将在那 15% 的基础上缴纳税款。如果税率是 10%，那么他的实际收益只有 13.5%。

对大多数投资者和小商人来说，税收是制定行业和投资决策的因素，但更为重要的终究是哪种投资或商业决策会使价值达到最大化。随着你财富的积累并逐渐成为经验老到的投资人，税收对于投资和行业决策的影响会变得越来越重要，而就如何减少税收负担，可以听从专业人士的意见。②

当一个国家的税收法规将税率置于高水平，这将导致抑制投资的趋势，甚至会发现不够清晰的税收法律将导致权利被滥用。同样地，投资人会犹豫是否启动自己的项目。因此，国家能否制定一个产生良性投资环境的税收政策便显得与之紧密相关。

举例来说，当基础设施、交通费用、政治与经济的稳定性基本处于平衡状态时，税收会显著左右投资者的选择。这种效果会由于税收手段、跨国公司的特征，以及税收机制在本土与接收国之间的关系而变化。当越来越多的国家开始竞争吸引跨国公司，财政刺激便成为了一种全球化趋势，并在 20 世纪 90 年代这一段时期激增。贫穷的非洲国家依靠免税期和进口免税，而西欧工业国家允许投资补贴或加速折旧。③

---

① Uche Ewelukwa Ofodile,Africa-China Bilateral Investment Treaties: A critique, http://repository.law.umich.edu/cgi/viewcontent.cgi?article=1027&context=mjil, accessed on 29th April 2016.

② http://business.lovetoknow.com/wiki/Impact_of_Tax_on_Investment_and_Business_Decisions.

③ Jacques Morisset and Neda Pirnia, How tax Policy and inccentives affects foreign Direct Investment, http://elibrary.worldbank.org/doi/abs/10.1596/1813-9450-2509.

（七）不支持农业融资的银行法规

项目融资构成投资中的又一主要方面。有意义的项目往往需要大量资金，通常不为投资人所具备，除非同贷款人合作。尽管在非洲农业中会遭遇其他紧急风险，特别是同气候相关，制定的银行法规和政策也同样不支持农业融资。

大多商业银行认为资助农业领域会带来很大风险，因为大多数的农民没有保险，而这将导致他们将一些不为农业设立的规则开放至这个领域[①]。正如 King Sooloo 所说的那样，这个领域难以扩张，无法为尼日利亚的经济发展带来贡献的根本原因在于不适当的融资难以推进农业信用。尼日利亚农业快速发展问题同时还表明，某些原因阻碍了扩大农村农民经济基础这一目标，即缺少或是限制取得贷款资金的途径。其中一个使得农业在经济中贡献降低的原因是缺少国家信用政策以及相应的农民资助信用机构。[②]

对所有国家而言，促使银行借贷给投资人以提供项目资金支持的法律机制必不可少，但保险公司也应同样富有创造力，为农业目的保障贷款提供相应方案和产品。

三、结论

总结来说，农业是大部分国家尤其非洲国家的支柱产业，这一点十分重要。因此，关键在于每个国家都应确保在投资农业领域时所面临的风险降到最低。

具体来说，法律风险源于那些对农业投资不友好的法律或是明确法律的缺失，而这些风险只有政府通过制定法规才能移除。如果政府不愿努力消除以上提及的风险，那么他们将永远面临注定失败的投资人和项目以及其他还未启动的局面。

结合采取了强有力措施以减轻妨碍投资风险的成功国家的案例，我们建议每一个非洲国家集中于移除投资壁垒，因为那将带给国家经济和国民幸福以积极的影响。

---

① Peterson Tumwebaze, Government, banks to fix agric financing challenges, http://www.newtimes.co.rw/section/article/2015-02-24/186274/.

② King Sooloo, The Role of Commercial Banks in Financing Agriculture, http://www.academia.edu/6694062, Accessed on 29th April 2016.

非洲拥有的资源足以推进农业投资，但政策的制定者同利益相关人合作时应努力降低投资者在农业中面临的风险。这将解决某些非洲国家长期面临的食物短缺的问题，同时在减轻贫困和缓解营养不良中扮演重要角色。

Legal Risks of Agricultural Investment in Africa

Author: David Furaha

Introduction

Agriculture is an important sector for every country as agricultural products are very essential for the life of citizen but also supply industries with raw materials.

The agriculture sector has a crucial role to play in the long-term development of most African countries. For many African countries, agriculture remains the most important source of employment, income and overall-wellbeing. The sector provides the largest contribution to national income; it is the biggest source of foreign exchange and is a major source of saving and investment.①

African Agriculture has been mainly on subsistence basis whereby the population strives to get food for their families. However more efforts have been mobilized to go from the subsistence agriculture towards industrial agriculture but this requires sufficient investment as it is characterized by a low fallow ratio and higher use of inputs such as capital and labour per unit land area②.

Investing in Agriculture is associated with certain risks and most of them are not different from those affecting other sectors. They include among others environmental risks, market risks, Legal Risks, etc. Our main focus in this paper shall be given to legal risks facing the investment in agriculture sector.

① Walter Odhiambo, Financing African Agriculture: Issues and Challenges, http://www.afdb.org/fileadmin/uploads/afdb/Documents/Knowledge/25120395-EN-ISSUES-AND-CHALLENGES-IN-FINANCIN-FINAL.PDF, Accessed on 27th April 2016.

② X, Industrial Agriculture, https://en.wikipedia.org/wiki/Intensive_farming, Accessed on 26th April 2016.

Legal Risks in Agricultural Investment

The legal risk is a term that encompasses both the legal consequences of business risk and business risks with legal origins (such as uncertain law or unsatisfactory legal work product)①.

We shall discuss risks related to immigration laws and policies, investment policies, banking laws, land acquisition and management laws and lack of Bilateral investment treaties, rules pertaining to control of capital freight, as well as lack of expropriation and concession law that are investor friendly.

1. Immigration laws and policies

Investing in agriculture in some African countries requires financial means which nationals may not have and this challenge may be resolved by allowing investors from foreign countries to come and start projects. To be able to do so, a country needs to have flexible immigration rules whereby getting work permits and entry documents does not involve long procedures and are not costly. We have noticed that a country that aspires to have foreign investors working on their land they have to ensure that their immigration laws and policies are flexible enough to attract investors.

For example in the USA, federal investment-based immigration law provides avenues for foreign investors to obtain investment or trade related visas, or investment-based green cards to come to the U.S. to establish, lead, manage, provide essential skills, or invest in certain types of businesses②.

Rwanda as a country that encourages foreign investors to come and do business has also tailored its immigration law towards investment based immigration laws and this has immensely helped in welcoming investors in the country including those in the Agriculture Sector. It is in line with the latter that the country has been able to have investors dealing with coffee and tea plantation, processing and export, agribusiness industries, etc.

2. Legal Risk pertaining to the acquisition and management of land

It is important to mention that one cannot talk of investing in agriculture leaving behind the regulation of land in the country because agriculture and land go hand in hand. Due to the fact that

① Professor Richard Moorhead and Dr. Steven Vaughan, Legal Risk, https://www.ucl.ac.uk/laws/law-ethics/research/papers/erc-executive-report-legal-risk-definition-management-ethics.pdf, Accessed on 27th April 2016.

② Ritter HALLIDAY LLP, Investment Based Immigration, http://ritterhalliday.com/services/investment-based-immigration, accessed on 27/04/2016.

investing in Agriculture requires massive land, the investor may need to acquire big portions of land either through purchasing them, leasing or concession from the Government.

It is therefore important for every country to have clear Laws the acquisition of land and its management. The absence of the Latter Laws may be a source of disputes which may jeopardize the investor's interests. Whenever an investor assesses the regulations governing land and realizes a potential risk in the management of Land he refrains from investing. Briefly, there are other risks facing agriculture in Africa related to basic infrastructure and weather and environment, the Countries' leadership should avoid adding on such legal risk.

For example in Rwanda, Land was not register in some year back and this caused a lot of disputes but also not body could give a portion of land as a collateral to the bank to get a loan but all these problems were solved when all land was registered and owners given titles. It did not stop there because different laws and regulations were put in place to determine clear and quick procedures on how to acquire the land and to manage it.

As a far as China is concerned, laws have been put in place to improve the way land is administered for the promotion of investment. In line with the latter, a law has been enacted in 1998 and different implementing regulations were put in place①.

This law grants the ownership of land in rural and suburban areas to the collectives. Such land must be registered and recorded by the Governments at the county level. State-owned land may be used by units or by individuals and is recorded by local People's Governments. A land survey and statistics system is introduced. The People's Governments at all levels are responsible for the preparation of plans for land utilization and urban planning must agree with the overall plan for land utilization. In the zones of rivers and lakes, utilization of land must be consistent with a comprehensive plan of development of rivers and lakes. People's Governments at all levels are required to adopt measures to protect cultivated, maintain irrigation and drainage installations, improve soil, prevent soil from desertification, control soil salinization and soil erosion. Whoever causes soil desertification or soil erosion must rectify the damage at his expense②.

The implementing regulations include the regulations on land-use management for foreign investment enterprises in Jiangsu province. The present regulations are made so as to enhance the management of land use by the equity or non-equity joint ventures and wholly foreign-owned enterprises and to encourage foreign investment in the province. The location and limits of the

① FAO, http://faolex.fao.org/cgi-bin/faolex.exe?rec_id=002201&database=faolex&search_type=link&table=result&lang=eng&format_name=@ERALL, accessed on 27th April 2016.

② FAO, http://faolex.fao.org/cgi-bin/faolex.exe?rec_id=002201&database=faolex&search_type=link&table=result&lang=eng&format_name=@ERALL, accessed on 27th April 2016.

site chosen by a foreign investment enterprise shall be subject to confirmation by local planning authorities①.

Procedures for the assignment initiate with an application for assignment by the foreign investment entity. When the application is approved, the applicant shall sign a land use contract, after which it will receive the land use certificate and the right over the use of the site. Land use rights do not include ownership of the land and are not transferable. The user of the land shall protect the water and mineral resources and other resources found within the borders of the site covered by the land use right and prevent any possible pollution or destruction. Remaining provisions deal with duration of the transfer, fees (agricultural, forestry, animal husbandry and fishery development projects shall benefit from a reduced fee), and dispute resolution.②

3. Legal Risk related to expropriation

Expropriation is another legal risk every investor should consider assessing, whether the investment concerns agriculture or not.

Expropriation is defined as the taking of a project/ property by the state, whether for public purposes or otherwise. At a basic level, expropriation can be divided into direct and indirect expropriation.

Direct expropriation is where the state exercises its sovereignty over a project either on an individual basis or as part of a wider scale nationalization program. Generally direct expropriation is a clear action by the state that transfers title of the project from the investors to the state and as such provides clear grounds for the deprived investors to seek compensation from the state.

Indirect expropriation is less specific and can be considered in the circumstances where a state may expropriate property, when it interferes with it, even though the state expressly disclaims any such intention, and even though a state may not purport to interfere with rights to property, it may, by its actions render those rights so useless that it will be deemed to have expropriated them."

Commentators have described indirect expropriation variously as disguised, creeping and consequential expropriation, for example the refusal to renew or the withdrawal of a licence (*Tecmed v Mexico*), undermining contractual arrangements (*CME v Czech Republic*) and termination of contracts for irrelevant reasons (*Azinan v Mexico*).

In a country where expropriation laws are not clear, the problem would be that no clear single

---

① FAO, http://faolex.fao.org/cgi-bin/faolex.exe?rec_id=002201&database=faolex&search_type=link&table=result&lang=eng&format_name=@ERALL, accessed on 27th April 2016.

② FAO, http://faolex.fao.org/cgi-bin/faolex.exe?rec_id=017262&database=faolex&search_type=link&table=result&lang=eng&format_name=@ER.

action by the state and as such the moment from which compensation should accrue may lack definition. The investor may therefore find itself in a position where it is unclear whether it should continue to operate the non-profitable project or abandon it and try to claim that expropriation has taken place due to the state's indirect interference①.

It is worth noting that not all changes to legislation or regulation by a state which are to the detriment of a project can be classified as expropriation. Non-discriminatory measures that are lawfully taken by a state, including the introduction of quotas, changes to taxation, environmental protection, labour laws and other measures may not be deemed to be expropriation despite the loss suffered by the investor and lenders and as such little or no compensation would be available to the investor and lenders in such circumstances. Such non-discriminatory measures however must be in line with international law and must not have the effect of "eviscerating" the rights of the investor (*Eureko v Poland*)[4].

It is therefore important for each country that aspires to see a lot of investment projects coming up to have clear laws on expropriation which indicate that nationalization, expropriation or requisitioning shall be based on grounds or reasons of public utility, security or the national interest which are recognized as overriding purely individual or private interests both domestic and foreign. In such cases the owner shall be paid appropriate compensation, in accordance with the rules in force in the State taking such measures in the exercise of sovereignty and in accordance with international law②.

Once the above is available investors will feel much safer and ready to invest in different projects including in agriculture.

4. Repatriation of capital investment and return on investment

Repatriation of capital is defined as the return of capital from abroad to the country of its origin, by the transfer to the homeland of capital invested abroad, as well as the profits on it, and by the transfer of foreign currency earned from the sale of goods and services.③

The most major factor, which could influence the inflow of investment into the economy by foreign investors, is the repatriation possibility of the investment and the returns thereon. Every foreign investor needs to assured that he will be able to take back home his money every time he needs to do so.

---

① Norton Rose Fulbright, Expropriation, http://www.nortonrosefulbright.com/knowledge/publications/30459/expropriation-investment-protection-and-mitigating-the-risks.

② August Reinisch, Expropriation in international investment Law, http://ils.univie.ac.at/fileadmin/user.

③ L. N. KRASAVINA, Repatriation of capital, http://encyclopedia2.thefreedictionary.com/Repatriation+of+Capital.

For example, Capital investment made in India can be fully repatriated along-with profits after completing certain formalities. Foreign investors desiring to receive back the value of their investment in India will necessarily have to first sell their shares in Indian companies to some resident in India. For this purpose, the foreign investors will be required to have the Reserve Bank of India's permission for which an application is to be made in Form TSI (Format available in R.B.I Manual) to the Chief General Manager, Exchange Control Department, Central Office, Foreign Investment Division (I), Reserve Bank of India, Mumbai-400001. After approval for dis-investment by Reserve Bank of India, repatriation can be made through an authorized dealer after fulfillment of certain formalities including No-Objection/Tax Clearance Certificate from the India Income-tax authorities[①].

Many of African countries don't have sufficient domestic investment and therefore need foreign investor to come and invest in different projects including agriculture and therefore need to consider putting fewer restrictions on capital repatriation so as to attract investors.

For example Rwanda has spent the past years working on its investment policies and banking regulation so as to put in place a friendly investment climate. In this regard an investment code have been enacted with very many facilities for investors but also banking regulation were refined to allow investors come with assurance that when they want to go back they will be able to take their investments. This has yielded a lot to the nation by bringing a big number of investors in the country and Rwanda has been ranked among African countries with the fastest economic growth.

5. Absence of Bilateral Investment Treaties

Bilateral investment treaties (BITs) are instruments that aim at promoting and protecting foreign direct investment (FDI)[②]. They are agreements between two countries for the reciprocal encouragement, promotion and protection of investments in each other's territories by companies based in either country. BITs are arguably the most important legal instruments for the governance of global foreign direct investment (FDI) flows and several studies illustrate the positive effect of BITs on FDI and on development.

When countries enter into a BIT, both countries agree to provide protections for the other country's foreign investments that they would not otherwise have. A BIT provides major benefits for investors in another country, including national treatment, fair and equitable treatment, protection from expropriation and performance requirements for investments, and access to neutral dispute

① Repatriation of Capital Investment and Return on Investment http://it4b.icsti.su/1000ventures_e/countries/india/india_reg_caprepatr.html, Accessed on 24th April 2016.

② Valentin Jentsch, the role of Bilateral investment treaties, http://papers.ssrn.com/sol3/papers.cfm?abstract_id=1400747, Accessed on 22nd April 2016.

settlement.

Taking the case of China-USA BITs, Chinese investments in the US are already granted most of these rights under US law, such as the right to due process and protection from expropriation, but the BIT gives Chinese investors a few additional benefits, such as access to neutral investor-state dispute settlement.

A BIT ensures that foreign governments will treat investors the same as domestic companies; this right is known as "national treatment." BITs also guarantee that investors are given the same types of preferences that other foreign investors are given in a market, also called "most-favored nation" treatment. For instance, under a strong US-China BIT, the Chinese government would treat US companies the same as Chinese companies, as well as companies from New Zealand, Germany, and Korea -- countries that already have investment agreements with China.

The promise of equal treatment applies to investments made prior to the time the BIT enters into force and to new investments in the market. That means that BITs bar foreign governments from using investment restrictions, like ownership caps, to prevent companies from investing in their markets. This is particularly important in China, which currently restricts investment in over 100 industry sectors, ranging from manufacturing to services to agriculture. By contrast, the United States restricts foreign investment outright in only five sectors, and maintains 24 mostly minor conditions or restrictions that would be removed if the US is given reciprocity in China's market.

Under a BIT, governments also commit to treating investors on a "fair and equitable" basis in accordance with international law. America already grants foreign investors these benefits, so a BIT would primarily serve to better protect American investors in China①.

A BIT would ensure that companies would not have to meet unfair investment requirements, like licensing requirements, that local companies are not required to meet. BITs also protect investors in several other ways. For example, BITs limit foreign governments' ability to take over US investments in their country. If such an expropriation does happen, BITs ensure governments compensate investors in a fair and timely manner. BITs also curb a government's ability to require that American investors meet burdensome conditions to operate in their markets. For example, under a BIT, governments cannot create rules mandating companies to use locally-made materials in their products or to transfer technology to a domestic company as a condition of investment. Finally, BITs ensure that American investors can move capital freely in and out of the country in which they have invested, as businesses do every day in the United States.

On a general note, any investor would feel safe to take his capital to a country that has a

① The US-China Business Council, https://www.uschina.org/reports/bilateral-investment-treaties-what-they-are-and-why-they-matter, Accessed on 25th April 2016.

Bilateral Investment Treaty with his home country than going where there is not such treaty to protect him.

As far as African countries are concerned, many BITs have been negotiated and signed with a view to attract investors that would help to economically develop these countries but some criticisms are being made against the signed BITs including the one saying that those agreements primarily reflect the interests of the latter. First, most BITs contain explicit provisions on investor protection but are usually silent when it comes to investor obligations. Furthermore, most BITs focus on the obligation of host states but pay scant attention to the rights of host communities. Second, there are concerns that most BITs afford foreign investors greater rights than domestic investors and force host governments to implement policies that either harm domestic investors or make it very difficult for them to compete vis-a-vis foreign corporations. Third, there are also concerns that BITs are used to limit the regulatory space of host governments.

According to South Africa's Department of Trade and Industry, Major issues of concern for developing countries are not being addressed in the BIT negotiating processes. BITs extend far into developing countries' policy space, imposing damaging binding investment rules with far-reaching consequences for sustainable development. New investment rules in BITs prevent developing country governments from requiring foreign companies to transfer technology, train local workers, or source inputs locally. Under such conditions, investment fails to encourage or enhance sustainable development.

In addition to concerns relating to the substance of BITs, developing countries are also concerned about the manner in which international investment disputes are handled. BITs typically provide for some type of investor-state dispute settlement (ISDS) mechanism. The effect is that BITs allow investors to bypass domestic courts and lodge claims against host governments directly with international arbitration tribunals. Thanks to the ISDS provisions in BITs, the number of investor-State claims has grown tremendously in the past two decades. Developing countries and civil society groups are concerned that giant corporations abuse this right and use it to cripple the economies of host States[①].

To summarize, Bilateral Investment treaties are very important for African countries to benefit from foreign investment despite the above criticism made to the BITs that are in existence.

6. Risks pertaining to taxation laws

Taxation is a vital aspect that every investor considers before injecting the money in the project.

① Uche Ewelukwa Ofodile, Africa-China Bilateral Investment Treaties: A critique, http://repository.law.umich.edu/cgi/viewcontent.cgi?article=1027&context=mjil, accessed on 29th April 2016.

He always wants to know the taxation rules and policies, how much tax in he going to pay to the tax administration in order to forecast his returns from investment.

This is because the taxes someone pays on the investments can reduce the amount of money he actually makes from a given investment. For example, if someone invests in a stock and make 15 percent on his money, he may be taxed on those gains. If he is taxed on the investment at 10 percent, then he really only makes 13.5 percent on your money.

For most investors and small business people, taxes play a role in how business and investment decisions are made, but ultimately the most important thing is to determine which investments or business decisions will have the best effect on your personal or businesses value. As you gain more money and become a more sophisticated investor, the impact of tax on investment and business decisions becomes more important and getting help from a professional to reduce your tax liability is usually advisable.①

In a country where laws on taxation have put taxes at a high rate there will be a tendency to refrain from investing. You might also find that taxation laws are not clear enough to guide the tax collector which may lead to some abuse. In the same way, investor will be hesitant to start up their projects. It is therefore relevant for the country to work on its taxation policies and make them investor friendly.

For instance, when other factors—such as infrastructure, transport costs, and political and economic stability—are more or less equal, the taxes in one location may have a significant effect on investors' choices. This effect varies, however, depending on the tax instrument used, the characteristics of the multinational company, and the relationship between the tax systems of the home and recipient countries. With an increasing number of governments competing to attract multinational companies, fiscal incentives have become a global trend that has grown considerably in the 1990s. Poor African countries rely on tax holidays and import duty exemptions, while industrial Western European countries allow investment allowances or accelerated depreciation②.

7. Banking Laws that do not favor Agriculture Financing.

Project Financing is another essential aspect for investment. Meaningful projects always require huge finances that the investor cannot afford unless he/she works with lenders. However, due to other imminent risks in African agriculture especially those pertaining to whether, banking regulations and

① http://business.lovetoknow.com/wiki/Impact_of_Tax_on_Investment_and_Business_Decisions.

② Jacques Morisset and Neda Pirnia, How tax Policy and inccentives affects foreign Direct Investment, http://elibrary.worldbank.org/doi/abs/10.1596/1813-9450-2509.

policies are written in a way that is not favorable to agricultural financing.

Most commercial banks say it is risky to fund the agriculture sector since majority of farmers are not insured and this leads them to put in place rules that are not open to agriculture①. As King Sooloo puts it, the inability of this sector to expand and as well contribute meaningfully to the growth of Nigerian economy as due to inadequate financing to improve on the situation that is, facilitating agricultural credit! Also, the problem of rapid agricultural development in Nigeria indicates that efforts directed at achieving expanded economic base of the rural farmers were frustrated by the scarcity of and restrictive access to loanable fund! one of the reasons for the decline in the contribution of agriculture to the economy is lack of formal National credit policy and paucity of credit institutions which can assist farmers②.

It is there for very essential for every state to put in place Legal mechanisms that will facilitate banks to issue loans to investors in order to finance their projects but also insurance companies should be creative enough to come up with products to secure the loans that are given for agricultural purposes.

Conclusion

To conclude it is important to note that Agriculture constitute the backbone of most of the countries in the world and more especially those of Africa. It is crucial for every country to therefore ensure that any risk that the investment in Agricultural sector may face is waived.

In particular, Legal risks result from laws that are not favorable to investment in Agriculture or the absence of some that are necessary to clear some matter and it is only the Government which enact laws that can remove those risks. Once the Government is not willing to work towards removing all the above mentioned risks, they will always be faced by investors and projects will fails while others are not started.

Following the success that is seen in countries that have taken at hard the alleviation of all risks hindering investment, we would recommend each African country to focus on removing barriers to investment and this will have a positive impact on the nation's economy and on the population's welfare.

Africa has enough resources that can facilitate agricultural investments but policy makers in

① Peterson Tumwebaze, Government, banks to fix agric financing challenges, http://www.newtimes.co.rw/section/article/2015-02-24/186274/.

② King Sooloo, The Role of Commercial Banks in Financing Agriculture, http://www.academia.edu/6694062, Accessed on 29th April 2016.

partnership with stakeholders should work hard to mitigate the risks that face investors in Agriculture. This will be a response to the problem of food scarcity that has become chronic in certain African countries but it will also play a big role in poverty alleviation and fighting malnutrition.

图书在版编目（CIP）数据

中非法律评论 . 第三卷 / 万猛，张海征主编 .—北京：中国法制出版社，2018. 1

ISBN 978-7-5093-8859-4

Ⅰ. ①中… Ⅱ. ①万… ②张… Ⅲ. ①法律—非洲—文集 Ⅳ. ① D94-53

中国版本图书馆 CIP 数据核字（2017）第 246677 号

责任编辑 马金风（editormjf@163.com） 封面设计 周黎明

中非法律评论（第三卷）

ZHONGFEI FALÜ PINGLUN (DISANJUAN)

主编 / 万 猛 张海征

经销 / 新华书店

印刷 / 北京九州迅驰传媒文化有限公司

开本 / 710 毫米 ×1000 毫米 16 印张 / 28.25 字数 / 504 千

版次 / 2018 年 1 月第 1 版 2018 年 1 月第 1 次印刷

中国法制出版社出版

书号 ISBN 978-7-5093-8859-4 定价：79.00 元

北京西单横二条 2 号 值班电话：66026508

邮政编码：100031 传真：66031119

网址：http://www.zgfzs.com 编辑部电话：66070046

市场营销部电话：66033393 邮购部电话：66033288

（如有印装质量问题，请与本社编务印务管理部联系调换。电话：010-66032926）